# The Legitimacy of the European Union through Legal Rationality

Third country nationals (TCNs) play an important part in the economy of the European Union (EU), reflected in the rights granted to them under EU law. Political expediency is, however, shaped by world, regional and domestic influences that in turn determine policy towards third country nationals and their legal rights to freedom of movement.

This book examines the concept of political legitimacy within the EU through the principles of legal rationality, focusing in particular on the EU's policy towards third country nationals. Richard Ball argues that for legal doctrine to be rational it must display the requirements of formal, instrumental and substantive rationality, each mutually exclusive and essential.

In taking this position of legal rationality, the book focuses on free movement rights of TCNs within EU treaties and implementing legislation, the 'area of freedom, security and justice' and association agreements. Ball concludes that the stance of EU law towards third country nationals lacks legitimacy, and suggests possible new directions that EU policy should take in the future.

**Richard Ball** is Senior Lecturer in Law at the University of the West of England, UK.

# Routledge Research in EU Law

Available titles in this series include:

**Criminal Law and Policy in the European Union**
*Samuli Miettinen*

**Local Government in Europe**
The 'Fourth Level' in the EU Multi-layered System of Governance
*Carlo Panara and Michael R. Varney*

**The Legitimacy of the European Union through
Legal Rationality**
Free Movement of Third Country Nationals
*Richard Ball*

Forthcoming titles in this series include:

**New Governance and the European Strategy for Employment**
*Samantha Velluti*

**Human Rights and Minority Rights in the European Union**
*Kirsten Shoraka*

# The Legitimacy of the European Union through Legal Rationality

Free Movement of Third Country Nationals

**Richard Ball**

Routledge
Taylor & Francis Group

LONDON AND NEW YORK

First published 2014
by Routledge
2 Park Square, Milton Park, Abingdon, Oxfordshire OX14 4RN

Simultaneously published in the USA and Canada
by Routledge
711 Third Avenue, New York, NY 10017

First issued in paperback 2015

*Routledge is an imprint of the Taylor & Francis Group, an informa business*

*British Library Cataloguing in Publication Data*
A catalogue record for this book is available from the British Library

*Library of Congress Cataloging-in-Publication Data*
A catalog record has been requested for this book

ISBN13: 978-1-138-93520-4 (pbk)
ISBN13: 978-0-415-50531-4 (hbk)


Typeset in Baskerville
by Keystroke, Station Road, Codsall, Wolverhampton

# Contents

# Acknowledgements

The research for this book started with a PhD study commenced too many years ago and completed in 2010 at the University of Birmingham, and is partly based on the thesis for this study. There are a number of people in specific groups without whom that PhD research and this book would not have been possible. Special thanks first to my PhD supervisor Professor Tony Arnull for his advice, help, recommendations, discussion, wise words and above all patience. Those thanks must also be extended to my external examiner, Professor Michael Dougan of the University of Liverpool, especially over his recommendations for the PhD thesis and his advice over this book. Thanks also to Professor Roger Brownsword, my academic inspiration.

Thank you to everyone at Routledge, who have given me advice and support throughout the process of my virgin book publication. Thanks especially to Katie Carpenter who has been so patient over so many years. I also thank the anonymous reviewers for their constructive comments and suggestions on the original book proposal.

Thanks also to my colleagues and friends at the University of the West of England for their support, encouragement and friendship.

Last but definitely not least I'd like to thank my family. Thanks to my parents who have supported me in all my endeavours, even when they were not necessarily in agreement with my decisions. Thanks to Nathan and Ella for just being themselves. However, my most heartfelt thanks is reserved for my partner Simone, without whom my PhD and thus this book would never have been completed. Her patience, support and absolute belief in me were invaluable whenever I faltered.

This book and the laws referred to are correct as of April 2013.

# 1   Introduction

The concept of political legitimacy within the European Union (EU) has gained considerable attention[1] since Weiler discussed it in his seminal article.[2] However, 'there are many ways to cut the conceptual cake of legitimacy in the European Union'[3] and so its meaning remains elusive,[4] compounded by a lack of structure to enable an analysis to be conducted[5] and with different approaches tending to be adopted by different doctrinal disciplines (political science targeting political power relationships[6] and law pursuing the law-making process[7] and its institutional structure[8]).

The traditional view of legitimacy within a democracy is based on popular sovereignty[9] where the consent of the governed is required to establish or disestablish governments and the power to govern is limited by delegation from the people.[10] As Yack points out, this is very much state based as the governed or 'the

---

1  See eg D Beetham, C Lord *Legitimacy and the European Union* (Longman 1998).

2  JHH Weiler 'The transformation of Europe' (1991) 100 *YLJ* 2403.

3  N Walker 'The white paper in constitutional context' in C Joerges, Y Mény and JHH Weiler (eds) *Mountain or Molehill? A Critical Appraisal of the Commission White Paper on Governance* (European University Institute, Harvard Law School and NYU School of Law 2001) 33, 34.

4  A Arnull 'Introduction: the European Union's accountability and legitimacy deficit' in A Arnull, D Wincott (eds) *Accountability and Legitimacy in the European Union* (OUP 2002) 3. See also G de Búrca 'The quest for legitimacy in the European Union' (1996) 59 *MLR* 349.

5  D Beetham *The Legitimation of Power* (Macmillan 1991) and D Beetham, C Lord 'Legitimacy and the European Union' in A Weale, M Nentwich (eds) *Political Theory and the European Union: Legitimacy, Constitutional Choice and Citizenship* (Routledge 1998) 15 use a structure of legality, normative justifiability and legitimation to analyse the political legitimacy of the European Union. It is submitted that, although a useful structure, it can be incorporated within, and then analysed more effectively, through the legal rationality lens.

6  Beetham (n 5). See also R Barker 'Legitimacy, legitimation, and the European Union: what crisis?' in P Craig, R Rawlings (eds) *Law and Administration in Europe: Essays in Honour of Carol Harlow* (OUP 2003) 157.

7  TM Franck *Fairness in International Law and Institutions* (Clarendon Press 1995) at 26 and 'Legitimacy in the international system' (1988) 82 *AJIL* 705, 706.

8  See G Majone *Dilemmas of European Integration: The Ambiguities and Pitfalls of Integration by Stealth* (OUP 2005) 28, criticised by M Dougan '"And some fell on stony ground . . .": a review of Giandomenico Majone's *Dilemmas of European Integration*' (2006) 31 *ELR* 865. See also M Singer 'Legitimacy criteria for legal systems' (2006) 17 *KCLJ* 229.

9  I Harden 'Democracy and the European Union' in P Hirst, S Khilnani (eds) *Reinventing Democracy* (Blackwells Publishers 1996) 132, 133.

10  B Yack 'Popular sovereignty and nationalism' (2001) 29 *Political Theory* 517, 519.

people' must constitute all of the people of the territory over which that government has power.[11] This then reinforces the notion of the state as the fundamental political institution within the international and global community.

It is an obvious statement to make that the EU is not a state[12] and, as Føllesdal illustrates, legitimacy for the EU is far more complex than the model described above.[13] The most well known model of complex legitimacy is that of Scharpf,[14] who has suggested that legitimacy has two aspects with different roles: input-orientated legitimacy (input legitimacy);[15] and output-orientated legitimacy (output legitimacy).[16] Other observers have suggested alternative theories of legitimacy but once they are analysed the theories can be broken down into Scharpf's legitimacy criteria and other non-legitimacy elements. A classic example of this is the model of Beetham and Lord,[17] who suggest that for a state to be legitimate it must demonstrate the necessary identity, democracy and performance[18] in meeting the needs and values of citizens, which they then transpose to the model of the EU. The second and third criteria can be equated to input and output legitimacy whilst identity itself is a much contested concept that can be viewed from an individualistic perspective (how a person views his or her own position in society) or from a community perspective (how society determines who belongs and who does not). Instead of being an element of legitimacy it determines the construction of the political community not its legitimacy.

Input-orientated legitimacy requires a clear accountability of political action to the citizens of the polity or, as Bellamy and Castiglione state: 'the normatively conditioned and voluntary acceptance by the ruled of the government of their rulers'.[19] This definition is close to that of the concept of popular sovereignty and, although Dahl suggests that it is impossible to provide a definition for democracy as the term is used in many different ways,[20] it also corresponds to a definition of

---

11  ibid.
12  Or at least not yet. For arguments for and against EU statehood see GF Mancini 'Europe: the case for statehood' (1998) 4 *ELJ* 29 and JHH Weiler 'Europe: the case against the case for statehood' (1998) 4 *ELJ* 43.
13  A Føllesdal 'Survey article: the legitimacy deficits of the European Union' (2006) 14 *Journal of Political Philosophy* 441, 445.
14  FW Scharpf 'Economic integration, democracy and the welfare state' (1997) 4 JEPP 18 and *Governing in Europe: Effective and Democratic?* (OUP 1999).
15  Scharpf *Governing in Europe* (n 14) 7.
16  ibid 10.
17  C Lord, D Beetham 'Legitimising the EU: is there a "post-parliamentary" basis for its legitimation?' (2001) 39 JCMS 443.
18  These three elements of a single theory can be contrasted with Horeth's three sources of legitimacy (M Horeth 'No way out for the beast? The unsolved legitimacy problem of European governance' (1999) 6 *JEPP* 249, 251 – democratic decision-making at the EU level, technocratic and utilitarian justification, indirect democratic legitimacy granted by Member States) and Eriksen and Fossum's three modes of legitimation (EO Eriksen, JE Fossum 'Europe in search of legitimacy: strategies of legitimation assessed' (2004) 25 *IPSR* 435, 438 – efficiency, collective and self-understanding, justice and norms of fairness).
19  R Bellamy, D Castiglione 'Legitimizing the Euro-"polity" and its "regime": the normative turn in EU studies' (2003) 2 *EJPT* 7, 10.
20  RA Dahl *On Democracy* (Yale University Press 1998) 37. He does, however, suggest an elementary principle for democracy of political equality and five criteria required for a democratic

democracy provided by Schmitter[21] and Schumpeter.[22] As such input legitimacy can be equated to democratic legitimacy and this has elicited considerable attention from EU commentators over the years, especially over the perception of the lack of democratic accountability of EU institutions and decision-making to the peoples of Europe.[23] Since the coining of the term 'democratic deficit' in 1979,[24] each treaty amendment has triggered another outbreak of academic writing on the existence of this democratic deficit and the failure to resolve it.[25] Menon and Weatherill[26] point out that many of these observers judge the limitations of the EU against a strict nation-state model and this model can change depending on which nation-state is chosen as the blueprint. Attempting to theorise the EU through a nation-state lens fails to take into account the supranational nature of the majority of the decision-making conducted by the EU's institutions, let alone the intergovernmentalism that remains a feature of the EU even after the Lisbon Treaty. The reality is that Europe is made up of many peoples rather than a single people, so that without 'the people' there can be no *demos* and, 'if there is no *demos*, there can be no democracy'[27] with few mechanisms to promote a *demos* such as a common language, centrally organised political parties,[28] harmonised education policies or

process: effective participation; voting equality; enlightened understanding; control of the agenda; and inclusion of all adults. This suggests a predominant reliance on popular sovereignty as the basis of democracy.

21 PC Schmitter, TL Karl 'What democracy is . . . and is not' (1991) 2 *Journal of Democracy* 75, 76: '. . . a system of governance in which rulers are held accountable for their actions in the public realm by citizens, acting indirectly through the competition and cooperation of their elected representatives'.

22 JA Schumpeter *Capitalism, Socialism and Democracy* (Routledge 1976) 269: '. . . the democratic method is that institutional arrangement for arriving at political decisions in which individuals acquire the power to decide by means of a competitive struggle for the people's vote'.

23 See A Moravcsik 'In defence of the "democratic deficit": reassessing legitimacy in the European Union' in I Begg, J Peterson and JHH Weiler (eds) *Reassessing the Fundamentals* (Blackwell Publishing 2003) 77. The 'democratic deficit' of the EU has seen considerable academic debate. For a comprehensive summary of the debates see JHH Weiler 'European democracy and its critics: polity and system' in *The Constitution of Europe: 'Do the New Clothes Have an Emperor?' and Other Essays on European Integration* (CUP 1999) 264; C Chalmers, G Davies and G Monti *European Union Law* (2nd edn CUP 2010) 125; P Craig 'Integration, democracy, and legitimacy' in P Craig, G de Búrca (eds) *The Evolution of EU Law* (2nd edn OUP 2011) 13, 28; and P Craig, G de Búrca *EU Law: Text, Cases and Materials* (5th edn OUP 2011) 154 (where input legitimacy and democratic accountability are combined into the term 'input democracy').

24 D Marquand *Parliament for Europe* (Jonathan Cape 1979) 64.

25 For example with the development of the Lisbon Treaty see M Nettesheim 'Developing a theory of democracy for the European Union' (2005) 23 *Berkeley Journal of International Law* 358; R Bellamy 'Still in deficit: rights, regulation, and democracy in the EU' (2006) 12 *ELJ* 725; A Etzioni 'The Community deficit' (2007) 45 *JCMS* 23; Y Devuyst 'The European Union's institutional balance after the Treaty of Lisbon: "Community method" and "democratic deficit" reassessed' (2008) 39 *Georgetown Journal of International Law* 247; D Jančić 'Caveats from Karlsruhe and Berlin: whither democracy after Lisbon?' (2010) 46 *Columbia Journal of European Law* 337; and P Lindseth *Power and Legitimacy: Reconciling Europe and the Nation-State* (OUP 2010).

26 A Menon, S Weatherill 'Transnational legitimacy in a globalising world: how the European Union rescues its states' (2008) 31 *Western Union Politics* 397, 400.

27 Weiler *The Constitution of Europe* (n 23) 337.

28 For a thorough analysis of electoral rights in the European Union see J Shaw *The Transformation of Citizenship in the European Union: Electoral Rights and the Restructuring of Political Space* (CUP 2007).

a European rather than national mass media. As input legitimacy relies on public support[29] or 'public control with political equality',[30] then the lack of *demos*, and thus lack of EU statehood,[31] creates significant hurdles to democratic accountability.[32]

However, as again noted by Menon and Weatherill,[33] this lack of democratic accountability or input-legitimacy should not create a 'counsel of despair' over the legitimacy of the EU as it opens up the possibility of alternative routes to establish the EU's legitimacy.

This alternative route can be discovered in Scharpf's concept of output-orientated legitimisation (henceforth output legitimacy). Here the determination of the legitimacy of the EU is perceived through reference to its output and Majone suggests that, as the Union is a 'regulatory State', then that regulation is the route to measuring legitimacy.[34] Much of the commentary on output legitimacy has focused on the economic side of the EU and in particular the internal market,[35] equating legitimacy with efficiency that has provided observers with considerable flexibility but without structure or a model for determining the legitimacy of the EU. The key then to analysing the legitimacy of the EU is to provide a model through which the EU's outputs can be evaluated. Once that model has been formulated then it can be applied to areas of regulatory output either on a micro or macro level.

The policy area to be examined through the lens of this model is the free movement rights of third country nationals (TCNs). Those ruled in Bellamy and Castiglione's definition,[36] when considered in the context of the EU, include all the peoples resident in the EU. These are made up of citizens of the EU[37] and TCNs. The position of the individual has been enhanced with

---

29  P Ehin 'Competing models of EU legitimacy: the test of popular expectations' (2008) 46 *JCMS* 619 at 621.
30  Lord, Beetham 'Legitimising the EU' (n 17) 444.
31  D Grimm 'Does Europe need a constitution?' (1995) 1 *ELJ* 282. See also the German Federal Constitutional Court's judgments in *Manfred Brunner and Others v The European Union Treaty* [1994] 1 CMLR 57 and *Re Ratification of the Lisbon Treaty* [2010] 3 CMLR 13.
32  Much of the commentary on democratic accountability and the EU focuses on the comitology process in decision-making. See FE Bignani 'The democratic deficit in European Community rulemaking: a call for notice and comment in comitology' (1999) 40 *Harvard International Law Journal* 451; E Fisher 'The European Union in the age of accountability' (2004) 24 *OJLS* 495; GJ Brandsma, D Curtin and A Meijer 'How transparent are EU "comitology" committees in practice?' (2008) 14 *ELJ* 819; J Blom-Hansen, GJ Brandsma 'The EU comitology system: intergovernmental bargaining and deliberative supranationalism?' (2009) 47 JCMS 719 and S Peers, M Costa 'Accountability for delegated and implementing acts after the Treaty of Lisbon' (2012) 18 *ELJ* 427.
33  Menon, Weatherill 'Transnational legitimacy' (n 26) 401.
34  G Majone 'Europe's "Democratic deficit": the question of standards' (1998) 4 *ELJ* 5.
35  See Scharpf *Governing in Europe* (n 14); Menon and Weatherill 'Transnational legitimacy' (n 26) and J Neyer 'Justice, not democracy: legitimacy in the European Union' (2010) 48 *JCMS* 903.
36  Bellamy, Castiglione 'Legitimizing the Euro-"polity"' (n 19) 10.
37  Article 20(1) TFEU provides that '[e]very person holding the nationality of a Member State shall be a citizen of the Union'.

the creation of citizenship of the Union and the rights that are correspondingly granted especially for free movement. Citizens of the EU are able to determine the extent of their rights to freedom of movement in a relatively logical and straightforward manner as the principle of free movement of persons was enshrined in the EC Treaty as one of the four fundamental freedoms. The Union, however, is not populated only by EU citizens, with an estimated 12.5 million[38] TCNs legally resident in the Union in 1997 that had increased to 16.2 million[39] by 2003 and approximately 20.1 million by 2010.[40] These TCNs do not form a homogenous group as their population is made up of peoples with many different national identities spread throughout the EU. As such, the citizens of this so-called 28th state[41] are a disparate group culturally, socially and economically, with the majority emanating from developing countries. However, from the sheer weight of numbers, it can be considered that TCNs have an important effect on, and play an important part in, the economy of the Union. They work, provide services, purchase goods, pay taxes and in general participate fully in the Europe-wide economy.[42] Demographic trends indicate that the steady population growth in developing countries is paralleled by falling birth rates in Western Europe.[43] This demographic pattern suggests that to ensure economic growth is sustained by the necessary workforce in the medium to long term, an increasing level of migration from third countries into the EU will be required.[44] Therefore, the TCN population in the EU is likely to increase in real and proportional terms as it increases in importance economically.[45] With this growing importance of TCNs to the EU it would be reasonable to assume that their free movement rights[46] would

---

38  S Veil et al *Report of the High Level Panel on the Free Movement of Persons* (Office for Official Publications of the European Communities 1998) 10.

39  Europa 'Integration of third country nationals' 1 September 2005 MEMO/05/290 http://europa.eu/rapid/press-release_MEMO-05-290_en.htm 4. These are the most up to date figures before the new round of EU accessions on 1 May 2004 and 1 January 2007.

40  Commission Communication of the annual report on immigration and asylum COM(2011) 291 final 1.

41  R Cholewinski 'The rights of non-EC immigrant workers and their families in EC countries of employment: a case for integration' in J Dine, B Watt (eds) *Discrimination Law: Concepts, Limitations and Justifications* (Longman 1996) 134, 135.

42  See T Hoogenboom 'Integration into society and free movement of non-EC nationals' (1992) 3 *EJIL* 36.

43  F Dell'Olio 'Immigration after Nice: from "zero immigration" to market necessity' in A Arnull, D Wincott (eds) *Accountability and Legitimacy in the European Union* (OUP 2002) 469 and P Stalker 'Migration trends and migration policy in Europe' (2002) 40 *International Migration* 151.

44  See United Nations *Replacement Migration: Is it a Solution to Declining and Aging Populations?* ST/ESA/SER.A/206 (United Nations Publications 2000); Commission Communication on a Community immigration policy COM(2000) 757 final Annex 1; European Union Committee *A Community Immigration Policy* (HL 2000–2001, 64) [21]–[27]; Commission Communication on immigration, integration and employment COM(2003) 336 final 12; Commission Communication on a policy plan on legal migration COM(2005) 669 final 4.

45  C Gamberale *European Citizenship and Political Identity* (University of Sheffield unpublished thesis No 9481 of 1998) 284.

46  See P Oliver 'Non-Community nationals and the Treaty of Rome' (1985) 5 *YEL* 57; W Alexander 'Free movement of non-EC nationals: a review of the case law of the Court of Justice' (1992) 3 *EJIL* 53; M Cremona 'Citizens of third countries: movement and employment of migrant workers within the European Union' (1995) 2 *LIEI* 87; M Hedemann-Robinson 'Third-country nationals,

be clearly defined, readily accessible and simple. This is not the case.[47] Moreover, the extent of such rights has altered over time, as has their political perception by the Member States, with certain TCNs receiving more favoured status than others as the political momentum swings.

## 1.1 Structure of the book

Chapter 2 constructs the measurable benchmark, that of legal rationality, through which the free movement rights of TCNs will be analysed. Politics is concerned with power,[48] the capacity of social agents to maintain or transform their social environment and the creation of a regulated order for managing human conflict and interaction. Law can be considered to be 'the enterprise of subjecting human conduct to the governance of rules'[49] or 'the human attempt to establish social order as a way of regulating and managing human conflict'.[50] As such, law deals with human action and human social action, is the method used to enact the rules required to regulate this human social action and is the final outcome of the political process. From these definitions politics and law are inevitably intertwined with the laws and rules of the polity providing the positive evidence of the policy stance of the polity. Therefore, to assess the political legitimacy of the outputs of the EU the laws and rules of the polity as the final embodiment of its policy must be analysed. It is the legal rationality model that provides the criteria for scrutiny of the law consisting of three elements, each mutually exclusive and essential: formal; instrumental; and substantive rationality. Formal rationality requires legal doctrine to be free from contradiction and for rules to be the same for everyone; instrumental rationality requires these rules and legal doctrine to be action guiding whilst substantive rationality necessitates the norms underlying legal doctrine to be justified. They are mutually exclusive as they are comprised of different factors and have different ends, namely the avoidance of conflict between laws, guidance for action and the justification for such action. They are essential as the failure of a desideratum of rationality leads to a conclusion that the law is defective. Legal rationality enables the outputs of political endeavour, the substantive law in action, to be scrutinised for legitimacy utilising practical reason that then reflects on politics. The methodology provides a structured analysis that enables specific recommendations to be made for improvement and reform when areas of concern are identified.

It must be acknowledged, however, that there are limitations to the extent that rationality can measure or enhance the ideas of legitimacy. The first is inherent in the main premise of the theory, namely to assess political or output legitimacy

---

European Union citizenship, and free movement of persons: a time for bridges rather than divisions' (1997) 12 *YEL* 321.

47  See S Peers 'Towards equality: actual and potential rights of third-country nationals in the European Union' (1996) 33 *CMLRev* 7.

48  D Held *Models of Democracy* (2nd edn Polity Press 1996) 309.

49  LL Fuller *The Morality of Law* (Yale University Press 1969) 96.

50  D Beyleveld, R Brownsword *Law as a Moral Judgment* (Sweet & Maxwell 1986) 2.

rather than democratic or input legitimacy. This can be criticised as the application of the term legitimacy to those who rule appears to require some input from those who are ruled. It is conceded that this would be a credible criticism if the focal point was to legitimise the accountability of the political process to the people. However, the focal point here is the final output of the political process that are the laws and rules of the polity, thereby assessing the law against a measurable benchmark. That measurable benchmark is the concept of legal rationality but this leads to a further limitation. The notion of legal rationality can be viewed as an ideal, abstract and precise scientific tool for analysis in a hermetically sealed, politically neutral world. In reality, however, the political world is not neutral and policy formation is influenced by a range of factors. Therefore, once the legal rationality assessment has been conducted it must be located within the policy purpose, which acts in the same manner as the doctrine of objective justification in the European Court of Justice's (ECJ) free movement jurisprudence and only comes into play when there is a finding of legal irrationality.

Chapters 3 to 5 are devoted to the examination of the free movement rights of TCNs in three specific and discrete fields. First, the free movement rights within the EU treaties and implementing legislation will be considered in Chapter 3. This will mainly be based on the provisions of the Treaty on the Functioning of the European Union (TFEU),[51] which will include consideration of European citizenship and discrimination, with the implementing legislation focus being on the Citizenship Directive.[52] Secondly, in Chapter 4 the Area of Freedom Security and Justice (AFSJ) will be investigated with consideration of the free movement provisions in Title V of the TFEU and AFSJ implementing legislation. Thirdly, association agreements signed with third countries that contain free movement of persons provisions will be the focus in Chapter 5. This will include the Agreement on the European Economic Area,[53] the Ankara Agreement with Turkey[54] and key stabilisation and association agreements, along with their respective implementing legislation.

Chapter 6 takes the findings from the previous three chapters and analyses them through the measurable benchmark of legal rationality that was constructed in Chapter 2 before Chapter 7 summarises, draws conclusions and provides recommendations for the direction of the EU's policy on free movement rights for TCNs.

51 Consolidated Versions of the Treaty on European Union and the Treaty on the Functioning of the European Union, Council Document 6655/7/08 62.
52 European Parliament and Council Directive 2004/38/EC on the right of citizens of the Union and their family members to move and reside freely within the territory of the Member States [2004] OJ L158/77.
53 Agreement on the European Economic Area [1994] OJ L1.
54 Agreement Establishing an Association between the European Economic Community and Turkey [1973] OJ C113/2.

# 2 The theory of rationality and objective justification

## 2.1 Legal rationality as a tool for analysis

The justifications for using legal rationality as a tool for analysis first need to be explored. As such the origins of the concept of rationality will be discussed, followed by a detailed examination of the factors involved in the rationality analysis, before considering alternatives and the reasons for employing legal rationality.

### 2.1.1 Philosophical rationality

Rationality is an extremely complex idea that could be considered to mean all things to all men.[1] Rationality conveys a two-dimensional notion in philosophical terms. The first is the broad or general view that all philosophers aspire to using reason to provide force for arguments and placing special emphasis on man's rational capacities.[2] Rationalism in the strict or narrow sense has caused considerably more debate as it has conflicted directly with the ideas of empiricism. Rationalists believe in the possibility of a priori knowledge, where a proposition is a priori if its truth can be established independently of any sensory observation.[3] The acquisition of this knowledge is achieved by employing reason. To establish pure truth, free from experiences, emotions and sensory input, pure reason needed to be applied. This position was attacked by empiricists who questioned the isolation of facts and truth and developed the belief that all human knowledge derived from the senses.[4] Rationalism approached human knowledge from a purely objective stance whilst empiricists employed a purely subjective approach. Following Hume, philosophers have attempted to synthesise empiricism within rationality. Kant[5] attempted to achieve this with his synthetic a priori

1 See JA Simpson, ESC Weiner (prepared) *The Oxford English Dictionary Vol XIII* (2nd edn Clarendon Press 1989) 220 for a multifaceted definition.
2 J Cottingham *Rationalism* (Thoemmes Press 1984) 2.
3 ibid 7; see eg the philosophical stance of René Descartes collected together in ES Haldane, GTR Ross *The Philosophical Works of Descartes* (CUP 1911).
4 See eg D Hume *A Treatise of Human Nature* (LA Selby-Bigge (ed) 3rd edn OUP 1975).
5 I Kant *The Critique of Pure Reason* (N Kemp Smith (ed) The Macmillan Press Ltd 1929).

truth, involving a transcendental deduction, that every event is determined by a cause so long as it is related to the empirical world of phenomena. In more recent times the search has turned to the use of practical reason rather than pure reason. The acquisition of knowledge is still considered to be a good, not in itself but as knowledge of human action. Reason is used to establish belief rather than pure truth and is shaped by the evidential nature of empirical facts.[6] As Nozick[7] states, this is a fusion of concepts allowing a priori knowledge to be supported by evidential facts. Modern day philosophical rationality then looks at practical reasons for human action. This has allowed philosophers to develop rational principles from human action.[8]

### 2.1.2 Sociological rationality

Rationality as advanced in sociology has its origins in the works of Max Weber. It is unfortunate, however, that Weber's thoughts are complex, dense and at times appear to be contradictory. Brubaker[9] identifies Weber's social thought on rationality as a relational concept where a thing can only be rational from a certain point of view and this thing cannot contain inherent rationality. Rationality as a relational notion is then applied to an analysis of social structure. Thus, formal rationality is a matter of fact referring primarily to the calculability of means and procedures. The action of calculation requires facts to be without contradiction to avoid the possibility of an irrational situation. Substantive rationality, on the other hand, is a matter of value referring principally to the worth of ends or results.[10] As this concept is value-laden, substantive rationality must be underpinned by morality.

In *Economy and Society*,[11] Weber suggests that human social action may be orientated in four ways.[12] The first is 'instrumental rationality', determined by expectations as to the behaviour of objects and other humans and used as conditions for the attainment of an individual's rationally pursued and calculated ends. This then is action guiding and can be connected to but not incorporate formal rationality.[13] The second is 'value-rationality', determined by a conscious belief in an absolute value and its implementation independently of the prospects for its successful realisation. As with substantive rationality, value rationality is value-laden and is thus imbued with moral concerns. The third is 'affectual orientation',

---

6  R Nozick *The Nature of Rationality* (Princeton University Press 1993) 112.
7  ibid 108.
8  See A Gewirth *Reason and Morality* (University of Chicago Press 1978).
9  R Brubaker *The Limits of Rationality* (Allen & Unwin 1984) 35.
10  ibid 36.
11  M Weber *Economy and Society: An Outline of Interpretative Sociology* (G Roth, C Wittich (eds) University of California Press 1968) 24.
12  See J Elster 'Rationality, economy, and society' in S Turner (ed) *The Cambridge Companion to Max Weber* (CUP 2000) 21, 31.
13  Weber equated legal legitimacy with this concept of formal rationality in Weber *Economy and Society* (n 11) 34 but this has been criticised by R Grafstein 'The failure of Weber's conception of legitimacy: its causes and implications' (1981) 43 *The Journal of Politics* 456, 467.

determined by an individual's specific effects and states of feeling, and the fourth is 'traditional orientation', determined by ingrained habituation. These latter two orientations are not considered rational as they lie on the borderline, often on the wrong side, of meaningfully orientated action.[14] So, from Weber's ideas on rationality we can identify three specific types: formal; instrumental; and substantive (equating this with value rationality). Other sociologists have attempted to add other kinds[15] but Weber's three rationalities remain dominant.

### 2.1.3   Legal rationality

As already observed, law can be considered to be 'the enterprise of subjecting human conduct to the governance of rules'[16] or 'the human attempt to establish social order as a way of regulating and managing human conflict'.[17] As such it deals with human action and human social action. Nozick[18] states that 'to term something rational is to make an evaluation; its reasons are good ones (of a certain sort), and it meets the standards (of a certain sort) that it should meet'. Law is built on judgment rather than chance[19] and thus the evaluation of the legal enterprise must be grounded by practical reason.[20] Academic writers, with the supposed advent of a political, and thus legal, legitimation crisis[21] across the Western world, have begun to explore rationality.[22] An important participant in the debate is Professor Roger Brownsword,[23] with his use of rationality as an instrument of analysis of contract law under the heads of formal, instrumental and substantive[24] rationality that represent 'the standards that we judge that

---

14  Weber *Economy and Society* (n 11) 25.
15  See eg J Habermas *Communication and the Evolution of Society* (Heinemann Educational 1979); *The Theory of Communicative Action Volume One* (Polity Press 1984) in which Habermas identifies perceived gaps left by Weber and attempts to fill them in by developing the concept of communicative rationality from human communicative action. Although an attractive theory, cogently argued, it is submitted that this simply takes elements of formal and substantive rationality to apply them to an ideal speech situation.
16  LL Fuller *The Morality of Law* (Yale University Press 1969) 96.
17  D Beyleveld, R Brownsword *Law as a Moral Judgment* (Sweet & Maxwell 1986) 2.
18  Nozick *The Nature of Rationality* (n 6) 98.
19  R Brownsword *Contract Law: Themes for the Twenty-First Century* (2nd edn OUP 2006) 273.
20  See S Toddington *Rationality, Social Action and Moral Judgment* (Edinburgh University Press 1993) ch 6, in which he confirms the claim of John Finnis (J Finnis *Natural Law and Natural Rights* (Clarendon Press 1980) chs 1, 2) that the practically reasonable point of view is the required viewpoint for social science. He goes on to agree with Finnis that this practically reasonable point of view can be shown to be a moral point of view but dismisses, it is submitted correctly, Finnis's attempts to do so.
21  J Habermas *Legitimation Crisis* (Heineman 1976).
22  Weber considered rationality of law but only approached this from the position of formal rationality. See Weber *Economy and Society* (n 11) 656.
23  Brownsword *Contract Law* (n 19) ch 11; R Brownsword 'Towards a rational law of contract' in T Wilhelmsson (ed) *Perspectives of Critical Contract Law* (Dartmouth 1993) 241; J Adams, R Brownsword *Key Issues in Contract* (Butterworths 1995) ch 10.
24  See G Teubner 'Substantive and reflexive elements in modern law' (1983) 17 *Law & Society Review* 239, 252, where he proffers the alternative labels of internal, system and norm rationality.

[the law] should meet and the reasons that we count as good ones',[25] where the 'we' is society in general.[26]

The practical application of legal rationality could be considered to be somewhat vague and uncertain.[27] Irrationality in English law is one of the grounds for judicial review in administrative law and is often used interchangeably with unreasonableness, although it is only one aspect of unreasonableness. In the *GCHQ*[28] case an irrational decision was one 'so outrageous in its defiance of logic or of accepted moral standards that no sensible person who had applied his mind to the question to be decided could have arrived at it'. In *Ex parte Smith*[29] it was held to be one which was 'beyond the range of responses open to a reasonable decision-maker'. From these two judgments we can glean that irrationality involves the lack of logic, reason and comprehensible justification for a decision made by a body with legislative powers that operates on the human social order.

In the USA there is a constitutional doctrine that legislative action must be rationally related to the accomplishment of some legitimate state purpose.[30] As Sunstein[31] notes, this only expressly prohibits the exercise of raw political power, as the review does not attempt to establish a separate category of impermissible government ends. However, some justification of legislative action is required that must be of some public value. Sunstein[32] identifies that a public value justifying the exercise of government power 'acts as a check on the danger of factional tyranny' and 'that the role of government is not to implement or trade off pre-existing private interests, but to select public values'. Once again rationality would appear to require the justification of a legislative political decision based on some value-laden societal norm.

The EU has been slow to elaborate a deliberately labelled concept of rationality.[33] Article 296 TFEU requires Union acts to 'state the reasons on which they are based'. Article 263 TFEU allows the ECJ to review the legality of legislative acts with paragraph 2 containing the grounds for review: lack of competence; infringement of an essential procedural requirement; infringement

---

25 Brownsword *Contract Law* (n 19) 273.
26 See J Gardner, T Macklem 'Reasons' in J Coleman, S Shapiro (eds) *The Oxford Handbook of Jurisprudence and Philosophy of Law* (OUP 2002) 440, who have questioned the existence of legal rationality as a separate concept. Their position, however, originates firmly within the area of philosophical rationality, considering the broad view of providing reasons in a narrow context that is grounded within empiricism.
27 See eg H Collins *Regulating Contracts* (OUP 1999) ch 6 entitled 'Rationality of contractual behaviour', in which no definition or explanation of the term 'rationality' is provided.
28 *Council of Civil Service Unions and Others v Minister for the Civil Service* [1985] AC 374 (HL), 410 (Lord Diplock).
29 *R v Ministry of Defence, ex parte Smith and Grady* and *R v Admiralty Board of the Defence Council, ex parte Beckett and Lustig-Prean* [1996] QB 517 (CA), 554 (Sir Thomas Bingham MR).
30 RW Bennett '"Mere" rationality in constitutional law: judicial review and democratic theory' (1979) 67 *California Law Review* 1029.
31 CR Sunstein 'Naked preferences and the constitution' (1984) 84 *Columbia Law Review* 1689, 1697.
32 ibid.
33 Commission Communication on a Community immigration policy COM(2000) 757 final [3.4.2] in which the concept of rationality is equated with transparency.

of the treaties or of any rule of law relating to its application; or misuse of powers. Again a concept of legal rationality could be constructed that requires legislative political action to be justified by reasons[34] with correct procedural fairness, under the rule of law and without the abuse of power. General principles of EU law are also applied by the Court and can be considered to provide an equivalent of the societal moral norm apparent in both English and US reviews.

### 2.1.3.1   Formal rationality

Formal rationality states the requirement that legal doctrine must be free from contradiction and that the rules should be the same for everyone. At first blush this would appear to repeat a traditional view of legal scholarship in which laws should be interpreted consistently and the irreconcilable avoided, provided laws apply to all. However, elevating boundaries between different legal disciplines (eg between rules in EU and international law or criminal and civil law) will not satisfy the requirements of formal rationality as the two legal positions may contradict one another. Furthermore, tension between two principles may not be contradictory where they complement decision-making rather than contradict it.

Formal irrationality then may arise in one of three ways.[35] First, doctrinal positions from outside Union law may contradict those within. Secondly, different doctrines within European law may be contradictory. Thirdly, situations within an area of EU law may be inconsistent.

### 2.1.3.2   Instrumental rationality[36]

Instrumental rationality can be sub-divided into two types: generic; and, specific. Generic instrumental rationality requires legal doctrine to be capable of guiding action and so, as Fuller observes, certain minimum principles must be presupposed.[37] This so-called 'inner morality of law' is made up of legal rules that should be general, promulgated, prospective, clear, non-contradictory and relatively constant. They should not require the impossible and there should be congruence between the law as officially declared and the law as administered. The Fullerian principles can be categorised as procedural matters as they are not underpinned by a moral conception and can be equated with the concept of the

---

34  Joined Cases C–71, 155 & 271/95 *Belgium v Commission* [1997] ECR I–687, para 53: 'It must show clearly and unequivocally the reasoning of the institution which adopted the measure so as to inform the persons concerned of the justification of the measure adopted . . . '.
35  Brownsword *Contract Law* (n 19) 275.
36  The term is not used in the same way as the philosophical debate over instrumental reasons for means and ends. See for example J Raz 'The myth of instrumental rationality' (2005) 1(1) *Journal of Ethics and Social Philosophy* http://www.jesp.org/PDF/6863_Raz-vol-1-no-1-rev.pdf.
37  Fuller *The Morality of Law* (n 16) 39.

rule of law.[38] Brownsword and Beyleveld,[39] Harden and Lewis,[40] Allan,[41] Simmonds,[42] Boyle,[43] Murphy[44] and Smith[45] have attempted to construct a substantive conception of the rule of law, with Fuller's procedural requirements infused with moral values, a position Fuller himself advocated. It is submitted that moral values may be sufficient but not necessary requirements for instrumental rationality, for which instrumentality is the key.[46] As legal rationality requires all three elements for justification of legislative action,[47] the moral issues can be analysed under the substantive element of rationality, thereby removing controversy and confusion[48] from the debate on the rule of law.

It must be noted that the principle of non-contradiction plays an important role in instrumental rationality, as well as being the basis of formal rationality, when it is set alongside the principles of clarity, constancy and promulgation. Furthermore, the distinction between contradiction and tension observed in formal rationality is of no importance in instrumental rationality as a legal matter will be clear or unclear without considering why the problem exists.

Generic instrumental rationality is a necessary, if not always sufficient, condition of action-guidance and is complemented by specific instrumental rationality. Legal intervention, either by legislation or by the judiciary, must display an

---

38  See FA Hayek *The Road to Serfdom* (Routledge 1944) 54, with analysis by Lord Neuberger in DE Neuberger 'General, equal and certain: law reform today and tomorrow' (2012) 33 *Statute Law Review* 323.

39  Beyleveld, Brownsword *Law as a Moral Judgment* (n 17) 314.

40  I Harden, N Lewis *The Noble Lie: The British Constitution and The Rule of Law* (Hutchinson 1986); P Birkinshaw 'Supranationalism, the rule of law, and constitutionalism in the draft Union constitution' (2004) 23 *YEL* 199, 203.

41  TRS Allan *Constitutional Justice: A Liberal Theory of the Rule of Law* (OUP 2001).

42  NE Simmonds *Central Issues in Jurisprudence* (3rd edn Sweet & Maxwell 2011) and 'Straightforwardly false: the collapse of Kramer's positivism' (2004) 63 *CLJ* 98.

43  J Boyle 'Legal realism and the social contract: Fuller's public jurisprudence of form, private jurisprudence of substance' (1993) 78 *Cornell Law Review* 371.

44  C Murphy 'Lon Fuller and the moral value of the rule of law' (2005) 24 *Law & Philosophy* 239.

45  T Smith 'Neutrality isn't neutral: on the value-neutrality of the rule of law' (2011) 4 *Washington University Jurisprudence Review* 49.

46  For an interesting academic discussion on whether the rule of law is infused with morality see the debate between Simmonds *Central Issues in Jurisprudence* and 'Straightforwardly false' (n 42), who argues for the infusion and MH Kramer *In Defense of Legal Positivism* (OUP 1999) and MH Kramer 'On the moral status of the rule of law' (2004) 63 *CLJ* 65, who argues against. For the purposes of this book the question of the moral underpinning of the rule of law is negated by the necessary requirement of substantive legal rationality.

47  This is a similar position to that taken by L Pech 'A Union founded on the rule of law': meaning and reality of the rule of law as a constitutional principle of EU law' (2010) 6 *European Constitutional Law Review* 359, 367, where he considers the rule of law as a standalone principle accompanied by liberty, respect for fundamental rights and democracy.

48  See T Bingham 'The rule of law' (2007) 66 *CLJ* 67 at 75 and *The Rule of Law* (Allen Lane 2010) ch 7, who it is submitted wrongly includes the protection of fundamental human rights in his list of elements for the rule of law. See also R Gosalbo-Bono 'The significance of the rule of law and its implications for the European Union and the United States' (2010) 72 *University of Pittsburgh Law Review* 229, 231 and 360, where the rule of law is described in procedural terms before the addition of 'the principle of respect for universal human rights as laid down in those international instruments and conventions accepted by the international community', without any reasoning to this position.

informed and competent attempt at promoting given ends. Legislative officials must consider which legal technique, or combination of techniques, would be most effective to achieve the task. Furthermore, if the legal act is intended to facilitate then it should do so; if it is intended to provide protection then it should protect. Finally, legislative officials and the judiciary will employ different ideologies, based on personal or normative beliefs, when drafting and interpreting legal instruments.

### 2.1.3.3   *Substantive rationality*

Substantive rationality requires that all rules of law should be based on good reasons. It is here that we encounter again the ideas of practical reason. First, there is a requirement that the empirical facts sustaining particular legal doctrines should be plausible. Secondly, and moving beyond empirical plausibility, the principle underpinning the doctrine must itself be defensible as legitimate. However, this requirement that the substance of legal doctrine should be justified or legitimate can be interpreted in at least three ways.[49] First, law may be substantively rational if its norms are by and large accepted as justified and legitimate. Problems occur if legal norms are not considered legitimate and so either have to be amended or public perception adjusted. Law may certainly be used to mould public opinion over time but it is extremely difficult to change public perception swiftly, unless in an emergency situation, and thus the acceptance of the law. Secondly, law is substantively rational if norms follow the first requirement but can also be shown to be a consistent set. This interpretation raises the same problems as the first but even if legal norms are considered to be legitimate they may fail the requirement of consistency. However, Brownsword[50] suggests that so long as this inconsistency is only noted by legal theorists then the law can still be effective. Thirdly, to be substantively rational law does not depend upon acceptance. If, and only if, its norms form a justified and legitimate set may law display substantive rationality. Thus, problems occur on this view when the legal norms cannot be coherently defended and justified, regardless of their acceptance. The interpretations involving acceptance include a substantial subjective element. It is submitted that if one is attempting to base rules of law on good reasons, the dictates of practical reason require an entirely objective approach. Thus, the only logical meaning of substantive rationality is that of the third interpretation. However, the justification of norms underlying legal doctrine is by definition value-laden and as such suffused with moral considerations.

Four options are available to establish how the determination of the moral criterion of substantive rationality is to be achieved.[51] First, it could be left to be determined by the judiciary to interpret the law, without outside direction on the

---

49  Brownsword 'Towards a rational law of contract' (n 23) 250; Adams, Brownsword *Key Issues in Contract* (n 23) 338.
50  ibid.
51  Brownsword *Contract Law* (n 19) 289.

positions to be taken. Judges with their training in fairness and impartiality combined with their separation from the legislative, political process could be considered to be an august and ideal body of moral deliberation.[52] However, as Griffith[53] has argued, the judiciary's social and educational background combined with their age and awareness of their position tend to make most judges susceptible to the adoption of highly conservative attitudes when faced with hard cases.[54] Dworkin[55] has answered Griffith by claiming that a rights culture would change the social base of the legal profession and that a professional judiciary steeped in such a culture would consider cases on the basis of social justice rather than social status quo. This is adequate as a general social observation and ideal but, as Griffith points out, the 'principal function of the judiciary is to support the institutions of government as established by law'[56] or to uphold the rule of law.[57] As such the principal value of the judiciary specifically and the legal profession in general is to 'preserve and protect the existing order',[58] thereby perpetuating the social status quo. Without some form of external moral guidance it is difficult to see how the judiciary could provide a socially just moral criterion for substantive rationality.[59] The equivalent position to that being advanced here is the situation in the UK before the Human Rights Act 1998 (HRA 1998) came into force with the Court of Appeal's judgment in *Ex parte Smith*[60] epitomising the limitations without an external moral guide. Dickson[61] highlights a similar situation in the House of Lords since the HRA 1998 in regard to international human rights standards that are unincorporated in UK law.

That external guidance could be provided by the second option,[62] the standards of fairness already recognised, either expressly or impliedly, in positive legal doctrine. Thus, Sir John Laws suggests that by following common law precedent, UK judges are able to uphold fundamental constitutional rights without a written constitution.[63] A system of precedent may limit judicial idiosyncrasy,

52 See N Browne-Wilkinson 'The infiltration of a bill of rights' [1992] PL 397; J Laws 'Is the High Court the guardian of fundamental constitutional rights?' [1993] PL 59.
53 JAG Griffith *The Politics of the Judiciary* (5th edn Fontana 1997) ch 9.
54 Cf R Dworkin *Taking Rights Seriously* (Duckworth 1978) ch 4.
55 R Dworkin *A Matter of Principle* (Clarendon Press 1985) 28–31.
56 Griffith *The Politics of the Judiciary* (n 53) 343.
57 A constitution would provide the external moral guidelines to direct the moral guidelines for substantive rationality. See GF Mancini 'Politics and the judges – the European perspective' (1980) 43 MLR 1 for a consideration of European judicial law-making in the shadow of a constitution and without a practising background, especially in the Italian legal system.
58 Griffith *The Politics of the Judiciary* (n 53) 342.
59 Dworkin *A Matter of Principle* (n 55) 30, where he appears to be suggesting such a situation with a conservative judge having to apply a principle of political morality if it is included in a legislative act.
60 *Smith* (n 29). Cf *A and Others v Secretary of State for the Home Department* [2005] 2 AC 68 (HL), 129 (Lord Hoffmann).
61 B Dickson 'Safe in their hands? Britain's law lords and human rights' (2006) 26 *LS* 329, 335.
62 Brownsword *Contract Law* (n 19) 290.
63 Laws 'High Court' (n 52). For a critical analysis of Laws's position see JAG Griffiths 'The brave new world of Sir John Laws' (2000) 63 *MLR* 159. See also T Poole 'Questioning common law constitutionalism' (2005) 25 *LS* 142.

indeed conforming to the requirements of formal rationality by limiting contradictions within the law, but substantive rationality is designed to evaluate the defensibility of legal doctrine. Establishing that a rule or procedure through precedent is employed at a particular time cannot be the reason for justifying that legal doctrine – that is, doctrine cannot validate itself as legitimate. Furthermore, the development of strict precedent, combined with the apparent conservative nature of the judiciary, leads to a diminution in the standards of fairness in recognised legal doctrine as the use of existing doctrine as the standard of legitimacy would curtail any proposal for reform or revision. If this were to be modified to allow some small improvements to existing doctrine then this suggests that there is a form of legitimacy outside the existing doctrine that can recognise such improvements and the need for them.

A logical progression from the second option to determine the moral criterion would be to consider background constitutional values[64] as a third option. These constitutional values are normally predicated through a written constitution that will display six characteristic features:[65] normative supremacy; judicial review; longevity; rigidity; a two-pronged content;[66] and a high degree of abstraction and generality. When political power is exercised in accordance with such a constitution then that power is justified.[67] However, as Michelman[68] points out, Rawls adopts a contractual contractarian mode of political justification, which requires either an actual or hypothetical unanimous agreement of the governed for it to be legitimate.[69] If this can be obtained, which is highly dubious, then there is either a 'content-independent' justification or a 'content-based' justification.[70] Content-independence would either be on the basis of the standing in society of those who authored the constitution or because of a general acquiescence of society.[71] If such a justification was available then a constitution would be inflexibly rigid with no opportunities to reform, revise or amend the constitution to take into account changing societal values, and society would be apathetic to such changes in any case. Content-basis derives justification from the substantive content of the constitution[72] and this suffers from the content of the constitution

---

64  Brownsword *Contract Law* (n 19) 291.
65  A Marmor 'Are constitutions legitimate?' (2007) 20 *Canadian Journal of Law and Jurisprudence* 69, 70.
66  ibid 71. This content will consist of details of how a state is to be governed, outlining the powers of the ruling institutions and limitations on those powers, and the delineation of important rights of individuals resident in the state, especially citizenship and fundamental rights.
67  J Rawls *Political Liberalism* (expanded edn Columbia University Press 2005) 217: '. . . our exercise of political power is proper and hence justifiable only when it is exercised in accordance with a constitution the essentials of which all citizens may reasonably be expected to endorse in the light of principles and ideals acceptable to them as reasonable and rational'.
68  F Michelman 'Rawls on constitutionalism and constitutional law' in S Freeman *The Cambridge Companion to Rawls* (CUP 2002) 394, 395.
69  RE Barnett 'Constitutional legitimacy' (2003) 103 *Columbia Law Review* 111, 123.
70  FI Michelman 'Is the constitution a contract for legitimacy?' (2003) 8 *Review of Constitutional Studies* 101, 125 and JM Balkin 'Respect-worthy: Frank Michelman and the legitimate constitution' (2004) 39 *Tulsa Law Review* 485, 486.
71  Michelman 'Contract for legitimacy' (n 70) 127.
72  FI Michelman 'Ida's way: constructing the respect-worthy governmental system' (2003) 72 *Fordham Law Review* 345, 358.

being employed to justify the constitution or doctrine validating itself as legitimate, an illegitimate action. Finally, as already alluded to, constitutions normally contain mechanisms for reform, revision or amendment and, as with the second option above, this indicates that there is a form of legitimacy outside the constitution that identifies the need for the changes and the content.

The fourth option is to invoke the standards of fairness recognised by the community.[73] This option raises two questions. What are the 'standards of fairness' and within which community are they to be recognised? Standards of fairness require some form of definitional elucidation. It is submitted that as the community is an arena for human social action then this is achieved through philosophical analysis using practical reason. As fairness is value-laden then the standards envisaged must be moral values[74] that are universal in nature, developed from a transcendental deduction, that can themselves be rationally justified and be grounded in practical reason. A modern neo-Kantian moral theory that answers these requirements is that advanced by Gewirth.[75] It is outside the scope of this volume to consider his theory in depth[76] but he argues from human action to a supreme principle of morality that he calls the principle of generic consistency (PGC). In essence, this states that on pain of contradiction of being a human being, every human being must act in accordance with the generic rights of other human beings as well as themselves, where the generic rights are freedom and wellbeing. As these generic rights are held equally by all human beings then they are human rights.[77] It is submitted that, even if Gewirth's argument to the PGC is disputed, the moral concept that underpins the principle of fairness is one that is embodied by the concept of human rights. Furthermore, if Gewirth's argument[78] of a supreme principle of morality derived from human action by practical reason is employed, then legal doctrine may be rationally justified using the PGC as the basis of human rights. The second question involving the determination of the community is as difficult as the first. Human rights are considered to be universal and so one could posit the notion that the community encompasses the whole of human kind. However, where legal doctrine is territorially delineated then it is logical to presume that the community will be likewise. Thus, EU law will be confined to the territory of the current 27 Member States. External agreements may extend this community reach in certain defined areas such as trade and immigration.

73 Brownsword *Contract Law* (n 19) 292.
74 See Toddington *Rationality* (n 20), where it is established that practical reason must be viewed from the moral point of view when used to analyse human social action.
75 Gewirth *Reason and Morality* (n 8).
76 See E Regis Jr (ed) *Gewirth's Ethical Rationalism: Critical Essays with a Reply by Alan Gewirth* (University of Chicago Press 1984); D Beyleveld *The Dialectical Necessity of Morality: An Analysis and Defence of Alan Gewirth's Argument to the Principle of Generic Consistency* (University of Chicago Press 1991).
77 A Gewirth *The Community of Rights* (University of Chicago Press 1986) ch 1.
78 Gewirth *Reason and Morality* (n 8).

*2.1.3.4   Reflexive rationality*

It must be queried, following the analysis of formal, instrumental and substantive rationality, whether any other type of legal rationality exists. Gunther Teubner[79] has argued that as there is scepticism over substantive rationality and a lack of desire for formal rationality then reflexive rationality may prevail. Reflexive rationality is used interchangeably by Teubner with procedural rationality[80] (or justice) and, according to John Rawls,[81] there are three types of procedural justice: pure; perfect; and imperfect. Pure procedural justice goes further than the ideas of formal rationality that rules are the same for all, so that the rules are not obviously for or against anyone. This is achieved by the ideas of equality of opportunity, chance or risk. However, pure procedural justice is not driven by any independent conception of a just outcome. Perfect and imperfect procedural justice concepts, on the other hand, are driven by the issue of outcomes. Perfect procedural justice deals with procedure guaranteed to generate a substantive, just outcome, and imperfect procedural justice with procedures that are blameworthy. A weak version of reflexive rationality can be equated with pure procedural justice and as there are no conceptions of substantively just outcomes as to the design of procedural conditions, then this topples into formal rationality. A strong version will be equated with the twin concepts of perfect and imperfect procedural justice. An independent theory of just outcomes will drive procedural conditions in a certain way, thus collapsing strong reflexive rationality into substantive rationality. As reflexive rationality attempts to chart a middle way between formal and substantive rationality it soon becomes apparent that it fails the very test of rationality that it attempts to resolve.

## 2.2   Legal rationality within the context of policy

The legal rationality tool that has been constructed provides an abstract construct through which to view policy. However, this precise scientific tool suffers from being something of a blunt instrument without some form of anchorage to policy considerations. To ensure that the legal rationality tool can be utilised to provide useful critical analysis, the findings of the critique must be set within the context of policy associated with the legal instruments examined. The aim is principally to determine whether the purposes of the policy[82] can 'objectively justify' any findings of legal irrationality so that there is political legitimacy but, as Tridimas states, the concept of objective justification is 'not easy to define in the abstract'.[83] As Spaventa notes, this objective justification is actually an objective reason for policy or a rule, 'an aim which is consistent with the values enshrined

---

79  Teubner 'Substantive and reflexive' (n 24).
80  Brownsword 'Towards a rational law of contract' (n 23) 242.
81  J Rawls *A Theory of Justice* (2nd edn OUP 1999) ch 14.
82  T Tridimas *The General Principles of EU Law* (2nd edn OUP 2006) 83.
83  ibid.

in a given system, that the rule seeks to pursue and which cannot be pursued otherwise than through that rule'.[84]

This principle of objective justification has been developed principally through the case law of the CJEU in three specific areas: discrimination; free movement; and competition. In discrimination law the ECJ in *Bilka-Kaufhaus*[85] determined that conduct that was discriminatory, albeit the indirect version could be excused by 'objectively justified factors which are unrelated to discrimination'. *Bilka-Kaufhaus*'s discrimination was on the basis of sex but the principle of objective justification has been recognised for other grounds of discrimination, such as age.[86] For free movement of persons, a similar statement as that in the *Bilka-Kaufhaus* case has been employed[87] but in cases involving free movement of goods different terminology is used, albeit with the same impact.[88] For the field of competition law objective justification is employed when analysing abuse of a dominant position under Article 102 TFEU but limiting objective justifications to economic rationales,[89] in contrast to the stance in the other two policy areas where objective justifications are linked to national interests of a 'non-economic character'.[90] For all three fields of Union law if the objective justification for the policy stance is deemed legitimate then it must be rigorously viewed through the perspective of proportionality.[91] This means that the conduct of the state must correspond to a real need on the part of the state, 'are appropriate with a view to achieving the objectives pursued and are necessary to that end'[92] or, as the ECJ stated in *Mangold*, 'the means used to achieve that legitimate objective are "appropriate and necessary"'.[93] As such the principle of proportionality contains four elements, two of which are tests.[94] The first element is the examination of the act to ensure that it pursues a legitimate aim. Second is the test of suitability, which 'requires that the means employed by a measure be suitable for, or reasonably likely, to achieve an interest or objective worthy of legal protection'.[95] The

84 E Spaventa 'On discrimination and the theory of mandatory requirements' (2000) 3 *CYELS* 457, 467.
85 Case 170/84 *Bilka-Kaufhaus GmbH v Weber von Hartz* [1986] ECR 1607 para 30.
86 Case C–144/04 *Werner Mangold v Rüdiger Helm* [2005] ECR I–9981 para 61.
87 Among others see Case C–237/94 *John O'Flynn v Adjudication Officer* [1996] ECR I–2617 para 20; Case C–274/96 *Criminal proceedings against Horst Otto Bickel and Ulrich Franz* [1998] ECR I–7637 para 27; and Case C–138/02 *Brian Francis Collins v Secretary of State for Work and Pensions* [2004] ECR I–2703 para 66. For a rare academic comment on objective justification under the free movement of persons see M Dougan 'Cross-border educational mobility and the exportation of student financial assistance' (2008) 33 *ELR* 723, 733.
88 Case 120/78 *Rewe-Zentral AG v Bundesmonopolverwaltung für Branntwein* [1979] ECR 649 para 8.
89 Case C–95/04P *British Airways plc v Commission* [2007] ECR I–2331 para 69.
90 A Albors-Llorens 'The role of objective justification and efficiencies in the application of Article 82 EC' (2007) 44 *CMLRev* 1727, 1734.
91 For a highly comprehensive study of the principle see A Barak *Proportionality: Constitutional Rights and their Limitations* (CUP 2012).
92 *Bilka* (n 85) para 36.
93 *Mangold* (n 86) para 62.
94 M Klatt, M Meister *The Constitutional Structure of Proportionality* (OUP 2012) 8.
95 E Rousseva 'The concept of "objective justification" of an abuse of a dominant position: can it help to modernise the analysis under Article 82 EC?' (2006) 2(2) *CompLRev* 27, 33.

third element is the test of necessity, which 'seeks to establish whether the measure is necessary to achieve the objective and whether there are less restrictive means capable of producing the same result'.[96] The final element is a balancing exercise, proportionality *stricto sensu* as described by Barak,[97] to determine if the act represents a beneficial gain 'when the reduction on employment of rights is weighed against the level of realisation of the aim'.[98] This then is a justificatory[99] analysis requiring the policy-maker to 'engage in theoretically informed practical reasoning'[100] that is underpinned by substantive justification.[101] This then corresponds to the requirements of substantive rationality such that the balancing exercise provides a form of hierarchical rights analysis with a moral, value-laden foundation of human rights.[102]

With the theoretical aspects of objective justification set out it can now be considered how the concept fits with legal rationality. There has been considerable academic discussion in the UK over the intensity of review of the proportionality test, especially over the question of deference of the judiciary to legislative intent[103] and the difference between the UK and European, be that ECJ or ECtHR, approach.[104] It could be assumed that as theory utilised in this book applies to EU law then the latter approach is to be preferred. However, the theory constructed is one that can be applied not just to EU law but also to any area of policy formation, and the principle of proportionality is being applied in a general rather than a judicial manner. As such, questions of deference and the absolute nature of rights can be set aside to enable a variable intensity of review[105] to be employed when fitting objective justification to the different elements of legal rationality. That variable intensity of review can be better

---

96  ibid.
97  Barak *Proportionality* (n 91) 340.
98  Klatt, Meister *Constitutional Structure* (n 94) 8.
99  M Cohen-Eliya, I Porat 'Proportionality and the culture of justification' (2011) 59 *American Journal of Comparative Law* 463.
100 M Kumm 'Political liberalism and the structures of rights: on the place and limits of the proportionality requirement' in G Pavlakos (ed) *Law, Rights and Discourse: The Legal Philosophy of Robert Alexy* (Hart Publishing 2007) 131, 145.
101 ibid.
102 This then counters the argument put forward by Tsakyakis that proportionality undermines human rights – see S Tsakyrakis 'Proportionality: an assault on human rights?' (2009) 7 *International Journal of Constitutional Law* 468 and the contrary position in K Möller 'Proportionality: challenging the critics' (2012) 10 *International Journal of Constitutional Law* 709.
103 For example on the side of deference see RA Edwards 'Judicial deference under the Human Rights Act' (2002) 65 *MLR* 859; M Taggart 'Proportionality, deference, Wednesbury' (2008) *NZLR* 423; AL Young 'In defence of due deference' (2009) 72 *MLR* 554; A Kavanagh 'Defending deference in public law and constitutional theory' (2010) 126 *LQR* 222. Against judicial deference see TRS Allan 'Human rights and judicial review: a critique of "due deference"' (2006) 65 *CLJ* 671; TRS Allan 'Deference, defiance, and doctrine: defining the limits of judicial review' (2010) 60 *University of Toronto Law Journal* 41; TRS Allan 'Judicial deference and judicial review: legal doctrine and legal theory' (2011) 127 *LQR* 96.
104 J Rivers 'Proportionality and variable intensity review' (2006) 65 *CLJ* 174, 180 for the UK approach and 182 for the European one.
105 For alternative approaches see ibid 202 and C Chan 'Proportionality and invariable baseline intensity of review' (2013) 33 *LS* 1, 16.

equated to the three levels model of review[106] to be found in US judicial review, rather than the sliding scale of models equated with Europe. Thus, any findings of formal irrationality will be value-neutral and so the balancing exercise used in the proportionality analysis can be equated to the 'rational basis test', allowing a wide scope of discretion[107] and will enable most good policy factors to be claimed as justification with different factors being arranged in order of importance as the polity determines. Instrumental rationality is likewise value-neutral but specific instrumental rationality contains within it the two tests of suitability and necessity in the principle of proportionality and so a more anxious scrutiny in the balancing exercise of the principle of proportionality, that can be equated to the US 'intermediate scrutiny test',[108] will be required. Finally, findings of substantive irrationality will be difficult to justify objectively as substantive rationality is value-laden with an underlying moral claim to the protection of human rights, a high standard of scrutiny equivalent to the US 'strict scrutiny test'.[109] As such, any justification for findings of substantive irrationality would need to be based on human rights standards.

## 2.3  Conclusions

The argument presented provides for a new method of analysing the rationality of policy from the EU. Starting from Scharpf's seminal theory of input and output legitimacy, it was found that input legitimacy, or democratic accountability as traditionally viewed through the lens of the nation-state model, was difficult to establish. Much of the academic commentary has been viciously circular, arguing for nation-state solutions from the starting point of a nation-state model, and failing to address the supranational, and at times intergovernmental, nature of the EU. However, output legitimacy, when considering the legal outputs of political action through the lens of legal rationality, could it is argued provide a measurable benchmark to evaluate the political legitimacy of the EU polity within a specific policy area. The unprocessed standard of legal rationality, however, is idealistic and sterile until set within the policy context of the polity. That policy context could objectively justify the finding of irrationality so long as it satisfies the requirements of the principle of proportionality. This is the reality check that brings the model into the real political world.

The question of the legitimacy of migration policy has recently been examined by Boswell[110] through four criteria that she claims are the vital elements of

---

106  S Greer '"Balancing" and the European Court of Human Rights: a contribution to the Habermas-Alexy debate' (2004) 63 *CLJ* 412, 432 suggests the introduction of a US style intermediate standard of review. See JH Gerards 'Intensity of judicial review in equal treatment cases' (2004) 51 *NILR* 135, 144.
107  Gerards 'Intensity' (n 106) 145.
108  ibid 147.
109  ibid 146.
110  C Boswell 'Theorizing migration policy: is there a third way?' (2007) 41 *International Migration Review* 75. The clear establishment of elements of legitimacy have been reconsidered, although

legitimacy: fairness; accumulation of wealth; security; and institutional legitimacy. This is a welcome development but it is submitted the analysis is fundamentally flawed. It can be observed that two of the criteria can be equated with two of the legal rationality *desiderata*, namely fairness with substantive legitimacy and institutional legitimacy with institutional rationality. However, the other two criteria of accumulation of wealth and security are not elements of legitimacy but are policy aims that are to be taken into consideration when setting rationality findings within a policy framework. The result is to confuse the basis of the assessment and to amalgamate policy aims into the legitimacy analysis under the cover of a legitimacy description.

not necessarily in a particularly clear way, by J Chia 'Immigration and its imperatives' (2009) 15 *ELJ* 683.

# 3 Free movement rights under the treaties and implementing legislation

To be capable of being claimed by an individual a right must be clearly identifiable, not only in its position within a legislative instrument but also who can claim it and its extent. The right to free movement is no exception to this rule. Chapter 1 established the economic importance of third country nationals (TCNs) to the EU, now and in the future, and as the free movement of persons is an economic right then it would be logical to presume that the right should apply to TCNs on an equal footing to that of nationals of Member States. Indeed as TCNs have already moved from a third country to a Member State in the EU then it is highly likely that they would be more willing to exercise a right of free movement within the EU than nationals of Member States because they are not as constrained by social, cultural or familial ties. Therefore it would be reasonable to presume that the free movement provisions of the EU Treaties or their implementing legislation should either outline the specific free movement rights for TCNs or should determine that the free movement provisions apply to both TCNs and Member State nationals. It is further reasonable to presume that such important rights should be clearly defined, readily accessible and simple.

This chapter outlines the objectives and principles of the EU applicable to free movement of persons before examining the concepts of discrimination, citizenship and the three free movement provisions of workers, establishment and services, and how they apply to TCNs. Chapter 4 will focus on the specific rights contained with the Area of Freedom, Security and Justice (AFSJ).

## 3.1 Objectives of the European Union

The policies or activities of the Union are set out in Article 3 TEU with Article 3(2) mandating the Union to 'offer its citizens an area of freedom, security and justice without internal frontiers, in which the free movement of persons is ensured in conjunction with appropriate measures with respect to external border controls, asylum, immigration', whilst Article 3(3) requires the Union 'to establish an internal market'. These objectives, introduced by the Lisbon Treaty, although similar to those in the EC Treaty, are somewhat different to the equivalent provisions in the EC Treaty that were in operation at the time of the development of most of the legal issues that will be analysed in this chapter.

The comparable provision to Article 3(3) TEU was Article 3(1)(c) EC that required the creation of 'an internal market characterised by the abolition, as between Member States, of obstacles to the free movement of . . . persons . . .'. This policy was predominantly economic in nature and as most TCNs, legally resident in the Union, were economically active persons then their reasonable expectations would have been for the EU to remove barriers to their own free movement within the Union. However, these expectations had to be considered in the light of the policy that was contained in Article 3(1)(d) EC that required 'measures concerning the entry and residence of persons as provided for in Title IV' to be enacted.

There is thus a subtle reordering of objectives in the new provisions with free movement of persons being tied to the AFSJ that is only offered to Union citizens rather than the internal market. Indeed, the aims and objectives of the internal market that are set out further in Article 3(3) TEU do not mention free movement of persons whatsoever. However, although the objectives provisions appear to have posited the free movement of persons as a citizenship right rather than an economic right, the detail of Article 26 TFEU promotes the previous posture of the EC Treaty.

Article 14 EC, inserted by the Single European Act 1986 (SEA), introduced the concept of the internal market and prescribed that '[t]he Community shall adopt measures with the aim of progressively establishing the internal market over a period expiring on 31 December 1992 . . . without prejudice to the other provisions of this Treaty'. This has been reworked by the Lisbon Treaty so that Article 26(1) TFEU states that '[t]he Union shall adopt measures with the aim of establishing or ensuring the functioning of the internal market, in accordance with the relevant provisions of the Treaties'. Article 26(2) TFEU defines the internal market as 'an area without internal frontiers in which the free movement of . . . persons . . . is ensured in accordance with the provisions of the Treaties'. Article 14 EC (now Article 26 TFEU) sat in juxtaposition with ex-Article 8 EEC's requirement for the progressive establishment of the common market by 1969.[1] Wyatt and Dashwood[2] suggested that 'common market' was just a term of art with 'internal market' being a more specific notion having a clearly defined objective. This objective of an internal market in Article 26(2) TFEU contains two elements.[3] The first is a measurable objective for the Union institutions of procuring the abolition of all frontier controls for intra-Member State movement of, inter alia, persons. The second, the realisation of the four freedoms, is more ethereal as the project has no immediate end. Indeed, Article 26(1) TFEU suggests that it is still not certain that an internal market has actually been established.

---

1  The Treaty of Amsterdam introduced a third paragraph to art 14 that reads '[t]he Council, acting by qualified majority voting on a proposal from the Commission, shall determine the guidelines and conditions necessary to ensure balanced progress in all the sectors concerned'. These provisions were contained in ex-art 7b EEC, repealed by the Treaty of Amsterdam.

2  AM Arnull, AA Dashwood, M Dougan, MG Ross, E Spaventa and DA Wyatt *Wyatt & Dashwood's European Union Law* (5th edn Sweet & Maxwell 2006) 921.

3  ibid 920.

The literal, and wide, reading of Article 26(2) TFEU implies the abolition of all frontier controls on all persons, irrespective of nationality,[4] although this is without prejudice to the other provisions of the treaties. The narrow view therefore would be that it must be interpreted in accordance with the EU 'free movement of persons' provisions and would only apply to migrant Member State nationals. Wyatt and Dashwood[5] suggest that the wider interpretation is to be preferred as this not only corresponds to the letter of Article 26(2) TFEU but 'is also necessary for the *effet utile* of the removal of internal frontiers since, if controls are retained for any categories of travellers, they are liable to be applied to all'. It would appear, therefore, if this supposition is correct, that Article 26 TFEU may provide a route for free movement rights across internal EU borders for all persons, including TCNs.

However, it must be determined what legal effects Article 26 TFEU has on both the EU institutions and Member States, thereby establishing the ability of individuals to prosecute a legal action. The Declaration on Article 14 EC, annexed to the Final Act of the SEA (but not included in any other revised treaties), appeared to suggest that the commitment to the date in the provision was purely political. It stated that: '[t]he Conference wishes . . . to express its firm political will to take before 1 January 1993 the decisions necessary to complete the internal market . . .' and '[s]etting the date of 31 December 1992 does not create an automatic legal effect'.

Wyatt and Dashwood[6] suggested that for EU institutions the Declaration had no effect on their obligations,[7] as declarations were not legally binding. The expression 'does not create an automatic legal effect' was addressed to the effects of Article 26 TFEU if the necessary implementing legislation had not been enacted by 31 December 1992. The ECJ in *Reyners*[8] held that a similar provision in ex-Article 52 EEC (now Article 49 TFEU) left the obligation intact beyond the period provided for its fulfilment as the progression required in ex-Article 52 EEC had not been adhered to. This was extended in the case of *van Binsbergen*,[9] where the Court held that ex-Article 59 EEC (now Article 54 TFEU) became unconditional following the expiry of the transition period and thus became directly effective. As such the mandatory obligation in ex-Article 14(1) EC must

---

4 See AG Toth 'The legal effects of the protocols relating to the United Kingdom, Ireland and Denmark' in T Heukels, N Blokker and M Brus (eds) *The European Union After Amsterdam* (Kluwer Law International 1998) 227, 249.

5 Arnull *Wyatt & Dashwood's* (n 2) 921.

6 ibid 922.

7 To determine if an action could be brought against either the Commission or Council under art 232 EC for failure to act, then the measures had to be capable of being defined with such precision as to be identified individually, and could be adopted in accordance with art 233 EC (Case 13/83 *European Parliament v Council* [1985] ECR 1513 paras 66–69). Where a provision provided a Community institution with discretionary power over the content of any implementing measures that required policy choices not included in the provision, then the subject-matter and nature of the provision could not be determined with such a sufficient degree of precision.

8 Case 2/74 *Reyners v Belgium* [1974] ECR 631 para 27.

9 Case 33/74 *Johannes Henricus Maria van Binsbergen v Bestuur van de Bedrijfsvereniging voor de Metaalnijverheid* [1974] ECR 1299 paras 24–27.

be given its plain and ordinary meaning, although the question of direct effect is more complex.

Article 26(2) TFEU contains two elements. The first provides a positive obligation to abolish internal frontier controls that is mandatory and precise. However, to abolish frontier controls for free movement of persons requires a considerable range of measures on asylum, immigration, visas, police matters, TCN rights etc to be implemented. Although, therefore, the original measure was mandatory, the implementing or flanking measures required to regulate it involve policy choices and the use of discretionary power. Furthermore, the second element of Article 26(2) TFEU ensuring the four freedoms is too general in its substance for the Court to be able to determine with precision the necessary legislative steps required.

Legal effects on the Member States need to be ascertained by determining whether Article 26 TFEU is capable of direct effect. For an individual to commence legal proceedings in a national court to enforce an individual right granted by a provision, that provision must be sufficiently clear, precise and unconditional.[10] From the foregoing discussion it is clear that to abolish internal frontiers and to ensure the four freedoms, implementing legislation will be required and until that is in place then the provision will remain conditional, thereby distinguishing ex-Article 59 EEC that *van Binsbergen* had found to have direct effect, and ex-Article 14(1) EC. Furthermore, it appears that this is consistent with the Declaration on Article 14 EC in which the Member States did not intend to be legally bound by the provision if implementing legislation had not been enacted by 31 December 1992. The Commission held the view for a period of time that, following 31 December 1992, the maintenance of internal frontier controls was absolutely prohibited.[11] As Wyatt and Dashwood[12] point out, this was an over-simplified position. Domestic border controls on free movement of persons could legitimately remain in place if they were required to safeguard interests sanctioned by the EU treaties. However, where measures had been implemented then Article 26 TFEU, Article 4(3) TEU and the principle of proportionality, would only permit retention of border controls if they were truly indispensable after 1 January 1993 and leaving the burden of proof on Member States to justify the retention of these controls.[13]

In *Wijsenbeek*[14] the ECJ was asked to consider this situation when a Dutch national refused to show a passport, or any other means of identification, on re-entry into Holland. Mr Wijsenbeek claimed that after 1 January 1993 he had a directly effective right of free movement across the EU's internal borders and any frontier controls were prohibited. The Court rejected his claim and held that ex-Article 14 EC 'cannot be interpreted as meaning that, in the absence of measures

---

10  See Case 41/74 *Yvonne van Duyn v Home Office* [1974] ECR 1337.
11  See the Commission's Communication of 18 May 1992 SEC(92) 877 final.
12  Arnull *Wyatt & Dashwood's* (n 2) 925.
13  ibid 926.
14  Case C–378/97 *Criminal proceedings against Florus Ariël Wijsenbeek* [1999] ECR I–6207; noted in
    D Martin 'Case note' (2000) 2 *EJML* 101.

adopted by the Council before 31 December 1992 requiring the Member States to abolish controls of persons at the internal frontiers of the Community, that obligation arises from expiry of that period'.[15] Such an obligation would require the full harmonisation of the Member States' laws in this area. The Court went on to emphasise that even if there was 'an unconditional right to move freely within the territory of the Member States, the Member States retained the right to carry out identity checks at the internal frontiers of the Community, requiring persons to present a valid identity card or passport . . . in order to be able to establish whether the person concerned is a national of a Member State, thus having the right to move freely within the territory of the Member States, or a national of a non-member country, not having that right'.[16] *Wijsenbeek* extinguished the possibility of TCNs being able to claim free movement rights through Article 26 TFEU.

Regulation 562/2006/EC[17] provides the legislation abolishing internal border controls. In Article 20 persons are authorised, whatever their nationality, to cross the internal borders of the EU at any point without checks being carried out. This does not provide a right of free movement across borders for everybody, including TCNs, but merely the abolition of checks at the internal borders. This is reinforced by recital 5, providing that these rules on the movement of persons across borders do not call into question or affect free movement rights of EU citizens and their family members, and free movement rights of TCNs and family members under association agreements. Furthermore, the legal base is the AFSJ rather than Article 26 TFEU, and so Chapter 4 will carry a more in depth analysis of the Regulation. However, it is submitted that these provisions do not create, nor extend, any free movement rights for TCNs. The rights provided are more subtle and are only directed at removing checks at the internal frontiers. As such, to claim rights of free movement TCNs will have to attempt either to bring themselves within the citizenship provisions, the original economic free movement rights, or through the AFSJ.

## 3.2 The principle of non-discrimination[18]

The principle of non-discrimination has been included in the concept of free movement since the original Treaty of Rome in 1957. The specific enunciations of this general notion will be considered below and so this section is designed to consider the general proposition and how it applies to free movement of TCNs as a standalone concept. The position today of TCNs is that there are a significant number who are legally resident in the EU, living and working side by side

---

15  ibid para 40.
16  ibid para 43.
17  European Parliament and Council Regulation 562/2006/EC establishing a Community Code on the rules governing the movement of persons across borders (Schengen Borders Code) [2006] OJ L105/1 (SBC).
18  See in particular E Ellis *EU Anti-Discrimination Law* (OUP 2005) for a comprehensive analysis of the principle of non-discrimination.

with nationals of Member States. The integration[19] of TCNs 'has gained increasing importance on the European agenda in recent years'[20] and Cholewinski advocates integration in order to achieve social justice, economic efficiency with a successful internal market and a vital element in the elimination of racial and ethnic discrimination.[21] One of the key ways of integrating TCNs into society, or at least those resident for a long period of time, would be to ensure TCNs were able to enforce rights of non-discrimination, particularly as they apply to free movement.

The Lisbon Treaty repositioned the provisions on non-discrimination from Part One of the EC Treaty on Principles into Part Two of the TFEU entitled 'Non-Discrimination and Citizenship of the Union'. The juxtapositioning of citizenship and non-discrimination in a specific part of the TFEU is a subtle attempt to move the right to non-discrimination from a general human rights based principle to a citizenship principle that is only applicable to Union citizens. However, even though there is an attempt to conflate the two principles into a general principle, the specific principles retain their independence.

Article 18 TFEU prohibits discrimination on the grounds of nationality but is 'merely a specific enunciation of the general principle of equality'.[22] It prohibits both direct and indirect discrimination,[23] although it is not absolute. The material scope of Article 18 TFEU must be 'without prejudice to any special provisions contained [in the Treaties]' and has been interpreted by the ECJ as applying 'independently only to situations governed by EU law in regard to which the Treaty lays down no specific rules prohibiting discrimination'.[24] The personal scope of Article 18 TFEU is such that the subject matter of the dispute must be brought 'within the scope of application of [the Treaties]'. In *Cowan*[25] the ECJ held that '[w]hen [EU] law guarantees a natural person the freedom to go to another Member State the protection of that person from harm in the Member State in question, on the same basis as that of nationals and persons residing there, is a corollary of that freedom of movement'.[26] Thus a national provision that refused criminal injury compensation to a national of another Member State who had exercised his free movement right was incompatible with Article 18

---

19  Commission Communication on immigration, integration and employment COM(2003) 336 final.
20  Commission Communication on a common agenda for integration: framework for the integration of third-country nationals in the European Union COM(2005) 389 final 3.
21  R Cholewinski 'The rights of non-EC immigrant workers and their families in EC countries of employment: a case for integration' in J Dine, B Watt *Discrimination Law: Concepts, Limitations and Justifications* (Longman 1996) 134, 136.
22  Case 810/79 *Peter Überschär v Bundesversicherungsanstalt für Angestellte* [1980] ECR 2747 para 16.
23  Case C–237/94 *John O'Flynn v Adjudication Officer* [1996] ECR I–2617 and Case C–274/96 *Criminal proceedings against Horst Otto Bickel and Ulrich Franz* [1998] ECR I–7637; noted in D Martin 'Case note' (1999) 1 *EJML* 149; M Bulterman 'Case note' (1999) 36 *CMLRev* 1325. For a recent UK case involving indirect discrimination see *Secretary of State for Work and Pensions v Carlos Bobezes* [2005] 3 All ER 497 (CA).
24  Case C–379/92 *Peralta* [1994] ECR I–3453 para 18.
25  Case 186/87 *Ian William Cowan v Le Trésor Public* [1989] ECR 195.
26  ibid para 17.

TFEU. Furthermore, the Court in *Collins*,[27] a case involving intellectual property rights, found that Article 18 TFEU required that 'persons in a situation governed by [EU] law be placed on a completely equal footing with nationals of the Member State concerned'.[28] Continuing, the ECJ confirmed that the first paragraph of Article 18 TFEU was directly effective.[29]

*Khalil*[30] involved a number of immigrants fleeing to Member States from third countries and settling in the host Member State but being refused recognition as political refugees. However, they were stateless persons and as such they claimed child benefit on the basis that they came within the personal scope of Regulation 1408/71. The ECJ pointed out that the legal base of Regulation 1408/71 in 1971 was Article 18 TFEU (and Article 48 TFEU)[31] and that Article 18 TFEU 'prohibits discrimination against [Union] nationals on the ground of nationality',[32] although in this case Article 18 TFEU 'is not relevant'. The statement in paragraph 39 could be interpreted as limiting the scope of Article 18 TFEU to the legal position in 1971 but the tense used in paragraph 40 is the present and it is submitted that this is the extant position. Therefore, it would appear that Article 18 TFEU does not provide direct rights for TCNs at the present time. However, if rights can be established within the TFEU, or implementing secondary legislation, that can be taken advantage of by a national of a Member State who has sufficient connection to the TCN, then they may be able to take advantage of this non-discrimination provision. This has, up to now, proven to be difficult.[33] With the introduction of the AFSJ (see Chapter 4) and the entering into force of the implementing measures, it is possible that TCNs may be brought under the personal scope of Article 18 TFEU[34] and so would be able to rely on it as a directly effective provision, unless limited to EU nationals by the ECJ. This has now been tested before the Court in two cases, one dealing with free movement of persons[35] and the other over the freedom of movement of goods.[36] In *Vatsouras* the ECJ, without any reasoning, found that Article 18 TFEU did not apply to situations where there were possible differences in treatment between nationals of Member States and TCNs and in

---

27  Joined Cases C–92/92 & 326/92 *Phil Collins and Others v Imrat Handelsgesellschaft mbH* [1993] ECR I–5145.
28  ibid para 32.
29  ibid.
30  Joined Cases C–95–98 & 180/99 *Mervett Khalil, Issa Chaaban, Hassan Osseili v Bundesanstalt für Arbeit, Mohamad Nasser v Landeshauptstadt Stuttgart and Meriem Addou v Land Nordrhein-Westfalen* [2001] ECR I–7413 para 25; noted in S Peers 'Case note' (2002) 39 *CMLRev* 1395.
31  ibid para 39.
32  ibid para 40.
33  Case C–105/89 *Ibrahim Buhari Haji v Institut national d'assurances sociales pour travailleurs indépendants* [1990] ECR I–4211.
34  C Hublet 'The scope of Article 12 of the Treaty of the European Communities vis-à-vis third-country nationals: evolution at last?' (2009) 15 *ELJ* 757, 770.
35  Joined Cases C–22 & 23/08 *Athanasios Vatsouras and Josif Koupatantze v Arbeitsgemeinschaft (ARGE) Nürnberg 900* [2009] ECR I–4585 para 52; noted in E Fahey 'Interpretive legitimacy and the distinction between "social advantage" and "work seekers allowance"' (2009) 34 *ELR* 933; D Damjanovic 'Case note' (2010) 47 *CMLRev* 847.
36  Case C–291/09 *Francesco Guarnieri and Cie v Vandevelde Eddy VOF* [2011] ECR I–2685 para 20.

*Guarnieri* it was found that a third country company could not usefully claim the benefit of Article 18 TFEU. As Muir argues,[37] this appears to be a conclusion that goes against the evidence of the actual 'scope of application of the Treaties' where the material scope of the AFSJ covers immigration and asylum as well as free movement of persons and thus the personal scope includes TCNs that come within the measures advanced in the AFSJ. Furthermore, the position of the ECJ is incompatible with the objectives of the EU set out in Article 3 TEU and expanded upon by the specific legislative measures enacted within the AFSJ.

A general non-discrimination provision was introduced by the Treaty of Amsterdam, (now Article 19 TFEU) that has been described by one commentator as an 'enigma'.[38] It specifies that:

> . . . [w]ithout prejudice to the other provisions of the Treaties and within the limits of the powers conferred by it upon the Union, the Council, acting unanimously in accordance with a special legislative procedure and after obtaining the consent of the European Parliament, may take appropriate action to combat discrimination based on sex, racial or ethnic origin, religion or belief, disability, age or sexual orientation.

This provision has attracted considerable attention from a number of commentators who have analysed the background to its introduction.[39] As Bell notes,[40] one of the principal reasons for Article 19 TFEU was to eliminate racism throughout the EU. As such, the Kahn Committee[41] recommended that the new provision should apply to all the peoples of the Union 'whether citizens of the European Union or not' but Article 19 TFEU fails to mention the legal position of TCNs. The forms of discrimination covered are 'sex, racial or ethnic origin, religion or belief, disability, age or sexual orientation' and this list is closed. The provision is not directly applicable,[42] unlike Article 18 TFEU, as it does not actually prohibit anything, although it may inform the general principle of equality.[43] From the exhaustive list in the Article, it can be deduced that measures may be adopted to protect all persons resident in the Union, including TCNs, against racial

---

37 E Muir 'Enhancing the protection of third-country nationals against discrimination: putting EU anti-discrimination law to the test' (2011) 18 *MJ* 136, 143.
38 E Szyszczak 'The new parameters of labour law' in D O'Keeffe, P Twomey (eds) *Legal Issues of the Amsterdam Treaty* (Hart Publishing 1999) 141, 152.
39 See L Waddington 'Article 13 EC: mere rhetoric or a harbinger of Change?' (1999) 1 *CYBELS* 175, 176; M Bell 'The new Article 13 EC: a sound basis for European anti-discrimination law?' (1999) 6 *MJ* 5, 6. See also L Flynn 'The implications of Article 13 EC – after Amsterdam, will some forms of discrimination be more equal than others?' (1999) 36 *CMLRev* 1127 for a comprehensive analysis of the implications of art 13 EC.
40 Bell 'The new Article 13 EC' (n 39) 19.
41 European Council Consultative Commission on Racism and Xenophobia 'Final Report' ref.6906/1/95 Rev 1 Limite RAXEN 24, General Secretariat of the Council of the European Union (1995) 59.
42 S Langrish 'The Treaty of Amsterdam: selected highlights' (1998) 23 *ELR* 3, 15; Waddington 'Article 13 EC' (n 39) 182.
43 Case C–144/04 *Werner Mangold v Rüdiger Helm* [2005] ECR I–9981.

discrimination. However, discrimination on the basis of nationality is not covered by Article 19 TFEU.[44] This is covered by Article 18 TFEU, but unlike the potential personal scope of Article 19 TFEU, TCNs are currently excluded.

The Commission issued a racism Action Plan[45] before the Treaty of Amsterdam came into force,[46] stating its intention to make 'early use of Article [19 TFEU], with a view to ensuring that concrete proposals are on the table for adoption before the end of 1999'.[47] To this end the Commission brought forward three proposals for implementing the discrimination provisions in Article 19 TFEU on 25 November 1999.[48] It was thought[49] that the requirement of a unanimous vote in the Council would limit the 'practical utility of this measure'.[50] However, within just over a year, the Council had concluded all three: the Race Directive;[51] the Employment Directive;[52] and the Action Programme Decision.[53]

Article 1 of the Race Directive states: '[t]he purpose of this Directive is to lay down a framework for combating discrimination on the grounds of racial or ethnic origin, with a view to putting into effect in the Member States the principle of equal treatment'. As Ellis notes, no definition of racial or ethnic origin is provided in the directive, although 'a few textual clues about its intended meaning can be garnered from the lengthy Preamble'.[54] She notes that recital 6 rejects any theoretical attempts to establish the existence of separate human races and recitals 7, 10 and 11 link the concept of racial origin with xenophobia. She suggests that the directive is primarily focused on discrimination against racial groups 'whose origin is outside the EU'.[55] It is submitted that this is too narrow a reading and that the directive is actually targeted at discrimination against racial groups of whatever origin. 'Ethnic origin' is perhaps an even more enigmatic term. Recital 8 refers to combating discrimination against groups such as ethnic minorities and Ellis reads 'ethnic origin' as pertaining to minorities within a state's

---

44 Bell 'The new Article 13 EC' (n 39) 20.
45 Commission Communication concerning a racism action plan COM(1998) 183 final.
46 On 1 May 1999.
47 Commission Communication (n 45) para 2.2.2.
48 Commission proposal for a Council Directive establishing a general framework for equal treatment in employment and occupation COM(1999) 565 final; Commission proposal for a Council Directive implementing the principle of equal treatment between persons irrespective of racial or ethnic origin COM(1999) 566 final; Commission proposal for a Council Decision establishing a Community Action Programme to combat discrimination 2001–2006 COM(1999) 567 final.
49 C Barnard 'Article 13: through the looking glass of Union citizenship' in O'Keefe, Twomey *Legal Issues* (n 38) 375, 393.
50 E Ellis 'Recent developments in European Community sex equality law' (1998) 35 *CMLRev* 379, 381.
51 Council Directive 2000/43/EC implementing the principle of equal treatment between persons irrespective of racial or ethnic origin [2000] OJ L180/22.
52 Council Directive 2000/78/EC establishing a general framework for equal treatment in employment and occupation [2000] OJ L303/16.
53 Council Decision 2000/750/EC Establishing a Community Action Programme to combat discrimination (2001 to 2006) [2000] OJ L303/23.
54 Ellis *EU Anti-Discrimination Law* (n 18) 30. See also E Guild 'The EC Directive on Race Discrimination: surprises, possibilities and limitations' (2000) 29 *ILJ* 416, 418.
55 Ellis *EU Anti-Discrimination Law* (n 18) 30.

population.[56] Thus 'race' refers to discrimination against individuals because of their origin external of the EU, whilst 'ethnic origin' is the EU internal dimension that corresponds to it. However, the vague nature of the term 'racial and ethnic origin' gives a wide margin of discretion to the ECJ to define the term.[57] The UK's case law in this area is, as Ellis notes, the most advanced across the EU and could therefore provide guidance to the ECJ.[58]

Article 2(1) determines that the principle of equal treatment means there must be no direct or indirect discrimination based on racial or ethnic origin. Direct discrimination is defined as 'where one person is treated less favourably than another is, has been or would be treated in a comparable situation on grounds of racial or ethnic origin'.[59] Indirect discrimination is defined as 'where an apparently neutral provision, criterion or practice would put persons of a racial or ethnic origin at a particular disadvantage compared with other persons, unless that provision, criterion or practice is objectively justified by a legitimate aim and the means of achieving that aim are appropriate and necessary'.[60] Harassment[61] and instructing someone to discriminate on the basis of racial or ethnic origin[62] are also brought under the meaning of discrimination in Article 2(1). Article 3(1) establishes an inclusive personal and expansive material scope, with the Race Directive applying to 'all persons, as regards both the public and private sectors, including public bodies, in relation to:' workplace practices;[63] social protection, including social security and healthcare; social advantages; education; and access to and supply of goods and services which are available to the public, including housing. Article 3(2), however, limits the inclusiveness of the personal scope such that the directive does not apply to 'difference of treatment based on nationality and is without prejudice to provisions and conditions relating to the entry into and residence of third-country nationals and stateless persons on the territory of Member States, and to any treatment which arises from the legal status of the third-country nationals and stateless persons concerned'. This is supported by recital 13[64] but appears to run counter to the statement in recital 16 that '[i]t is important to protect all natural

---

56  ibid.
57  ibid 31. See also M Barbera 'Not the same? The judicial role in the new Community anti-discrimination law context' (2002) 31 *ILJ* 82.
58  See in particular *Mandla (Sewa Singh) and Another v Dowell Lee and Others* [1983] AC 548 (HL), 558 (Lord Fraser), *Gwynedd County Council v Jones and Another* [1986] ICR 833 (EAT) and *Crown Suppliers (Property Services Agency) v Dawkins* [1993] ICR 517 (CA).
59  Council Directive 2000/43 (n 51) art 2(2)(a).
60  ibid art 2(2)(b).
61  ibid art 2(2)(c) with harassment defined as 'when an unwanted conduct related to racial or ethnic origin takes place with the purpose or effect of violating the dignity of a person and of creating an intimidating, hostile, degrading, humiliating or offensive environment'.
62  ibid art 2(2)(d).
63  ibid art 3(1)(a)–(d).
64  'This prohibition of discrimination should also apply to nationals of third countries, but does not cover differences of treatment based on nationality and is without prejudice to provisions governing the entry and residence of third-country nationals and their access to employment and to occupation.'

persons against discrimination on grounds of racial or ethnic origin'. The Race Directive therefore 'is intended to apply to all within the EU irrespective of their nationality',[65] which, as it has been estimated that two-thirds of the EU's ethnic minorities are TCNs,[66] is positive. However, by limiting the scope of the Race Directive so that it does not apply to the entry, residence or status of TCNs then, by implication, it excludes the non-discrimination principle from a significant number of ethnic minorities in three particularly important areas of policy and exacerbates indirect discrimination of TCNs.[67] In most situations to claim under the Race Directive TCNs will be relying on their legal status as TCNs and their treatment on the basis of that status, which Article 3(2) specifically prohibits and thus most TCNs will fall outside the scope of the directive.[68] Furthermore, Hepple[69] argues that the exclusion of nationality from the scope of the Race Directive, and as Article 18 TFEU does not apply to TCNs, then this undermines the fundamental human right to be free from discrimination. An individual who is a member of an ethnic minority or a racial group but who is a TCN, cannot claim discrimination on the basis of his or her nationality, nor in the three policy areas that are likely to concern him or her in a significant manner. By limiting the scope of the Directive with the exclusion of nationality discrimination and certain aspects of policy towards TCNs, combined with the exclusion of TCNs from the scope of Article 18 TFEU, the principle of non-discrimination shifts from a human right to a citizen right.[70] As Chalmers points out,[71] this provision permits discrimination against, and negates the effects of the Directive for, TCNs. In 2008 a Framework Decision[72] was adopted under the third pillar decision-making process, designed to combat, through domestic

---

65  Ellis *EU Anti-Discrimination Law* (n 18) 290; P Watson 'Equality between Europe's citizens: where does the Union now stand?' (2012) 35 *Fordham International Law Journal* 1426, 1462.

66  TK Hervey 'Migrant workers and their families in the European Union: the pervasive market ideology of Community law' in J Shaw, G More (eds) *New Legal Dynamics of European Union* (Clarendon Press 1995) 101; M Bell 'Article 13 EC: The European Commission's anti-discrimination proposals' (2000) 29 *ILJ* 79, 84.

67  C Brown 'The Race Directive: towards equality for all the peoples of Europe?' (2002) 21 *YEL* 195, 211.

68  Case C–571/10 *Servet Kamberaj v Istituto per l'Edilizia sociale della Provincia autonoma di Bolzano (IPES), Giunta della Provincia autonoma di Bolzano and Provincia autonoma di Bolzano* [2012] 2 CMLR 43 paras 47–50; noted in S Peers 'The Court of Justice lays the foundations for the Long-term Residents Directive' (2013) 50 *CMLRev* 529, 531.

69  B Hepple 'Race and law in Fortress Europe' (2004) 67 *MLR* 1, 7.

70  See M Bell 'Beyond European labour law? Reflections on the EU Racial Equality Directive' (2002) 8 *ELJ* 384, 388; R Whittle, M Bell 'Between social policy and Union citizenship: the Framework Directive on Equal Treatment in Employment' (2002) 27 *ELR* 677, 688. In C Barnard, 'The United Kingdom, the "social chapter" and the Amsterdam Treaty' (1997) 26 *ILJ* 275, 280, Barnard describes the introduction of art 13 EC into the EC Treaty as the creation of a 'social dimension of Union citizenship'.

71  D Chalmers 'The mistakes of the good European?' in S Fredman (ed) *Discrimination and Human Rights: The Case of Racism* (OUP 2001) 193, 219.

72  Council Framework Decision 2008/913/JHA on combating certain forms and expressions of racism and xenophobia by means of criminal law [2008] OJ L328/55. See JJ Garman 'The European Union combats racism and xenophobia by forbidding expression: an analysis of the Framework Decision' (2008) 39 *University of Toledo Law Review* 843.

criminal measures, certain forms and expressions of racism and xenophobia. It should be noted that no rights of enforcement were granted to individuals, including TCNs.

The Employment Directive presents a framework for 'combating discrimination on the grounds of religion or belief, disability, age or sexual orientation as regards employment and occupation, with a view to putting into effect in the Member States the principle of equal treatment'.[73] It follows a similar pattern to the Race Directive but with the concept of indirect discrimination slightly modified for individuals with a disability[74] and the material scope limited to workplace practices.[75] Article 3(2) replicates Article 3(2) of the Race Directive but recital 12 excludes nationality discrimination, provisions governing entry and residence of TCNs, and access by TCNs to employment and occupation from the scope of the Employment Directive. Lahuerta[76] criticises the Race and Employment Directives and the interpretation of Article 18 TFEU by the ECJ as the result is to move away from a singular concept of equality to a hierarchy of equalities and peoples.

The path of fundamental rights might prove to be a route that could open up for TCNs to claim a human right to the principle of non-discrimination.[77] Article 14 of the European Convention on Human Rights (ECHR) prohibits any 'discrimination on any ground such as sex, race, colour, language, religion, political or other opinion, national or social origin, association with a national minority, property, birth or other status' but this is only complementary to securing the other rights in the ECHR and cannot be used as a stand-alone legal ground for a discrimination complaint. Article 1 of Protocol 12 to the ECHR does provide this stand-alone general non-discrimination clause with the same grounds of discrimination as Article 14 ECHR but a number of Member States, including the UK,[78] have yet to ratify it, even though it has been open for ratification since 2000[79] and so it is unlikely to be used as the basis of human rights judgments until it is ratified.

The Charter of Fundamental Rights could provide an alternative route at the purely EU level as since the entry into force of the Lisbon Treaty it has 'the same legal value as the Treaties' according to Article 6(1) TFEU. As such, Article 21(1)

---

73 Council Directive 2000/78 (n 52) art 1. It does not cover racial or ethnic origin discrimination in the work place as the Race Directive already covers this (recital 10).
74 ibid arts 2(2)(b)(ii) at 5 and recitals 20, 21.
75 ibid art 3(1)(a)–(d).
76 SB Lahuerta 'Race equality and TCNs, or how to fight discrimination with a discriminatory law' (2009) 15 *ELJ* 738, 747.
77 E Howard *The Race Directive: Developing the Protection Against Racial Discrimination Within the EU* (Routledge 2010) 92.
78 N Grief 'Non-discrimination under the European Convention on Human Rights: a critique of the United Kingdom Government's refusal to sign and ratify Protocol 12' (2002) 27 *ELR* (Human Rights Survey) 3.
79 See R Wintamute '"Within the ambit": how big is the "gap" in Article 14 European Convention on Human Rights? Part 1' (2004) *EHRLR* 366 and 'Filling the Article 14 "gap": government ratification and judicial control of Protocol No 12 ECHR: Part 2' (2004) *EHRLR* 484.

of the Charter of Fundamental Rights prohibits discrimination on grounds 'such as sex, race, colour, ethnic or social origin, genetic features, language, religion or belief, political or any other opinion, membership of a national minority, property, birth, disability, age or sexual orientation'. It should be noted first that the list is non-exhaustive and so further grounds could be added in the future. Secondly, the provision is clear, precise and unconditional and is likely to be directly effective. Thirdly, nationality discrimination is not included but is provided for in Article 21(2). Unfortunately a caveat is applied so nationality discrimination is only prohibited within 'the scope of application of the Treaties and without prejudice to the special provisions of those Treaties'. Before the Charter gained legal effect the ECJ utilised it simply to reaffirm the provisions of the ECHR[80] and other human rights law instruments.[81] Since the Lisbon Treaty came into force the Court has maintained this approach but supplemented it by using the Charter either to read provisions of the Treaty through the lens of the Charter[82] or, more interestingly, as the basis of the judgment itself,[83] although this is as yet rare. Article 21(2) of the Charter echoes Article 18(1) TFEU[84] and the ECJ would almost certainly interpret it in the same manner by observing Article 18(1) TFEU through the lens of the Charter's equivalent provision. Thus the fundamental rights route for a TCN to claim a right to non-discrimination on the basis of his or her nationality appears to be closed.

An alternative model to claims based on the general non-discrimination clause could be to introduce further protection of non-discrimination into the TFEU based on the General Agreement on Tariffs and Trade's (GATT) provisions on most-favoured-nation (MFN)[85] and national[86] treatments. MFN treatment requires any advantage, favour, privilege or immunity granted to products originating in one country must be granted immediately and unconditionally to like products originating in the territories of all other World Trade Organization (WTO) Member States, whereas national treatment necessitates a Member State to treat imported goods no less favourably than it treats domestic goods. These principles are replicated in the General Agreement on Trade in Services (GATS),[87]

---

80 Case C–432/05 *Unibet (London) Ltd and Unibet (International) Ltd v Justitiekanslern* [2007] ECR I–2271.
81 Case C–540/03 *European Parliament v Council* [2006] ECR I–5769.
82 Case C–400/10PPU *J McB v LE* [2010] ECR I–8965 para 60; Case C–491/10PPU *Joseba Andoni Aguirre Zarraga v Simone Pelz* [2010] ECR I–14247 para 60; Case C–141/11 *Torsten Hörnfeldt v Porsten Meddelande AB* [2012] 3 CMLR 37 para 37.
83 Case C–279/09 *DEB Deutsche Energiehandels- und Beratungsgesellschaft mbH v Germany* [2010] ECR I–13849; noted in P Oliver 'Case note' (2011) 48 *CMLRev* 2023.
84 Howard *The Race Directive* (n 77) 93.
85 General Agreement on Tariffs and Trade (adopted 15 April 1994, entered into force 1 January 1995) 1867 UNTS 187 (GATT 1994) art I.
86 ibid art III.
87 General Agreement on Trade in Services (adopted 15 April 1994, entered into force 1 January 1995) 1869 UNTS 183 (GATS). For a discussion on the GATS coverage of temporary migration measures in bilateral labour and economic integration agreements see R Grynberg, V Qalo 'Migration and the World Trade Organisation' (2007) 41 *Journal of World Trade* 751.

although with more exceptions than that in the GATT.[88] The effect of the MFN treatment should be to accelerate the process of trade barrier elimination,[89] although, as well as the GATT exceptions, Member States have developed policies as means to avoid their GATT obligations,[90] whilst the national treatment provision ensures that goods once they have entered the Member State are subjected to the same policy as domestic goods.[91] The advantage of such an approach would be two-fold. First, MFN treatment would ensure that immigration policies were standardised across the EU and, secondly, national treatment would ensure that a TCN upon entry to the EU would receive the same rights as Union citizens, including the right to freedom of movement. This is similar to the position of the free movement of goods in EU law[92] and if people were simply factors of production, from an economic viewpoint, then it is submitted this approach could be justified and could create a beneficial position for TCNs. However, people are not just factors of production and as such the situation becomes far more complex.

## 3.3   Citizenship

The first 50 years of the 20th century were lean times for the study of citizenship until Marshall's 1949 seminal treatise.[93] Over the last 20 years citizenship has experienced a remarkable upsurge in popularity amongst policy-makers and academic commentators of many different disciplines, which is even more remarkable when it is considered how elusive the concept has been to define and to contain within set parameters and boundaries. This ephemeral nature means that there is a danger of viewing citizenship as purely symbolic and the concept incoherent.[94] Lack of conceptual clarity, however, is countered, and it is submitted 'trumped',[95] by the normative value of citizenship. Indeed, Bosniak suggests that because of this normative value, and its resonance with people, citizenship creates such profound disagreements, arguments and discussions over its meaning, application and implications for normal life.

88  See Y Wang 'Most-favoured-nation treatment under the General Agreement on Trade in Services – and its application in financial services' (1996) 30 *Journal of World Trade* 91; AK Abu-Akeel 'The MFN as it applies to service trade: new problems for an old concept' (1999) 33 *Journal of World Trade* 103.
89  FM Abbott 'The North American integration regime and its implications for the world trading system' in JHH Weiler (ed) *The EU, the WTO and the NAFTA: Towards a Common Law of International Trade* (OUP 2000) 169, 173.
90  JH Jackson *The Jurisprudence of GATT and the WTO: Insights on Treaty Law and Economic Relations* (CUP 2000) 59.
91  BM Hoekman, MM Kostecki *The Political Economy of the World Trading System* (OUP 1995) 26.
92  L Ehrling '*De facto* discrimination in world trade law: national and most-favoured-nation treatment – or equal treatment?' (2002) 36 *Journal of World Trade* 921, 948.
93  TH Marshall *Citizenship and Social Class* (CUP 1949) reprinted in TH Marshall, T Bottomore *Citizenship and Social Class* (Pluto Press 1992).
94  L Bosniak 'Citizenship' in P Cane, M Tushnet (eds) *The Oxford Handbook of Legal Studies* (OUP 2003) 183.
95  R Dworkin *Taking Rights Seriously* (Duckworth 1977) 85.

Citizenship of the Union,[96] as a form of postnationalism[97] or transnationalism,[98] offers an opportunity to cast citizenship in an alternative way to that envisaged in traditional citizenship dialogue where citizenship has become inexorably linked to nationality,[99] and the nation to the state. Nationality is the 'ideological glue'[100] that binds a group of individuals around a set of shared institutions and a common political culture with sovereignty over a specific territorial area.[101] The resultant identity includes citizens and excludes non-citizens, with rights being granted to citizens by the nation-state. The formation of citizenship of the Union, a form of citizenship external to the nation-state, provided an opportunity to 're-imagine communities'[102] and to delineate the nation, constituted by an affinity group with shared genealogical origins, language, historic myths and culture, from the state, constituted by a civil society, politics and the law.[103] This would enable an alternative European identity to be forged to create 'an ever closer Union among the peoples of Europe', complementary to national identity[104] and inclusive of all the 'peoples of Europe', which could potentially include legally resident TCNs. If this new citizenship was truly novel, inclusive and post-national then this could be demonstrated by an inclusive citizenship possibly focused on the internal market, the economic benefits to the EU provided by TCNs and the application of the right to freedom of movement to all legally resident people in the Union, regardless of nationality. Indeed Articles 21–24 TFEU provide a catalogue of rights for Union citizens with Article 21(1) TFEU stating that '[e]very citizen of the Union shall have the right to move and reside freely within the territory of the Member States, subject to the limitations and conditions laid down in the Treaties and by the measures adopted to give them effect'. Therefore a TCN must ascertain the material and personal scope of the Union citizenship provisions to determine if it is possible to claim any of the catalogue of rights, including the free movement right in Article 21(1) TFEU.

---

96 For a recent analysis of the academic debate on EU citizenship see D Kochenov 'The essence of EU citizenship emerging from the last ten years of academic debate: beyond the cherry blossoms and the moon?' (2013) 62 *ICLQ* 97.

97 J Shaw 'Citizenship of the Union: towards post-national membership?' in European University Institute (ed) *Collected Courses of the Academy of European Law Vol VI-1* (Nijhoff 1998) 237; J Shaw 'Postnational constitutionalism in the European Union' (1999) 6 *JEPP* 579.

98 Y Soysal *Limits of Citizenship – Migrants and Postnational Membership in Europe* (University of Chicago 1994) 148.

99 D Miller *Citizenship and National Identity* (Polity Press 2000) ch 5.

100 D Curtin *Postnational Democracy: The European Union in Search of a Political Philosophy* (Kluwer Law International 1997) 52.

101 R Bellamy, D Castiglione 'The Communitarian ghost in the cosmopolitan machine: constitutionalism, democracy, and the reconfiguration of politics in the new Europe' in R Bellamy (ed) *Constitutionalism, Democracy and Sovereignty: American and European Perspectives* (Avebury 1996) 111.

102 The phrase is adapted from B Anderson *Imagined Communities* (Verso 1991).

103 TM Franck 'Clan and superclan: loyalty, identity and community in law and practice' (1996) 90 *AJIL* 359, 362.

104 See R Aron 'Is multinational citizenship possible?' (1974) 41 *Social Research* 638, who argued that an individual could not belong to several polities and enjoy multiple identities. The situation has moved on since 1974 and Benhabib now describes 'a dialectic of rights and identities' across multiple polities in S Benhabib *The Rights of Others: Aliens, Residents and Citizens* (CUP 2004) 168.

The preamble to the TEU launches EU citizenship by stating that the Member States are 'resolved to establish a citizenship common to nationals of their countries', which the TEU then fleshes out in a general manner in Article 9 TEU. The Union is mandated in 'all its activities' to 'observe the principle of equality of its citizens, who shall receive equal attention from its institutions, bodies, offices and agencies'. This connection of citizenship with equality is reflected in Part II of the TFEU, entitled 'Non-Discrimination and Citizenship of the Union', the former concept examined above.[105] The conceptual basis for Union citizenship is established by Articles 9 TEU and 20 TFEU, which declare '[e]very person holding the nationality of a Member State shall be a citizen of the Union'. This is an area that caused Denmark serious concerns during its first referendum on the Maastricht Treaty, so to ease these concerns[106] and complement EU citizenship a Decision[107] of the heads of state and government, meeting within the European Council, and a Unilateral Declaration[108] by Denmark were agreed by the European Council to be 'associated with the Danish act of ratification' of the TEU, and no other existing or acceding Member State. Section A of the Decision stated in categorical fashion that the Union citizenship provisions did not 'in any way take the place of national citizenship' and that the determination of individual nationality was a matter exclusively for the Member States' domestic law. The Unilateral Declaration expanded this by declaring that Union citizenship was a political and legal concept that was different to the Danish concept of citizenship and did not equate to citizenship of a nation-state, which meant that a national of another Member State could not use citizenship of the Union to claim Danish citizenship or the attendant rights. This Danish position was further supported by the introduction of '[c]itizenship of the Union shall complement and not replace national citizenship' by the Treaty of Amsterdam into ex-Article 17(1) EC (now Article 20(1) TFEU). This has undergone a further revision under the Lisbon Treaty with Articles 9 TEU and 20(1) TFEU, now reading that '[c]itizenship of the Union shall be additional to and not replace national citizenship'. The result of this rewording is as yet unclear but it is possible that, as suggested by de Waele,[109] the development of Union citizenship could float free of the anchor of nationality of Member States and start to create a dynamic model to the benefit of all citizens of the EU. However, the material

---

105 The ECJ does not appear to draw a distinction between the twin concepts of equality and non-discrimination – see Case C–115/08 *Land Oberösterreich v ČEZ as* [2009] ECR I–10265 para 89: 'Article [18 TFEU], which prohibits any discrimination on grounds of nationality, is a specific expression of the general principle of equality, which itself is one of the fundamental principles of [Union] law'.
106 Denmark and the Treaty on European Union [1992] OJ C348/1.
107 Decision of the heads of state and government, meeting within the European Council, concerning certain problems raised by Denmark on the Treaty on European Union [1992] OJ C348/2.
108 Unilateral Declarations of Denmark, to be associated to the Danish Act of Ratification of the Treaty on European Union and of which other Member States will take cognizance [1992] OJ C348/4.
109 H de Waele 'EU citizenship: revisiting its meaning, place and potential' (2010) 12 *EJML* 319, 322.

scope of Union citizenship appears on the wording of Articles 9 TEU and 20(1) TFEU to be exclusionary, limiting Union citizenship to nationals of Member States and ignoring the situation of TCNs, either economically active or at least legally resident within the territory of the EU. This conclusion has been confirmed by subsequent case law, strengthening the principle of Union citizenship but not necessarily clarifying its reach.

At the time of the Maastricht Treaty, Declaration 2 attached to the Final Act[110] reserved the right to determine nationality exclusively to the domestic law of the Member States, which (as the ECJ confirmed in *Micheletti*[111]) meant that the Member States retained the exclusive competence to determine who could be one of their nationals.[112] However, in the recitals of the judgment,[113] the ECJ inserted a proviso or *obiter dictum* that the Member States must exercise this power 'having due regard to [Union] law'. O'Leary[114] claimed that this, when coupled with the principle of sincere cooperation in Article 4(3) TFEU, could have a considerable impact on the Member States' competence to determine EU citizenship through domestic nationality law, thereby theoretically bringing TCNs within the material scope of Union citizenship and potentially coming within the personal scope of the direct citizenship rights, especially freedom of movement. In *Kaur*,[115] it was argued that the EU could intercede in the determination of nationality if there was a breach of fundamental rights, a suggestion first put forward by Hall.[116] As fundamental rights were part of the general principles of EU law then if the Member State failed to respect them, power would not have been exercised in accordance with EU law and the Union could enter this field of competence. The Advocate General and the Court chose not to address this point, deciding the matter on a separate issue, without addressing the proviso.

The cases of *Spain v UK*[117] and *Eman and Sevinger*[118] appeared to have opened a chink in the door of Union citizenship to TCNs by identifying rights in the EU Treaties that enjoyed a personal scope that was not exclusive to Union citizens. In 1999 the European Court of Human Rights (ECtHR) in *Matthews v United*

---

110 See also the declarations on nationality made by several states (eg Germany and the United Kingdom) at the time of the signing of the EC Treaty or on accession, and their subsequent alterations with the changes in domestic nationality laws.

111 Case C–369/90 *Mario Vicente Micheletti and Others v Delegación del Gobierno en Cantabria* [1992] ECR I–4239 para 10; noted in HUJ d'Oliveira 'Case note' (1993) 30 *CMLRev* 623 (see ch 5 for discussion of *Micheletti* as it applies to the EEC-Maghreb Agreements).

112 S O'Leary *The Evolving Concept of Community Citizenship* (Kluwer Law International 1996) 57; S O'Leary 'Nationality law and Community competence: a tale of two uneasy bedfellows' (1992) 12 *YEL* 353, 378.

113 *Micheletti* (n 111) para 10.

114 O'Leary (n 112).

115 Case C–192/99 *R v Secretary of State for the Home Department, ex parte Manjit Kaur* [2001] ECR I–1237; noted in P Shah 'British nationals under Community law: the *Kaur* case' (2001) 3 *EJML* 271; H Toner 'Case note' (2002) 39 *CMLRev* 881.

116 S Hall 'Loss of Union citizenship in breach of fundamental rights' (1996) 21 *ELR* 129.

117 Case C–145/04 *Spain v United Kingdom* [2006] ECR I–7917.

118 Case C–300/04 *MG Eman and OB Sevinger v College van burgemeester en wethouders van Den Haag* [2006] ECR I–8055; noted in LFM Besselink 'Case note' (2008) 45 *CMLRev* 787 and J Shaw 'The political representation of Europe's citizens: developments' (2008) 4 *EuConst* 162.

*Kingdom*[119] had found that the decision of the UK to exclude British citizens resident in Gibraltar from voting in elections to the European Parliament was an infringement of Article 3 of the First Protocol to the ECHR, that requires Member States to conduct free elections for their people to choose representatives for the national legislature. The UK enabled Gibraltar residents to vote in European parliamentary elections with the enactment of the European Parliament (Representation) Act 2003. Although Spain and the UK had come to a bilateral agreement over this matter, Spain brought an action against the UK, under Article 259 TFEU, before the ECJ. In a similar action, Mr Eman and Mr Sevinger objected to the Dutch rejection of their application to vote in European parliamentary elections, even though they were Dutch nationals resident in Aruba. The ECJ found, inter alia, that although Article 20(2) TFEU provided that '[c]itizens of the Union shall enjoy the rights and be subject to the duties provided for in the Treaties', the EU treaties also recognised rights that were not linked to Union citizenship or even to nationality of the Member States. Thus the rights identified in the EU treaties were not limited to Union citizens.[120] Furthermore, it was for the Member State to decide who was to vote in European parliamentary elections[121] and did not exclude an individual who was not a Union citizen from voting or indeed standing for election.[122] It was possible, therefore, to envisage the proviso in *Micheletti* being used potentially to enable TCNs to bring themselves within the material scope of the Union citizenship provisions in the event of other rights in the EU treaties or fundamental rights being breached.

This proviso though was specifically addressed again in *Rottmann*,[123] a case involving an Austrian national under criminal investigation in Austria who left the country for Germany and acquired German nationality without informing the authorities of the criminal investigation. Germany wished to strip Mr Rottmann of his acquired German nationality and, as he had lost his Austrian nationality when he became German, this would make him stateless. The ECJ

---

119  *Matthews v United Kingdom* (1999) 28 EHRR 361; noted in HG Schermers 'Case note' (1999) 36 *CMLRev* 673. See also AS Reid, M Doherty 'Voting rights for the European Parliament: whose responsibility?' (1999) *EHRLR* 420; T King 'Ensuring human rights review of intergovernmental Acts in Europe' (2000) 25 *ELR* 7; I Canor '*Primus inter pares*: who is the ultimate guardian of fundamental rights in Europe?' (2000) 25 *ELR* 3.
120  *Eman and Sevinger* (n 118) paras 73, 74.
121  *Matthews v United Kingdom* (n 119) para 45.
122  *Eman and Sevinger* (n 118) para 70.
123  Case C–135/08 *Janko Rottmann v Freistaat Bayern* [2010] ECR I–1449; noted in D Kochenov 'Case note' (2010) 47 *CMLRev* 1831; T Konstadinides 'La fraternité Européene? The extent of national competence to condition the acquisition and loss of nationality from the perspective of EU citizenship' (2010) 35 *ELR* 401; GR de Groot, A Seiling 'The consequences of the *Rottmann* judgment on Member State autonomy – the European Court of Justice's avant-gardism in nationality matters' (2011) 7 *EuConst* 150; HUJ d'Oliveira 'Decoupling nationality and Union citizenship' (2011) 7 *EuConst* 138; R Morris 'European citizenship: cross-border relevance, deliberate fraud and proportionate responses to potential statelessness' (2011) 17 *EPL* 417. For an excellent overall analysis of recent developments in Union citizenship see D Kochenov 'A real European citizenship: a new jurisdiction test: a novel chapter in the development of the Union of Europe' (2011) 18 *Columbia Journal of European Law* 55.

found that the proviso in this instance meant that for citizens of the Union, particularly when a decision to withdraw naturalisation was being made, the decision had to be 'amenable to judicial review carried out in the light of European Union law'.[124] Thus a domestic court undertaking such a review had to review the consequences in light of the situation of the individual themselves, as well as national law through the lens of proportionality.[125] The Court made it clear[126] that this case fell within the ambit of Union law due to Mr Rottmann's Union citizenship, which he would lose if German nationality was withdrawn. Thus to be able to undertake an examination of the personal scope of Union citizenship, the threshold of material scope, actual Union citizenship, had to be crossed. In *Chen* the ECJ held that 'it is for each Member State, having due regard to [Union] law, to lay down the conditions for the acquisition and loss of nationality'[127] but that 'it is not permissible for a Member State to restrict the effects of the grant of the nationality of another Member State by imposing an additional condition for recognition of that nationality with a view to the exercise of the fundamental freedoms provided for in the Treaty'.[128] The Member States therefore retain their competence to determine the nationality of their own citizens but they are not able to impose any unilateral restrictions on the EU rights that are attached to nationality of a Member State, in particular freedom of movement. The ECJ's judgment in *Chen* and *Rottmann* negatively resolved any possibility of TCNs being able to claim direct national citizenship status through a Union route as TCNs cannot fall within the material scope of Union citizenship, on the basis that they are not EU citizens. As the determination of national citizenship is a matter solely within the competence of the Member States any claims on the basis of a breach of fundamental rights as general principles of EU law or of other rights in the EU Treaties would have little purchase on which to bite. Therefore, instead of being an inclusive concept separating nationality from citizenship, Union citizenship could be characterised as a derived 'condition of nationality'.[129] However, the retention of the phrase 'having due regard to [Union] law' in the *Kaur* judgment from *Micheletti*, and its examination in *Rottmann*, would appear to maintain some element of EU competence in the determination by the Member States of their citizens' nationality. However, the extent of such competence remains unresolved[130] and the possibility of TCNs claiming to be included within the material scope of Union citizenship is tenuous.

---

124  ibid para 48.
125  ibid para 55.
126  ibid para 42.
127  Case C–200/02 *Kunqian Catherine Zhu and Man Lavette Chen v Secretary of State for the Home Department* [2003] ECR I–9925 para 37.
128  Case C–148/02 *Carlos Garcia Avello v Belgium* [2003] ECR I–11613 para 28 (noted in T Ackerman 'Case note' (2007) 44 *CMLRev* 141) and ibid para 39.
129  C Closa 'Citizenship of the Union and nationality of the Member States' (1995) 32 *CMLRev* 487, 510.
130  C Jacqueson 'Union citizenship and the Court of Justice: something new under the sun? Towards social citizenship' (2002) 27 *ELR* 260, 261.

The exclusive nature of Union citizenship, however, may have been mitigated by further case law of the ECJ. Unfortunately the Court has developed links between Articles 20 and 21 TFEU and Article 18 TFEU that has advanced the status of citizens[131] of the Union and correspondingly diminished that of TCNs. In *Martínez Sala*,[132] the first case involving EU citizenship, a child-raising allowance was denied to a Spanish woman legally resident in Germany, but without a residence permit, on the basis that she was not a worker. She had not worked for seven years. The ECJ held, inter alia, that such a refusal was direct discrimination on grounds of nationality and 'a citizen of the European Union, such as the appellant in the main proceedings, lawfully resident in the territory of the host Member State, can rely on Article [18 TFEU] in all situations which fall within the scope *ratione materiae* of [Union] law'.[133] In *Grzelczyk*,[134] a French national worked in Belgium to pay for his studies there. In his final year he ceased work to concentrate on his studies and applied for a maintenance grant, that was only available to Belgian nationals and aliens if covered by Regulation 492/11, and was refused. The Court decided that to determine the scope of application of Article 18 TFEU it would have to be read in conjunction with the citizenship provisions.[135] By pursuing university studies in a Member State other than the state of which he is a national, a citizen of the Union is exercising his EU free movement right and cannot be deprived of the possibility of relying on Article 18 TFEU. The ECJ found that the conditions imposed upon non-Belgian Member State nationals for the maintenance grant violated both Articles 18 and 20 TFEU. In a bold statement the Court declared that 'Union Citizenship is destined to be the fundamental status of nationals of the Member States, enabling those who find themselves in the same situation to enjoy the same treatment in law irrespective of their nationality', although this was 'subject to such exceptions as are expressly provided for'.[136] The ECJ went on to hold that those situations included 'those involving the exercise of the fundamental freedoms guaranteed by the Treaty and those involving the exercise of the right to move and reside freely in another Member State, as conferred by Article [21(1) TFEU]'.[137] This statement

---

131  It is not intended to expand on the definition and concept of citizenship in this thesis. Suffice to say that 'citizenship' implies a process of inclusion and exclusion of rights to individuals commonly on the basis of nationality. See MJ Elsmore, P Starup 'Union citizenship – background, jurisprudence, and perspective: the past, present, and future of law and policy' (2007) 26 *YEL* 57.

132  Case C–85/96 *María Martínez Sala v Freistaat Bayern* [1998] ECR I–2691; noted in S O'Leary 'Putting flesh on the bones of European Union citizenship' (1999) 24 *ELR* 68; C Tomuschat 'Case note' (2000) 37 *CMLRev* 449. See also S Fries, J Shaw 'Citizenship of the Union: first steps in the European Court of Justice' (1998) 4 *EPL* 533.

133  *Sala* (n 132) para 61.

134  Case C–184/99 *Rudy Grzelczyk v Centre public d'aide D'Ottignies-Louvain-la-Neuve* [2001] ECR I–6193; noted in AP van der Mei 'Freedom of movement and financial aid for students' (2001) 3 *EJSS* 181; D Martin 'Case note' (2002) 4 *EJML* 127; A Iliopoulou, H Toner 'Case note' (2002) 39 *CMLRev* 609.

135  *Grzelczyk* (n 134) para 30.

136  ibid para 31.

137  ibid para 33.

on the fundamental nature of Union citizenship has been repeated in subsequent case law[138] but has yet to be employed as the basis of a judgment.

As the case law has developed so the ECJ's reasoning over the relationship between citizenship and discrimination has appeared to become clearer. The first stage of the Court's analysis was to determine if the facts of the case fell within the material scope of Union law and whether the individuals concerned were covered by its personal scope. If so, then Article 21(1) TFEU's right to freedom of movement and residence could be exercised to establish the material scope, 'subject to the limitations and conditions laid down in the Treaties and by the measures adopted to give it effect'. At this point Article 18 TFEU was engaged requiring freedom of movement to be exercised without discrimination on the basis of nationality. It is certainly the case that the Court's approach has been striking, imaginative and inclusive but the Court has recently taken citizenship in a new direction that can be described as revolutionary.[139] In *Rottmann* Mr Rottmann had exercised his right of free movement to move from Austria to Germany. Advocate General Poiares Maduro had brought Mr Rottmann's situation within the material scope of the EU Treaties by finding that he exercised his right of freedom of movement[140] as the traditional approach demanded. However, the Court did not follow the Advocate General's route and instead found that the mere fact of Mr Rottmann holding Union citizenship brought him within the material scope of the EU treaties.[141] This break with the requirement for freedom of movement to establish the material scope of the EU treaties was reinforced in *Ruiz Zambrano*.[142] Mr Ruiz Zambrano was a Colombian national with a Belgian

---

138 Case C–224/98 *Marie-Nathalie D'Hoop v Office National d'Emploi* [2002] ECR I–6191 para 28 (noted in D Martin 'Case note' (2003) *EJML* 143 and A Iliopoulou, H Toner 'A new approach to discrimination against free movers' (2003) 28 *ELR* 389). The statement that 'citizenship of the Union is destined to be the fundamental status of nationals of the Member States' has appeared frequently since in the ECJ's case law on Union citizenship. See Case C–413/99 *Baumbast v Secretary of State for the Home Department* [2002] ECR I–7091 para 82 (noted in D Martin 'Case note' (2003) 5 *EJML* 155 and AP van der Mei 'Residence and the evolving notion of European Union citizenship' (2003) 5 *EJML* 419). For more in depth analysis see M Dougan, E Spaventa 'Educating Rudy and the (non-)English patient: a double bill on residency rights under Article 18 EC' (2003) 28 *ELR* 699; O Golynker 'Partial migration in the EU after the *Baumbast* case: bringing social and legal perspectives together' (2004) 15 *KCLJ* 367; M Dougan 'The constitutional dimension to the case law on Union citizenship' (2006) 31 *ELR* 613; Case C–138/02 *Brian Francis Collins v Secretary of State for Work and Pensions* [2003] ECR I–2703 para 61 (noted in M Dougan 'The Court helps those who help themselves: the legal status of migrant work-seekers under Community law in the light of the *Collins* judgment' (2005) 7 *EJSS* 7; O Golynker 'Jobseekers' rights in the European Union: challenges of changing the paradigm of social solidarity' (2005) 30 *ELR* 111; H Oosterom-Staples 'Case note' (2005) 42 *CMLRev* 205); *Zhu and Chen* (n 127) para 25, *Garcia Avello* (n 128) para 22, Case C–224/02 *Heikki Antero Pusa v Osuuspankkien Keskinäinen Vakuutusyhtiö* [2003] ECR I–5763 para 16, Case C–76/05 *Herbert Schwarz and Marga Gootjes-Schwarz v Finanzamt Bergisch Gladbach* [2007] ECR I–6849 para 86, Case C–524/06 *Heinz Huber v Bundesrepublik Deutschland* [2008] ECR I–9705 para 69.
139 Kochenov 'A real European citizenship' (n 123) 70.
140 *Rottmann* (n 123) paras 10, 11.
141 ibid para 42.
142 Case C–34/09 *Gerardo Ruiz Zambrano v Office National de l'Emploi (ONEm)* [2011] ECR I–1177; noted in K Hailbronner, D Thym 'Case note' (2011) 48 *CMLRev* 1253; A Hinarejos 'Extending citizenship and the scope of EU law' (2011) 70 *CLJ* 309; A Lansbergen, N Miller 'European

visa who, with his wife, applied for refugee status in Belgium. This was refused but they were unable to be returned to Colombia because of the civil war in that country. Mrs Ruiz Zambrano gave birth to two children who acquired Belgian nationality, and thus Union citizenship, upon birth. In a short judgment, lacking reasoning (unlike Advocate General Sharpston's Opinion), the ECJ began by reiterating that Article 21 TFEU confers Union citizenship on all individuals who are nationals of a Member State and that the two children were Belgian nationals and had Union citizenship.[143] The Court then repeated the statement that EU citizenship was intended to be the fundamental status of nationals of Member States[144] and that Article 20 TFEU precluded 'national measures which have the effect of depriving citizens of the Union of the genuine enjoyment of the substance of the rights conferred by virtue of their status as citizens of the Union'.[145] Such an effect occurred by not conferring a residence right or a work permit to a TCN with dependent minor children who are Union citizens.[146] The effect of both of these restrictions would be that the parents, and thus the children, would be forced to leave the territory of the Union, thereby ensuring that they were unable to exercise the substance of the rights conferred on them.[147] However, the question prevails following the case as to the substance of the term 'deprivation of the genuine enjoyment of the substance of the rights associated with the status of Union citizen'.[148] In *McCarthy*,[149] the Court conducted both a traditional analysis of requiring the Union citizen to have exercised his or her right of freedom of movement to establish an EU nexus and then a *Ruiz Zambrano* style evaluation, determining that there had been no movement across borders and that the national measure did not deprive Mrs McCarthy of the substance of her rights. The most recent judgment of the ECJ involving this new approach is *Dereci*.[150] Here the Court again found that the right to freedom of movement was not

Citizenship in internal situations: an ambiguous revolution?' (2011) 7 *EuConst* 287; R Morris 'Case note' (2011) 18 *MJ* 179; NN Shuibhne 'Seven questions for seven paragraphs' (2011) 36 *ELR* 161; H van Eijken, SA de Fries 'A new route into the promised land? Being a European citizen after *Ruiz Zambrano*' (2011) 36 *ELR* 704; I Solanke 'Using the citizen to bring the refugee in' (2012) 75 *MLR* 78.

143   *Zambrano* (n 142) para 40.
144   ibid para 41.
145   ibid para 42.
146   ibid para 43.
147   ibid para 44.
148   D Kochenov, R Plender 'EU citizenship: from an incipient form to an incipient substance? the discovery of the treaty text' (2012) 37 *ELR* 369, 395.
149   Case C–434/09 *Shirley McCarthy v Secretary of State for the Home Department* [2011] ECR I–3375; noted in S Cox 'Case comment' (2011) 25 *JIANL* 293; P van Elsuwege 'European Union citizenship and the purely internal rule revisited' (2011) 7 *EuConst* 308; A Wiesbrock 'Disentangling the "Union citizenship puzzle"? The *McCarthy* case' (2011) 36 *ELR* 861.
150   Case C–256/11 *Murat Dereci, Vishaka Heiml, Alban Kokollari, Izunna Emmanual Maduike & Dragica Stevic v Bundesministerium für Inneres* [2012] 1 CMLR 45; noted in S Adam, P van Elsuwege 'Citizenship rights and the federal balance between the European Union and its Member States: comment on Dereci' (2012) 37 *ELR* 176; A Hinarejos 'Citizenship of the EU: clarifying "genuine enjoyment of the substance" of citizenship rights' (2012) 71 *CLJ* 279; S Mantu 'European Union citizenship anno 2011: *Zambrano, McCarthy* and *Dereci*' (2012) 26 *JIANL* 40; NN Shuibhne '(Some of) the kids are all right' (2012) 49 *CMLRev* 349.

required to be exercised for a Union citizen to come within the material scope of the EU Treaties, that Union citizenship was intended to be the fundamental status of nationals of the Member States and that Article 20 TFEU precludes national measures which have the effect of depriving EU citizens of the genuine enjoyment of the substance of the rights conferred by Union citizenship.[151] However, it was held that the 'criterion relating to the denial of the genuine enjoyment of the substance of the rights conferred by virtue of European Union citizen status refers to situations in which the Union citizen has, in fact, to leave not only the territory of the Member State of which he is a national but also the territory of the Union as a whole'.[152] In a confused paragraph the Court appeared to summarise the right of residence that could be claimed in a *Ruiz Zambrano* scenario[153] before finding that desirability by a Union citizen for a TCN family member to be granted such a right, whether for economic reasons or for family unification, was not sufficient 'in itself to support the view that the Union citizen will be forced to leave Union territory if such a right is granted'.[154]

The result of these cases on citizenship, and on the relationship between citizenship and non-discrimination is two-fold. First, by limiting the material scope of EU citizenship to nationality of a Member State, TCNs are excluded from any rights that could arise as a consequence, in particular those concerning freedom of movement. Furthermore, by limiting the determination of nationality solely to the competence of the Member States, albeit with a requirement to 'having due regard to [Union] law', any refinement of a Union concept of citizenship that would be favourable to TCNs would appear to be curtailed, although its effects on Member State nationals has been clarified by the ECJ's jurisprudence. This has created two types of resident within the Union: those with access to the full range of EU rights through citizenship of the Union; and those with extremely limited access to EU rights as a TCN. The second is the transformation of the right to non-discrimination as a right in itself into a right dependent upon citizenship of the Union,[155] thereby developing it as a citizen rather than a human right and confirming the conclusion reached on the Race Directive above. Such a right is granted to a Union citizen but not to a TCN, unless a sufficient connection to a Union citizen can be established. This undermines the principle of non-discrimination, a principle designed to give substantive effect to the right to equality,[156] so that TCNs are denied access to protection when they are in a similar situation to citizens of the Union.

---

151 *Dereci* (n 150) paras 61–64.
152 ibid para 66.
153 ibid para 67.
154 ibid para 68.
155 M Bell *Anti-Discrimination Law and the European Union* (OUP 2002) 39.
156 See C Barnard 'The principle of equality in the Community context: *P, Grant, Kalanke* and *Marschall*: four uneasy bedfellows?' (1998) 57 *CLJ* 352, who argues that the principle of non-discrimination provides the substantive filling for the vacuum of formal equality suggested by P Westen 'The empty idea of equality' (1982) 95 *HLR* 537.

### 3.3.1   *The Citizenship Directive*

In 2004 EU citizenship developed a new phase with the enactment of Directive 2004/38/EC.[157] This provides a single legislative instrument to regulate the free movement rights of citizens of the Union but importantly for TCNs it also provides rights for family members as well. The recitals begin by providing the rationale for the directive. First, it is confirmed that '[c]itizenship of the Union confers on every citizen of the Union a primary and individual right to move and reside freely within the territory of the Member States' but that is subject to limitations and conditions in the EU treaties and secondary legislation (recital 1). Furthermore, free movement of persons is one of the fundamental freedoms of the internal market and that when people exercise this fundamental freedom, and the right to reside, their fundamental status should be citizens of the Union (recitals 2 and 3). Importantly for TCNs, recital 5 declares that for the right of Union citizens to move and reside freely within the territory of the Member States to be exercised under objective conditions of freedom and dignity, then the right to free movement and residence must also be granted to their family members, *irrespective of nationality*.[158] The right to family reunification is an important principle in Europe,[159] let alone the Union, evidenced by the Family Reunification Directive,[160] although family members of Union citizens are outside its personal scope (Article 3(3)). In *Commission v Germany*[161] it was held that the facilitation of freedom of movement contained two elements: first, 'the importance, from a human point of view, of having his entire family with him'; and, secondly, 'the importance, from all points of view, of the integration of the worker and his family into the host Member State without any difference in treatment in relation to nationals of that State'. Family reunion therefore has an individual and Union importance. In *Commission v Spain*[162] the latter importance was stressed when the Court stated 'that the [Union] legislature has recognised the importance of ensuring protection for the family life of nationals of the Member States in order to eliminate obstacles to the exercise of the fundamental freedoms guaranteed by the [Treaties]'. In this case two EU nationals were exercising their right of freedom of movement from their home Member States to Spain. Spain refused residence permits for their TCN spouses on the basis that they should have applied for visas at the Spanish Consulate in the home Member State. The

---

157  European Parliament and Council Directive 2004/38/EC on the right of citizens of the Union and their family members to move and reside freely within the territory of the Member States [2004] OJ L158/77. See RCA White 'Free movement, equal treatment, and citizenship of the Union' (2005) 54 *ICLQ* 885; K Hailbronner 'Union citizenship and access to social benefits' (2005) 42 *CMLRev* 1245.

158  Recital 5, emphasis added.

159  See art 8 ECHR. For commentary on this right to family life and the ECtHR case law see H Lambert 'The European Court of Human Rights and the right of refugees and other persons in need of protection to family reunion' (2000) 11 *IJRL* 427.

160  Council Directive 2003/86/EC on the right to family reunification [2003] OJ L251/12. See ch 4 for a detailed analysis.

161  Case 249/86 *Commission v Germany* [1989] ECR 1263 para 11.

162  Case C–157/03 *Commission v Spain* [2005] ECR I–2911 para 26.

Court stated that 'the right of entry into the territory of a Member State granted to a third country national who is the spouse of a national of a Member State derives from the family relationship alone'.[163] Thus, the right of entry is derived from a TCN's status as a family member of a Member State national[164] not as a right owned by the TCN in his or her own right.

Two sets of definitions of family members are provided in Articles 2(2)[165] and 3(2) of Directive 2004/38. The difference between the two is that the directive applies in full to EU citizens and their family members as defined in Article 2(2) who move to or reside in another Member State (Article 3(1)), whereas Member States must only facilitate entry and residence for family members in Article 3(2) in accordance with that Member State's domestic law. A TCN maybe a family member under Article 2(2) but to be a 'beneficiary' of the directive Article 3(1) requires that they must have accompanied or joined the Union citizen who has moved to or resided in another Member State.[166] Therefore there is no right of entry or residence in the directive for persons covered by Article 3(2)[167] but Member States must set out the criteria in their domestic law that the competent authorities would use to examine an application from a TCN[168] and, although granted a wide discretion when choosing that criteria, that can 'impose particular requirements relating to the nature and duration of dependence',[169] they 'must be consistent with the normal meaning of the term 'facilitate' and of the words relating to dependence used in Article 3(2) and must not deprive that provision of its effectiveness'.[170] Article 2(2) family members are: (a) the spouse; (b) the partner[171] with whom the Union citizen has contracted a registered partnership, on the basis of the legislation of a Member State, if the legislation of the host Member State treats registered partnerships as equivalent to marriage and in accordance with the conditions laid down in the relevant legislation of the host Member State; (c) the direct descendants who are under the age of 21 or are dependents and those of the spouse or partner;[172] and (d) the dependent direct

---

163  ibid para 28.
164  Case C–503/03 *Commission v Spain* [2006] ECR I–1097 para 42; noted in E Brouwer 'Case note' (2008) 45 *CMLRev* 1251.
165  For previous definitions see Council Regulation 1612/68/EEC on freedom of movement for workers within the Community [1968] OJ Sp Ed L257/2 art 10; Council Directive 73/148/EEC on the abolition of restrictions on movement and residence within the Community for nationals of Member States with regard to establishment and the provision of service [1973] OJ L172/14 art 1(1); Council Directive 90/364/EEC on the right of residence [1990] OJ L180/26 art 1(2); Council Directive 90/365/EEC on the right of residence for employees and self-employed persons who have ceased their occupational activity [1990] OJ L180/28 art 1(2); and Council Directive 93/96/EEC on the right of residence for students [1993] OJ L317/59 art 1(2).
166  Case C–40/11 *Yoshikazu Iida v Stadt Ulm* (ECJ 8 November 2012) para 61.
167  See recital 6 of the directive and Case C–83/11 *Secretary of State for the Home Department v Muhammad Sazzadur Rahman, Fazly Rabby Islam & Mohibullah Rahman* [2012] 3 CMLR 55 para 21.
168  *Rahman* (n 167) paras 22–23.
169  ibid para 40.
170  ibid para 24.
171  Incorporating the judgment in Case 59/85 *Netherlands v Ann Florence Reed* [1986] ECR 1283.
172  The ECJ held in Case C–291/05 *Minister voor Vreemdelingenzaken en Integratie v RNG Eind* [2007] ECR I–10719 (noted in JB Bierbach 'Case note' (2008) 4 *EuConst* 344; D Martin 'Case note'

relatives in the ascending line and those of the spouse or partner. Article 3(2) includes persons who are: (a) any other family members, irrespective of their nationality, not falling under the definition in Article 2(2) who, in the country from which they have come, are dependents or members of the household of the Union citizen having the primary right of residence, or where serious health grounds strictly require the personal care[173] of the family member by the Union citizen; and (b) the partner with whom the Union citizen has a durable relationship, duly attested. 'Dependent' as defined in *Jia*[174] is determined by 'having regard to their financial and social conditions, [when] they are not in a position to support themselves. The need for material support must exist in the state of origin of those relatives or the state whence they came at the time when they apply to join the [Union] national'. The host Member State must carry out an extensive examination of their personal circumstances and any refusal of entry must be justified. In *Rahman*, the Court held that even though the wording of Article 3(2) was 'not sufficiently precise to enable an applicant for entry or residence to rely directly on that provision in order to invoke criteria which should in his view be applied when assessing his application, the fact remains that such an applicant is entitled to a judicial review of whether the national legislation and its application have remained within the limits of the discretion set by that directive'.[175] Article 3(2) does not require a dependent family member to have been resident with the Union citizen before the Union citizen moved to the host Member State[176] or have been dependent on that Union citizen shortly before or at the time that the Union citizen moved to the host Member State.[177] However, at the time the dependent family member applies to join the Union citizen in the host Member State then that individual must be dependent on the Union citizen.[178]

The personal scope of Directive 2004/38 ensures that the rights prescribed for TCNs are not enjoyed on the basis of their own individual capacity but are derived from, or piggy-backed on, the rights of another person where the right holder must have exercised a freedom of movement Union right for the derivative right to be claimed. In *Morson and Jhanjan*,[179] two Dutch nationals of Surinamese extraction were working in the Netherlands. They brought their

---

(2008) 10 *EJML* 365, 373) that this includes TCNs who did not have a right of residence in the Union citizen's home Member State and was not affected by the fact that the Union citizen was not economically active.

173   The terms 'serious health grounds', 'strictly' and 'personal care' have been interpreted reasonably generously by the UK Asylum and Immigration Tribunal in *TR v Secretary of State for the Home Department* [2008] UKAIT 4 (AIT).

174   Case C–1/05 *Yunying Jia v Migrationsverket* [2007] ECR I–1 para 37; noted in D Martin 'Case note' (2007) 9 *EJML* 457; B Olivier, JH Reestman 'Case note' (2007) 3 *EuConst* 463; M Elsmore, P Starup 'Case note' (2007) 44 *CMLRev* 787; S Currie 'Case note' (2007) 51(Sum) *SLR* 28.

175   *Rahman* (n 167) para 25.

176   ibid paras 31, 33.

177   ibid para 33.

178   ibid.

179   Joined Cases 35 & 36/82 *Elestina Esselina Christina Morson and Sweradjie Jhanjan v Netherlands* [1982] ECR 3723 paras 14–16.

Surinamese mothers to visit them as tourists and asked the Dutch authorities for permission for them to stay as the women were dependent on their sons. The Dutch authorities refused and the mothers sought to rely on Article 18 TFEU to take advantage of Article 10(1)(b) of Regulation 1612/68 (now replaced by Article 2(2)(d) of Directive 2004/38) which permitted 'dependent relatives in the ascending line of the worker' to install themselves with nationals of a Member State, irrespective of their own nationality. The ECJ held that the objective of Regulation 1612/68 was to facilitate free movement of workers as an essential factor in the establishment of a common market and unfortunately Article 10(1) of Regulation 1612/68 only applied where 'a worker who is a national of one Member State . . . is employed in the territory of another Member State'. The ECJ thus concluded that there was no factor linking the women with EU law, as their sons, on whom they were dependent, had not exercised their right to free movement within the Union.[180] The reality of this situation then is that these persons become subordinated to the will of the right holder and the polity as a whole and, as Weiler[181] has observed, they become a 'thing which serves the purpose of ensuring free movement'. Therefore, a claim to an indirect right by a TCN requires the two elements of a Union relationship and movement of the primary right holder.[182] Whether the *Rottmann* and *Ruiz Zambrano* line of cases has an impact here or not remains to be seen, although it is suggested that their effect is likely to be negligible in the vast majority of situations.[183]

Article 5 of Directive 2004/38 governs the right of entry to a Member State, although it is without prejudice to the provisions on travel documents applicable to national border controls.[184] Union citizens must be granted leave to enter a Member State's territory with a valid identity card or passport, and without the requirement of an entry visa, or an equivalent formality. Family members who are TCNs must also be granted leave to enter a Member State's territory with a valid passport. However, family member TCNs will be required to have an entry visa in accordance with Regulation 539/01[185] or, where appropriate, in accordance with national law. In such circumstances the Member States must grant every facility to obtain the necessary visas,[186] free of charge and as soon as possible through an accelerated procedure. Where individuals in this situation present a valid residence card in accordance with Article 10 of Directive 2004/38 then they

---

180 See also Joined Cases C–64/96 & 65/96 *Land Nordrhein-Westfalen v Kari Uecker* and *Vera Jacquet v Land Nordrhein-Westfalen* [1997] ECR I–3171.
181 JHH Weiler 'Thou shalt not oppress a stranger: on the judicial protection of the human rights of non-EC nationals' (1992) 3 *EJIL* 65, 90.
182 M Cremona 'Citizens of third countries: movement and employment of migrant workers within the European Union' (1995) 2 *LIEI* 87.
183 *Iida* (n 166) para 67.
184 See SBC (n 17).
185 Council Regulation 539/2001/EC listing the third countries whose nationals must be in possession of visas when crossing the external borders and those whose nationals are exempt from that requirement (subsequently amended by Regulations 2414/2001/EC, 453/2003/EC, 851/2005/EC, 1791/2006/EC, 1932/2006/EC, 1244/2009/EC, 1091/2010/EU, 1211/2010/EU) [2001] OJ L81/1. See ch 4 for analysis.
186 *Commission v Germany* (n 161) para 33.

will be exempted from the visa requirement and their passports will not be stamped with an entry or exit stamp. If Union citizens or family member TCNs do not have the necessary travel documentation then they must be given every reasonable opportunity to obtain them, have them brought to them in a reasonable time period, or to prove by other means that they are covered by the right of free movement, before the Member State refuses them entry. However, family members accompanying a Union worker without a valid identity card or passport or, where necessary, a visa, cannot be denied entry to a Member State where they can prove their identity and conjugal ties.[187] Article 5(5) sanctions the Member State to require an individual to report his or her presence on the Member State's territory within a reasonable and non-discriminatory time period. If the individual fails to comply with this requirement then the Member State can impose proportionate and non-discriminatory sanctions.[188] A complementary right to exit the territory of a Member State is included in Article 4 for Union citizens with a valid passport or identity card and family member TCNs holding a valid passport but without the imposition of an exit visa or equivalent formality. Member States must issue and renew identity cards and passports to their own nationals, stating their nationality, in accordance with their national laws. The passport must be valid for a minimum renewal period of five years for all Member States and countries that a passport holder must transit when travelling between Member States, and for states that do not issue identity cards.

The right of entry creates a distinction between nationals of a Member State, who can move either as Union citizens in their own right or as family members of an EU citizen, and TCN family members, who must hold or be given every opportunity to obtain a visa.[189] Although, after *MRAX*, the possession of a visa is a purely administrative requirement if there are alternative ways to prove a TCN's identity and relationship with the Union citizen, it nevertheless creates a perception of difference or exclusion based purely on nationality.[190]

Chapter III of Directive 2004/38 provides details of the complex system for establishing an individual's right of residence. The right of residence is accompanied by the issuing of a residence permit, card or certificate by the national authorities. This is a purely administrative measure that does not provide rights for the holder and only establishes the position of the individual with regard to provisions of Union law.[191] The effect is that if a person can prove his or her identity and nationality unequivocally by other means other than a valid identity card or passport then failure to present the passport or identity card cannot lead to a

---

187  Case C–459/99 *Mouvement contre le racisme, l'antisémitisme et la xénophobie ABSL (MRAX) v Belgium* [2002] ECR I–6591 para 62.
188  In Case 157/79 *R v Stanislaus Pieck* [1980] ECR 2171 and Case 118/75 *Italy v Lynne Watson and Alessandro Belmann* [1976] ECR 1185, the ECJ found that the proportionate and non-discriminatory sanctions should be administrative and the equivalent to that for minor offences. A penalty of deportation was disproportionate.
189  S Carrera 'What does free movement mean in theory and practice in an enlarged EU?' (2005) 11 *ELJ* 699, 716.
190  NW Barber 'Citizenship, nationalism and the European Union' (2002) 27 *ELR* 241.
191  *Commission v Spain* (n 162) para 28.

residence application being refused.[192] A Member State cannot refuse to issue a residence permit and to issue an expulsion order on the sole reason that the TCN family member has entered the Member State unlawfully where that TCN family member is able to prove his or her identity and relationship with a national of a Member State.[193] Furthermore, a Member State cannot refuse to issue a residence permit to a TCN family member who has entered the territory of that Member State lawfully, nor issue an expulsion order, on the sole ground that the family member's visa has expired before he or she applied for a residence permit.[194]

The conditions for residence now apply to three types of residence: short term; long term; and permanent. Article 6 applies to short term residency of up to three months[195] so that a Union citizen and his or her TCN family members have a right of residence on the territory of another Member State without any conditions or formalities other than holding a valid passport or identity card, so long as they do not become an unreasonable burden on the social assistance system of the host Member State (Article 14(1)). However, recourse to the social assistance system of the host Member State must not lead to expulsion as the automatic consequence (Article 14(3)).

Articles 7–11 deal with the right of residence for the longer term residency of greater than three months and the administrative formalities associated with that stay. Article 7(1) provides that right of residence for Union citizens on the territory of another Member State so long as they satisfy the criteria in that Article. These are that they are workers, individuals with sufficient resources[196] and comprehensive sickness insurance not to become a burden on the host Member State, students with sufficient resources and comprehensive sickness insurance, and their family members. For this longer term of residency, the host Member State may require Union citizens to register with the relevant national authorities (Article 8(1)). Article 9 provides the right to a residence card for TCN family members of a Union citizen to be issued no later than six months after the application submission, with a certificate of application being issued immediately (Article 10(1)) that will be valid for five years from the date of issue or for the length of residence of the Union citizen if it is less than five years (Article 11(1)). Its validity cannot be affected by temporary absences of less than six months in a

---

192 Case C–215/03 *Salah Oulane v Minister voor Vreemdelinganzaken en Integratie* [2005] ECR I–1215 paras 25–26.
193 ibid para 80.
194 ibid para 91.
195 In *EA v Secretary of State for the Home Department* [2008] UKAIT 17 (AIT) it was held that this three month period commences from the date of entry to the host Member State, not from when the initial leave to remain expires.
196 Article 8(4) provides: 'Member States may not lay down a fixed amount which they regard as "sufficient resources" but they must take into account the personal situation of the person concerned. In all cases this amount shall not be higher than the threshold below which nationals of the host Member State become eligible for social assistance or, where this criterion is not applicable, higher than the minimum social security pension paid by the host Member State'.

year, longer absences for compulsory military service or one absence of a maximum 12 month period for important reasons.[197]

The right of residence for family members can now be retained on the death or departure of the Union citizen, or in the event of divorce, annulment of the marriage or the termination of the registered partnership (henceforth collectively known as divorce). Article 12 deals with the former and Article 13 the latter with paragraph 1 of both Articles providing this right for family members who are themselves nationals of a Member State, although they must meet the conditions set out in Article 7(1). Where the Union citizen dies and the TCN family member has been resident in the host Member State for at least a year, then he or she retains the right of residence (Article 12(2)) that can be permanent if the TCN can meet the conditions in Article 12(1). Furthermore, if the Union citizen dies or departs the host Member State then the right of residence will be retained for the Union citizen's children, and the parent with custody of the children, whilst the children are in full time education, regardless of nationality (Article 12(3)).[198] Where the Union citizen divorces then a TCN family member as defined in Article 2(2) will retain the right of residence where: (a) prior to initiation of the divorce the marriage has lasted at least three years, including one year in the host Member State; or (b) by agreement or court order the TCN spouse has custody of the Union citizen's children; or (c) this is warranted by particularly difficult circumstances, such as having been a victim of domestic violence during the marriage; or (d) by agreement or court order, the TCN spouse has the right of access to a minor child in the host Member State (as ordered by the court) and for as long as is required (Article 13(2)).[199] The right of permanent residence for TCN family members upon the divorce, death or departure of a Union citizen is conditional on them continuing to show that they are a worker or self-employed person, they are self-sufficient or they are a member of the family, already constituted in the host Member State, of a person satisfying these requirements. The right of residence for family members is retained exclusively on a personal basis so this becomes a directly owned right by that person, although obtaining such a right is dependent on continued accompaniment of the Union citizen.[200] TCN family members, to whom Articles 12(2) and 13(2) apply, acquire the right of permanent residence after living legally for five consecutive years in the host Member State.[201]

---

197  Article 11(2) gives a non-exhaustive list of examples such as 'pregnancy and childbirth, serious illness, study or vocational training, or a posting in another Member State or a third country'.

198  It should be noted that art 12(3) is not expressly premised on the condition of self-sufficiency, unlike art 12(2). See Case C–310/08 *London Borough of Harrow v Nimco Hassan Ibrahim & Secretary of State for the Home Department* [2010] ECR I–1065 para 57 and Case C–480/08 *Maria Teixeira v London Borough of Lambeth & Secretary of State for the Home Department* [2010] ECR I–1107 para 68; noted in P Starup, MJ Elsmore 'Taking a logical step forward? Comment on *Ibrahim* and *Teixeira*' (2010) 35 *ELR* 571; C O'Brien 'Case note' (2011) 48 *CMLRev* 203.

199  For a recent interpretation of these positions by a domestic court see *Amos & Theophilus v Secretary of State for the Home Department* [2011] 3 CMLR 20 (CA); noted in M Gill, NS Ahluwalia 'Case comment' (2011) 25 *JIANL* 304.

200  *Iida* (n 166), Opinion of AG Trstenjak paras 46–47 – this was not addressed by the ECJ in its judgment.

201  Article 18, which is in Chapter IV of Directive 2004/38.

Where the conditions for the right to remain in Articles 12 and 13 are not satisfied, the residence document of the TCN can be withdrawn by the host Member State. This is because the purpose for the TCN family member's presence in the host Member State is to ensure the freedom of movement of the EU citizen and does not provide a primary or direct right for the TCN family member but merely a derivative or indirect right.[202] However, where the marriage is intact, even though the relationship has ended, the couple have separated and are not even living together anymore, the right of residence remains. In *Diatta v Land Berlin*[203] a Senegalese national had married a French national and both lived and worked in Berlin. After a period of time the marriage broke down and the Senegalese wife moved out of the matrimonial home. The German authorities refused her a residence permit on the basis that she was no longer a family member of an EC national. The ECJ held that the spouse's right of residence was not lost where the couple separated as long as they remained married. There was no requirement that residence had to be under the same roof. However, the ECJ made clear that there was no independent right of residence for a TCN if the relationship with the EU worker failed. In *Singh*[204] an Indian national had married a UK national and they had both moved to Germany to work. They remained for a number of years before returning to the UK. The ECJ held that individuals may be deterred from leaving their own state to undertake economic activities in another Member State if they were treated less favourably on their return than they would have been if they had entered another Member State. Thus, a TCN family member could enter a Member State as a family member of a Union citizen under EU rather than national law. In *Akrich*,[205] Mr Akrich was a Moroccan national who entered the UK on a tourist visa, was denied leave to remain as a student and a few months later was convicted of criminal offences and deported. He returned illegally, married Mrs Akrich and applied for leave to remain that was refused. He asked to be deported to Dublin where Mrs Akrich had moved to work in order then to move back to the UK and take advantage of the *Singh* ruling. The Court held, in a somewhat elliptical judgment, that:

> ... [i]n order to benefit in a situation such as that at issue in the main proceedings from the rights provided for in Article 10 of Regulation 1612/68 [and now Article 2(2) of Directive 2004/38], the national of a non-Member State, who is the spouse of a citizen of the Union, must be lawfully resident

---

202  *R v Secretary of State for the Home Department, ex parte Sandhu (Amirjit Singh)* [1983] 3 CMLR 131 (CA); *LB and MB v Secretary of State for the Home Department* [2006] UKAIT 15 (AIT); *DA v Secretary of State for the Home Department* [2006] UKAIT 27 (AIT).

203  Case 267/83 *Aissatou Diatta v Land Berlin* [1985] ECR 567; noted in L Woods 'Family rights in the EU – disadvantaging the disadvantaged?' (1999) 11 *Child & Family LQ* 17.

204  Case C–370/90 *R v Immigration Appeal Tribunal and Surinder Singh, ex parte Secretary of State for the Home Department* [1992] ECR I–4265.

205  Case C–109/01 *Secretary of State for the Home Department v Hacene Akrich* [2003] ECR I–9607; noted in AP van der Mei 'Case note' (2004) 6 *EJML* 277; C Schiltz '*Akrich*: a Clear delimitation without limits' (2005) 12 *MJ* 241; E Spaventa 'Case note' (2005) 42 *CMLRev* 225.

in a Member State when he moves to another Member State to which the citizen of the Union is migrating or has migrated.[206]

Where the Union citizen, established in a Member State and married to a TCN with a right to remain in that Member State, moves to another Member State to work, that move must not result in the loss of the opportunity lawfully to live together. This is the reason why Article 10 of Regulation 1612/68 (and now Article 2(2) of Directive 2004/38) conferred on spouses the right to install themselves in that other Member State.[207] The motives for the Union citizen to exercise his or her right to free movement are irrelevant, and they cannot be taken into account when assessing the legal situation of the couple. However, a marriage of convenience would constitute an abuse of EU law.[208] When considering Union citizens returning to their home Member State after exercising their free movement rights, accompanied by their TCN spouse with whom they have resided in the other Member State, and the marriage is genuine although the residence of the TCN spouse has not been lawful, due regard must be had to the right to family life in Article 8 ECHR.[209]

Unsurprisingly this difficult judgment has resulted in further cases coming before the Court, the first focusing on the meaning of a dependent and the term 'lawfully resident'. Mrs Jia[210] was a retired Chinese national whose Chinese son lived with his German wife in Sweden. Mrs Jia's German daughter-in-law was self-employed in Sweden, had exercised her right to free movement under Article 43 EC and was in possession of a valid residence permit, as was Mrs Jia's son as her spouse. Mrs Jia entered Sweden on a visitor's permit and, before its expiry, applied for a residence permit on the basis of her family member status, particular that of a dependent. The Court distinguished Mrs Jia's position from that of Mr Akrich by finding that Mrs Jia was residing lawfully in Sweden and had submitted her application for a residence permit in a perfectly correct manner.[211] The Court reaffirmed previous case law as to the definition of 'dependent': 'The status of "dependent" family member is the result of a factual situation characterised by the fact that material support for that family member is provided by the [Union] national who has exercised his[or her] right of free movement or by his[or her] spouse'.[212] As the right to free movement must be interpreted broadly and uniformly, the status of dependent family member does not presuppose the existence of a right to maintenance, the need to determine the

---

206   ibid para 50.
207   ibid para 52.
208   ibid paras 55–57. See the UK cases of *Adetola v First Tier Tribunal (Immigration and Asylum Chamber) and Secretary of State for the Home Department* [2011] 2 FLR 611 (QB) and *Entry Clearance Officer, Nicosia v Lindita Papajorgji* [2012] Imm AR 447(IAC) for examples of marriages not of convenience.
209   ibid para 58.
210   *Jia* (n 174).
211   ibid para 31.
212   ibid para 35; Case 316/85 *Centre public d'aide sociale de Courcelles v Marie-Christine Lebon* [1987] ECR 2811 paras 20–22; *Zhu & Chen* (n 127) para 43.

reasons for recourse to that support nor to question if that individual is able to support him or herself by taking up paid employment.[213]

*Akrich* has now been examined again in *Metock*,[214] where the ECJ held that the judgment in *Akrich* requiring a TCN spouse of an EU citizen to be lawfully resident in a Member State when the Union citizen exercised his or her right of freedom of movement had to be reconsidered. In a straight overruling of the *Akrich* case, the Court found that prior lawful residence of a TCN spouse of an EU citizen in another Member State was not required for establishing rights under Directive 2004/38.[215] Furthermore, the ECJ in *Sahin*[216] found that where a TCN had entered the host Member State independently of the Union citizen and only after entering that Member State had acquired family member status or had started to lead a family life with that Union citizen then the TCN comes within the personal scope of Directive 2004/38, can claim rights of residence[217] and must be issued with a residence card on the basis of being a family member of a Union citizen.[218]

The right to permanent residence is outlined in Chapter IV of Directive 2004/38 and is not subject to the conditions in Chapter III. A Union citizen, and a TCN family member legally residing with him or her, acquires this after residing legally[219] in the host Member State for five continuous years (Article 16(1) and (2)) or shorter if the criteria in Article 17(1) are fulfilled. The continuous period (Article 16(3)) is not broken by temporary absences and, once acquired, permanent residence can only be lost by an absence from the host Member State exceeding two continuous years. Article 17(4) confronts the dilemma for family members if the worker or self-employed person dies before the permanent residence conditions

---

213  ibid para 36.
214  Case C–127/08 *Blaise Baheten Metock and Others v Minister for Justice, Equality and Law Reform* [2008] ECR I–6241; noted in N Berkowitz 'Case comment' (2008) 22 *JIANL* 371; N Cambien 'Case note' (2009) 15 *Columbia Journal of European Law* 321; C Costello '*Metock*: free movement and "normal family life" in the Union' (2009) 46 *CMLRev* 587; S Currie 'Accelerated justice or a step too far: residence rights of non-EU family members and the Court's ruling in *Metock*' (2009) 34 *ELR* 310; A Lansbergen '*Metock*, implementation of the citizens' rights directive and lessons for EU citizenship' (2009) 31 *Journal of Social Welfare & Family Law* 285; S Peers 'Free movement, immigration control and constitutional conflict' (2009) 5 *EuConst* 173; A Tryfonidou 'Family reunification rights of (migrant) Union citizens: towards a more liberal approach' (2009) 15 *ELJ* 634.The UK has been particularly concerned over the effect of the *Metock* judgment (Council Document 15903/08), although the other Member States do not appear to share these concerns (Council Document 16151/1/08), confirmed in the November 2008 JHA Council's Conclusions (Council Document 16325/08). See also the Commission Communication of the report on the application of Directive 2004/38/EC on the right of citizens of the Union and their family members to move and reside freely within the territory of the Member States COM(2008) 840 final.
215  ibid para 58.
216  Case C–551/07 *Deniz Sahin v Bundesminister für Inneres* [2008] ECR I–10453.
217  ibid para 33.
218  ibid para 40.
219  'Have resided legally' was defined in Joined Cases C–424 & 425/10 *Thomas Ziolkowski, Barbara Szeja, Maria-Magdalena Szeja & Marlon Szeja v Land Berlin* (ECJ, 21 December 2011) para 46 as 'a period of residence which complies with the conditions laid down in the directive, in particular those set out in Article 7(1)'.

have been achieved. In such a situation family members gain the right to permanent residence if: (a) the worker or self-employed person had, at the time of death, resided continuously on the territory of that Member State for two years; or (b) the death resulted from an accident at work or an occupational disease; or (c) the surviving spouse lost the nationality of that Member State following marriage to the worker or self-employed person. A certification document of the right to permanent residence must be issued to a Union citizen as soon as possible upon application (Article 19) with a permanent residence card issued to TCN family members within six months of an application, renewable automatically every 10 years (Article 20(1)).

The right of residence has been transformed by Directive 2004/38 from a mere complement to the right of entry to containing significant elements and providing a substantive right to the person it is granted to. There is a notable delineation again between citizens of the Union, who are granted the right directly and therefore hold it in their own right, and TCN family members, who are granted their right on a derivative basis as belonging to the EU citizen's family. However, the retention of the right of residence upon the death of a Union citizen or divorce and the right to permanent residence after five years residing with the EU citizen in the host Member State are advances for TCN family members. Furthermore, the fact that these are personal rights, owned by the TCN, even though they derive originally from the relationship of the TCN and the EU citizen, creates a more inclusive spirit, if not a significant substantive effect, to the concept of Union citizenship.

Article 23 provides that the family members of Union citizens, regardless of nationality, who have the right of residence or permanent residence, are entitled to take up employment or self-employment there.

A right to equality for Union citizens and family members is included in Article 24(1) but Article 24(2) allows the host Member State to refuse to provide social assistance during the first three months of residence or, where appropriate, during the long term period of residence provided for in Article 14(4)(b). Furthermore, prior to acquisition of the right of permanent residence, the host Member State is not obliged to grant maintenance aid for studies, including vocational training, in the form of student grants or loans, to individuals other than workers or self-employed persons, those who retain such status and their family members.

Article 24(1) links the right to equality, and thus the principle of non-discrimination, with the concept of citizenship and puts the ECJ's case law on citizenship and non-discrimination into legislative effect. However, the directive goes further by providing a general equal treatment provision that is not defined, thereby requiring all forms of non-discrimination between nationals of Member States and citizens of the EU in all areas of Union competence to be eliminated. It is only limited by Article 24(2), which is a derogation from the general right specified in Article 24(1) and thus must be interpreted narrowly. This could have a major effect not only citizenship but also on the equal treatment of persons in host Member States, and can be equated to the national treatment provision of

GATT, discussed above. It is also significant for TCNs as well, although only for family members of EU citizens, as they must not be discriminated against in comparison with a Member State national. However, there is only a requirement of equal treatment in comparison with nationals of the host Member State and so there is no obligation on the host Member State to respect any higher standard right that the individual could possess in his or her home Member State before exercising his or her free movement right if the national standard is lower.

The derogation in Article 24(2) appears to create problems as there is some difficulty over consistency with the ECJ's case law in this area. *Collins*[220] concerned an Irishman with dual American nationality who spent one semester in the UK in 1978 as part of his college studies and returned for a little less than a year in 1980 where he did part-time and casual work. He travelled to the USA, working there and in Africa, before he returned to the UK in 1988 to seek work in the social services sector, but after a week he claimed jobseeker's allowance, a benefit classified as social assistance. The ECJ held that following the introduction of citizenship of the Union and the interpretation by the case law of the ECJ of the right to equal treatment, it was no longer possible to exclude from the scope of equal treatment a benefit of a financial nature intended to facilitate access to employment in the labour market of a Member State.[221] The UK's legislation was indirectly discriminatory but could be objectively justified by requiring that a genuine link existed between the person seeking work and the employment market of that state.[222] In *Ioannidis*,[223] a case involving a Belgian tide-over allowance for helping young people to move from education into employment, the Court approved the reasoning in *Collins*, although the case was decided under the free movement of workers provisions. In *Vatsouras*[224] the ECJ was asked if Article 24(2) could be reconciled with Article 18 TFEU but by finding that benefits intended to facilitate access to the labour market could not be regarded as constituting social assistance and therefore falling outside Article 24(2)[225] the Court did not have to answer the specific question.

The rights of Member State nationals to enter and reside on another Member State's territory, and the same complementary rights for TCN family members, are not unconditional.[226] Chapter VI of Directive 2004/38[227] outlines the derogations from, or restrictions on, the right to freedom of movement that,

---

220 *Collins* (n 138).
221 ibid para 63.
222 ibid para 69.
223 Case C–258/04 *Office national d'emploi v Hoannis Ioannidis* [2005] ECR I–8275; noted in N Berkowitz 'Case comment' (2006) 20 *IANL* 51; A Cygan, E Szyszczak 'Case note' (2006) 55 *ICLQ* 977; D Martin 'Case note' (2006) 8 *EJML* 231.
224 *Vatsouras* (n 35).
225 ibid para 45.
226 *Commission v Spain* (n 163) para 43 and Case C–441/02 *Commission v Germany* [2006] ECR I–3449 para 32.
227 See NN Shuibhne 'Derogations from the free movement of persons: when can EU citizens be deported?' (2006) 8 *CYELS* 187; A Harvey 'Expulsion and exclusion' (2007) 21 *JIANL* 208.

as they are derogations from a general right, must be applied narrowly.[228] Thus, Article 27(1) provides the exhaustive list of grounds of public health, public security and public health, as set out in Articles 45(3) and 52(1) TFEU, that can be used to restrict the right to freedom of movement and residence for a Union citizen and a family member, irrespective of nationality. Again these grounds cannot be invoked 'to serve economic ends'. Restrictions based on public policy or public security (Article 27(2))[229] must be proportionate[230] and based exclusively on the personal conduct of the individual,[231] and previous criminal convictions[232] cannot in themselves constitute grounds for taking measures. The personal conduct of the person must 'represent a genuine, present and sufficiently serious threat affecting one of the fundamental interests of society. Justifications that are isolated from the particulars of the case or that rely on considerations of general prevention shall not be accepted'.[233] Article 28 provides for a three-part hierarchy of tests for expulsion[234] that is based on the degree of integration of individuals in the host Member State such that the greater the degree of integration then the greater the protection against expulsion.[235] As such there is a non-exhaustive list of factors to be taken into account before the Member State takes any expulsion decision (Article 28(1)), a permanently resident Union citizen or family member, irrespective of nationality, only to be expelled if there are serious grounds of public policy or public security (Article 28(2)), or a minor or a Union citizen resident for more than 10 years only to be expelled if there are imperative grounds of national security (Article 28(3)). As such it is for the domestic court to determine

---

228  *Commission v Germany* (n 226) para 34.

229  The ground of public health is covered by art 29.

230  This is an additional requirement to the same provision in the previous legislation, art 3(1) of Directive 64/221/EEC on the coordination of special measures concerning the movement and residence of foreign nationals which are justified on grounds of public policy, public security or public health [1964] OJ Sp Ed 850/64/117. In Case C–33/07 *Ministerul Administrației și Internelor – Direcția Generală de Pașapoarte București v Gheorghe Jipa* [2008] ECR I–5157 para 29, the ECJ did not expand any further.

231  The definition of individual personal conduct has been fleshed out by the ECJ in a series of cases, although this is outside the area of this book. See Case 67/74 *Carmelo Angelo Bonsignore v Oberstadtdirektor der Stadt Köln* [1975] ECR 297, Case 30/77 *R v Pierre Bouchereau* [1977] ECR 1999, Case 131/79 *R v Secretary of State for Home Affairs, ex parte Mario Santillo* [1980] ECR 1585 and Case C–348/96 *Criminal proceedings against Donatella Calfa* [1999] ECR I–11; noted in M Doppelhammer 'Expulsion: a test case for European Union citizenship' (1999) 24 *ELR* 621; CG Rotaeche, FB Lloréns 'Case note' (1999) 1 *EJML* 357; C Costello 'Case note' (2000) 37 *CMLRev* 817.

232  Article 17(3) allows the host Member State to request the individual's police record from the original country or other Member States in certain circumstances. However, such an enquiry is not to be a matter of routine.

233  This is a new provision not previously included in Directive 64/221 and amalgamates the previous case law of the ECJ. The position in the UK (see *R v Secretary of State for the Home Department, ex parte Marchon* [1993] 2 CMLR 132 (CA)) where particularly disgraceful criminal conduct could itself merit the deportation of an individual, without reference to any propensity to reoffend, is not now compatible with art 27. See *MG and VC v Secretary of State for the Home Department* [2006] Imm AR 619 (AIT) and *LC v Secretary of State for the Home Department* (IAT, 17 August 2007).

234  *LG (Italy) v Secretary of State for the Home Department* [2008] EWCA Civ 190 (CA) [19] (Carnwath LJ).

235  Case C–145/09 *Land Baden-Württemberg v Panagiotis Tsakouridis* [2010] ECR I–11979 para 25.

the length of time that the Union citizen or family member has been resident in the host Member State, taking all the resident factors into consideration in each individual case and in particular: the duration of each period of absence from the host Member State; the cumulative duration and the frequency of those absences; and the reasons why that individual left the host Member State.[236] It is also a matter for the domestic court to determine the effect of a prison sentence on actual residence within the host Member State to determine if previously forged integrating links are broken.[237] The term 'serious'[238] is not defined in the directive and neither are 'imperative grounds' as Member States are given the competence to determine these. The ECJ has provided some guidance to domestic courts for interpreting these terms in *Tsakouridis*. The Court first identifies that 'imperative grounds' are considerably stricter than 'serious grounds' and that the intention of the European legislature was to limit measures based on Article 28(3) to 'exceptional circumstances' as stated in recital 24.[239] 'Imperative grounds' then presuppose not just the existence of a threat to public security but that such a threat is of a particularly high degree of seriousness, reflected in the use of 'imperative reasons'.[240] 'Public security' must be interpreted in this context, extending to both external and internal security, and demonstrated inter alia by a threat to the functioning of institutions and essential public services and the survival of the population, a serious disturbance to foreign relations or to the peaceful coexistence of nations, or a risk to military interests.[241] Thus, the fight against crime in connection with dealing in narcotics as part of an organised group[242] and the sexual exploitation of children[243] can, if the domestic court decides, be covered by either Article 28(2) or 28(3). Individuals excluded on the grounds of public policy or public security can apply for the lifting of the exclusion order after a reasonable period, depending on the circumstances, and in any event after three years from the valid enforcement of the final exclusion order by arguing that there has been a material change in the circumstances that justified the original decision (Article 32). The Member State must reach a decision within six months of the submission of the application and during this period the individual has no right of entry to the host Member State.

---

236 ibid para 33.
237 ibid para 34. In *HR (Portugal) v Secretary of State for the Home Department* [2009] 3 CMLR 9 (CA) the UK Court of Appeal held that a Union citizen whilst held in prison was not resident in the UK.
238 The Court of Appeal in *Bulale v Secretary of State for the Home Department* [2009] QB 536 (CA) was invited to make a reference to the ECJ under art 267 TFEU to clarify the term 'serious' but decided against it on the basis that the legislation was designed only to provide general guidance, leaving the question to be determined by national courts on a case by case basis (Buxton LJ) para 31.
239 *Tsakouridis* (n 235) para 40.
240 ibid para 41.
241 ibid paras 42–44.
242 ibid para 56.
243 Case C–348/09 *PI v Oberbürgermesterin der Stadt Reimscheid* (ECJ, 22 May 2012) para 28; noted in L Azoulai, S Coutts 'Restricting Union citizens' residence rights on grounds of public security: where Union citizenship and the AFSJ meet' (2013) 50 *CMLRev* 553.

Chapter VI represents a significant advancement on the provisions of Directive 64/221 for the protection of individuals, including TCN family members, from disproportionate and unfair restrictions on the right of free movement, more commonly known as expulsion, imposed by the host Member State, although much of the improved Articles are based on ECJ jurisprudence. The guidance provided on personal conduct and on the protections against expulsion in Article 28 clarifies the factors to be considered by a national court and gives some legal certainty to individuals. The inclusion of the requirement of seriousness, although undefined, for the grounds of expulsion for those having the right of permanent residence creates a higher threshold that reflects the implications for an individual if permanence is rescinded and the level of integration into the society of the host Member State. The final material addition, and one that reflects the more inclusive nature of Union citizenship and the prevention of Member States excluding persons from their territory for life (recital 27), is the duration limitation of three years imposed upon an exclusion order. There is no indication as to how this is to be analysed by the national authorities, and ultimately the courts, other than there must be a 'material change in the circumstances', which justified the exclusion, and this term is not defined. However, in Article 33(2) if an exclusion order is not enforced two years after it was issued then the Member State must check to see if the individual is still a genuine threat to public policy or security and if there has been any material change in the circumstances. Therefore it is submitted the 'material change in circumstances' must be such that the person is not currently, or likely to be in the future, a genuine threat to public policy or security.

A final provision in Directive 2004/38 that may affect TCNs is Article 35, supported by recital 28, that enables Member States to adopt measures to remove any rights provided under the directive in cases of fraud or abuse of rights with the specific example given of marriages of convenience.[244]

## 3.4   Free movement of workers

The first paragraph of Article 45 TFEU, stipulates '[f]reedom of movement for workers shall be secured within the Union' without any mention of nationality or European citizenship.[245] It had been considered by some commentators that this may have provided a legal base for direct rights for TCNs,[246] and indeed Plender[247] suggested that this was the intention of the founding fathers. However, secondary legislation implementing Article 45 TFEU limited this direct free movement right

---

244  See *IS (Serbia) v Entry Clearance Officer, Skopje* [2008] UKAIT 31 (AIT).
245  O'Leary 'Nationality law' (n 112) 356. This can be contrasted with art 49 TFEU where the right to freedom of establishment is limited to 'nationals of a Member State in the territory of another Member State'.
246  R Plender 'Competence, European Community law and nationals of non-Member States' (1990) 39 *ICLQ* 599, 604.
247  ibid.

to nationals of the Member States,[248] subsequently confirmed by the ECJ in *Meade*[249] in a somewhat ambiguous judgment. The ECJ conclusively decided the matter in favour of nationals of Member States in *Awoyemi*.[250] In comparison to the first paragraph, the second paragraph of Article 45 TFEU specifically states that this freedom of movement is to entail the prohibition of discrimination based on nationality 'between workers of the Member States'. Article 45(3) TFEU lays out the more specific rights included within the general right of freedom of movement of workers. These are the rights to accept and move freely to take up offers of employment, and to reside in a Member State during and following employment. Limitations to these rights can only be justified by recourse to public policy, public security or public health, the details of which are provided in Chapter VI of Directive 2004/38.

Regulation 1612/68 was one of the first pieces of secondary legislation that implemented the principle of free movement of workers enunciated in Article 45 TFEU that has recently been codified as Regulation 492/11 to take into account the numerous amendments over the years. The principal aim of Regulation 492/11 is to ensure that in each Member State workers from other Member States receive treatment which is not discriminatory by comparison with that of national workers by providing for the systematic application of the rule of national treatment as far as all conditions of employment and work are concerned.[251] Many of the clauses in Regulation 1612/68 provided exclusive rights for nationals of Member States and therefore only a small number of the provisions affected TCNs and their free movement. These were those dealing with family members of workers (Article 10), the right to employment (Article 11), the right to education (Article 12) and the right to equal treatment contained in Article 7(2) with Directive 2004/38 now repealing Articles 10 and 11. Regulation 492/11 maintains Article 7(2) but has renumbered the right to education as Article 10.

Article 10 of Regulation 492/11 provides that migrant Union workers' children, resident in the host Member State, have a right to be admitted to that Member State's 'general educational, apprenticeship and vocational training courses'. Indeed Member States are exhorted to 'encourage all effort to enable such children to attend these courses under the best conditions'. As Oliver[252] remarks, the ECJ has interpreted Article 10 broadly,[253] both in the kinds of course covered and in the definition of 'access to courses' to include such facilitative measures as grants.[254] In *Gaal*[255] the ECJ held that ex-Article 12 of Regulation

---

248 See eg Regulation 1612/68 (n 165) art 1; Council Directive 68/360/EEC on the abolition of restrictions on movement and residence within the Community for workers of Member States and their families [1968] OJ Sp Ed L253/13 art 1.
249 Case 238/83 *Caisse d'Allocations Familiales v Mr and Mrs Richard Meade* [1984] ECR 2631.
250 Case C–230/97 *Criminal proceedings against Ibiyinka Awoyemi* [1998] ECR I–6781 para 29.
251 Case 110/79 *Una Coonan v Insurance Officer* [1980] ECR 1445.
252 P Oliver 'Non-Community nationals and the Treaty of Rome' (1985) 5 *YEL* 57, 69.
253 See Case 76/72 *Michel S v Fonds National de Reclassement Social des Handicapés* [1973] ECR 457.
254 Case 9/74 *Donato Casagrande v Landeshaupstatdt München* [1974] ECR 773.
255 Case C–7/94 *Landesamt für Ausbildungsförderung Nordrhein-Wesfalen v Lubor Gaal* [1996] ECR I–1031.

1612/68 had a wider remit than ex-Article 10[256] so that non-dependent children over the age of 21 could complete their education successfully. Although most cases in this area have dealt with family members who were EU nationals, the ECJ stated in *Baumbast*[257] that TCNs, coming within the definition of Article 2(2) of Directive 2004/38, could also rely on Article 10 of Regulation 492/11. However, *Baumbast* was pre-Directive 2004/38 and with its introduction of the condition of self-sufficiency for continuing residence of TCN family members if the Union citizen departs from the host Member State, there were doubts over whether the previous case law was still relevant. In *Ibrahim* the ECJ found that the children of a national of a Member State who works or has worked in the host Member State, and the parent who is the children's primary carer can claim a right of residence on the basis of Article 10 without it being conditional on having sufficient resources and comprehensive sickness insurance.[258] In *Teixeira* the Court went further, finding that there was a right of residence for the primary carer on the sole basis of Article 10: without recourse to the residence conditions in Directive 2004/38;[259] not conditional on having sufficient resources not to become a burden on the social assistance system of that Member State and having comprehensive sickness insurance;[260] not dependent on one of the child's parents working in the host Member State on the date that the child started education;[261] and ends when the child reaches the age of maturity.[262] In *Olarape*,[263] Advocate General Bot has suggested that where a person completes periods of residence on the sole basis of Article 10, such that the criteria of Article 7(1) of Directive 2004/38 are not satisfied, then those periods should not be taken into account for the purpose of determining the right of permanent residence in Articles 16 and 18 of Directive 2004/38.

---

256 Article 10 stated: '1. The following shall, irrespective of their nationality, have the right to install themselves with a worker who is a national of one Member State and who is employed in the territory of another Member State:

(a) his spouse and their descendants who are under the age of 21 years or are dependants;
(b) dependent relatives in the ascending line of the worker and his spouse.

2. Member States shall facilitate the admission of any member of the family not coming within the provisions of paragraph 1 if dependent on the worker referred to above or living under his roof in the country whence he comes.
3. For the purposes of paragraphs 1 and 2, the worker must have available for his family housing considered as normal for national workers in the region where he is employed; this provision, however must not give rise to discrimination between national workers and workers from the other Member States'.

257 *Baumbast* (n 138) para 56.
258 *Ibrahim* (n 198).
259 *Teixeira* (n 198) paras 53–54.
260 ibid paras 67–68.
261 ibid para 75.
262 ibid para 86.
263 Case C–529/11 *Olaitan Ajoke Alarape and Olukayode Azeez Tijani v Secretary of State for the Home Department* (Opinion of AG Bot, 15 January 2013) para 95.

There is no mention in the EU treaties or secondary legislation of a right to education for family members other than children. In *Forcheri*[264] the Italian wife of an Italian Commission official, who worked and resided in Belgium, enrolled for a vocational course and was required to pay a special fee demanded from all foreign students but not Belgian students. Mrs Forcheri's status was not included in Article 10 of Regulation 492/11. The ECJ held that 'to require a national of another Member State *lawfully established* in the first Member State to pay an enrolment fee which is not required of its own nationals ... constitutes discrimination by reason of nationality, which is prohibited by Article [18] of the Treaty'.[265] In *Gravier*[266] the ECJ extended this approach. Ms Gravier was a French student studying at a Belgian art college and, like Mrs Forcheri, she had to pay an enrolment fee that Belgian nationals did not. The Court found the EU had competence in the field of education and vocational training on a basis that included Articles 7 and 10 of Regulation 492/11. Moreover, access to vocational training was directly linked to the promotion of the free movement of persons[267] and so fell within the scope of the EU Treaty. Ms Gravier's treatment was held to discriminate against her on the basis of her nationality as prohibited by Article 18 TFEU. In *Blaizot*[268] this was extended to the majority of university courses[269] and *Humbel*[270] concluded that secondary education must be treated as vocational if it forms an integral part of an overall programme of vocational education, even with an element of general education.[271] It was argued before, but not commented on by, the Court in *Gravier* that as Ms Gravier was not a worker nor the spouse or a child of a migrant worker then she could not be lawfully established in Belgium. In *Raulin*[272] the ECJ utilised the principle of non-discrimination on the grounds of nationality to establish a right of entry to another Member State for students admitted to a course of vocational training. A right of residence for the duration of the course complemented this right of entry. A TCN lawfully established in a Member State would find it difficult to employ this ECJ jurisprudence to establish a right to education complemented by rights of entry and residence in another Member State, as the right to non-discrimination on the basis of nationality is not available to TCNs.[273]

---

264  Case 152/82 *Sandro Forcheri and his wife Marisa Forcheri, née Marino v Belgium and asbl Institut Supérieur de Sciences Humaines Appliqués – Ecole Ouvrière Supérieure* [1983] ECR 2323.
265  ibid para 18, emphasis added.
266  Case 293/83 *Françoise Gravier v City of Liège* [1985] ECR 593.
267  ibid para 24.
268  Case 24/86 *Vincent Blaizot v University of Liège and Others* [1988] ECR 379.
269  ibid para 20 for exceptions.
270  Case 263/86 *Belgium v René Humbel and Marie-Thérèse Edel* [1988] ECR 5365.
271  See Arnull *Wyatt & Dashwood's* (n 2) 96. The introduction of arts 149 and 150 EC, provisions dealing with education and vocational training, would appear to have removed any distinction between general education and vocational training. They are both now within the scope of the EU Treaties and subject to the application of art 18 TFEU.
272  Case C–357/89 *VJM Raulin v Netherlands Ministry for Education and Science* [1992] ECR I–1027 para 34.
273  See section 3.2 above.

An alternative way to establish a right to education for the worker's family members has been suggested by Oliver[274] by utilising Article 7(2) of Regulation 492/11.[275] The ECJ has not so far followed this approach. However, an indirect path to establish rights to social security may be available under Article 7(2), as may a right to social assistance for education.[276] This provision entitles the migrant worker to 'the same social and tax advantages as national workers'. The Court held in *Even*[277] that the social advantages encompassed by Article 7(2) were:

> . . . all advantages which, whether or not linked to a contract of employment, are generally granted to national workers primarily because of their objective status as workers or by virtue of the mere fact of their residence on the national territory and the extension of which to workers who are nationals of other Member States therefore seems suitable to facilitate their mobility within the [EU].

This is known as the *Even* formula and has been applied subsequently by the Court. In *Deak*[278] it was held that although Mr Deak, a Hungarian national living with his Italian mother, could not claim unemployment benefit under Regulation 1408/71 the principle of equal treatment in Article 7(2) of Regulation 492/11 was designed to prevent discrimination against descendants of a worker who were dependent on him, regardless of their nationality. He could therefore claim the special unemployment benefit under Article 7(2) as the benefit was also available to Belgian nationals. In *Taghavi*,[279] however, the handicapped persons' allowance was only available to Belgians resident in Belgium. As a Belgian worker's spouse who was a TCN could not claim the allowance then there was no social advantage for national workers for Article 7(2) to attach to and so Mr Taghavi, an Iranian married to an Italian residing in Belgium, could not claim.

Rights of access to education and vocational training were considered above. However, the ECJ has created a more complex and contrived position over rights to the payment of maintenance and training grants for students who are Member State nationals. The ECJ in *Brown*[280] considered that the payment of maintenance grants to students fell outside the scope of Article 18 TFEU as it was a matter of combined educational policy, which was not as such included in the Community's competence, and social policy that remained within the Member States' competence. However they could be considered to be a social advantage

---

274  Oliver 'Non-Community nationals' (n 252) 72.
275  In the territory of a Member State, a worker who is a national of another Member State 'shall enjoy the same social and tax advantages as national workers'.
276  See E Ellis 'Social advantages: a new lease of life?' (2003) 40 *CMLRev* 639 for a comprehensive analysis of the concept of social advantages.
277  Case 207/78 *Ministère Public v Gilbert Even and ONPTS* [1979] ECR 2019 para 22.
278  Case 94/84 *Office Nationale de l'Emploi v Joszef Deak* [1985] ECR 1873 paras 22–25.
279  Case C–243/91 *Belgian State v Noushin Taghavi* [1992] ECR I–4401 paras 10–11.
280  Case 197/86 *Steven Malcolm Brown v Secretary of State for Scotland* [1988] ECR 3205 para 18.

and thus fall within the ambit of Article 7(2) of Regulation 492/11, so long as the student had been employed in the state where he was to attend university in a manner that was not ancillary to the studies.[281] Moreover, the host Member State could not impose conditions requiring the student to undertake a minimum period of employment there before taking up a study position.[282] The ambit of Article 7(2) includes grants for study abroad[283] and, unlike Article 10 of Regulation 492/11, is not confined to children of migrant workers who are resident in the host Member State. Thus, in *Meeusen*[284] a Belgian student resident in Belgium, whose Belgian parents were also resident in Belgium, could claim study finance to study in the Netherlands from the Netherlands authorities. This was based on the fact that her father was the director and sole shareholder of a company established in the Netherlands, for whom her mother worked. Furthermore, a home Member State could not impose a residence requirement for obtaining study finance that made it necessary for a non-home student to have lived in the home territory for three out of six years prior to enrolling at a foreign university.[285] An alternative way of reading the two cases of *Brown* and *Meeusen* is to consider the relationship of the claimant to the right. In *Brown* the individual was claiming a direct right himself, which was a primary right, whilst in *Meeusen* the right was based on the relationship of the child with a migrant worker who was her mother. Therefore, Miss Meeusen had an indirect or secondary right that enabled the worker to exercise her right to freedom of movement.

With the establishment of Union citizenship, the ECJ's ruling in *Martinez Sala*,[286] and the extension of the EU's competence at Maastricht to include a chapter on education and vocational training in the EC Treaty[287] calls were made[288] for the position in *Brown* to be reviewed by the ECJ, which it has been in *Grzelczyk*.[289] A French national, studying in Belgium, had worked there to pay for his studies. In his final year he gave up work to concentrate on those studies and claimed a maintenance grant available to Belgian nationals and citizens of the Union to whom Regulation 492/11 applied, for which he was refused. The ECJ held, inter alia, '[t]he fact that a Union citizen pursues university studies in a Member State other than the State of which he is a national cannot, of itself, deprive him of the possibility of relying on the prohibition of all discrimination

---

281 ibid para 27.
282 Case C–3/90 *MJE Bernini v Minister van Onderwijs en Wetenschappen* [1992] ECR I–1071.
283 Case 235/87 *Annunziata Matteucci v Communauté française of Belgium and Commissariat général aux relations internationales of the Communauté française of Belgium* [1988] ECR 5589.
284 Case C–337/97 *CPM Meeusen v Hoofddirectie van de Informatie Beheer Groep* [1999] ECR I–3289.
285 Case C–542/09 *Commission v Netherlands* [2012] 3 CMLR 27.
286 *Sala* (n 132).
287 Now Title XII of Part Three of TFEU. See M Dougan 'Fees, grants, loans and dole cheques: who covers the costs of migrant education within the EU?' (2005) 42 *CMLRev* 943; S Jørgensen 'The right to cross-border education in the European Union' (2009) 46 *CMLRev* 1567 for comprehensive analysis of migrant education.
288 Arnull *Wyatt & Dashwood's* (n 2) 783; J Shaw 'From the margins to the centre: education and training law and policy' in P Craig, G de Búrca (eds) *The Evolution of EU Law* (1st edn OUP 1999) 555, 569.
289 *Grzelczyk* (n 134).

on grounds of nationality laid down in Article [18] of the Treaty'.[290] Thus Union citizenship, as the 'fundamental status of nationals of the Member States'[291] provided the basis for Article 18 TFEU to bite and thus excluded any direct rights for TCNs. However, if a TCN family member of a migrant worker, who is a national of a Member State, is installed with that worker in accordance with Article 2 of Directive 2004/38, then the worker may claim a maintenance grant on the family member's behalf if it is available to nationals of the host state.

The position was reconsidered again in the case of *Bidar*,[292] with *Brown* being looked at specifically. Bidar was a French national, who came with his sick French mother, when he was a boy, to live in the UK with his grandmother. His mother died soon after they arrived and his grandmother supported him, as he pursued and completed his secondary education, on the basis that he was her dependent. On completion of his secondary education he started a university course and applied for a student loan but his application was rejected. The ECJ first held that maintenance costs, whether in the form of grants or loans, fell within the scope of application of the TFEU[293] and therefore it had to be determined if the refusal of an application for such costs was discriminatory under Article 18 TFEU. The Court pointed out that there was a requirement for a Member State, in the organisation and application of its social assistance systems, to show a certain amount of financial solidarity with nationals of other Member States but that should not become an unreasonable burden on the Member State's finances.[294] As such it was legitimate for a Member State only to grant assistance to students who had demonstrated a certain degree of integration into the society of the Member State,[295] that could be evidenced either by a link with the employment market[296] or by a certain period of residence.[297] Thus, as Barnard comments,[298] '*Bidar* makes clear that migrant citizens can in principle have access to maintenance loans and grants on the same terms as nationals but only if they have been lawfully resident in the host State for a certain time or have a residence permit'. In *Förster* the ECJ found that a five year residence requirement was not excessive to ensure the necessary degree of integration into the society of the host Member State.[299] The Court also drew attention to Article 24(2) of Directive

290  ibid para 36.
291  ibid para 31.
292  Case C–209/03 *R v London Borough of Ealing and Secretary of State for Education, ex parte Dany Bidar* [2005] ECR I–2119; noted in C Barnard 'Case note' (2005) 42 *CMLRev* 1465; AP van der Mei 'Union citizenship and the 'de-nationalisation' of the territorial welfare state' (2005) 7 *EJML* 203; O Golynker 'Student loans: the European concept of social justice according to *Bidar*' (2006) 31 *ELR* 390.
293  ibid para 48.
294  ibid para 56.
295  ibid para 57.
296  ibid para 58 where the ECJ observes that this cannot be required for a student whose university course does not assign him or her to a particular geographical market.
297  ibid para 59.
298  Barnard 'Case note' (n 292) 1473.
299  Case C–158/07 *Jacqueline Förster v Hoofddirectie van de Informatie Beheer Groep* [2008] ECR I–8507 para 54; noted in O Golynker 'Case note' (2009) 46 *CMLRev* 2021; D Martin 'Case note' (2009)

2004/38 not requiring the host Member State to grant maintenance assistance for studies to students who had not acquired the right of permanent residence in Article 16(1) and thus equating the five year Dutch residence requirement in *Förster* and the provisions of Directive 2004/38.[300] Thus, if students move to another Member State not as students but in some other capacity then maintenance grants or loans are available to migrants and the situation in *Brown* is overturned. However, if a student moves to another Member State to study at university[301] or to take preparatory courses to prepare for university, then he or she will not satisfy the requirement of integration into society and so will not qualify for assistance with maintenance costs, although the student will with maintenance fees. As such, 'the legacy of *Brown/Lair* lives on'.[302] For a TCN, this case appears to confirm the position established in *Grzelczyk*.

A further stage in the development of the case law involving education and EU citizenship appears to have started with the joined cases of *Morgan & Bucher*[303] that is again of benefit to citizens of the Union but of little assistance to TCNs. German rules provided financial assistance to students to study at a university in another Member State and was awarded to all students resident in Germany so long as the student had studied for one year at a German university and was now undertaking the same education or training abroad. Morgan was studying in the UK and Bucher was studying at university in Holland but had moved closer to the Dutch border whilst retaining residence in Germany. Both students were denied the financial assistance they applied for. In Morgan's case this was because she had not completed a year's university education in Germany and for Bucher it was the same reason but supplemented by the fact that she had moved residence purely for educational reasons and therefore she could not take advantage of the generous assistance for students who commuted. The ECJ found that this rule was contrary to Article 21 TFEU, especially as Article 21 TFEU prohibits measures that disadvantage the Member State's own nationals for exercising their right to freedom of movement,[304] of even more relevance in the field of education as ex-Articles 3(1)(q) and 149(2) EC (now Article 165(2) TFEU) referred to the objective of encouraging the free movement of students and teachers.[305] As such, where a Member State provided a system of financial assistance to pursue studies in another Member State, it had to ensure that the

---

11 *EJML* 95; S O'Leary 'Equal treatment and EU citizens: a new chapter on cross-border educational mobility and access to student financial assistance' (2009) 34 *ELR* 612; C Marzo 'A new method of interpretation linked to European citizenship' (2010) 3 *Web JCLI*.

300 *Förster* (n 299) para 55.

301 *Bidar* (n 292) para 45.

302 Barnard 'Case note' (n 292) 1473.

303 Joined Cases C–11 & 12/06 *Rhiannon Morgan v Bezirksregierung Köln and Iris Bucher v Landrat des Kreises Düren* [2007] ECR I–9161; noted in M Dougan 'Cross-border educational mobility and the exportation of student financial assistance' (2008) 33 *ELR* 723. See now Joined Cases C–523 & 585/11 *Lawrence Prinz v Region Hannover and Philipp Seeberger v Studentenwerk Heidelberg* (Opinion of AG Sharpston, 21 February 2013).

304 *Morgan & Bucher* (n 303) paras 25–26.

305 ibid para 27.

detailed rules for their award did not create an unjustified restriction to the right to free movement.[306] The German rules were, because of personal inconvenience, additional costs and possible delays, liable to discourage Union citizens from leaving Germany to study at a university in another Member State and therefore stop them from availing themselves of their right to freedom of movement conferred by Article 21(1) TFEU.[307] This was even more pronounced when the year studying in Germany was not taken into account for calculating the duration of studies in other Member States.[308] Thus, only through objective justification based on considerations of public interest independent of the nationality of the persons concerned and the satisfaction of the proportionality criteria could the German rules be acceptable,[309] which on the facts of these cases they were found not to be.[310] As Dougan[311] establishes, the finding in this case suggests 'a real prospect of enhancing the practical value of EU citizenship for a broader category of its potential beneficiaries'; those beneficiaries however, would not include TCNs.

Measures in the field of social security to facilitate freedom of movement for 'workers' were to be adopted by the Council, acting unanimously on a proposal from the Commission, under Article 48 TFEU. Regulation 1408/71/ EEC,[312] with Regulation 574/72/EEC[313] implementing and supplementing it, was introduced to achieve the objectives of Article 48 TFEU, with Article 4 setting out its material scope, such that social security provisions of the Member States were not harmonised but coordinated to ensure that claimants' contributions were aggregated for the purposes of Article 48(a) TFEU and able to be collected wherever they were resident in the Union. Article 2 established the regulation's personal scope and contained two components. The first was positive for TCNs as it included family members of employed or self-employed persons. Furthermore, Article 3(1) articulated a non-discrimination provision for persons covered by Regulation 1408/71 and resident in the territory of a Member State, subject to the special provisions in it. However, the ECJ in *Kermaschek*[314] distinguished between social security benefits granted by domestic law as a personal right and derived rights, acquired only as a consequence of the claimant's position as a member of the worker's family. Only the latter could be claimed by family

---

306  ibid para 28.
307  ibid para 30.
308  ibid para 31.
309  ibid para 33.
310  ibid paras 35–50.
311  Dougan 'Cross-border educational mobility' (n 303) 726.
312  Council Regulation 1408/71/EEC on the application of social security schemes to employed persons, to self-employed persons and to members of their families moving within the Community [1971] OJ L149/2.
313  Council Regulation 574/72/EEC laying down the procedure for implementing Regulation 1408/71/EEC on the application of social security schemes to employed persons, to self-employed persons and to their families moving within the Community [1972] OJ L74/1.
314  Case 40/76 *Slavica Kermaschek v Bundesanstalt für Arbeit* [1976] ECR 1669. The case involved a Yugoslav national married to a German working and residing in Germany who attempted to aggregate periods of insurance or employment to claim unemployment benefit.

members on the basis of the non-discrimination provision of Regulation 1408/71. In *Deak*[315] a Hungarian national living with his Italian mother who worked and resided in Belgium claimed a special unemployment benefit available to Belgian nationals but not to Mr Deak on the basis of his nationality. The ECJ held that unemployment benefit was a personal right and could not be claimed by Mr Deak through his position as a member of the worker's family. *Taghavi*[316] concerned an Iranian national, married to an Italian residing in Belgium, claiming his entitlement to handicapped persons' allowances. The Court found that these handicapped persons' allowances were classified by Belgian domestic law as a personal right and so Mr Taghavi could not claim them on the basis of his membership of a worker's family. The ECJ reconsidered this case law in *Cabanis-Issarte*.[317] Mrs Cabanis-Issarte was a French national who had never worked but who had lived with her late husband in Holland for a period of time before returning to France. She claimed the right to pay voluntary social security contributions at the same rate as Dutch nationals, which was clearly a personal right as classified by Dutch domestic law. The ECJ held that maintaining the distinction between personal and derived rights would 'adversely affect freedom of movement of workers'.[318] Moreover, it would 'undermine the fundamental [EU] law requirement that its rules should be applied uniformly, by making their applicability to individuals depend on whether the national law relating to the benefits in question treats the rights concerned as rights in person or derived rights, in the light of specific features of the domestic social security scheme'.[319] Finally, the Court considered that national social security systems tended to blur the distinction 'in view of the tendency for social security cover to be universal'.[320] Thus the earlier jurisprudence was specifically limited to personal rights that were aimed at the worker, such as those in Articles 67–71 of Regulation 1408/71 concerning unemployment benefits.[321] At first blush the consequences for TCNs do not appear significant as these consequences seem to be equivalent to those of citizens of the Union. However, the ability to claim an 'owned' direct right to non-discrimination on the grounds of nationality, which is the logical effect of *Cabanis-Issarte*, is a step towards the establishment of universal social security across the Union based on need and residence rather than nationality. Thus, national social security systems that tended to exclude TCNs from the benefits of social security through inventive drafting of rights now have to comply with the requirement of non-discrimination.

It has already been stated that if Article 48 TFEU was to be read literally then there would appear to be no differentiation between TCNs and nationals of

---

315 *Deak* (n 278).
316 *Taghavi* (n 279).
317 Case C–308/93 *Bestuur van de Sociale Verzekeringsbank v JM Cabanis-Issarte* [1996] ECR I–2097; noted in M Moore 'Case note' (1997) 34 *CMLRev* 727.
318 *Cabanis-Issarte* (n 317) para 30.
319 ibid para 31.
320 ibid para 33.
321 ibid paras 23–24, 34.

Member States but the second component of the personal scope of Regulation 1408/71/EEC limited this to employed or self-employed persons 'who are nationals of one of the Member States or who are stateless persons or refugees residing within the territory of one of the Member States' (Article 2). Thus, stateless persons or refugees were able to take advantage of the rights enunciated in Regulation 1408/71, but other TCNs were excluded. However, the ECtHR in the far-reaching case of *Gaygusuz*[322] held that a social security provision was a pecuniary right for the purpose of Article 1 of Protocol No 1[323] and that denying the applicant this right on the grounds of nationality was in breach of Article 14 ECHR.[324] As a consequence, the Commission submitted proposals in 1998 for a new regulation to replace Regulation 1408/71,[325] with the aim of simplifying and modernising the law. The personal scope was to be extended in Article 1 to 'persons who are or have been subject to the social security legislation of one or more Member States' and recital 13 of the preamble outlined the aim of extending equality of treatment to 'all persons occupied in the territory of a Member State', thereby incorporating legally resident TCNs within the personal scope of the new regulation. This was a 'radical and comprehensive attempt to extend the scope of the Regulation'[326] but the Council did not adopt this proposal.

The problems with the 1998 Proposal were significant, both politically[327] and legally. First, Article 48 TFEU itself presented difficulty as agreement in the Council on secondary legislation had to be unanimous and both the UK[328] and Denmark voiced considerable objections. Secondly, decision-making under Article 48 TFEU followed the ordinary legislative procedure under Article 294 TFEU and the European Parliament adopted 47 amendments to the 1998 Proposal.[329] It was, however, the intervention of the ECJ that ensured that the 1998 Proposal was abandoned. In *Khalil*,[330] the Court was asked if Regulation

---

322  *Gaygusuz v Austria* (1996) 23 EHRR 364; see H Verschueren 'EC social security co-ordination excluding third country nationals: still in line with fundamental rights after the *Gaygusuz* judgment?' (1997) 34 *CMLRev* 991. This has been confirmed, and extended, by the ECtHR in *Koua Poirrez v France* (2005) 40 EHRR 2. The ECHR extended the concept of a pecuniary right from paid contributions to non-contributory social benefits. For an analysis of recent developments see MB Dembour '*Gaygusuz* revisited: the limits of the European Court of Human Rights' equality agenda' (2012) 12 *HRLR* 689.

323  'Every natural or legal person is entitled to the peaceful enjoyment of his possessions. No one shall be deprived of his possessions except in the public interest and subject to the conditions provided for by law and by the general principles of international law'.

324  'The enjoyment of the rights and freedoms set forth in this Convention shall be secured without discrimination on any ground such as sex, race, colour, language, religion, political or other opinion, national or social origin, association with a national minority, property, birth or other status.'

325  Commission proposal for a Council Regulation (EC) on coordination of social security systems COM(1998) 779 final.

326  F Pennings 'Inclusion and exclusion of persons and benefits in the new co-ordination regulation' in M Dougan, E Spaventa (eds) *Social Welfare and EU Law: Essays in European Law* (Hart Publishing 2005) 243.

327  See F Pennings 'The European Commission proposal to simplify Regulation 1408/71' (2001) 3 *EJSS* 45.

328  S Roberts '"Our view has not changed": the UK's response to the proposal to extend the co-ordination of social security to third country nationals' (2000) 2 *EJSS* 189.

329  Pennings 'Inclusion and exclusion' (n 326).

330  *Khalil* (n 30).

1408/71 applied to stateless persons and members of their families if they had no right to free movement under the EU treaties. The ECJ recast this to enquire if Regulation 1408/71 was valid by including stateless persons and refugees resident in the territory of a Member State and their family members within the personal scope of Regulation 1408/71, even though they did not enjoy the right to freedom of movement under the EU treaties.[331] The Court answered this question in the timeframe of 1971, when the regulation was created, conducting an historic analysis of the international obligations towards stateless persons and refugees of the Member States at that time, and finding that Regulation 1408/71 was not invalid.[332] The ECJ then considered the second question asked by the German court, holding that the regulation only applied to refugees and stateless persons who had moved within the EU,[333] rather than from a third country to a Member State. As a result of this case the Council[334] concluded that Article 48 TFEU would not be a suitable legal basis for the new regulation.

In 2002 the Commission tried an alternative approach to rectify this conflict by putting forward a new proposal[335] to bring TCNs within the coverage of Regulation 1408/71. This was enacted as Regulation 859/03/EC,[336] with Article 1 extending the provisions of Regulation 1408/71 to all TCNs, their family members and survivors who were not already covered solely on the ground of their nationality. Regulation 859/03 only governs coordination of social security and the radical equal treatment for TCNs in the original proposal has been removed.[337] The recipients of these new rights must be legally resident in a Member State and must be in a situation, which is not confined in all respects within a single Member State (Article 1). It is submitted therefore that a cross-border EU nexus must be established before the provisions of Regulation 859/03 can bite (recital 12) and as such it fails fully to implement the *Gaygusuz* judgment. Furthermore, the legal basis chosen was ex-Article 63(4) EC of the AFSJ[338] and, although the UK and Ireland have opted in (recital 18), Denmark has opted out (recital 19). The outcome means that, in Member States where the regulation applies, TCNs must move between Member States for the provisions of Regulation 859/03 to take effect, a particularly difficult criterion to achieve where there is a lack of a general right to free movement for TCNs.[339]

---

331  ibid para 29.
332  ibid para 58.
333  ibid para 72.
334  Council Document 15056/01 at 3.
335  Commission proposal for a Council Regulation extending the provisions of Regulation 1408/71/ EEC to nationals of third countries who are not covered by these provisions solely on the ground of their nationality COM(2002)59 final.
336  Council Regulation 859/2003/EC extending the provisions of Regulation 1408/71/EEC and Regulation 574/72/EEC to nationals of third countries who are not already covered by these provisions solely on the ground of their nationality [2003] OJ L124/1.
337  Peers 'Case note' (n 30) 1401.
338  See ch 4.
339  Peers 'Case note' (n 30) 1401. See also DS Martinson 'Who has the right to intra-European social security? From market citizens to European citizens and beyond' EUI Working Paper, Law, 2003/13 at 33.

Regulation 1408/71 has now been replaced by the new Regulation 883/04/EC,[340] implemented by Regulation 987/09/EC[341] and amended by Regulation 988/09/EC,[342] which replicates the personal scope of Regulation 1408/71 in Article 2. Regulation 859/03 has now been replaced by Regulation 1231/10/EU,[343] with the same material and personal scope. However, as the legal base is Article 79(2)(b) TFEU of the AFSJ both the UK and Denmark have chosen to opt out of adopting this regulation. The result is that for Denmark, Regulation 883/04 is applicable but does not extend to TCNs not covered solely on the basis of their nationality. For the UK, Regulation 883/04 applies for Union citizens and TCNs who are within the scope of Article 2. However, for TCNs that are not covered by Article 2 solely on the basis of their nationality then Regulation 859/03 continues to apply, along with Regulation 1408/71. This complicated situation also retains the limitations for TCNs from the previous regime as outlined above and frustrates any calls for simplicity.[344]

## 3.5   Freedom of establishment

The wording of Article 49 TFEU may be contrasted with that in Article 45 TFEU as the right to freedom of establishment is limited to 'nationals of a Member State in the territory of another Member State' and specifically excluding TCNs from the Article's scope. Furthermore, there is no equivalent provision to the second paragraph of Article 56 TFEU, on freedom to provide services (see below), enabling the extension of this right to TCNs through secondary legislation. However, if a citizen of the Union exercises the right to establish him or herself in another Member State then his or her family, regardless of their nationality, will be able to accompany or join that person in accordance with Directive 2004/38.

## 3.6   Freedom to provide services

The right to provide services in another Member State, other than one's own, is specified in Article 56 TFEU and, similar to Article 49 TFEU, is limited to nationals of Member States. However, unlike Article 49 TFEU, the Parliament and Council, acting in accordance with the ordinary legislative procedure,

---

340 European Parliament and Council Regulation 883/2004/EC on the coordination of social security systems [2004] OJ L166/1.
341 European Parliament and Council Regulation 987/2009/EC laying down the procedure for implementing Regulation 883/2004/EC on the coordination of social security systems [2009] OJ L284/1.
342 European Parliament and Council Regulation 988/2009/EC amending Regulation 883/2004/EC on the coordination of social security systems, and determining the content of its Annexes [2009] OJ L284/43.
343 European Parliament and Council Regulation 1231/2010/EU extending Regulation 883/2004/EC and Regulation 987/2009/EC to nationals of third countries who are not already covered by these Regulations solely on the ground of their nationality [2010] OJ L344/1.
344 E Eichenhofer 'How to simplify the co-ordination of social security' (2000) 2 *EJSS* 231.

may extend this right to TCNs established in the Union and who provide services.

Companies or firms when exercising their rights to provide cross-border services under Article 56 TFEU are entitled to use their own employees in this process even if they are not EU nationals.[345] Article 56 TFEU requires:

> . . . not only the elimination of all discrimination on grounds of nationality against service providers who are established in another Member State, but also the abolition of any restriction, even if it applies without distinction to national providers of services and to those of other Member States, which is liable to prohibit, impede or render less advantageous the activities of a service provider established in another Member State, where he lawfully provides similar services.[346]

If, however, a national legislative measure applied equally to all persons and undertakings operating in that Member State's territory in a legislative area that was not harmonised by EU law, then it may 'be justified where it meets an over-riding requirement relating to the public interest and that interest is not already safeguarded by the rules to which the service provider is subject in the [home] Member State'.[347] However, it must comply with the requirement of proportionality so that 'it is appropriate for securing the attainment of the objective which it pursues and does not go beyond what is necessary in order to attain it'.[348] Thus, it is contrary to Article 56 TFEU for the host Member State to require the employer to obtain work permits,[349] to set the duration of employment with the company prior to posting to the host Member State,[350] to require the service providers to provide a bank guarantee[351] or to pay social security contributions where they have already been paid in the home Member State.[352] Indeed, the ECJ held in *Commission v Germany*[353] that a simple prior declaration by the service provider certifying the legality of the workers concerned would be enough to satisfy any checks that the host Member State may be justified in conducting.[354]

---

345 Case C–113/89 *Rush Portugesa Lda v Office National d'Immigration* [1990] ECR I–1417.
346 Case C–244/04 *Commission v Germany* [2006] ECR I–885, para 30.
347 ibid para 31.
348 ibid.
349 Case C–43/93 *Raymond Vander Elst v Office des Migrations Internationales* [1994] ECR I–3803, where Moroccan nationals legally resident, with work permits, in Belgium had already obtained entry visas to carry out services in France. See S Peers 'Indirect rights for third-country service providers confirmed' (1994) 19 *ELR* 303. See also Case C–445/03 *Commission v Luxembourg* [2004] ECR I–10191.
350 *Commission v Luxembourg* (n 349) and *Commission v Germany* (n 346).
351 *Commission v Luxembourg* (n 349).
352 Joined Cases 62 & 63/81 *Société anonyme de droit français Seco and Société anonyme de droit français Desquenne & Giral v Etablissement d'assurance contre la vieillesse et l'invalidité* [1982] ECR 223, where it was discriminatory for French construction companies working in Luxembourg to pay employer's social security contributions in Luxembourg when already paying similar contributions in France.
353 *Commission v Germany* (n 346) para 41.
354 *Rush Portugesa* (n 345) para 17.

Two Commission proposals[355] for directives attempted to clarify and formalise the position of TCNs in this field, although, somewhat confusingly, the first, on the posting of workers who are TCNs for the provision of cross-border services, had a legal basis in Article 53 TFEU. In both proposals, the Member State in which the service provider was established would have had to issue an 'EC Service Provision Card' at the request of the service provider when it was wished to post an employed worker who was a TCN to another Member State (Article 2(1)). The recipient Member State would have provided a right of entry and residence on production of the card, an identity card or passport, and a statement from the service provider detailing the probable duration of stay (Article 3(1)). Visas, residence permits or work permits would not have been required (Article 3(2)). Unfortunately, these proposals have not progressed any further.

The Union has passed secondary legislation to harmonise some aspects of the cross-border provision of services. The first was the Posting of Workers Directive[356] that, as Davies[357] points out, does not specifically apply to TCNs but nor does it exclude them and, therefore, it is suggested that Article 56 TFEU case law continues to apply. The second is the Services Directive,[358] the scope of which applies to services supplied by providers established in a Member State (Article 2(1)). The extensive and exhaustive list (Article 2(2)[359]) of activities that the directive does not apply to and the list (Article 3) of legislation that takes precedence over the directive, do not mention TCNs and thus by implication does not exclude TCNs from the scope of the directive. Furthermore, the application of the directive by the Member States is to comply with the free movement of establishment and services Treaty rules (Article 3(3)), thereby once again suggesting that the Article 56 TFEU case law will apply.

In 2002 the ECJ gave a striking and, at the time, a possibly far-reaching judgment, particularly for TCNs, on the interpretation of Article 56 TFEU. In *Carpenter*,[360] Mrs Carpenter was a Philippine national who entered the UK on a

---

355 Commission proposal for a Directive of the European Parliament and Council on the posting of workers who are third country nationals for the provision of cross-border services and Commission proposal for a Council Directive extending the freedom to provide cross-border services to third country nationals established within the Community COM(1999) 3 final/2. Now amended COM(2000) 271 final.

356 Parliament and Council Directive 96/71/EC concerning the posting of workers in the framework of the provision of services [1997] OJ L18/1. See recently the Commission proposal for a Regulation on the enforcement of Directive 96/71/EC concerning the posting of workers in the framework of the provision of services COM(2012) 131 final.

357 P Davies 'Posted workers: single market or protection of national labour law systems?' (1997) 34 *CMLRev* 571, 589.

358 Parliament and Council Directive 2006/123/EC on services in the internal market [2006] OJ L376/36. See G Davies 'The Services Directive: extending the country of origin principle, and reforming public administration' (2007) 32 *ELR* 232 for a comprehensive analysis of the new measure.

359 See also art 17.

360 Case C–60/00 *Mary Carpenter v Secretary of State for the Home Department* [2002] ECR I–6279; noted in H Toner 'Case note' (2003) 5 *EJML* 163; A Tryfonidou 'The beginning of a new era in the European Union?' (2003) 14 *KCLJ* 81; Editorial 'Freedoms unlimited? Reflections on *Mary*

six month visitor's permit, overstayed her leave to remain and, 20 months after her initial entry, married Mr Carpenter. She applied for leave to remain in the UK as the spouse of a UK national but this was refused and she was served a deportation notice. Upon referral to the ECJ, it was found that Mr Carpenter ran a business, established in the UK, selling advertising space in journals in which a significant proportion of his business was conducted with advertisers established in other Member States of the EU and that Mr Carpenter travelled often in Europe on business. The Court held that Mr Carpenter was exercising his right freely to provide services under Article 56 TFEU by offering cross-border services and thus fell under the material scope of the EU Treaties, even though he had not actually moved. The importance of ensuring the protection of the family life of nationals of the Member States in order to eliminate obstacles to the exercise of the fundamental freedoms guaranteed by the EU treaties, was apparent from the provisions of the free movement implementing legislation (see now Directive 2004/38). The effect of deporting Mrs Carpenter would be to separate Mr and Mrs Carpenter, which would be detrimental to their family life and 'to the conditions under which Mr Carpenter exercises a fundamental freedom. That freedom could not be fully effective if Mr Carpenter were to be deterred from exercising it by obstacles raised in his country of origin to the entry and residence of his spouse'.[361] A Member State could not justify a national measure to obstruct the exercise of the freedom to provide services for reasons of public interest if it was not compatible with fundamental rights. The right to family life was a fundamental right, as outlined in Article 8 ECHR, and the decision to deport Mrs Carpenter was disproportionate to the aim of maintenance of public order and public safety. It must be noted that, although the ECJ constructed an argument against the deportation of Mrs Carpenter on the basis of fundamental rights and Article 8 ECHR, the right that was protected was that of Mr Carpenter. Therefore, Mrs Carpenter held a secondary or derived right only on the basis of her relationship with a Union citizen who was exercising a free movement right. With 10 years' hindsight this case can be bracketed with further cases of the ECJ such as *Metock* and *Ruiz Zambrano* that ensured the position of the TCN was guaranteed through protecting the Union citizenship or free movement rights of the Union citizen that the TCN enjoyed a relationship with.

## 3.7 Conclusion

TCNs are not granted any direct free movement rights under the TFEU, or the implementing legislation. The rights that have been granted are derivative, secondary or indirect rights based on the relationship that the TCN has with a citizen of the Union and the fact that the citizen of the Union has exercised his or her free movement rights. The principle of non-discrimination on the basis of

---

*Carpenter v Secretary of State'* (2003) 40 *CMLRev* 537; S Acierno 'The *Carpenter* judgment: fundamental rights and the limits of the Community legal order' (2003) 28 *ELR* 398.
361 *Carpenter* (n 360) para 39.

nationality can only apply if there is an EU nexus, a condition that a TCN who does not have free movement rights will find difficult to satisfy. Even the possibility that the inclusion of TCNs within the provisions of the AFSJ could have brought at least some TCNs within the Union criterion appears to have been thwarted by the judgment in *Vatsouras* that Article 18 TFEU does not apply to TCNs. The Race and Ethnic Origin Directive adopted under Article 19 TFEU is, it is submitted, significantly flawed through the failure to include the prohibition of discrimination on the basis of nationality. An example from recent European history can illustrate this: a TCN who was a Bosnian Serb living in an EU Member State could gain protection if he was discriminated against on the basis of his Serb ethnicity but not on the basis of his Bosnian nationality. European citizenship has garnered few advantages for TCNs, especially as the basis for citizenship of the Union is nationality of a Member State,[362] creating a citizenship that is predominantly formulated on inclusion and exclusion, entrenching the 'preexisting status between EU nationals and third country nationals'.[363] The extent of the rights that a TCN can claim following the judgment in *Ruiz Zambrano* is uncertain, especially with the high threshold required to activate such rights as specified in *Dereci*. Directive 2004/38 provides some major advances for TCNs when they are family members of citizens of the Union, although once again the rights are derivative of the relationship with an EU citizen and the exercising of the free movement right. These derivative rights have been furthered by the jurisprudence of the ECJ, particularly in *Singh, Metock, Jia, Chen, Baumbast* and *Carpenter*. It should be noted, however, that the rights provided were secondary rights designed to enhance the position of the Union citizen and his or her ability to move freely.

362  J Shaw 'The interpretation of European Union citizenship' (1998) 61 *MLR* 293.
363  M Bell 'Civic citizenship and migrant integration' (2007) 13 *EPL* 311, 314.

# 4   The area of freedom, security and justice (AFSJ)

The second area to be examined in this book is the AFSJ[1] and the free movement rights provided within it for third-country nationals (TCNs). The AFSJ was introduced into the EC Treaty at the Treaty of Amsterdam by moving the provisions concerning free movement of persons from the third pillar (Title VI TEU) into the first pillar (Title IV EC). With the adoption of the Lisbon Treaty the Union's pillar structure has been replaced by a single supranational edifice with Article 67(1) TFEU requiring the constitution of 'an area of freedom, security and justice with respect for fundamental rights and the different legal systems and traditions of the Member States'. Article 67(2) TFEU offers the possibility of free movement rights for TCNs by mandating the absence of internal border controls for persons, which notably does not limit this to Union citizens. Furthermore, a common policy on asylum, immigration and external border control, based on solidarity between Member States, is required, that has a single aim to be 'fair towards third country nationals'. Article 77(1) TFEU identifies two policy areas (free movement across internal borders for all persons 'whatever their nationality'; and the control and management of the Union's external borders) for which legislation can be adopted concerning visas, checks when crossing external borders, conditions for short period free movement for TCNs, a management for external borders and the 'absence of any controls on persons, whatever their nationality, when crossing internal borders' (Article 77(2) TFEU). Articles 78 and 79 TFEU then identify two different types of TCNs towards whom the Union's policies are directed: those requiring international protection; and immigrants. This has reduced the types of TCNs originally identified in ex-Article 63 EC (those claiming asylum, refugees and immigrants) from three to two.

The two principal international legal instruments that are relevant when dealing with TCNs in the AFSJ, particularly asylum-seekers and refugees, are the

---

1   See P Boeles 'Introduction: freedom, security and justice for all' in E Guild, C Harlow (eds) *Implementing Amsterdam: Immigration and Asylum Rights in EC Law* (Hart Publishing 2001) 1 for an analysis of the meaning of the term AFSJ. For a comprehensive description of the development of the AFSJ and of the EU's asylum policy see I Boccardi *Europe and Refugees: Towards an EU Asylum Policy* (Kluwer Law International 2002).

Geneva Convention on the Status of Refugees 1951 and the 1967 Protocol (Geneva Convention, Article 78(1) TFEU), and the European Convention on Human Rights (ECHR, Article 6 TEU). Article 33(1) of the Geneva Convention prevents the *refoulement* of a refugee to a state where his life or freedom would be threatened on account of race, religion, nationality, membership of a particular social group or political opinion. This must be coupled in Europe with Article 3 ECHR, which prevents anyone being subjected to torture or to inhumane or degrading treatment or punishment. The European Court of Human Rights (ECtHR) has held that this provides a similar protection to Article 33(1) of the Geneva Convention, as *refoulement* must be prevented if there is a real risk of being subjected to treatment contrary to Article 3 ECHR in the receiving country.[2] Furthermore, Addo and Grief have argued[3] that this Article 3 ECHR right is an absolute right, without any derogation,[4] particularly for extradition,[5] so long as there is a real risk rather than a mere possibility of ill-treatment[6] and thus extends further than Article 33(1) of the Geneva Convention.[7] It is also incumbent upon each Contracting State of the ECHR, in accordance with Article 13 ECHR, to ensure that an investigation of a risk of breach of Article 3 ECHR

2  *Chahal v United Kingdom* (1997) 23 EHRR 413; noted in Anon 'Case comment' [1997] EHRLR 172; S Foster 'Case comment' (1997) 31 *Law Teacher* 238; CJ Harvey 'Expulsion, national security and the European Convention' (1997) 22 *ELR* 626. *Chahal* was recently confirmed in strong language by the ECtHR in *Saadi v Italy* (2009) 49 EHRR 30; noted in Anon 'Case comment' [2008] EHRLR 422; D Feldman 'Deporting suspected terrorists to face torture' (2008) 67 *CLJ* 225; JL Cernic 'National security and expulsion to a risk of torture' (2008) 12 *Edin LR* 486. See *NA v UK* (2009) 48 EHRR 15 paras 109–113 for a summary of the general principles applicable to expulsion cases, and repeated in *SH v United Kingdom* (2012) 54 EHRR 4 para 68.

3  MK Addo, N Grief 'Does Article 3 of the European Convention on Human Rights enshrine absolute rights?' (1998) 9 *EJIL* 510; MK Addo, N Grief 'Some practical issues affecting the notion of absolute right in Article 3 ECHR' (1998) 23 Supp (Human Rights Survey) *ELR* 17; MK Addo, N Grief 'Is there a policy behind the decisions and judgments relating to Article 3 of the European Convention on Human Rights?' (1995) 20 *ELR* 178. See also H Battjes 'In search of a fair balance: the absolute character of the prohibition of *refoulement* under Article 3 ECHR reassessed' (2009) 22 *Leiden Journal of International Law* 583 and N Mavronicola 'What is an 'absolute right'? Deciphering absoluteness in the context of Article 3 of the European Convention on Human Rights' (2013) 12 *HRLR* 723.

4  *Ireland v United Kingdom* (1979–80) 2 EHRR 25 and more recently *Mubilanzila Mayeka and Kaniki Mitunga v Belgium* (2008) 46 EHRR 23 para 48.

5  *Soering v United Kingdom* (1989) 11 EHRR 439. See J Yorke 'Europe's judicial inquiry in extradition cases: closing the door on the death penalty' (2004) 29 *ELR* 546; A Lester, K Beattie 'Risking torture' [2005] EHRLR 565; J Yorke 'The right to life and abolition of the death penalty in the Council of Europe' (2009) 34 *ELR* 205; J Yorke 'Inhuman punishment and abolition of the death penalty in the Council of Europe' (2010) 16 *EPL* 77. For an in-depth analysis of the *Soering* case see M den Heijer 'Whose rights and which rights? The continuing story of *non-refoulement* under the European Convention on Human Rights' (2008) 10 *EJML* 277; H Battjes 'The *Soering* threshold: why only fundamental values prohibit *refoulement* in ECHR case law' (2009) 11 *EJML* 205.

6  *Vilvarajah v United Kingdom* (1992) 14 EHRR 248; A Sherlock 'Asylum seekers and the Convention' (1992) 17 *ELR* 281.

7  *Chahal* (n 2) para 80: 'protection afforded by Article 3 is . . . wider than that provided by Articles 32 and 33 of the United Nation's 1951 Convention on the Status of Refugees' and supported by H Lambert 'Protection against *refoulement* from Europe: human rights law comes to the rescue' (1999) 48 *ICLQ* 515; A Duffy 'Expulsion to face torture? *Non-refoulement* in international law' (2008) 20 *IJRL* 373, 379.

can be carried out rigorously and independently[8] so that it can have suspensive effect of the extradition process,[9] particularly when the effect of the extradition, where it is contrary to the ECHR, is potentially irreversible.[10] Indeed, in cases involving Article 3 ECHR the importance that the ECtHR attaches to Article 3 ECHR and the potential for irreversible consequences if the individual is extradited despite the extradition contravening Article 3 ECHR, the ECtHR has held that Article 13 ECHR requires appeals to be suspensive as a matter of law.[11] Article 5(1) ECHR provides for the right of liberty and security of the person that applies to everyone and Article 5(1)(a)–(f) ECHR provides an exhaustive list of permissible grounds for deprivation of a person's liberty.[12] Article 5(1)(f) ECHR allows the state to control the liberty of aliens in an immigration situation such that there can be a 'lawful arrest or detention of a person to prevent his effecting an unauthorised entry into the country or . . . against whom action is being taken with a view to deportation or extradition'. This does not call into question the decision to deport an individual[13] but the detention must be lawful,[14] non-arbitrary[15] and proportionate,[16] and the detention will be justified 'only for as long as deportation proceedings are in progress'.[17] Finally, an individual has the right to family life as outlined in Article 8 ECHR and the ECtHR's jurisprudence.[18]

8  *Assenov v Bulgaria* (1999) EHRR 652; noted in Anon 'Case comment' [1999] EHRLR 225 (for a more in-depth analysis see JA Goldston 'Race discrimination in Europe: problems and prospects' [1999] EHRLR 462). See also *R (on the application of Nasseri) v Secretary of State for the Home Department* [2008] 2 WLR 523 (QB), although overturned on appeal in *R (on the application of Nasseri) v Secretary of State for the Home Department* [2008] 3 WLR 1386 (CA), confirmed by the House of Lords in *R (on the application of Nasseri) v Secretary of State for the Home Department* [2010] 1 AC 1 (HL).

9  *Jabari v Turkey* [2001] INLR 136.

10  *Conka v Belgium* (2002) 34 EHRR 54; noted in Anon 'Case comment' [2002] EHRLR 691.

11  *Gebremedhin v France* (2010) 50 EHRR 29; noted in Anon 'Case comment' [2007] EHRLR 468; P Boeles 'Case reports of the European Court of Human Rights, the Human Rights Committee and the Committee against torture' (2008) 10 *EJML* 105, 112.

12  *A v United Kingdom* (2009) 49 EHRR 29 paras 162–63.

13  *Chahal* (n 2) para 112.

14  ibid para 118; *Medvedyev and Others v France* (2010) 51 EHRR 39 paras 79–80.

15  *Saadi v United Kingdom* (2008) 47 EHRR 17 paras 67–68.

16  ibid para 70.

17  *Chahal* (n 2) para 113.

18  See R Cholewinski 'The protection of the right of economic migrants to family reunion in Europe' (1994) 43 *ICLQ* 568; A Sherlock 'Deportation of aliens and Article 8 ECHR' (1998) 23 *ELR* HR62; H Lambert 'The European Court of Human Rights and the right of refugees and other persons in need of protection to family reunion' (2000) 11 *IJRL* 427; D Thym 'Respect for private and family life under Article 8 ECHR in immigration cases: a human right to regularize illegal stay?' (2008) 57 *ICLQ* 87. For the principles involving art 8 ECHR and the expulsion of long-term immigrants see *Boultif v Switzerland* (2001) 33 EHRR 50 (see Anon 'Case comment' [2002] EHRLR 276; N Rogers 'Immigration and the European Convention on Human Rights: are new principles emerging?' [2003] EHRLR 53), recently expanded in *Üner v Netherlands* (2007) 45 EHRR 14 (noted in N Berkowitz 'Case comment' (2007) 27 *JIANL* 43; Anon 'Case comment' [2007] EHRLR 103; P Boeles, M Bruins 'Case reports of the European Court of Human Rights and the Human Rights Committee' (2007) 9 *EJML* 253, 263; C Steinorth 'Case comment' (2008) 8 *HRLR* 185) and applied in *Keles v Germany* (2007) 44 EHRR 12, *Maslov v Austria* (2008) 47 EHRR 20 and subsequent case law.

This chapter picks up the investigation of free movement of persons in Chapter 3 but considers the entitlement to free movement of TCNs as specifically detailed in Title V TFEU. The introduction of the AFSJ with the Treaty of Amsterdam and its continuing development ever since has seen, as Toth[19] has pointed out, free movement of persons move away from a purely economic purpose to become the foundation on which the AFSJ is based. The chapter will commence with a short overview of the introduction of the AFSJ, that includes an analysis of the different positions of the UK, Ireland and Denmark, before then considering the positions of asylum-seekers, refugees and immigrants and their free movement rights.[20]

## 4.1 The introduction of the AFSJ

The Treaty of Amsterdam attempted to rationalise the labyrinthine structure that had been created through the intergovernmental structures of the Schengen Agreement and Schengen Implementing Convention (SIC) and to communitarise the decision-making process without resorting to supranationalism.[21] The objectives of the EU were amended from the close cooperation on justice and home affairs to the maintenance and development of the Union as an 'area of freedom, security and justice' (ex-Article 2 TEU). Free movement of persons was to be assured 'in conjunction with appropriate measures with respect to external border controls, asylum, immigration and the prevention and combating of crime'. This was compatible with the main premise of the SIC, which was to establish an area among the Schengen signatory states that had fully implemented free movement of persons such that '[i]nternal borders may be crossed at any point without any checks on persons being carried out' (Article 2(1) SIC). The Schengen Protocol annexed to both the TEU and the EC Treaty laid out the

---

19 AG Toth 'The legal effects of the protocols relating to the United Kingdom, Ireland and Denmark' in T Heukels, N Blokker and M Brus (eds) *The European Union after Amsterdam* (Kluwer Law International 1998) 227, 248; A Wiener 'Forging flexibility – the British "no" to Schengen' (2000) 1 *EJML* 441.

20 Note the adoption and development of the global approach to migration in Council Document 15914/1/05 at 2, 9; Commission Communication on priority actions for responding to the challenges of migration: First follow-up to Hampton Court COM(2005) 621 final; Commission Communication on the Global Approach to Migration one year on: towards a comprehensive European migration policy COM(2005) 735; Commission Communication on applying the Global Approach to Migration to the Eastern and South-eastern regions neighbouring the European Union COM(2007) 247; Commission Communication on strengthening the Global approach to Migration: Increasing coordination, coherence and synergies COM(2008) 611 final.

21 See E Wagner 'The integration of Schengen into the framework of the European Union' (1998) 25 *LIEI* 1; PJ Kuijper 'Some legal problems associated with the communitarisation of policy on visas, asylum and immigration under the Amsterdam Treaty and incorporation of the Schengen *acquis*' (2000) 37 *CMLRev* 345; M den Boer, L Corrado 'For the record or off the record: comments about the incorporation of Schengen into the EU' (1999) 1 *EJML* 397.

process of integrating the Schengen *acquis*[22] with Council Decisions 1999/435[23] and 1999/436,[24] defining it and assigning the legal base for each provision. This Schengen Protocol and a series of other protocols attached to the EC Treaty and/ or the TEU regulated the complex position of the UK, Ireland and Denmark in reference to Schengen, Article 14 EC and Title IV EC Treaty, whilst Article 69 EC limited the application of Title IV EC to the UK, Ireland and Denmark in accordance with these protocols. With the adoption of the Lisbon Treaty, Title IV EC has become Title V of Part Three of the TFEU, incorporating the old Title IV EC and the Justice and Home Affairs (JHA) provisions of the third pillar and with the protocols revised. The position of these opt-outs in the protocols are now correctly summarised by Peers as 'fiendish'.[25] Article 1 of the Schengen Protocol[26] (Protocol 19) lists the Member States authorised to establish closer cooperation over matters dealing with the Schengen *acquis*, which does not include the UK or Ireland. Article 4 then establishes the possibility for the UK and Ireland to opt in to some or all of the Schengen *acquis* provisions with the approval of the unanimous vote in the Council, which both the UK and Ireland have taken up for specific measures.[27] Article 5(1) specifies that any proposals or initiatives to build on the Schengen *acquis* are to be subject to the EU treaties' provisions and if Ireland and the UK have not notified the Council, in writing, within a reasonable period of time, then enhanced cooperation authorisation to go ahead with the legislation will have been granted, as stipulated in Article 329 TFEU. Article 5(2) creates a new right for the UK and Ireland to be able to opt-out of these Schengen-building measures even when they had opted in to the underlying Schengen *acquis*. This new right, however, is heavily procedural, with the special procedure in Article 5(3), (4) and (5) only coming into play after the suspension of the normal

22  See Protocol Integrating the Schengen *acquis* into the framework of the European Union, attached to the Treaty of Amsterdam [1997] OJ L340/93. The *acquis* is defined in the annex to the Protocol as the Schengen Agreement, the Schengen Implementing Convention, the Accession Protocols and Agreements to the Schengen Agreement and the Decisions and Declarations of the Schengen Executive Committee. These are published in [2000] OJ L239.

23  Council Decision 1999/435/EC concerning the definition of the Schengen *acquis* for the purpose of determining, in conformity with the relevant provisions of the Treaty establishing the European Community and the Treaty on European Union, the legal basis for each of the provisions or decisions which constitute the *acquis* [1999] OJ L176/1.

24  Council Decision 1999/436/EC determining, in conformity with the relevant provisions of the Treaty establishing the European Community and the Treaty on European Union, the legal basis for each of the provisions or decisions which constitute the Schengen *acquis* [1999] OJ L176/17.

25  S Peers 'In a world of their own? Justice and home affairs opt-outs and the Treaty of Lisbon' (2008) 10 *CYELS* 383, 411.

26  Protocol (No 19) on the Schengen *acquis* integrated into the framework of the European Union [2012] OJ C326/290.

27  Council Decision 2000/365/EC concerning the request of the United Kingdom of Great Britain and Northern Ireland to take part in some of the provisions of the Schengen *acquis* [2000] OJ L131/43; Council Decision 2002/192/EC concerning Ireland's request to take part in some of the provisions of the Schengen *acquis* [2002] OJ L64/20; T Tayleur 'Schengen: opting in – but how far?' (2001) 151 *NLJ* 482. The UK's participation has been put into effect by Council Decision 2004/926/EC on the putting into effect parts of the Schengen *acquis* by the United Kingdom of Great Britain and Northern Ireland [2004] OJ L395/70 but it should be noted there is no equivalent legal measure for Ireland.

decision-making procedure. The price to be paid for this right is that the Council could decide that the underlying Schengen *acquis* no longer applies, either wholly or in part, with a balancing test being employed of the widest possible participation against coherence and serious effect on practical operability.[28] This then grants a right of choice to the UK and Ireland to opt in to the development of new legal measures of the Schengen *acquis*[29] if the legislative measure falls into the category of Schengen measures agreed under Article 4 of the Protocol, that is, those included in Decisions 2000/365 and 2002/192. If, however, the new Schengen *acquis* measure is not within that category the UK and Ireland can only opt in to develop it if it can be applied autonomously.[30] Furthermore, any decision by the UK and Ireland to opt out of these Schengen-building measures after initially opting in could see either state excluded from the Schengen decision-making process and *acquis*.

Two further protocols elaborate the position of the UK and Ireland with respect to immigration. In Protocol 20,[31] Article 1 entitles the UK, notwithstanding the absolute statement in Articles 26 and 77 TFEU, any other provision of the TFEU or the TEU, or any international convention, to maintain external border controls to verify and determine whether to grant the right of entry to the UK. This is extended to Ireland by Article 2 maintaining the Common Travel Area (CTA), the bilateral arrangement founded upon administrative agreements between the two countries relating to the movement of persons between them[32] and now endorsed in a public agreement.[33] As a consequence, Article 3 allows the other Member States to maintain border controls between 'Schengenland'[34] and the UK and Ireland. Articles 1 and 2 of Protocol 21[35] secure an opt-out for the UK and Ireland from the provisions of Title V and any implementing measures. However, if within three months after a proposal or initiative for a Title V implementing measure, either the UK or Ireland notifies the Council in writing that it wishes to take part in the adoption and application of this measure,

28 M Fletcher 'Schengen, the European Court of Justice and flexibility under the Lisbon Treaty: balancing the United Kingdom's "ins" and "outs"' (2009) 5 *EuConst* 71, 91.
29 Cases C–137/05 *United Kingdom v Council* [2007] ECR I–11593 para 50 and C–77/05 *United Kingdom v Council* [2007] ECR I–11459 para 68, where the UK brought two art 263 TFEU actions for annulment of two Schengen legal measures; noted in JJ Rijpma 'Case note' (2008) 45 *CMLRev* 835.
30 Case C–137/05 (n 29) Opinion of AG Trstenjak para 101 and Case C–77/05 (n 29) Opinion of AG Trstenjak para 107.
31 Protocol (No 20) on the Application of Certain Aspects of Article 26 TFEU to the UK and Ireland [2012] OJ C326/293.
32 See B Ryan 'The common travel area between Britain and Ireland' (2001) 64 *MLR* 855.
33 Home Office 'Joint Statement of Mr Damien Green UK Minister of State for Immigration and Mr Alan Shatter Ireland Minister for Justice and Equality Regarding Co-operation on Measures to Secure the External Common Travel Area Border' December 2011 http://www.homeoffice. gov.uk/about-us/freedom-of-information/released-information1/foi-archive-immigration/ 21197-mea-sec-trav/21197-mea-sec-trav?view=Binary.
34 The term is used in K Hailbronner, C Thierry 'Schengen II and Dublin: responsibility for asylum applications in Europe' (1997) 34 *CMLRev* 957, 959.
35 Protocol (No 21) on the Position of the UK and Ireland in Respect of the AFSJ [2012] OJ C326/295.

then it will be entitled to do so (Article 3). It is clear that this may not be used by the UK or Ireland to block the implementation of the measure as the Council is authorised to adopt measures on its own if agreement cannot be reached with the UK or Ireland within 'a reasonable time' (Article 3(2)). If after a measure has been adopted by the Council the UK or Ireland notifies the Council and Commission that it wishes to accept that measure then the Commission will decide within four months whether it can or cannot and determine the arrangements required (Article 4). The new Article 4a specifies that Protocol 21 provisions are to apply to measures proposed or adopted amending an existing measure to which the UK and Ireland are bound. However, where the non-participation of the UK or Ireland would make the application of the measure inoperable for other Member States a further two months of negotiation can be allowed to attempt to persuade either state to come on board (Article 4a(2)). If on expiry of the two month period the UK or Ireland do not opt in to the new measure the UK or Ireland can be expelled from the existing measure. The Council, acting by qualified majority voting (QMV) (notably without special participation rules so involving the UK and Ireland) 'may determine that the UK or Ireland should bear the direct financial consequences, if any, necessarily and unavoidably incurred as a result of the cessation of its participation in the existing measure' (Article 4a(3)). Article 4a(4) allows the UK or Ireland to opt in to an adopted measure in accordance with Article 4. Under Article 8, Ireland has the possibility of unilaterally withdrawing from Protocol 21, further emphasised by Ireland's Declaration No 56,[36] which declares its intention to engage fully in Title IV EC developments as far as the CTA with the UK allows. In general, the provisions of the *acquis* that the UK and Ireland opted into were the restrictive, control and order flanking measures in the areas of police and judicial cooperation in criminal matters, the Title VI TEU aspects of the Schengen Information System (SIS), the fight against drugs, asylum and air carrier sanctions (Articles 26 and 27 SIC), rather than the liberalising free movement of persons provisions. Thus, in an area of freedom, security and justice the UK and Ireland participate in security and justice but opt out of freedom.

The Schengen Protocol (Protocol 19) has attempted to create a slightly more straightforward opt-out procedure for Denmark than the previous regime under the EC Treaty,[37] although the new Protocol 22[38] creates opacity and has been described by Adler-Nissen as 'bizarre'.[39] Article 1 of Protocol 19 includes Denmark within the Schengen Member States with Article 3 providing for the adoption of measures constituting a development of the Schengen *acquis*, their

---

36  Declaration (No 56) by Ireland on Article 3 of the Protocol on the Position of the UK and Ireland in respect of the AFSJ [2012] OJ L326/358.
37  M Hedemann-Robinson 'The area of freedom, security and justice with regard to the UK, Ireland and Denmark: the "opt-in opt-outs" under the Treaty of Amsterdam' in D O'Keeffe, P Twomey (eds) *Legal Issues of the Amsterdam Treaty* (Hart Publishing 1999) 289, 300.
38  Protocol (No 22) on the Position of Denmark [2012] OJ C326/299.
39  R Adler-Nissen 'Behind the scenes of differentiated integration: circumventing national opt-outs in justice and home affairs' (2009) 16 *JEPP* 62, 75.

implementation and application to Denmark to be governed by Protocol 22. With the earlier equivalent Protocol, similar to that for the UK and Ireland, Denmark had attempted to secure a politically acceptable opt-out to Title IV TFEU (Article 2) and measures implemented under it (Article 1). The new proto-col attempts to achieve a similar position with an opt-out to Title V TFEU in Article 2 that is complemented by an opt-out from measures adopted under Title V through both Articles 1 and 2, although Article 6 provides for Denmark's participation in measures dealing with visas. Article 2 also excludes any judgments of the European Courts on Title V or measures adopted under it from having any effect in Denmark. This latter opt-out from the jurisprudence of the ECJ must be read with Article 4(1), which enables Denmark to opt in to any Schengen-building proposal or initiative within six months of its adoption, without an ability to opt in at the proposal stage, but the measure would then create an international legal obligation on Denmark rather than a Union duty. There is a heavy incentive to implement these decisions, however, as Article 4(2) allows the Member States and Denmark to take 'appropriate measures' that is effectively a justification for the erection of border controls at the Danish border.[40] The situa-tion with Denmark has been complicated by an addition of the Lisbon Treaty and a recent development, Article 8, which was added by the Lisbon Treaty enabling Denmark, if it chooses, to introduce a similar opt-out regime, with the possibility of individual opt-in, similar to that applicable to the UK and Ireland. In 2011 the newly elected Danish prime minister, Helle Thorning-Schmidt, announced the intention of her government to hold a referendum to withdraw from Protocol 22 using the right set out in Article 7,[41] although this has yet to be enacted. The effect of Protocol 22 on Denmark has been minimal, as Denmark has chosen within a short period of time to sign up to all the measures that have been passed under Title V TFEU, a situation reflected in the proposal of the prime minister. The position with reference to the jurisprudence of the ECJ is far more worrying, as there does not appear to be the possibility of individuals being able to clarify the law, question the law or rely on their rights before the ECJ.

## 4.2   Asylum-seekers

The EU policy on asylum has been in development since Schengen in 1985, through the Tampere Conclusions and Hague Programme to the creation of a future Common European Asylum System (CEAS) as a constituent part of the AFSJ as formulated in the Commission's Green Paper on the future CEAS[42] and on to the Stockholm Programme and European Pact on Asylum and Immigration.

---

40  Hedemann-Robinson 'The area of freedom, security and justice' (n 37) 299.
41  V Pop 'New Danish Government rolls back border controls' 4 October 2011 http://euobserver. com/justice/113809.
42  Commission Green Paper on the future Common European Asylum System COM(2007) 301 final. See also the Commission Communication on a policy plan on asylum: an integrated approach to protection across the EU COM(2008) 360 final.

The authority for the adoption of legislative measures dealing with asylum is set out in Article 78(1) TFEU and must comply with the Geneva Convention. A debate on asylum was originally initiated through a Communication[43] in which the Commission set out its policy on asylum[44] for a common procedure and a uniform status of asylum-seekers. In a forward thinking assessment it raised the issue of the integration of asylum-seekers with the possibility of access to Member State nationality or, in the alternative, the development of a concept of civic citizenship.[45] The asylum policy of the EU has now been encapsulated in the three objectives set out in the 2003 Commission Communication:[46]

(1) the orderly and managed arrival of persons in need of international protection in the EU from the region of origin;
(2) burden and responsibility sharing within the EU as well as with regions of origin enabling them to provide effective protection as soon as possible and as closely as possible to the needs of persons in need of international protection; and,
(3) the development of an integrated approach to efficient and enforceable asylum decision-making and return procedures.

The emphasis therefore of this asylum policy is on the movement of TCNs across the external borders of the EU rather than the internal movement of such persons. However, the legislative measures that have been adopted have an impact on the internal dimension and must therefore be considered when analysing the free movement rights of TCNs and in particular asylum-seekers. The difference between an asylum-seeker and an individual with refugee status is hard to determine as the international community has determined the meaning and regulated refugees through the Geneva Convention but no international agreement has been forthcoming on asylum-seekers. The clearest international statement on asylum is that laid down in Article 18 of the EU Charter of Fundamental Rights, that 'the right of asylum shall be guaranteed with due respect for the rules of the Geneva Convention and in accordance with the [TEU] and [TFEU]',[47] although Article 14(1) of the 1948 Universal Declaration of Human Rights stated that '[e]veryone has the right to seek and to enjoy in other countries asylum from persecution'. Its inclusion in the EU Charter imbues the right with fundamental rights status and the Lisbon Treaty inserted the new Article 6(1) TEU that gave the EU Charter the same legal value as the EU

---

43 Commission Communication towards a common asylum procedure and a uniform status, valid throughout the Union, for persons granted asylum COM(2000)755 final.
44 For a discussion of the theories on asylum see N Nathwani 'The purpose of asylum' (2000) 12 *IJRL* 354.
45 Commission Communication towards a common asylum procedure (n 43) para 3.4. See M Bell 'Civic citizenship and migrant integration' (2007) 13 *EPL* 311.
46 Commission Communication towards more accessible, equitable and managed asylum systems' COM(2003) 315, 13.
47 C Harvey 'The right to seek asylum in the European Union' [2004] EHRLR 17, 32.

Treaties. It is submitted that the provision, when the ECJ considers it, is likely to be found to be sufficiently clear, precise and unconditional, when compared with provisions such as Articles 18 and 157 TFEU, for the Court to find it directly effective. The effect of such a right on TCNs is uncertain, particularly with the restrictive implementing legislation that has been adopted. It is also uncertain with reference to citizens of the Union as the Protocol on Asylum[48] affords safe country of origin status to all Member States.

An asylum-seeker will travel to the EU and make an application in a specific state on the basis of subjective reasons applicable to that particular applicant. It may be that the person applies at the first opportunity as soon as he or she has arrived in the EU, or the applicant may favour a particular Union Member State because of family connections or a supportive community, cultural, linguistic or historical connections or individual preference that the applicant has for the receiving country.[49] The EU has, however, created a system of allocating the Member State responsible for assessing the applicant's claim in a one-stop-shop objective system. This was originally laid down in Articles 28–38 SIC and then replaced by the Dublin Convention[50] of 1990. This intergovernmental arrangement had the objective of ensuring not only that one Member State was responsible for the investigation of an asylum application from a TCN but that a Member State did actually take responsibility for processing the asylum application and so asylum-seekers did not 'orbit'[51] from country to country in a process known as asylum shopping. Article 2 required it to be applied in accordance with the Geneva Convention. Article 3(1) required Member States 'to examine the application of any alien who applies at the border or in the territory to any one of them for asylum' with a hierarchical catalogue of conflict rules determining the Member State with responsibility for examining the asylum application. These rules were applied in descending priority of: the Member State where refugee status had already been granted to a specified family member who was legally resident in the Member State;[52] the Member State that had already issued a residence permit or a visa; the Member State where the applicant had first entered illegally from outside the EU; the Member State with responsibility for controlling the entry of the applicant across the external borders of the Member States; and, in all other cases, the Member State where the first application for asylum was made in the EU, including any previous applications for asylum that had been refused (Articles 4–8). Thus, the default position for

---

48  Protocol (No 24) on Asylum for Nationals of Member States of the European Union [2012] L326/305.

49  N Blake 'The Dublin Convention and rights of asylum seekers in the European Union' in Guild, Harlow (eds) *Implementing Amsterdam* (n 1) 95, 99.

50  Convention determining the State responsible for examining applications for asylum lodged in one of the Member States of the European Communities [1997] OJ C254/1.

51  R Byrne, A Shacknove 'The safe third country notion in European asylum law' (1996) 9 *Harvard Human Rights Journal* 185, 207; R Marx 'Adjusting the Dublin Convention: new approaches to Member State responsibility for asylum applications' (2001) 3 *EJML* 7, 10.

52  The concept of 'family member' in art 4 was narrowly defined to include only the reunification of spouses and of parents with their unmarried children under 18 years of age.

application examination was for the 'first country of entry' in Article 8 unless the applicant could bring him or herself within Articles 4–7. A sovereignty clause, Article 3(4), enabled a Member State to examine the asylum application where the Member State did not have responsibility under the conflict rules and a negative decision had already been determined in another Member State, and Article 9 enabled another state to take the application by mutual consent. However, Article 3(5) provided that a Member State could decide that a non-Community country was responsible for the application in accordance with the state's own laws and practices.

In 1992, at the London Council meeting of the ministers responsible for immigration, the 'safe third country' concept required under Article 3(5) of the Dublin Convention was fleshed out, to be incorporated into national law as soon as possible. Thus: the life and freedom of the asylum applicant could not be threatened within the meaning of Article 33 of the Geneva Convention; there must be no risk of torture or inhuman or degrading treatment; the applicant must either have been granted protection or had an opportunity to claim protection in the third country before entering the EU, or there is clear evidence of his admissibility to a third country; and there must be effective protection available within the meaning of the Geneva Convention.[53]

The Dublin Convention and the use of the safe third country concept aroused considerable criticism. First, the Dublin Convention did not achieve its objective as a Member State would not substantively assess and process the application. A Member State would first determine if the asylum applicant had passed through a non-Member State before entering the EU. If so then that country would be assessed on the safe third country criteria in the London Resolutions and if it fulfilled the criteria then the person would be returned to that third country without considering the application made.[54] Secondly, if the asylum applicant had passed through a number of third countries, particularly as third countries followed the EU example and incorporated the safe third country definition into their own domestic law, or had passed through several Member States then the individual could remain in orbit without his or her application being assessed.[55] Thirdly, there was evidence that the end of the chain resulted in *refoulement* in

---

53 Council Document 10579/92. The three non-legally binding instruments in this document became known as the London Resolutions. See J van Selm 'Access to procedures: "safe third countries", "safe countries of origin" and "Time limits"' June 2001 UNHCR http://www.unhcr.org/protect/PROTECTION/3b39a2403.pdf 10.

54 A Achermann, M Gattiker 'Safe third countries: European Developments' (1995) 7 *IJRL* 19, 22 and G Borchelt 'The safe third country practice in the European Union: a misguided approach to asylum law and a violation of international human rights standards' (2002) 33 *Columbia Human Rights Law Review* 473, 497. See also H Lambert '"Safe third country" in the European Union: an evolving concept in international law and implications for the UK' (2012) 26 *JIANL* 318.

55 Borchelt 'The safe third country practice' (n 54) 501; GI Coman 'European Union policy on asylum and its inherent human rights violations' (1998) 64 *Brooklyn Law Review* 1217, 1235. See also R Dunstan 'Playing human pinball: the Amnesty International United Kingdom Section Report on UK Home Office "safe third country" practice' (1995) 7 *IJRL* 606.

breach of Article 33(1)[56] of the Geneva Convention[57] (chain *refoulement*). Fourthly, the Geneva Convention obligates each signatory state[58] to make its own judgment about the recognition or refusal and eventual deportation of individual applicants for asylum. By failing to assess an application a Member State was therefore in breach of the Geneva Convention.[59] Fifthly, applications for asylum on humanitarian grounds that were not based on the Geneva Convention were not considered and the family reunification provisions (Article 4) were too strict.[60] Furthermore, the evidential rules that required proof of the travel route of asylum-seekers were often impossible to satisfy that, in Hurwitz's opinion,[61] rendered the Dublin Convention virtually useless in many cases. Finally, the Member States applied different standards for the determination of 'protection' within Article 33 of the Geneva Convention with the UK following the 'internal protection' approach in which an individual can fear persecution from non-state actors as well as state actors, and Germany and France following the 'accountability theory' that only considered state actors.[62] In *TI v UK*[63] a Sri Lankan Tamil travelled from Sri Lanka to Germany and then entered the UK, claiming asylum in the UK. He claimed that he feared persecution from the Tamil Tigers, a non-state terrorist group, and that if he was returned to Germany in accordance with the Dublin Convention the UK would be in breach of Article 3 ECHR as he would be returned to Sri Lanka where he would be tortured or suffer inhumane treatment. The ECtHR held that by returning TI to Germany the UK would be in breach of Article 3 ECHR if there was a real risk that that he would be removed to Sri Lanka where he would be subjected to treatment contrary to Article 3 ECHR. As there were alternative methods for assessing his return other than that for asylum then TI could be returned to Germany, even though there was previous evidence of *refoulement* of Tamils in fear of Tamil Tiger persecution.

---

56  Article 33(1) Geneva Convention: 'No Contracting State shall expel or return ("*refouler*") a refugee in any manner whatsoever to the frontiers of territories where his life or freedom would be threatened on account of his race, religion, nationality, membership of a particular social group or political opinion'.

57  Borchelt 'The safe third country practice' (n 54) 502; D Joly 'The porous dam: European harmonisation on asylum in the nineties' (1994) 6 *IJRL* 159, 170; S Weidlich 'First instance asylum proceedings in Europe: do bona fide refugees find protection?' (2000) 14 *Georgetown Immigration Law Journal* 643, 657.

58  UNHCR *Handbook on Procedures and Criteria for Determining Refugee Status under the 1951 Convention and the 1967 Protocol relating to the Status of Refugees HCR/IP/4/Eng/REV.1* (2nd edn United Nations Publications 1992) Foreword.

59  M-CSFG Foblets 'Europe and its aliens after Maastricht: the painful move to substantive Harmonisation of Member States' policies towards third country nationals' (1994) 42 *American Journal of Comparative Law* 783, 794.

60  A Hurwitz 'The 1990 Dublin Convention: a comprehensive assessment' (2000) 11 *IJRL* 464.

61  ibid.

62  See J Moore 'Whither the accountability theory: second-class status for third-party refugees as a threat to international refugee protection' (2001) 13 *IJRL* 32; D Wilsher 'Non-state actors and the definition of a refugee in the United Kingdom: protection, accountability or culpability?' (2003) 15 *IJRL* 68.

63  *TI v United Kingdom* [2000] INLR 211.

In *Adan and Aitseguer*[64] the House of Lords held that returning two asylum-seekers to France and Germany in accordance with the Dublin Convention would be in breach of Article 33 of the Geneva Convention as the French and German courts did not accept non-state agents as agents of persecution. The two asylum-seekers could ultimately be returned to their country of origin and face persecution there.[65] The result of the failure to take into account the Member States' different definitions of protection[66] meant that 'the system is fundamentally flawed as the same individual who seeks asylum in different Member States is likely to have a different outcome as regards protection'.[67]

Probably the most damning flaw of the Dublin Convention was that it simply did not work.[68] This was confirmed in two working papers the Commission issued on the operation of the Dublin Convention.[69] The result was the replacement of the intergovernmental Dublin Convention with Regulation 343/2003/EC,[70] which has become known either as the Dublin Regulation or Dublin II. Dublin II did not apply to Denmark, which continued to follow the Dublin Convention procedures[71] until Decision 2006/188/EC[72] was adopted. Much of the Dublin Regulation mirrors the Dublin Convention. Article 3 continues to require Member States to examine an asylum application of a TCN, the examination being carried out by a single state determined by the criteria laid down in Chapter III of the regulation. Article 3(2) also enables a Member State to examine an application even if it is not the responsible state as determined by the Chapter III criteria (the sovereignty clause). This is coupled with Article 15 that sanctions any Member State, on humanitarian grounds, to bring together family members, as well as other dependent relatives, based in particular on family or cultural considerations

---

64 *R v Secretary of State for the Home Department, ex parte Adan, Subaskaran and Aitsegeur* [2001] 2 AC 477 (HL).
65 ibid 515 (Lord Steyn): 'It is accepted, and rightly accepted, by the Secretary of State that it is a long standing principle in English law that if it would be unlawful to return the asylum seeker directly to his country of origin where he is subject to persecution in the relevant sense, it would be unlawful to return him to a third country which is known will return him to his country of origin . . .'.
66 G Noll 'Formalism vs empiricism: some reflections on the Dublin Convention on the occasion of recent European case law' (2001) 70 *NJIL* 161.
67 E Guild 'Seeking asylum: storm clouds between international commitments and EU legislative measures' (2004) 29 *ELR* 198, 207.
68 Blake 'The Dublin Convention' (n 49) 95.
69 Revisiting the Dublin Convention: developing Community legislation for determining which Member State is responsible for considering an asylum application submitted in one of the Member States SEC(2000) 522 final, and Evaluation of the Dublin Convention SEC(2001) 756 final.
70 Council Regulation 343/2003/EC establishing the criteria and mechanisms for determining the Member State responsible for examining an asylum application lodged in one of the Member States by a third-country national [2003] OJ L50/1. A further regulation has been adopted fleshing out the detail of Dublin II – Council Regulation 1560/2003/EC laying down detailed rules for the application of Regulation 343/2003 [2003] OJ L222/3.
71 S Adamo 'The legal position of migrants in Denmark: assessing the context around the "cartoon crisis"' (2007) 9 *EJML* 1.
72 Council Decision 2006/188/EC on the conclusion of the agreement between the European Community and Denmark extending to Denmark the provisions of Regulation 343/2003 and Regulation 2725/2000 [2006] OJ L66/37. The agreement is at [2006] OJ L66/38.

and with the consent of the persons concerned. Special cases where the person concerned is dependent on assistance of another person because of pregnancy, a newborn child, serious illness, severe handicap or old age, should normally be kept or brought together with another relative in a Member State, so long as there were family ties in the country of origin. Where a TCN has already moved from the initial Member State of entry to another Member State in accordance with the dependency requirement of Article 15(2) then the second Member State takes responsibility for assessing the claim for asylum.[73] Furthermore, dependency for family reunification purposes can either be of the asylum-seeker on the already established TCN, or vice versa.[74] If an unaccompanied minor has relatives in a Member State who can care for him or her then there should be reunification if possible and if it is in the best interests of the child. Article 3(3) still enables a Member State under domestic law to return an asylum-seeker to a third country, so long as the Geneva Convention is complied with. The hierarchy of criteria for the allocation of the state responsible for examining the asylum claim are set out in Chapter III, are similar to the Dublin Convention criteria with some additions and still have a descending order of priority. By default, if the criteria cannot designate the Member State responsible, the first Member State in which the asylum application was lodged shall be responsible (Article 13). Where a number of family members lodge asylum applications at a similar time they are to be assessed together by the Member State who is responsible for examining the applications of the largest number of them or, failing this, is responsible for examining the application of the oldest of them (Article 14). Chapter V outlines the procedures for taking charge and taking back, an important matter as the two processes involve different time limits. For both taking charge and taking back the request must be made within three months of the asylum application and the asylum-seeker will be transferred within six months of the acceptance of responsibility.[75] However, a decision must be made within two months of the request for the taking charge procedure, whilst for taking back the decision will be made within a month of the request, or a fortnight if the request is based on Eurodac (that is, fingerprint comparison database) information. If a Member State establishes through the hierarchical criteria that another Member State is responsible for determining the application, then it can request the latter Member State to take back or take charge of the asylum-seeker. The request to take charge occurs where the asylum-seeker did not make an application in the Member State that is considered to be responsible in accordance with the criteria, whilst a request to take back means that an application had previously been lodged, withdrawn or rejected in another Member State.

73 Case C–245/11 *K v Bundesasylamt* (ECJ 6 November 2012) para 30.
74 ibid paras 32–33.
75 See Case C–19/08 *Migrationsverket v Edgar Petrosian and Others* [2009] ECR I–495 clarifying the time limits.

The Dublin Regulation maintains 'the same hereditary weaknesses which bedevilled the Dublin Convention',[76] particularly the possibility of 'chain *refoulement*', asylum-seekers in orbit and the return of an asylum-seeker to a safe third country without assessing the safety of the third country or the asylum-seeker if returned there. However, although the weaknesses remain there are improvements. The first is that the legislative measure is a regulation and so has direct applicability in the Member States. Domestic courts can rely directly on it and are able to refer questions of interpretation to the ECJ under Article 267 TFEU. As a consequence, the ECJ can provide the harmonisation that Guild[77] calls for on definitional issues, in particular the determination of the meaning of protection in the Geneva Convention. Indeed, the issue of the difference of protection may now have receded with the House of Lords' acceptance that Germany does indeed provide sufficient guarantees over the level of protection required for the Geneva Convention[78] and the ECHR,[79] and evidence by Phuong[80] that French legislation and case law has now come into line with the British position. Battjes[81] suggests that the position that a Member State does not have to consider the merits of an asylum application before an applicant is returned to either another Member State or a safe third country is in compliance with the Member State's obligations under Article 33(1) of the Geneva Convention, so long as the applicant is given the opportunity upon application to present evidence specific to his or her case that could rebut that presumption. The introduction of a humanitarian clause alongside the 'sovereignty clause' of Article 3(2) provides some greater protection for family members and more vulnerable persons over the examination of the asylum application and transfer to another Member State. Also, the family reunification criteria at the head of the hierarchy of criteria emphasises the importance of family reunification within the EU, which has now been broadly interpreted by the ECJ in *K v Bundesasylamt*.

However, problems remain with the Dublin Regulation. The first is that there is an automatic presumption that all EU Member States are safe for the return of asylum applicants (recital 2). Thus it is possible that domestic courts and immigration authorities will ignore the specific circumstances of the individual.[82] Secondly, the definition of family member in Article 2(i) is limited to an asylum applicant's spouse (or partner if the national law recognises this), their minor

---

76 Guild 'Seeking asylum' (n 67) 207.
77 ibid 208.
78 *R (on the application of Zeqiri) v Secretary of State for the Home Department* [2002] Imm AR 296 (HL); *R (on the application of Yogathas and Thangarasa) v Secretary of State for the Home Department* [2003] 1 AC 920 (HL).
79 *Yogathas and Thangarasa* (n 78) 942 (Lord Hutton) where his lordship equated the protection under art 3 ECHR with the scope of protection required under art 33(1) of the Geneva Convention. See *R (on the application of Razgar) v Secretary of State for the Home Department* [2004] 2 AC 368 (HL), where a similar position was adopted for art 8 ECHR.
80 C Phuong 'Persecution by non-state agents: comparative judicial interpretation of the 1951 Refugee Convention' (2003) 4 *EJML* 521.
81 H Battjes 'A balance between fairness and efficiency? The Directive on International Protection and the Dublin Regulation (2002) 4 *EJML* 159, 188.
82 See *Nasseri* (HL) (n 8).

children as long as they are unmarried and dependent, and the father, mother or guardian when the applicant is a minor and unmarried. This is considerably truncated when compared with the definition for family members of an EU citizen in Article 2(2) of Directive 2004/38. In a research paper for the UNHCR in 2006,[83] Kok investigated the operation of the Dublin Regulation and found three significant issues of concern. The first[84] was that some Member States do not conduct a full and fair assessment of a returnee's asylum application, treating certain claims as implicitly withdrawn and failing to comply with the *non-refoulement* principle. Secondly,[85] some asylum-seekers are returned or deported to a safe third country before the full legal process is completed as the right to suspensive effect of appeals is not automatic. Thirdly,[86] there is an inconsistent approach to family reunification that does not give full effect to the right to family life in Article 8 ECHR. Furthermore, the limited definition of 'family member' creates significant hardships for some families and difficulties for Member States when processing asylum applications. The first Commission Report[87] on the evaluation of the Dublin Regulation confirmed the first and third of Kok's findings,[88] whilst also noting the increased use of custodial measures before the transfer of the asylum-seeker and procedural irregularities, particularly with time limits.[89]

The position of Greece in relation to the Dublin Regulation has caused considerable concern with low rates of granting refugee status to applicants[90] as well as allegations of persecution of asylum-seekers by non-state actors[91] and, indeed, state actors[92]. However, of more concern are the procedures for assessing applications for asylum[93] and the possibility of the *refoulement* of TCNs.[94] In particular, where an asylum-seeker applies for asylum in Greece but then leaves for another Member State before the assessment procedure is concluded, then the application will be withdrawn and the applicant notified as a person whose whereabouts are unknown. That individual, if returned to Greece under

---

83  L Kok *The Dublin II Regulation* (UNHCR 2006).
84  ibid 2.
85  ibid 3.
86  ibid.
87  Commission Report on the evaluation of the Dublin system COM(2007) 299 final.
88  ibid 6.
89  ibid 8.
90  A Skordas, N Sitaropoulos 'Why Greece is not a safe host country for refugees' (2004) 16 *IJRL* 25, 27.
91  ibid 32.
92  PRO ASYL 'The truth may be bitter, but it must be told: the situation of refugees in the Aegean and the practices of the Greek coast guard' October 2007 http://www.statewatch.org/news/2007/oct/greece-proasyl-refugees.pdf; PRO ASYL 'The situation in Greece is out of control' October 2008 http://www.proasyl.de/fileadmin/proasyl/fm_redakteure/Asyl_in_Europa/Griechenland/Out_of_contol_Eng_END.pdf.
93  Amnesty International 'Out of the spotlight: the rights of foreigners and minorities are still a grey area' EUR 25/005/2006 http://www.amnesty.org/en/library/asset/EUR25/016/2005/en/dom-EUR250162005en.html.
94  For an analysis of recent developments see J Mink 'EU asylum and human rights protection: revisiting the principle of *non-refoulement* and the prohibition of torture and other forms of ill-treatment' (2012) 14 *EJML* 119.

the Dublin Regulation, will be unable to have the process reopened unless the TCN presents him or herself to the authorities within three months of the notification and can adduce evidence that any absence was as the result of force majeure.[95] The problems with Greece have been addressed by the UK courts[96] with the Court of Appeal refusing to stay the removal of TCNs to Greece until the outcome of a House of Lords or ECtHR judgment. In *KRS v United Kingdom*[97] the ECtHR held that, despite some concerns, the Dublin Regulation provided a satisfactory system for processing asylum applications and any human rights complaints could be raised in Greece. Therefore, the UK could remove TCNs to Greece legally, a position confirmed by the House of Lords in *Nasseri*.[98] However, in *MSS v Belgium and Greece*[99] the ECtHR held that the detention and living conditions of asylum-seekers in Greece infringed Article 3 ECHR and Article 13 ECHR in combination with Article 3. Furthermore, Belgium had infringed Article 3 ECHR by returning the asylum claimant to Greece, thereby exposing him to the detention and living conditions in Greece that were in breach of Article 3, and Article 13 ECHR in combination with Article 3. In December 2011 the ECJ in *NS and ME*[100] referred[101] to the case of *MSS v Belgium and Greece*, finding that there was a presumption that the treatment of asylum-seekers in all Member States complied with the requirements of the Charter of Fundamental Rights, the Geneva Convention and the ECHR[102] but that presumption was not conclusive[103] and was thus rebuttable.[104] Thus the Member States, including domestic courts, could not transfer asylum-seekers to another Member State where they

---

95 See UNHCR 'UNHCR position on the return of asylum-seekers to Greece under the "Dublin Regulation"' 15 April 2008 http://www.unhcr.org/cgi-bin/texis/vtx/refworld/rwmain?docid=4805bde42.
96 *Nasseri* (QB) and (CA) (n 8); *R (on the application of Zego) v Secretary of State for the Home Department* [2008] EWHC 302 (Admin); *AH (Iran), Zego (Eritrea) & Kadir (Iraq) v Secretary of State for the Home Department* [2008] EWCA Civ 985 (CA); *R (on the application of Malik) v Secretary of State for the Home Department* [2008] EWHC 888 (Admin); *R (on the application of Hardini) v Secretary of State for the Home Department* [2008] EWHC 1942 (Admin).
97 *KRS v United Kingdom* (2009) 48 EHRR SE8.
98 *Nasseri* (HL) (n 8).
99 *MSS v Belgium and Greece* (2011) 53 EHRR 2. See M Bossuyt 'Belgium condemned for inhuman or degrading treatment due to violations by Greece of EU asylum law' [2011] EHRLR 582; M Bossuyt 'The Court of Strasbourg acting as an asylum court' (2012) 8 *EuConst* 203; G Clayton 'Asylum seekers in Europe' (2011) 11 *HRLR* 758; C Costello 'Courting access to asylum in Europe: recent supranational jurisprudence explored' (2012) 12 *HRLR* 287; P Mallia 'Case note' (2011) 30(3) *RSQ* 107; V Moreno-Lax 'Dismantling the Dublin system' (2012) 14 *EJML* 1.
100 Joined Cases C–411 & 493/10 *NS v Secretary of State for the Home Department* and *ME, ASM, MT, KP and EH v Refugee Applications Commissioner and Minister for Justice, Equality and Law Reform* [2012] 2 CMLR 9; noted in G de Baere 'Case note' (2012) 106 *AJIL* 616; J Buckley 'Case comment' [2012] EHRLR 205; M den Heijer 'Case note' (2012) 49 *CMLRev* 1735; C Costello 'Dublin case *NS/ME*: finally, an end to blind trust across the EU?' [2012] Asiel & Migrantenrecht 83; S Lieven 'Case comment' (2012) 14 *EJML* 223; A Pickup 'Case comment' (2012) 26 *JIANL* 289. See also E Brouwer 'Mutual trust and the Dublin Regulation: protection of fundamental rights in the EU and the burden of proof' (2013) 9 *Utrecht Law Review* 135.
101 *NS* (n 100) paras 88–90.
102 ibid para 80.
103 ibid para 99.
104 ibid para 104.

'cannot be unaware that systemic deficiencies in the asylum procedure and in the reception conditions of asylum seekers in that Member State amount to substantial grounds for believing that the asylum seeker would face a real risk of being subjected to inhuman or degrading treatment within the meaning of Article 4 of the Charter'.[105] Where the host Member State decides to examine further criteria to determine if another Member State is responsible for examining the asylum-seeker's application, that Member State must not take an unreasonable amount of time. If that time does becoming unreasonable then that Member State must examine the asylum application itself under the sovereignty clause.[106]

Probably the most serious criticism of the Dublin Regulation is the same as that identified by Blake over the Dublin Convention, in that it does not work effectively or efficiently. In a European Council on Refugees and Exiles (ECRE) report,[107] low transfer rates,[108] the continuance of multiple asylum applications[109] and the lengthy and cumbersome nature of the Dublin procedure at the beginning of an asylum application[110] were identified as establishing the inefficiency and ineffectiveness of the system, leading to concerns over the best use of public money.[111] The ECRE also examined the disproportionate effect of the Dublin Regulation on southern and eastern Member States compared with northern and western countries[112] and the negative effect on applicants for refugee status themselves in the EU's 'asylum lottery'.[113]

Complimentary to Dublin II, Eurodac[114] was established to compare the fingerprints of asylum-seekers[115] and was designed to combat the problem of asylum-seekers arriving in the EU without any documentation.[116] Article 4 requires all Member States to take the fingerprints of all the fingers of every asylum-seeker of at least 14 years of age and persons suspected of irregularly crossing the border and transmit the data[117] to a central database where a comparison is made with

---

105   ibid para 94.
106   ibid para 98.
107   ECRE 'Sharing responsibility for refugee protection in Europe: Dublin reconsidered' March 2008 http://www.ecre.org/files/Sharing%20Responsibility_Dublin%20Reconsidered.pdf; the findings of this report have recently been confirmed in a further report by ECRE – ECRE 'Dublin II Regulation: lives on hold' February 2013 http://www.ecre.org/component/content/article/56-ecre-actions/317-dublin-ii-regulation-lives-on-hold.html.
108   ECRE 'Sharing responsibility' (n 107) 10.
109   ibid 11.
110   ibid.
111   ibid 12.
112   ibid.
113   ibid 14.
114   Council Regulation 2725/2000/EC concerning the establishment of 'Eurodac' for the comparison of fingerprints for the effective application of the Dublin Convention [2000] OJ L316/1 art 1. Further details of the system are set out in Council Regulation 407/2002/EC laying down certain rules to implement Regulation 2725/2000 [2002] OJ L62/1. The Eurodac provisions have been extended to Denmark by Council Decision 2006/188/EC [2006] OJ L66/37.
115   See ER Brouwer 'Eurodac: its limitations and temptations' (2002) 4 *EJML* 231; JP Aus 'Eurodac: a solution looking for a problem?' ARENA Working Paper 9/06.
116   Guild 'Seeking asylum' (n 67) 209.
117   Article 5(1) provides an exhaustive list of data to be stored in the central database: '(a) Member State of origin, place and date of the application for asylum; (b) fingerprint data; (c) sex;

other fingerprints held on the database. If there is a 'hit' then that asylum-seeker can be returned to the Member State from where the hit came from.[118] Fingerprint data of asylum-seekers is stored for 10 years, whilst that from those illegally crossing the external border is only stored for two years and can only be used for future comparisons. Fingerprints from persons illegally present in the Member States is not stored. If a person is given refugee status then data relating to that person is to be blocked in the Central Unit but not erased until the time limit is reached.

Guild[119] has criticised Eurodac for failing to comply with the requirements of Directive 95/46/EC[120] on the grounds of a failure of the principle of proportionality and not including the concerns of Article 6(1) of Directive 95/46. In accordance with Article 6(1), data can only be stored on an individual if it is for specified, explicit and legitimate purposes and the data retained is not excessive in relation to the purposes for which it is collected. Furthermore, the storage of data for 10 years could be seen as excessive under Article 8 ECHR. Brouwer[121] has also criticised Eurodac as this data taken and then stored from an asylum-seeker appears to criminalise that person, thereby possibly breaching Article 31 of the Geneva Convention.

In 2008 the Commission put forward proposals for a Recast Dublin Regulation[122] (Dublin III) and a Recast Eurodac Regulation.[123] The Commission aimed to address six issues with Dublin III:[124] extension of the scope to all claimants of international protection; greater efficiency of the system, mainly through increased information gathering and sharing; improved legal safeguards for individuals claiming international protection; strengthened right to family unity and a clarified sovereignty and humanitarian clause; improved protection safeguards for unaccompanied minors and vulnerable groups; and a new procedure to suspend the operation of transfers in cases of significant pressure on certain Member States with limited reception and absorption capacities. These received guarded approval from the ECRE with the suggestion that the proposals needed

---

(d) reference number used by the Member State of origin; (e) date on which the fingerprints were taken; (f) date on which the data were transmitted to the Central Unit; (g) date on which the data were entered in the central database; (h) details in respect of the recipient(s) of the data transmitted and the date(s) of transmission(s)'.

118  For an example of the working of the system see *RZ v Secretary of State for the Home Department* [2008] UKAIT 7 (AIT).
119  Guild 'Seeking asylum' (n 67) 210.
120  Council Directive 95/46/EC on the protection of individuals with regard to the processing of personal data and on the free movement of such data [1995] OJ 1995 L281/31.
121  Brouwer 'Eurodac' (n 115) 243.
122  Commission proposal for a European Parliament and Council Regulation establishing the criteria and mechanisms for determining the Member State responsible for examining an application for international protection lodged in one of the Member States by a third-country national or a stateless person (recast) COM(2008) 820 final.
123  Commission proposal for a European Parliament and Council Regulation concerning the establishment of 'Eurodac' for the comparison of fingerprints for the effective application of the Dublin Regulation (recast) COM(2008) 825/3 final.
124  Commission proposal for Dublin III (n 122) 7–10.

to go further[125] and a similar response from the UNHCR.[126] In 2011 the Commission withdrew the proposal after difficulties in the Council and issued a new proposal that now addressed a different range of issues. These were: to make implementation of the regulation easier for Member States; the introduction of clear and strict rules on detention; the benchmarking of dignified standards of living to measurable national standards; and the enhancement of the self-sufficiency of asylum-seekers. The principles for Dublin III were agreed in the Council in April 2012[127] and negotiations between the European Parliament and Council finalised the substance of the text,[128] which has now been released to the public[129] with the UK and Ireland opting in. Dublin III contains some significant changes to the previous regulation. First, Article 3(2) has incorporated the *MSS* and *NS and ME* case law[130] and greater clarity of rights for asylum-seekers is presented with a right to information (Article 4), a right to a personal interview (Article 5) and guarantees for minors (Article 6). Chapter III is renamed from 'Hierarchy of Criteria' to 'Criteria for Determining the Member State Responsible' and the criteria themselves remain basically the same as those in Dublin II but with increased consideration for minors in Article 8. Chapter IV deals with dependents, the contents of which are discretionary depending on the circumstances of the case but are a notable improvement on the family member provisions of Dublin II. There are some minor amendments to the obligations of the state responsible for examining an application and the procedures for taking charge requests but a new taking back request procedure has been adopted. The most significant changes in Dublin III are beneficial to TCNs. The first is the introduction of Article 26, providing the right to a remedy for asylum-seekers. This is complemented by detailed rules and limitations on the use of detention during the Dublin III procedure. In Article 29 costs of transfers are allocated, mainly to the transferring state, thereby introducing a limited element of burden sharing. Article 31 provides an opportunity for the Member States to put in place a detailed procedure in the case of problems encountered in a Member State through pressure on a Member State's asylum system and/or through the functioning of that Member State's asylum system. However, Article 31 only envisages the drawing up and implementation of a preventive action plan, or if that fails a crisis management action plan. Finally, for the first time under Article 40A the Commission is provided with delegated powers, with the power to adopt delegated acts covering Articles 8 (minors) and 16A (dependents). Although many of the changes are significant improvements on Dublin II it is difficult to see

---

125 ECRE 'Comments from the European Council on refugees and exiles on the European Commission proposal to recast the Dublin Regulation' April 2009 http://www.ecre.org/topics/areas-of-work/introduction/133.html.
126 UNHCR 'UNHCR Comments on the Commission's proposals for recast Dublin and Eurodac Regulations' March 2009 http://www.unhcr.org/refworld/docid/49c0ca922.html.
127 Council Document 9179/12, 11.
128 Council Document 15389/12, 7.
129 Council Document 16332/12.
130 Albeit without *NS* (n 100) para 98 on unreasonable length of time and use of the sovereignty clause by the host Member State.

that the problems with the system will be alleviated and, indeed, it is likely that the inefficiencies and ineffectiveness that Blake originally identified for the Dublin Convention will be perpetuated. Dublin III does not adequately address the problems that many Southern European Member States are experiencing of paying for the domestic asylum system that is under significant pressure from large numbers of asylum-seekers at the same time as the economy is suffering from the worst downturn since the Great Depression. This will, it is suggested, only be ameliorated once an effective burden-sharing system is introduced.

With the proposal to recast the Eurodac Regulation the aims of the Commission were to improve the efficiency and effectiveness of Eurodac and were mainly technical in nature. However, in 2009 the original recast proposal was withdrawn and two new proposals were adopted: one as a replacement for the original regulation;[131] and the other as a decision[132] enabling the Member States' law enforcement authorities and Europol to access and compare data held by Eurodac. With the coming into force of the Lisbon Treaty these proposals lapsed and a replacement recast regulation was adopted in 2010,[133] dropping the provisions on access to Eurodac data for law enforcement purposes. However, in May 2012 this was withdrawn and a new proposal[134] was put forward by the Commission that re-enacted the provisions allowing Member States' law enforcement authorities and Europol to access Eurodac's central database to prevent, detect and investigate terrorist offences and other serious crimes, and enabled the European Agency[135] for the management of large-scale IT systems in the AFSJ to supervise Eurodac data. No impact assessment was undertaken as it was considered that the original 2008 and 2009 impact assessments were still extant.[136] The proposal has been heavily criticised by the European Data Protection Supervisor,[137] UNHCR,[138] the Meijers

---

131 Commission proposal for a European Parliament and Council Regulation concerning the establishment of 'Eurodac' for the comparison of fingerprints for the effective application of the Dublin Regulation (recast) COM(2009) 342 final.

132 Commission proposal for a Council Decision on requesting comparisons with EURODAC data by Member States' law enforcement authorities and Europol for law enforcement purposes COM(2009) 344 final.

133 Commission proposal for a European Parliament and Council Regulation concerning the establishment of 'Eurodac' for the comparison of fingerprints for the effective application of the Dublin Regulation (recast) COM(2010) 555 final.

134 Commission proposal for a European Parliament and Council Regulation concerning the establishment of 'Eurodac' for the comparison of fingerprints for the effective application of the Dublin Regulation (recast) COM(2012) 254 final.

135 European Parliament and Council Regulation 1077/2011/EU establishing a European Agency for the operational management of large-scale IT systems in the area of freedom, security and justice [2011] OJ L286/1.

136 ibid 3.

137 EDPS 'Opinion on the amended proposal for a European Parliament and Council Regulation concerning the establishment of "Eurodac" for the comparison of fingerprints for the effective application of the Dublin Regulation (recast)' September 2012 http://www.edps.europa.eu/EDPSWEB/webdav/site/mySite/shared/Documents/Consultation/Opinions/2012/12-09-05_EURODAC_EN.pdf.

138 UNHCR 'An efficient and protective Eurodac' November 2012 http://www.unhcr.org/refworld/pdfid/50ad01b72.pdf.

Committee[139] and the Joint Supervisory Body of Europol,[140] with complaints ranging from the lack of hard evidence on the proposal to breaches of fundamental rights over privacy, data retention and transfer and a significant change in the rationale for Eurodac. It is submitted, however, that a major fault with this proposal is the linking of asylum-seeking and criminality, which breaches the fundamental structure of the Geneva Convention of non-criminalisation of refugees and claimants of international protection.

Once it has been clarified which Member State has responsibility to determine the asylum application, there must be at least minimum reception conditions and rights provided for asylum-seekers. Directive 2003/9/EC[141] applies to all TCNs and stateless persons who apply for asylum either at the border or in the Member State's territory, as long as they are allowed to remain on that territory as asylum-seekers, and to family members, if they are covered by the same asylum application according to national law. When asylum-seekers apply for asylum the Member State, according to Article 13(1), must grant the right to material reception conditions from when their asylum applications are made, to ensure a standard of living that is adequate for the health of the applicants and is capable of ensuring their subsistence (Article 13(2)), the aim being to secure the human dignity of asylum-seekers.[142] Member States' obligations to grant material reception conditions to asylum-seekers continue throughout the asylum claimants' stay on the Member State's territory, even if they are to be transferred to another Member State under the Dublin Regulation.[143] These material reception conditions include housing, food and clothing, provided in kind, or as financial allowances or in vouchers, and a daily expenses allowance (Article 2(j)). Where housing is provided 'in kind' Article 14 ensures that it must be: (a) premises used to house applicants during the examination of an asylum application lodged at the border; (b) accommodation centres which guarantee an adequate standard of living; (c) private properties adapted for housing applicants. The housing must protect the applicant's family life, including the current family unity if the asylum-seeker agrees, ensure safety from assault within the premises and enable communications with relatives, legal advisers, representatives of the UNHCR and non-governmental organisations. Alongside these 'material reception conditions' Member States must ensure asylum-seekers receive adequate health care

139 Standing Committee of Experts on International Immigration, Refugee and Criminal Law 'Note of the Meijers Committee on the proposal for a Regulation on the establishment of Eurodac' October 2012 http://www.statewatch.org/news/2012/oct/eu-meijers-committee-eurodac-proposal.pdf.
140 Joint Supervisory Body of Europol 'Opinion 12/52with respect to the amended proposal for a Regulation of the European Parliament and of the Council on the establishment of EURODAC' October 2012 http://www.statewatch.org/news/2012/oct/europol-jsb-opinion-eurodac.pdf.
141 Council Directive 2003/9/EC laying down the minimum standards for the reception of asylum seekers [2003] OJ L31/18 art 3.
142 See the Explanatory Memorandum in the Commission proposal for a Council Directive laying down the minimum standards for the reception of asylum seekers COM(2001) 181 final 3, 4, 15 and 16.
143 Case C-179/11 *Cimade, Groupe d'information et de soutien des immigrés (GISTI) v Ministre de l'Intérieur, de l'Outre-mer, des Collectivités territoriales et de l'Immigration* [2013] 1 CMLR 11 para 58.

that includes at least emergency care, essential treatment of illness and the protection of special needs (Article 15), although asylum-seekers may be required to be medically screened on public health grounds (Article 9).

After providing for the 'material reception conditions' the directive considers other rights for asylum-seekers, including the right to free movement. Article 7(1) states that asylum-seekers may move freely within the host Member State's territory, or within an area assigned to them by that Member State. The scope of this assigned area is not defined in the directive but it cannot affect the unalienable sphere of private life nor impinge upon access to all the benefits under the directive. Applicants must inform the competent authorities of their current address and notify any change as soon as possible (Article 7(6)). Article 7(2) provides that Member States can decide on the residence for the asylum-seeker because of public interest, public order or for the swift processing and effective monitoring of the application. Member States may also, when it proves necessary (for example for legal reasons or reasons of public order), confine an applicant to a particular place in accordance with domestic law (Article 7(3)).[144] However, Article 7(5) enables Member States to provide for the possibility of granting applicants temporary permission to leave their place of residence or assigned area, with decisions taken individually, objectively and impartially and reasons provided if the decision is negative. Member States must also specify a time period, from the date of application, during which time an applicant is not able to work (Article 11(1)) but after a year without an initial decision on the application the Member State must provide conditions for granting access to the labour market, a right that cannot be lost during an appeal process. However, Member States can prioritise jobs to EU citizens and other legally resident TCNs if the labour market demands (Article 11(4)). In *Negassi and Lutalo*,[145] Maurice Kay LJ identified Article 11(1) as a negative right rather than a positive right of access to the labour market that did not set out a time period beyond which a positive obligation to grant work could be imposed on Member States. Although as a literal reading of this provision Maurice Kay LJ's approach cannot be faulted, a more purposive approach or, for the ECJ, a teleological approach, would possibly result in a judgment that did not empty the measure of any effect.

The 'material reception conditions' appear, from Article 13(1) and (2), to be concrete rights essential for the human dignity of the asylum-seeker. However, Member States can make the provision of the material reception conditions subject to actual residence by the applicants in a specific place, as determined by the Member State (Article 7(4)). Furthermore, they may be reduced or withdrawn where the asylum-seeker inter alia abandons the subscribed place of residence without informing the competent authorities, or without gaining permission if the move had been requested (Article 16(1)(a)). The only benefit that the Member

144 See K Hailbronner 'Detention of asylum seekers' (2007) 9 *EJML* 159.

145 *R (on the application of Negassi and Lutalo) v Secretary of State for the Home Department* [2013] EWCA Civ 151 (CA) [25]–[32] (Maurice Kay LJ).

States cannot withdraw is an asylum-seeker's access to emergency health care (Article 16(4)).

It should be noted from the outset that the standards outlined are the minimum[146] required and Member States can choose to retain higher standards (Article 4). However, these minimum norms are markedly 'minimum'[147] and Member States have the option to lower them further if the asylum-seeker is found to be in breach of the directive's requirements. As the material reception conditions are supposedly the minimum standards required to enable an asylum-seeker to retain his or her human dignity, their withdrawal must breach the requirement that '[h]uman dignity is inviolable' (Article 1 Charter) and could lead to the risk of the individual becoming destitute in breach of Article 3 ECHR.[148] This is particularly so where an asylum-seeker moves from his or her place of residence without informing or receiving permission from the authorities, especially, as Rogers[149] notes, only Germany restricted the freedom of asylum-seekers in such a way before the directive was adopted and the German Basic Law protects the human dignity of individuals. The restriction of the free movement of asylum-seekers, at least within the territory of the host Member State, appears to be unnecessary, affects significantly the quality of life of the individual concerned, and requesting permission to move residence is demeaning and likely to cause even more stigmatisation of asylum-seekers.[150] Furthermore, an asylum-seeker's free movement can be totally curtailed by his or her confinement to a particular place. Even though this is an exception to the norm,[151] it must be justified on the grounds in the directive and would be interpreted by the ECJ narrowly; there are no minimum conditions or safeguards on the use of detention by Member States in the directive.[152]

In 2008 the Commission put forward a proposal for a Recast Reception Conditions Directive[153] following a critical report,[154] with the main objective

---

146 PJ Kuijper 'The evolution of the third pillar from Maastricht to the European Constitution: institutional aspects' (2004) 41 *CMLRev* 609, 614 notes that a minimum standards directive 'does exactly what the title announces, namely laying down rather minimal standards'.

147 D O'Keeffe 'Can the leopard change its spots? Visas, immigration and asylum following Amsterdam' in O'Keeffe, Twomey (eds) *Legal Issues of the Amsterdam Treaty* (n 37) 271, 272.

148 N Rogers 'Minimum standards for reception' (2002) 4 *EJML* 215, 228; see *R (on the application of Limbuela, Tesema and Adam v Secretary of State for the Home Department* [2006] 1 AC 396 (HL); noted in A Mackenzie 'Case comment' [2006] EHRLR 67; A Hardiman-McCartney 'Absolutely right: providing asylum seekers with food and shelter under Article 3' (2006) 65 *CLJ* 4. See also K Puttick 'Strangers at the welfare gate: asylum seekers, "welfare" and Convention rights after *Adam*' (2005) 19 *IANL* 214; S Palmer 'A wrong turning: Article 3 ECHR and proportionality' (2006) 65 *CLJ* 438; S York, N Fancott 'Enforced destitution: impediments to return and Access section 4 "hard cases" support' (2008) 22 *JIANL* 5.

149 N Rogers 'Minimum standards for reception' (n 148) 227.

150 ibid 229.

151 Guild 'Seeking asylum' (n 67) 214.

152 N Rogers 'Minimum standards for reception' (n 148) 229.

153 Commission proposal for a European Parliament and Council Directive laying down minimum standards for the reception of asylum-seekers COM(2008) 815 final.

154 Commission Communication of the report on the application of Directive 2003/9/EC laying down the minimum standards for the reception of asylum seekers COM(2007) 745 final.

being 'to ensure higher standards of treatment for asylum-seekers with regard to reception conditions that would guarantee a dignified standard of living, in line with international law'.[155] This was to be achieved by extending the scope to include those claiming international protection, facilitating greater access to the labour market, improving and standardising the material reception conditions, limiting detention of asylum-seekers by the use of the principles of necessity and proportionality and the underlying principle that a person seeking international protection should not be held in detention solely for that reason, protecting persons with special needs, and improving monitoring and reporting systems.[156] These proposals were greeted with some enthusiasm by the UNHCR[157] and the ECRE[158] but in 2011 the Commission issued an amended proposal with a general dilution of all the suggested improvements, protections and increased rights.[159] In September the revised text was agreed by the Council and European Parliament's Civil Liberties, Justice and Home Affairs (LIBE) Committee, with the LIBE Committee recommending the adoption of the text by the European Parliament in a second reading vote.[160] The final text does extend the personal scope to all applicants for international protection but does little to advance the rights of claimants for international protection from the position in Directive 2003/9 apart from new provisions on detention (Articles 8–11), a right of access to the labour market no later than nine months after an application for international protection is lodged (new Article 15(1)) and a requirement for Member States to ensure access to health care and a dignified standard of living for all asylum-seekers (new Article 20(5)).[161] Furthermore, it maintains considerable flexibility for Member States and fails to enhance standardised protections for TCNs. The minimum standards outlined retain a very 'minimum' status, although 'minimum' is removed from the title of the measure. Finally, the UK and Ireland have opted out of this measure (recitals 28 and 29) and so the former Directive 2003/9 will continue to apply in these Member States.

Asylum-seekers, as the first class of TCNs covered by the AFSJ, are granted little in the way of free movement rights. Under the Dublin Regulation they have

155 ibid 4.
156 ibid 4–7.
157 UNHCR 'UNHCR Comments on Commission Proposal for a European Parliament and Council Directive laying down minimum standards for the reception of asylum seekers' March 2009 http://www.unhcr.org/cgi-bin/texis/vtx/refworld/rwmain?docid=49ba8a192.
158 ECRE 'ECRE Comments on Commission Proposal for a European Parliament and Council Directive laying down minimum standards for the reception of asylum seekers' April 2009 http://www.ecre.org/topics/areas-of-work/protection-in-europe/142.html.
159 Commission Amended Proposal for a European Parliament and Council Directive laying down minimum standards for the reception of asylum seekers COM(2011) 320 final; see ECRE 'ECRE comments on Amended Commission Proposal to recast Reception Conditions Directive' September 2011 http://www.ecre.org/component/content/article/57-policy-papers/253-ecre-comments-and-recommendations-on-the-amended-commission-proposal-to-recast-the-reception-conditions-directive-com2011-320-final.html.
160 Council Document 14112/1/12 at 2.
161 This replaces the original art 16(4) and the term 'asylum seekers' here should mean 'applicants for international protection'.

limited choice as to which Member State can assess their application as the default position is that the first country of entry is the responsible Member State. The exceptions to this are narrow, and narrowed further by the use of a truncated definition of family member. As will be explained later, air carrier sanctions limit the movement of asylum-seekers into the EU and therefore necessity drives opportunity with asylum-seekers either crossing the EU external borders clandestinely by road or by boat from nearby states. As the majority of neighbour countries are safe third countries then the asylum-seeker can be returned there. The alternative is to entrust entry into the EU into the hands of human traffickers or human smugglers, entering the EU illegally and without documentation or a travel evidence trail. The provision of minimum reception standards in Directive 2003/9, the restriction of free movement to the host Member State or to part of the territory or an assigned place, the detention of asylum-seekers and the withdrawal of the material reception conditions for exercising free movement, demeans, stigmatises and breaches the human dignity of asylum-seekers. It is submitted that the effect on people who have left their country of origin in desperation is likely to be severe and could lead to asylum-seekers choosing to remain covertly in the EU rather than claiming asylum.

## 4.3   Refugees

The difference between asylum and refugee law is not easy to determine. As was considered above, there is international recognition of refugee status and the rights associated with it, but no international treaty has been adopted on international protection on the basis of asylum (the international conference designed to do this was abandoned in 1977 when no agreement could be found between the participating states). It is certainly the case that they are 'intimately connected'[162] but the refugee regime is centrally concerned with humanitarian concerns, whilst the asylum system tends to be more of a balancing exercise that includes humanitarian issues, costs, systemic abuse and equity between Member States. Although the Lisbon Treaty has conflated the two concepts into one of international protection this analysis will continue to differentiate between the two on the basis of principle and the practicalities of legislation adopted under the previous regime still being applicable today.

Union refugee law protects three groups of persons, two of which, those with refugee and subsidiary protection status, are covered by the Qualification Directive 2004/83/EC,[163] now partially replaced by Directive 2011/95/EU[164] and the

---

162  C Chalmers, G Davies and G Monti *European Union Law* (2nd edn CUP 2010) 525.

163  Council Directive 2004/83/EC on minimum standards for the qualification and status of third country nationals or stateless persons as refugees or as persons who otherwise need international protection and the content of the protection granted [2004] OJ L304/12 art 1. See Commission Report on the application of Directive 2004/83/EC COM(2010) 465 final.

164  European Parliament and Council Directive 2011/95/EU on standards for the qualification of third-country nationals or stateless persons as beneficiaries of international protection, for a

other, the temporary mass influx of persons, is detailed in the Temporary Protection Directive 2001/55/EC.[165] The Qualification Directive lays down minimum standards for the qualification of TCNs as refugees such that Member States can choose to retain or introduce more favourable standards (Article 3). A TCN or stateless person has the right to be granted refugee status if he or she qualifies as a refugee in accordance with Chapters II and III of Directive 2004/83 (Article 13). A refugee is defined as a TCN who 'owing to a well-founded fear of being persecuted for reasons of race,[166] religion,[167] nationality,[168] political opinion[169] or membership of a particular social group,[170] is outside the country of nationality and is unable or, owing to such fear, is unwilling to avail himself or herself of the protection of that country, or a stateless person, who, being outside of the country of former habitual residence for the same reasons as mentioned above, is unable or, owing to such fear, unwilling to return to it'. It is not necessary for the applicant actually to possess the characteristic of persecution, merely that the actor of persecution is attributing that characteristic to the applicant (Article 10(2)). According to Article 9, acts of persecution as defined by Article 1A of the Geneva Convention must: '(a) be sufficiently serious by their nature or repetition as to constitute a severe violation of basic human rights, in particular the rights from which derogation cannot be made under Article 15(2) of the [ECHR]; or (b) be an accumulation of various

uniform status for refugees or for persons eligible for subsidiary protection, and for the content of the protection granted [2011] OJ L337/9.

165 Council Directive 2001/55/EC on minimum standards for giving temporary protection in the event of a mass influx of displaced persons and on measures promoting a balance of efforts between Member States in receiving such persons and bearing the consequences thereof [2001] OJ L212/12.

166 Article 10(1)(a) 'the concept of race shall in particular include considerations of colour, descent, or membership of a particular ethnic group'.

167 Article 10(1)(b) 'the concept of religion shall in particular include the holding of theistic, non-theistic and atheistic beliefs, the participation in, or abstention from, formal worship in private or in public, either alone or in community with others, other religious acts or expressions of view, or forms of personal or communal conduct based on or mandated by any religious belief'.

168 Article 10(1)(c) 'the concept of nationality shall not be confined to citizenship or lack thereof but shall in particular include membership of a group determined by its cultural, ethnic, or linguistic identity, common geographical or political origins or its relationship with the population of another State'.

169 Article 10(1)(e) 'the concept of political opinion shall in particular include the holding of an opinion, thought or belief on a matter related to the potential actors of persecution mentioned in art 6 and to their policies or methods, whether or not that opinion, thought or belief has been acted upon by the applicant'.

170 Article 10(1)(d) 'a group shall be considered to form a particular social group where in particular: — members of that group share an innate characteristic, or a common background that cannot be changed, or share a characteristic or belief that is so fundamental to identity or conscience that a person should not be forced to renounce it, and — that group has a distinct identity in the relevant country, because it is perceived as being different by the surrounding society; depending on the circumstances in the country of origin, a particular social group might include a group based on a common characteristic of sexual orientation. Sexual orientation cannot be understood to include acts considered to be criminal in accordance with national law of the Member States: Gender related aspects might be considered, without by themselves alone creating a presumption for the applicability of this Article'.

measures, including violations of human rights which is sufficiently severe as to affect an individual in a similar manner as mentioned in (a)'. These can include: physical or mental violence, including sexual violence; discriminatory legal, administrative, police and/or judicial measures; disproportionate or discriminatory prosecution or punishment or denial of judicial redress resulting in this; prosecution of punishment for refusal to perform military service in a conflict where acts in such a situation would fall under the Article 12(2) exclusion clauses; and acts of a gender or child-specific nature (Article 9(2)). The ECJ has recently provided guidance as to the requirements for persecution on the basis of religious belief in *Germany v Y and Z*.[171] As such not all interference with the right to freedom of religion, as set out in Article 10(1) of the Charter of Fundamental Rights, is capable of constituting an 'act of persecution'.[172] Such an act 'must be a "severe violation" of religious freedom having a significant effect on the person concerned'.[173] It is the severity of the measures and sanctions against the individual which will determine if there is persecution[174] such that if a refugee applicant was to exercise his right to religious freedom in country of origin then he would run 'a genuine risk of, *inter alia*, being persecuted or subject to inhuman or degrading treatment or punishment'[175] by one of the actors of persecution or serious harm set out in Article 6. Furthermore, an applicant's fear of being persecuted is well founded if the exercise of such a right would expose that individual to a real risk of persecution: 'In assessing an application for refugee status on an individual basis, [the competent] authorities cannot reasonably expect the applicant to abstain from those religious practices'.[176]

Directive 2004/83 also introduces a right to subsidiary protection status (Article 18) if a TCN or stateless person is eligible according to the assessment criteria in Chapter II, that is the same for refugee status, and the qualification criteria in Chapter V. Recital 24 specifies that the aim of subsidiary protection is complementary and additional to the refugee protection enshrined in the Geneva Convention. A person eligible for subsidiary protection is defined as a TCN or stateless person 'who does not qualify as a refugee but in respect of whom substantial grounds have been shown for believing that the person concerned, if returned to his or her country of origin, or in the case of a stateless person, to his or her country of former habitual residence, would face a real risk of suffering serious harm as defined in Article 15 . . . and is unable, or, owing to

---

171  Joined Cases C–71 & 99/11 *Germany v Y and Z* [2013] 1 CMLR 5.
172  ibid para 58.
173  ibid para 59.
174  ibid para 66.
175  ibid para 67.
176  ibid para 80. See *HJ (Iran) and HT (Cameroon) v Secretary of State for the Home Department* [2011] 1 AC 596 (SC) and *RT, SM, AM and KM (Zimbabwe) v Secretary of State for the Home Department* [2013] 1 AC 152 (SC) in which the UK Supreme Court adopts a similar approach when considering the Refugee Convention.

such risk,unwilling to avail himself or herself of the protection of that country' (Article 2(e)). The definition of serious harm in Article 15 consists of:

(a) death penalty or execution; or
(b) torture or inhuman or degrading treatment or punishment of an applicant in the country of origin; or
(c) serious and individual threat to a civilian's life or person by reason of indiscriminate violence in situations of international or internal armed conflict.

Article 15(a) replicated Protocols 6 and 13 of the ECHR and Article 15(b) was almost an exact replica of Article 3 ECHR[177] but Article 15(c) appeared to be something new. McAdam[178] argued that Article 15(c) was a type of serious harm additional in scope to Article 15(b) and thus an extension to Article 3 ECHR. Battjes[179] also suggested that, as Article 15(c) required only that a person must face a 'threat', then this was wider in scope than the substantial grounds required for Article 15(a) and (b). Storey,[180] however, contended that this was not the intention of the Member States during the adoption process, when they wished to confine Article 15 to the scope of Article 3 ECHR. The ECJ has now provided an interpretation of Article 15(c) after a number of Member States' courts[181] attempted to interpret it themselves. In *Elgafaji*[182] an Iraqi husband and wife claimed subsidiary protection status in Holland on the basis of Article 15(c). The Court began by addressing the differences between the three types of harm outlined in Article 15. Article 15(a) and (b) 'cover situations in which the applicant for subsidiary protection is specifically exposed to the risk of a particular type of harm'[183] with Article 15(b) corresponding to Article 3 ECHR and Article 15(c) having different content to Article 3 ECHR and thus requiring, albeit through the lens of fundamental rights, independent EU interpretation,[184] which as Lambert and Farrell suggest[185] also dismisses an international humanitarian law reading of Article 15(c).[186] The

---

177 H Storey 'EU Refugee Qualification Directive: a brave new world?' (2008) 19 *IJRL* 1, 32.

178 J McAdam *Complementary Protection in International Refugee Law* (OUP 2007) 83.

179 H Battjes *European Asylum Law and International Law* (Brill 2006) 239.

180 Storey 'EU Refugee Qualification Directive' (n 177) 34.

181 See UNHCR 'UNHCR statement on subsidiary protection under the EC Qualification Directive for people threatened by indiscriminate violence' January 2008 http://www.unhcr.org/refworld/docid/479df7472.html for an overview of cases before domestic courts of the Member States.

182 Case C–465/07 *Meki Elgafaji and Noor Elgafaji v Staatssecretaris van Justitie* [2009] ECR I–921; noted in R Errera 'The CJEU and subsidiary protection: reflections on *Elgafaji* – and after' (2010) 23 *IJRL* 93. See also P Tiedemann 'Subsidiary protection and the function of Article 15(c) of the Qualification Directive' (2012) 31(1) *RSQ* 123.

183 *Elgafaji* (n 182) para 32.

184 ibid para 28.

185 H Lambert, T Farrell 'The changing character of armed conflict and the implications for refugee protection jurisprudence' (2010) 22 *IJRL* 237, 246.

186 However, in H Storey, 'Armed conflict in asylum law: the "war-flaw"' (2012) 31 *Refugee Survey Quarterly* 1, Storey argues that whenever the subject matter of fear of persecution or serious harm is armed conflict then the international humanitarian law should be applied as *lex specialis*. This,

harm in Article 15(c) covered a more general form of harm,[187] which the Court underpinned through the wording of the provision of 'a threat . . . to a civilian's life or person' instead of specific acts of violence, the general situation of 'international or internal armed conflict' that is inherent in the 'threat', and the 'indiscriminate' nature of the violence that leads to that 'threat', 'which implies that it may extend to people irrespective of their personal circumstances'.[188] The ECJ held the word 'individual' in 'individual threat' covered:

> . . . harm to civilians irrespective of their identity, where the degree of indiscriminate violence characterising the armed conflict taking place – assessed by the competent national authorities before which an application for subsidiary protection is made, or by the courts of a Member State to which a decision refusing such an application is referred – reaches such a high level that substantial grounds are shown for believing that a civilian, returned to the relevant country or, as the case may be, to the relevant region, would, solely on account of his presence on the territory of that country or region, face a real risk of being subject to the serious threat referred in Article 15(c) of the Directive.[189]

Thus, the individual threat was not merely purely personal but also situational or geographical.[190] As Lambert and Farrell explain,[191] in situations of low level indiscriminate violence the individual would have to establish that he is 'specifically affected by reason of factors particular to his personal circumstances',[192] although not actually targeted or singled out.[193] On the other hand, in situations of high level indiscriminate violence 'the fact that the applicant comes from that geographical location would be sufficient to establish the existence of "substantial grounds" that s/he would be subjected "individually" to the risk in question'.[194] A serious indication of real risk, such as that outlined in Article 4(4),[195] or past exposure to an armed conflict,[196] would lower the level of indiscriminate violence required for subsidiary protection. Since *Elgafaji* it is domestic courts that have then applied the ECJ's judgment without any further references for interpretation

---

it is submitted, is not the approach of the ECJ or indeed some national courts following *Elgafaji* (see *QD and AH (Iraq) v Secretary of State for the Home Department* [2011] 1 WLR 689 (CA)) and has been argued as flawed by JF Durieux 'Of war, flows, laws and flaws: a reply to Hugo Storey' (2012) 31 *Refugee Survey Quarterly* 161.

187  *Elgafaji* (n 182) para 33.
188  ibid para 34.
189  ibid para 35.
190  Lambert, Farrell 'The changing character of armed conflict' (n 185) 245.
191  ibid 246.
192  *Elgafaji* (n 182) para 39.
193  ibid para 43.
194  Lambert, Farrell 'The changing character of armed conflict' (n 185) 246.
195  *Elgafaji* (n 182) para 40.
196  Lambert, Farrell 'The changing character of armed conflict' (n 185) 246.

to the Court.[197] In *Sufi and Elmi*[198] the ECtHR, after noting that it would not be appropriate to comment on Article 15(c) as the jurisdiction of the ECtHR was to interpret the ECHR, then went on to suggest that Article 3 ECHR offers comparable protection to Article 15(c). This has been considered by the UK Immigration and Asylum Upper Tribunal,[199] which held that general violence that is so serious and intense as to cross the threshold for Article 3 ECHR would also cross the threshold for Article 15(c). However, *Elgafaji* makes it clear that crossing the threshold for Article 15(c) would not necessarily mean that the threshold for Article 3 ECHR would be crossed. It is logical, therefore, that the nature of the harm required to engage Article 15(c) will be less severe than that for Article 15(b)/Article 3 ECHR.

The two types of protection share common elements. First, the assessment of facts and circumstances will be in accordance with Article 4, and where a Member State has two separate procedures for the two types of international protection then there is a separate right to be heard for each procedure.[200] Secondly, the fear of harm or persecution according to Article 5 may be based on events that take place or activities that have been engaged in[201] after the individual has left the country of origin, unless by the applicant's own decision. Actors of persecution or serious harm as set out in Article 6 include:

(a)  the State;
(b)  parties or organisations controlling the, or a substantial part of the, State;
(c)  non-State actors if the actors in (a) and (b), including international organisations, are unwilling or unable to provide the protection against persecution or serious harm as defined in Article 7.

Actors of protection are those in (a) and (b), the latter including international organisations (Article 7(1)) so long as they have taken reasonable steps to prevent the persecution or harm by operating an effective legal system for the detection and punishment of the acts causing harm or persecution (Article 7(2)). If there is a part of the country of origin where there would be no well founded fear of being persecuted, or no real risk of suffering serious harm and the claimant can reasonably be expected to stay in that part of the country, then this can lead to a finding that there will not be a need for international protection (Article 8(1)).

197  See Errera 'The CJEU and subsidiary protection' (n 182) 105–112; Lambert, Farrell 'The changing character of armed conflict' (n 185) 247–256; UNHCR 'Safe at last? Law and practice in selected EU Member States with respect to asylum-seekers fleeing indiscriminate violence' July 2011 http://www.unhcr.org/refworld/pdfid/4e2ee0022.pdf for analysis of some domestic case law on art 15(c)
198  *Sufi and Elmi v United Kingdom* (2012) 54 EHRR 9 para 226.
199  *AMM and Others v Secretary of State for the Home Department* [2011] UKUT 445 (IAC) para 334; noted in G Loughran, H Short 'Somalia: indiscriminate risk' (2012) 26 *JIANL* 175.
200  Case C–277/11 *MM v Minister for Justice, Equality and Law Reform, Ireland and Attorney General* (ECJ 22 November 2012) para 91.
201  In particular if they constitute the expression and continuation of convictions or orientations held in the country of origin.

These two limbs have been described as the 'safety limb' and the 'reasonableness limb' and both must be assessed in accordance with the criteria[202] in Articles 4, 9 and 10 for refugee status or Articles 4 and 15 for subsidiary protection status.

An individual with refugee or subsidiary protection status can suffer from the cessation and exclusion of both, as well as having the status revoked, ended or refused to be renewed. For those with refugee status the circumstances leading to the grant of that status must have changed so significantly and permanently that the well founded fear of persecution does not exist anymore. These circumstances, set out in Article 11, are:

(a)   has voluntarily re-availed himself or herself of the protection of the country of nationality;

(b)   having lost his or her nationality, has voluntarily reacquired it;

(c)   has acquired a new nationality, and enjoys the protection of the country of his or her new nationality;

(d)   has voluntarily re-established himself or herself in the country which he or she left or outside which he or she remained owing to fear of persecution;

(e)   can no longer, because the circumstances in connection with which he or she has been recognised as a refugee have ceased to exist, continue to refuse to avail himself or herself of the protection of the country of nationality; or

(f)   being a stateless person with no nationality, he or she is able, because the circumstances in connection with which he or she has been recognised as a refugee have ceased to exist, to return to the country of former habitual residence.

Article 12 outlines the circumstances when a TCN or stateless person is excluded from refugee status. Paragraph 1 provides this exclusion for individuals who fall within the scope of Article 1D of the Geneva Convention, relating to protection of assistance from UN agencies or organs other than the UNHCR,[203] and persons who attain citizenship of the Member State, along with the associated rights and duties. Paragraph 2 states:

1.   A third country national or a stateless person is excluded from being a refugee where there are serious reasons for considering that:

   (a)   he or she has committed a crime against peace, war crime or crime against humanity;

---

202 *AK (Afghanistan) v Secretary of State for the Home Department* [2012] UKUT 163 (IAC) [228]–[231].

203 See C–31/09 *Nawras Bolbol v Bevándorlási és Állampolgársági Hivatal* [2010] ECR I–5539, noted in PJ Caldwell 'Case comment' (2011) 36 *ELR* 135, for interpretation of this provision and thus of art 1D of the Geneva Convention. For a reiteration of that interpretation see Case C–364/11 *Abed El Karem El Kott and Others v Bevándorlási és Állampolgársági Hivatal* (ECJ 19 December 2012).

(b)  he or she has committed a serious non-political crime[204] outside the country of refuge prior to admission as a refugee[205] . . .;

(c)  he or she has been guilty of acts contrary to the purposes and principles of the UN . . .

Membership of an organisation that, because of its involvement in terrorist acts, is on a UN list of persons, groups and entities does not automatically mean that the claimant falls within Article 12(b) or (c), even though a terrorist acts fall within the definition of Article 12(b) and (c).[206] Rather, the competent authorities of the Member States must undertake an assessment for each individual case of the specific facts to determine if the acts committed by the individual concerned would come within the exclusion clauses.[207] As such it must be possible to attribute to the person concerned 'a share of the responsibility for the acts committed by the organisation in question while that person was a member'.[208] Factors to be taken into consideration include: 'the true role played by the person concerned in the perpetration of the acts in question; his position within the organisation; the extent of the knowledge he had, or was deemed to have, of its activities; any pressure to which he was exposed; or, other factors likely to have influenced his conduct'.[209] There is, however, a danger in the intersection between criminal law and refugee law where a person claiming refugee status is criminalised and stigmatised as a 'guilty' asylum-seeker or refugee claimant, contrary to the Geneva Convention's aims.[210]

Refugee status will be revoked, ended or refused to be renewed if the person has ceased to be a refugee in accordance with Article 11[211] (Article 14(1)) with the burden of proof on the state that granted protection to establish that refugee status has ceased or should never have been granted (Article 14(2)). The status will also be withdrawn if the person was excluded from being a refugee in accordance with Article 12 or had misrepresented, or omitted, facts decisive to the grant of

---

204  Particularly cruel acts, even if committed with an allegedly political objective, may be classified as serious non-political crimes.

205  Classed as the time a residence permit was issued confirming refugee status.

206  Joined Cases C–57 & 101/09 *Germany v B and D* [2010] ECR I–10979 paras 81–84. As noted by the UK Supreme Court in *Al-Sirri and DD (Afghanistan) v Secretary of State for the Home Department* [2012] 3 WLR 1263 (SC) [15], this is consistent with the UK approach to interpreting art 1F of the Geneva Convention in *JS (Sri Lanka) v Secretary of State for the Home Department* [2011] 1 AC 184 (SC). For guidance on interpreting art 1F see UNHCR 'Statement on Article 1F of the 1951 Convention' July 2009 http://www.unhcr.org/refworld/pdfid/4a5de2992.pdf and academic comment on national case law interpreting art 1F see SS Juss 'Complicity, exclusion, and the "unworthy" in refugee law' (2012) 31 *Refugee Survey Quarterly* 1.

207  *Germany v B and D* (n 206) para 87.

208  ibid para 95.

209  ibid para 97.

210  J Bond 'Excluding justice: the dangerous intersection between refugee claims, criminal law, and "guilty" asylum seekers' (2012) 24 *IJRL* 37.

211  See Joined Cases C–175, 176, 178 & 179/08 *Aydin Salahadin Abdulla and Others v Germany* [2010] ECR I–1493, noted in R Errera 'Case comment' (2011) 23 *IJRL* 521. For a critical analysis of the approach of the EU see M O'Sullivan 'Acting the part: can non-state entities provide protection under international refugee law?' (2012) 24 *IJRL* 85.

refugee status (Article 14(3)). Member States may withdraw the status if there are reasonable grounds for believing the person is a danger to the security of the host Member State or, having been convicted of a particularly serious crime, constitutes a danger to the community of that Member State (Article 14(4)). Article 14(5) then introduces Article 14(4) as a further exclusion for granting the right.

For persons benefiting from subsidiary protection the right ceases, according to Article 16, once the circumstances leading to the grant of the right abate or change, significantly and permanently, such that the protection is no longer required. An individual will be excluded from the benefit of subsidiary protection if they commit or instigate: (a) a crime against peace, war crime or crime against humanity; (b) a serious crime; (c) acts contrary to the purposes and principles of the UN; and (d) are a danger to the community or the security of the host Member State (Article 17(1)). Furthermore, the person can be excluded if a crime was committed before entering the host Member State that would be punishable by imprisonment if it had been committed in the Member State concerned (Article 17(3)). Subsidiary protection status will be revoked, ended or refused to be renewed if the person has ceased to be eligible for subsidiary protection in accordance with Article 16 (Article 19(1)). The status will also be withdrawn if the person was excluded from being a refugee in accordance with Article 17(1) and (2) or had misrepresented, or omitted, facts decisive to the grant of refugee status (Article 19(3)). Article 19(2) allows Member States, at their discretion, to withdraw subsidiary protection status if the individual should have been excluded in accordance with Article 17(3). The burden of proof is on the state that granted protection to establish that subsidiary protection status has ceased or the person was not eligible for such status (Article 19(4)).

Once the right to refugee status or subsidiary protection status has been granted, further rights and benefits flow. Article 32 provides the right to freedom of movement within the territory of the host Member State under the same conditions and restrictions as those provided for other TCNs legally resident in the Member State. Refugees have the right to obtain travel documents to travel outside the Member State's territories and a similar right for persons with subsidiary protection status if they are unable to obtain a national passport, at least when serious humanitarian reasons occur that require their presence in another state (Article 25). Article 24 provides the right to a renewable residence permit of at least three years for refugees, a renewable residence permit of less than three years for family members and a renewable one year residence permit for persons with subsidiary protection status. According to Article 23, Member States should ensure the maintenance of family unity, where the family member is the spouse, or partner as recognised under domestic law, and the unmarried and dependent minor children, present in the same Member State as the refugee or beneficiary of subsidiary protection. Beneficiaries of both refugee and subsidiary protection status must be authorised to engage in employed or self-employed activity, although Member States can take into account the situation of the labour market possibly to prioritise access to the labour market for a limited period of time for persons with subsidiary protection (Article 26). Member States must also respect the principle of *non-refoulement* in accordance with their international obligations (Article 21). Where international obligations do not prohibit, a Member State may refoule refugees if there are reasonable grounds for considering they are a danger to the security of the host Member State or they have been convicted of a particularly serious crime that constitutes a danger to the community of that Member State.

In December 2011 Directive 2011/95 was adopted to replace Directive 2004/83.[212] The aim was to confirm the principles underlying Directive 2004/83[213] but also, by making substantive changes[214] and on the basis of higher standards,[215] to achieve a higher level of approximation of the rules on the recognition and content of international protection.[216] Unfortunately, the UK and Ireland have opted out of the new directive and Denmark has not as yet opted in, so Directive 2004/83 will remain in force for those Member States. The first major change is in the title with the removal of the term 'minimum', the increased prominence of international protection and the emphasis of a uniform status for refugees or for persons eligible for subsidiary protection. Article 2(j) extends the definition of 'family member' and there are a number of minor changes to the definitions in Article 2. Article 3 on the retention of more favourable standards by Member States is retained, and no amendments are made to Articles 4 to 6. As Peers points out,[217] the references in the new clauses of the preamble to 'confirm the principles underlying' Directive 2004/83 mean that owing to the principle of continuity of interpretation non-amended Articles will be interpreted in the same way as those from Directive 2004/83. Article 7 on actors of protection has been amended to provide that protection against persecution or serious harm can only be provided by the state or parties or organisations, including international organisations, controlling the, or a substantial part of the, state, thereby tacitly outlawing non-state actors from being able to provide such protection. The test for such protection is now 'provided they are willing and able to offer protection in accordance with paragraph 2', which includes that this protection 'must be effective and of a non-temporary nature'. Article 8 on internal protection has been extended, cross-referenced to other provisions and clarified. First, Article 8(1) allows the option for denying international protection status to an applicant if there is no well founded fear of being persecuted or is not at real risk of suffering serious harm, or has access to protection against persecution or serious harm as defined in Article 7, and can safely travel to and gain admittance to that part of the country and can

---

212 See S Peers 'Legislative update 2011, EU immigration and asylum law: the recast Qualification Directive' (2012) 14 *EJML* 199 for a detailed breakdown of changes made by Directive 2011/95.
213 Recital 10.
214 Recital 1.
215 Recital 10.
216 ibid.
217 Peers 'Legislative update 2011' (n 212) 207 and 209.

reasonably be expected to settle there.[218] In both situations the individual must be able safely and legally to travel to and gain admittance to that part of the country and can reasonably be expected to settle there. Article 8(2), on guidance for examination of a claim, has been clarified by cross-referencing to Article 4 and examples provided from where to garner accurate, precise and up-to-date information. Article 9 on acts of persecution has been amended somewhat opaquely to provide that the country's failure to protect an individual against actions of private parties can be regarded as an act of persecution so long as the omission is linked to a Geneva Convention ground.[219] The extended explanations of the reasons for persecution in Article 10 have mainly stayed the same, except when determining a particular social group, gender related aspects, including gender identity, must be given due consideration when determining the membership or characteristic of the group (Article 10(1)(d)).[220] Under the cessation clauses of Articles 11 and 16, if the conditions requiring protection cease to exist, the individual can still claim international protection by invoking 'compelling reasons arising out of previous persecution' (Articles 11(3) and 16(3)). The rights associated with international protection have been strengthened somewhat with the deletion of the provisions providing Member State discretion to reduce benefits for individuals whose refugee or subsidiary protection status was self-induced by their own actions (Article 20(6) and (7) of Directive 2004/83), and an improved family unity provision (Article 23). A significant change is the removal of the distinction between persons with refugee and subsidiary protection status such that the remaining rights are applicable equally to those with international protection in general. Thus, for persons with subsidiary protection these include an extended duration of residence permits (Article 24(2)), a right to travel documents if they are unable to obtain a passport from their country of origin (Article 25(2)) and a possible improved access to employment educational opportunities, although Member States only have to 'endeavour to facilitate full access' (Article 26(3) and a new right to equal treatment of recognition of qualifications (Article 28(1)), along with a requirement in Article 28(2) for Member States to 'endeavour to facilitate full access for beneficiaries of international protection who cannot provide documentary evidence of their qualifications to appropriate schemes for the assessment, validation and accreditation of their prior learning'. Article 31(5) provides for an enhanced procedure for tracing family members for unaccompanied minors and Article 32(2) almost provides for a right to non-discrimination and equality of opportunities regarding access to accommodation but Member States are merely required to 'endeavour to implement policies' with this objective.

---

218  For a highly critical analysis of the original art 8 and its replacement see J Eaton 'The internal protection alternative under European Union law: examining the recast Qualification Directive' (2012) 24 *IJRL* 765.

219  Peers 'Legislative update 2011' (n 212) 212–13.

220  See UNHCR 'Guidance note on refugee claims relating to sexual orientation and gender identity' November 2008 http://www.unhcr.org/refworld/pdfid/48abd5660.pdf; N LaViolette '"UNHCR guidance note on refugee claims relating to sexual orientation and gender identity": A critical commentary' (2010) 22 *IJRL* 173.

The Refugee Procedures Directive, Directive 2005/85/EC,[221] provides detailed rules and procedures for the application of Directive 2004/83 but does not impact upon the procedures contained in Regulation 343/2003. Article 6 ensures a right to apply for asylum for each adult having legal capacity on his or her own behalf and a possible right, depending on whether a Member State allows it, for the applicant also to claim for his or her dependents. Article 7 provides the right to remain in the Member State, for the sole purpose of the procedure, until at least the completion of the application procedure, unless a subsequent application will not be further examined under Article 32 or where the person will be surrendered or extradited to another Member State in accordance with the European Arrest Warrant (EAW),[222] to a third country or to international criminal courts or tribunals (Article 34). This right to remain does not constitute an entitlement to a residence permit. Article 18 details a right to not be held in detention for the sole purpose that the applicant is an asylum applicant.

The directive does not contain any provisions on free movement of persons and does not delineate between an asylum-seeker and a refugee but it does define four particularly important concepts that are common in all EU asylum and immigration measures: the first country of asylum; the safe third country; the safe country of origin; and the European safe third country. According to Article 26, an individual can have a country considered to be a first country of asylum based on personal circumstances if that applicant: (a) has been recognised in that country as a refugee and protection is still available there; or (b) otherwise enjoys sufficient protection in that country, including benefiting from the principle of *non-refoulement*, and may take into account the safe third country concept in Article 27. This safe third country concept applies to a country so long as:

(a)   life and liberty are not threatened on account of race, religion, nationality, membership of a particular social group or political opinion;
(b)   the principle of *non-refoulement* in accordance with the Geneva Convention is respected;
(c)   the prohibition of removal, in violation of the right to freedom from torture and cruel, inhuman or degrading treatment as laid down in international law, is respected; and
(d)   the possibility exists to request refugee status and, if found to be a refugee, to receive protection in accordance with the Geneva Convention are available to a claimant in it.[223]

---

221  Council Directive 2005/85/EC on minimum standards on procedures in Member States for granting and withdrawing refugee status [2005] OJ L326/13; see ECRE 'ECRE information note on Council Directive 2005/85/EC' October 2006 http://www.ecre.org/topics/areas-of-work/protection-in-europe/118.html.
222  Council Framework Decision 2002/584/JHA on the European Arrest Warrant and the surrender procedures between Member States [2002] OJ L190/1.
223  Article 27(2) also requires the concept to be subject to rules laid down in national legislation that include a nexus between the applicant and the third country, methodology for applying the safe

These two concepts of 'first country of asylum' and 'safe third country' are utilised in the criteria for determining if the asylum application is admissible in Article 25(2). It will be inadmissible if:

(a)   another Member State has granted refugee status;
(b)   a country which is not a Member State is considered as a first country of asylum for the applicant;
(c)   a country which is not a Member State is considered as a safe third country for the applicant;
(d)   the applicant is allowed to remain in the Member State concerned on some other grounds and as result of this he/she has been granted a status equivalent to the rights and benefits of refugee status by virtue of Directive 2004/83;
(e)   the applicant is allowed to remain in the territory of the Member State concerned on some other grounds which protect him/her against *refoulement* pending the outcome of a procedure for the determination of status pursuant to point (d);
(f)   the applicant has lodged an identical application after a final decision;
(g)   a dependant of the applicant lodges an application, after he/she has, in accordance with Article 6(3), consented to have his/her case be part of an application made on his/her behalf, and there are no facts relating to the dependant's situation, which justify a separate application.

Article 29[224] enables the Council, acting by QMV and using the consultation decision-making procedure, to adopt a minimum common list of third countries that are considered to be safe countries of origin when examining asylum applications. However, Article 30 allows Member States to maintain their own list, over and above the minimum common list. A country of origin will only be safe for a particular applicant in Article 31 if the applicant is a national of that country, or he/she is a stateless person who was formally habitually resident in that country, and no grounds have been submitted that the country is not safe in the applicant's particular case. Article 36 takes the 'safe country of origin' concept one stage further, by introducing the 'European safe third country' concept if the country has ratified and observes the Geneva Convention without geographical limitations, has an asylum procedure in national law, has ratified the ECHR and observes its provisions and the Council has designated it as a safe country of origin. According to Article 36(1), this applies where the asylum-seeker has entered or attempted to enter the Member State illegally and means that it is at the Member State's discretion whether to examine the asylum application in full, in part or at all.

third country concept to the third country and the applicant, and methodology for determining the safety of the third country for that particular applicant.
224  In Case C–133/06 *European Parliament v Council* [2009] ECR I–9687 the ECJ annulled the adoption by the Council of lists of countries in arts 29(1) and(2) and 36(3) on the basis that secondary legal bases were tantamount to according that institution a legislative power which exceeds powers provided for by the EU Treaties; noted in R Ball, C Dadomo 'Case comment' (2009) 15 *EPL* 335; P Craig 'Case note' (2009) 46 *CMLRev* 1265.

In 2009 the Commission put forward a proposal[225] for a recast of the Procedures Directive with the aim of improving the efficiency and quality of the decision-making procedures,[226] simplifying and consolidating procedures[227] and improving coherence between asylum instruments.[228] This was withdrawn and then put forward again in 2011.[229] Informal agreement has now been reached between the European Parliament and the Council on an agreed text,[230] although this has yet to be made public.

The war in the Former Republic of Yugoslavia in the early 1990s, and in particular the ethnic cleansing of Bosnian Muslims and Croats by Bosnian Serbs (and the more limited ethnic cleansing of Bosnian Muslims by Bosnian Croats) within Bosnia and Herzegovina, created a sudden movement of significant numbers of persons into the EU.[231] In 1997 two separate articles[232] called for the revision of the international protection regime to replace the 'existing individualised system for assessing and granting claims for refugee protection and its replacement by a collective framework emphasising temporary protection in the region of origin rather than asylum'.[233] A similar situation to that of Bosnia occurred in 1999 in the Serbian region of Kosovo, with both scenarios being dealt with in an ad hoc manner by domestic immigration law.[234] The Temporary Protection Directive (TPD) is the legal instrument that provides EU temporary protection[235] rights for

225 Commission proposal for a European Parliament and Council Directive on minimum standards on procedures in Member States for granting and withdrawing international protection (recast) COM(2009) 554 final; see UNHCR 'Comments on the European Commission's proposal for a Directive of the European Parliament and of the Council on minimum standards on procedures in Member States for granting and withdrawing international protection' August 2010 http://www.unhcr.org/4c640eee9.pdf.
226 Commission proposal on minimum standards on procedures (n 225) 4.
227 ibid 5.
228 ibid.
229 Commission amended proposal for a European Parliament and Council Directive on minimum standards on procedures in Member States for granting and withdrawing international protection (recast) COM(2011) 319 final; see ECRE 'Amended Commission Proposal to recast the Asylum Procedures Directive' September 2011 http://www.ecre.org/component/content/article/57-policy-papers/248-ecrecommentsrecastapd2011.html and UNHCR 'Comments on the European Commission's Amended Proposal for a Directive of the European Parliament and of the Council on common procedures for granting and withdrawing international protection status' January 2012 http://www.unhcr.org/4f35256c9.pdf. See also the Commission Report on the application of Directive 2005/85/EC COM(2010) 314 final.
230 Council Document 7715/13, 2.
231 K Koser, M Walsh and R Black 'Temporary protection and the assisted return of refugees from the European Union' (1998) 10 *IJRL* 444.
232 JC Hathaway, RA Neve 'Making international refugee law relevant again: a proposal for collectivised and solution-orientated protection' (1997) 10 *Harvard Human Rights Journal* 115; PH Schuck 'Refugee burden-sharing: a modest proposal' (1997) 22 *Yale Journal of International Law* 243.
233 D Anker, J Fitzpatrick and A Shacknove 'Crisis and cure: a reply to Hathaway/Neve and Schuck' (1998) 11 *Harvard Human Rights Journal* 295.
234 K Kerber 'Temporary protection in the European Union: a chronology' (1999) 14 *Georgetown Immigration Law Journal* 35.
235 Article 2(a): '"temporary protection" means a procedure of exceptional character to provide, in the event of a mass influx or imminent mass influx of displaced persons from third countries who are unable to return to their country of origin, immediate and temporary protection to such persons, in particular if there is also a risk that the asylum system will be unable to process this

those persons who are part of the mass influx[236] of displaced persons[237] as determined by the Council but is not designed to prejudge recognition of refugee status under the Geneva Convention. The duration of temporary protection is one year, renewable for a further year, in six month steps, as decided by the Council, unless the Council decides that the situation in the country of origin permits the safe and durable return of those granted temporary protection (Article 6).

There is no right to freedom of movement to another Member State, unless that Member State has a bilateral agreement with the other state, with the host Member State ensuring the return of the individual after the visit (Article 11). There is a right to a residence permit and visa for the duration of the temporary protection in Article 8. A beneficiary of temporary protection can engage in employed and self-employed activities, although Member States can prioritise jobs for EU citizens and other legally resident TCNs if the labour market warrants it (Article 12). Any person provided with temporary protection has the right to claim asylum at any time, although Member States may provide that the status of 'asylum-seeker' shall not run concurrently with that of 'temporary protection', whilst the application is being processed. At the end of the period of temporary protection, persons will be repatriated to their country of origin either voluntarily or by force.[238] However, these individuals retain the right to respect for their human dignity. If the period of temporary protection has not ended and the persons have exercised their right to return to their home state, Member States must give favourable consideration to requests to return to the host Member State depending on the circumstances prevailing in the country of origin.

The continued influx of TCNs to the EU and in particular the possibilities for mass influx either from military action, for example in Iraq and Afghanistan, or economic or environmental degradation, in particular from Africa and Albania, or from revolutionary uprisings, such as those in North Africa in early 2011 (the Arab Spring),[239] produced concerns over the working of the global asylum and refugee system. The UK circulated a 'concept paper' within the European Council in 2003, after informal intergovernmental discussions with the

---

influx without adverse effects for its efficient operation, in the interests of the persons concerned and other persons requesting protection'.

236  Article 2(d): '"mass influx" means arrival in the Community of a large number of displaced persons, who come from a specific country or geographical area, whether their arrival in the Community was spontaneous or aided, for example through an evacuation programme'.

237  Article 2(c): '"displaced persons" means third-country nationals or stateless persons who have had to leave their country or region of origin, or have been evacuated, in particular in response to an appeal by international organisations, and are unable to return in safe and durable conditions because of the situation prevailing in that country, who may fall within the scope of Article 1A of the Geneva Convention or other international or national instruments giving international protection, in particular: (i) persons who have fled areas of armed conflict or endemic violence; (ii) persons at serious risk of, or who have been the victims of, systematic or generalised violations of their human rights'.

238  Articles 20–23.

239  B Nascimbene, A Di Pascale 'The "Arab Spring" and the extraordinary influx of people who arrived in Italy from North Africa' (2011) 13 *EJML* 341.

Dutch and Danish governments and within the Council of Ministers,[240] suggesting proposals to achieve 'better management of the asylum process globally'[241] through improved regional management and transit processing centres (TPCs). The improved regional management would result from: the prevention of conditions that cause population movement; better regional protection and resources; setting quotas for more managed resettlement arrangements from source regions to Europe; and raising awareness and acceptance of state responsibility to accept returns. The Commission[242] interpreted the UK's proposal as the development of regional protection areas (RPAs) and TPCs that necessitated 'effective protection' for claimants of international protection.[243] RPAs would be set up near to an area of population displacement, enabling displaced persons a 'safe haven' close to their country of origin, whilst TPCs would be situated on the transit routes of displaced persons, outside the EU, where they could make an application for international protection and wait until it was fully processed. As the House of Lords EU Select Committee observed,[244] at the Thessaloniki Council meeting in June 2003 there was strong opposition to these proposals from several Member States such that the UK dropped its ideas on TPCs. In parallel with the EU and UK initiatives the UNHCR launched the Convention Plus[245] initiative to improve global refugee protection, develop a normative framework for global burden-sharing and resolve refugee problems through multilateral agreements and the 'three-prong' proposal.[246] This latter proposal envisaged in the 'EU prong', EU based reception centres where claimants would be registered and pre-screened at the EU, rather than the national, level. The Commission responded to the debate with a Communication[247] in 2004 that rejected the idea of any moves towards external processing, RPAs and TPCs. This appeared to be conclusive but, as Noll observed, these proposals for extra-territorial processing remained on the EU agenda and were 'moving targets for analysis, as the political debate within the EU and beyond still is in a formative phase'.[248] The German Interior Minister at the Brussels Justice and Home Affairs meeting in July 2004[249]

240  G Noll 'Visions of the exceptional: legal and theoretical issues raised by transit processing centres and protection Zones' (2003) 5 *EJML* 303.
241  European Union Committee *Handling EU Asylum Claims: New Approaches Examined* (HL 2003–2004 74) Annex 5, 54.
242  Commission Communication towards more accessible, equitable and managed asylum systems COM(2003) 315 final at 5.
243  ibid 6.
244  European Union Committee *Handling EU Asylum Claims* (n 241) 22.
245  UNHCR 'Convention plus at a glance' http://www.unhcr.org/cgi-bin/texis/vtx/protect/opendoc.pdf?tbl=PROTECTION&id=403b30684.
246  European Union Committee *Handling EU Asylum Claims* (n 241) Annex 7, 60. For an analysis of the initiative and its eventual failure see M Zieck 'Doomed to fail from the outset? UNHCR's Convention plus initiative revisited' (2009) 21 *IJRL* 387.
247  Commission Communication on the managed entry in the EU of persons in need of international protection and enhancement of the protection capacity of the regions of origin: improving access to durable solutions COM(2004) 410 final.
248  Noll 'Visions of the exceptional' (n 240) 303.
249  Reported by M Garlick 'The EU discussions on extraterritorial processing: solution or conundrum?' (2006) 18 *IJRL* 601, 619.

raised the issue again and called for 'safe zones' or 'camps' to be set up in North Africa to process claimants for international protection, a suggestion to which the Austrian Interior Minister responded with a call for an Eastern European facility to deal with Chechen asylum-seekers. Although no proposal was advanced, the German Interior Minister went further still in 2005[250] by suggesting the interception of asylum-seekers' vessels in international waters, so that the Geneva Convention would not be applicable, and the rejection of full formal asylum assessments for a process of screening. The response of the Commission was to issue a Communication proposing the establishment of Regional Protection Programmes (RPPs) to 'enhance the capacity of areas close to regions of origin to protect refugees'.[251] The chosen pilot RPP was to be set up in the Western newly independent states (Ukraine, Moldova and Belarus)[252] with future RPPs for sub-Saharan Africa (Great Lakes and East Africa, centred on Tanzania), North Africa, Afghanistan and the Horn of Africa.[253] It is notable that there are no plans for 'camps', 'zones' or TPCs in the Commission Communication,[254] although there were discussions with Libya over possible sites before the recent revolution. RPPs were eventually set up for Ukraine, Moldova and Belarus, and Tanzania[255] with a third in the Horn of Africa (Kenya, Djibouti and Yemen), with close cooperation from the UNHCR in September 2010[256] and a fourth in Egypt, Tunisia and Libya in September 2011,[257] although there remains very little information published about them. In early 2011, with the Arab Spring popular revolutions in Tunisia and especially Libya creating significant outflow of migrants from those countries, some of whom reached Malta and Italy, Italy applied to activate the TPD and to establish a plan for burden sharing to include the disbursement of refugees throughout the EU.[258] However, at the April JHA Council meeting[259] the request was rejected by the Council on the basis that the number of displaced persons was not enough to be a 'mass influx'.[260]

---

250  ibid 621.
251  Commission Communication on regional protection programmes COM(2005) 388 final.
252  ibid 6.
253  ibid 7.
254  O Lynskey 'Complementing and completing the common European asylum system: a legal analysis of the emerging extraterritorial elements of EU refugee protection policy' (2006) 31 *ELR* 230; C Levy 'Refugees, Europe, camps/state of exception: "into the Zone", the European Union and extraterritorial processing of migrants, refugees, and asylum-seekers (theories and practice)' (2010) 29 *Refugee Survey Quarterly* 92.
255  Commission first annual report on immigration and asylum COM(2010) 214 final at 6.
256  Commission second annual report on immigration and asylum COM(2011) 291 final at 6.
257  Commission third annual report on immigration and asylum COM(2012) 250 final at 16.
258  Nascimbene, Di Pascale 'The "Arab Spring"' (n 239) 346; G Campesi 'The Arab Spring and the crisis of the European border regime: manufacturing emergency in the Lampedusa crisis' EUI Working Papers RSCAS 2011/59 November 2011 at 13; S Carrera, E Guild, M Merlino and J Parkin 'A race against solidarity: the Schengen regime and the Franco-Italian affair' April 2011 http://www.ceps.eu/book/race-against-solidarity-schengen-regime-and-franco-italian-affair 14.
259  Council Document 8692/11. It is noticeable that no mention was made of the request by Italy in this press release.
260  Carrera, Guild, Merlino and Parkin 'A race against solidarity' (n 258) 15.

The development of European refugee law in the EC Treaty was an essential complementary policy to ensuring the free movement of persons (Article 61(a) EC), and with the amendments in the Lisbon Treaty to the equivalent provision (Article 67 TFEU) that is a requirement to 'frame a common policy on asylum' linked to the 'absence of border controls for persons' (Article 67(2) TFEU). This evolution, with Article 78 TFEU as the legal base, could be viewed optimistically as having a positive impact on refugees by providing a fair and efficient assessment of claims, by treating any individuals returning to their country of origin with dignity and ensuring their safety, and by the development and democratisation of regions beyond the EU that have a propensity to produce asylum-seekers.[261] Furthermore, by harmonising the standards required for the qualification of refugee status and introducing the rights to subsidiary and temporary protection, common values become standardised across the EU, different forms of international protection are introduced to cater for different situations thereby raising levels of protection, filling gaps that had been filled in an ad hoc manner by Member States acting on their own and ensuring the end to forum shopping.[262] The rejection of the 'accountability theory' as favoured by Germany and France by including non-state actors as potential perpetrators of persecution or serious harm in Article 6 of the Qualification Directive is a welcome higher standard that should provide greater protection for refugees.[263] Furthermore, this should ensure that the concerns with the standards of protection in Member States, when asylum-seekers are returned through the operation of the Dublin Regulation, should be reduced.

However, considerable concerns have been raised over the three legislative measures. The first involves the compatibility with the Geneva Convention that itself involves a number of issues. The first is the definition of 'refugee' in the Qualification Directive in comparison to that in Article 1A of the Geneva Convention and the scope of the directive. The term 'refugee' is only available for TCNs and stateless persons in Article 2(c) of the directive, as is also the case for those 'eligible for subsidiary protection' in Article 2(e), whereas the definition in the Geneva Convention applies to 'any person'. Therefore EU citizens are excluded from the capacity to claim refugee status in other EU Member States,[264] which also applies to subsidiary protection (Article 2(f)). This is embedded further by Protocol 24 attached to the EU treaties that with the level of protection for fundamental rights and freedoms by the Member States, Member States are safe countries of origin for asylum purposes, with only limited exceptions. As

---

261  GS Goodwin-Gill 'The individual refugee, the 1951 Convention and the Treaty of Amsterdam' in Guild, Harlow (eds) *Implementing Amsterdam* (n 1) 141.

262  S Boutillon 'The interpretation of Article 1 of the 1951 Convention Relating to the Status of Refugees by the European Union: toward harmonisation' (2003) 18 *Georgetown Immigration Law Journal* 111, 117.

263  European Union Committee *Defining Refugee Status and Those in Need of International Protection* (HL 2001–2002, 156) 21.

264  This complies with Protocol (No 24) (n 48).

Gilbert[265] and Boutillon[266] observe, Article 1 of the Geneva Convention, through the utilisation of Article 27 of the Vienna Convention on the Law of Treaties,[267] is non-derogable and the exclusion of nationals of Member States would breach Article 3 of the Geneva Convention that requires states to apply the Convention's provisions to refugees without discrimination as to inter alia country of origin. It also contravenes Article 42 of the Geneva Convention that prohibits reservations to Article 1.[268] Boutillon[269] suggests a reason for this exclusion is that the right of free movement for citizens of the Union enables individuals to move to another Member State without the need to claim refugee status. However, there are limitations with this argument, in particular over the transition arrangements of the new Member States, where free movement is limited for seven years after accession, and the treatment of the Roma people in some of these new Member States.[270] The second compatibility issue involves the relationship of Article 14(4) and (5) of the Qualification Directive and Article 33(2) of the Geneva Convention. Article 33(1) provides the right to, and conditions for, the principle of *non-refoulement* that Member States must respect (Article 21(1) of the Qualification Directive) and Article 33(2) allows *refoulement* of refugees on the basis of national security and public safety, given effect by Article 21(2) of the Qualification Directive. Article 33(2) does not envisage the withdrawal of, or the refusal to, grant refugee status for an individual but simply the possibility of allowing *refoulement*. Article 14(4) of the Qualification Directive enables Member States to withdraw refugee status and Article 14(5) allows Member States to refuse to grant refugee status to individuals on the basis of the reasons in Article 33(2) of the Geneva Convention. This is a misreading of Article 33(2) of the Geneva Convention that the directive has interpreted as an exclusion clause for the grant of refugee status but is in fact an exception to the principle to *non-refoulement* of a refugee already granted that status.[271] Thirdly, although recital 3 provides that the Geneva Convention is the

265  G Gilbert 'Is Europe living up to its obligations to refugees?' (2004) 15 *EJIL* 963, 975.
266  Boutillon 'The interpretation of Article 1' (n 262) 136.
267  Vienna Convention on the Law of Treaties between States and International Organisations or International Organisations 1986 art 27(1): 'A State party to a treaty may not invoke the provisions of its internal law as justification for its failure to perform the treaty'. As a directive is not a treaty it would not fall within the scope of arts 30 and 41 dealing with obligations in Treaties but upon transposition into domestic law it would come within the definition in art 27(1), prohibiting Member States to limit their obligations in international treaties through their national law.
268  A Klug 'Harmonization of asylum in the European Union – emergence of an EU refugee system?' (2004) 47 *GYIL* 594, 600; H Lambert 'The EU Asylum Qualification Directive, its impact on the jurisprudence of the United Kingdom and international law' (2006) 55 *ICLQ* 161, 178.
269  Boutillon 'The interpretation of Article 1' (n 262) 140.
270  Gilbert 'Is Europe living up' (n 265) 975. Ill-treatment of the Roma people is not confined to the new Member States; see CJ Chido 'Peril of movement: migrating Roma risks expulsion as EU Member States test the limits of the Free Movement Directive' (2011) 20 *Tulane Journal of International and Comparative Law* 233 and J Parra 'Stateless Roma in the European Union: reconciling the doctrine of sovereignty concerning nationality laws with international agreements to reduce and avoid statelessness' (2011) 34 *Fordham International Law Journal* 1666.
271  Lambert 'The EU Asylum Qualification Directive' (n 268) 178; C Teitgen-Colly 'The European Union and asylum: an illusion of protection' (2006) 43 *CMLRev* 1503, 1555.

'cornerstone of the international legal regime for the protection of refugees' the Qualification Directive fails to include significant elements of the Geneva Convention. Thus Article 4, regarding the freedom to practise religion and religious education of refugees' children, and Articles 12–16, on the rights attached to juridical status, are not included in the directive.[272] However, Article 16 on the right to access to courts is provided for in the Procedures Directive. Fourthly, Article 34 of the Geneva Convention, compels states, as far as possible, to facilitate the assimilation and naturalisation of refugees, swiftly and with the minimum charges and costs. This naturalisation provision has been replaced with a general requirement for Member States to provide integration programmes without any reference to naturalisation.[273] Fifthly, as Teitgen-Colly notes,[274] the exclusion clauses to the grant of refugee status set out in Article 1F of the Geneva Convention are required to be interpreted restrictively as they are exclusions to the general right of international protection[275] but they have been interpreted broadly by Article 14(3) of the directive and the wording, in particular in Article 14(2)(b), has been significantly extended from that in Article 1F.

The second concern features the introduction of subsidiary protection status in the Qualification Directive and once again involves a number of issues. The first is that by definition (Article 2(e)) subsidiary protection is only to be granted if a person does not qualify for refugee status. There is a danger, therefore, that states will provide claimants with the lower protection, and the subsequent lower benefits and rights, rather than the status of refugee. The new Qualification Directive goes some way to addressing this concern by removing the Member States' discretion to award lower benefits and has attempted generally to equalise rights around international protection status. However, Directive 2004/83 remains in force for the UK, Ireland and Denmark. Secondly, the elements of 'serious harm' included in Article 15 are an exhaustive list that does not allow any development or flexibility of protection for violation of other human rights apart from those listed in Article 15.[276] McAdam's point is though now rather muted, particularly with the judgment in *Elgafaji*. Teitgen-Colly[277] has also criticised Article 15 for its limited nature and clarity, but it is submitted that her criticisms of the imprecise scope of subsidiary protection and serious harm are not reflected in the elements of Article 15. Thirdly, the exclusion clause in Article 17 is broader than that for refugee status in Article 12 and Article 1F of the Geneva Convention,

---

272 Lambert 'The EU Asylum Qualification Directive' (n 268) 179.
273 ibid.
274 Teitgen-Colly 'The European Union and asylum' (n 271) 1557.
275 UNHCR *Handbook on Procedures* (n 58) para 149 – the objective of the handbook is to provide practical guidelines to Member States but lacks binding force.
276 J McAdam 'The European Union Qualification Directive: the creation of a subsidiary protection regime' (2005) 18 *IJRL* 461, 492; McAdam *Complementary Protection* (n 178) 83. Article 15 in the original Commission proposal for the Qualification Directive (COM(2001) 510 final) had included a broad human right provision that provided that serious harm would include 'violation of a human right, sufficiently severe to engage the Member State's international obligations'.
277 Teitgen-Colly 'The European Union and asylum' (n 271) 1533.

as Article 17(1)(b) only requires that there be serious reasons for believing that 'he or she has committed a serious crime', rather than a 'serious non-political crime'.[278] Furthermore, Article 17(1)(d) includes the Article 33(2) exemption from *non-refoulement* as an exclusion of protection clause. Article 17(3) also enables Member States to exclude individuals from subsidiary protection status if they have carried out a crime not included in Article 17(1) that would have been capable of being punished by imprisonment in the host Member State and they have left their country of origin to escape such punishment. There is no parallel to this provision in the Geneva Convention.[279] Although Directive 2011/95 includes some welcome improvements, as Peers notes,[280] it could have gone further and the possibility of Member States retaining higher standards under Article 3 means that harmonisation will not be achieved, emphasised even more by the continued operation of Directive 2004/83 for the UK, Ireland and Denmark.

The Procedures Directive raises the third concern with a number of further issues as outlined by Costello.[281] The first issue is the diminished standard of the requirement of 'sufficient protection' in a first country of asylum for Article 26, rather than the higher standard of 'effective protection'.[282] Secondly, the safe third country concept is considered to be flawed as there should be a requirement that the third country should provide a fair and efficient determination procedure and that there must be a meaningful link between the applicant and the third country.[283] More concerning is the concept of European safe third country, where no examination need be carried out by the Member State concerned of the application before the applicant is returned to that state. Lists of safe third countries, safe countries of origin and European safe third countries mean that it is possible for the applicant to be returned to that country without the country being assessed for safety as applicable to the personal circumstances of that individual. As Costello observes,[284] the inevitable consequence of this is chain *refoulement* and refugees in orbit.

The fourth concern is levelled at the TPD. Temporary protection has been described by Fitzpatrick as 'like a magic gift, assuming the desired form of its enthusiasts' policy objectives. Simultaneously, it serves as a magic mirror of its observers' fears'.[285] This is reflected in the three issues that are raised over the

---

278  Gilbert 'Is Europe living up' (n 265) 979.
279  McAdam 'The European Union Qualification Directive' (n 276) 497.
280  Peers 'Legislative update 2011' (n 212) 220.
281  C Costello 'The Asylum Procedures Directive and the proliferation of safe country practices: deterrence, deflection and the dismantling of international protection?' (2005) 7 *EJML* 35.
282  Commission Communication towards more accessible, equitable and managed asylum systems COM(2003) 315 final 6, identifying the minimum conditions for 'effective protection'; S Legomsky 'Secondary refugee movements and the return of asylum seekers to third countries: the meaning of effective protection' (2003) 16 *IJRL* 567.
283  Costello 'The Asylum Procedures Directive' (n 281) 60.
284  ibid 61.
285  J Fitzpatrick 'Temporary protection of refugees: elements of a formalised regime' (2000) 94 *AJIL* 279, 280.

directive. First, the power rests with the Council to open a temporary protection scheme[286] in which the Council is given a 'blank cheque'[287] as to the definition of 'mass influx of displaced persons', even with guidance provided by Article 5(4). As the situation of the Arab Spring demonstrates, determining what can be considered to be a mass influx is highly political, extremely delicate and could seriously damage relationships between Member States. Secondly, the availability of temporary protection enables states to put off assessment of a claim for either refugee or subsidiary protection status. Thirdly, the length of protection is finite up to a maximum of two years (Article 4(1)).[288] Many, if not most, conflicts last for a considerably longer period than two years,[289] raising concerns over decisions concerning individuals after two years and their final destination.

The fifth concern is raised over the concepts of 'safe havens', 'camps', RPAs and TPCs but, as these proposals have not become concrete legal measures, only a brief outline will be provided. The first issue is who has responsibility for these areas. The Geneva Convention requires the Contracting States to process applications for international protection but if TPCs are established outside the EU then it is uncertain who would have this responsibility. Secondly, there could be a breach of the principle of *non-refoulement* if a national of a state is returned to a TPC or RPA situated within that state. Thirdly, detention within a TPC would probably violate Article 31(2) of the Geneva Convention and Article 5(1) ECHR. Finally, the German Interior Minister's suggestion of intercepting applicants for international protection before they enter EU Member States' territorial waters in order to circumvent the principle of *non-refoulement* in the Geneva Convention is likely to be illegal if, as has been cogently argued,[290] it has *jus cogens* status and would also be, just as importantly, immoral.[291] In 2009 the Italian Revenue Police

---

286  Guild 'Seeking asylum' (n 67) 211.
287  N Arena 'The concept of "mass influx of displaced persons" in the European Directive Establishing the Temporary protection scheme' (2005) 7 *EJML* 435, 438.
288  Guild 'Seeking asylum' (n 67) 211.
289  For example the Bosnian civil war lasted from 1991 until 1995.
290  See Borchelt 'The safe third country practice' (n 54) 480; J Allain 'The *jus cogens* nature of *non-refoulement*' (2002) 13 *IJRL* 534; E Lauterpacht, D Bethlehem 'The scope and content of the principle of *non-refoulement*: Opinion' in E Feller, V Türk and F Nicholson (eds) *Refugee Protection in International Law: UNHCR's Global Consultations on International Protection* (CUP 2003) 87, 149. For alternative views see J Pirjola 'Shadows in paradise – exploring *non-refoulement* as an open concept' (2007) 19 *IJRL* 639; Duffy 'Expulsion to face torture' (n 7). For recent consideration of the EU position see S Klepp 'A contested asylum system: the European Union between refugee protection and border control in the Mediterranean Sea' (2010) 12 *EJML* 1 and GS Goodwin-Gill 'The right to seek asylum: interception at sea and the principle of *non-refoulement*' (2011) 23 *IJRL* 443.
291  However, see the US Supreme Court's judgment in *Sale, Acting Commissioner, Immigration and Naturalization Service v Haitian Centers Council* 509 US 155 (1993), where it was held legal for the US coastguard to intercept Haitian refugees on the high seas and turn them back towards Haiti and that the Geneva Convention was only relevant within the borders of a state. This has been criticised by academics (for example TD Jones 'Case note' (1994) 88 *AJIL* 114, 122; GL Neuman 'Extraterritorial violations of human rights by the United States' (1994) 9 *American University Journal of International Law and Policy* 213; SH Legomsky 'The USA and the Caribbean interdiction program' (2006) 18 *IJRL* 677; A Roberts 'Righting wrongs or wronging rights? The United States and human rights post-September 11' (2004) 15 *EJIL* 721; M Pallis 'Obligations of states towards

and Coastguard intercepted three vessels off the Italian coast filled with, mainly, Somali and Eritrean nationals who had left the Libyan coast with the aim of landing in Italy and claiming asylum, but who were then not allowed to make a claim. The occupants were returned to Tripoli on Italian military ships, handed over to the Libyan authorities in Tripoli and had all their possessions, including identity and travel documents, confiscated by the Italians. The ECtHR in *Hirsi Jamaa v Italy*[292] held that Italy's actions infringed Article 3 ECHR, due to the risk of inhuman and degrading treatment in Libya and the risk of arbitrary repatriation to Eritrea and Somalia, Article 4 of Protocol 4 ECHR, due to collective expulsion without any formal examination of each applicant's situation, and Article 13 ECHR, as they had no opportunity to put their case for an asylum claim or for a breach of Articles 3 and 4 of Protocol 4 ECHR. Indeed, they had been led to believe by the Italian personnel on the vessels that they were being taken to Italy.

There are also concerns that are collective issues that cover all three directives. First, the directives provide minimum standards. The aim is to allow Member States to retain and adopt higher levels of protection in areas of their discretion and even though the new Qualification Directive has deleted the word 'minimum' in the title, Article 1 makes it quite clear that the standards remain mimimal. However, it is difficult to see Member States retaining international protection standards higher than those of other Member States, as the very presence of a more liberal regime is likely to open up that Member State to the possibility of increased applications for that protection.[293] Secondly, the definition of 'family member' is considerably narrower than that included in Article 2(2) of Directive 2004/38. As such, a spouse met or a child born after the applicant had left the country of origin would not be able to claim protection. Neither would a family member who arrived in the host Member State after the applicant received protection nor a child who was not a minor, unmarried and dependent. Thirdly, there is either no right to freedom of movement or an extremely limited right and the ability to travel to other states is dependent on the type of international protection that the individual enjoys.

---

asylum seekers at sea: interactions and conflicts between legal regimes' (2002) 14 *IJRL* 329), the UNHCR (UNHCR 'Advisory Opinion on the extraterritorial application of *non-refoulement* obligations under the 1951 Convention relating to the status of refugees and its 1967 Protocol' [2007] EHRLR 484) and judicially (see *R (on the application of European Roma Rights Centre and Others) v Immigration Officer, Prague Airport* [2004] QB 811 [34] (Simon Brown LJ) but cf *R (on the application of European Roma Rights Centre and Others) v Immigration Officer, Prague Airport* [2005] 2 AC 1 (HL) [68]–[71] (Lord Hope)). In Case 10.675 *The Haitian Centre for Human Rights v United States* Report 51/96 [1998] 5 IHRR (Inter-American Commission for Human Rights) it was held that the USA had acted illegally with regard to its obligations under the Geneva Convention.

292  *Hirsi Jamaa and Others v Italy* (2012) 55 EHRR 21; noted in M Giuffre 'Case comment' (2012) 61 *ICLQ* 728; E Guild 'The European geography of refugee protection – exclusions, limitations and exceptions from the 1967 Protocol to the present' [2012] EHRLR 413; S York 'Case comment' (2012) 26 *JIANL* 283.

293  R Piotrowicz, C van Eck 'Subsidiary protection and primary rights' (2004) 53 *ICLQ* 107, 114.

## 4.4  Immigration

The third type of TCN whose movement is regulated by the measures implementing Article 79 TFEU of the AFSJ is the migrant. The relationship between migration and asylum is close, being labelled the 'migration-asylum nexus',[294] constituted by the distinction between forced and economic migration, and the blurring of this distinction.[295] This nebulous distinction between asylum-seekers or refugees and immigrants has led to national immigration policies treating their international movement as similar[296] and erasing the line between migration control and refugee protection,[297] whilst dehumanising immigrants through the use of terminology such as 'floods' and 'invasions'.[298] The Commission has attempted to steer a steady course through these confused waters by developing a distinct Union immigration policy that splits immigration into two discrete areas: legal and illegal immigration.[299] This has now been recognised and accepted by the Council in the European Pact on Immigration and Asylum[300] and is utilised as the basis for the Commission's Annual Reports on Immigration and Asylum.[301] In 2012 Peers[302] put forward proposals for an EU Immigration Code, which is a possible way forward for the Union in this area, although nothing has yet been brought forward by the Commission.

### *4.4.1  Legal immigration*

The difference between legal and illegal immigration is difficult to determine with precision. However, legal migrants will tend to have obtained the requisite documents for travel before entering the EU and retain these during their time in the EU, whilst illegal migrants are unlikely to hold these genuine documents.

---

294  K Koser 'New approaches in asylum?' (2001) 39 *International Migration* 85, 87.
295  A Betts 'Towards a Mediterranean solution? Implications for the region of origin' (2006) 18 *IJRL* 652, 655.
296  R Hansen 'Asylum policy in the European Union' (2000) 14 *Georgetown Immigration Law Journal* 779, 793.
297  E Feller 'Asylum, migration and refugee protection: realities, myths and the promise of things to come' (2006) 18 *IJRL* 510, 515.
298  G Brochman 'The current traps of European immigration policies' Willy Brandt Series of Working Papers in International Migration and Ethnic relations 1/03; J Banks 'Unmasking deviance: the visual construction of asylum seekers and refugees in English national newspapers' (2012) 20 *Critical Criminology* 293.
299  Commission Communication on a Community immigration policy COM(2000) 757 final; Commission Communication on a common immigration policy for Europe: Principles, actions and tools COM(2008) 359 final.
300  Council Document 13440/08 adopted at the Brussels European Council Meeting of 15 and 16 October 2008; Council Document 14368/08 at 9.
301  See Commission Annual Reports to the European Parliament and Council on Immigration and Asylum COM(2010) 214 final and COM(2011) 291 final. An alternative more dialogic approach was adopted for the latest report COM(2012) 250 final.
302  S Peers 'An EU immigration code: towards a common immigration policy' (2012) 14 *EJML* 33 and supplemented by S Peers 'A proposal for an EU immigration code' *Statewatch Analysis* (No 167) January 2012 http://www.statewatch.org/analyses/no-167-immigration-code-steve-peers.pdf.

Secondly, they are likely to comply with the requisite admission procedures for their entry. Upon their successful entry they will be granted certain rights that should be broadly the same as those of EU nationals[303] and facilitate their integration into the host society as the essential corollary of admission policies.[304] To that end the family is an important element of integration policies,[305] in particular the right to family reunification.[306] It is logical, therefore, to analyse these four elements as they apply to the legal immigration of TCNs and in particular their freedom of movement.

### 4.4.1.1   *EU common visa policy*[307]

Two types of visa for entry of TCNs into Schengenland were introduced in the SIC: the short term visa; and, the long term visa, with Regulation 539/2001/EC[308] providing lists of third countries whose nationals have to be in possession of visas when crossing the external borders of the Union or need not be in possession of a visa for stays of less than three months. Article 10(1) SIC required the introduction of a uniform 'Schengen short term visa' that could be issued for visits not exceeding three months. This was further delineated into travel and transit visas. Travel visas would be 'valid for one or more entries, provided that neither the length of a continuous visit nor the total length of successive visits exceeds three months in any half-year, from the date of first entry' (Article 11(1)(a) SIC). Transit visas enabled the holder to pass through the Member State's territory en route to a third country, so long as the transit was less than five days (Article 11(1)(b) SIC). Regulation 1683/95/EC,[309] augmented by Regulation 333/2002/EC,[310] laid down a uniform format for these short term visas. In 2006 the

---

303  Commission Communication on a Community immigration policy (n 299) 15.
304  ibid 16.
305  ibid 20.
306  ibid 12.
307  A Meloni 'The development of a common visa policy under the Treaty of Amsterdam' (2005) 42 *CMLRev* 1357.
308  Council Regulation 539/2001/EC listing the third countries whose nationals must be in possession of visas when crossing the external borders and those whose nationals are exempt from that requirement [2001] OJ L81/1, as amended by Regulation 2414/2001/EC [2001] OJ L327/1, Regulation 453/2003/EC [2003] OJ L69/10, Regulation 851/2005/EC [2005] OJ L141/3, Regulation 1791/2006/EC [2006] OJ L363/1, Regulation 1932/2006/EC [2007] OJ L29/10, Regulation 1244/2009/EC [2009] OJ L336/1, Regulation 1091/2010/EU [2010] OJ L329/1 and Regulation 1211/2010/EU [2010] OJ L339/6. The Commission proposed a new codified Regulation in 2008 to replace the much amended Regulation 539/2001 but this was not adopted – see Commission proposal for a Regulation listing the third countries whose nationals must be in possession of visas when crossing the external borders and those whose nationals are exempt from that requirement (Codified version) COM(2008) 761 final.
309  Council Regulation 1683/95/EC laying down a uniform format for visas [1995] OJ L164/1 as amended by Regulation 334/2002/EC, Regulation 1791/2006/EC and Regulation 856/2008/EC.
310  Council Regulation 333/2002/EC on a uniform format for affixing the visa issued by Member States to persons holding travel documents not recognised by the Member State drawing up the form [2002] OJ L53/4.

Commission brought forward a proposal[311] for a regulation to establish a Community Code on Visas (Visa Code) that was adopted in 2009[312] so that the Union Common Visa Policy and its provisions are now contained in four consolidated measures, namely Regulations 1683/95, 539/2001, 333/2002 and 810/2009,[313] with the SIC provisions and attendant legislative measures repealed (Visa Code Article 56). This Common Visa Policy provides for a unified visa application, examination and processing procedure for short stay visas where stays do not exceed three months in a six month period (Article 1). Again, there are two types of visa with the procedures for airport transit visas set out in Article 3 and standard visas in Title III. For the latter, applications must be examined and decided upon by consulates (Article 4(1)) unless the exceptional conditions of Articles 35 and 36 are satisfied, which enables visas to be dealt with at the Union's external borders (Article 4(2)). TCNs must apply for a visa in their country of residence unless they are lawfully resident in another country and have a legitimate reason for not applying in their country of residence (Article 6). The application must be made in person (Article 10(1)), unless the applicant is known to the consulate for his integrity and reliability (Article 10(2)). Article 10(3) requires the presentation of the application form (Article 11), a travel document (Article 12), a photograph or a set of fingerprints for biometric identification (Article 13),[314] the fee (Article 16), supporting documents (Article 14) and proof of adequate and valid travel medical insurance (Article 15) with a minimum amount of €30,000. A visa can be limited territorially under the conditions in Article 25, refused (Article 32), extended (Article 33) or annulled and revoked (Article 34).

Article 18 SIC provided that long term visas for stays exceeding three months were to remain national visas so long as the person meets the criteria for entry to the Schengen area in Article 5 SIC, and Regulation 1091/2001/EC[315] enables these national long term visas to be used for travel between Member States. The long term visa is still regulated by national law as no Union legislation has been adopted.

The importance of visas to the right of free movement becomes apparent when considering Articles 19–21 SIC. Article 19(1) states that '[a]liens[316] who hold uniform visas and who have legally entered the territory of a Contracting Party may move freely within the territories of all the Contracting Parties during the

---

311 Commission proposal for a Regulation of the European Parliament and Council establishing a Community Code on Visas COM (2006) 403 final.
312 European Parliament and Council Regulation 810/2009/EC establishing a Community Code on Visas (Visa Code) [2009] OJ L243/1; S Peers 'Legislative update, EC immigration and asylum law: the new visa code' (2010) 12 *EJML* 105, 108.
313 A Meloni 'The Community code on visas: harmonisation at last?' (2009) 34 *ELR* 671, 679.
314 For a recent analysis of biometrics see A Farraj 'Refugees and the biometric future: the impact of biometrics on refugees and asylum seekers' (2011) 42 *Columbia Human Rights Law Review* 891.
315 Council Regulation 1091/2001/EC on Freedom of Movement with a long-stay visa [2001] OJ L150/4.
316 'Alien' was the term used in Schengen and the SIC that is now replaced with the more politically correct term TCN.

period of validity of their visas', unless limited territorially by a Member State. Articles 20 and 21 enable TCNs, not subject to visa requirements or who hold valid residence permits, to move freely within the territories of the Contracting Parties for a maximum period of three months during the six months following the date of first entry. The ECJ in *Bot*[317] held that the term 'first entry' refers not only to the very first entry into Schengen territory but also to any other first entry after the expiry of any new period of six months. However, Article 30 of the Visa Code makes it clear that '[m]ere possession of a uniform visa or a visa with limited territorial validity does not confer an automatic right of entry' for TCNs.

As Gilbert[318] and Guild[319] note, visas are complemented by the provisions on carrier sanctions that work 'in combination to place decision-making about entry back with the State of departure'. These carrier sanctions are laid down in Articles 26 and 27 SIC, complemented and supplemented by three directives that have the objective of curbing migratory flows and combating illegal immigration.[320] Article 26(1)(a) SIC requires the air, sea or land carrier that brought the TCN to the EU to assume responsibility again for that TCN immediately upon the refusal of entry to the EU and return that TCN to the third country they came from, or they obtained the travel document from or that will certainly admit them. Furthermore, the carrier must take all the necessary measures to ensure that a TCN travelling by sea or air is in possession of the travel documents necessary for entry to the EU (Article 26(1)(b) SIC). Article 26(2) and (3) SIC requires sanctions to be levied against air, sea or land carriers for breaches of their obligations, whilst Article 27 SIC requires the levy of appropriate sanctions against individuals for assisting or trying to assist a TCN illegally to enter or reside in the EU for financial gain. Directive 2001/51/EC[321] supplements Article 26 SIC. If a TCN is refused entry in transit, then the obligations of carriers remain even if they refuse to take the TCN on board for onwards flight to the country of destination or if the state of destination has refused the TCN entry and the TCN has been returned to the transit Member State (Article 2). The level of sanctions for carriers under Article 26(2) and (3) must be a maximum of €5000 and a minimum of €3000 per person, with a maximum lump sum for each infringement of €500,000 (Article 4). Directive 2003/110/EC[322] specifies in Article 3(1) that the preferred means of returning a TCN by air is by a direct flight to the country of destination.

---

317 Case C–241/05 *Nicolae Bot v Préfet du Val-de-Marne* [2006] ECR I–9627 para 43.
318 Gilbert 'Is Europe living up' (n 265) 971.
319 E Guild 'Between persecution and protection: refugees and the new European asylum policy' (2000) 3 *CYELS* 169, 179. See also VL Lax 'Must EU borders have doors for refugees? On the compatibility of Schengen visas and carriers' sanctions with EU Member States' obligations to provide international protection to refugees' (2008) 10 *EJML* 315; E Feller 'Carrier sanctions and international law' (1999) 1 *IJRL* 48.
320 European Union Committee *Fighting Illegal Immigration: Should Carriers Carry the Burden?* (HL 2003–2004, 29).
321 Council Directive 2001/51/EC supplementing the provisions of Article 26 of the Convention implementing the Schengen Agreement [2001] OJ L187/45.
322 Council Directive 2003/110/EC on assistance in cases of transit for the purposes of removal by air [2003] OJ L321/26.

However, if this is not reasonably practicable then the Member State can request to use a transit flight through another Member State along with assistance during the transit (Articles 3(2) and 5(2)). Finally, Article 3(1) of Directive 2004/82/EC[323] places obligations on carriers to transmit in advance (by the end of check-in) information on passengers when they are going to enter the territory of a Member State at an authorised border crossing point. Where the carrier has negligently transmitted incomplete or false data then the Member State can fine that carrier a maximum of €5000 or a minimum of €3000 per journey (Article 4(1)). The duties and sanctions imposed on carriers can be objected to on a number of grounds. The first is that a public service obligation, being the duty of customs and immigration officials, should not be imposed on private service providers,[324] the transport carriers, and backed up by penalties. As a consequence, internal border checks, the removal of which was the principal aim of Schengen, have increased with checks being conducted by both national custom police and transport carriers, the latter to avoid legal sanctions.[325] The second is that carrier sanctions are likely to act as a block on legitimate attempts by genuine asylum-seekers or refugees to leave their country of residence as these individuals, by the nature of their desperate situation, are unlikely to have the opportunity to obtain the appropriate travel documentation before fleeing.[326] Therefore, asylum-seekers and refugees are likely to become frustrated, further disenfranchised, more desperate, and fall into the hands of organised illegal immigration organisations, a situation that the Common Visa Policy is supposedly designed to avoid.

### 4.4.1.2   Admission requirements for entry

Article 3(1) SIC states that '[e]xternal borders may in principle only be crossed at border crossing points and during the fixed opening hours'. This general provision required legislative measures to be adopted to enable the second element of an EU immigration policy, to provide common admission requirements for the entry of TCNs to the EU, to be achieved. This has proven to be difficult to achieve for the Member States as this impinges on a fundamental element of national sovereignty.

Two directives were adopted in this area without too many difficulties: Directive 2004/114/EC[327] and Directive 2005/71/EC.[328] They were perceived as being

---

323  Council Directive 2004/82/EC on the obligation of carriers to communicate passenger data [2004] OJ L261/24.

324  Although contracting out responsibilities of the state to private corporations is now quite common, the duties of customs and immigration officials would appear to go to the heart of sovereignty and power.

325  European Union Committee *Fighting Illegal Immigration* (n 320) 8.

326  Foblets 'Europe and its aliens after Maastricht' (n 59).

327  Council Directive 2004/114/EC on the conditions of admission of third-country nationals for the purposes of studies, pupil exchange, unremunerated training or voluntary service [2004] OJ L375/12.

328  Council Directive 2005/71/EC on a specific procedure for admitting third-country nationals for the purposes of scientific research [2005] OJ L289/15.

advantageous to the Member States without creating significant enforceable rights for TCNs, especially those of free movement.[329] The former directive provides the conditions and procedures for the admission of TCNs to the territory of the Member States for a period exceeding three months in order to carry out study, pupil exchange, unremunerated training or voluntary service. Articles 12–15 provide for the right to a residence permit for at least a year for: a student that is capable of renewal; for no more than a year for a school pupil; for the duration of the placement for unremunerated trainees up to a maximum of a year (renewable only once and exclusively for the time to acquire a vocational qualification); and for a year for volunteers, although in exceptional cases this can be extended to the duration of the voluntary project. The conditions for the acquisition of the right to a residence permit are specific to each category of person and are contained in Articles 7–11, with Article 6 providing general conditions applicable to all. Only students are provided with a limited right to freedom of movement in Article 8 so that a student who has already been admitted as a student in one Member State can apply to follow part of the commenced studies, or to complement them with a related course of studies in another Member State. Providing the criteria in Article 8(1) are met then the second Member State must admit the student within a period that does not hamper the pursuit of the relevant studies. The latter directive provides the conditions for the admission of TCN researchers to Member States for more than three months to carry out a research project under hosting agreements with research organisations (Article 1). A renewable one year residence permit will be issued under Article 8 so long the criteria in Articles 5–7 are complied with on application. However, family members may join or accompany the TCN researcher at the Member State's discretion and have a right to a residence permit for the same duration as the researcher (Article 9), although 'family members' are not defined. Article 13 provides the right of mobility to a researcher, such that the researcher may be admitted to another Member State to carry out part of the research there. This right to mobility is a highly restricted right of movement that is notably only available for the researcher and not for his or her family members.

A third directive was adopted for highly-skilled migrants after a long gestation period, Directive 2009/50/EC,[330] better known as the Blue Card Directive. Article 1 sets out the purpose of the directive, being to provide the conditions of entry and residence of highly qualified TCNs as EU Blue Card holders and their families for longer than three months into a Member State's territory (Article 1(a)) and residence in Member States other than the first Member State (Article 1(b)). A clear and straightforward scope of the directive is outlined in Article 3(1) as applying 'to third country nationals who apply to be admitted to the territory of

---

329  See the two 2011 Commission Reports on the Directives, Commission Report on the application of Directive 2004/114/EC COM(2011) 587 final and Commission Report on the application of Directive 2005/71/EC COM(2011) 901 final.

330  Council Directive 2009/50/EC on the conditions of entry and residence of third country nationals for the purposes of highly qualified employment [2009] OJ L155/17; YK Gümüs 'EU blue card scheme: the right step in the right direction?' (2009) 11 *EJML* 435.

a Member State for the purpose of highly qualified employment under the terms of this Directive'. Paragraph 2 provides for 10 exempted classes of individuals, some of which are reasonable, expected and covered by other EU legislation (TCNs migrating to the EU to study, conduct scientific research, as family members of Union citizens who have exercised their free movement rights, posted workers and long-term resident TCNs). However, there are a further three classes that are more problematic. The first is the exclusion of beneficiaries of international or temporary protection (Article 3(2)(a)–(c)) from the scope of the directive, even though they may be highly skilled and qualified individuals. The second is the exclusion of seasonal workers (Article 3(2)(h)), where the term 'seasonal workers' is not defined and thus the rights associated with the acquisition of a blue card could be circumvented by classifying an individual as a 'seasonal worker'. Thirdly, the exemption for TCNs whose expulsion has been suspended because of fact or law where the term 'suspended' would appear to indicate the expulsion to be temporary but again the directive does not provide a definition. Article 3(3) introduced a general exemption for future bilateral agreements between the EU and/or the Member States and third countries to ensure ethical recruitment of employees in areas of labour shortages by listing professions falling outside the scope of the directive in order to protect human resources in those developing countries. Finally, on exemptions to the general scope of the directive and controversially,[331] Article 3(4) enables Member States to maintain national systems for granting residence rights to TCN highly qualified employees under different terms to those in the directive and without the rights of residence in other Member States conferred on TCNs by the directive. Article 3(4) should be read alongside Article 4, which enables Member States to retain more favourable provisions under EU law, and bilateral agreements made between the Union, or Member States and third countries (Article 4(1)). Article 4(2) maintains the fragmentary nature of the directive by allowing Member States to adopt or retain more favourable provisions in respect of important elements of the directive. Article 5 lays out the criteria for admission, with paragraph 1 specifying the necessary documentary evidence and paragraph 2 enabling Member States to require a blue card applicant to provide his or her address in the Member State concerned. Article 5(3) outlines a salary threshold for TCNs where the migrant's gross annual salary resulting from the monthly or annual salary specified in the work contract or binding job offer must not be inferior to a relevant salary threshold of at least 1.5 times the average gross annual salary as determined and published by that Member State. This salary threshold can be reduced through the derogation in paragraph 5 to 1.2 for employment in professions in particular need of TCN workers and which belong to the major groups 1 and 2 of the International Standard Classification of Occupation (ISCO-88), those groups consisting of legislators, senior officials and managers, and professionals. Member States retain the right under Article 6 to control the volume of admission of highly qualified

---

331 S Peers 'Legislative update: EC immigration and asylum law attracting and deterring labour migration: the Blue Card and Employer Sanctions Directives' (2009) 11 *EJML* 387, 391.

TCNs entering their territory. When a TCN fulfils the Article 5 criteria and is issued with a positive decision in accordance with Article 8 by the competent authority of the Member State concerned, he or she will be issued with a blue card (Article 7) that entitles the TCN the right to enter, re-enter and reside in the Member State issuing the blue card and the rights in the directive. These rights that come with the blue card are contained in Chapter IV. Access to the labour market is outlined in Article 12 with a restrictive approach for the first two years of legal employment that requires the conditions of Article 5 to be met and changes in employment only allowed with the prior authorisation in writing of the competent authorities of the host Member State. After two years the Member State has the discretion to grant equal treatment with nationals for access to highly qualified employment but if it does not the TCN concerned must communicate changes that affect the conditions of Article 5 to the host Member State's competent authorities, in accordance with domestic procedures. A public service restriction on access to the labour market can be retained by the Member States, as can restrictions reserving employment to nationals, Union citizens or EEA citizens in accordance with national or Union law. Loss of employment cannot automatically lead to withdrawal of the blue card, unless unemployment lasts for longer than three months, or if it occurs more than once during the period of validity of the blue card (Article 13). Article 14 provides a right of equal treatment for blue card holders with nationals of the host Member State with regard to: working conditions; trade union rights; education and vocational training; recognition of qualifications; social security; state pension; access to public goods and services; and free movement within the host Member State's territory. Member States can limit this right to equal treatment when it comes to study and maintenance grants and access to further and higher education may be subject to specific prerequisites as specified by domestic law. The Family Reunification Directive provides the appropriate rights for families of blue card holders, according to Article 15, with a number of minor amendments and the Long Term Residents Directive is also to apply, but again with derogations set out in Article 16. Importantly, the five year continuous residence requirement in the host Member State in Article 4(1) of the Long Term Residents Directive (see below) is reduced to two years, with five years of continuous legal residence in the territory of the EU as a blue card holder. A limited right to move between Member States is provided for in Chapter V, although this right is so constrained there is no right to free movement. After 18 months of legal employment in the first Member State, the blue card holder and his family may move to another Member State to take up further highly qualified employment. A full application must be made again to the second Member State's authorities, who determine whether to approve the application or not. Such an application can be made within a month of moving to the second Member State, which can refuse to allow the applicant to work until a decision has been taken, or from the first Member State. If the application is refused, and this can be on the basis of the volumes of admission in accordance with Article 6, the first Member State must immediately readmit the blue card holder and family members without formalities.

The fourth and more difficult area to legislate is on the general rights of entry of TCNs to the EU, and the rights that should pertain to these persons upon entry. This is a key element in the EU's policy to integrate TCNs.[332] Two attempts were made to legislate in this area before a third was eventually successful. The first was the External Frontiers Convention (EFC)[333] of 1993, drafted to complement both the SIC and the Dublin Convention but, even after the original proposal was heavily amended[334] to incorporate three Council resolutions on the entry requirements of TCNs,[335] the EFC was never signed because of the continuing dispute between Spain and the UK over Gibraltar. Interestingly, Article 35 of the revised EFC provided a right to freedom of movement to a TCN to take up an offer of employment where there was a vacancy or to enrol in a higher education course of study. The Commission put forward a second proposal in 2001[336] concerning the conditions of entry and residence of TCNs for employed and self-employed economic activities with a notable absence of a right to freedom of movement within the EU. The proposal, although receiving support from the European Parliament, stalled in the Council and so the Commission initiated a debate on the subject of the integration of legally resident TCNs in 2003 with a Communication[337] followed by a Green Paper,[338] Communication[339] and Policy Plan[340] in 2005. The Policy Plan proposed five new legislative measures: a general framework directive to guarantee a common framework of rights to all TCNs in legal employment already admitted into a

332  See T Kostakopoulou 'Integrating" non-EU migrants in the European Union: ambivalent legacies and mutating paradigms' (2002) 8 *Columbia Journal of European Law* 181; K Groenendijk 'Legal concepts of integration in EU migration law' (2004) 6 *EJML* 111; R Cholewinski 'Migrants as minorities: integration and inclusion in the enlarged European Union' (2005) 43 *JCMS* 695; T Gross 'Integration of immigrants: the perspective of European Community law' (2005) 7 *EJML* 145; S Velluti 'What European Union strategy for integrating migrants? The role of OMC: soft mechanisms in the development of an EU immigration policy' (2007) 9 *EJML* 53; K Rosenow 'The Europeanisation of integration policies' (2009) 47 *International Migration* 133 for detailed discussions on the integration of immigrants.

333  Commission Communication on a proposal for a Decision, based on Article K3 of the Treaty on European Union, establishing the Convention on the crossing of the external frontiers of the Member States COM(1993) 684 final.

334  Commission proposal for a Council Act establishing the Convention on rules for the admission of third-country nationals to the Member States COM(1997) 387 final.

335  Council Resolution on limitation on admission of third-country nationals to the territory of the Member States for employment [1996] OJ C274/3; Council Resolution relating to the limitations on the admission of third-country nationals to the territory of the Member States for the purpose of pursuing activities as self-employed persons [1996] OJ C274/7; and Council Resolution on the admission of third-country nationals to the territory of the Member States for study purposes [1996] OJ C274/10.

336  Commission proposal for a Council Directive on the conditions of entry and residence of third-country nationals for the purpose of paid employment and self-employed economic activities COM(2001) 386 final.

337  Communication from the Commission on immigration, integration and employment COM(2003) 336 final.

338  Commission Green Paper on an EU approach to managing economic migration COM(2004) 811 final.

339  Communication from the Commission on a common agenda for integration – framework for the integration of third-country nationals in the European Union COM(2005) 389 final.

340  Commission Communication on a policy plan on legal migration COM(2005) 669 final.

Member State, but not yet entitled to long term residence status (the Single Permit Directive);[341] and four specific directives on the conditions of entry and residence for highly skilled workers, which became the Blue Card Directive, seasonal workers[342] and remunerated trainees,[343] as well as the procedures regulating the entry into, the temporary stay and residence of, intra-corporate transferees (ICTs).[344]

The Single Permit Directive[345] was adopted in December 2011 and provides for a single application procedure for a single permit for TCNs to reside for the purpose of work in a Member State combined with a common set of rights for TCN workers legally residing in a Member State, irrespective of the purposes of their initial admittance, and based on equal treatment with that Member State's nationals (Article 1(1)). However, Member States retain their powers vis-à-vis the admission of TCNs to their labour markets. It applies to TCNs who apply to reside in a Member State to work, who have been admitted to a Member State for purposes other than work but who are allowed to work and hold a residence permit to that effect, and who have been admitted to a Member State for the purpose of work (Article 3(1)). Article 3(2), however, substantially curtails the directive's scope by excluding 12 categories of TCNs, including inter alia ICTs, seasonal workers, beneficiaries and applicants for international protection status, or those with long-term resident status. It is particularly disappointing that the directives on seasonal workers and ICTs have not been adopted before the adoption of the Single Permit Directive, thus leaving these TCNs without any Union law rights. To obtain the single permit (Article 6) the TCN must be able to apply in a single application procedure (Article 4) to a competent authority nominated by the Member State (Article 5). Under Article 11 the single permit provides at least the minimum rights of entry and residence in the Member State issuing the single permit, free movement within the territory of that Member State, work as authorised under the single permit and information on the holder's rights conferred by the directive, although these will not be uniform EU-wide rights as they are determined in accordance with national law. Article 12(1) also grants the right to equal treatment with nationals of the Member State for working conditions, membership of a trade union, education and vocational training, recognition of

---

341  Commission proposal for a Council Directive on a single application procedure for a single permit for third-country nationals to reside and work in the territory of a Member State and on a common set of rights for third-country workers legally residing in a Member State COM(2007) 638 final.

342  Commission proposal for a European Parliament and Council Directive on the conditions of entry and residence of third-country nationals for the purposes of seasonal employment COM(2010) 379 final.

343  No proposal put forward by the Commission at this time.

344  Commission proposal for a European Parliament and Council Directive on conditions of entry and residence of third-country nationals in the framework of an intra-corporate transfer COM(2010) 378 final.

345  European Parliament and Council Directive 2011/98/EU on a single application procedure for a single permit for third-country nationals to reside and work in the territory of a Member State and on a common set of rights for third-country workers legally residing in a Member State [2011] OJ L343/1.

qualifications, social security, tax benefits, access to and supply of goods and services made available to the public, and advice services afforded by employment offices. However, these rights of equal treatment can be severely limited at a Member State-wide discretion by the restrictions listed in Article 12(2), these limitations driven by Germany that, as Brinkmann[346] notes, wanted the directive to resemble a Recommendation, which Member States could follow or not as they wished. It is again notable that there is no right to any form of freedom of movement within the EU.

The lack of significant legislative measures detailing the entry and residence requirements of TCNs entering the EU created a vacuum in the AFSJ at the Union level that continued to be filled by the domestic law of the Member States. The case for Union legislation in this area was compelling and had been made on a number of occasions by the Commission in numerous Communications issued on immigration policy.[347] Eventually, two significant directives, the Blue Card and Single Permit Directives, were adopted but the entry of persons, in particular TCNs, to the territory of a state is a matter that goes to the heart of the concept of national sovereignty and, as such, both directives are heavily restrictive on rights for TCNs with considerable discretion given to domestic law. The failure to adopt the seasonal workers or ICTs Directives and these TCNs' exclusion from the Single Permit Directive creates a class of TCNs unprotected under Union law. Furthermore, the legal instruments lack, or at best grant a highly attenuated form of, a right of free movement for TCNs who have entered the EU legally. This would appear to be at variance with the Tampere Conclusions, where it was stated that the lack of this freedom 'would be in contradiction with Europe's traditions to deny such freedom to those whose circumstances lead them justifiably to seek access to our territory'.[348] The result is fragmentary EU legislative instruments, that do little to integrate TCNs or indeed make them feel wanted, whilst ensuring that they are unable to move legally between Member States in search of employment.

### 4.4.1.3 Long term residents

Directive 2003/109 on the status of Long Term Resident (LTR) TCNs, as amended by Directive 2011/51,[349] determines the minimum requirements for the grant and withdrawal of LTR status for TCNs, the rights associated with such status and rights of residence in other Member States (Article 1). According to Article 3, the directive applies to TCNs residing legally in the Member State's

---

346 G Brinkmann 'Opinion of Germany on the single permit proposal' (2012) 14 *EJML* 351, 365.
347 The latest is the Commission Communication on the European Agenda for the integration of Third-Country Nationals COM(2011) 455 final.
348 Tampere European Council Presidency Conclusions SN200/99 at 1 para 3.
349 European Parliament and Council Directive 2011/51/EU amending Council Directive 2003/109/EC to extend its scope to beneficiaries of international protection [2011] OJ L132/1; S Peers 'Legislative update EU immigration and asylum law 2010: extension of long-term residence rights and amending the law on trafficking in human beings' (2011) 13 *EJML* 201.

territory except those: pursuing studies or vocational training; residing, or apply-ing to reside, in a Member State on the basis of a national form of pro-tection not covered by the definition of international protection in Article 2(f); applying for residence on the basis of international protection as defined in Article 2(f); being employed on temporary grounds, for the purposes of cross-border services, or having their residence permit formally limited as such;[350] and enjoying diplomatic protection. Article 4 specifies that long term residency status must be granted to TCNs who have resided legally and continuously in the Member State's territory for five years,[351] so long as they have stable resources above the social assistance level of the Member State and sickness insurance (Article 5), and was applied for with documentary evidence to the appropriate authorities (Article 7). However. in Article 6, Member States may refuse to grant LTR status on grounds of public policy or public security. If the Articles 4 and 5 criteria are met and the individual does not pose a threat within the meaning of Article 6 then, according to Article 7(3), a Member State must grant the TCN concerned LTR status.[352] When this long term residency is granted, it must be permanent, unless withdrawn in accordance with Article 9. The LTR has the right to a renewable residence permit valid for at least five years (Article 8). According to Article 9(1)(a)–(c) it can be withdrawn if the TCN has acquired the status fraudulently, has been expelled or has left the territories of the EU for a year. Consequently, LTRs should receive equal treatment with nationals on a range of measures laid down in Article 11 that includes free access to the territory of the Member State concerned, within national legislative limits for reasons of security and access to employment and self-employed activity. In *Kamberaj*[353] the ECJ was asked to determine whether housing benefit was included within the criteria set out in Article 11(1)(d) of 'social security, social assistance and social protection'. The Court left the question to the domestic court to determine as the criteria of Article 11(1)(d) were stated to be 'defined by national law'[354] but in a highly nuanced judgment the national court was warned, after referring to the right to social and housing assistance in Article 34(3) of the Charter[355] that any

---

350 Case C–502/10 *Staatssecretaris van Justitie v Mangat Singh* [2013] 1 CMLR 36 para 51 – a formally limited residence permit prevents long term residence of the TCN concerned.

351 Article 4 also limits the five year general rule in certain situations. Where international protection is revoked, ended or refused then LTR status is not to be granted (art 4(1)(a)). Periods of residence on the basis of being employed on temporary grounds, for the purposes of cross-border services, or having their residence permit formally limited as such and enjoying diplomatic protection are not counted and only 50% of the prior residence as a student counts. For those with international protection status at least half the period from application to the issue of a residence period in accordance with the Qualification Directive is to count, or the whole period if that period exceeds 18 months.

352 Case C–40/11 *Yoshikazi Iida v Stadt Ulm* (ECJ 8 November 2012) para 39.

353 Case C–571/10 *Servet Kamberaj v Istituto per l'Edilizia sociale della Provincia autonoma di Bolzano (IPES), Giunta della Provincia autonoma di Bolzano and Provincia autonoma di Bolzano* [2012] 2 CMLR 43; noted in S Peers 'The Court of Justice lays the foundations for the long-Term residents Directive' (2013) 50 *CMLRev* 529.

354 ibid para 77.

355 ibid para 80.

interpretation must not undermine the effectiveness of the directive[356] and take into account the integration objective pursued by the directive.[357] Furthermore, the derogation provided in Article 11(4) had to be interpreted strictly,[358] noting that recital 13 was a non-exhaustive list of 'core benefits' so that its lack of reference to housing benefit did not mean it was excluded from equal treatment[359] and with due reference to the right to social and housing assistance in Article 34(3) of the Charter.[360] Member States can expel the LTR but only if he or she constitutes an actual and sufficiently serious threat to public policy and public security and a decision must not be taken on economic grounds (Article 12). There appears to be a possible contradiction in the legal position of a TCN here in that LTR status may be refused on the grounds of public policy or public security (Article 6(1)) but expulsion can only take place if there is an 'actual and sufficiently serious threat' to public policy and public security. Furthermore, Article 9(7) provides that a TCN can remain in the Member State's territory if there is withdrawal or loss of LTR status if the TCN complies with domestic legislation and is not a threat to public policy or public security, but this does not cover the refusal of granting LTR status. The factors to be taken into consideration before an expulsion decision is taken include the duration of residence, the age of the LTR, the consequences for the LTR and family members, and the links with the country of residence or the absence of links with the country of origin. Where a Member State decides to expel a TCN with LTR status, granted through international protection by another Member State, that Member State must be asked to confirm that the individual still has international protection status (Article 12(3)(a)). If so then the individual must be expelled to that Member State, and the Member State must immediately admit that person and his or her family members without formalities (Article 12(3)(b)). It is notable that according to recital 9, the transfer of responsibility for the protection of beneficiaries of international protection falls outside the scope of Directive 2011/51.[361] The LTR has the right to appeal in a court of law and the right to equal treatment as nationals for the grant of legal aid (Article 12(4) and (5)).

LTRs are also provided in Article 14 with the right to exercise the right of residence in another Member State's territory for more than three months if exercising an economic activity in an employed or self-employed capacity, pursuing studies or vocational training or for other (unspecified) purposes. Where the TCN moves to the second Member State on the grounds of exercising an economic activity in an employed or self-employed capacity, the Member State can examine the situation of their labour market and apply their national procedures regarding the requirements for filling a vacancy or for exercising self-employed activities. As such Member States can give preference to Union citizens,

356  ibid para 78.
357  ibid para 81.
358  ibid para 86.
359  ibid para 85.
360  ibid para 92.
361  See S Peers 'Transfer of international protection and European Union law' (2012) 24 *IJRL* 527.

TCNs who come within Union Agreements with third countries, and unemployed TCNs already lawfully resident in the Member State for reasons of labour market policy. Member States can derogate from this right through setting quotas for granting the right of residence for TCNs if domestic legislation did so when the directive was adopted. Member States may require that these LTR TCNs should have adequate resources not to be a burden on the state and sickness insurance and comply with integration measures and attend language courses as set out in national law (Article 15). As soon as entering the territory of the second Member State, or at least within three months, the LTR must apply for a residence permit. That second Member State may, at its discretion, allow the LTR to submit an application for a residence permit whilst the LTR is still residing in the first Member State (Article 15(1)). However, as Peers observes,[362] the right of residence is not dependent on the issue of the residence permit as applications for residence can only be refused on the grounds of public policy, public security and public health (Articles 17 and 18) and its declaratory nature can be inferred from Article 9(6), which specifies that the expiry of the residence permit 'shall in *no case* entail withdrawal or loss of LTR status' (emphasis added). An LTR TCN exercising his right under Article 14 also has the right to family reunification for his family members under Article 16 so that they may join or accompany the TCN, so long as the family was already constituted in the first Member State. Family members are as defined in Article 4(1) of Directive 2003/86. Member States may levy charges for residence permits for TCNs or family members but they must not be set so high as to create a significant financial impact and have either the object or effect of creating an obstacle to obtaining LTR status, contrary to the objective of the directive.[363] Articles 17 and 18 enable the Member States to refuse applications for residence only where the person constitutes a threat to public policy, public security or public health. The analysis by the Member State of the threat to public health follows a similar analysis for citizens of the Union in Directive 2004/38 and it is submitted is an equivalent provision. For the threat to public policy and public security the Member State must consider the severity or type of offence or the danger that emanates from the person concerned, which is different wording to that in Article 27(2) of Directive 2004/38 but it is suggested would most likely be construed by the ECJ in a similar manner.[364] The application for residence must be processed within four months, with a possibility of a maximum extension of a further three months, according to Article 19 and a renewable residence permit must then be issued for the individual and family members providing access to the rights outlined in Article 11 so long as the criteria for issue have been met. If the application for a residence permit is refused, the directive specifies that the TCN can mount a legal

---

362  S Peers 'Implementing equality? The directive on long term resident third country nationals' (2004) 29 *ELR* 437, 456.

363  Case C–508/10 *Commission v Netherlands* [2012] 2 CMLR 48 paras 68–70.

364  See PJ Slot, M Bulterman 'Harmonization of legislation on migrating EU citizens and third country nationals: towards a uniform evaluation framework?' (2006) 29 *Fordham International Law Journal* 747, 784 for criticism of this different wording.

challenge (Article 20(2)) but there is nothing in the directive to indicate the outcome for the TCN. If the residence permit is merely declaratory then the reasons for refusal can only be for public policy, public security or public health. As such, the TCN will continue to enjoy long term residency status in the first Member State and so should be able to return. The position upon return to the first Member State may mean, however, that the TCN cannot be expelled from that state as the threat in Article 12 must constitute 'an actual and sufficiently serious' threat, rather than a mere threat. If the long term TCN resident remains in the second Member State then, on satisfying the same qualifying criteria, the individual can claim the right of LTR status in the second Member State (Article 23). At that point the TCN will lose LTR status in the first Member State (Article 9(4)).

The LTR Directive is to be welcomed as it provides the strengthening of positive rights for TCNs across the EU when compared with their previous weak position. Furthermore, the introduction of a right of mobility for LTR TCNs beyond the short term, three-month SIC permitted travel, although significantly less than a right to freedom of movement, is an improvement on the previous situation.[365] However, there are significant faults with the directive. First, is its sheer complexity, a matter that can confuse the sharpest legal analyst,[366] let alone a TCN without legal training. Secondly, although Peers argues that any ambiguity in the directive's text should be resolved in favour of the TCN and family members, based on the inclusion of the Tampere Conclusions requirement of equal treatment for LTR TCNs in comparison to EU citizens in the preamble (recital 2) and that Article 61 EC stated that an objective of the AFSJ was to safeguard the rights of TCNs (replaced now in Article 67(3) by a requirement for 'a common policy on asylum, immigration and external border control . . . which is fair to third country nationals'), this 'line of reasoning is not entirely obvious'.[367] It is submitted that the considerable discretion given to the Member States in many provisions, as well as the, at times, convoluted, contradictory and often confusing drafting would not necessarily see the matter resolved in favour of the TCN. Thirdly, this convoluted, contradictory and confusing drafting creates considerable uncertainty as to the meaning and extent of the rights granted. Fourthly, some terms are undefined, in particular the third ground for residence in a second Member State in Article 14(2)(c), 'other purposes', and does not specify whether the other purposes are to be defined by the TCN, the Member State or objectively by the ECJ. Fifthly, TCNs' right to equal treatment with nationals (whether these

---

365  Peers 'Implementing equality' (n 362) 442.
366  ibid 458, where Peers highlights the possibility of the loss of LTR status in the first Member State if there is a delay in the processing of the residence permit application in the second Member State. Although not stated, it is submitted that Peers misreads art 9(1)(c) as meaning that loss will occur if the TCN is absent from the first Member State's territory for a period of 12 consecutive months rather than the 'territory of the Community'. Article 9(4) provides loss of LTR status if absent from the first Member State's territory for six years – a very long delay in processing the permit.
367  L Halleskov 'The Long-term Residents Directive: a fulfilment of the Tampere objective of near-equality?' (2005) 7 *EJML* 181, 188.

are nationals of the first, second or any Member State is not specified) in Article 11 can be extensively derogated[368] from by Member States. Peers suggests that these derogations should be interpreted narrowly[369] but the derogations are drafted in such a way as to give the Member States considerable discretion in this area that may not allow a narrow reading. Sixthly, the UK and Ireland have opted out of the LTR Directive and Directive 2011/51, thereby creating fragmentation, complexity and confusion. Seventhly, even with the amendment of Directive 2011/51 the personal scope of the directive is quite significantly limited by Article 3(2). Eighthly, although the introduction of mobility rights for TCNs is a step forward, these rights are unfortunately far removed from free movement rights.[370] Finally, and most extraordinarily, is the lack of a provision prohibiting discrimination on the basis of nationality. Recital 3 provides that the directive respects fundamental rights, particularly those recognised in the ECHR and the Charter, and recital 5 tells Member States to give effect to the provisions of the directive without discrimination on the basis of sex, race, colour, ethnic or social origin, genetic characteristics, language, religion or beliefs, political or other opinions, membership of a national minority, fortune, birth, disabilities, age or sexual orientation,[371] but there is no mention of nationality. Boelaert-Suominen[372] is optimistic that Member States will not be able to discriminate against TCNs on the basis of their nationality; however, such an omission, whilst mentioning all other forms of discrimination would suggest otherwise. The Tampere Conclusions, which set out the guiding principles for the EU institutions when adopting legislation implementing the AFSJ at the time that the directive was adopted, made clear that a TCN, lawfully resident in a Member State and holding a long term resident permit 'should be granted in that Member State a set of uniform rights which are as near as possible to those enjoyed by EU citizens'. The directive purposefully distinguishes between different classes of TCNs, ensures by the significant derogations and provisions with Member State discretion that there cannot be a uniform set of rights (especially when considering the situation with the UK and Ireland) and affords rights that are nowhere near those enjoyed by EU citizens. Finally, the Tampere Conclusions endorsed the aim of the naturalisation of LTR TCNs, a notable omission from the LTR Directive.

In September 2011 the Commission delivered its first report on the application of the LTR Directive in accordance with the requirements of Article 24 of the

---

368  S Boelaert-Suominen 'Non-EU nationals and Council Directive 2003/109/EC on the status of third-country nationals who are long-term residents: five paces forward and possibly three paces back' (2005) 42 *CMLRev* 1011, 1026.

369  Peers 'Implementing equality' (n 362) 443.

370  SI Sánchez 'Free movement of third country nationals in the European Union? Main features, deficiencies and challenges of the new mobility rights in the area of freedom, security and justice' (2009) 15 *ELJ* 791, 801; A Wiesbrock 'Free movement of third-country nationals in the European Union: The illusion of inclusion' (2010) 35 *ELR* 455, 462.

371  This mirrors art 21 Charter, rather than art 19 TFEU.

372  Boelaert-Suominen 'Non-EU nationals' (n 368) 1028.

directive.[373] In very strong language the Commission concluded that 'the weak impact of the LTR Directive in many Member States is to be deplored'.[374] Indeed, many of the findings reflected the concerns raised above, especially over derogations for Member States and the use of the mobility provisions that from the data suggested were less than 50 per Member State.

### 4.4.1.4 Family reunification

Directive 2003/86/EC provides the right to family reunification for TCNs residing lawfully in a Member State with a residence permit valid for at least a year who have reasonable prospects of obtaining the right of permanent residence (Article 3(1)). However, Article 3(2) and (3) provides an exhaustive list of individuals to whom the directive does not apply: a TCN applying for refugee status; a TCN applying for or who has obtained temporary or subsidiary protection status; or family members of a Union citizen. Article 4(1) is the heart of the directive as it defines family members. They include the applicant's spouse and the minor children of the applicant or his spouse, including where one of them has custody and the children are dependent, and that also includes adopted children. Minor children must be below the national age of majority and be unmarried. Where a minor child over the age of 12 arrives independently of the family, the Member State may verify if the child meets a condition for integration provided for by its existing legislation before allowing entry and residence. This limitation is intended to 'reflect the children's capacity for integration at early ages and shall ensure that they acquire the necessary education and language skills in school' (recital 12). The ECJ[375] has interpreted this final paragraph of Article 4(1) and the explanation in recital 12 in an Article 263 TFEU challenge by the European Parliament. The Parliament suggested[376] that the reasoning in recital 12 was not convincing, with the Council confusing the concepts 'condition for integration' and 'objective of integration'. As one of the most important means of successfully integrating a minor child is through family reunification, it was inconsistent to impose a condition for integration before the child joined the sponsor that rendered family reunification unachievable and negated the right, and as the concept of integration was undefined by the directive Member States could significantly restrict the right to family reunification. This right was protected by Article 8(1) ECHR, could only be derogated from by one of the specific conditions in

---

373 Commission Report on the application of Directive 2003/109/EC concerning the status of third-country nationals who are long-term residents COM(2011) 585 final.
374 ibid 10.
375 Case C–540/03 *European Parliament v Council* [2006] ECR I–5769; noted in AM Arnull 'Family reunification and fundamental rights' (2006) 31 *ELR* 611; D Martin 'Case note' (2007) 9 *EJML* 144; R Lawson 'Case note' (2007) 3 *EuConst* 324; E Drywood 'Giving with one hand, taking with the other: fundamental rights, children and the Family Reunification Decision' (2007) 32 *ELR* 396; M Bulterman 'Case note' (2008) 45 *CMLRev* 245. See also Commission Communication of the report on the application of Directive 2003/86/EC on the right to family reunification COM(2008) 610/3 final.
376 *European Parliament v Council* (n 375) paras 40–45.

Article 8(2) ECHR, which the final paragraph of Article 4(1) did not fall into, and the final paragraph of Article 4(1) did not require any weighing of the respective interests at issue and so was not justified or proportionate. Parliament further argued that the directive was contradictory as it did not provide for any limitation founded on a condition for integration so far as concerned the sponsor's spouse, was discriminatory as the condition was based exclusively on a child's age, which was not objectively justified and contrary to Article 14 ECHR and the standstill clause was not as strict as customary standstill clauses. The Court found that the right to respect for family right within the meaning of Article 8 ECHR was one of the fundamental rights protected in EU law.[377] After investigating the ECtHR case law the ECJ found that Article 8 ECHR did not provide an individual right to be allowed to enter the territory of a state, as Member States retained a margin of appreciation when they examined applications for family reunification.[378] Article 4(1) of the directive goes beyond Article 8 ECHR by removing the margin of appreciation, defining precise positive obligations on Member States and clearly defining rights for individuals.[379] The final paragraph of Article 4(1) partially preserved that margin of appreciation for the Member States, did not breach the right to respect for family life and the Court rejected Parliament's arguments.[380]

Article 4(2) gives the Member States discretion to authorise the entry and residence of dependent relatives in the ascending line of the applicant or spouse without family support in the country of origin, and of children of full age of the applicant or spouse who are incapable of supporting themselves through ill-health. Member States also have discretion to authorise the entry and residence of the unmarried TCN partner of the applicant where there is an evidentially annotated stable long term relationship or registered partnership, along with their unmarried minor children, including those adopted, and adult unmarried children who are incapable of supporting themselves through ill-health. Member States can also decide that registered partners can be treated equally as spouses with respect to family reunification (Article 4(3)). Article 4(4) prohibits the entry of a spouse if the applicant is in a polygamous marriage and the sponsor already has a spouse resident on the Member State's territory. Furthermore, the reunification of minor children can be limited in such a situation. Paragraph 5 allows Member States to demand the applicant and/or his or her spouse to be a minimum age, up to a maximum age of 21, before reunification. This is to ensure better integration and to prevent forced marriages. Finally, Article 4(6) allows a Member State to require applications for family reunification of minor children to be submitted before the age of 15, if the Member State's legislation provides for this at the time of the adoption of the directive. Member States that decide to apply this derogation must authorise the entry and residence of these minor children on grounds

---

377  ibid para 52.
378  ibid para 59.
379  ibid para 60.
380  ibid paras 61 and 62.

other than family reunification. This latter provision was also questioned by the Parliament[381] using a similar argument to that used for Article 4(1), which received a similar reply from the Court.[382]

The Member State decides whether an application for family reunification should be submitted by the sponsor or the family members (Article 5(1)). Article 5(3) requires that the application be made when the family members are resident outside the Member State's territory where the sponsor is resident, although Member States may accept an application when the family members are already in its territory, in appropriate circumstances. 'Appropriate circumstances' are not defined. According to Article 6, Member States may reject an application for entry and residence for family members, and can withdraw or refuse to renew a family member's residence permit, on the grounds of public policy, public security or public health, considering the severity or type of offence committed, the considerations in Article 17[383] and the dangers that are emanating from the individual (Article 6(2)). Article 6(3) specifies that the issuing of a residence permit cannot be delayed, nor the individual expelled, on the sole ground of illness or disability suffered after the issue of the residence permit. When the application is submitted the Member State may require the applicant to prove that there is adequate and appropriate housing available for the family, the family members are covered by sickness insurance, have stable and regular resources which are sufficient to maintain himself or herself and the members of his or her family, without recourse to the social assistance system of the Member State concerned (Article 7(1)). The latter element was examined by the ECJ in *Chakroun*.[384] The Court held that Article 7(1)(c) must be interpreted strictly and that the margin of appreciation for Member States contained within it must not be used to undermine the objective of the directive, namely the promotion of family reunification, and the effectiveness of that.[385] As such, the term 'recourse to the social assistance system' in Article 7(1)(c) had to be interpreted as:

> precluding a Member State from adopting rules in respect of family reunification which result in such reunification being refused to a sponsor who has proved that he has stable and regular resources which are sufficient to maintain himself and the members of his family, but who, given the level of his resources, will nevertheless be entitled to claim special assistance in order

---

381  ibid para 77.
382  ibid para 90.
383  'Member States shall take due account of the nature and solidity of the person's family relationships and the duration of his residence in the Member State and of the existence of family, cultural and social ties with his/her country of origin where they reject an application, withdraw or refuse to renew a residence permit or decide to order the removal of the sponsor or members of his family'.
384  Case C–578/08 *Rhimou Chakroun v Minister van Buitenlandse Zaken* [2010] ECR I–1839; noted in B Kunoy, B Mortansson 'Case comment' (2010) 47 *CMLRev* 1815; A Wiesbrock 'Case comment' (2010) 6 *EuConst* 462. See also Joined Cases C–356 & 357/11 *O & S v Maahanmuuttovirasto* and *Maahanmuuttovirasto v L* (ECJ 6 December 2012).
385  *Chakroun* (n 384) para 43.

to meet exceptional, individually determined, essential living costs, tax refunds granted by local authorities on the basis of his income, or income-support measures in the context of local-authority minimum-income policies.[386]

Furthermore, the definition of family reunification in Article 2(d) 'must be interpreted as precluding national legislation which, in applying the income requirement set out in Article 7(1)(c) of the directive, draws a distinction according to whether the family relationship arose before or after the sponsor entered the territory of the host Member State'.[387] Article 7(2) also provides a margin of appreciation for Member States to require TCNs to comply with integration measures in accordance with national law. Article 8 gives the Member States discretion to require the applicant to have stayed lawfully in the Member State's territory for not more than two years before family reunification. However, where the Member State's legislation on the date of adoption of the directive takes into account its reception capacity, the Member State may provide for a waiting period of no more than three years between submission of the application and the issue of a residence permit to the family members. The European Parliament also questioned this provision in relation to the right to respect for family life,[388] and once again the Court gave a similar finding to that for Article 4(1).[389]

The right to reunification for refugees is treated as a special case in Chapter V. Article 9 provides the right to reunification, although Member States may confine this to family relationships before the refugee's entry. Article 10(1) defines family members in accordance with Article 4, except that the minor children of the refugee, including adopted children, who are dependent on him, are not included within this definition. Member States are authorised, however, to provide family reunification of other family members not referred to in Article 4 if they are dependent on the refugee (Article 10(2)). If the refugee is an unaccompanied minor the Member State must authorise the entry and residence of the first-degree relatives in the direct ascending line for family reunification, or may authorise the entry and residence of the legal guardian or any other family member, where the refugee has no relatives in the direct ascending line or they cannot be found (Article 10(3)). Article 11 requires the documentary evidence outlined in Article 5, although if this is not available to prove the family relationship, other evidence, determined by national law, should be taken into account. A decision rejecting the application for reunification must not be based solely on the fact that documentary evidence was not available. Article 12 enables derogations from Articles 7 and 8. Evidence as required for Article 7 will not be required for a refugee and/or family members, unless there is a third country where

---

386  ibid para 52.
387  ibid para 66.
388  *European Parliament v Council* (n 375) para 91.
389  ibid paras 97 and 98.

reunification is possible and with which the sponsor and/or family members have special links, or the application for family reunification is not submitted within three months of granting refugee status (Article 12(1)). Also derogating from Article 8, Member States must not require a period of residence in their territory before authorising family reunification (Article 12(2)).

Once the right to family reunification has been granted, the Member State must authorise the entry of the family members, grant them every facility to obtain the requisite visas and must provide a renewable residence permit for at least one year (Article 13). Article 14 provides rights to access to education, employment and self-employment, vocational guidance, initial and further training and retraining, to the same extent as the sponsor. Member States may set conditions for family members when exercising employment or self-employment, which can mean that family members are not able to work for a maximum of 12 months. Member States may also restrict access to employment or self-employment for first-degree relatives in the direct ascending line or adult unmarried children. After five years of residence the spouse, unmarried partner or child can claim the right to a residence permit independent of the original applicant, although this can be limited to the spouse or unmarried partner in the case of the breakdown of the relationship (Article 15(1)). Autonomous residence permits may also be issued to adult children and relatives in the direct ascending line but without time limit so long as the conditions in Article 4(2) apply, as they may in the event of widowhood, divorce, separation or death of first-degree relatives in the direct ascending or descending line (Article 15(2) and (3)). Where there are particularly difficult circumstances the issue of the autonomous residence permit becomes obligatory (Article 15(4)).

The right to family reunification is a particularly important right to TCNs separated from their homes, culture and society. Although it does not include a right to freedom of movement, it is an essential corollary to that right. As such the Family Reunification Directive is notable for its far-reaching effect,[390] extending the right to respect for family life further than that outlined in Article 8 ECHR,[391] and it must be commended. However, a notable omission in the scope of the directive is for individuals benefiting from subsidiary and temporary protection (Article 3(2)(b) and (c))[392] that should be rectified at the earliest opportunity.[393]

---

390 See K Groenendijk 'Family reunification as a right under Community law' (2006) 8 *EJML* 215 for a particularly eulogising account of the directive.

391 ibid; see Lambert 'The European Court of Human Rights' (n 18) for a comprehensive account of the ECtHR case law on art 8 ECHR.

392 McAdam 'The European Union Qualification Directive' (n 276) 503.

393 See the Commission Green Paper on the right to family reunification of third-country nationals living in the European Union COM(2011) 735 final 6.

### 4.4.2  *Illegal immigration*

It would appear to be a trite statement that the corollary to legal immigration is illegal immigration. However, the concept of illegal immigration is the key area where the concepts of asylum/refugee and immigrant become conjoined as it applies to immigrants within the Union and also those applicants who have been refused international protection status, as well as what has become known as 'bogus' or 'failed' asylum-seekers. There has been considerable policy activity in the area of illegal immigration starting with the Commission Communication[394] on a common policy, a Comprehensive Plan[395] to combat illegal immigration and trafficking of human beings, a Commission Communication[396] on a Community return policy following a Green Paper,[397] a return action programme[398] and another Commission Communication[399] on the development of a common policy. In 2006 the Commission published another Communication[400] outlining its policy priorities in the area of illegal immigration of TCNs. These are: cooperation with third countries; secure external borders; human trafficking; secure travel and identity documents; illegal employment; return policy; exchange of information; and carriers' liability. The European Pact on Immigration and Asylum focused on the return policy for illegal migrants[401] but a more balanced approach was evident in the 2011 Commission Communication on Migration.[402] Much of the debate about policy and policy development involves criminal activity involving illegal immigration, which as Goodwin-Gill observes sees asylum-seekers suffering the 'imputation of double criminality'[403] as they enter the EU illegally and invariably consort with criminals to do so. These criminal aspects fall outside the scope of this book and therefore will not be considered. Furthermore, as the very nature of illegal immigration cannot involve the right to freedom of movement, only the policy involving movement or the repatriation[404] of TCNs will be analysed, which in particular deals with the expulsion of TCNs, the return

394 Commission Communication on a common policy on illegal immigration COM(2001) 672 final.
395 Commission proposal for a comprehensive plan to combat illegal immigration and trafficking of human beings in the European Union [2002] OJ C142/23.
396 Commission Communication on a Community return policy on illegal residents COM(2002) 564 final.
397 Commission Green Paper on a Community return policy on illegal residents COM(2002) 175 final.
398 Danish Presidency's proposal for a return action programme, Council Document 14673/02. This was approved by the JHA Council of 28–29 November 2002, Council Document 14817/02 at 10.
399 Commission Communication on the development of a common policy on illegal immigration, smuggling and trafficking of human beings, external borders and the return of illegal residents COM(2003) 323 final.
400 Commission Communication on policy priorities in the fight against illegal immigration of third-country nationals COM(2006) 402 final.
401 Council Document 13440/08 at 7.
402 Commission Communication on migration COM(2011) 248 final 8.
403 GS Goodwin-Gill 'The international protection of refugees: what future?' (2000) 12 *IJRL* 1, 4.
404 See JC Hathaway 'The meaning of repatriation' (1997) 9 *IJRL* 551.

of TCNs to third countries and partnerships between the EU and third countries.

### 4.4.2.1 Expulsion

Expulsion of TCNs is predominantly regulated by national law, or on the basis of the returns procedures analysed below. However, Directive 2001/40/EC[405] enables the mutual recognition of decisions of the competent authorities of the Member States on the expulsion of TCNs in two cases outlined in Article 3. The first is where it is based 'on a serious and present threat to public order or to national security and safety' if convicted of an offence punishable by at least one year in jail or the existence of serious evidence pointing to the commitment or intention to commit serious criminal offences. The second is based on the 'failure to comply with national rules on the entry or residence of aliens'. The directive does not apply to 'family members of citizens of the Union who have exercised their right of free movement' (Article 1(3)).

### 4.4.2.2 Returns policy [406]

Many of the situations involving returns to Member States and third countries are dealt with by the Dublin Regulation, the Qualification Directive and the Procedures Directive. However, the Commission brought forward a proposal[407] with the objective of harmonising Member States' standards and procedures for the return of TCNs staying illegally in 2005, which was adopted as the Returns Directive, 2008/115.[408] The scope of the directive is set out in Article 2(1) and it applies to TCNs illegally staying in the territory of the Member States but with considerable discretion in Article 2(2) for Member States not to apply the directive to TCNs. These include individuals who have been refused entry in accordance with the Schengen Borders Code (SBC)[409]Article 13 and TCNs who have illegally crossed the external border of a Member State and not then

---

405 Council Directive 2001/40/EC on the mutual recognition of decisions on the expulsion of third country nationals [2001] OJ L149/34; see also Council Decision 2004/191/EC setting out the criteria and practical arrangements for the compensation of the financial imbalances resulting from the application of Directive 2001/40 [2004] OJ L60/55.
406 For a critical analysis of returns policy, and in particular forced returns of asylum seekers in the UK, see C Phuong 'The removal of failed asylum seekers' (2005) 25 *LS* 117.
407 Commission proposal for a Directive on common standards and procedures in Member States for returning illegally staying third-country nationals COM(2005) 391 final; E Canetta 'The EU policy on return of illegally staying third-country nationals' (2007) 9 *EJML* 435.
408 European Parliament and Council Directive 2008/115/EC on common standards and procedures in Member States for returning illegally staying third-country nationals [2008] OJ L348/98; see A Baldaccini 'The return and removal of irregular migrants under EU law: an analysis of the Returns Directive' (2009) 11 *EJML* 1 for an examination of the adoption procedure and final directive.
409 European Parliament and Council Regulation 562/2006/EC establishing a Community Code on the rules governing the movement of persons across borders (Schengen Borders Code) [2006] OJ L105/1.

regularised their stay (Article 2(2)(a)), although in accordance with Article 4(4) Member States must ensure certain levels of treatment and protection and must respect the principle of *non-refoulement*. TCNs who are subject to criminal law sanctions and TCNs who are subject to extradition procedures (Article 2(2)(b)) can also be excluded from the scope of the directive but they do not enjoy the protection guaranteed in Article 4(4). Furthermore, the Returns Directive does not apply to TCNs who enjoy the EU right to free movement as defined in Article 2(5) of the SBC. Definitions are included in Article 3 with 'TCN' defined by a negative reference to citizenship of the Union and Article 2(5) of the SBC, and 'illegal stay' by a negative reference to Article 5 of the SBC. The concept of 'return' means the process of a TCN going back, either voluntarily[410] or as enforced, to the TCN's country of origin or a transit country under EU or bilateral readmission agreements or other arrangements. Returning to another third country can only happen if the TCN concerned so decides and that third country also agrees to take the TCN. Article 4 enables Member States to retain more favourable provisions than those of the directive if EU or individual country bilateral or multilateral agreements with third countries, or the EU *acquis* on immigration and asylum, so specify, or if a Member State chooses to do so. When implementing the directive the Member States must take due account of three factors: the best interest of the child,[411] family life[412] and the state of health of the TCN and must also respect the principle of non-refoulement.[413] Article 6 provides for a return decision[414] to be issued by a Member State that can then be enforced in accordance with Article 8, unless the TCN voluntary departs the territory of the Member State (Article 7). The period specified for voluntary departure ranges from seven to 30 days (Article 7(1)), with the possibility of the TCN leaving sooner, although this period can be extended depending on individual circumstances (Article 7(2)).[415] If coercive measures are used, as a last resort, for the removal of a TCN who resists removal then they must be proportionate, not exceed reasonable force, be in accordance with fundamental rights and must respect the dignity

---

410  See J van Selm 'Return seen from a European perspective: an impossible dream, and improbable reality, or an obstruction to refugee policy?' (2005) 28 *Fordham International Law Journal* 1504, who argues that most individuals claiming international protection would voluntarily return to their country of origin if it was safe to do so and safety could be guaranteed.

411  Article 5 does not mention the United Nations Convention on the Rights of the Child 1989 but recital 22 does refer to it when considering the best interests of the child that is described as a primary consideration of Member States when implementing the directive.

412  It is only in recital 22 that the right to respect for family life, in line with the ECHR, is mentioned as a primary consideration of the Member States when implementing the directive.

413  Recital 23: 'Application of this directive is without prejudice to the obligations resulting from the Geneva Convention relating to the Status of Refugees of 28 July 1951, as amended by the New York Protocol of 31 January 1967'.

414  Defined in art 3(4): 'means an administrative or judicial decision or act, stating or declaring the stay of a third-country national to be illegal and imposing or stating an obligation to return'.

415  Such as the length of stay, children attending school and other family and social links.

and physical integrity of the TCN concerned (Article 8(4)).[416] Article 9 provides for the postponement of the removal of the TCN for inter alia humanitarian grounds and to protect the principle of *non-refoulement*. The return decision must be accompanied by an entry ban of up to five years if no period for voluntary departure has been granted or if the obligation to return has not been complied with, and in all other situations a return decision may be accompanied by a five year entry ban (Article 11(1)).[417] This entry ban can be extended if the TCN represents a serious threat to public policy, public security or to national security (Article 11(2)). Finally, when preparing to return or carry out the removal process, and in particular if there is a risk of the TCN absconding or if the TCN avoids or hampers the preparation of return or the removal process, then the Member State can keep the TCN in detention for up to six months, with the possibility of extending this to 18 months (Article 15). Article 16 sets out the conditions for this detention.

The provisions on detention have been contentious, with the ECJ carefully picking its way through delicate issues and providing clarification for national courts. In the first judgment on the Returns Directive the Court in *Kadzoev*[418] found that the period of detention for the purposes of return before the directive became applicable had to be taken into account when calculating the maximum period of detention.[419] Furthermore, the period that a TCN was kept in detention whilst judicial review procedures were ongoing concerning the deportation order, and the deportation process had been suspended during the judicial review process, had to be counted in the calculation of the period of detention,[420] although a period of detention whilst an asylum application was processed was not to be counted.[421] Where it is unlikely that a third country will admit the returning TCN then there is no reasonable prospect of removal, as there is no real prospect that the removal can be carried out successfully, and this must be taken into consideration for the calculation of the periods of permissible detention.[422] Detention cannot be extended beyond the maximum permitted in the directive, on the basis of lack of valid documents, aggressive conduct or absence of supporting means, including accommodation or state support.[423] As such, the grounds of public order or safety cannot be used to detain a TCN under the directive.[424]

---

416 The provisions of the directive do not refer to the Committee of Ministers of the Council of Europe 'Twenty guidelines on forced return' (adopted 4 May 2005) COM(2005) 40, although it is mentioned in recital 3.

417 For an analysis of this provision on children see ME Kalverboer, AE Zijlstra and EJ Knorth 'The development consequences for asylum-seeking children living with the prospect for five years or more of enforced return to their home country' (2009) 11 *EJML* 41.

418 Case C–357/09PPU *Said Shamilovich Kadzoev (Huchbarov)* [2009] ECR I–11189; noted in E Mincheva 'Case comment' (2010) 12 *EJML* 361; G Cornelisse 'Case comment' (2011) 48 *CMLRev* 925.

419 *Kadzoev* (n 418) para 39.

420 ibid para 48.

421 ibid para 57.

422 ibid para 67.

423 ibid para 70.

424 ibid.

In *El Dridi*,[425] it was held that the Returns Directive did not preclude national law from classifying an illegal stay as a criminal offence and imposing criminal sanctions to deter and penalise such an offence.[426] However, criminal law rules must not undermine the application of the common standards and procedures established by the Returns Directive.[427] As such, a penalty of imprisonment cannot be imposed upon a TCN when coercive measures for the TCN's removal have failed on the sole ground that the TCN continues to stay illegally on the territory of the Member State,[428] as the effect of the sanction is to frustrate the purpose of the directive and delay the enforcement of the return decision.[429] In *Sagor* the ECJ held that a fine that could be replaced by an expulsion order was an acceptable criminal sanction[430] but a home detention order would not contribute to the removal of the TCN from the Member State and would not be acceptable.[431]

The Returns Directive has encountered considerable criticism from a range of sources. The original proposal was considered to be deeply flawed by the House of Lords EU Select Committee, as it failed to enable 'persons to be returned to their country of origin safely and humanely, with respect for their human rights and dignity'.[432] In particular, the House of Lords called for clearer drafting of the term 'illegal stay',[433] removal of the upper fixed time limit for voluntary returns,[434] application of strict limits on the use of detention,[435] extension and more precise drafting on the conditions of temporary custody to include all situations dealing with custody and the needs of vulnerable people,[436] greater safeguards for the treatment of children,[437] clarification of the legal status of an illegally staying TCN whose removal was impossible[438] and a limitation on re-entry bans so they apply only to persons convicted of a serious criminal offence.[439] The final directive created a clear definition of 'illegal stay' but few of the other concerns were addressed. Indeed, from the reaction of

---

425  Case C–61/11PPU *Hassen El Dridi, alias Karim Souffi* [2011] ECR I–3015; noted in R Raffaelli 'Criminalizing irregular immigration and the Returns Directive: an analysis of the *El Dridi* case' (2011) 13 *EJML* 467. The reasoning in *El Dridi* was confirmed in Case C–329/11 *Alexandre Achughbabian v Préfet du Val-de-Marne* [2012] 1 CMLR 52 and Case C–430/11 *Criminal proceedings against Md Sagor* (ECJ 6 December 2011).
426  *El Dridi* (n 425) para 53.
427  ibid para 55.
428  ibid para 58.
429  ibid para 59.
430  *Sagor* (n 425) paras 35–38.
431  ibid paras 44–45.
432  European Union Committee *Illegal Immigrants: Proposals for a Common EU Returns Policy* (HL 2005–2006, 166) 48.
433  ibid 15.
434  ibid 22.
435  ibid 27.
436  ibid 29–30.
437  ibid 31–33.
438  ibid 34.
439  ibid 47.

states from other parts of the world, especially South America,[440] the directive is a disturbing legal instrument, with much of the criticism directed at the European Parliament's[441] inability to ameliorate the position of the Council, supported by the Commission. Furthermore, the ECRE in a 2009 Information Note[442] was highly critical of the discretion left to the Member States on many issues, including the treatment of unaccompanied children, the imposition of re-entry bans, the lack of procedural protections for TCNs and the low level of protection against destitution under Article 14. The most disturbing aspect of the directive it is submitted is the arbitrary use of detention, with considerable discretion given to the Member States over the period of incarceration and the persons covered, thereby effectively criminalising asylum-seeking. For some TCNs the lack of a legal status causes considerable problems, both for the TCN and the Member State. In *Kadsoev* Mr Kadsoev was unable to be removed from Bulgaria as he had no papers to establish his identity and so at the end of his period of detention he had to be released but without any legal status. His lack of legal status meant that he could not obtain identity documentation, which meant that he could be detained if questioned for not having identity documents. As Mincheva[443] points out, this situation could not be resolved as Bulgaria had no domestic law for issuing documents to a person such as Mr Kadsoev and no legal route to regularisation of his position.

### 4.4.2.3   Readmission agreements

Cooperation with third countries is essential for the effective and efficient operation of a returns programme, of which the most important is the negotiation of special bilateral agreements with third countries to enable mutual return of illegal immigrants. Bouteillet-Paquet[444] traces three generations of these agreements: the first generation in the 1960s between Member States to control the irregular movement of persons; the second generation in the 1990s with the CEECs; and now the third generation. The Council empowered the Commission to negotiate these third generation bilateral readmission agreements,[445] which it

---

440  See A Baldaccini 'The EU Directive on Return: principles and protests' (2010) 28 *Refugee Survey Quarterly* 114, 136.
441  D Acosta 'The good, the bad and the ugly in EU migration law: is the European Parliament becoming bad and ugly? (The adoption of Directive 2008/115: the Returns Directive)' (2009) 11 *EJML* 19.
442  ECRE 'Information note on the Returns Directive' January 2009 http://www.ecre.org/topics/areas-of-work/returns/171.html.
443  Mincheva 'Case comment' (n 418) 369.
444  D Bouteillet-Paquet 'Passing the buck: a critical analysis of the readmission policy implemented by the European Union and its Member States' (2003) 5 *EJML* 359.
445  For critical analysis of readmission agreements in general see NA Abell 'The compatibility of readmission agreements with the 1951 Convention Relating to the Status of Refugees' (1999) 11 *IJRL* 60.

has done[446] with Hong Kong,[447] Macao,[448] Sri Lanka,[449] Albania,[450] Russia,[451] Ukraine,[452] the former Republic of Macedonia,[453] Bosnia and Herzegovina,[454] Montenegro,[455] Serbia,[456] Moldova,[457] Pakistan,[458] Georgia[459] and Turkey.[460] The Commission has also been granted a mandate to negotiate readmission agreements with Azerbaijan, Algeria, Armenia, Belarus, China, Cape Verde[461] and

446 Commission Communication on the evaluation of EU Readmission Agreements COM(2011) 76 final.
447 Council Decision 2004/80/EC concerning the conclusion of the Agreement between the European Community and the Government of the Hong Kong Special Administrative Region of the People's Republic of China on the readmission of persons residing without authorisation [2004] OJ L17/23.
448 Council Decision 2004/424/EC concerning the conclusion of the Agreement between the European Community and the Macao Special Administrative Region of the People's Republic of China on the readmission of persons residing without authorisation [2004] OJ L143/97.
449 Council Decision 2005/372/EC concerning the conclusion of the Agreement between the European Community and the Democratic Socialist Republic of Sri Lanka on the readmission of persons residing without authorisation [2005] OJ L124/41.
450 Council Decision 2005/809/EC concerning the conclusion of the Agreement between the European Community and the Republic of Albania on the readmission of persons residing without authorization [2005] OJ L304/14; I Kruse 'EU readmission policy and its effects on transit countries – the case of Albania' (2006) 8 *EJML* 115; LI Caraoshi, N Ndoci 'Do EU Member States need readmission agreements? Analysis of the EC-Albania readmission agreement' (2011) 25 *JIANL* 12.
451 Council Decision 2007/341/EC on the conclusion of the Agreement between the European Community and the Russian Federation on readmission [2007] OJ L129/38.
452 Council Decision 2007/839/EC concerning the conclusion of the Agreement between the European Community and Ukraine on readmission of persons [2007] OJ L332/46.
453 Council Decision 2007/817/EC on the conclusion of the Agreement between the European Community and the former Yugoslav Republic of Macedonia on the readmission of persons residing without authorisation [2007] OJ L334/1.
454 Council Decision 2007/820/EC on the conclusion of the Agreement between the European Community and Bosnia and Herzegovina on the readmission of persons residing without authorisation [2007] OJ L334/65.
455 Council Decision 2007/818/EC on the conclusion of the Agreement between the European Community and the Republic of Montenegro on the readmission of persons residing without authorisation [2007] OJ L334/25.
456 Council Decision 2007/819/EC on the conclusion of the Agreement between the European Community and the Republic of Serbia on the readmission of persons residing without authorisation [2007] OJ L334/45.
457 Council Decision 2007/826/EC on the conclusion of the Agreement between the European Community and the Republic of Moldova on the readmission of persons residing without authorisation [2007] OJ L334/148.
458 Council Decision 2010/649/EU on the conclusion of the Agreement between the European Community and the Islamic Republic of Pakistan on the readmission of persons residing without authorisation [2010] OJ L287/50.
459 Council Decision 2011/118/EU on the conclusion of the Agreement between the European Union and Georgia on the readmission of persons residing without authorisation [2011] OJ L52/45.
460 Council Decision 2012/499/EU on the signing, on behalf of the European Union, of the Agreement between the European Union and the Republic of Turkey on the readmission of persons residing without authorisation [2012] OJ L244/4. See A Bürgin 'European Commission's agency meets Ankara's agenda: why Turkey is ready for a readmission agreement' (2012) 19 *Journal of European Public Policy* 883.
461 Council Decision 2013/77/EU on the signing, on behalf of the European Union, of the Agreement between the European Union and the Republic of Cape Verde on the readmission of persons residing without authorisation [2013] OJ L37/1. The draft agreement has been agreed

Morocco.[462] The stumbling block for some of the negotiations of these agreements has been the inclusion of a clause not just for the readmission of nationals of the third country but also for the readmission of TCNs who have stayed in, or merely transited through, the territory of the third country.[463] These agreements therefore treat third countries not just as a safe country of origin but also a safe country of transit.[464] With the entering into force of the Lisbon Treaty, Article 79(3) TFEU provides the Union with the competence to conclude readmission agreements with third countries.[465]

The policy on movement as it applies to illegal immigrants remains predominantly the domain of the Member States. The problems with the Returns Directive highlight the difficulties on reaching agreement on legislative measures in this area that go to the heart of a nation's sovereignty and for political reasons make it hard to give substantive rights to individuals. The readmission agreements are part of the strategy to secure the external frontiers of the EU but, as Bouteillet-Paquet observes,[466] the second generation agreements did not see great numbers of readmissions, did not dissuade human traffickers or organised criminals and had a detrimental effect on bona fide refugees. There is no reason to believe that the third generation agreements are going to be different, particularly as they do not address the root causes of the reasons for migrant flow of poverty, inequality, warfare and human rights violations[467] and arguably work solely in the EU's interest. The difficult area of negotiations with Pakistan, Morocco and Turkey has been the readmission of TCNs who can often have little connection with the country to which they are returning. The consequences of the readmission agreements are therefore a considerable risk of chain *refoulement* and refugees in orbit but, as recognised in recital 23 of the Returns Directive, the Member States' international human rights obligations must be observed,[468] in particular the principle of *non-refoulement* in Article 33(1) of the Geneva Convention, which applies to all returnees whether enjoying refugee status or not, and Article 3 ECHR. In the light of the protection of human rights in some

---

but has yet to be signed – see Commission proposal for a Council Decision concerning the signing of the Agreement between the European Union and the Republic of Cape Verde on the readmission of persons residing without authorisation COM(2012) 558 final 7 for the draft agreement.

462 See EA Mrabet 'Readmission agreements: the case of Morocco' (2003) 5 *EJML* 379.

463 See for example art 3 of the EU-Albania readmission agreement.

464 A Roig, T Huddleston 'EC readmission agreements: a re-evaluation of the political impasse' (2007) 9 *EJML* 363, 366.

465 For analysis of this new competence see C Billet 'EC readmission agreements: a prime instrument of the external dimension of the EU's fight against irregular immigration: an assessment after ten years of practice' (2010) 12 *EJML* 45, 59; M Panizzon 'Readmission agreements of EU Member States: a case for EU subsidiarity or dualism?' (2012) 31 *Refugee Survey Quarterly* 101. For the Council conclusions defining the EU strategy on readmissions see Council Document 122501/12.

466 Bouteillet-Paquet 'Passing the buck' (n 444) 365.

467 S Peers 'Readmission agreements and EC external migration law' *Statewatch Analysis* (No 17) May 2003 http://www.statewatch.org/news/2003/may/readmission.pdf.

468 C Phuong 'Minimum standards for return procedures and international human rights law' (2007) 9 *EJML* 105; SH Legomsky 'Secondary refugee movements and the return of asylum seekers to third countries: the meaning of effective protection' (2003) 15 *IJRL* 567, 612; M Bradley 'Back to basics: the conditions of just refugee returns' (2008) 21 *JRS* 285.

countries that the EU has negotiated readmission agreements with and those it is negotiating or wishes to negotiate with,[469] and the instability and novelty of democracy in others, then there is a significant risk of the return of persons through the use of readmission agreements contravening the principle of *non-refoulement*. Furthermore, the considerable weakening during negotiations of the already minimal standards in the Returns Directive is likely to exacerbate this situation.

## 4.5   Free movement of persons

Article 2(1) SIC provided that '[i]nternal borders may be crossed at any point without any checks on persons being carried out'. This applied to both nationals of Member States, including non-Schengen states, and TCNs. The SBC, replacing Article 2 SIC, 'provides for the absence of border control of persons crossing . . . internal borders' and 'establishes rules governing border control of persons crossing . . . external borders' (Article 1). Article 3 states that the SBC applies to anyone crossing the internal or external borders of Member States without prejudice to '(a) the rights of persons enjoying the [Union] right of free movement;[470] (b) the rights of refugees and persons requesting international protection, in particular as regards *non-refoulement*'. Title II provides detailed conditions and procedures for the crossing of the external borders of the EU. Article 5(1) sets out the entry conditions for TCNs. For stays not exceeding three months in a six month period the entry criteria are that:

(a)   they are in possession of valid travel documents authorising them to cross the border;

(b)   they are in possession of a valid visa, if required by Regulation 539/2001 [. . .], except where they hold a valid residence permit [or a valid long-stay visa];[471],[472]

469   See Amnesty International *The State of the World's Human Rights Report 2007* (Amnesty International 2007); S Hamood 'EU-Libya cooperation on migration: a raw deal for refugees and migrants?' (2008) 21 *JRS* 19.

470   Defined in art 2(5) as (a) 'Union citizens within the meaning of Article 17(1) of the Treaty, and third-country nationals who are members of the family of a Union citizen exercising his or her right to free movement to whom Directive 2004/38/EC of the European Parliament and of the Council of 29 April 2004 on the right of citizens of the Union and their family members to move and reside freely within the territory of the Member States applies; (b) third-country nationals and their family members, whatever their nationality, who, under agreements between the Community and its Member States, on the one hand, and those third countries, on the other hand, enjoy rights of free movement equivalent to those of Union citizens'.

471   Added by European Parliament and Council Regulation 265/2010/EU amending the Convention Implementing the Schengen Agreement and Regulation 562/2006/EC as regards movement of persons with a long-stay visa [2010] OJ L85/1 art 2.

472   See art 2(15) for the definition of residence permit and Commission Information, list of residence permits referred to in art 2(15) of the SBC [2006] OJ C247/1 that is amended frequently.

(c) they justify the purpose and conditions of the intended stay,[473] and have sufficient means of subsistence; [. . .];[474]

(d) they are not persons for whom an alert has been issued in the SIS for the purposes of refusing entry; and

(e) they are not considered to be a threat to public policy, internal security, public health or the international relations of any of the Member States, in particular where no alert has been issued in Member States' domestic data bases refusing entry on [these] grounds.

After the judgment in *Bot*[475] the Commission put forward a proposal to clarify the first part of Article 5(1) and Article 5(1)(a).[476] The entry conditions[477] for TCNs for intended stays of more than three months in any six month[478] period from the date of first entry in the territory of the Member States were to include: (a) possession of a valid travel document or a document authorising them to cross the border, so long as (i) its validity extends at least three months after the intended date of departure and (ii) it was issued within the previous 10 years. Article 5(4) would allow three derogations from the strict conditions laid down in Article 5(1). First, if TCNs held a residence permit and/or a re-entry visa issued by a Member State[479] they could transit other Member States' territories to reach the territory of the Member State that issued the document. A re-entry visa was:

1. ... an authorisation which can be issued by a Member State to a third-country national who does not hold either a residence permit or a visa or a visa with limited territorial validity within the meaning of the Visa Code and which allows him to leave that Member State for a specific purpose before then returning to the same State.[480]

Such a visa could not be limited solely under the first derogation to points of entry to national territory of the Member State that issued it as this was a matter for the third derogation.[481] Secondly, if TCNs only failed to fulfil the condition in Article 5(1)(b) but presented themselves at the border then they could be issued

---

473 Article 5(2) specifies that Annex 1 sets out a non-exhaustive list of documents that can provide justification for the stay.

474 Article 5(3) specifies the method of calculation for the means of subsistence that each Member State must notify to the Commission in accordance with art 34.

475 *Bot* (n 317).

476 Commission proposal for a European Parliament and Council Regulation amending Regulation 562/2006/EC COM(2011) 118 final 3.

477 ibid 15.

478 In the latest draft (Council Document 18006/12 at 16) the period has now been quantified in days so that three months now reads 90 days and six months is 180 days.

479 Commission proposal amending Regulation 562/2006 (n 476) 15 where these documents are 'a residence permit or a long-stay visa'.

480 Case C–606/10 *Association nationale d'assistance aux frontiers pour les étrangers (ANAFE) v Ministre de l'Intérieur, de l'Outre-mer, des Collectivités territoriales et de l'Immigration* (ECJ 14 June 2012) para 52.

481 ibid paras 54–55.

with a border visa in accordance with Regulation 415/2003.[482] Thirdly, TCNs could be authorised by a Member State to enter its territory, but only its territory, on humanitarian grounds, on grounds of national interest or because of international obligations, but if they were subject to an SIS national alert then the Member State had to inform other Member States of the decision. As a derogation from Regulation 562/2006, Regulation 1931/2006/EC[483] creates a local border traffic regime at the external land borders of the Member States in order to facilitate the continued movement of local populations in border areas but does not establish any free movement rights.

Title III of Regulation 562/2006 deals with internal borders with Chapter I outlining the rules for the abolition of internal border controls across the EU. Article 20 states that '[i]nternal borders may be crossed at any point without a border check on persons, irrespective of their nationality, being carried out', although this does not affect the exercise of police powers by the competent authorities of the Member States under national law (Article 21). The exercise of police powers may not be considered equivalent to the exercise of border checks when the police measures:

1.   ... do not have border control as an objective; are based on general police information and experience regarding possible threats to public security and aim, in particular, to combat cross-border crime; are devised and executed in a manner clearly distinct from systematic checks on persons at the external borders; and, lastly, are carried out on the basis of spot-checks.[484]

Controls within a Member State are only prohibited when they have an effect equivalent to border controls.[485] Member States are also required to remove all road traffic obstacles to fluid traffic flow at internal border crossing points, although arrangements must be in place to reinstate facilities for checks in the event of reintroducing internal border controls (Article 22). Chapter II concerns the temporary reintroduction of internal border controls[486] with the basic rule, set out in Article 23(1), that a Member State may exceptionally reintroduce internal border controls where there is a serious threat to public policy or internal security for a limited period of no more than 30 days or for the foreseeable duration of the

---

482   Commission proposal amending Regulation 562/2006 (n 476) 15 where Regulation 415/2003 is replaced with 'Articles 35 and 36 of Regulation 810/2009/EC'.
483   European Parliament and Council Regulation 1931/2006/EC laying down rules on local border traffic at the external land borders of the Member States and amending the provisions of the Schengen Convention [2006] OJ L405/1.
484   Joined Cases C–188 & 189/10 *Aziz Melki and Sélim Abdeli* [2010] ECR I–5667 para 70; Case C–278/12PPU *Atiqullah Adil v Minister voor Immigratie, Integratie in Asiel* (ECJ 19 July 2012).
485   *Melki* (n 484) para 69.
486   See K Groenendijk 'Reinstatement of controls at the internal borders of Europe: why and against whom?' (2004) 10 *ELJ* 150 for an analysis of the position before the introduction of Regulation 562/2006.

serious threat if greater than 30 days.[487] although the scope and duration must not exceed what is strictly necessary to respond to the serious threat.[488] Where the threat demands urgent action then according to Article 25 controls may be reintroduced immediately. If the threat persists then the reintroduction of controls can be prolonged for renewal periods of up to 30 days, taking into account any new elements (Article 23(2)).[489] Checks on the Member State's actions have been introduced with the Member State required to notify the Commission and other Member States as soon as possible under Article 24(1), the Commission entitled to issue an opinion (Article 24(2)) and consultations to take place between the Member State planning to reintroduce controls and other Member States and the Commission to organise mutual cooperation or examine the proportionality of the measures (Article 24(3)). Furthermore, the European Parliament is to be kept informed and, after three consecutive prolongations of controls, the Member State must report to the European Parliament on the need for controls, if requested (Article 27). The Member State reintroducing internal border controls must confirm the date of their lifting and at the same time, or soon afterwards, report to the European Parliament, Council and Commission outlining, in particular, the operation and effectiveness of the checks (Article 29). In April 2011 first France threatened to reintroduce border controls as a result of Italy granting Tunisian migrants with temporary visas free movement within the Schengen area and then Denmark announced the reintroduction of border controls.[490] The result was a Commission proposal[491] to amend significantly the rules on the temporary reintroduction of border controls, replacing Articles 23–27 and 29–30 that has yet to be adopted. The new Article 23 would instigate a detailed general framework for the reintroduction of border controls at internal borders, with the maximum period being six months (Article 23(4)), unless persistent serious deficiencies related to external border control or return procedures were identified under the new Schengen evaluation and monitoring mechanism (Article 26).[492] The criteria and procedures for the temporary reintroduction of border controls at internal borders were set out in Articles 23a and 24 respectively.[493]

---

487  Article 24 provides the procedure for the reintroduction of internal border controls.

488  See Commission Report on the application of Title III (Internal Borders) of Regulation 562/2006/EC COM(2010) 554 final 8.

489  Article 26 provides the procedure for prolonging internal border controls.

490  See P Hobbing 'A farewell to open borders? The Danish approach' November 2011 http://www. ceps.eu/book/farewell-open-borders-danish-approach; M Wind 'The blind, the deaf and the dumb! How domestic politics turned the Danish Schengen controversy into a foreign policy crisis' in N Hvidt, H Mouritzen *Danish Foreign Policy Yearbook 2012* (Danish Institute for International Studies 2012).

491  Commission proposal for a European Parliament and Council Regulation amending Regulation 562/2006/EC in order to provide for common rules on the temporary reintroduction of border control at internal borders in exceptional circumstances COM(2011) 560 final.

492  Commission amended proposal for a European Parliament and Council Regulation on the establishment of an evaluation and monitoring mechanism to verify the application of the Schengen acquis COM(2011) 559 final.

493  See CW Jorgensen, KA Sorensen 'Internal border controls in the European Union: recent challenges and reforms' (2012) 37 *ELR* 249.

At first blush Regulation 562/2006 provides a general free movement right across the internal borders of the EU for all persons, whether they are citizens of the Union or TCNs, that appears potentially to open up freedom of movement to all and significantly enhance the rights of TCNs. However, there is no mention of this right of free movement in the regulation and, on more careful examination, the actual right is more nuanced, only providing that persons, regardless of nationality, may cross the internal borders at any point without border checks being carried out. The implication therefore is that free movement rights are provided in other legislative instruments (such as Articles 21 and 45 TFEU) and restrictions on that freedom of movement are also contained in other legislation. As soon as the meaning of the regulation is appreciated then its effect for TCNs diminishes significantly because the restrictions in the other legislation analysed above will be retained.

## 4.6 The jurisdiction of the ECJ in Title IV of the EC Treaty

Title IV of the EC Treaty saw an explosion in the adoption of legislative measures that has continued after the changes wrought by the Lisbon Treaty. The AFSJ, as a new area of EU competence with many new terms, rights and obligations, required interpretation by the EU and national institutions including courts and tribunals and, in order to ensure the uniform interpretation of these provisions and to clarify the law, it was essential that courts or tribunals of Member States should be able to make a preliminary reference to the ECJ at the earliest opportunity.[494] The importance of this interpretative mechanism takes on greater significance when it is considered that the legal measures involved affect some of the most vulnerable individuals in society. Unfortunately, the jurisdiction of the ECJ in Title IV of the EC Treaty was highly restricted.

Article 68 EC first extended the jurisdiction of the ECJ to give a preliminary ruling under Article 234 to Title IV but then went on to limit severely the ECJ's oversight in this area.[495] Article 68(1) EC provided that national courts of last resort had to seek a ruling on the interpretation of Title IV, or on the validity or interpretation of measures based on Title IV, if it considered that a decision on the question was necessary to enable it to give judgment. However, lower courts were excluded from seeking such a ruling. Advocate General Fennelly,[496] writing extrajudicially on the subject, highlighted the problems that could be encountered in some cases. Lower courts would retain the right to request a preliminary ruling on all aspects of the EC Treaty except Title IV. Thus, a national court could refer

---

494 For a detailed analysis of the ECJ's jurisprudence on the AFSJ see V Hatzopoulos 'With or without you: . . . judging politically in the field of area of freedom, security and justice' (2008) 33 *ELR* 44.
495 See A Arnull 'Taming the beast? The Treaty of Amsterdam and the Court of Justice' in O'Keeffe, Twomey (eds) *Legal Issues of the Amsterdam Treaty* (n 37) 109, 115.
496 N Fennelly 'The area of "freedom, security and justice" and the European Court of Justice – a personal view' (2000) 49 *ICLQ* 1, 5.

a question on the free movement of persons with a legal base outside the AFSJ but would not be able to make a reference questioning free movement of persons measures adopted under the AFSJ. The position was complicated further by the protocols attached to the EU treaties where the UK, Ireland and Denmark had various opt-outs, opt-ins and the ability to opt in to an area where they had an opt-out. The outcome was that the free movement of persons could be interpreted in different ways by courts in the UK, Ireland and Denmark, or other Member States' courts, or by the ECJ.

Article 68(2) EC went on to limit the ECJ's jurisdiction further. It excluded the ECJ from having any jurisdiction to rule on any measure or decision taken pursuant to Article 62(1) EC relating to the maintenance of law and order and the safeguarding of internal security. This was a curious provision as Article 62(1) EC did not mention law and order or internal security, but merely the abolition of internal borders in accordance with Article 14 EC for EU citizens and TCNs. Advocate General Fennelly[497] suggested that at first blush it could be considered that there was an error in transcription[498] and that the reference to Article 62(1) EC should have referred to Article 64(1) EC. This would be logical as Article 64(1) EC referred directly to law and order and internal security. However, excluding ECJ jurisdiction from an area of competence already reserved exclusively to the Member States did not make sense and the English and French versions of the original Treaty of Amsterdam, the consolidated EC Treaty and the version printed in the Official Journal maintained the identical provision. Furthermore, the Treaty of Nice did not correct the 'error' if it was an error. Advocate General Fennelly concluded that at the very least the 'drafting lacks clarity'.[499]

Article 68(3) EC also allowed the Council, Commission or a Member State to request the ECJ to provide an interpretative ruling on Title IV or implementing measures of Title IV.

The European Parliament was consulted during the process of adoption of Decision 2004/927/EC,[500] which extended the codecision-making procedure in Title IV, and Parliament proposed the removal of limitations under Article 68 EC by the abolition of Article 68(1) and (2),[501] which the Council ignored. The matter was raised again by the Commission in a Communication in 2006.[502] In a closely reasoned explanatory section the Commission made out a case for abolishing Article 68, which was then proposed in a draft decision. This was discussed at the

---

497 ibid.
498 As suggested by E Guild, S Peers 'Deference or defiance? The Court of Justice's jurisdiction over immigration and asylum' in Guild, Harlow (eds) *Implementing Amsterdam* (n 1) 273, 279.
499 Fennelly 'The area of "freedom, security and justice"' (n 496) 6.
500 Council Decision 2004/927/EC providing for certain areas covered by Title IV of Part Three of the Treaty establishing the European Community to be governed by the procedure laid down in art 251 of that Treaty [2004] OJ L396/45 art 1.
501 European Parliament Document P6_TA(2004)0105.
502 Commission Communication on adaptation of the provisions of Title IV of the Treaty establishing the European Community relating to the jurisdiction of the Court of Justice with a view to ensuring more effective judicial protection COM(2006) 346 final.

JHA Council meeting on 24 July 2006[503] and gained the approval of the European Parliamentary Committee on Legal Affairs[504] but it was not advanced any further. The overall position of the ECJ and the preliminary reference procedure under Title IV EC Treaty was unfortunate as limitations on the jurisdiction of the ECJ impinged significantly on the efficacy of EU law, its uniformity and the ability of individuals to realise their rights[505] in a timely fashion.[506]

The Lisbon Treaty removed the limitations on the ECJ's jurisdiction to interpret measures in the AFSJ by removing Article 68 EC,[507] thus enabling all courts or tribunals to make a preliminary reference under Article 267 TFEU to the Court. The move is a significant advancement for the efficiency and uniformity of the law and for individuals, in particular TCNs, to be able to clarify their rights and position within the Union. It is suggested that the ECJ is likely to use Article 25 of the Statute of the Court[508] to ask the UNHCR to provide expert opinions when considerations of international law and the Geneva Convention are raised in judicial proceedings.

## 4.7   The European arrest warrant

The remnants of the old Title VI TEU, JHA pillar, that did not concern the free movement of persons remained in the new Title VI TEU after the Treaty of Amsterdam, which was renamed Provisions on Police and Judicial Co-operation in Criminal Matters. These provisions were considered to be in juxtaposition with the 'directly related flanking measures' of Article 61(a) EC and, although they did not provide additional direct rights for citizens of the Union or TCNs, they did impinge directly on an individual's freedoms. As such the jurisdiction of the ECJ over Title VI TEU, as outlined in ex-Article 35 TEU, was even more constrained than under Article 68 EC. Ex-Article 35(1) empowered the ECJ to give preliminary rulings on the validity and inter-pretation of legislative measures adopted under Title VI TEU, although for the Court to have this jurisdiction ex-Article 35(2) TEU required Member States to make a declaration to that effect and to state whether the ability to refer was limited to the highest

---

503   Council Document 11556/06.
504   European Parliament Document A6-0082/2007.
505   For an alternative viewpoint see J Komarek 'In the court(s) we trust? On the need for hierarchy and differentiation in the preliminary ruling procedure' (2007) 32 *ELR* 467.
506   A Rosas 'Justice in haste, justice denied? The European Court of Justice and the area of freedom, security and justice' (2009) 11 *CYELS* 1, 8.
507   MV Garlick 'The common European asylum system and the European Court of Justice: new jurisdiction and new choices' in E Guild, S Carrera and A Eggenschwiler (eds) *The Area of Freedom, Security and Justice Ten Years On: Successes and Future Challenges Under the Stockholm Programme* (Centre for European Policy Studies 2010) 49, 60; K Lenaerts 'The contribution of the European Court of Justice to the area of freedom, security and justice' (2010) 59 *ICLQ* 255, 265.
508   Protocol (No 3) on the Statute of the Court of Justice of the European Union [2012] OJ L326/210.

national court[509] or was extended to any court or tribunal.[510] Any Member State, however, irrespective of whether it had made a declaration or not, could submit statements of case or written observations to the Court (ex-Article 35(4)) and Member States or the Commission could ask the ECJ to review legislation on the same grounds and within the same time limit as Article 230 EC (now Article 263 TFEU).

The first case to be heard in the ECJ on the interpretation of a Title VI Framework decision[511] was the case of *Pupino*,[512] described as 'remarkable' by Peers.[513] The framework decision involved was the Victims Decision,[514] the details of which are outside the scope of this book. Mrs Pupino was an Italian nursery school teacher charged under Italian criminal law with the 'misuse of disciplinary measures' against some of her pupils who were aged less than five years old. These amounted to striking them regularly, threatening to give them tranquilisers and sticking plaster over their mouths, preventing them from going to the toilet and inflicting serious injuries by hitting a pupil and causing swelling to the forehead. The public prosecutor asked the judge, during pre-trial procedures, to take pre-trial evidence from the children using a 'special inquiry procedure'. The aim of this procedure was to protect the dignity, modesty and character of the minor witnesses and to secure the authenticity of their evidence. However, Italian law only allowed this special procedure for certain closed categories of case, all of them involving sexual offences or offences with a sexual background. Mrs Pupino successfully argued that her case did not fall into these categories and the judge referred the case to the ECJ, questioning the compatibility of the Italian closed category of cases and the Victims Decision, especially as the national court must 'interpret its national law in the light of the letter and the spirit of Community provisions'.[515] The Court first noted that the wording of ex-Article 34(2)(b) TEU was very closely inspired by Article 249(3) EC, concerning directives, and this

509 Council Information concerning the declarations by the French Republic and the Republic of Hungary on their acceptance of the jurisdiction of the Court of Justice to give preliminary rulings on the acts referred to in Article 35 of the Treaty on European Union [2005] OJ C318/1 and L327/19. Declarations were made to this effect by Belgium, the Czech Republic, Germany, Greece, France, Italy, Luxembourg, Holland, Austria, Portugal, Finland, Sweden, Cyprus and Romania.

510 ibid. Declarations were made to this effect by Spain and Hungary.

511 Article 34(2)(b) provides that a framework directive 'shall be binding upon the Member States as to the result to be achieved but shall leave to the national authorities the choice of form and methods. They shall not entail direct effect'.

512 Case C–105/03 *Criminal proceedings against Maria Pupino* [2005] ECR I–5285; noted in M Fletcher 'Extending "indirect effect" to the third pillar: the significance of *Pupino*' (2005) 30 *ELR* 862; E Herlin-Karnell 'In the wake of *Pupino*' (2007) 8 *German Law Journal* 1147; C Lebeck 'Sliding towards supranationalism? The constitutional status of EU framework decisions after *Pupino*' (2007) 8 *German Law Journal* 501; E Spaventa 'Opening Pandora's box: some reflections on the constitutional effects of the decision in *Pupino*' (2007) 3 *EuConst* 5.

513 S Peers 'Salvation outside the church: judicial protection in the third pillar after the *Pupino* and *Segi* judgments' (2007) 44 *CMLRev* 883, 909.

514 Council Framework Decision 2001/220/JHA on the standing of victims in criminal proceedings [2001] OJ 2001 L82/1.

515 *Pupino* (n 512) para 18.

identical binding character of framework decisions and directives created an obligation to interpret national law in conformity.[516] This principle of indirect effect[517] was not invalidated by the jurisdiction of the ECJ being less extensive under Title VI than under the EC Treaty by virtue of ex-Article 35 TEU or by the fact that there was no complete system of action and procedures to ensure the legality of the acts of the institutions in the context of Title VI.[518] The Court found that it was perfectly comprehensible that the authors of the TEU should have considered it useful to provide legal instruments in Title VI with similar effects to those in the EC Treaty to contribute effectively to the pursuit of the Union's objectives, notwithstanding the degree of integration envisaged by the Treaty of Amsterdam in the process of creating an ever closer union among the peoples of Europe within the meaning of Article 1 TEU.[519] The Court confirmed its importance to give preliminary rulings under ex-Article 35 TEU because of the Member States' ability to refer statements or written observations to the ECJ under ex-Article 35(4) TEU, even if they had not made a declaration as to jurisdiction under ex-Article 35(2) and this jurisdiction would be deprived of most of its useful effect if an individual could not obtain a conforming interpretation of national law with framework decisions before the national courts.[520] The Court observed that the principle of loyal cooperation in Article 10 EC applied just as equally to Title VI, which was entirely based on cooperation between the Member States and the institutions, as it did to the EC Treaty, as it was required for the Union to carry out its task efficiently.[521] The Court concluded that:

> ... the principle of conforming interpretation is binding in relation to Framework Decisions adopted in the context of Title VI of the [TEU]. When applying national law, the national court that is called upon to interpret it must do so as far as possible in the light of the wording and purpose of the Framework Decision in order to attain the result which it pursues and thus comply with Article 34(2)(b) [TEU].[522]

The Court went on to note the limitations to the principle of indirect effect already provided in EU case law. The judgment in *Pupino* has been confirmed in *Dell'Orto*[523] and *Goicoechea*.[524]

---

516  ibid paras 33, 34.
517  For the same principle utilised in judgments of the ECJ in the first pillar see Case 14/83 *Sabine von Colson and Elisabeth Kamann v Land Nordrhein-Westfalen* [1984] ECR 1891; Case 106/89 *Marleasing SA v La Comercial Internacional de Alimentacion SA* [1990] ECR 4135; Joined Cases C–397–403/01 *Bernhard Pfeiffer and Others v Deutsches Rotes Kreuz, Kreisverband Waldshut eV* [2004] ECR I–8835. See S Preschal *Directives in EC Law* (2nd edn OUP 2005) ch 8 on the principle of indirect effect.
518  *Pupino* (n 512) para 35.
519  ibid para 36.
520  ibid paras 37, 38.
521  ibid para 42.
522  ibid para 43.
523  Case C–467/05 *Criminal proceedings against Dell'Orto* [2007] ECR I–5557.
524  Case C–296/08PPU *Extradition proceedings against Ignacio Pedro Santesteban Goicoechea* [2008] ECR I–6307.

Most of the provisions adopted under Title VI TEU do not affect free movement of persons directly, except for the EAW Framework Decision.[525] This legislative measure was adopted to enable suspected offenders to be extradited or surrendered between Member States and therefore limits an individual's freedom of movement by imposing movement on that person between Member States. The EAW is defined in Article 1(1) as 'a judicial decision issued by a Member State with a view to the arrest and surrender by another Member State of a requested person, for the purposes of conducting a criminal prosecution or executing a custodial sentence or detention order'. It is to be executed on the basis of the principle of mutual recognition,[526] a high level of confidence between Member States (recital 10) and in accordance with the EAW Framework Decision. Article 2(1) provides that the EAW may be issued for acts punishable by the law of the issuing Member State by a custodial sentence or a detention order for a maximum period of at least 12 months or, where a sentence has been passed or a detention order has been made, for sentences of at least four months. If, however, the offences listed in Article 2(2) are punishable in the issuing Member State by a custodial sentence or a detention order for a maximum period of at least three years and as they are defined by the law of the issuing Member State, then there is a mandatory requirement to surrender the suspected criminal under the terms of the EAW Framework Decision and without verifying the double criminality of the act. The list of offences in Article 2(2) is exhaustive but extensive, although if the offence is not covered, then surrender of the suspect may still occur if the act constitutes an offence under the law of the executing Member State, whatever the constituent elements or however it is described (Article 2(4)). Grounds for non-execution of the EAW are outlined in Articles 3 and 4, with Article 3 providing the mandatory grounds and Article 4 at the Member States' discretion. The mandatory grounds are: where there is an amnesty for the offence in the executing Member State; a limited form of the *ne bis in idem* principle, where the requested person has been sentenced;[527] or where the subject of the EAW is below the age of criminal responsibility under the law of the executing state. The

---

525 See Council Document 5598/08 involving an initiative by Member States to extend the scope of the EAW Framework Decision to criminal judgments given *in absentia*.

526 On mutual recognition see in particular S Peers 'Mutual recognition and criminal law in the European Union: has the Council got it wrong?' (2004) 41 *CMLRev* 5; V Mitsilegas 'The constitutional implications of mutual recognition in criminal matters in the EU' (2006) 43 *CMLRev* 1277; I Bantekas 'The principle of mutual recognition in EU criminal law' (2007) 32 *ELR* 365.

527 This has been considered and expanded upon by the ECJ with reference to arts 54 and 55 SIC in Joined Cases C–187 & 385/01 *Criminal proceedings against Hüseyin Gözütok and Klaus Brügge* [2003] ECR I–1345 (noted in M Fletcher 'Some developments to the *ne bis in idem* principle in the European Union' (2003) 66 *MLR* 769; A Tchorbadjiyska 'Case note' (2004) 10 *Columbia Journal of European Law* 549); Case C–469/03 *Criminal proceedings against Filomeno Mario Miraglia* [2005] ECR I–2009; Case C–436/04 *Criminal proceedings against Leopold Henri van Esbroek* [2006] ECR I–2333; Case C–467/04 *Criminal proceedings against Giuseppe Francesco Gasparini and Others* [2006] ECR I–9199; Case C–150/05 *Jean Leon van Straaten v Holland and Italy* [2006] ECR I–9327; Case C–288/05 *Criminal proceedings against Jürgen Kretzinger* [2007] ECR I–6441; Case C–367/05 *Criminal proceedings against Norma Kraaijenbrink* [2007] ECR I–6619; Case C–297/07 *Klaus Bourquain* [2008] ECR I–9425; Case C–261/09 *Gaetano Mantello* [2010] ECR I–11477. For analysis of the

Article 4 grounds can be included in domestic law when transposing the EAW Framework Decision at the Member State's discretion and are: double criminality outside the Article 2(2) offences; ongoing proceedings for the same offences in the executing state; the full *ne bis in idem* principle; the offence is committed in whole or in part in the executing Member State's territory; and the offence is committed outside the issuing Member State's territory and the executing Member State's law does not allow prosecution for that offence when committed outside its territory.[528] Framework Decision 209/299/JHA[529] amended the EAW Framework Decision by inserting Article 4a, which allowed the refusal of execution of an EAW following a trial at which the individual concerned did not appear in person, although this is highly limited. Article 5 provides a discretionary list of guarantees that the issuing Member State may provide.

Chapter 2 details the surrender procedures and contains a number of rights for the requested person including a right to information on the EAW and its contents (Article 11) and the possibility of consenting to surrender (Article 13), as well as a right to legal assistance and an interpreter, and a judicial hearing if the person does not consent to surrender (Article 14). It is the executing judicial authority that decides whether the person is to be surrendered and to reach such a decision then it can call for supporting information from the issuing Member State (Article 15). Article 17 sets out the time limits for the execution of the EAW, with a requirement that it be dealt with and executed as a matter of urgency. If a person has consented to surrender a decision on execution should be given within 10 days after the consent was given, whilst in other cases the time limit is 60 days and in exceptional circumstances both time limits may be extended a further 30 days. Article 19 provides the requested person with the right to be heard before a

---

*ne bis in idem* principle see S Peers 'Double jeopardy and EU law: time for a change?' (2006) 8 *Eur JL Reform* 199. An analysis of the concept is outside the scope of this book.

528  The terms 'staying' and 'resident' utilised in art 4(6) have been interpreted by the ECJ in Case C–66/08 *Proceedings concerning the execution of a European arrest warrant issued against Szymon Kozlowski* [2008] ECR I–6041; noted in M Fichera 'Case note' (2009) 46 *CMLRev* 241. Both were considered to be (EU) terms requiring uniform interpretation (para 43) with 'reception' meaning that the individual has 'established his actual place of residence in the executing Member State' and 'staying' the acquisition 'following a stable period of presence in that State, certain connections with that State which are of a similar degree to those resulting from residence' (para 46). The Court went on to determine those connections as 'in particular, the length, nature and conditions of his presence and the family and economic connections which that person has with the executing Member State' (para 48). In Case C–123/08 *Dominic Wolzenburg* [2009] ECR I–9621 (noted in E Herlin-Karnell 'European arrest warrant cases and the principles of non-discrimination and EU citizenship' (2010) 73 *MLR* 824) it was held that a residence requirement for a non-national EU citizen of five years infringed the principle of non-discrimination on the basis of nationality in art 18 TFEU but could be objectively justified and was proportionate. Such a limitation is acceptable but an automatic and absolute exception of the nationals of other Member States staying or residing in the executing State from the exception of art 4(6) would not be allowed – see Case C–42/11 *João Pedro Lopes Da Silva Jorge* [2012] 3 CMLR 54.

529  Council Framework Decision 2009/299/JHA amending Framework Decisions 2002/584/JHA, 2005/214/JHA, 2006/783/JHA, 2008/909/JHA and 2008/947/JHA, thereby enhancing the procedural rights of persons and fostering the application of the principle of mutual recognition to decisions rendered in the absence of the person concerned at the trial [2009] OJ L81/24 art 2.

judicial authority, not necessarily the executing judicial authority, pending the decision to execute the EAW. The time limits for surrender are provided for in Article 23. The individual should be surrendered as soon as possible on a date agreed between the authorities concerned, but should be no later than 10 days after the final decision on the execution of the EAW. Where circumstances outside the authorities' control conspire, the time limit can be extended by a further 10 days and for serious humanitarian reasons, such as endangering the requested person's life or health, the surrender may exceptionally be temporarily postponed. When the grounds for postponement have passed then a new date should be set and the time limits apply. Upon expiry of these time limits and the person is still in custody Article 23(5) orders his release.

The Member States had until 31 December 2003 to transpose the EAW into national law, which they all did eventually,[530] although as the Commission observes not consistently. With domestic law adopted with the aim of transposing the EAW Framework Decision and the application of the principle of indirect effect in accordance with the *Pupino* judgment then it is incumbent upon national courts to interpret domestic law consistently with the EAW Framework Decision, enabling inconsistencies to be smoothed out.

Most academic commentators were initially positive about the new measure[531] and Mackarel concluded that the 'initial phase of the EAW indicates that the new scheme for surrender in the EU is functioning effectively on a practical level'.[532] Indeed, Herlin-Karnell[533] has recently concluded that the case law of the ECJ establishes that the EAW Framework Decision has now successfully been established as a supranational instrument rather than an intergovernmental measure. In the UK the courts appeared to approach the EAW Framework Decision in the way described above, where the judiciary attempted to use a purposive approach to interpret the new law.[534] This was particularly apparent in

---

530 See Commission Report based on art 34 of the EAW Framework Decision COM(2006) 8 final. The implementing acts of all Member States are available at http://www.eurowarrant.net and http://www.law.uj.edu.pl/~kpk/eaw.

531 See W Wagner 'Building an internal security community: the democratic peace and the politics of extradition in Western Europe' (2003) 40 *Journal of Peace Research* 695; M Plachta 'European arrest warrant: revolution in extradition?' (2003) 11 *European Journal of Crime, Criminal Law and Criminal Justice* 178; JR Spencer 'The European arrest warrant' (2003–2004) 6 *CYELS* 201; J Wouters, F Naert 'Of arrest warrants, terrorist offences and extradition deals: an appraisal of the EU's main criminal law measures against terrorism after "11 September"' (2004) 41 *CMLRev* 909; Z Deen-Racsmány, R Blekxtoon 'The decline of the nationality exception in European extradition?' (2005) 13 *European Journal of Crime, Criminal Law and Criminal Justice* 317. A negative position towards the EAW and the principle of mutual recognition are adopted by Peers 'Mutual recognition' (n 526); S Alegre, M Leaf 'Mutual recognition in European judicial co-operation: a step too far too soon? Case study – the European arrest warrant' (2004) 10 *ELJ* 200.

532 M Mackarel 'The European arrest warrant – the early years: implementing and using the warrant' (2007) 15 *European Journal of Crime, Criminal Law and Criminal Justice* 37, 63.

533 E Herlin-Karnell 'From mutual trust to the full effectiveness of EU law: 10 years of the European arrest warrant' (2013) 38 *ELR* 79, 86.

534 See in particular *Office of the King's Prosecutor, Brussels v Cando Armas and Another* [2006] 2 AC 1 (HL); *Dabas v High Court of Justice, Madrid* [2007] 2 AC 31 (HL); *Hilali v Governor of Whitemoor Prison and Another* [2008] 1 AC 805 (HL); *Pilecki v Circuit Court of Legnica, Poland* [2008] 1 WLR 325 (HL); *Caldarelli v Judge for Preliminary Investigations of the Court of Naples, Italy* [2008] 1 WLR 1724 (HL).

*Dabas*, *Hilali* and *Caldarelli*, where the House of Lords relied on the *Pupino* judgment and considered the purpose of the EAW Framework Decision. However, in *Assange*,[535] the Supreme Court changed direction significantly, the ramifications of which are yet to be clarified. Lord Mance, with whom the other six members of the court agreed, held that the EAW Framework Decision was an intergovernmental legislative measure that fell outside the definition of EU law in the European Communities Act 1972.[536] As such the EAW Framework Decision, *Pupino* and the principle of conforming interpretation[537] were not part of UK law,[538] a major constitutional issue over the relationship between UK and EU law as it applies to the EAW[539] and in particular the relationship between national courts and the ECJ. There have been other major constitutional challenges to the EAW in several other Member States concerning the extradition of Member State nationals.[540] The first case came before the Polish Constitutional Tribunal (the Trybunal Konstytucyjny) in April 2005[541] when the Gdansk Circuit Court asked the tribunal if the Polish law transposing the EAW Framework Decision was compatible with Article 55(1) of the Polish Constitution that stated '[t]he extradition of a Polish citizen shall be prohibited'. The tribunal found that it was not compatible but took advantage of Article 190(3) of the Polish Constitution that allowed the binding effect of the judgment to be delayed for 18 months, until 6 November 2006. A new Article 55 was adopted on 7 November 2006 that enabled Polish nationals to be extradited but, as Lazowski notes,[542] the revised Article 55 appears to be contrary to the EAW Framework Decision as it requires full protection of the principle of double criminality.

The second successful constitutional challenge came before the German Federal Constitutional Court (the Bundesverfassungsgericht, BVerfG) in July 2005.[543] A German national opposed his extradition to Spain through an EAW

---

See further M Mackarel '"Surrendering" the fugitive – the European arrest warrant and the United Kingdom' (2007) 71 *Journal of Criminal Law* 362; N Padfield 'The implementation of the European arrest warrant in England and Wales' (2007) 3 *EuConst* 253.

535  *Assange v Swedish Prosecution Authority (Nos 1 and 2)* [2012] 2 AC 471 (SC).

536  ibid [210].

537  ibid [202] (Lord Mance) uses this term rather than 'indirect effect'.

538  ibid [217].

539  ibid [210].

540  For a general overview see Z Deen-Racsmány 'The European arrest warrant and the surrender of nationals revisited: the lessons of constitutional challenges' (2006) 14 *European Journal of Crime, Criminal Law and Criminal Justice* 271; J Komárek 'European constitutionalism and the European arrest warrant: in search of the limits of "contrapunctual principles"' (2007) 44 *CMLRev* 9; O Pollicino 'The new relationship between national and European courts after the enlargement of Europe: towards a unitary theory of jurisprudential supranational law? (2010) 29 *YEL* 65.

541  Case P1/05 *Re Enforcement of a European Arrest Warrant* [2006] 1 CMLR 36; noted in A Lazowski 'Poland: constitutional tribunal on the surrender of Polish citizens under the European arrest warrant' (2005) 1 *EuConst* 569; K Kowalik-Bańczyk 'Should we polish it up? The Polish constitutional tribunal and the idea of supremacy of EU law' (2005) 6 *German Law Journal* 1355; D Leczykiewicz 'Case note' (2006) 43 *CMLRev* 1181.

542  A Lazowski 'Conformity of the Accession Treaty with the Polish constitution. Decision of 11 May 2005' (2007) 3 *EuConst* 148, 160.

543  *Re Constitutionality of German Law Implementing the Framework Decision on a European Arrest Warrant* (2BvR 2236/04) [2006] 1 CMLR 16; noted in S Mölders 'European arrest warrant is void – the

issued by Spain on the basis that the German EAW implementing legislation[544] was contrary to Article 16(2) and Article 19(4) of the Basic Law. Article 16(2)[545] of the German Basic Law had been amended to enable German citizens to be extradited to EU Member States so long as 'constitutional principles are observed'. The BVerfG found that the right to remain in the citizen's legal system in the first sentence of Article 16(2) was of high constitutional importance and that it could only be derogated from in accordance with the Article 16(2) proviso in the second sentence. This proviso was not unconstitutional as it complied with other provisions of the Basic Law. When the legislator implemented the EAW into German law it had to ensure not only that the objective of the EAW Framework Decision was included but also that the legislation was proportionate to the proviso. Furthermore, the rule of law had to be guaranteed in the Member State where the suspect was to be extradited and the implementation had to respect all other provisions of the Basic Law. These considerations meant that for the implementing legislation to be constitutional, it had to take account of the opportunities for discretion outlined in Article 4 of the EAW Framework Decision, which it did not do, so that the proviso would be proportionate to the constitutional right.[546] Furthermore, the BVerfG found that the lack of judicial review in the German EAW law was contrary to the right to recourse to the courts in Article 19(4) of the Basic Law.[547] For inter alia these reasons, the BVerfG found the German EAW law to be void in its entirety. Thus, German citizens were unable to be extradited until the new implementing legislation was adopted on 20 July 2006,[548] which incorporates all the recommendations of the BVerfG.[549] In a second BVerfG judgment[550] on the extradition of a Danish citizen to Spain, the Court confirmed the first judgment and utilised the judgment in *Pupino* to enable the German authorities to refer directly to the EAW Framework Decision, even though a

---

decision of the German Federal Constitutional Court of 18 July 2005' (2005) 7 *German Law Journal* 45; C Tomuschat 'Inconsistencies – the German Federal Constitutional Court on the European arrest warrant' (2006) 2 *EuConst* 209; AH Parga 'Case note' (2006) 43 *CMLRev* 583; N Nohlen 'Germany: The European arrest warrant case' (2008) 6 *IJCL* 153. See also H Satzger, T Pohl 'The German Constitutional Court and the European arrest warrant: "cryptic signals" from Karlsruhe' (2006) 4 *JICC* 686; C Lebeck 'National constitutional control and the limits of European integration – the European arrest warrant in the German Federal Constitutional Court' [2007] PL 23.

544 European Arrest Warrant Act 2004 [2004] BGBl.I 1748.
545 '(2) No German may be extradited to a foreign country. A different regulation to cover extradition to a Member State of the European Union or to an international court of law may be laid down by law, provided that constitutional principles are observed.' The second sentence was added in 2000 to enable German citizens to be extradited to stand trial at the International Criminal Court.
546 *Re Constitutionality* (n 543) [70]–[95].
547 ibid [101]–[107].
548 European Arrest Warrant Act 2006 [2006] BGBl.I 1721.
549 A Sinn, L Wörner 'The European arrest warrant and its implementation in Germany – its constitutionality, laws and current developments' [2007] ZIS 204, 211.
550 *Decision of the German Constitutional Court* 2 BvR 1667/05 24 November 2005 (no English translation); noted in Sinn, Wörner 'The European arrest warrant' (n 549) 208.

framework decision cannot have direct effect and there was no German legislation implementing it.

The third successful challenge to national EAW implementing legislation came from the Supreme Court of Cyprus (SCC) on 7 November 2005[551] when it upheld a judgment of the Limassol District Court to refuse extradition of a Cypriot national to the UK. Appendix D, Article 14 of the Constitution of Cyprus states that '[n]o citizen shall be banished or excluded from the Republic under any circumstances'. The SCC was unable to locate a provision of the Constitution that provided a legal base for the arrest and surrender of a Cypriot national, as Appendix D, Article 11 provided an exhaustive list of circumstances when a person can be arrested and only the arrest for extradition is mentioned in Article 11(2) with regard to aliens. Therefore, the Constitution could not be interpreted in accordance with *Pupino* to give effect to the EAW Framework Decision. Furthermore, in the SCC's opinion, the fact that framework decisions do not have direct effect meant that framework decisions do not have supremacy over national constitutions. The Cypriot government moved swiftly following the judgment and amended the Constitution with a new Appendix D, Article 11 that enables Cypriot nationals to be arrested for extradition to another EU Member State but is time limited to 1 May 2004, the date of the Cypriot accession to the Union.

There have also been unsuccessful challenges in Greece,[552] the Czech Republic[553] and Ireland.[554] However, a further problem arose in Greece, where Article 11(f) of the Greek implementing legislation prohibited the extradition of a Greek national if the warrant was to enforce a custodial sentence imposed by final decision of another Member State's criminal courts, as allowed by Article 4(6) EAW. The provision required the executing judicial authority to order sentence to be carried out in the Greek prison system, which the Court of Appeal of Athens has complied with.[555] In Belgium the authorities brought an action for annulment of the EAW Framework Decision before the ECJ on the grounds that the EAW ought to have been implemented by a Convention rather than a framework decision,[556] as Article 34(2)(b) TEU stated that framework decisions could only be adopted for the approximation of the laws and regulations of the Member States.

---

551 *Attorney General of the Republic of Cyprus v Konstantinou* [2007] 3 CMLR 42.
552 *Re Execution of a German Arrest Warrant: Tsokas and Another* [2007] 3 CMLR 24. The Supreme Court of Greece nevertheless quashed the orders for extradition in this case because of Germany annulling the national implementing EAW legislation, thereby creating direct conflict with the principle of reciprocity. For an alternative approach to this problem see the UK case of *Oliver v Secretary of State for the Home Department* [2006] 3 CMLR 46 (QB).
553 *Re Constitutionality of Framework Decision on the European Arrest Warrant* [2007] 3 CMLR 24.
554 *Minister for Justice, Equality and Law Reform v Stapleton* [2007] IESC 30.
555 *Re Enforcement of a European Arrest Warrant Against Tzoannos* [2008] 2 CMLR 38.
556 Case C–303/05 *Advocaten voor de Wereld VZW v Leden van de Ministerrad* [2007] ECR I–3633; noted in C Janssens 'Case note' (2007) 14 *Columbia Journal of European Law* 169; D Sarmiento 'The European arrest warrant and the quest for constitutional coherence' (2008) 6 *IJCL* 171. See also A Hinarejos 'Recent human rights developments in the EU courts: the Charter of Fundamental Rights, the European arrest warrant and terror lists' (2007) 7 *HRLR* 793; D Leczykiewicz 'Constitutional conflicts and the third pillar' (2008) 33 *ELR* 230.

The Court quickly rejected this as, in the ECJ's view, the EAW Framework Decision did precisely what a framework decision was supposed to do.[557] The Belgian court also questioned whether the EAW Framework Decision was valid as Article 2(2) dispensed with verification of the principle of double criminality and therefore allegedly breached Article 6(2) TEU over the fundamental principles of the legality of criminal offences and penalties and of equality and non-discrimination, as reaffirmed by the Charter of Fundamental Rights.[558] The ECJ held that the EAW Framework Decision did not harmonise the Member States' criminal offences or penalties and so the definition of both remained within the competences of the Member States and the EAW Framework Decision did not breach Article 6(2) TEU.[559]

The EAW Framework Decision and the Member States' constitutional courts' interpretation of it raise a number of concerns over EU law in general and an individual's rights that impinge on freedom of movement. The Polish constitutional tribunal's judgment appears to be a rational result considering the wording of Article 55 of the Polish Constitution at the time, the fact that the *Pupino* case had yet to be decided and the suspension of the judgment for 18 months to enable new legislation to be passed. However, the resulting amendment to Article 55 appears to contravene Article 2(2) of the EAW Framework Decision that could see further legal challenges. The two German BVerfG judgments raise several points of concern. The first is the failure to refer in the first case to the judgment of the ECJ in *Pupino* that had been given over a month earlier, except in the dissenting Opinion of Judge Gerhardt.[560] Parga[561] argues persuasively that this should have featured strongly and would, if interpreted in the correct manner, have resulted in a different finding. Secondly, the use of *Pupino* by the BVerfG in the second case, even though the first judgment was confirmed, led to an unusual conclusion that is difficult to support on the basis of EU law. Framework decisions do not have direct effect and therefore a national authority cannot refer to them directly without implementing legislation. There was no implementing legislation in force, as the first judgment had declared it void in its entirety, and so the *Pupino* judgment should not have been able to bite. Thirdly, the result of the two cases appears to have seen a difference in the treatment of the two individuals, both notably citizens of the Union, purely on the basis of their nationality, discrimination that is prohibited by Article 18 TFEU. Fourthly, Germany had made a declaration, as Arnull notes,[562] on the jurisdiction of the ECJ in accordance with Article 35 TEU that the highest court in the land could make a reference to the Court for a preliminary ruling. The BVerfG is the highest court in Germany and, it would appear from the judgment, making a reference did not appear to have been considered by the court. The SCC judgment would at first blush appear to be logical. The

557 *Advocaten voor de Wereld* (n 556) para 30.
558 ibid paras 45, 46.
559 ibid paras 52–54 and 57–60.
560 *Re Constitutionality* (n 543) [88] (Judge Gerhardt).
561 Parga 'Case note' (n 543) 586–90.
562 A Arnull 'Arrested development' (2005) 30 *ELR* 605, 606.

Constitution, as worded at the time, did not enable the extradition of a Cypriot national and was incapable of being interpreted in line with *Pupino* and so therefore the individual could not be extradited. However, the finding that as a framework decision was not directly effective so that it could not have supremacy over national constitutions muddles the separate and distinct principles of direct effect and primacy. Direct effect simply means that an individual can enforce his or her individual rights, as provided in European law, in the national courts so long as the provision is clear, precise, unconditional[563] and, in the case of directives and, it is submitted, Framework decisions after the judgment in *Pupino*, has passed the transposition date.[564] The principle of supremacy, or primacy, provides simply that European law takes precedence over domestic law[565] that includes national constitutional law.[566] It is submitted that the Cypriot court confused itself on this issue and thus interpreted European law incorrectly. Finally, the UK Supreme Court's interpretation in *Assange* is at odds with the ECJ's suggested approach in *Pupino* and subsequent case law, even though Lord Mance attempted to justify his finding in the wording of the ECJ's *Pupino* judgment.[567] The discussion based on the European Communities Act 1972 rather than on the principle of supremacy resulted in a highly literal judgment rather than the purposive approach that had been followed previously by the House of Lords.

The position of the individual vis-à-vis the EAW also provides some concerns. First, as the partial abolition of the principle of double criminality has been held by the ECJ not to be in breach of fundamental rights as the EAW Framework Decision did not harmonise the definition of criminal offences or penalties and so they remain within the competence of the Member States, the fact that they do remain within the competence of the Member States raises the possibility of a challenge before the ECtHR.[568] Secondly, as the list of offences in Article 2(2) is

---

563  Case 41/74 *Yvonne van Duyn v Home Office* [1974] ECR 1337.
564  Case 148/78 *Pubblico Ministero v Tullio Ratti* [1979] ECR 1629.
565  Case 6/64 *Flaminio Costa v ENEL* [1964] ECR 585.
566  Case 11/70 *Internationale Handelsgesellschaft mbH v Einfuhr- und Vorratsstelle für Getreide und Futtermittel* [1970] ECR 1125.
567  *Assange* (n 535) [216] (Lord Mance).
568  See *Matthews v United Kingdom* (1999) 28 EHRR 361 (noted in RS Reid, M Doherty 'Voting rights for the European Parliament: whose responsibility?' [1999] EHRLR 420; HG Schermers 'Case note' (1999) 36 *CMLRev* 673; I Canor '*Primus inter pares*: who is the ultimate guardian of fundamental rights in Europe?' (2000) 25 *ELR* 3; T King 'Ensuring human rights review of intergovernmental acts in Europe' (2000) 25 *ELR* 79) and *Bosphorus Hava Yolları Turizm ve Ticaret Anonim Şirketi v Ireland* (2006) 42 EHRR 1 (noted in C Banner, A Thomson 'Human rights review of state acts performed in compliance with EC law' [2005] EHRLR 649; C Costello 'The *Bosphorus* ruling of the European Court of Human Rights: fundamental rights and blurred boundaries in Europe' (2006) 6 *HRLR* 87; S Douglas-Scott 'Case note' (2006) 43 *CMLRev* 243; AH Parga '*Bosphorus v Ireland* and the protection of fundamental rights in Europe' (2006) 31 *ELR* 251; C Eckes 'Does the European Court of Human Rights provide protection from the European Community?' (2007) 13 *EPL* 47). The ECtHR in *Matthews* found that although it was not able to examine EU law directly, because the Member States had transferred some sovereignty to the Union then they retained their responsibility for it and so the ECtHR was able to consider EU law indirectly. In *Bosphorus* the ECtHR held that although there was a presumption of equivalent human rights protection between the EU's fundamental rights and the ECHR, this presumption

extensive, can be added to at the Member State's discretion (Article 2(1) allows Member States to create disproportionate sentences for minor crimes that would bring the offence within the EAW Framework Decision), and is defined in domestic legislation then there is no uniformity across the EU leading to the possibility of Member States increasing the severity of criminal sanctions for offences in order to avoid forum shopping.[569] Thirdly, the restrictions on the right of freedom of movement for citizens of the Union and their family members are laid down in Chapter VI of Directive 2004/38 that the ECJ has interpreted narrowly as they derogate from the general right of freedom of movement (see Chapter 3 of this book). Although the EAW Framework Decision does not mention Directive 2004/38, nor the case law on restrictions to the right of free movement, as the execution of an EAW will restrict an individual's right to entry and residence in a Member State then it submitted that there is a possibility to challenge the execution of an EAW through Chapter VI of Directive 2004/38. Fourthly, although there is a general reference to Article 6(2) TEU in Article 1(3) and recital 12 provides that the framework decision respects fundamental rights and observes the principles recognised by Article 6 TEU and reflected in the Charter, in particular Chapter VI entitled 'Justice', there is no explicit reference to the ECHR or the individual provisions of the ECHR, in particular Article 5 ECHR on the right to liberty and security of the person and Article 6 ECHR on the right to a fair trial, within the text of the EAW Framework Decision.[570] It could be argued that by providing interpretive guidance in recital 12 and as Chapter VI of the Charter contains Article 47 on the right to an effective remedy and fair trial then there is no need to specify the ECHR itself or any provision of it.[571] However, by highlighting Chapter VI of the Charter the framework decision creates a rod for its own back as the partial abolition of the *non bis in idem* principle in Article 2(2) would appear to contravene Article 50[572] of the Charter, which prohibits a person being tried and punished twice in criminal proceedings for the same criminal offence. Fifthly, there was disunity over the jurisdiction of the ECJ to give a preliminary ruling on the interpretation of the EAW Framework Decision or its validity, as some Member States had not given the declaration required in ex-Article 35 TEU, some had but had then limited references to the highest court in the land, and some had enabled any court or tribunal to make a reference. The

could be rebutted depending on the circumstances of a particular case where the protection of the rights in the ECHR was 'manifestly deficient' (para 156).

569 M Fichera 'The European arrest warrant and the sovereign state: a marriage of convenience?' (2009) 15 *ELJ* 70, 96 suggests that the list of crimes in art 2(2) should be reduced to a few core offences that can be clearly defined to ensure legal certainty and to eliminate forum shopping.

570 S Douglas-Scott 'The rule of law in the European Union – putting the security into the "area of freedom, security and justice"' (2004) 29 *ELR* 219, 226.

571 See Case C–399/11 *Stefano Melloni v Ministerio Fiscal* (ECJ 26 February 2013) and Case C–396/11 *Ministerul Public – Parchetul de pe lângă Curtea de Apel Constanţa v Ciprian Vasile Radu* (Opinion of AG Sharpston 18 October 2012), where the Grand Chamber and Advocate General respectively interpret the EAW Framework Directive in accordance with the Charter and the ECHR.

572 'No one shall be liable to be tried or punished again in criminal proceedings for an offence for which he or she has already been finally acquitted or convicted within the Union in accordance with the law.'

failure to provide an ECJ jurisdiction clause in the framework decision led to a lack of uniformity in the law with contradictory national court judgments, legal uncertainty, opacity and incongruence between the law as specified in the EAW Framework Decision and the 27 ways of interpreting it. As Douglas-Scott observed,[573] this did not bode well for the principle of mutual trust and recognition which the EAW Framework Decision was built on and which was intended to operate as the cornerstone of the AFSJ. Finally, the time limits[574] in the framework decision are notably short and, although the EAW Framework Decision does not expressly limit the right to appeal, such short time limits are likely to put grave impediments in the way of access to the full judicial process for cases that can often be highly complex in nature.

The Lisbon Treaty moved the majority of Title VI of the TEU from the third pillar into the first pillar, extended the ECJ's jurisdiction to its full competence in Article 267 TFEU and removed any distinction between decision-making under the third pillar and the first pillar. Protocol 36 on Transitional Provisions detailed the approach to be followed for the previous third pillar provisions.[575] Article 9 maintained the legal effect of the measures adopted before the Lisbon Treaty and Article 10(1) maintained the pre-Lisbon powers of the institutions. If a legal measure was amended, such as the EAW Framework Decision being given a new legal base, becoming a directive or being recast, then the full EU Treaty provisions would take effect (Article 10(2)). However, the transitional measures of Article 10(1) cease to have effect on 1 December 2014, five years after the Lisbon Treaty entered into force (Article 10(3)). Article 10(4) provides an opt-out for the UK from all legal measures adopted under the third pillar before the Lisbon Treaty. The UK must notify the Council by 1 June 2014 of its intentions with the possibility of opting back into specific legal instruments using the procedure set out in Protocol 19. It is unfortunate[576] for the unanimity of European law that the Home Secretary, in an oral statement to the House of Commons setting out the thinking of the government,[577] suggested that the UK would exercise its option to opt out of all pre-Lisbon measures and then attempt to negotiate opt-ins to individual measures. It is therefore uncertain whether the EAW Framework Decision will be given effect as a directive or if a new instrument will have to be adopted, or indeed whether the UK will take part. Whatever the answer the result will standardise the juridical issues, creating uniformity and removing legal uncertainty for those that

---

573  Douglas-Scott 'The rule of law' (n 570) 227; S Douglas-Scott 'The EU's area of freedom, security and justice: a lack of fundamental rights, mutual trust and democracy' (2009) 11 *CYELS* 53, 77.
574  Douglas-Scott 'The rule of law' (n 570) 226.
575  Protocol (No 36) on transitional provisions [2012] OJ L326/322; S Peers 'Finally "fit for purpose"? The Treaty of Lisbon and the end of the third pillar legal order' (2008) 27 *YEL* 47 for an analysis of the transitional provisions.
576  For a highly critical report of this approach by the UK see A Hinarejos, J R Spencer and S Peers 'Opting out of criminal law: what is actually involved?' CELS Working Paper New Series 1 September 2012 http://www.cels.law.cam.ac.uk/Media/working_papers/Optout%20text%20 final.pdf.
577  Right Hon Theresa May MP, Secretary of State for the Home Department HC Deb 15 October 2012 vol 551 cols 34–45.

take part. However, the Charter may see legal challenges to the EAW Framework Decision or the issuing of EAWs[578] and, when the Union accedes to the ECHR, similar challenges may result through Articles 5 and 6 ECHR.

## 4.8   Conclusion

The AFSJ is a vast[579] and highly complex new field of competence for the EU, made even more complex by the difficult and different opt-outs for the UK, Ireland and Denmark. The creation of this AFSJ from the Treaty of Amsterdam onwards must be built on solid foundations if it is to be credible for the citizens of the Union and attuned to the needs of the EU itself. Those foundations are clearly set out in Title I of the TEU, entitled Common Provisions and include the values of, inter alia, human dignity, freedom, equality, the rule of law and human rights (Article 2 TEU), free movement of persons (Article 3(2) TEU) and the establishment of an internal market (Article 3(3) TEU). However, the free movement rights of TCNs under the AFSJ as seen in this chapter are highly restrictive, with different TCNs treated in different ways depending on their status, leading to a hierarchical arrangement of rights, including free movement rights, for TCNs. The pledge by the European Council at Tampere in October 1999 not to deny the right to move freely throughout the Union to 'those whose circumstances lead them justifiably to seek access to our territory', as it 'would be in contradiction with Europe's traditions',[580] weighs heavily when considering TCNs' rights to freedom of movement.

The hierarchy of TCNs can clearly be illustrated when examining their status as asylum-seekers, illegal immigrants and individuals with temporary protection who have no right to free movement (and even freedom itself can be curtailed), claimants for international protection who have a right to travel or legal migrants and especially LTR TCNs, who have a right to move to a second EU Member State under limited circumstances. However, the UK's and Ireland's opt-out from Regulation 2011/95 means that the hierarchy is maintained within the single policy area of international protection where TCNs are treated differently according to their status so that refugees have a right to travel and beneficiaries of subsidiary protection can travel if there are serious humanitarian reasons for their presence in another Member State. Even when rights of movement are granted, such as those in the LTR TCN Directive and Blue Card Directive, they are limited, have complex and difficult criteria for the establishment of the right and do not lead to any further rights of movement or freedom. The rights granted to TCNs in the Single Permit Directive can easily be attenuated through wide

---

578  See TP Marguery 'The protection of fundamental rights in European criminal law after Lisbon: what role for the Charter of Fundamental Rights?' (2012) 37 *ELR* 444.

579  The vastness can be visualised by comparing the size of Steve Peers first edition and latest edition of his authoritative work on the AFSJ; S Peers *EU Justice and Home Affairs Law* (Longman 2000) cf S Peers *EU Justice and Home Affairs Law* (3rd edn OUP 2011).

580  Presidency Conclusions of the Tampere European Council 15–16 October 1999 SN 200/1/99 para 3.

discretion granted to Member States, especially when it comes to equality of treatment and must be considered carefully against the Union's commitment to grant to TCNs 'rights and obligations comparable to those of EU citizens'.[581] The lack of a TCN right to freedom of movement for persons must be contrasted with the ease to transfer TCNs between Member States under the EAW Framework Directive and the Dublin Regulation system. From the analysis in this chapter it is clear that the area of freedom, security and justice applies security to the case of TCNs but without a great deal of freedom or justice.

581  ibid para 18.

# 5 Free movement rights under association agreements

We have so far examined the rights of third country nationals (TCNs) that flow directly from the EU treaties and legislative measures implementing the provisions of them, including the AFSJ. The EU has also concluded a large number of international agreements with an array of third countries, some of which grant direct rights to the nationals of those third countries. These rights do not flow directly from the EU treaties but indirectly through an agreement negotiated with a legal base in the EC Treaty, and now the TEU and TFEU. There is no uniform rationale that applies to the negotiation of these agreements as each is entered into for reasons specific to that state and its relationship with the EU. Thus an agreement could be concluded with a European state with the aim of eventually acceding to the Union, or the state concerned might not satisfy the criteria for accession to the EU[1] but is strategically important because of its geographical, cultural or historical relationship with the EU, a group of states in the EU or just a single EU Member State. It is not the aim of this book to carry out a definitive analysis of all these agreements,[2] but to investigate a number of them and to highlight the disparities within them for the right of free movement for TCNs. Therefore this chapter will briefly outline the procedural aspects of agreement formation and the interpretative principles of the ECJ before analysing the different agreements in a roughly descending hierarchical order of free movement rights.

## 5.1 Procedural aspects of the agreements

Article 47 (TEU) provides the Union with legal personality, with Article 8 TEU providing a general mandate to the EU to 'develop a special relationship with neighbouring countries' by concluding 'specific agreements with the countries concerned' and the TFEU setting out the specific requirements for the implementation of this general obligation. As such, Article 217 TFEU gives the Union

---

1 Article 49 TEU states that '[a]ny European State which respects the principles set out in art 6(1) may apply to become a member of the Union'.
2 See D Martin, E Guild *Free Movement of Persons in the European Union* (Butterworths 1996) and N Rogers, R Scannell *Free Movement of Persons in the Enlarged European Union* (Sweet & Maxwell 2005).

specific external competence to conclude 'association' agreements with third countries that include 'reciprocal rights and obligations, common action and special procedure'. Article 218 TFEU lays down the procedure that applies for the conclusion and implementation of agreements concluded under Article 217 TFEU that will be binding both on EU institutions and Member States.[3] The provisions of these agreements form an integral part of the Union legal system[4] and the ECJ has jurisdiction to interpret them in order to ensure uniform application throughout the EU.[5] They have been interpreted by the ECJ on a significant number of occasions, with the frequency of referrals over the free movement of persons provisions increasing as migration to the EU has become more attractive. However, even where the terms used in an agreement are the same as those used in the EU treaties, the understanding of such terms in the EU treaties may not be directly transposed onto those of the international agreement, as the purpose, objective and spirit of the agreement may be different.[6] The four categories of agreement to be analysed provide different levels of free movement rights that initially appear to depend only on the nationality of the individual concerned. However, this is merely one of the factors that is dependent on the purpose and objective of the agreement.

## 5.2   Agreement on the European Economic Area (EEA)[7]

The EEA Agreement is, to date, the most ambitious association agreement concluded by the EU and Member States with third countries under Article 217 TFEU.[8] Initially concluded with Austria, Sweden, Finland, Norway and Iceland in October 1991 and coming into force on 1 January 1994,[9] the first three countries subsequently joined the EU, whilst Liechtenstein signed up to the EEA Agreement.[10] Therefore the nationals of Norway, Iceland and Liechtenstein remain subject to the provisions of the EEA Agreement. Nationals of Austria,

---

3   Case 104/81 *Hauptzollamt Mainz v CA Kupferberg & Cie KG aA* [1982] ECR 3641 para 11.
4   Case 181/73 *R & V Haegeman v Belgium* [1974] ECR 449, 459; *Kupferberg* (n 3) para 13. See I Cheyne 'International agreements and the European Community legal system' (1994) 19 *ELR* 581.
5   *Kupferberg* (n 3) para 14. See MT Karayigit 'Why and to what extent a common interpretative position for mixed agreements?' (2006) 11 *EFAR* 445.
6   Case 270/80 *Polydor Ltd and RSO Records Inc v Harlequin Record Shops Ltd and Simons Records Ltd* [1982] ECR 329 paras 15–18.
7   Agreement on the European Economic Area [1994] OJ L1/3.
8   *Opinion 1/91* [1991] ECR I–6079 para 2.
9   Council and Commission Decision 94/1/ECSC & EC on the conclusion of the Agreement on the European Economic Area between the European Communities, the Member States and the Republic of Austria, the Republic of Finland, the Republic of Iceland, the Principality of Liechtenstein, the Kingdom of Norway, the Kingdom of Sweden and the Swiss Confederation [1994] OJ L1/1.
10   Treaty of Accession – Finland, Austria and Sweden [1994] OJ C241 and Decision of the EEA Council 1/95 on the entry into force of the Agreement on the European Economic Area for the Principality of Liechtenstein [1995] OJ L86/58.

Sweden and Finland who remain in those countries and who wish to enforce their EEA rights that arose before accession to the Union must bring an action in their national courts that then refer questions to the European Free Trade Association (EFTA) Court,[11] rather than the ECJ. Substantively, Article 1(2) EEA specifies the four freedoms, including the free movement of persons, as objectives of the EEA that are implemented by the provisions in Part III, entitled 'Free Movement of Persons, Services and Capital'. Although the wording of these measures is slightly different to that of the TFEU it is submitted that such differences are inconsequential and are necessitated by a requirement to set in place the free movement of persons without subsequent implementing legislation. Thus nationals of EEA Member States have the same rights to free movement of workers, social security,[12] freedom of establishment[13] and freedom to provide services[14] as those of citizens of the Union throughout the EEA. Furthermore, Article 4 EEA prohibits discrimination on grounds of nationality in the same words as that of paragraph 1 of Article 18 TFEU.

The EEA Agreement is built on two pillars of equal standing: the EU pillar; and the EFTA pillar. To resolve disputes between these pillars, and the pillars and Member States, the original plan was to create an EEA Court staffed by three judges from the EFTA states and two ECJ judges.[15] However, the ECJ rejected this approach in *Opinion 1/91*[16] and so the EFTA court was created[17] to rule on matters dealing with the EFTA pillar. This reformulation of the Court structure won approval from the ECJ in *Opinion 1/92*.[18]

The aim of the EEA Agreement, as laid down in Article 1(1), is to create a dynamic and homogenous EEA supported by the twin pillars of the EU and EFTA. As Forman[19] notes, this is based on a free trade agreement. However, both the General Count (hereafter GC) and the EFTA Court have subsequently

11 Case C–321/97 *Ulla-Brith Andersson and Susanne Wåkerås-Anderson v Swedish State* [1999] ECR I–3551 paras 28–31.
12 Case E–3/04 *Tsomakas Athanasios and Others v Norway* [2004] EFTA Court Report 97.
13 Case E–3/98 *Herbert Rainford-Towning v Liechtenstein* [1998] EFTA Court Report 205; Case E–2/01 *Dr Franz Martin Pucher v Liechtenstein* [2002] EFTA Court Report 44; Case E–8/04 *EFTA Surveillance Authority v Liechtenstein* [2005] EFTA Court Report 48; Case E–1/06 *EFTA Surveillance Authority v Norway* [2007] EFTA Court Report 7 and Case E–3/06 *Ladbrokes Ltd v Norway* [2007] EFTA Court Report 86.
14 Case E–1/03 *EFTA Surveillance Authority v Iceland* [2003] EFTA Court Report 143. See also Case E–1/07 *Criminal proceedings against A* [2007] EFTA Court Report 246.
15 C Baudenbacher 'The EFTA Court – an example of the judicialisation of international economic law' (2003) 28 *ELR* 880, 881; C Baudenbacher 'The EFTA Court: an actor in the European judicial dialogue' (2005) 28 *Fordham International Law Journal* 353; C Baudenbacher 'The EFTA Court, the ECJ, and the latter's Advocates General – a tale of judicial dialogue' in A Arnull, P Eeckhout and T Tridimas (eds) *Continuity and Change in EU Law* (OUP 2008) 90.
16 *Opinion 1/91* (n 8) para 51. See B Brandtner 'The drama of the "EEA": comments on Opinions 1/91 and 1/92' (1992) 3 *EJIL* 300 for a full analysis of Opinion 1/91.
17 Article 108(2) EEA and Part IV of the Surveillance and Court Agreement (SCA) [1994] OJ L344/3.
18 *Opinion 1/92* [1992] ECR I–2821.
19 J Forman 'The EEA Agreement five years on: dynamic homogeneity in practice and its implementation by the two EEA courts' (1999) 36 *CMLRev* 751, 755.

concluded that it is one stage further than this,[20] although it is not a customs union and has no external competence. Indeed, the EFTA Court in *Sveinbjörnsdóttir*[21] has concluded that the 'EEA Agreement is an international treaty *sui generis* which contains a distinct legal order of its own', although there has been no 'transfer of legislative powers'.[22] On the basis of the latter point the ECJ in *Opinion 1/91*[23] inferred that the principles of primacy and direct effect did not apply to the EEA Agreement when applied in the EU or the EFTA states. However, since then the GC in *Opel Austria*[24] has found a provision in the EEA Agreement to be sufficiently clear, precise and unconditional to have direct effect in the Union and in its first ruling the EFTA Court in *Restamark*[25] found that Article 16 EEA was unconditional and sufficiently precise for Protocol 35[26] to apply.[27] Furthermore, the EFTA Court in *Sveinbjörnsdóttir*[28] has held that the principle of state liability is applicable in EFTA states. Much academic debate has surrounded the context of primacy and direct effect within the EEA.[29] The rulings in *Opel Austria*, *Restamark* and *Sveinbjörnsdóttir* and two recitals of the preamble appear to support the supposition that for the EEA Agreement to achieve its objectives throughout the EEA, the provisions must be capable of being relied on by individuals in their own national courts. First, recital 8 stresses the importance of the individuals' role in the EEA 'through the exercise of the rights conferred upon them by this Agreement and through the judicial defence of these rights'. Secondly, recital 15 determines that there is to be equal treatment of individuals with regard to the four freedoms. Thus for individuals to enforce their rights the EEA Agreement must create a new legal order in which it has primacy over national law and individuals in national courts must rely on provisions within it. The EFTA Court appeared initially to

---

20   Case T–115/94 *Opel Austria GmbH v Council* [1997] ECR II–39 para 107: 'the EEA Agreement involves a high degree of integration, with objectives which exceed those of a mere free trade agreement'; Case E–2/97 *Mag Instrument Inc v California Trading Company (Maglite)* [1997] EFTA Court Report 127 para 27: 'the aim of the EEA Agreement . . . is to create a fundamentally improved free trade area'; Case E–9/97 *Erla Maria Sveinbjörnsdóttir v Iceland* [1998] EFTA Court Report 95 para 59: 'the EEA Agreement . . . establish[es] . . . an enhanced free trade area'; noted in M Eyjólfsson 'Case note' (2000) 37 *CMLRev* 191.

21   *Sveinbjörnsdóttir* (n 20).

22   ibid para 63.

23   *Opinion 1/91* (n 8) paras 20–22.

24   *Opel Austria* (n 20) para 102.

25   Case E–1/94 *Ravintoloitsijain Liiton Kustannus Oy Restamark* [1994] EFTA Court Report 1 para 80.

26   Protocol 35 to the EEA Agreement requires EFTA states to introduce a statutory provision to the effect that implemented EEA rules are to take primacy over conflicting domestic statutory provisions.

27   The Court did not actually state that art 16 had direct effect.

28   *Sveinbjörnsdóttir* (n 20) para 63.

29   Those against include AT Laredo 'The EEA Agreement: an overall view' (1992) 29 *CMLRev* 1199, 1206; M Cremona 'The "dynamic and homogenous" EEA: Byzantine structures and variable geometry' (1994) 19 *ELR* 508, 519–22. Those for include W van Gerven 'The genesis of EEA law and the principles of primacy and direct effect' (1992) 16 *Fordham International Law Journal* 955, 967–989; L Sevon, M Johansson 'The protection of the rights of individuals under the EEA Agreement' (1999) 24 *ELR* 373. Those sitting on the fence include D O'Keefe 'The Agreement on the European Economic Area' (1992) 19(1) *LIEI* 1; J Forman 'The EEA Agreement five years on' (n 19).

confirm this position in *Einarsson*[30] on direct effect and the principle of primacy, but in more recent cases[31] the Court has explicitly rejected the application of both principles in the EEA. Furthermore, the EFTA Court has gone out of its way to examine the criteria for state liability in *Karlsson*,[32] whilst finding that state liability arose without any contingent recognition of a corollary principle of direct effect.[33]

Although some of the terms used in the EEA Agreement are identically worded to those used in the TFEU, the understanding of such terms in the TFEU may not be directly transposed onto those of this international agreement. Rather, as with the other association agreements, and as already discussed, the purpose, objective and spirit of the agreement must first be considered.[34] However, under Article 6 EEA, if the provisions of the EEA Agreement are identically worded to those of the TFEU then they will be interpreted in accordance with the ECJ's jurisprudence given prior to the signature of the agreement.[35] Furthermore, there is a need to ensure that the provisions of the EEA Agreement that are identical in substance to the TFEU are interpreted uniformly.[36] However, as there is no requirement to follow the jurisprudence decided after the date of signature, then the *Polydor* formula will continue to apply. A court or tribunal of an EFTA state is entitled to make a preliminary reference to the EFTA Court for interpretation of the EEA Agreement, although national law can limit this to a court or tribunal from which there is no judicial remedy (Article 34 SCA). However, to ensure the uniformity of the application of EU law, Protocol 34 to the EEA Agreement enables a court or tribunal of an EFTA state to make a preliminary reference to the ECJ for interpretation where the provisions of the EEA Agreement and the TFEU are identically worded.

The EEA Agreement extends much of EU legislation and protection of that legislation to certain third countries without the obligation on these states to join the Union. In particular rights to freedom of movement, and especially Directive 2004/38,[37] are identical for EEA nationals as they are for EU citizens. This appears to be a remarkable situation considering that the three countries

---

30 Case E–1/01 *Hörður Einarsson v Iceland* [2002] EFTA Court Report 1 paras 53–55; *Criminal proceedings against A* (n 14) paras 37–39.

31 Case E–4/01 *Karl K Karlsson hf v Iceland* [2002] EFTA Court Report 240 para 28; *Criminal proceedings against A* (n 14) para 40.

32 ibid paras 37–48. See HP Graver 'Mission impossible: supranationality and national legal autonomy in the EEA Agreement' (2002) 7 *EFAR* 73. See also Case E–8/07 *Celina Nguyen v Norway* [2008] EFTA Court Report 224 and Case E–2/10 *Þór Kolbeinsson v Iceland* [2010] EFTA Court Report 234.

33 *Karlsson* (n 31) para 29.

34 ibid para 14; *Polydor* (n 6).

35 Case C–286/02 *Bellio F Illi Srl v Prefettura di Treviso* [2004] ECR I–3465 para 34.

36 See Case C–452/01 *Margarethe Ospelt v Schlössle Weissenberg Familienstiftung* [2003] ECR I–9743 para 29; Case E–1/03 *EFTA Surveillance Authority v Iceland* [2003] EFTA Court Report 143 para 27. See also *Bellio* (n 35) para 34; Case C–471/04 *Finanzamt Offenbach am Main-Land v Keller Holding* [2006] ECR I–2107 para 48.

37 See Case E–4/11 *Arnulf Clauder* [2011] EFTA Court Report 216 for the first EFTA Court judgment on the interpretation of provisions of Directive 2004/38.

involved are not Member States of the Union and, indeed, the citizens of Norway have rejected the chance to join the Union twice in referenda in 1972 and 1994. As Fredriksen[38] points out, much of the homogeneity between EU and EEA law, especially on free movement and the internal market, is as a direct result of the ECJ and EFTA Court's teleological interpretation of the EU Treaties and the EEA Agreement. However, the EEA Agreement remains limited to the creation of an EFTA between the EEA states and the EU and the EFTA states are isolated from the decision-making process of Union legislation. It can be argued that the states involved are integral European states that historically should be integrated as fully as possible into the 'ever closer Union amongst the peoples of Europe' and as they are reasonably small then it is probably in the best interests of the Union and the EFTA states. On the other hand, they have chosen positively not to join the Union and it must be questioned why their citizens should receive the same free movement rights as EU citizens.

## 5.3   EEC-Turkey Association Agreement and Council Decisions[39]

The EEC-Turkey Association Agreement or 'Ankara' Agreement was concluded in 1963[40] with the aim of establishing a customs union (Articles 2 and 10) as a preliminary to Turkey's membership of the EU (Recital 4 and Article 28). Article 6 empowered an Association Council to take appropriate measures for the fulfilment of the agreement's obligations. The resulting decisions of the Association Council are international legal instruments that must be brought within EU law by the enactment of implementing Union legislation, usually in the form of a regulation. Articles 12–14 envisaged that the Contracting Parties would be guided by the TFEU's provisions on the free movement of workers, freedom of establishment and freedom to provide services in order progressively to secure freedom of movement of workers and abolish restrictions on freedoms of establishment and provision of services.

In 1970 a protocol[41] was added to the agreement that set out arrangements and the timescale for the establishment of the customs union. Article 9 set out the principle of non-discrimination on the basis of nationality, that referred to

---

38  HH Fredriksen 'The EFTA Court 15 years on' (2010) 59 *ICLQ* 731; HH Fredriksen 'Bridging the widening gap between the EU Treaties and the Agreement on the European Economic Area' (2012) 18 *ELJ* 868.

39  For full details and analysis see N Rogers *A Practitioner's Guide to the EC-Turkey Association Agreement* (Kluwer Law International 2000); B Cicekli 'The rights of Turkish migrants in Europe under international law and EU law' (1999) 33 *IMR* 300; N Tezcan/Idriz 'Free movement of persons between Turkey and the EU: to move or not to move? The response of the judiciary' (2009) 46 *CMLRev* 1621; MT Kurayigit 'Vive la clause de standstill: the issue of first admission of Turkish nationals into the territory of a Member State within the context of economic freedoms' (2011) 13 *EJML* 411.

40  Agreement Establishing an Association between the European Economic Community and Turkey [1973] OJ C113/2.

41  Additional Protocol [1973] OJ C113/18.

Article 18 TFEU (ex-Article 7 EEC). In *Sürül*,[42] the ECJ appeared to give a wide interpretation to the provision, equating it with ex-Article 7 EEC. Advocate General La Pergola, in his second Opinion in the case, suggested that Article 9 had direct effect.[43] Although the ECJ by inference agreed with the Advocate General[44] it did not comment directly on this matter. Advocate General Colomer in *Kochak*[45] noted that Article 9 was similar to ex-Article 7 EEC, in that it only applied where there was no more specific non-discrimination rule. This was confirmed by the ECJ in *Öztürk*,[46] although the matter of the direct effect of Article 9 remains to be judicially confirmed.

Other provisions included a standstill clause for services and establishment in Article 41(1) that the ECJ in *Savas*[47] declared was directly effective. The Court made it clear that Article 41(1) 'precludes a Member State from adopting any new measure having the object or effect of making the establishment, and, as a corollary, the residence of a Turkish national in its territory subject to stricter conditions than those which applied at the time when the Additional Protocol entered into force with regard to the Member State concerned'.[48] In *Abatay*[49] the Court held that the same interpretation applied to the freedom to provide services. However, Article 41(1) did not encroach upon the competence of the Member States to regulate entry to their territory and conditions for taking up first employment. Article 41(1) regulated the situation where Turkish workers were already integrated into the work force.[50] In *Tum and Dari*[51] two Turkish men claimed asylum in the UK and were restricted or prohibited from taking employment. They both set up businesses in the UK and applied to enter the UK, after their asylum applications were rejected, in a self-employed capacity. In Advocate General Geelhoed's Opinion[52] the rules applicable to entry of Turkish nationals onto the territory of a Member State remained exclusively within the competence of the Member States. Thus, the UK rules fell outside the material scope of Article 41(1) and the UK was free to adapt, liberalise or make more

42 Case C–262/96 *Sema Sürül v Bundestantalt für Arbeit* [1999] ECR I–2685 para 64; noted in H Verschueren 'The *Sürül* judgment: equal treatment for Turkish workers in matters of social security' (1999) 1 *EJML* 371.
43 ibid; Opinion of AG La Pergola paras 6–12.
44 ibid para 68.
45 Joined Cases C–102 & 211/98 *Ibrahim Kocak v Landesversicherungsanstalt Oberfranken und Mittelfranken* and *Ramazan Örs v Bundesknappschaft* [2000] ECR I–1287; Opinion of AG Colomer para 28.
46 Case C–373/02 *Sakir Öztürk v Pensionsversicherungsanstalt der Arbeiter* [2004] ECR I–3605 para 49.
47 Case C–37/98 *R v Secretary of State for the Home Department, ex parte Abdulnasir Savas* [2000] ECR I–2927 paras 46–54. See A Ott 'The *Savas* case – analogies between Turkish self-employed and workers?' (2000) 2 *EJML* 445.
48 ibid para 69.
49 Joined Cases C–317 & 369/01 *Erin Abatay and Others, and Nadi Sahin v Bundesanstalt für Arbeit* [2003] ECR I–12301 paras 66–68.
50 *Savas* (n 47) para 58; ibid para 63.
51 Case C–16/05 *R v Secretary of State for the Home Department, ex parte Veli Tum and Mehmet Dari* [2007] ECR I–7415.
52 ibid; Opinion of AG Geelhoed para 58.

restrictive these entry rules.[53] Rogers[54] criticised this Opinion as appearing to undermine the ECJ's judgment in *Savas*. The ECJ judgment began by stating that Mr Tum and Mr Dari were regarded, by national legislation, as not having entered the UK, as their physical presence on the UK's territory did not amount to actual clearance for entry to the UK.[55] The Court then reaffirmed its previous case law on Article 41(1)[56] before holding that the previous case law did not refer expressly to the first admission of Turkish nationals into the territory of the host Member State[57] and the ECJ in *Savas* and *Abatay* had not ruled on this issue as the two men in these cases had actually entered the territory of the Member States concerned.[58] Returning to that previous case law, the Court found that the 'standstill' clause in Article 41(1), and Article 41(1) itself, was incapable of conferring upon a Turkish national a right of establishment, a corollary right of residence or a right of first entry into the territory of a Member State. However, it prohibited Member States from introducing any new measures that would either have the objective or the effect of making the establishment of Turkish nationals subject to stricter conditions than those in force at the time that the Protocol came into force in the Member State, which for the UK was 1 January 1973.[59] The ECJ concluded this part of the judgment by holding that Article 41(1) did not have the effect of conferring on Turkish nationals a right of entry into the territory of a Member State, as no such positive right could be inferred from EU rules currently applicable, and it remained governed by national rules. Therefore the 'standstill' clause did not operate in the same way as a substantive rule by rendering inapplicable the law it replaced but operated as a quasi-procedural law that stipulated, on a temporary basis, the Member State's legislative provisions that must be referred to when assessing the freedom of establishment of a Turkish national in a Member State.[60] The Court dismissed the UK's assertion that the 'standstill' clause called into question the competence of a Member State to conduct its national immigration policy as it simply limited Member States' room to manoeuvre and did not undermine their sovereign competence in respect of aliens. The Court also pointed out that Article 41(1) refers in a general way to new restrictions inter alia on the freedom of establishment, so does not restrict its scope of application, like Article 13 of Decision 1/80, and ensures that no further obstructions to the gradual implementation of freedom of establishment are adopted. Thus the 'standstill' clause is also applicable to rules relating to the first admission of Turkish nationals into a Member State where

---

53  ibid; Opinion of AG Geelhoed para 59. This appears to be in line with the reasoning of LJ Sedley in *R (on the application of A) v Secretary of State for the Home Department* [2002] 3 CMLR 14 (CA) para 12.
54  N Rogers 'Turkish association agreement applications – a myriad of problems and some solutions' (2006) 20 *Journal of Immigration Asylum and Nationality Law* 283, 286.
55  *Tum and Dari* (n 51) para 45.
56  ibid paras 46–49.
57  ibid para 50.
58  ibid para 51.
59  ibid paras 52–53.
60  ibid paras 54–55.

they intend to exercise their freedom of establishment, and it is irrelevant whether the Turkish national is legally resident or not at the time of the application for establishment.[61] Finally, the ECJ rejected the UK argument that allowing failed asylum-seekers to rely on Article 41(1) was tantamount to endorsing fraud or abuse, as there was no evidence that either Mr Tum or Mr Dari were acting fraudulently, were using the 'standstill' clause with the sole aim of wrongfully benefiting from advantages provided for by EU law, the protection of a legitimate national interest, such as public policy, public security or public health, was at issue or the scope of Article 41(1) was restricted by excluding failed asylum-seekers.[62]

The judgment in *Tum and Dari* confirmed the previous case law on Article 41(1) and significantly extended the 'standstill' provision in Article 41(1) to rules on the first admission of Turkish nationals to a Member State's territory. The Court notably did not follow Advocate General Geelhoed's Opinion and instead forged a teleological path advocated by Rogers.[63] The implications are that the rules on first entry to a Member State must be those that were in place at the time of the Protocol taking effect in the Member State concerned, which in the UK's case would be 1 January 1973, when the Turkish national applies to exercise the right to freedom of establishment.[64] This must also be the case if a Turkish national is exercising the freedom to provide services, as Article 41(1) also covers services but does not apply to the free movement of workers. For workers there is no standstill clause in the Protocol and Article 13 of Decision 1/80 only provides a standstill on the conditions of access to employment. Furthermore, because Article 41(1) is not limited, unlike Article 13 of Decision 1/80, to 'legally resident and employed' workers and their families then the legality of the entry of the Turkish national cannot be taken into consideration when assessing the application to exercise the right of freedom of establishment, or to provide services. Finally, so long as a failed Turkish asylum-seeker does not claim the right to freedom of establishment fraudulently then the fact that his or her asylum application has been rejected cannot be used as evidence of fraud or abuse of the system. In effect the ECJ is refusing to criminalise asylum-seekers. However, in a series of cases[65] before UK courts the failure of an asylum claim had been considered to be an aspect of fraud or abuse with 'false' asylum applications being equated with fraud.[66] This appeared contrary to the position taken by the ECJ in

---

61  ibid paras 59–63.
62  ibid paras 64–68.
63  Rogers 'Turkish association agreement applications' (n 54).
64  This implication is applied in *R (on the application of Yusuf Aldogan) v Secretary of State for the Home Department* [2007] EWHC 2586 (Admin) para 14.
65  *R (on the Application of Ozman Taskale) v Secretary of State for the Home Department* [2006] EWHC 712 (Admin), *R (on the application of Ibrahim Aksoy) v Secretary of State for the Home Department* [2006] EWHC 1487 (Admin) and *R (on the application of Temiz) v Secretary of State for the Home Department* [2006] EWHC 2450 (Admin).
66  *IY (Ankara Agreement – Fraud and Abuse) Turkey* [2008] UKAIT 81 (AIT) [32].

*Tum and Dari* and indeed, the Court of Appeal in *Sonmez*[67] had found that abuse or fraudulent conduct could be taken into account and could defeat the effect of Article 41(1). In *Oguz*[68] the ECJ found that the standstill clause applied 'to a stage before the merits of the case are assessed and before an assessment is made as to whether there is any abuse of rights'[69] and thus the legal residence of the Turkish national at the time of application for establishment was irrelevant for applying Article 41(1).[70] Consequently, non-compliance with conditions attached to a residence permit was irrelevant for applying the standstill clause.[71] Rix LJ in *KA*[72] held that *Oguz* swept away the previous UK judgments on fraud or abuse of right, such that 'even in a true case of fraud or abuse of rights, the standstill clause still applies'.[73] If an applicant, as in Mr KA's position, set up his business ahead of official approval to do so then this need neither be fraudulent, an abuse of rights or tantamount to either. An abuse of rights only arises where the right is claimed by virtue of its abuse.[74]

The extent of Article 41(1) is well illustrated in the case of *Soysal*,[75] where the introduction of a visa requirement for Turkish nationals by Germany that had not been required before 1 January 1973 was held to be a 'new restriction' within the meaning of Article 41(1).[76]

Article 41(2) states a requirement for the Association Council to adopt measures for the progressive abolition of restrictions on freedom of establishment and provision of services. No such measures have yet been adopted and the Court has held that Article 41(2) does not have direct effect.[77]

The first chapter of Title II of the Protocol set out provisions for workers. Article 36 fixed a timescale of between 12 and 22 years from the date of the Ankara Agreement (30 November 1974 to 30 November 1986) to secure freedom of movement of workers in accordance with Article 12 of the Ankara Agreement. The Association Council was mandated to decide on the rules to achieve this objective. Moreover, Article 37 prohibited discrimination for Turkish workers employed in a Member State, over conditions of work and remuneration, when compared to workers who were nationals of Member States, which has been held to be directly effective.[78] Article 38 allowed the Association Council to make

---

67  *Filiz Sonmez and Others v Secretary of State for the Home Department* [2010] 1 CMLR 7 (CA) [59] (Dyson LJ).
68  Case C–186/10 *Tural Oguz v Secretary of State for the Home Department* [2012] 1 WLR 709.
69  ibid para 32.
70  ibid para 33.
71  ibid para 34.
72  *KA (Turkey) v Secretary of State for the Home Department* [2013] 1 CMLR 2 (CA) at [32] (Rix LJ).
73  ibid [51].
74  ibid.
75  Case C–228/06 *Mehmet Soysal & Ibrahim Savatli v Germany* [2009] ECR I–1031 at para 56; noted in S Peers 'Turkish visitors and Turkish students: new rights from the European Court of Justice' (2009) 29 *JIANL* 197; S Peers 'EC immigration law and association agreements: fragmentation or integration' (2009) 34 *ELR* 628.
76  ibid para 57.
77  *Tum and Dari* (n 51) para 62.
78  Case C–152/08 *Real Sociedad de Fútbol SAD and Nihat Kahveci v Consejo Superior de Deportes and Real Federación Española de Fútbol* [2008] ECR I–6291.

recommendations to the Member States over matters including residence and work permits to facilitate Turkish workers' employment in Member States, while Article 39 envisaged the adoption of social security measures for Turkish workers by the Association Council within a year of the Protocol coming into force. The Association Council has adopted a number of decisions to implement the provisions in the Ankara Agreement and Additional Protocol.

In *Demirel*[79] the ECJ considered the Ankara Agreement and Additional Protocol for the first time and held that, as in *Haegeman*,[80] they were an integral part of EU law and as such the ECJ had jurisdiction to interpret them,[81] particularly in respect of the freedom of movement of workers.[82] This was extended to Association Council Decisions in *Sevince*.[83] However, Article 12 of the Ankara Agreement and Article 36 of the Protocol were held in *Demirel* to set out a programme and not be sufficiently clear, precise and unconditional to be directly effective.[84] The ECJ has yet to rule on the expiry of the full implementation of freedom of movement for workers timescale, although Advocate General Darmon, in his Opinion in *Demirel*,[85] believed it had no legal implications of binding effect.

No provisions in the Ankara Agreement, the Additional Protocol or the Association Council Decisions establish a right of entry for Turkish nationals. Thus, a Member State may regulate the entry of Turkish workers to its territory, and the conditions under which they may take up their first employment.[86] It is notable, unlike in *Tum and Dari*, that there is no equivalent 'standstill' clause for the free movement of workers to Article 41(1) for freedom of establishment so Member States can introduce new restrictive measures for the first entry of Turkish workers.

The first Association Council Decision relevant to the question of the free movement of workers was Decision 2/76,[87] adopted as a first step with a duration of four years. Under Article 2, a Turkish worker who had been in legal employment for three years in a Member State could respond to an offer of employment from an employer in the same occupation, subject to the priority of nationals of Member States. Furthermore, after five years of legal employment in a Member State, a Turkish worker was free to take any paid employment in the Member State without limitation. Article 5 established an employment hierarchy

---

79 Case 12/86 *Meryem Demirel v Stadt Schwäbisch Gmünd* [1987] ECR 3719; noted in N Neuwahl 'Freedom of movement for workers under the EEC Treaty association agreement' (1988) 13 *ELR* 360.
80 *Haegeman* (n 4).
81 *Demirel* (n 79) para 7.
82 ibid para 12.
83 Case C–192/89 *SZ Sevince v Staatssecretaris van Justitie* [1990] ECR I–3461 paras 7–12.
84 *Demirel* (n 79) para 23.
85 ibid; Opinion of AG Darmon para 23.
86 Case C–237/91 *Kazim Kus v Landeshauptstadt Wiesbaden* [1992] ECR I–6781, noted in N Burrows 'The rights of Turkish workers in the Member States' (1994) 19 *ELR* 305; A Weber 'Case note' (1994) 31 *CMLRev* 423. See also H Lichtenberg 'The rights of Turkish workers in Community law' (1995) 24 *ILJ* 90.
87 See Rogers *A Practitioner's Guide* (n 39) 53.

of nationals of Member States, Turkish workers and then other TCNs. The standstill provisions of Article 7 prohibited Member States from introducing new restrictions on legally resident and employed workers' conditions of access to employment.

Decision 2/76 was replaced on 1 December 1980 by Decision 1/80, which is unconstrained by a time limit on applicability. The provisions constitute 'one stage further . . . towards securing freedom of movement for workers' and to achieve this aim it is 'essential to transpose . . . the principles in Articles [46, 47 and 48] of the [TFEU] to Turkish workers who enjoy the rights conferred by Decision 1/80'.[88] Various provisions of Decision 1/80 have consistently been held to be directly effective[89] and capable of establishing rights for Turkish nationals resident in Member States' territory.

Article 6 was the first provision of Decision 1/80 to be considered by the ECJ and has repeatedly been held to be capable of having direct effect.[90] A Turkish national may obtain rights by satisfying three main conditions:[91] being a worker and in legal employment; being duly registered as belonging to the labour force; and being legally employed for one of three specified time periods. No definition of 'worker' is provided but the ECJ has equated the concept of a 'Turkish worker' with that of 'EU worker'.[92] Thus in *Kurz*[93] the Court found that:

> . . . [a]ny person who, even in the course of vocational training and whatever the legal context of that training, pursues a genuine and effective economic activity for and under the direction of an employer and on that basis receives remuneration which can be perceived as the consideration for that activity must be regarded as a worker for the purposes of Community law.

If a Turkish national enters the host Member State for another purpose but then takes up employment and satisfies the second and third conditions then he or she can rely on Article 6(1).[94] 'Legal employment' is an EU concept that must be 'defined objectively and uniformly in the light of the spirit and the purpose of the provision'.[95] 'The legality of employment . . . must be determined in the light of the legislation of the host State governing the conditions under which the Turkish worker entered the national territory and is employed there.'[96] It has

88  Case C–434/93 *Ahmet Bozkurt v Statssecretaris van Justitie* [1995] ECR I–1475 paras 19–20, noted in S Peers 'Case note' (1996) 33 *CMLRev* 103.
89  *Sevince* (n 83) para 21.
90  *Sevince* (n 83) para 26; *Kus* (n 86) para 28.
91  See Rogers *A Practitioner's Guide* (n 39) 17.
92  Case C–1/97 *Mehmet Birden v Stadtgemeinde Bremen* [1998] ECR I–7747 paras 24–25; noted in D Martin 'Case note' (1999) 1 *EJML* 151. See also Case C–14/09 *Hava Genc v Land Berlin* [2010] ECR I–931 para 18.
93  Case C–188/00 *Bülent Kurz, né Yüce v Land Baden-Württemberg* [2002] ECR I–10691 para 34.
94  Case C–294/06 *R (on the application of Ezgi Payir, Burhan Akyuz and Birol Ozturk) v Secretary of State for the Home Department* [2008] ECR I–203 para 38.
95  Case C–98/96 *Kasim Ertanir v Land Hessen* [1997] ECR I–5179 para 59; noted in G Brinkmann 'Case note' (1999) 1 *EJML* 131.
96  *Bozkurt* (n 88) para 27.

consistently been held to 'presuppose a stable and secure situation as a member of the labour force',[97] thus 'there must be an undisputed right of residence, for any dispute as to that right must lead to instability in the worker's situation'.[98] As such the worker must not have entered the Member State on false documentation, nor have entered employment fraudulently.[99] However, having legally entered the Member State, taken up employment and completed one of the time requirements in Article 6(1), a Member State cannot limit the rights obtained under this provision, even where these limitations were a precondition for the issue of a residence permit.[100] Indeed, the issuing of a residence or work permit is purely administrative, not a condition precedent,[101] and legal employment in a Member State implies a right of residence, as without it Article 6(1) would be deprived of all effect.[102] Where a Turkish worker requires the time from refusal of a residence permit to his appeal hearing to bring him within Article 6(1), he will be considered to have failed to meet the requirements of 'legal employment'.[103] Thus he must find legal employment before his application for a residence permit has been determined.

'Being duly registered as belonging to the labour force' has no equivalent meaning for Union workers, as it does not appear in the TFEU. To satisfy this criterion three further conditions are required. First, the worker must be in an employment relationship or available for work. The ECJ has interpreted the first section of this requirement broadly and in line with the meaning of 'worker' and 'employed person' in EU jurisprudence.[104] However, where the Turkish worker 'has definitely ceased to belong to the labour force of a Member State', either by reaching retirement age or becoming totally and permanently incapacitated for work, then the rights obtained under Article 6(1) are forfeited, including the right of residence.[105] The right of residence that he claims has no link even with future employment.[106] Where the worker is temporarily incapacitated, then providing the break remains temporary, it will not affect his fitness to continue to exercise his right to work. This may include a short provision of prison detention.[107] Secondly, the worker must be engaged in employment which can be located within the territory of the Member State or retain a sufficiently close link with that territory. The ECJ has held that this is a matter for national courts to determine. However,

97 *Birden* (n 92) para 30.
98 Rogers *A Practitioner's Guide* (n 39) 19.
99 Case C–285/95 *Suat Kol v Land Berlin* [1997] ECR I–3069.
100 Case C–36/96 *Faik Günaydin v Freistaat Bayern* [1997] ECR I–5143 paras 37–39; *Ertanir* (n 95) para 56. See also Case C–187/10 *Baris Unal v Staatssecretaris van Justitie* (ECJ 29 September 2011); Case C–268/11 *Atilla Gülbahce v Freie und Hansestadt Hamburg* (ECJ 8 November 2012).
101 *Bozkurt* (n 88) para 29.
102 *Birden* (n 92) para 20.
103 *Sevince* (n 83) para 32; *Kus* (n 86) para 15.
104 See Case 53/81 *DM Levin v Staatssecretaris van Justitie* [1982] ECR 1035; Case 139/85 *RH Kempf v Staatssecretaris van Justitie* [1986] ECR 1741; Case C–292/89 *R v IAT ex parte Gustaff Desiderius Antonissen* [1991] ECR I–745.
105 *Bozkurt* (n 88) para 39.
106 ibid para 40.
107 Case C–340/97 *Ömer Nazli and Others v Stadt Nürnberg* [2000] ECR I–957 paras 37–42.

three non-exhaustive factors can be taken into account: where the worker was hired; the territory on which the paid employment was based; and the applicable national legislation in the field of employment and social security law.[108] Thirdly, the worker must have completed the formalities applicable under national law.

The third main condition for qualification for direct rights is the fulfilment of specific time periods of legal employment. Article 6(1) first indent provides for the renewal of the Turkish worker's work permit when he has been legally employed with the same employer[109] for one year. The second indent establishes that the Turkish worker may, after three years' legal employment, change employers and respond to any offer of employment 'for the same occupation'. As yet there is no ECJ jurisprudence on the meaning of this latter term. The third indent entitles the Turkish worker, after four years of legal employment, to free access to any paid employment in that Member State. In the case of *Kurz*,[110] where Mr Kurz had entered Germany on a visa only for the purpose of vocational training which had subsequently been amended to vocational training with a specific employer and he had then worked for that employer for an uninterrupted period of greater than four years, he enjoyed the right of free access to any paid employment and a corresponding right of residence. Furthermore, if a Turkish worker subsequently becomes unemployed, he may claim an extension to his residence authorisation to exercise his right of free access to any paid employment of his choice 'not only by responding to job offers actually made but also by seeking a new job over a reasonable period'.[111]

Article 6(2) provides for periods of annual holidays, maternity leave, absence caused by accidents at work or short illnesses to be treated as legal employment, to which the ECJ has added short periods without a valid residence or work permit.[112] In *Sedef*[113] the Court found that periods of unemployment that were due to breaks between individual fixed-term contracts of employment in the merchant navy were not under the control of Mr Sedef and therefore were the same kind of interruptions in employment laid down in Article 6(2).[114] Long absences owing to sickness or periods of involuntary unemployment are not treated as legal employment, but rights already obtained as the result of previous employment are not affected. Article 6(2) only applies whilst Article 6(1) applies restrictions to employment.[115] Once a Turkish worker has satisfied the conditions laid down in Article 6(1) third indent then Article 6(2) becomes redundant. In that situation national authorities can only restrict the rights provided for by the third indent of Article 6(1) on the basis of Article 14(1),[116] to be considered below.

---

108 *Bozkurt* (n 88) paras 23–24.
109 See Case C–386/95 *Süleyman Eker v Land Baden-Württemberg* [1997] ECR I–2697.
110 *Kurz* (n 93) para 58.
111 ibid para 59; Case C–171/95 *Recep Tetik v Land Berlin* [1997] ECR I–329 para 48.
112 *Payir* (n 94).
113 Case C–230/03 *Mehmet Sedef v Freie und Hansestadt Hamburg* [2006] ECR I–157.
114 ibid para 55.
115 Case C–383/03 *Ergül Dogan v Sicherheitsdirektion für das Bundesland Vorarlberg* [2005] ECR I–6237 para 16.
116 ibid para 23.

As with Article 6, the ECJ has consistently found Article 7 to be sufficiently clear, precise and unconditional to have direct effect within the Member States.[117] Decision 1/80 does not specify a nationality condition for family members[118] and therefore family members of a Turkish worker may obtain the rights of Article 7 regardless of nationality.[119] There is no right to family reunification, as the entry of a Turkish worker's family to the territory of a Member State is dependent on domestic law, subject to the observance of fundamental rights and in particular Article 8 ECHR.[120] However, the Court has found that the aim of Article 7 is 'to create conditions conducive to family unity in the host Member State, first by enabling family members to be with the migrant worker and then after some time by consolidating their position there by granting them the right to obtain employment in that State'.[121] To achieve this, Article 7(1) provides employment rights directly to family members of the Turkish worker after a specific time of residence, which domestic law may require to be evidenced by cohabitation with the worker.[122] There is then a necessarily implied right of residence,[123] with residence and work permits having only administrative application.[124] Thus, a member of a Turkish workers' family can respond to any employment offer after three years of legal residence, subject to the priority of an EU worker, and without any conditions attached to residence.[125] That legal residence will not depend on the worker being employed for those three years; only that the worker continues to be duly registered as belonging to the labour force of the host Member State for the whole period.[126] Furthermore, after five years of legal residence workers have free access to any paid employment of their choice, again without any conditions attached relating to residence.[127] The rights provided by Article 7(1) will be retained by the family members of the Turkish national even if they attain nationality of the host Member State whilst retaining their Turkish nationality[128] or if the same family member marries within the timescales of Article 7(1) but continues to live under the roof of the Turkish national.[129] Once a family member has acquired

---

117 Case C–355/93 *Hayriye Eroglu v Land Baden-Württemburg* [1994] ECR I–5113 para 17; noted in M Zuleeg 'Case note' (1996) 33 *CMLRev* 93; Case C–351/95 *Selma Kadiman v Freistaat Bayern* [1997] ECR I–2133 para 28.

118 For an analysis of the case law on family members see AP van der Mei 'The *Bozkurt*-interpretation rule and the legal status of family members of Turkish workers under Decision 1/80 of the EEC-Turkey Association Council' (2009) 11 *EJML* 367.

119 Case C–451/11 *Natthaya Dülger v Wetteraukreis* [2012] 3 CMLR 50.

120 Case C–325/05 *Ismail Derin v Landkreis Darmstadt-Dieburg* [2007] ECR I–6495 para 64.

121 Case C–275/02 *Engin Ayaz v Land Baden-Württemberg* [2004] ECR I–8765 para 41; *Kadiman* (n 117) paras 34–36.

122 *Ayaz* (n 121) para 40.

123 *Eroglu* (n 117) para 20.

124 Case C–329/97 *Sezgin Ergat v Stadt Ulm* [2000] ECR I–1487 para 61.

125 Case C–373/03 *Ceyhun Aydinli v Land Baden-Württemburg* [2005] ECR I–6181 para 24.

126 Case C–337/07 *Ibrahim Altun v Stadt Böblingen* [2008] ECR I–10323 para 32.

127 Case C–453/07 *Hakan Er v Wetteraukreis* [2008] ECR I–7299 para 28.

128 Joined Cases C–7 & 9/10 *Staatssecretaris van Justitie v Tayfun Kahveci and Osman Inan* (ECJ 29 March 2012).

129 Case C–484/07 *Fatma Pehlivan v Staatssecretaris van Justitie* (ECJ 16 June 2011).

the rights under Article 7(1) he or she is independent of the relationship with the Turkish national.[130]

As noted above there is no definition of 'family member' provided in Article 7 but the Court has held[131] that the aim of Article 7 is the same objective as that pursued by Article 10(1) of Regulation 1612/68[132] and as now provided for in Article 2(2) of Directive 2004/38.[133] Therefore, 'family member' in Article 7 is likely to have an analogous definition to that in Article 2(2) of Directive 2004/38.[134] However, in *Dülger* the ECJ notably avoids mentioning Article 2(2) of Directive 2004/38 whilst mentioning other provisions of the directive[135] and employs Article 7 of the Charter of Fundamental Rights on the right to respect for private and family life to support the right to family reunification, no matter the nationality of the family member.[136] Furthermore, where the spouse has been granted a right of entry for the purpose of family unity under Article 7(1), then a period of cohabitation outside of wedlock must be aggregated to that of marriage to establish the appropriate length of residence.[137]

Under Article 7(2), the children of such workers, having completed a course of vocational training in the Member State, may take up any employment in the host state without a length of residence requirement, so long as a parent has been legally resident there for at least three years, which is again a directly effective right.[138] In *Akman*,[139] the ECJ held that the objectives of the two paragraphs in Article 7 were different. Article 7(1) was to facilitate family reunification and thus only intended to benefit family members authorised to join the Turkish worker. Article 7(2) was a more favourable provision than the first, aiming to provide specific treatment for children as opposed to other members of the family in order to assist the objective of the free movement of Turkish workers.[140] As Peers notes,[141] this gives children of Turkish workers two bites of the cherry. The first

---

130  Case C–303/08 *Land Baden-Württemberg v Metin Bozkurt* [2010] ECR I–13445 para 40.
131  *Ayaz* (n 121) para 42.
132  Council Regulation 1612/68/EEC on freedom of movement for workers within the Community [1968] OJ Sp Ed L257/2.
133  European Parliament and Council Directive 2004/38/EC on the right of citizens of the Union and their family members to move and reside freely within the territory of the Member States [2004] OJ L158/77.
134  See *Ayaz* (n 121), where a Turkish worker's stepson was considered to be a family member.
135  *Dülger* (n 119) para 51.
136  ibid para 53.
137  Case C–65/98 *Safet Eyüp v Landesgeschäftstelle des Arbeitsmarktservice Vorarlberg* [2000] ECR I–4747 paras 36–38. This appears to go further than the Union concept of 'spouse' that only applies to marital relationships (Case 59/85 *Netherlands v Ann Florence Reed* [1986] ECR 1283 para 15), although this has now been extended in art 2(2) of Directive 2004/38 and would appear to be in line with this new definition. Advocate General La Pergola at paras 13–24, had suggested a rethink of the Union definition of the term 'spouse' to take into account art 8 ECHR jurisprudence and provide rights for cohabitees but the Court did not consider this.
138  *Eroglu* (n 117) para 17; Case C–502/04 *Ergün Torun v Stadt Augsburg* [2006] ECR I–1563 para 19; Case C–462/08 *Ümit Bekleyen v Land Berlin* [2010] ECR I–5053 para 16.
139  Case C–210/97 *Haydar Akman v Oberkreisdirektor des Rheinisch-Bergischen-Kreises* [1998] ECR I– 7519; noted in S Peers 'Case note' (1999) 39 *CMLRev* 1027; D Martin 'Case note' (1999) 1 *EJML* 150.
140  ibid para 38.
141  Peers 'Case note' (n 139) 1037.

is where they fail to complete their vocational training, or a parent has yet to complete three years' employment. In this situation, they may have rights under Article 7(1), subject to compliance with its provisions. However, where children are born in a Member State they can only obtain rights under Article 7(2). In order to benefit from the provisions of Article 7(2), the parent of the child need not still be in employment or even be resident in the Member State.[142]

The Court has held that there are only two kinds of restrictions on the rights conferred by Article 7.[143] The first is that laid down in Article 14(1), to be considered below, and the second is where the individual has left the territory of the host Member State for a significant length of time without a legitimate reason. A custodial sentence[144] or a period of drug rehabilitation[145] does not permit the rights conferred by Article 7 to be limited.

For some time Article 9 suffered from a lack of judicial interpretation from the ECJ, although the right created was potentially extensive. The first sentence provides that a Turkish child residing legally with his or her parents in a Member State, who are or have been legally employed in that Member State 'will be admitted to courses of general education, apprenticeship and vocational training under the same educational entry qualifications as the children of nationals of the Member States'. In *Gürol*[146] the ECJ held that this first sentence of Article 9 was directly effective and that a Turkish child who was residing legally with his Turkish parents but on commencement of his studies transferred his residence to the place of his educational establishment, was meeting the residence conditions laid down in Article 9.[147] Thus, the first sentence of Article 9 confers a 'right of access without discrimination to education and training'[148] for a Turkish child living away from his or her parents with, as Peers suggests,[149] a right of residence[150] at the place of the educational or training institute. Furthermore, the personal scope of Article 9 is wider than Article 7(1), incorporating the situation envisaged by Article 7(2). However, the right did not appear to provide for equal treatment with EU nationals over maintenance grants or tuition fees as entry was limited to the 'same educational qualifications' rather than the 'same conditions'[151] as laid down in Regulation 492/11 Article 10.[152] Moreover, according to the second

---

142 *Akman* (n 139) paras 47–48; *Bekleyen* (n 138) para 31.
143 Case C–467/02 *Inan Cetinkaya v Land Baden-Württemberg* [2004] ECR I–10895 para 36 and *Aydinli* (n 125) para 27 for art 7(1) and *Torun* (n 138) para 25 for art 7(2).
144 *Torun* (n 138) para 26; Case C–325/05 *Ismail Derin v Landkreis Darmstadt-Dieburg* [2007] ECR I–6495 para 56.
145 *Derin* (n 144) para 28.
146 Case C–374/03 *Gaye Gürol v Bezirksregierung Köln* [2005] ECR I–6199 paras 20–26.
147 ibid para 29.
148 *Akman* (n 139) para 41.
149 Peers 'Case note' (n 139) 1040.
150 Cf Case C–357/89 *VJM Raulin v Netherlands Ministry for Education and Science* [1992] ECR I–1027 discussed in ch 3.
151 See Case 9/74 *Donato Casagrande v Landeshaupstadt München* [1974] ECR 773 in ch 3 where the ECJ's interpretation of this term is examined.
152 S Peers 'Towards equality: actual and potential rights of third-country nationals in the European Union' (1996) 33 *CMLRev* 7, 26.

sentence of Article 9, Turkish children 'may in that Member State be eligible to benefit from advantages provided for in national legislation' that did not appear to be sufficiently clear, precise or unconditional to exercise direct effect. The Court in *Gürol* interpreted the provision very widely. It found that the second sentence of Article 9 was directly effective[153] and that where the legislation of a Member State provides for educational advantages, such as grants, 'intended to cover the costs of the student's access to education and maintenance, Turkish nationals may be entitled to them in just the same way as the nationals of the Member State'.[154] Although the Court used the word 'may' it made it clear that non-discriminatory access for Turkish children to courses of education or training would be purely illusory if they were not assured equal rights to advantages such as grants. Furthermore, the interpretation provided by the ECJ was the only one that made it possible to attain the objective laid down in Article 9 to guarantee equal opportunities for both Turkish and Member State national children in the sphere of education and vocational training.[155] Finally, the Court concluded that this right of equal treatment applied even when education was pursued in Turkey.[156]

Under Article 10, where a Turkish worker is duly registered as belonging to the labour force,[157] the Member State must not discriminate over remuneration and other conditions of work on the basis of nationality. Article 10(1) is directly effective[158] and when determining the scope of Article 10, reference should be made to the equivalent provision of the TFEU, namely Article 45(2)[159] and the case law associated with it. Furthermore, although Article 10(1) does not establish a principle of free movement of Turkish workers within the EU, once a Turkish worker is legally employed within the territory of a Member State, Article 10(1) provides a right of equal treatment to Turkish workers as regards conditions of work and remuneration to the same extent as Article 45(2) TFEU provides for Member State nationals.[160] As Advocate General Bot points out in *Gülbache*,[161] Article 10(1) only comes into play if the Turkish worker has satisfied the conditions in Article 6(1). It does not create a right of access to the territory of the host Member State or a complementary right of residence.[162] Article 10(2) also provides that Turkish workers and their family members must be granted the same assistance as EU workers from the employment services to obtain employment.

---

153　*Gürol* (n 146) para 43.
154　ibid para 38.
155　ibid paras 39, 40.
156　ibid para 44.
157　See Case C–4/05 *Hasan Güzeli v Oberbürgermeister der Stadt Aachen* [2006] ECR I–10279 para 48, where the ECJ held that the term 'duly registered as belonging to the labour market of the Member State' had the same meaning as that laid down in art 6(1).
158　Case C–171/01 *Wählergruppe 'Gemeinsam Zajedno/Birlikte Alternative und Grüne GewerkschafterInnen/UG' and Others* [2003] ECR I–4301 at paras 57, 58.
159　ibid paras 73, 74.
160　ibid para 89.
161　*Gülbahce* (n 100); Opinion of AG Bot para 76.
162　ibid paras 77–80.

Article 13 is a standstill provision that prohibits the Member States and Turkey from introducing new restrictions on access to employment conditions applicable to workers and family members.[163] In *Sevince*[164] the ECJ found this standstill clause and Article 7 of Decision 2/76 to be 'unequivocal' and to have direct effect. Thus, a Turkish worker may enjoy the conditions of access to employment as they applied on 20 December 1976, as Decision 1/80 simply reiterates Decision 2/76's standstill provision for workers. However, family members may only rely on the conditions as they stood on 1 December 1980, as they were not incorporated in Decision 2/76. Article 13 does not require the acquisition of rights under Articles 6 or 7[165] and so applies to Turkish nationals who do not yet qualify for the employment and residence rights of Article 6[166] or, it has been suggested, who no longer benefit from them.[167] Rogers goes on to suggest that it is those who do not enjoy 'a stable and secure position in the labour force' who would benefit. These would include asylum seekers with work permission and a Turkish national married to a settled Turkish worker whose marriage ended within a year of legal employment. In these situations the introduction of administrative charges for residence permits or the extension of residence permits that are disproportionate as compared with those paid by EU nationals is precluded.[168] Furthermore, Member States are not permitted to tighten provisions for Turkish nationals that can be equivalent to a 'new restriction'.[169]

Article 14(1) uses almost identical wording to that found in Article 45(3) TFEU. Thus, the provisions of Decision 1/80 are to be applied 'subject to limitations justified on grounds of public policy, public security or public health' and in *Nazli*[170] the ECJ interpreted the provision analogously to Article 45(3) TFEU.[171] The concept of public policy therefore presupposes the existence of a genuine and sufficiently serious threat to one of the fundamental interests of society.[172] As the provision is a derogation from the basic rules laid down in the agreement, it must be interpreted restrictively. Thus, a criminal conviction can only justify expulsion if the circumstances leading to that conviction are evidence of personal conduct constituting a personal threat to the requirements of public policy.[173] The concept of public policy 'presupposes the existence, in addition to the pertur-

163 In *Abatay* (n 49) para 70 the ECJ held that the art 13 standstill clause was to have the same meaning as art 41(1) of the Additional Protocol.
164 *Sevince* (n 83) paras 18, 26.
165 *Abatay* (n 49) paras 75–84; Case C–242/06 *Minister voor Vreemdelingenzaken en Integratie v T Sahin* [2009] ECR I–8465 para 50.
166 *Sahin* (n 165) para 51.
167 Rogers *A Practitioner's Guide* (n 39) 28.
168 *Sahin* (n 165); Case 92/07 *Commission v Netherlands* [2010] ECR I–3683; noted in A Hoogenboom 'Moving forward by standing still? First admission of Turkish workers: comment on *Commission v Netherlands* (Administrative Fees)' (2010) 35 *ELR* 707.
169 Joined Cases C–300 & 301/09 *Staatssecretaris van Justitie v F Toprak and I Oguz* [2010] ECR I–12845.
170 *Nazli* (n 107) paras 56, 60.
171 See *Polydor* (n 6).
172 Case 30/77 *R v Pierre Bouchereau* [1977] ECR 1999 para 35.
173 *Nazli* (n 107) para 58.

bation of the social order which any infringement of the law involves, of a genuine and sufficiently serious threat to a fundamental interest of society'.[174] Thus expulsion of an EU or Turkish national is precluded on general preventive grounds in order to deter other aliens.[175] 'A Turkish national can be denied, by means of expulsion, the rights which he derives from Decision 1/80 only if that measure is justified because his personal conduct indicates a specific risk of new and serious prejudice to the requirements of public policy'.[176] Furthermore, as the Court has interpreted Article 14(1) analogously to Article 45(3) TFEU, it has also found that the provisions of Directive 64/221 are to be applied[177] to both Turkish workers and their family members such that protection must be no lower than that laid down in Articles 8 and 9 of Directive 64/221.[178] Directive 2004/38 has repealed Directive 64/221 and Chapter VI incorporates similar provisions to Directive 64/221 as well as the ECJ's case law (see Chapter 3) and so it would be logical to believe that this would also apply to Turkish nationals, especially as it was adopted with the intention of bringing together and updating the previous law. However, in *Ziebell*[179] the ECJ found that it was not possible to equate it with Article 14(1) as the EEC-Turkey Agreement 'pursues a purely economic objective and is restricted to the gradual achievement of the free movement of workers',[180] whilst Directive 2004/38 on the basis of the very concept of citizenship itself justified the limitation of Chapter VI to Union citizens alone.[181] As Peers points out, this is highly questionable reasoning as the directive applies to EEA nationals and TCN family members as well as Union citizens.[182] The Court went on to attempt to provide guidance for the interpretation of Article 14(1) by first equating the position of a Turkish national who had resided lawfully and consistently with the minimum protection against expulsion for any LTR TCN set out in Article 12 of Directive 2003/109.[183] The conditions then are set out by the ECJ: first, the LTR concerned can only be expelled where he/she constitutes a genuine and sufficiently serious threat to public policy or public security; secondly, economic considerations cannot provide the basis for the expulsion decision; and, thirdly, before a decision is taken the host state's competent authorities must take account of the duration of residence, the age of the person, the consequences of expulsion for that person and family members, links with the country of residence or lack of

---

174  Case C–349/06 *Murat Polat v Stadt Rüsselsheim* [2007] ECR I–8167 para 34.
175  ibid para 35; *Nazli* (n 107) para 59; Case 67/74 *Carmelo Angelo Bonsignore v Oberstadtdirektor der Stadt Köln* [1975] ECR 297 para 7.
176  *Nazli* (n 107) para 61; *Dogan* (n 115) para 24; *Derin* (n 120) para 74.
177  *Cetinkaya* (n 143) para 44; *Polat* (n 174) para 31 where the Court referred to art 3 of Directive 64/221.
178  Case C–136/03 *Georg Dörr v Sicherheitsdirektion für das Bundesland Kärnten* and *Ibrahim Ünul v Sicherheitsdirektion für das Bundesland Vorarlberg* [2005] ECR I–4759 para 68.
179  Case C–371/08 *Nural Ziebell v Land Baden-Württemberg* [2012] 2 CMLR 35 para 60; noted in S Peers 'Expulsion of Turkish citizens: a backward step by the Court of Justice' (2012) 26 *JIANL* 56.
180  ibid para 72.
181  ibid para 74.
182  Peers 'Expulsion of Turkish citizens' (n 179) 61.
183  *Ziebell* (n 179) para 79.

links with the country of residence.[184] The Court then went on to reiterate its previous case law on Article 14(1),[185] which was the equivalent of that for Directive 64/221, to provide a further set of criteria as guidance for national courts. Finally, the national court would have to weigh up the planned interference with the individual's right of residence in order to safeguard the legitimate interest pursued by the host Member State against actual integration factors enabling that person to reintegrate into society in the host Member State.[186] The result is extremely confusing for Turkish nationals and for domestic courts. As the provisions of Directive 2004/38 do not apply then it is the previous case law from Directive 64/221 that provides the criteria for guidance for domestic courts, thus creating a ghost legislative situation as Directive 64/221 has been repealed. Equating Article 14(1) with Article 12 of Directive 2003/109 appears illogical, confused and 'in principle objectionable',[187] as it suggests there is no difference between Turkish nationals under the Ankara Agreement and LTR TCNs, which is clearly against the objectives of the Ankara Agreement.

Article 39 of the Protocol envisaged the Association Council adopting social security measures for Turkish workers and their families within a year of the Protocol coming into effect. The subject area is highly sensitive politically and so only over a decade later did the Association Council belatedly complete its task. As with Regulation 1408/71, Decision 3/80 aims to coordinate the social security schemes of Member States to enable Turkish workers employed or formerly employed in the Union, their family members, and survivors to qualify for benefits. As Peers[188] points out, Decision 3/80 is closely connected to Regulation 1408/71, either by copying large portions of it or incorporating provisions by making reference to it. Regulation 1408/71 required an extremely lengthy and detailed implementing measure, namely Regulation 574/72, to give it effect. The Commission waited three years before submitting a proposed regulation to implement Decision 3/80, which the Council promptly refused to adopt.[189] The resulting ECJ case law has proved controversial.

In *Taflan-Met*[190] the ECJ, on a request for a preliminary ruling, was asked to rule on the applicability and direct effect of Decision 3/80 without an implementing measure. The ECJ held that, on the first point, decisions of the Association Council were binding without any further implementing measures. Therefore, Decision 3/80 came into force on the date on which it was adopted, 19 September 1980, and the Contracting Parties had been bound by it from that date.[191]

---

184  ibid para 80.
185  ibid paras 81–84.
186  ibid para 85.
187  Peers 'Expulsion of Turkish citizens' (n 179) 61.
188  S Peers 'Social security equality for Turkish nationals' (1999) 24 *ELR* 624, 625.
189  Commission proposal for a Council Regulation to implement Decision 3/80 COM(1983) 13 final.
190  Case C–277/94 *Z̧ Taflan-Met and Others v Bestuur van de Social Verzekeringsbank* and *O Akol v Bestuur van de Algemene Bedrijfsvereniging* [1996] ECR I–4085; noted in M Bulterman 'Case note' (1997) 34 *CMLRev* 1497; S Peers 'Equality, free movement and social security' (1997) 22 *ELR* 342.
191  *Taflan-Met* (n 190) paras 17–21.

However, on the matter of direct effect, the ECJ held that although some provisions of Decision 3/80 were sufficiently clear and precise, they could not be directly effective until the Council had adopted supplementary measures.[192] It is clear from the judgment, and is suggested by extrajudicial writing,[193] that the ECJ intended for no provision of Decision 3/80 to have direct effect. Thus, even the non-discrimination provision of Article 3(1) guaranteeing equal access for Turkish claimants as with EU claimants to their host state's security system was not directly effective.[194]

Three years later in *Sürül*[195] the ECJ was invited to reconsider its judgment in *Taflan-Met* by ruling on the direct effect of Article 3(1). The ECJ first distinguished *Taflan-Met* by finding that the previous ruling had not considered Article 3(1). Indeed, it was found that an implementing measure was not required to give Article 3(1) direct effect,[196] it simply being the specific enunciation of the non-discrimination principle in Article 9 of the Protocol,[197] thereby enabling it to be relied on by Turkish nationals.[198] The Court's interpretation, especially considering the apparent categorical nature of the requirement of implementing measures in *Taflan-Met*, was bold, imaginative and far more in keeping with the spirit of Decision 3/80. The ECJ then defined the personal scope of Article 3(1) broadly, equating Decision 3/80 with Regulation 1408/71 to establish whether Mrs Sürül was a worker or the family member of a worker. As such, under the case law of Regulation 1408/71,[199] a person has the status of a worker where he is covered, even if only in respect of a single risk, by a social security scheme, irrespective of an employment relationship.[200] Mrs Sürül would also be covered when she was not affiliated to a social security scheme as a member of the family of a Turkish worker if Mr Sürül was likewise insured for just one risk.[201] The ECJ then conventionally applied the non-discrimination principle to the German requirement for Turkish nationals to produce a residence document to obtain social security, unlike German nationals.[202] Finally, the ECJ found that as this was the first time the ECJ had had to interpret Article 3(1) and because the *Taflan-Met* judgment may have created uncertainty the temporal effect of the judgment would be restricted.[203]

---

192  ibid para 37.
193  D Edward 'Direct effect, the separation of powers and the judicial enforcement of obligations' in C Gulman (ed) *Scritti in Onore di Federico Mancini, Volume II* (Guiffrè 1998) 423, 436–37. Judge Edward's opinion carries considerable weight, as he was also the *Judge-Rapporteur* responsible for drafting the judgment.
194  Peers 'Social security' (n 188) 626.
195  *Sürül* (n 42).
196  ibid paras 55–58.
197  ibid para 68.
198  ibid para 63.
199  Case C–85/96 *María Martínez Sala v Freistaate Bayern* [1998] ECR I–2691 para 36; Case C–275/96 *Anne Kuusijärvi v Riksförsäkringsverket* [1998] ECR I–3419 para 21 (see ch 3).
200  *Sürül* (n 42) para 93.
201  ibid para 94.
202  ibid paras 101–102.
203  ibid paras 109–111.

A Turkish national would appear, therefore, to be able to rely in national courts on the direct effect of Article 3(1) but would not be able to rely on other provisions of Decision 3/80 without supplementary implementing measures. Indeed, Advocate General Colomer has suggested that Decision 3/80 Article 3(1) should be interpreted in the same way as Regulation 1408/71 Article 3(1), as Article 37 of the Protocol was very similar to Article 45(2) TFEU.[204] The position, however, remains politically sensitive, which the ECJ is aware of. As such the two explanations that the Court used to justify its temporal limitations to judgments in *Sürül* appear to be novel adaptations of its previous practices. As Peers points out, however, this reasoning is problematic. The principles underlying the two reasons appear to be contradictory in that the first reason justifies a new line of case law by the Court and the second justifies a marked change in direction in existing case law. Furthermore, the first reason is surprising as the Court is often called upon to interpret provisions of EU law for the first time and the second reason, for the first time, justifies temporal limitations on the basis of uncertainty 'for which the Court is wholly responsible'.[205] Now that the ECJ has extended the reasoning for temporal limitations, this practice is likely to continue, limiting the rights of Turkish nationals to social security benefits. This ambiguity is likely to lead to confusion and uncertainty and, as a direct consequence, an ever-burgeoning case law. It is submitted, however, that the outcome in *Sürül* is to be preferred to that in *Taflan-Met*.

In *Öztürk*[206] the Court held that a Turkish national who had previously worked and paid old-age insurance contributions in Austria, but who had then worked and now resided in Germany, could rely on Article 3(1) against the Austrian authorities to secure his entitlement to a pension based on the periods of insurance completed by him in Austria.

In *Akdas*[207] the ECJ took a bold step forward by declaring the first paragraph of Article 6(1) of Decision 3/80, which prohibits any restriction on the export of rights acquired by Turkish nationals under the host Member State's legislation, as being directly effective.[208] Furthermore, if benefits are obtained under a Member State's legislation and the Turkish national has to return involuntarily to Turkey,[209] then those benefits retain their portability and can still be claimed from Turkey.[210]

The EU enacted Regulation 859/03[211] to extend the coverage of Regulation 1408/71 to all TCNs, family members and survivors not covered by the latter

---

204 *Kocak* (n 45); Opinion of AG Colomer para 43.

205 Peers 'Social security' (n 188) 630.

206 *Öztürk* (n 46).

207 Case C–485/07 *Rand van bestuur van het Uitvoeringsinstituut werknemersverzekeringen v H Akdas and Others* [2011] ECR I–4499; noted in K Eisele, AP van der Mei 'Portability of social benefits and reverse discrimination of EU citizens vis-à-vis Turkish nationals: comment on *Akdas*' (2012) 37 *ELR* 204.

208 ibid para 69.

209 ibid para 94.

210 ibid para 88.

211 Council Regulation 859/03/EC extending the provisions of Regulation 1408/71/EEC and Regulation 574/72/EEC to nationals of third countries who are not already covered by these provisions solely on the ground of their nationality [2003] OJ L124/1.

regulation's provisions solely on the basis of nationality, with further measures adopted to replace both regulations.[212] However, a cross-border EU nexus must be established before the new provisions can bite. Thus Decision 3/80, with its inconsistent case law, will retain its importance for those Turkish nationals who only have links with Turkey and the host Member State. In 2012 the Commission put forward a proposal[213] that was accepted by the Council in December 2012[214] for the EU's position on a new regulation to be negotiated in the EU-Turkey Association Council that would see Decision 3/80 repealed and replaced by a new decision. The Commission's aim is 'to provide legal certainty and to give effect to the principles of social security coordination contained in the Ankara Agreement and the Additional Protocol'[215] and it is envisaged that the new decision would not need any further implementing measures. It is expected that this will be on the table for debate at the 51st EU-Turkey Association Council in June 2013.

## 5.4   EEC-Maghreb Agreements

In 1976 the EEC entered into cooperation agreements with Algeria,[216] Morocco[217] and Tunisia,[218] the aim of which was laid down in Article 1 of the agreements to 'promote overall cooperation between the Contracting Parties' in order to assist the Maghreb countries to develop economically and socially. In 1995 the EU negotiated new Euro-Mediterranean Agreements (EMAs) with Tunisia[219] and Morocco.[220] The difficult political situation in Algeria delayed the negotiations for an EMA with Algeria, although a draft EMA was agreed in December 2001 so the 1976 Cooperation Agreement continued to apply. The EMA with Algeria was finally signed in 2005.[221] Peers[222] states that the EMAs do not substantively alter the rules of the cooperation agreements relied on by individuals. However, Martin and Guild[223] suggest that the strengthening of relationships between the parties envisaged in Article 1 might have consequences for the interpretation of some of the provisions. It must be pointed out that, unlike the Ankara Agreement,

---

212   See ch 3 for the complicated situation with social security instruments.
213   Commission proposal for a Council Directive on the position to be taken on behalf of the European Union within the Association Council set up by the Agreement establishing an association between the European Economic Community and Turkey with regard to the provisions on the coordination of social security systems COM(2012) 152 final.
214   Council Decision 2012/776/EU on the position to be taken on behalf of the European Union within the Association Council set up by the Agreement establishing an association between the European Economic Community and Turkey, with regard to the adoption of provisions on the coordination of social security systems [2012] OJ L340/19.
215   Commission proposal (n 213) 2.
216   Cooperation Agreement – Algeria [1978] OJ L263.
217   Cooperation Agreement – Morocco [1978] OJ L264.
218   Cooperation Agreement – Tunisia [1978] OJ L265.
219   Euro-Mediterranean Agreement – Tunisia [1998] OJ L97.
220   Euro-Mediterranean Agreement – Morocco [2000] OJ L70.
221   Euro-Mediterranean Agreement – Algeria [2005] OJ L265.
222   Peers 'Social security' (n 188) 625.
223   Martin, Guild (eds) *Free Movement of Persons* (n 2) 282.

which had the ultimate objective of Turkish membership of the EU, there is no possibility at the present time of any of the three countries becoming members of the Union. This is a direct consequence of a candidate country needing to be a 'European State' as required in Article 49 TEU. In 2003 the Commission published a Communication[224] on the European neighbour countries with the aim of establishing a policy to 'develop a zone of prosperity and friendly neighbourhood – "a ring of friends" – with whom the EU enjoys close, peaceful and co-operative relations'.[225] The result is the European Neighbourhood Policy (ENP).[226] This involved negotiating action plans for incorporating a set of agreed priorities for action with 16 neighbour countries.[227] With the beginning of the Arab Spring in December 2010 the Commission, alongside the High Representative of the European Union for Foreign Affairs and Security Policy, suggested a new direction for the ENP based on democratic transformation and institution building, a stronger partnership with the people, and sustainable and inclusive growth and economic development.[228] This has resulted in a new approach to the ENP,[229] with the Commission proposing a new financial instrument for all states[230] but which has yet to see any changes to the EMAs.

The EMAs with the Maghreb states are part of this ENP and it is these that will be examined as they are the longest standing of the EU's neighbourhood relationships. The ECJ has not directly addressed the question of whether it has jurisdiction to interpret the agreements, simply presuming from its case law that it does.[231] As the EMAs are predominantly the same, the provisions of the Tunisian EMA will be studied to investigate the rights available to Maghreb nationals and interpret the case law relating to all three countries.

---

224 Commission Communication on wider Europe – neighbourhood: a new framework for relations with our Eastern and Southern neighbours COM(2003) 104 final.
225 ibid 4.
226 Commission Communication on European Neighbourhood Policy: strategy paper COM(2004) 373 final. See RA Del Sarto, T Schumacher 'From EMP to ENP: What's at stake with the European neighbourhood policy towards the southern Mediterranean' (2005) 10 *EFAR* 17; S Pardo, L Zemer 'Towards a new Euro-Mediterranean neighbourhood space' (2005) 10 *EFAR* 39; B van Vooren 'A case-study of "soft law" in EU external relations: the European neighbourhood policy' (2009) 34 *ELR* 696 for analysis of the ENP.
227 Action plans have been agreed with Algeria, Armenia, Azerbaijan, Belarus, Egypt, Georgia, Israel, Jordan, Lebanon, Libya, the Republic of Moldova, Morocco, the occupied Palestinian territory, Syria, Tunisia and Ukraine. Kazakhstan has expressed an interest in the ENP and Russia has opted for an alternative arrangement with the formation of the EU-Russia Common Space for Freedom, Security and Justice.
228 Commission and High Representative of the European Union for Foreign Affairs and Security Policy Joint Communication on a partnership for democracy and shared prosperity with the Southern Mediterranean, COM(2011) 200 final 3.
229 Commission and High Representative of the European Union for Foreign Affairs and Security Policy Joint Communication on a new response to a changing Neighbourhood, COM(2011) 303 final and Commission and High Representative of the European Union for Foreign Affairs and Security Policy Joint Communication on delivering on a new European Neighbourhood Policy JOIN(2012) 14 final.
230 Commission proposal for a Regulation establishing a European Neighbourhood Instrument COM(2011) 839 final.
231 See Case C–18/90 *Office National de l'emploi v Bahia Kziber* [1991] ECR I–199 but for analysis see Opinion of AG van Gerven para 5.

Title III entitled 'Right of Establishment and Services' has been included by the EMA and was not included in the former cooperation agreements. Article 31(1) provides for the reciprocal right of establishment of a firm in the Contracting Party's territory and the 'liberalisation of the provision of services by one Party's firms to consumers in the other'. Article 31(2) empowers the Association Council to make recommendations for achieving this objective. It is submitted that this provision does not have direct effect, Article 31(1) simply outlining a programme and objective, and Article 31(2) authorising the Association Council to implement supporting measures.

The following area in Title VI, called 'Cooperation in Social and Cultural Matters', includes several chapters with Chapter 1 dealing with the position of workers. The agreements provide no definition of the term 'workers' and it is submitted that it should be defined in line with EU jurisprudence.[232] Article 64(1)[233] is a nationality non-discrimination clause regarding working conditions, remuneration and dismissal. Dismissal as a third object of the non-discrimination requirement has been added by the EMA, although this does not apply to temporary workers.[234] Rights under Article 64(1) are attached to the 'worker' status of a Tunisian national not his 'nationality',[235] so a Tunisian national who is not a worker would not be able to take advantage of Article 64(1). The equivalent provision, Article 40, in the old Morocco Cooperation Agreement has been interpreted by the ECJ. In *El-Yassini*,[236] Mr El-Yassini entered the UK on a visitor's permit with a prohibition on employment. In 1990 he married a UK national and the restriction prohibiting his employment was removed the following year. He took up employment but some time later the couple separated. Mr El-Yassini applied for an extension of leave to remain in the UK. The Court[237] held that Article 40 was capable of having direct effect. However, the ECJ then interpreted the scope very narrowly, in particular refusing to apply by analogy the case law of the Ankara Agreement.[238] Thus, the principle of equal treatment as regards working conditions and remuneration in Article 40(1) cannot ipso facto 'have the effect of prohibiting the authorities of the host Member State from refusing to extend the residence permit of a Moroccan migrant worker employed on its territory, even though such a measure could not, by its very nature, be taken against a national of the Member State concerned'.[239] Furthermore, the national authorities can refuse to extend a residence permit, where the initial reason for its issue has expired, even though this may mean the employment contract could be terminated early.[240] However, the

---

232  *Levin, Kempf, Antonissen* (n 104).
233  Article 64(1) for Morocco and art 67(1) for Algeria.
234  Article 64(2).
235  *R v Director of Labour and Social Security, ex parte Mohamed* [1992] 2 CMLR 481 (Supreme Court of Gibraltar) para 20.
236  Case C–416/96 *Nour Eddline El-Yassini v Secretary of State for the Home Department* [1997] ECR I–1209; noted in B Melis 'Case note' (1999) 36 *CMLRev* 1357; N Rogers 'Case note' (1999) 1 *EJML* 365.
237  ibid paras 27–28.
238  ibid para 61.
239  ibid para 46.
240  ibid paras 62–63.

ECJ provided an exception with an example.[241] The exception was where the 'Member State had granted the Moroccan migrant worker specific rights in relation to employment which were more extensive than the rights of residence conferred on him'. For example, where a residence permit is issued for a shorter time than a work permit, the Member State may not refuse to extend the residence permit to cover the temporal effect of the work permit, unless it is for the protection of a legitimate national interest. The extension of the equality principle in Article 64(1) to dismissal may provide a directly effective right to those in a similar position to Mr El-Yassini, thereby allowing the EU case law on residence permits to be applied to Maghreb nationals. In *Gattoussi*[242] the ECJ interpreted Article 64(1) of the Tunisian EMA in the same manner as Article 40(1) of the Moroccan Cooperation Agreement, although the Court provided the non-exhaustive list of public policy, public security and public health as examples of a 'legitimate national interest' that were to be interpreted in accordance with EU case law.[243]

Article 65(1) extends the nationality non-discrimination principle to social security, for workers and their family members. The ECJ has consistently held this provision, as provided for in the corresponding provisions of the cooperation agreements with Morocco (Article 65(1)) and Algeria (Article 68(1)), to be capable of having direct effect[244] and that the previous case law on the cooperation agreements is fully transposable to the EMAs.[245] This broad interpretation has been further extended by the ECJ to the personal and material scope of the provision. The personal scope applies first and foremost[246] or primarily[247] to Algerian, Moroccan or Tunisian nationals, 'which encompasses[248] both active workers and those who have left the labour market, in particular after reaching the age required for receipt of an old-age pension'.[249] Furthermore, the provision 'also applies to members of those workers' families living with them in the Member State in which they are or have been employed'.[250] However, if the worker's dependent children reside outside the Union then neither they nor the worker may claim social security in the form of study finance.[251] The persons covered by

---

241 ibid paras 64–66.
242 Case C–97/05 *Mohamed Gattoussi v Stadt Rüsselsheim* [2006] ECR I–11917.
243 ibid paras 40, 41.
244 *Kziber* (n 231) para 17; Case C–58/93 *Zoubir Yousfi v Belgian State* [1994] ECR I–1353 paras 17–19 (the German request for the ECJ to reconsider *Kziber* was swiftly rejected); Case C–103/94 *Zoulika Krid v Caisse nationale d'assurance vieillesse des travailleurs salariés (CNAVTS)* [1995] ECR I–719 para 24.
245 Case C–336/05 *Ameur Echouikh v Secrétaire d'État aux Anciens Combattants* [2006] ECR I–5223 para 40.
246 Case C–113/97 *Henia Babahenini v Belgian State* [1998] ECR I–183 para 20.
247 Case C–126/95 *A Hallouzi-Choho v Bestuur van de Sociale Verzekeringsbank* [1996] ECR I–4807 para 22; noted in N Burrows 'Non-discrimination and social security in co-operation agreements' (1997) 22 *ELR* 166.
248 *Kziber* (n 231) para 27; *Yousfi* (n 244) para 21; *Krid* (n 244) para 26.
249 *Babahenini* (n 246).
250 ibid para 21.
251 Case C–33/99 *Hassan Fahmi and M Esmoris Cerdeiro-Pinedo Amado v Bestuur van de Sociale Verzekeringsbank* [2001] ECR I–2415 paras 52–58; noted in AP van der Mei 'Freedom of movement and financial aid for students; (2001) 3 *EJSS* 181.

the provision are different from those covered by Article 2 of Regulation 1408/71. As such, the case law distinguishing between derived family rights and personal family rights in the context of Regulation 1408/71 cannot be applied to the EMAs.[252] The material scope of 'social security' is considered to bear the equivalent meaning as the identical term used in Regulation 1408/71.[253] This extremely broad interpretation of the personal scope of Article 65(1) has received what appears to be a partial reversal in *Mesbah*.[254] Mrs Mesbah was the mother-in-law of a Moroccan worker, the latter having acquired Belgian nationality by naturalisation and thereby enjoying dual nationality. Mrs Mesbah claimed disability allowance on the basis of the non-discrimination principle of Article 65(1). The ECJ, in convoluted and difficult reasoning, distinguished and refused to apply by analogy the seminal case of *Micheletti*.[255] In *Micheletti* the Court held that when a migrant worker of Member State nationality held dual nationality, other Member States were not entitled to challenge the worker's use of his status of national of a Member State on the ground that he also held the nationality of a non-Member State. This constituted an unjustified limitation on his right of freedom of movement. However, in *Mesbah* the Court found that there was no objective of creating free movement of Moroccan nationals within the Union but simply to consolidate the social security position of workers and their family members.[256] As such a Member State could prevent a national from relying on his Moroccan dual nationality to take advantage of the principle of equal treatment in Article 65(1) on the sole ground that under domestic legislation the worker is considered to be a national of the Member State alone. Thus, the national court was the appropriate forum to apply its domestic law to determine the nationality of the claimant.[257] As Peers[258] suggests, allowing the claimant to use his Moroccan nationality would have assisted in consolidating the social position of Moroccan workers and their families within the host state. Thus in Union law a national of a Member State with dual nationality may rely on his Member State nationality to take advantage of EU rights but not his non-Member State nationality. The ECJ then ruled that the phrase 'member of the family' was of general application that incorporated relatives in the ascending line and was not confined to blood relatives, thereby including in-laws if they in fact lived with the worker.[259]

---

252   *Krid* (n 244) para 39.
253   *Yousfi* (n 244) para 32; *Krid* (n 244) para 24. See also Case C–23/02 *Office national de l'emploi v Mohamed Alami* [2003] ECR I–1399 confirming previous case law, in particular *Kziber*.
254   Case C–179/98 *Belgium v Fatna Mesbah* [1999] ECR I–7955.
255   Case C–369/90 *Mario Vicente Micheletti and Others v Delegación del Gobierno en Cantabria* [1992] ECR I–4239.
256   *Mesbah* (n 254) para 36.
257   ibid paras 39–41.
258   S Peers 'ILPA European update' December 1999 23.
259   *Mesbah* (n 254) paras 44–46.

## 5.5   EC-CEEC Agreements

Since the fall of the Berlin Wall in 1989 and the escape of the former Communist bloc from Soviet influence, the EU and Member States entered into many association agreements with Central and Eastern European Countries (CEEC).[260] On 1 May 2004 the CEEC states, the Czech Republic, Estonia, Latvia, Lithuania, Hungary, Poland, Slovenia and Slovakia, along with Malta and Cyprus, joined the EU[261] and, on 1 January 2007, Bulgaria and Romania acceded to the Union.[262] Although this means the agreements have little effect for these countries, apart from legal situations that arise prior to accession and during the transition arrangements, new candidate countries have already emerged in Croatia,[263] the Former Yugoslav Republic of Macedonia,[264] the Republic of Montenegro[265] and Serbia,[266] who have entered into stabilisation and association agreements (SAAs) with the European Communities. Albania[267] entered into a SAA that entered into force on 1 April 2009 but has yet to be granted candidate country status and

---

260 Association Agreement with Central and Eastern European Country – Hungary [1993] OJ L347; Association Agreement with Central and Eastern European Country – Poland [1993] OJ L348; Association Agreement with Central and Eastern European Country – Romania [1994] OJ L357; Association Agreement with Central and Eastern European Country – Bulgaria [1994] OJ L358; Association Agreement with Central and Eastern European Country – Slovak Republic [1994] OJ L359; Association Agreement with Central and Eastern European Country – Czech Republic [1994] OJ L360; Association Agreement with Central and Eastern European Country – Slovenia [1996] OJ L344; Association Agreement with Central and Eastern European Country – Latvia [1998] OJ L26; Association Agreement with Central and Eastern European Country – Lithuania [1998] OJ L51; Association Agreement with Central and Eastern European Country – Estonia [1998] OJ L68.

261 Treaty of Accession – The Czech Republic, Poland, Hungary, Slovenia, Estonia, Latvia, Lithuania, Slovakia, Cyprus and Malta [2003] OJ L236/17. See the following for detailed analysis of the Accession Treaty and transitional arrangements: NN Shuibhne 'Legal implications of EU enlargement for the individual: EU citizenship and free movement of persons' (2004) 5 *ERA Forum* 355, 362; C Hillion 'The European Union is dead. Long live the European Union: a commentary on the Treaty of Accession 2003' (2004) 29 *ELR* 583; A Adinolfi 'Free movement and access to work of citizens of the new Member States: The Transitional measures' (2005) 42 *CMLRev* 469.

262 Treaty of Accession – Bulgaria and Romania [2005] OJ L157/11. See A Lazowski 'And then they were Twenty-seven . . . a legal appraisal of the Sixth Accession Treaty' (2007) 44 *CMLRev* 401.

263 Stabilisation and Association Agreement between the European Communities and their Member States, of the one part, and the Republic of Croatia, of the other part [2005] OJ L26/3 that entered into force on 1 February 2005.

264 Stabilisation and Association Agreement between the European Communities and their Member States, of the one part, and the Former Yugoslav Republic of Macedonia, of the other part [2004] OJ L84/13 that entered into force on 1 April 2004.

265 Stabilisation and Association Agreement between the European Communities and their Member States of the one part, and the Republic of Montenegro, of the other part [2010] OJ L108/3 that entered into force on 1 May 2010.

266 Stabilisation and Association Agreement between the European Communities and their Member States of the one part, and the Republic of Serbia, of the other part, Council Document 16005/07 yet to enter force, although candidate country status was granted at the European Council meeting of 1–2 March 2012 Council Document 128520/12 at 14.

267 Stabilisation and Association Agreement between the European Communities and their Member States, of the one part, and the Republic of Albania, of the other part [2009] OJ L107/166.

Bosnia and Herzegovina[268] has also signed and ratified a SAA that awaits EU ratification. These SAAs[269] possess inherent similarities to the former CEEC Agreements as the overall objective of accession is the same, although not included in the body of the SAA, and therefore the previous agreements and the Court's interpretation of them will continue to wield significant influence. Croatia has now completed the accession procedure and will accede to the EU on 1 July 2013.[270] Until then the SAA will retain significance and for free movement of persons the transition measures will be particularly important.[271]

The original CEEC Agreements were predominantly similar with only minor variations, although a preamble requirement to 'respect the rights of persons belonging to minorities' was inserted into the agreements concluded after those of Hungary and Poland. Therefore, the Polish Agreement will be utilised as a blueprint to assess the rights of CEEC nationals in the EU.

A major objective, set out in the preamble, recital 15, and Article 1, was to integrate the CEECs into a 'new Europe' but this did not stretch as far as accession to the EU as an aim for all the parties, just the CEECs. However, the European Council at the Copenhagen Summit in June 1993 also made accession of the CEECs a political commitment of the EU.[272] On this basis, there-fore, the agreements could have been interpreted by the ECJ in a more liberal manner to agreements with states that were either unlikely to or could not accede to the Union. The ECJ has now given judgment in a number of cases and it is suggested that the Court has followed this interpretation.[273] It is notable that the Macedonian and Croatian SAAs do not include this objective in Article 1(2) or the preamble and so there is a possibility of a more limited interpretation by the ECJ.

As with the other association agreements considered, apart from the EEA Agreement, there was no right of entry for Polish nationals. Domestic law deter-mined entry conditions. Member States also controlled initial access to the labour market with legal residents having no legal right to a work permit. Member States in accordance with Article 41(3), which was unique to the Poland Agreement, were merely obliged to 'examine the possibility of granting work permits to Polish nationals already having residence permits'. Tourists and visitors were excluded from this possibility. Indeed, Article 41 provided no rights to Polish nationals,

---

268  Stabilisation and Association Agreement between the European Communities and their Member States, of the one part, and Bosnia and Herzegovina, of the other part, Council Document 8226/08.

269  See C Pippan 'The rocky road to Europe: The EU's stabilisation and Association process for the Western Balkans and the principle of conditionality' (2004) 9 *EFAR* 219.

270  Treaty of Accession – Croatia [2012] OJ L112/10 – for commentary see K Ott 'Croatia and the European Union: accession as Transformation' in K Ott (ed) *Croatian Accession to the European Union: Facing the Challenges of Negotiation* (Institute of Public Finance 2005) ch 1.

271  See M Kapural 'Freedom of workers in the enlarged European Union and its effect on Croatia' in K Ott (ed) *Croatian Accession to the European Union* (n 270) ch 4.

272  Conclusions of the Presidency *Bull. EC* 6-1993 at 12.

273  See in particular Case C–162/00 *Land Nordrhein-Westfalen v Beata Pokrzeptowicz-Meyer* [2002] ECR I–10491 paras 39–45.

merely a policy statement on the desirability of bilateral agreements on access to employment between a Member State and Poland in Article 41(1) and the possibility of the Association Council creating greater access to professional training. The Association Council was further limited by Article 42 only granting it the right to introduce recommendations and not decisions in the second transition stage to full implementation of the association agreement set out in Article 6, which commenced on 1 February 1999, to improve the movement of workers.

Article 37 first indent provided a general nationality non-discrimination provision that, as with the Tunisian EMA, was applicable to 'working conditions, remuneration or dismissal' for legally employed workers. However, this equal treatment was 'subject to the conditions and modalities applicable in each Member State'. This exception would appear to subordinate the principle of equality to the discretionary power of the individual Member State. Martin and Guild[274] contended that this could not have been the intention of the Contracting Parties and should be read to mean that equal treatment does not have a uniform EU content but was to be filled by appropriate national law. As such, this provision was likely to be capable of having direct effect.[275] This was the finding in *Pokrzeptowicz-Meyer*.[276] Mrs Pokrzeptowicz-Meyer was a Polish national, living in Germany and working as a part-time Polish language assistant at the University of Bielefeld, employed on a fixed term contract. She claimed that her employment contract could not be terminated at the end of its fixed term, as German legislation could not justify the imposition of a limit on the duration of that contract. It was argued that, as the Court had held that this provision could not be applied to EU nationals because of its discriminatory character,[277] the same should be applied in the case of Polish nationals. The ECJ held that Article 37(1) was capable of direct effect and the exception could not allow Member States to set conditions or discretionary limitations, as that would render it meaningless and deprive it of any practical effect.[278] Indeed, the objectives of the agreement required the interpretation of Article 45(2) TFEU to be transposed to Article 37(1). In *Kolpak*[279] a Slovakian handball player employed in Germany was able to take advantage of the direct effect of the Slovakian Agreement's equivalent provision (Article 38(1)) so that the handball league's regulations on the number of non-EU players in a team did not apply to him. However, in *Pavlov*[280] the ECJ

274 Martin, Guild (eds) *Free Movement of Persons* (n 2) 297.
275 M Cremona 'Movement of persons, establishment and services' in M Maresceau (ed) *Enlarging the European Union: Relations between the EU and Central and Eastern Europe* (Longman 1997).
276 *Pokrzeptowicz-Meyer* (n 273) paras 19–30.
277 Case C–272/92 *Maria Chiara Spotti v Freistaat Bayern* [1993] ECR I–5185.
278 *Pokrzeptowicz-Meyer* (n 273) para 24.
279 Case C–438/00 *Deutscher Handballbund e V v Maros Kolpak* [2003] ECR I–4135; noted in S van den Bogaert 'And another uppercut from the European Court of justice to nationality requirements in sports regulations' (2004) 29 *ELR* 267; A Ott 'Case note' (2004) 10 *Columbia Journal of European Law* 379; J-P Dubey 'Case note' (2005) 42 *CMLRev* 499.
280 Case C–101/10 *Gentcho Pavlov and Gregor Famira v Ausschuss der Rechtsanwaltskammer Wien* [2011] 3 CMLR 34 para 28.

found that the Bulgarian provision (Article 38(1)) did not extend to national rules on access to the regulated profession of lawyer.

The second indent of Article 37 authorised the spouse and children of the Polish worker to have access to the Member State's labour market whilst the worker was employed, so long as the worker was not seasonal or covered by a bilateral agreement.

Article 38 contained the social security provisions of the agreement. There was no general equal treatment clause and it only contained three specific benefits: aggregation of time for pensions, annuities and medical care; family benefits; and the ability to transfer benefits. However, the Commission proposed an EU position within the Association Council[281] on social security provisions to bring them into line with the EC-Turkey Association Council Decision 3/80 and Regulation 1408/71. This proposal was withdrawn by the Commission in 2005 upon accession to the EU by the CEECs.[282] For Croatia and Macedonia draft decisions of the SAA Council were published in the Official Journal[283] along with decisions of the Council[284] on the position of the EU within the SAA Council. However, they have yet to be adopted and it is likely that the Croatian situation will replicate that of the formers CEECs.

The provisions on establishment and services were considered to be particularly important by the Union as the CEECs offer new and expansive opportunities for business. Article 44(1) and (3) required Poland and the Member States of the EU to grant a treatment no less favourable to that of their own companies and nationals in the establishment of the other Party's companies and nationals. Furthermore, this 'no less favourable' treatment was extended to companies and nationals already established. In a declaration annexed to the Final Act the Contracting Parties appeared to define 'no less favourable' in a similar manner to

---

281 COM(1999)675, 676–82 and 684 final.
282 Communication from the Commission to the Council and the European Parliament on the outcome of the screening of legislative proposals pending before the legislator COM(2005) 462 final.
283 Draft — Decision No . . . / . . . of the Stabilisation and Association Council established by the Stabilisation and Association Agreement between the European Communities and their Member States, of the one part, and the former Yugoslav Republic of Macedonia, of the other part, of . . . with regard to the provisions on the coordination of social security systems contained in the Stabilisation and Association Agreement [2010] OJ L306/29; Draft — Decision No . . . / . . . of the Stabilisation and Association Council established by the Stabilisation and Association Agreement between the European Communities and their Member States, of the one part, and the Republic of Croatia, of the other part, of . . . with regard to the provisions on the coordination of social security systems contained in the Stabilisation and Association Agreement [2010] OJ L306/36.
284 Council Decision on the position to be taken by the European Union within the Stabilisation and Association Council established by the Stabilisation and Association Agreement between the European Communities and their Member States, of the one part, and the former Yugoslav Republic of Macedonia, of the other part, with regard to the adoption of provisions on the coordination of social security systems [2010] OJ L306/28; Council Decision on the position to be taken by the European Union within the Stabilisation and Association Council established by the Stabilisation and Association Agreement between the European Communities and their Member States, of the one part, and the Republic of Croatia, of the other part, with regard to the adoption of provisions on the coordination of social security systems [2010] OJ L306/35.

the non-discrimination principle. The boundary between the rights of establishment and movement of workers was stressed in Article 44(4)(a)(i), which provided that 'self-employment and business undertakings by nationals shall not extend to seeking or taking employment in the labour market or confer a right of access to the labour market of the other party'. In *Gloszczuk*,[285] the Court held that Article 44(3) was capable of having direct effect, notwithstanding the fact that the Member State's authorities remained competent to apply their own national laws and regulations regarding entry, stay and establishment, in accordance with Article 58(1).[286] This right of establishment meant that there must be complementary rights of entry and residence to pursue activities of an industrial or commercial character, of craftsmen or of the professions in the Member State.[287] However, from Article 58(1) they were not absolute privileges as they could be limited in some circumstances by the rules of the host Member State.[288] These national rules could not be such as to make the exercise of the Article 44(3) rights impossible or excessively difficult.[289] The Court found that after considering the objectives of the Poland Agreement the right of establishment in Article 44(3) was not equivalent to that of Article 43 EC and so the latter's case law could not be applied.[290] The ECJ, however, in *Jany*[291] found that the term 'economic activities as self-employed persons' in Article 44(4)(a)(i) had the same meaning and scope as the 'activities as self-employed persons' referred to in Article 49 TFEU.

In *Gloszczuk*,[292] Mr and Mrs Gloszczuk, both Polish nationals, entered the UK as tourists, with their entry visas containing an express condition prohibiting them from entering employment or engaging in any business or profession in a self-employed capacity. Instead of leaving, as they had stated they intended to do to the immigration authorities on entry, they remained. Mrs Gloszczuk gave birth to a son and Mr Gloszczuk began working as a self-employed building contractor.

285 Case C–63/99 *R v Secretary of State for the Home Department, ex parte Wieslaw Gloszczuk and Elzbieta Gloszczuk* [2001] ECR I–6369. See Case C–235/99 *R v Secretary of State for the Home Department, ex parte Eleanora Ivanova Kondova* [2001] ECR I–6427; Case C–257/99 *R v Secretary of state for the Home Department, ex parte Julius Barkoci and Marcel Malik* [2001] ECR I–6557 for corresponding judgments on the Bulgarian and Czech agreements respectively. Noted in B Bogusz 'Regulating the right of establishment for accession state nationals: reinforcing the "buffer zone" or improving labour market flexibility?' (2002) 27 *ELR* 474; A Pedain 'A hollow Victory: The ECJ rules on direct effect of freedom of establishment provisions in Europe agreements' (2002) 61 *CLJ* 284; A Pedain '"With or without me": The ECJ adopts a pose of studied neutrality Towards EU enlargement' (2002) 51 *ICLQ* 981; R van Ooik 'Freedom of movement of self-employed persons and the Europe agreements' (2002) 4 *EJML* 377; C Hillion 'Case note' (2003) 40 *CMLRev* 465.

286 ibid paras 29–38. Article 58(1) reads '. . . nothing in the Agreement shall prevent the Parties from applying their laws and regulations regarding entry and stay, work, labour conditions and establishment of natural persons, and supply of services, provided that, in so doing, they do not apply them in a manner as to nullify or impair the benefits accruing to any Party under the terms of a specific provision of this Agreement . . . ".

287 ibid para 42.

288 ibid para 51.

289 ibid para 56.

290 ibid paras 47–52.

291 Case C–268/99 *Aldona Malgorzata Jany and Others v Staatssecretaris van Justitie* [2001] ECR I–8615 paras 32–50.

292 *Gloszczuk* (n 285).

Mr Gloszczuk applied to claim a right of establishment under Article 44 with Mrs Gloszczuk and his son as his family members. The UK was found to be acting legally in having immigration rules that required the checking of employment and self-employment visa applications before the individuals left their home state. However, where in *Panayotova*[293] a similar Dutch system required the individual to obtain a temporary residence permit before leaving the home state, the ECJ held that the procedural rules for obtaining such a permit must not make it impossible or excessively difficult to exercise the right of establishment. The Court in both *Gloszczuk*[294] and *Panayotova*[295] found that a Member State was acting compatibly with Article 58(1) by rejecting an application under Article 44(3) if the applicant was residing illegally in that state by making false representations on initial entry or failing to comply with an express condition attached to that initial entry.

Article 52(1) allowed companies or nationals exercising their right of establishment to employ key personnel, as defined in Article 52(2), from their home country, for which the personnel would receive residence and work permits for the duration of employment.

Article 55 dealt with the supply of services and was considerably less comprehensive than the provisions dealing with establishment. Articles 55(1) envisaged the attainment of the free movement of services but only 'progressively' and after the Parties had taken the 'necessary steps'. Although clear and precise it was conditional and therefore not directly effective. Article 55(2) provided for the employment of key personnel or the service provider in the other Party's country but only when the liberalisation process of Article 55(1) had been realised. Thus, it was deprived of direct effect until Article 55(1) was fully applied.

The transition arrangements for the 1 May 2004 and 1 January 2007 accession states created a complex structure for the phasing in of rights of free movement of workers applicable to nationals of the new Member States. The Treaty of Accession (TA)[296] was a short declaratory document that provided in Article 1(2) (Article 2(2) for the Bulgarian and Romanian TA and Article 1(3) for the Croatian TA) for the Act of Accession (AA)[297] to be an integral part of it. It is the AA that

293  Case C–327/02 *Lili Georgieva Panayotova and Others v Minister voor Vreemdelingenzaken en Integratie* [2004] ECR I–11055 para 26. The case also confirmed the judgment in *Gloszczuk*.
294  *Gloszczuk* (n 285) para 57.
295  *Panayotova* (n 293) paras 31, 32.
296  Treaty of Accession – the Czech Republic, Poland, Hungary, Slovenia, Estonia, Latvia, Lithuania, Slovakia, Cyprus and Malta (n 261), Bulgaria and Romania (n 262) and Croatia (n 270).
297  Act concerning the conditions of accession of the Czech Republic, the Republic of Estonia, the Republic of Cyprus, the Republic of Latvia, the Republic of Lithuania, the Republic of Hungary, the Republic of Malta, the Republic of Poland, the Republic of Slovenia and the Slovak Republic and the adjustments to the Treaties on which the European Union is founded [2003] OJ L236/33; Act concerning the conditions of accession of the Republic of Bulgaria and Romania and the adjustments to the treaties on which the European Union is founded [2005] OJ L157/203; Act concerning the conditions of accession of the Republic of Croatia and the adjustments to the Treaty on European Union, the Treaty on the Functioning of the European Union and the Treaty establishing the European Atomic Energy Community [2012] OJ

provided the detail for the accession and transitional arrangements, the details of the latter then outlined for each country in the Annexes. There were no restrictions applied to the right to free movement of citizens of the Union in Article 21 TFEU, although internal border controls were to be maintained. Article 8 of the Schengen Protocol required all new Member States to accept the Schengen *acquis* in full. However, Article 3(1) AA provided that only the provisions in Annex I (Article 4(1) AA and Annex II for Bulgaria, Romania and Croatia) would be binding and applicable in the new Member States from the date of accession. The remaining provisions would only apply when given effect by a Decision passed by the Council and internal border controls would be lifted when a Council Decision verified that all of the Schengen *acquis* was being applied in that new Member State (Article 3(2) AA and Article 4(2)A for Bulgaria, Romania and Croatia).[298] The final pieces of the Schengen *acquis* jigsaw were put in place in June[299] and December 2007[300] for the first wave of CEECs or Accession 8 (A8), enabling the removal of internal land and sea borders on 8 December 2007 and air borders on 30 March 2008.[301] As yet, Bulgaria and Romania have not satisfied the European Council that they are ready fully to accede to Schengen and therefore internal border controls have yet to be lifted.[302] The European Council was to assess this readiness again in September 2012[303] but it has been repeatedly delayed,[304] with a number of Member States raising concerns over progress on the fight against organised crime and corruption. The earliest date for entry is now expected to be the end of 2013.[305]

The transition measures for each acceding state are set out in the AA's Annexes, a separate Annex for each A8 state. For Cyprus and Malta there were no transition arrangements for the free movement of workers into the old EU Member States but Malta could suspend until 30 April 2011 the application of Articles 1–6 of Regulation 492/11 if there were, or possible threats of, disturbances to its labour market. For the other new Member States, the A8 states, the

L112/21. The three Acts of Accession are similar and so it is intended to refer to the former unless there are substantial differences.

298 Adinolfi 'Free movement' (n 261) 472.

299 Council Decision 2007/471/EC on the application of the provisions of the Schengen *acquis* relating to the Schengen Information System in the Czech Republic, the Republic of Estonia, the Republic of Latvia, the Republic of Lithuania, the Republic of Hungary, the Republic of Malta, the Republic of Poland, the Republic of Slovenia and the Slovak Republic [2007] OJ L179/46.

300 Council Decision 2007/801/EC on the full application of the provisions of the Schengen *acquis* in the Czech Republic, the Republic of Estonia, the Republic of Latvia, the Republic of Lithuania, the Republic of Hungary, the Republic of Malta, the Republic of Poland, the Republic of Slovenia and the Slovak Republic [2007] OJ L323/34.

301 ibid art 1.

302 This is despite reports to the contrary – see Council Documents 9166/4/11 and 9167/4/11.

303 See Novinite.com 'Dutch Govt stalls Bulgaria, Romania Schengen bids till 2013' 17 September 2012 http://www.novinite.com/view_news.php?id=143320.

304 See The Sofia Globe 'Decision on Bulgaria and Romania joining Schengen visa zone unlikely before Autumn' 7 March 2013 http://sofiaglobe.com/2013/03/07/decision-on-bulgaria-and-romania-joining-schengen-visa-zone-unlikely-before-autumn/.

305 See Novinite.com 'Dutch Govt to block again Bulgaria, Romania Schengen bids – Report' 9 January 2013 http://www.novinite.com/view_news.php?id=146699.

Annexes outlined identical provisions for the free movement of workers. A seven year transition period for the full implementation of free movement of persons was put in place because of concerns over the adequacy of the labour markets in the old Member States to absorb the expected flow of migrants from the East. As Currie observed,[306] national flexibility was the essential factor in the transitional arrangements, with Member States given significant discretion to decide unilaterally the length and scope of the derogations from the principle of free movement. For the first two years, until 30 April 2006, Member States could maintain their national measures to regulate access to their labour markets for nationals from the former CEECs and derogate from Articles 1–6 of Regulation 492/11. On the basis of a Commission Report[307] the Council reviewed those measures before the end of the two year period and Member States notified the Commission on their intentions to lift the restrictions, ease the restrictions or retain the restrictions until 30 April 2009. Old Member States could even continue to apply their restrictions until 30 April 2011 where there were, or there were possible threats of, serious disturbances to the labour market. For Member States who decided to open up their labour markets fully there was a safeguard clause that enabled Member States to request authorisation from the Commission to suspend the free movement of workers if there were actual or foreseeable disturbances to their labour market, which could seriously threaten the standard of living or level of employment in a given region or occupation. A standstill clause ensured that no more restrictive measures could be introduced than were in place on 1 May 2004.

The transitional arrangements for family members were problematic. If the family member was residing with the worker in the EU on 1 May 2004 then the family member would have immediate access to the labour market. However, if the family member was not resident with the worker on 1 May 2004 then he or she was not able to enter the labour market until the family member had resided with the worker for 18 months or from 1 May 2007, whichever was the earlier. The CEEC Agreements did not contain any time limitations for family members entering the labour market and it is difficult to see how the AA could impose a more restrictive regime than was in place before, particularly when the standstill clause was factored into the equation.[308] Furthermore, the Family Reunification Directive[309] (see Chapter 4) authorised Member States to set a time limit that could not exceed 12 months for TCN family members of TCN workers to take up employment, although the Member States had the discretion to require the worker to have been resident in the Member State for up to two years. The ECJ

---

306  S Currie '"Free" movers? The post-accession experience of accession–8 migrant workers in the UK' (2006) 31 *ELR* 207, 210.

307  Commission Report on the functioning of the transitional arrangements set out in the Accession Treaty 2003 (period 1 May 2004–30 April 2006) COM(2006) 48 final.

308  Hillion 'The European Union is dead' (n 261) 598.

309  Council Directive 2003/86/EC on the right to family reunification [2003] OJ L251/12 art 14 – see ch 4 for analysis of this measure.

was not called upon to interpret these arrangements but Adinolfi suggested[310] that, following the case of *Peskeloglou*,[311] the Court would probably have treated any of the transition arrangements as derogations from the fundamental right of the free movement of workers and interpreted such a restriction narrowly.

Bulgaria and Romania's accession to the Union on 1 January 2007 involved similar transitional arrangements to the A8 states but with the date of the first period ending on 31 December 2008,[312] the second period on 31 December 2011,[313] full application on 31 December 2013 and the family reunification requirement on 31 December 2009.[314] In August 2011[315] Spain activated the safeguard clause to reintroduce Articles 1–6 of Regulation 492/11 for Romanian nationals until 31 December 2012, now extended to 31 December 2013[316] owing to the economic recession being experienced by Spain since 2008 leading to unemployment exceeding 20 per cent, which was further perpetuated in the Romanian community resident in Spain.

For the Croatian accession similar transition measures will apply with the date of the first period ending on 30 June 2015, the second period on 30 June 2018, full application on 30 June 2020 and the family reunification requirement on 30 June 2016.

## 5.6 Conclusion

The agreements that the EU has entered into with third countries create a divergent spread of rights for TCNs that depend in particular on the purpose of the agreement, the geographical location of the third country (that is, is it European?) and the long term intentions of the third country and the EU. The EEA implementing a free trade area with fellow European states that may eventually accede to the Union allows full free movement rights for nationals of EEA countries. The Ankara Agreement, EMAs and CEEC Association Agreements do not allow free movement of persons either on the entry of the state's nationals into the EU or within the EU when they have been granted access to the Member

---

310  Adinolfi 'Free movement' (n 261) 490.
311  Case 77/82 *Anastasia Peskeloglou v Bundesanstalt für Arbeit* [1983] ECR 1085.
312  Commission Report on the first phase (1 January 2007–31 December 2008) of the Transitional Arrangements set out in the 2005 Accession Treaty and as requested according to the Transitional Arrangement set out in the 2003 Accession Treaty COM(2008) 765 final.
313  Commission Report on the Functioning of the Transitional Arrangements on Free Movement of Workers from Bulgaria and Romania COM(2011) 729 final.
314  See J Traser 'Who's afraid of the EU's latest enlargement? The impact of Bulgaria and Romania joining the Union on free movement of persons' ECAS Report 2008 http://www.ecas-citizens.eu/content/view/84/178.
315  Commission Decision 2011/503/EU authorising Spain to temporarily suspend the application of arts 1 to 6 of Regulation (EU) No 492/2011 of the European Parliament and of the Council on freedom of movement for workers within the Union with regard to Romanian workers [2011] OJ L207/22 art 1.
316  Commission Decision 2012/831/EU authorising Spain to temporarily suspend the application of arts 1 to 6 of Regulation (EU) No 492/2011 of the European Parliament and of the Council on freedom of movement for workers within the Union with regard to Romanian workers [2012] OJ L356/90 art 1.

State's territory, but there are provisions enabling access to the labour market and non-discrimination. The later agreements appear to be less generous over rights for TCNs than the earlier arrangements, particularly comparing the CEEC Association Agreements and the new SAAs with the Ankara Agreement. However, the ECJ has interpreted the provisions teleologically and it is possible to discern a more generous approach to states that, with the signing of a SAA, are candidate countries. The liberal judgments in *Pokrzeptowicz-Meyer*, *Gloszczuk* and *Panayotova* involving the CEEC states can be contrasted with the restrictive rulings in *El-Yassini* and *Mesbah* concerning the EMA Agreements.

The international agreements entered into by the Union with third countries have created rights for some TCNs that place these TCNs in a novel position. They do not have the full rights of Union citizenship but the rights they do have are targeted towards enabling their market access once they have entered the territory of the host Member State. They are in effect equivalent to 'denizens'[317] who acquire 'market citizenship'[318] upon accession to the Union but do not acquire full Union citizenship until seven years after accession.[319]

---

317 T Hammer *Democracy and the Nation State: Aliens, Denizens and Citizens in a World of International Migration* (Avebury 1990).
318 M Everson 'The legacy of the market citizen' in J Shaw, G More (eds) *New Legal Dynamics of European Union* (Clarendon Press 1995) 73.
319 N Reich, S Harbacevica 'Citizenship and family on Trial: a fairly optimistic overview of recent Court practice with regard to free movement of persons' (2003) 40 *CMLRev* 615, 616 and N Reich 'The constitutional relevance of citizenship and free movement in an enlarged Union' (2005) 11 *ELJ* 675, 690.

# 6 The practical application of rationality

The purpose of this chapter is threefold. The first objective is to consider the attitudes that have shaped the EU's policy towards third country national (TCNs). The second objective is to analyse these attitudes towards the movement of persons to determine the predominant policy considerations when dealing with TCNs. The third objective is to analyse the findings from Chapters 3–5 through the lens of legal rationality, and to position them within the policy context to determine if any findings of legal irrationality can be objectively justified.

## 6.1 EU policy concerns towards TCNs

The area of freedom, security and justice (AFSJ) was first recognised at the Treaty of Amsterdam in 1997 where an objective of the EU was the maintenance and development of the 'Union as an area of freedom, security and justice' and Article 61 EC considered the progressive establishment of an AFSJ. The political concerns over the treatment of TCNs were discussed at the meeting of the European Council at Tampere in October 1999. In the Presidency Conclusions[1] it was declared that European integration was to be underpinned by the common values of 'freedom based on human rights, democratic institutions and the rule of law' that had proven 'necessary for securing peace and developing prosperity in the European Union' and would 'serve as a cornerstone for the enlarging Union'.[2] This freedom, which included the right to move freely throughout the Union, was not to be regarded as the exclusive preserve of the Union's own citizens and that it 'would be in contradiction with Europe's traditions to deny such freedom to those whose circumstances lead them justifiably to seek access to our territory'.[3] To this end a common approach had to be developed to ensure the integration into the Member States' societies of TCNs lawfully resident in the Union. Further on in the Tampere Conclusions a section was dedicated to the fair treatment of TCNs. The EU had to 'ensure fair treatment of TCNs who reside legally on the territory of its Member States' through a

1 Presidency Conclusions of the Tampere European Council (15–16 October 1999) SN 200/1/99.
2 ibid para 1.
3 ibid para 3.

'more vigorous integration policy' with the aim of 'granting them rights and obligations comparable to those of EU citizens'.[4] Furthermore, '[t]he legal status of TCNs should be approximated to that of Member States' nationals' and a set of uniform rights granted for those who have resided in a Member State for a specified time period whilst holding a long-term resident's permit. Finally, the European Council supported the ability of a long-term TCN being able to obtain nationality of that Member State by naturalisation.[5]

The development of the AFSJ and EU policy towards asylum and immigration, which appeared to conflate the two concepts, meant that six years after the Tampere European Council Conclusions the Hague Programme[6] was agreed by the European Council[7] with similar objectives and topics to those of the Tampere Conclusions. However, the common values of the Tampere Conclusions encountered a marked shift in emphasis in the Hague Programme. The cornerstone of the Union of 'freedom based on human rights, democratic institutions and the rule of law' was not now a cornerstone of the Union in the Hague Programme,[8] as the starting point now was for the AFSJ to respond 'to a central concern of the peoples of the States brought together in the Union'. This central concern was then spelt out as security, replacing the accent on freedom in the Tampere Conclusions. It could be considered that this high priority on security is understandable with the increased terrorist threat following 9/11, the Madrid train bombings on 11 March 2004 and the London attacks of 7 July 2005, but the shift was noted with concern by the House of Lords.[9] Security[10] meant that the citizens of Europe expected the Union, 'while guaranteeing respect for fundamental freedoms and rights, to take a more effective, joint approach to cross border problems', such as illegal migration, human trafficking, terrorism and organised crime,[11] with the internal dimension linked to the external. In the Tampere Conclusions the rule of law appeared in the first paragraph and was linked to the idea of freedom, whilst in the Hague Programme the rule of law was relegated to paragraph 9[12] and was linked to security with the AFSJ being 'vital to securing safe communities, mutual trust and the rule of law throughout the Union'. An

---

4  ibid para 18.
5  ibid para 21.
6  Council Document 'The Hague Programme: Strengthening freedom, Security and Justice in the European Union' [2005] OJ C53/1.
7  The Hague Programme: Strengthening Freedom, Security and Justice in the European Union [2005] OJ C53/1; C Elsen 'From Maastricht to The Hague: the politics of judicial and police cooperation' (2007) 8 *ERA Forum* 13.
8  T Balzacq, S Carrera 'The Hague Programme: the long road to freedom, security and justice' in T Balzacq, S Carrera (eds) *Security Versus Freedom? A Challenge for Europe's Future* (Ashgate 2006) 1, 5.
9  European Union Committee *The Hague Programme: A Five Year Agenda for EU Justice and Home Affairs* (HL 2004–2005, 84) 11.
10  The Hague Programme (n 7) 1 para 4.
11  AN Pratt 'Human trafficking: the nadir of an unholy trinity' (2007) 13 *European Security* 55 amalgamates these four elements into three in what he describes as a very 'unholy trinity' – terrorism, corruption and international organised crime.
12  The Hague Programme (n 7) 2.

Action Plan[13] was adopted by the Council and Commission and, in 2009,[14] the Commission declared that progress had been mixed but there had been visible achievements.[15]

A re-evaluation of policy concerns towards the AFSJ on a more limited approach took place with the French presidency's initiative in the latter half of 2008 to create the European Pact on Immigration and Asylum,[16] adopted at the Brussels European Council meeting[17] in October 2008 as a prelude to the third programme for the AFSJ after Tampere and the Hague. The document is a notably strong statement on the management of migration flows with five basic commitments[18] centred on: legal migration based on integration of migrants; illegal migration based on the removal of illegal immigrants; effective border controls; construction of a Europe of asylum; and partnerships with third countries to 'encourage the synergy between migration and development'.[19] As Carrera and Guild[20] note, there is a notable intergovernmental sense to the pact,[21] positing the stance of the Council (and the French in particular) and possibly conflicting with the Commission[22] in its 2008 Communication on Immigration.[23] Furthermore, like the Hague Programme before it, there is much spoken about security but little on freedom, justice or the rights and liberties of TCNs.[24]

The third programme for the AFSJ, taking over from the Hague Programme, is the Stockholm Programme[25] adopted in 2009,[26] which is heavily influenced by the European Pact on Immigration and Asylum. The resulting programme is far more structured than the Tampere and Hague Programmes and starts by laying

---

13   Council Document 'Council and Commission Action Plan Implementing the Hague Programme on Strengthening Freedom, Security and Justice in the European Union' [2005] OJ C198/1.

14   Commission Communication on Justice, Freedom and Security in Europe Since 2005: an evaluation of the Hague Programme and Action Plan COM(2009) 263 final.

15   ibid 3. This should be compared with the finding of a general overall assessment on the implementation of the Hague Programme as 'rather unsatisfactory' in the Commission Communication of the report on the implementation of the Hague Programme for 2007 COM(2008) 373 final 2, 'mixed' for 2006 (Commission Communication of the report on the implementation of the Hague Programme for 2006 COM(2007) 373 final 2), and 'a broadly positive assessment' for 2005 (Commission Communication of the report on the implementation of the Hague Programme for 2007 COM(2006) 333 final 2).

16   Council Document 13440/08.

17   Council Document 14368/08, 8.

18   Council Document 13440/08 (n 16) 4.

19   ibid.

20   S Carrera, E Guild 'The French Presidency's European Pact on Immigration and asylum: intergovernmental vs. Europeanisation? Security vs rights?' September 2008 http://www.ceps. be/book/french-presidency%E2%80%99s-european-pact-immigration-and-asylum-intergovernmentalism-vs-europeanisatio.

21   ibid 5.

22   ibid 7.

23   Commission Communication on a common immigration policy for Europe: principles, actions and tools (COM)2008 359 final.

24   Carrera, Guild 'The French Presidency's European Pact on Immigration and Asylum' (n 20) 9.

25   European Council Document 'The Stockholm Programme – an open and secure Europe serving and protecting citizens' [2010] OJ C115/1; see European Union Committee *The Stockholm Programme: Home Affairs* (HL 2008–2009, 175).

26   Council Document EUCO 6/09.

out the political priorities[27] of the Stockholm Programme and the tools of implementation.[28] Those political priorities are then set out in detail.[29] The first priority[30] is 'Promoting Citizens' Rights: A Europe of Rights' that equates the protection of rights, and in particular fundamental rights, with citizenship rather than with all persons resident in the EU.[31] Even where there are opportunities for a broader agenda to include TCNs, for example on the right to free movement, racism and xenophobia, rights of the child and vulnerable groups, the emphasis on citizenship is retained. The second priority[32] focuses on justice, the third[33] and fourth[34] policy priorities deal with internal and external security and the sixth[35] with external relationships, be that external security as formulated by foreign policy, bilateral agreements with third countries, the European Neighbourhood Policy or the external dimensions of human rights. Interestingly this latter field emphasises the interlinked nature of the internal and external aspects of human rights,[36] providing two examples including the principle of *non-refoulement*. Priority five[37] deals with a 'dynamic and comprehensive migration policy' and '[a]sylum: a common area of protection and solidarity', which reintroduces the Tampere distinction between migration and asylum. The former initially focuses on the Global Approach to Migration and maintenance of a balance in the three areas of promotion of mobility and legal migration, optimisation of the link between migration and development, and the prevention and action to combat illegal migration.[38] This is followed by considerations for migration and development,[39] and immigration centred on the requirements of the national labour market.[40] It is only then that 'proactive policies for migrants and their rights'[41] are considered, which resemble the aims set out in the Tampere Conclusions. Thus the Union 'must ensure fair treatment of third country nationals who reside legally on the territory of the Member States'.[42] TCNs need to be integrated by 'granting them rights and obligations comparable to those of citizens of the Union' with an implementation date of no later than 2014.[43] Indeed, it is stated that the 'successful integration of legally residing third country nationals remains the key to maximising the benefits of immigration'.[44] Again

27  The Stockholm Programme (n 25) 4.
28  ibid 5.
29  ibid 8–37.
30  ibid 8.
31  See S Carrera, A Wiesbrock 'Whose European citizenship in the Stockholm Programme? The enactment of citizenship by third country nationals in the EU' (2010) 12 *EJML* 337.
32  The Stockholm Programme (n 25) 11.
33  ibid 17.
34  ibid 26.
35  ibid 33.
36  ibid 34.
37  ibid 27.
38  ibid 28.
39  ibid 29.
40  ibid.
41  ibid 30.
42  ibid.
43  ibid.
44  ibid.

there is an emphasis on the 'objective of granting comparable rights, responsibilities, and opportunities for all' but with an assertion that integration is a two-way process of rights and duties, and efforts by national, regional and local authorities alongside greater commitments by the host community and immigrants.[45] The second policy concern in this section is asylum, which says little about the protection of TCNs, except for a commitment to the Geneva Convention as the basis of a Common Policy on Asylum with a further commitment for the Union to seek accession to it.[46] The remainder of the section focuses on responsibilities and solidarity between Member States and the external dimension of asylum, which can be linked to issues of security. In 2010[47] the Commission put forward an Action Plan to implement the Stockholm Programme.

The Stockholm Programme and the Action Plan are certainly ambitious but it is difficult to establish a thread that could define them as there are a considerable number of policy priorities in the Stockholm Programme that are then added to by the Action Plan.[48] A recurring theme is the protection of fundamental rights but this appears to be equated with Union citizenship, and thus citizenship rights rather than human rights. This is a similar conflation of the principle of equality and Union citizenship in Part Two of the TFEU. It should also be noted that unlike the Tampere Conclusions and the Hague Programme there is no mention of the rule of law in the Stockholm Programme, and since the Tampere Conclusions there has been no reference to the possibility of obtaining national citizenship status through naturalisation. However, it is quite clear from the Stockholm Programme that of the three aspects of the AFSJ, the dominant policy concern is security. Indeed, Bunyan has summed up the Stockholm Programme and the Action Plan as 'a bit more freedom and justice but a lot more security'.[49]

## 6.2   Underlying policy considerations towards TCNs

The immediate conclusion that can be taken from this analysis above is that the underlying policy towards TCNs is highly complex[50] and, secondly, that it has changed over time. Furthermore, the factors that feed into this policy matrix are not controlled solely by the EU but can be dictated by global, regional and national events and, indeed, an individual's actions. Policy formation when dealing with TCNs must manage two concerns: the movement of TCNs into the EU from a third country (the migration issue); and the position of TCNs once

---

45  ibid.
46  ibid 32.
47  Commission Communication on delivering an area of freedom, security and justice for Europe's citizens: an Action Plan implementing the Stockholm Programme COM(2010) 171 final.
48  Editorial 'The EU as an area of freedom, security and justice: implementing the Stockholm Programme' (2010) 47 *CMLRev* 1307, 1314.
49  T Bunyan 'Commission: Action Plan on the Stockholm Programme – a bit more freedom and justice and a lot more security' http://www.statewatch.org/analyses/no-95-stockholm-action-plan.pdf.
50  SA Espinoza, C Moraes 'The law and politics of migration and asylum: the Lisbon Treaty and the EU' in D Ashiagbor, N Countouris and I Lianos (eds) *The European Union After the Treaty of Lisbon* (CUP 2012) 156, 166.

they have entered the EU (the rights issue). A further complication arises over the fact that the EU is not a state, although it is acting with state-like qualities when it is conducting policy towards TCNs. Furthermore, the fractured nature[51] of TCN policy within the AFSJ with the opt-outs of the UK and Ireland, and the difficult position of Denmark, adds an additional layer of difficulty to policy formation. As such, a mere critical analysis of migration policy formation at the state level[52] does not consider all the factors that have to be taken into account when dealing with TCNs at a supranational level, although some elements will be consistent. It is suggested that the following factors in particular are involved in policy formation towards the treatment of TCNs.

### 6.2.1   *Legal*

The legal position for TCNs is highly complex, involving the interaction of international, regional and national questions. At the international level, the legal question that is central to the position of TCNs is whether there is a general right to free movement for individuals or not. The question of 'open borders'[53] has become a much debated issue in recent years with philosophical,[54] historical,[55] ethical[56] (including human rights)[57] and economic[58] arguments deployed for the

---

51   See D Curtin 'The constitutional structure of the Union: a Europe of bits and pieces' (1993) 30 *CMLRev* 17.

52   For example S Castles 'Why migration policies fail' (2004) 2 *ERS* 205; S Castles 'The factors that make and unmake migration policies' (2004) 38 *IMR* 852.

53   See A Pécoud, P de Guchteneire (eds) *Migration Without Borders: Essays on the Free Movement of People* (UNESCO Publishing/Berghahn Books 2007) for a recent comprehensive collection on this subject. See also KR Johnson 'Open borders?' (2003) 51 *UCLA Law Review* 193.

54   See in particular JH Carens 'Aliens and citizens: the case for open borders' (1987) 49 *Review of Politics* 250; JH Carens 'Migration and morality: a liberal egalitarian perspective' in B Barry, RE Goodin (eds) *Free Movement: Ethical Issues in the transnational Migration of People and of Money* (Harvester Wheatsheaf 1992) 25; JH Carens 'Realistic and idealistic approaches to the ethics of migration' (1996) 30 *IMR* 156; JH Carens *Culture, Citizenship and Community* (OUP 2000); JH Carens 'Who should get in? The ethics of immigration admissions' (2003) 17 *Ethics & International Affairs* 95, who has argued consistently for open borders from a liberal egalitarian perspective that considers the interests of individuals prior to community or society. An alternative argument where the interests of the community are considered prior to those of individuals and thus supporting closed borders was put forward by M Walzer *Spheres of Justice: A Defence of Pluralism and Equality* (Basic Books 1983) and more recently by PC Meilaender *Toward a Theory of Immigration* (Palgrave 2001).

55   JAR Nafziger 'The general admission of aliens under international law' (1983) 77 *AJIL* 804.

56   See M Weiner 'Ethics, national sovereignty and the control of immigration' (1996) 30 *IMR* 171; T Hayter *Open Borders: The Case Against Immigration Controls* (Pluto Press 2000); SS Juss *International Migration and Global Justice* (Ashgate 2006); M Ugur 'The ethics, economics and governance of free movement' in Pécoud, de Guchteneire (eds) *Migration Without Borders* (n 53) 65. For a review of the literature see J Seglow 'The ethics of immigration' (2005) 3 *Political Studies Review* 317.

57   See SS Juss 'Free movement and the world order' (2004) 16 *IJRL* 289; A Pécoud, P de Guchteneire 'International migration, border controls and human rights: assessing the relevance of a right to mobility' (2006) 21 *Journal of Borderlands Studies* 69; R Nett 'The civil right we are not ready for: the right of free movement of people on the face of the Earth' (1971) 81 *Ethics* 212; EM Bruch 'Open or closed: balancing border policy with human rights' (2007) 96 *Kentucky Law Journal* 197.

58   See B Hamilton, J Whalley 'Efficiency and distributional implications of global restrictions on labour mobility: calculations of policy implications' (1984) 14 *Journal of Development Economics* 61,

right to free movement of persons across borders. Indeed, freedom of movement has been described as 'the first and most fundamental of man's liberties'.[59] However, the legal position is clear and at odds with the pro-open borders position. Article 13(2) of the Universal Declaration of Human Rights 1948 (UDHR) specifies that '[e]veryone has the right to leave any country, including his own, and to return to his country'.[60] This is a right to emigration but there is no complementary right to immigration and thus there is no human right to free movement of persons at the international level, notwithstanding the logical 'absurdity'[61] of a human right to leave a state that fails to be complemented by a right of entry to another state, creating a 'fundamental contradiction between the notion that emigration is widely regarded as a matter of human rights while immigration is regarded as a matter of national sovereignty'.[62]

National sovereignty is the key legal factor in the policy matrix for the treatment of TCNs. There is no specific provision of international law that specifies that it is the state that determines the entry and exit of persons from that state, although it is recognised and accepted by the international community.[63] The EU, however, is a unique international organisation where sovereignty has been voluntarily pooled or transferred by the Member States, thereby enabling the EU to act in certain specified policy areas. A difficulty then is to determine if

who calculated estimated worldwide efficiency gains ranging from \$4.7 trillion to \$16 trillion (worldwide GNP at that time was \$7.82 trillion). This study has recently been reworked using updated figures by WJ Moses, B Letnes 'If people were money: estimating the gains and scope of free movement' in GJ Borjas, J Crisp (eds) *Poverty, International Migration and Asylum* (Palgrave 2005) 188; WJ Moses, B Letnes 'The economic costs to international labor restrictions: revisiting the empirical discussion' (2004) 32 *World Development* 1609, who come to a figure of \$34.08 trillion. A similar position has been suggested by other economists – see GJ Borjas 'Economic theory and international migration' (1989) 23 *IMR* 457; GJ Borjas 'The economics of immigration' (1994) 32 *Journal of Economic Literature* 1667; GJ Borjas 'The economic benefits from immigration' (1995) 9 *Journal of Economic Perspectives* 3; M Wolf *Why Globalisation Works* (Yale University Press 2004) 117. Open borders have also been suggested by MJ Trebilcock 'The law and economics of immigration policy' (2003) 5 *American Law & Economics Review* 271 but with mandatory private insurance to protect social welfare schemes and the raising of revenues through tariffs by HF Chang 'Migration as international trade: the economic gains from the liberalized movement of labor' (1998) 3 *UCLA Journal of International Law & Foreign Affairs* 371; HF Chang 'The economics of international labor migration and the case for global distributive justice in liberal political theory' (2008) 41 *Cornell International Law Journal* 1.
59 M Cranston *What are Human Rights?* (2nd edn Bodley Head 1973) 31, 33.
60 See also art 12(2) of the International Covenant on Civil and political rights 1966 and art 2(2) of Protocol 4 to the ECHR. See J McAdam 'An intellectual history of freedom of movement in international law: the right to leave as a personal liberty' (2011) 12 *Melbourne Journal of International Law* 27 for a comprehensive analysis of the historical development of the right to emigrate rather than the right of freedom of movement.
61 A Dummett 'The transnational migration of people seen from within a natural law tradition' in Barry, Goodin (eds) *Free Movement* (n 54) 169, 173.
62 Weiner 'Ethics' (n 56) 171.
63 See K Anan 'International migration and development: report of the Secretary General' A/60/871, 18 May 2006 http://www.un.org/esa/population/migration/hld/Text/ReportoftheSGJune2006_English.pdf para 76: 'States have the sovereign right to decide who enters and stays in their territory, subject to treaty obligations and obligations deriving from customary international law'. See also GCIM 'Migration in an interconnected world: new directions for action – Report of the Global Commission on International migration' GCIM 2005 http://www.gcim.org 66.

the EU should be classified as a state for international law purposes when dealing with the migration issue. If the EU does act in such a way (see Chapters 3 and 4) then the legal position of TCNs is complicated by Article 13(1) of the UDHR that '[e]veryone has the right to freedom of movement and residence within the borders of each State'.[64] It should be noted here that Article 13(1) differs from Article 13(2) by specifying state rather than country. This, it is submitted, appears to focus on the political construct that is the state enabling a wide definition to be applied that could possibly include the EU, which would mean that TCNs would have the right of freedom of movement within the EU. However, the opt-outs of the UK, Ireland and Denmark from the AFSJ create a further complication in the basic legal position as these Member States have not agreed to transfer their sovereignty on such matters to the supranational EU except in certain areas (see Chapter 4).

### 6.2.2   *Economic*

The second policy consideration is the economic factor of the migration issue of immigration into the EU and then the rights issue involving migration within the Union. The open borders debate has produced a raft of economic reports[65] suggesting that global free movement of persons would produce considerable advantages not just for developed countries but also for developing and least developed countries. However, this debate is a sterile one when applied to the EU as it calls for a global rather than a regional commitment. Thus the economic factors for immigration into the EU are more nuanced. The key to this economic policy component is the perceived necessity in the modern capitalist world for economies at least to maintain if not increase economic growth rates. In the EU the projected population for 2060[66] will see total numbers increasing, the average age increasing and birth rates continuing to decline; the increase in overall population is due mainly to an assumption that migration into the Union will increase. The result is that the working age population is expected to be reduced by 50 million people if historical immigration rates are maintained or by 110 million if this immigration was curtailed. This loss of the working age population coupled with the expected tendency for people to live longer will have a significant impact on the EU's economic performance[67] and public expenditure on pensions, long-term care, health and education.[68] The policy implication from

---

64  See also art 12(1) of the International Covenant on Civil and Political Rights 1966 and art 2(1) of Protocol 4 to the ECHR.
65  Note 58.
66  Commission Demography Report 2008: Meeting social needs in an ageing society SEC(2008) 2911, 54.
67  Commission Communication on a common immigration policy for Europe: principles, actions and tools (COM)2008 359 final 2.
68  Economic Policy Committee and the European Commission (DG ECFIN) 'The impact of ageing on public expenditure: projections for the EU25 Member States on pensions, health care, long term care, education and unemployment transfers (2004–2050)' Special Report 1/2006 http://ec.europa.eu/economy_finance/publications/publication6654_en.pdf.

these statistics is that the EU will need to allow significant immigration from third countries to enable the continuing growth of the region and ensure that sufficient resources are produced to manage the care of the aging population.

The migration of TCNs within the EU provides another dimension to the economic factor, this time one dominated by the right to freedom of movement for persons and the internal market. The economic logic of the internal market views individuals as labour and thus factors of production that can move any-where within the EU so that supply can satisfy demand for labour. From a purely economic perspective all units of labour are simply that, devoid of other characteristics such as nationality, race, sex or indeed humanity. The reality, however, is far more complex and one that is explored in Chapter 3.

A related economic feature, supporting the previous two, is the effect of migration on the cost of Member States' social welfare systems. It is considered that large scale immigration from third countries could cause significant problems for the working of the welfare state,[69] particularly if this immigration was indiscriminate.[70] If the receiving state provides a comprehensive and universal benefit system then theory suggests that this is likely to act as a 'welfare magnet'[71] for immigrants, although recent empirical evidence calls this theory into question.[72] However, if this immigration was targeted and managed then the impact on the welfare state could be beneficial rather than negative with TCNs working, providing services, purchasing goods, paying taxes and fully participating in the host Member State's economy.[73] This positive aspect of TCN involvement in the host Member State is reflected in the position of TCNs migrating between Member States where migration would enable available labour to move to Member States, or indeed specific regions within Member States, to satisfy the demand for labour. The fact that TCNs had already migrated from outside the EU would suggest that social, cultural and economic ties to a host community would be less strong than those of citizens of the host Member State and thus TCNs would have a greater propensity to embrace such movement.

---

69  M Gibney *The Ethics and the Politics of Asylum: Liberal Democracy and the Response to Refugees* (CUP 2004) 69.

70  H Entzinger 'Open borders and the welfare state' in Pécoud, de Guchteneire (eds) *Migration Without Borders* (n 53) 119, 132.

71  GJ Borjas 'Immigration and welfare magnets' (1999) 17 *Journal of Labor Economics* 607; JD Hansen 'Immigration and welfare redistribution in welfare states' (2003) 19 *European Journal of Political Economy* 735; P Nannestad 'Immigration and welfare states: a survey of 15 years of research' (2007) 23 *European Journal of Political Economy* 512.

72  PJ Pedersen, M Pytlikova and N Smith 'Selection and network effects: migration flows into OECD countries 1990–2000' (2008) 52 *European Economic Review* 1160; G De Giorgi, M Pellizzari 'Welfare migration in Europe' (2009) 16 *Labour Economics* 353; C Giulietti, M Guzi, M Kahanec and KF Zimmerman 'Unemployment benefits and immigration: evidence from the EU' (2013) 34(1) *International Journal of Manpower* 24–38.

73  Entzinger 'Open borders' (n 70) 127; this appears to be supported by the evidence presented in (n 72).

### 6.2.3  *Status*

The status of TCNs, or their classification, when compared with that of nationals of Member States is another strong factor that underpins policy formation of treatment of TCNs, particularly when dealing with the rights issue. Peers[74] suggests there are three models for the classification of TCNs. The citizen, or human, model would see immigrants granted the same rights and assimilated with EU citizens, whilst the alien model would be at the opposite end of the spectrum with few rights granted with little assimilation. The third model is that of the worker where the TCN is equated with, and granted the rights equivalent to, a guest-worker. Classifying TCNs into alien, citizen or worker would help determine the formation of policy towards TCNs and their level of rights.

A fourth model of status classification, entitled denizenship by Hammar,[75] could also be utilised to determine policy formation over the treatment of TCNs. By being considered as denizens, TCNs could be granted rights as a form of 'half-way house' status between worker and citizen that could encourage greater integration of TCNs into the host society with the added advantage of providing the opportunity for TCNs to step up through the status classifications.[76]

### 6.2.4  *Security*

The Hague Programme, and now the Stockholm Programme, saw a shift in the factors underpinning policy formation from the Tampere Conclusions with the introduction of securitisation of migration. As Huysmans[77] notes, much debate over large scale migration has centred on the destabilising effect of this immigration on integrated communities, public order through the increased threat of terrorism from third country sources and the need to control this new perceived danger. The result is to create an identity in the migrant that is removed from the centre,[78] in contrast with the model of the European Citizen[79] and capable of being marginalised through minimal rights, which potentially raises claims of racialisation.[80] The ultimate result of such marginalisation is to dehumanise the individual and to lead to elimination of 'the other' as a form of survival.[81]

---

74  S Peers 'Aliens, workers, citizens or humans? Models for Community immigration law' in E Guild, C Harlow (eds) *Implementing Amsterdam: Immigration and Asylum Rights in EC Law* (Hart Publishing 2001) 291.

75  T Hammar *Democracy and the Nation State, Aliens, Denizens and Citizens in a World of International Migration* (Avebury 1990).

76  For a consideration of the effect of denizenship on the future of the EU see N Walker 'Denizenship and the deterritorialization in the EU' EUI Working Paper Law 2008/08.

77  J Huysmans 'The European Union and the securitization of migration' (2000) 38 *JCMS* 751.

78  J Huysmans 'Migrants as a security problem: dangers of "securitizing" societal issues' in R Miles, D Thränhardt (eds) *Migration and European Integration: The Dynamics of Inclusion and Exclusion* (Pinter Publishers 1995) 53, 59.

79  I Ward 'Identifying the European other' (2002) 14 *IJRL* 219.

80  M Ibrahim 'The securitization of migration: a racial discourse' (2005) 43 *International Migration* 163.

81  Huysmans 'Migrants as a security problem' (n 78) 64.

A more positive slant on the securitisation of migration is possible if the definition of security is expanded so that the concept moves from national security to human security.[82] Afzal notes that the term human security has been used in an ad hoc manner,[83] with disagreement about its precise scope.[84] However, three general approaches can be observed.[85] The first is a narrow one[86] that categorises human security as the protection of the individual against violent threats such as war, genocide and terrorism or, as Oberleitner suggests, an 'approach that relies on natural rights and the rule of law anchored in basic human rights'.[87] The broad approach[88] instead seeks to protect people from threats that include hunger, disease and natural disasters, can encompass economic deprivation and threats to human dignity[89] and links human security with 'the state of the global economy, development and globalisation'.[90] A middle way or 'humanitarian approach' understands human security 'as a tool for deepening and strengthening efforts to tackle issues such as war crimes or genocide', thus 'preparing the ground for humanitarian intervention'.[91] An alternative methodology has been suggested by Owen,[92] who advocates a threshold approach by first defining human security as 'the protection of the vital core of all human lives from critical and pervasive threats'[93] and then separating and categorising those threats as 'environmental, economic, food, health, personal and political'.[94] The result of all these approaches is that by considering security as including human security, instead of just national security, the emphasis is switched towards protection of the individual rather than merely that of the state. The effect of such a switch is, at the least, to require the protection of an individual's human rights to

---

82  The term 'human security' was first used in 1994 – see United Nations Development Programme (UNDP) *New Dimensions of Human Security* (OUP 1994) 22. However, the history of the concept can be traced back to the Helsinki Accords of 1975 and it has attracted considerable academic discussion – see for example G King, CJL Murray 'Rethinking Human security' (2002) 116 *Political Science Quarterly* 585.

83  M Afzal 'Rethinking asylum: the feasibility of human security as new ratione personae protection' (2005) 3 *Journal of International Law & Policy* 2:1, 2:24.

84  R Paris 'Human security: paradigm shift or hot air?' (2001) 26 *International Security* 87.

85  G Oberleitner 'Human security: a challenge to international law?' (2005) 11 *Global Governance* 185, 187.

86  See Human Security Centre *Human Security Report 2005: War and Peace in the 21st Century* (OUP 2005).

87  ibid.

88  UNDP *New Dimensions of Human Security* (n 82) 22 and in general the Commission on Human Security *Human Security Now* (Commission on Human Security 2003).

89  H van Ginkel, E Newman 'In quest of "Human security"' (2000) 14 *Japan Review of International Affairs* 79.

90  Oberleitner 'Human security' (n 85) 188.

91  ibid; N Thomas, WT Tow 'The utility of human security: sovereignty and humanitarian intervention' (2002) 33 *Security Dialogue* 177.

92  T Owen 'Human security – conflict, critique and consensus: colloquium remarks and a proposal for a threshold-based definition' (2004) 35 *Security Dialogue* 373, 381.

93  ibid 382.

94  ibid 383.

ensure his or her security.[95] Howard-Hassman[96] warns, however, that an overly broad interpretation of human security is a potential threat to the protection of human rights, as human rights could be subordinated to human security. In the European Security Strategy (ESS),[97] adopted in December 2003 at the Brussels European Council meeting,[98] the EU equated human security with external threats and protection of the territory, the traditional concern of security policy. However, in the Barcelona Report of 2004,[99] the Study Group on Europe's Security Capabilities reporting to the EU High Representative for Common Foreign and Security Policy, Javier Solana, attempted to flesh out the ESS. The study group put forward six principles on which European security doctrine should be built[100] with the first principle, the primacy of human rights,[101] underpinning all others.[102] By prioritising human rights, the concerns of Howard-Hassman recede and, as Edwards[103] suggests, the European human security policy applies to all individuals, be they EU citizens or TCNs resident within the territory of the Union. However, Oberleitner[104] correctly notes that whilst there is room for interaction between human rights and human security, interchangeable use of the two concepts would damage both. Indeed, the danger is threefold:[105] a possible dilution of the legal character of human rights; a potential securitisation of human rights; and governments able to choose to defy human rights obligations in favour of human security.

### 6.2.5   *Human rights*

Some supporters of open borders deploy an ethical or humanitarian argument for the free movement of persons across all frontiers. The human rights factor in policy formation in the treatment of TCNs has a more limited role than this but is equally as significant and important. There are again two layers: the international and the internal. At the international level dealing with immigration or movement of persons into the EU, the UDHR provides the basis for any human rights considerations. However, as we have seen above, there is no right of immigration

---

95  RE Howard-Hassman 'Human security: undermining human rights?' (2012) 34 *Human Rights Quarterly* 88, 90.
96  ibid 99.
97  Council Document 15895/03.
98  Council Document 5381/04 para 84.
99  Study Group on Europe's Security Capabilities 'Barcelona Report: a human security doctrine for Europe' September 2004 http://www2.lse.ac.uk/internationalDevelopment/research/CSHS/humanSecurity/barcelonaReport.pdf.
100  ibid 8.
101  ibid 14.
102  M Kaldor, M Martin and S Selchow 'Human security: a new strategic narrative for Europe' (2007) 83 *International Affairs* 273, 283.
103  A Edwards 'Human security and the rights of refugees: transcending territorial and disciplinary borders' (2009) 30 *Michigan Journal of International Law* 763.
104  G Oberleitner 'Porcupines in love: the intricate convergence of human rights and human security' [2005] EHRLR 588, 605.
105  ibid 606.

under the UDHR or equivalent international treaties. For refugees the basis of international protection is provided by the Geneva Convention on the Status of Refugees 1951 and the 1967 Protocol (the Geneva Convention).[106] It must be noted that this is only directed at a limited category of TCNs and therefore only affects policy formation dealing with refugees.

Once a TCN has entered a Member State, whether that is by legal or illegal means, human rights are protected at the domestic level by the European Convention on Human Rights (ECHR) and national policy formation must take account of the rights protected by the ECHR. In the EU the Charter of Fundamental Rights according to Article 6(1) TEU has the 'same legal value as the Treaties', thereby ensuring that the Charter is the dominant human rights instrument determining policy formation in the EU.[107] However, it must also be noted that Article 6(2) TEU provides authority for the EU to accede to the ECHR, thereby eventually enabling the ECHR to influence policy formation at the Union level as it does presently at the national level.

### 6.2.6  *Cultural*

The final major policy formation factor is the cultural dimension and the idea of identity formation.[108] Nationals of third countries have diverse cultural backgrounds that can range from educated, Christian and relatively wealthy individuals (for example citizens of the former UK dominions, Canada, Australia, South Africa and New Zealand) to uneducated, Muslim and poor (for example Afghan or Somalian refugees or asylum-seekers). The former individuals could be considered to be closer to the dominant European culture than to that of the latter and as such it is possible to perceive the immigration of the former more favourably than that of the latter. Indeed, the migration of significantly culturally diverse individuals could be seen as a threat to the stability of the host society and the perception of the society's identity formation. Once the TCN has entered the EU this perceived threat can be dealt with in one of two ways. The first is to require assimilation of the culture of the TCN to that of the culture of the host state, or the dominant European culture. The second is to respect the culture of the TCN and to accommodate a multicultural[109] approach to cultural diversification. Article 15(1)(a) of the International Covenant on Economic, Social and Cultural Rights 1966 (ICCPR) recognises that everyone has the right to 'take part in cultural life' but this could be interpreted to provide for assimilation or multiculturalism.

---

106  Examined further in ch 4.
107  See K Lenaerts 'Exploring the limits of the EU Charter of Fundamental Rights' (2012) 8 *EuConst* 375.
108  K Xuereb 'European cultural policy and migration: why should cultural policy in the European Union address the impact of migration on identity and social integration?' (2011) 49 *International Migration* 28.
109  See in particular W Kymlicka *Multicultural Citizenship: A Liberal Theory of Minority Rights* (OUP 1995); J Raz 'Multiculturalism' (1998) 11 *Ratio Juris* 193.

A further element in the cultural consideration is the issue of family reunification. The right to found a family is stated in Article 16(1) of the UDHR with the limitation of arbitrary or unlawful interference with the family by Article 17(1) ICCPR as it is the 'natural and fundamental group unit of society'.[110] An actual right to family reunification can be found in two international conventions. The first is the United Nations Convention on the Rights of the Child 1989 (CRC), where Article 8(1) creates an obligation on states to preserve 'family relations, as recognized by law without unlawful interference' and to ensure that a child is not involuntarily separated from his or her parents[111] and that 'applications by a child or his or her parents to enter or leave a State Party for the purpose of family reunification shall be dealt with by States Parties in a positive, humane and expeditious manner'.[112] The second is in Article 44 of the International Convention on the Protection of the Rights of All Migrant Workers and Members of Their Families 1990. Paragraph 1 requires states to 'take appropriate measures to ensure the protection of the unity of the families of migrant workers', whilst in paragraph 2 states must 'facilitate the reunification of migrant workers with their spouses . . . as well as with their minor dependent unmarried children'. From these international conventions a factor to be considered when formulating policy for the treatment of TCNs is family reunification.

## 6.3   Legal rationality

It will be recalled that legal rationality consists of three elements: formal; instrumental; and substantive rationalities. These are the measurable benchmarks against which the outcomes from Chapters 3–5 will be set. Any results of rationality or irrationality must be given a practical grounding, which is provided by outlining the underlying policy considerations towards TCNs in the Union on this topic and locating the legal rationality assessment within these policy purposes. This is applied through the doctrine of objective justification.

The three elements of legal rationality each contain their own distinct components that were outlined in Chapter 2. For formal rationality the law must be consistent. Inconsistency can occur in any combination of three ways: doctrinal positions from outside EU law; different doctrinal positions within Union law; and cases within a particular area of EU law. Instrumental rationality is constituted by two elements: generic and specific. The Fullerian procedural principles provide the framework for the investigation of the generic element of instrumental rationality. It requires legal doctrine to be capable of guiding action for which the generic qualities of instrumental rationality are necessary but not sufficient. Sufficiency is provided by the inclusion of specific instrumental rationality. As such, generic instrumental rationality is compatible with the concept of the rule of law, relying on the principle of effectiveness rather than morality. Generic

---

110  Article 23(1) ICCPR.
111  Article 9(1) CRC.
112  Article 10(1) CRC.

instrumental rationality requires legal rules to be general, promulgated, prospective, clear, non-contradictory and relatively constant. They should not require the impossible and there should be congruence between the law as officially declared and the law as administered. Specific instrumental rationality creates sufficiency for action-guidance when complementing the generic version and contains three factors. The first is that legitimate ends or goals must be promoted in a good faith manner or attempt by the legislative bodies or judiciary when acting within the legal enterprise. Thus, the 'law abiding citizen . . . does not *apply* legal rules to serve specific ends set by the law-giver, but rather *follows* them in the conduct of his own affairs, the interests he is presumed to serve in following legal rules being those of society generally'.[113] The second factor is that legal officials must utilise the most effective legal technique to achieve societal ends, ensuring that the function of the legal act matches its effect. The third factor is the acknowledgement that legislative officials and the judiciary will employ different ideologies, based on personal or normative beliefs, when drafting and interpreting legal instruments. Substantive rationality requires that all rules of law must be based on good reasons so that legal doctrine can be sustained on plausible empirical facts and that the underlying principle can be justifiable or legitimate. Such justification takes place through the application of standards of fairness recognised by the community. As fairness is value-laden then the standards envisaged must be moral through the application of human rights norms within the Union. Such human rights norms are possessed by individuals on the basis of their innate humanity.

Once the legal rationality analysis has been conducted any findings of irrationality must be construed by the principle of objective justification, such that the policy must be a legitimate aim, it must satisfy the tests of suitability and necessity and the balancing exercise must come down on the side of the policy, for it to be justified. It is here that rationality and policy come together as it must be considered which of the general policy concerns described above best fit which element of rationality. That best fit has to apply to TCNs in general rather than to specific categories such that a purely economic benchmark would fail adequately to consider asylum-seekers or refugees, or indeed illegal immigrants. It has been established that the elements of formal and instrumental rationality are value-neutral. They both need to take account of the six factors above but they do so in a way that is strictly neutral and so some factors are likely to be of greater importance than others, such as the legal, economic, status, 'national' security and 'assimilation' model of culture elements. However, substantive rationality in comparison is value-laden as it is determined by the protection of human rights within the Union. As such the value-laden elements of policy formation will be significantly more important, with human rights, 'human' security and multiculturalism as the dominant elements for policy formation. The EU policy benchmarks from which the necessary elements are extracted

---

113 LL Fuller *The Morality of Law* (Yale University Press 1969) 207 (Fuller's emphasis).

are of course laid down by the Tampere Conclusions, the Hague Programme and now the Stockholm Programme, which are voluntary commitments by the EU to improve the position of TCNs. The policy factors outlined above and set out in the latest version of the policy benchmarks, the Stockholm Programme, become the legitimate aims that attempt objectively to justify any findings of irrationality.

### 6.3.1   Free movement rights under the treaties and implementing legislation

#### 6.3.1.1   Formal legal rationality

As outlined above, there are three possible avenues for legal irrationality to occur in a formal setting. These are all evident when considering the analysis conducted in Chapter 3.

The first issue involves contradiction between an international legal system, namely that of the ECHR and the judgments of the ECtHR, which co-exists with this substantive area of EU law, and creates a separate and possibly contradictory legal doctrine. In Chapter 3 of this book it was established that Regulation 1408/71,[114] implementing Article 48 TFEU, included stateless persons and refugees within its scope of application but other TCNs were excluded. The ECtHR in *Gaygusuz*[115] held that a social security provision was a pecuniary right for the purpose of Article 1 of Protocol No 1 and that denying the applicant this right on the grounds of nationality was in breach of Article 14 ECHR. It is certainly the case that Member States as signatories to Protocol No 1 would be bound to comply with this ruling under international law. The contradictory position between the two legal positions of the Union and the ECHR appeared to have been resolved with the enactment of Regulation 859/03/EC.[116] However, a cross-border EU nexus had to be established before its provisions could bite and thus it failed fully to implement the *Gaygusuz* judgment. Moreover, with a legal basis of Article 64(3) EC and Denmark's opt-out of the regulation's adoption, inconsistency was retained. Regulation 1408/71 and Regulation 859/03 have now been replaced by Regulation 883/04[117] and Regulation 1231/10[118] respectively that replicate the personal scope of the

---

114  Council Regulation 1408/71/EEC on the application of social security schemes to employed persons, to self-employed persons and to members of their families moving within the Community [1971] OJ L149/2.

115  *Gaygusuz v Austria* (1996) 23 EHRR 364.

116  Council Regulation 859/03/EC extending the provisions of Regulation 1408/71/EEC and Regulation 574/72/EEC to nationals of third countries who are not already covered by these provisions solely on the ground of their nationality [2003] OJ L124/1.

117  European Parliament and Council Regulation 883/2004/EC on the coordination of social security systems [2004] OJ L166/1.

118  European Parliament and Council Regulation 1231/2010/EU extending Regulation 883/2004/EC and Regulation 987/2009/EC to nationals of third countries who are not already covered by these Regulations solely on the ground of their nationality [2010] OJ L344/1.

previous measures. The latter regulation has a legal base of Article 79(2)(b) TFEU and it does not apply to the UK or Denmark, thus making a confused situation even more confused. It was the case that for Regulation 1408/71 to bite there had to be a cross-border element,[119] and this remains the case for Regulation 883/04. It could therefore be argued that on the basis of requiring movement between Member States TCNs and European citizens are treated the same without contradiction. However, the contradiction lies between the ECHR judgment and the scope of Regulations 1408/71 and 859/03, and Regulations 883/04 and 1231/10. A person whose situation is confined in all respects within a single Member State may still be discriminated against on the basis of nationality over the allocation of a social security provision under EU legislation but not in accordance with the ECHR. As such the two legal doctrines are contradictory.

For the examination of objective justification the objectives underpinning the policy formation in this area provide a complex structure of interests. The legal element itself comprises three factors: the necessary requirement for the Member States to comply with judgments of the ECtHR; the legal fact that the EU has yet to accede to the ECHR and therefore has no binding commitment to comply with the ECHR; and the question of national sovereignty. The latter point is a difficult area, particularly when considering the position of social security. The Member States have transferred their sovereignty over social security for citizens of the EU to the extent that Regulation 1408/71, and now Regulation 883/04, coordinates the social security schemes of Member States and have extended this for Regulation 859/03 and for Regulation 1231/10, except for the UK and Denmark. However, the lacuna, identified by the ECtHR, remains and can only be resolved by loosening sovereignty further by enabling TCNs to be able to claim social security without taking into account nationality, in accordance with the *Gaygusuz* judgment. The question of social security leads to the second underlying factor affecting policy, the economic element. The full implication of the *Gaygusuz* judgment could have a significant impact on the social welfare schemes of Member States, as all TCNs migrating into the EU from a third country would be able to claim. With the estimated number of TCNs resident in the EU standing at 20.1 million, theoretically all of these TCNs would be able to claim, which would potentially have a greater impact on some Member States, particularly those with significant TCN populations, such as Germany, Spain and the UK. Furthermore, it has been suggested that welfare acts as a magnet for migration,[120] leading to even greater numbers coming to the EU and claiming. However, the majority of the 20.1 million TCNs resident in the EU are in employment and would not require social security and recent empirical evidence suggests that welfare has little magnetic effect.[121] However, even if welfare does act as a magnet then this would act as a factor to encourage the inflow of TCNs, an essential requirement for the EU to enable

119  Case C–153/91 *Camille Petit v Office National des Pensions* [1992] ECR I–4973 para 10.
120  Borjas 'Immigration and welfare Magnets' (n 71).
121  Giulietti 'Unemployment benefits' (n 72).

economic growth and the production of sufficient resources to manage the care of an aging population.

It must be determined whether these aims behind the policy are legitimate. As the policy on social security is a specific policy of the EU and at this time the EU has still not acceded to the ECHR then it has to be concluded that the legal aim is legitimate, and also satisfies the tests for suitability and necessity. Furthermore, the economic aim, when assessed with the wide discretion of the rational basis test, must also be considered as legitimate, the potential impact on the Member States' social security systems being so extreme. The limitation of social security applying to TCNs without exercising free movement does potentially contribute to the achievement of the economic goal, thereby satisfying the requirement of suitability,[122] and it is difficult to perceive a less restrictive approach, thus satisfying the test for necessity.[123] After finding that the aims are legitimate and there is satisfaction of the suitability and necessity tests the wide discretion available to policy-makers enables the balancing exercise, taking into account the opposing economic rationale for freedom of movement of TCNs, to come down on the side of justifying the policy.

The second issue lies in the area of contradiction within European law between different doctrinal positions in the EU legal pantheon. The first possibility of contradiction between EU doctrines lies between the principle of non-discrimination and both citizenship of the Union and right to free movement of workers. Article 18 TFEU provides for the right to non-discrimination on the basis of nationality and, by its wording, if TCNs can bring themselves within the scope of application of the EU treaties then they could expect to rely on its protection. However, the scope of Union law does not include TCNs, as they are not citizens of the Union or workers within the parameters of Article 45 TFEU, and so they cannot enjoy the rights conferred by the EU treaties through the possession of the status of worker or EU citizen. They thus suffer discrimination on the basis of their nationality and there is contradiction between two legal doctrines twice: first, the principle of non-discrimination and Union citizenship; and secondly, non-discrimination and free movement of workers. The citizenship jurisprudence of the ECJ has exacerbated the former contradiction by transforming the right to non-discrimination as a right in itself and a human right into a right linked to citizenship of the Union, and thus a citizen right. This is exacerbated by the creation of Part Two of the TFEU, which brings together the treaty provisions on non-discrimination with those on Union citizenship. The AFSJ (see Chapter 4) now brings TCNs within the scope of Union law and so they may fall within the scope *ratione personae* of Article 18 TFEU, depending on the jurisprudence of the ECJ, in which case the contradiction between the two doctrines of non-discrimination and citizenship would be removed. This does not remove the apparent contradiction between free movement of workers and

122  K Möller 'Proportionality: challenging the critics' (2012) 10 *International Journal of Constitutional Law* 709, 713.
123  ibid.

discrimination of TCNs on the basis of nationality. It must be questioned, however, whether there is tension between the two doctrines as TCNs cannot exercise a right of freedom of movement as they do not have the right in the first place. This lack of right is on the basis of their nationality, but it is not discriminatory and so there is no contradiction between the two doctrines.

A further contradiction exists between two forms of the non-discrimination principle, which it could also be argued is also a contradictory position within a single area of Union law, namely non-discrimination. The two are the prohibitions on race and ethnic origin, and nationality discrimination. The Race and Ethnic Origin Directive[124] limits its material scope so that non-discrimination on the basis of nationality is not included and it does not apply to the entry, residence or status of TCNs. It therefore excludes the non-discrimination principle from a significant number of ethnic minorities in three particularly important areas of policy and permits Member States to discriminate against TCNs on the basis of their nationality in these policy areas, effectively discriminating on the basis of race or ethnic origin. This is a contradiction both between doctrines and within a single area of EU law.

Article 6(1) TEU provides that the Charter of Fundamental Rights will have the same legal value as the EU Treaties and its provisions will be capable of being utilised by persons as the basis of a legal action. Article 21(1) is a general non-discrimination clause that is clear, precise and unconditional and, it is submitted, capable of having direct effect. The non-discrimination grounds are extensive, non-exhaustive and appear to be without restriction. This contradicts the more limited and non-directly effective Article 19 TFEU. It could also contradict the limited scope of the Race Directive and the Employment Directive.[125] These provisions of the Charter must, however, comply with the horizontal provisions of the Charter found in Chapter VII and Article 52(2) requires Charter rights based on the EU treaties to be 'exercised under the conditions and within the limits defined by those Treaties'. It is uncertain until the ECJ rules on these provisions the extent of this limitation but it is conceivable that instead of contradictions within the principle of non-discrimination there are merely tensions between different legal instruments that require interpreting by the Court. Furthermore, as Blackstock notes,[126] for the wider rights in Article 21(1) of the Charter, if Article 19 TFEU action has not been taken in those areas then Article 52(2) might be inapplicable such that Article 21(1) would apply and again there would be no contradiction between doctrines, or within the doctrine of non-discrimination.

Contradictions between different doctrines or within the doctrine of non-discrimination, rather than merely tensions, will amount to formal irrationality

---

124 Council Directive 2000/43/EC implementing the principle of equal treatment between persons irrespective of racial or ethnic origin [2000] OJ L180/22.

125 Council Directive 2000/78/EC establishing a general framework for equal treatment in employment and occupation [2000] OJ L303/16.

126 J Blackstock 'The EU Charter of Fundamental Rights: scope and competence' 18 April 2012 http://eutopialaw.com/2012/04/18/the-eu-charter-of-fundamental-rights-scope-and-competance-2/.

requiring to be objectively justified to legitimise the policy. The aims of the policy are cultural, status based or for the protection of human rights and an aim itself can be legitimate or the matrix of objectives can be legitimate. The question of culture is grounded in assimilation or multiculturalism – should TCNs assimilate with the dominant European culture or should Europe accept the culture of TCNs on a multiculturalist basis? The integration of TCNs 'has gained increasing importance on the European agenda in recent years'[127] but whether this integration should be by assimilation or multiculturalism is not addressed[128] and is a highly controversial issue. A less controversial way of looking at the cultural issue would be to focus simply on the issue of integration of TCNs in a particular area, with a key way of integrating TCNs into society, or at least those resident for a long period of time, being to ensure TCNs were able to enforce rights of non-discrimination, particularly as they apply to free movement. In Cholewinski's opinion,[129] this would aid the achievement of social justice, economic efficiency with the successful completion of the internal market and would be a vital element in the elimination of racial and ethnic discrimination. As integration of TCNs is a legitimate aim and a key issue on the policy agenda then classifying the status of TCNs is another important policy factor. Discrimination on the basis of nationality when compared to citizens of the EU immediately bestows an inferior status on TCNs and a limitation on the rights that flow from it. If it is accepted that by definition TCNs cannot be citizens of the EU then an alternative status needs to be considered. If the status chosen is that of alien then there would appear little incentive to grant rights to individuals as there is no intention for integration to take place, clearly at odds with EU policy stance in the Stockholm Programme. Granting worker status would enable individuals to be granted rights and to enable integration. However, for individuals to achieve the full benefits of worker status they must be able to enjoy the benefits of the principle of non-discrimination, something that the EU has limited to Union citizens and their family members. It could be that TCNs can be classified as denizens without the right to non-discrimination but again this appears to be at odds with the aim of integration. The final objective is the protection of human rights and the status of the principle of non-discrimination itself. The principle of non-discrimination is designed to give substantive effect to the right to equality.[130] As such it is a human right that should be available to all individuals to enable them to claim their right to equality. The case law of the ECJ has removed the universality of the principle

---

127  Commission Communication on a common agenda for integration: framework for the integration of third-country nationals in the European Union COM(2005) 389 final 3.
128  This is still not addressed in the Commission Communication on a European agenda for the integration of third-country nationals COM(2011) 455 final.
129  R Cholewinski 'The rights of non-EC immigrant workers and their families in EC countries of employment: a case for integration' in J Dine, B Watt *Discrimination Law: Concepts, Limitations and Justifications* (Longman 1996) 134, 136.
130  See C Barnard 'The principle of equality in the Community context: *P, Grant, Kalanke* and *Marschall*: four uneasy bedfellows?' (1998) 57 *CLJ* 352, who argues that the principle of non-discrimination provides the substantive filling for the vacuum of formal equality suggested by P Westen 'The empty idea of equality' (1982) 95 *HLR* 537.

through the link created between citizenship and non-discrimination and re-crafted it as a citizen right taking it away from its actual purpose, which has now been more formally recognised in Part Two of the TFEU. As such therefore the aim, instead of being one designed to protect human rights, is targeted at the protection of citizen rights.

Turning to objective justification, the first thing to note is that it is uncertain whether there is a contradictory position for TCNs and the personal scope of Article 18 TFEU with the introduction of the AFSJ, and the relationship between Article 19 TFEU and Article 21(1) of the Charter. Much will depend on the interpretation of the ECJ. Furthermore, apparent contradictions could merely be tensions between doctrinal positions, as there is between rights of free movement and the principle of non-discrimination. However, the limitation on the material scope of the Race and Ethnic Origin Directive excluding discrimination of the basis of nationality effectively enables discrimination to take place on the basis of race or ethnic origin. This is clearly a contradictory stance and thus formally irrational. The cultural and status policy aims identified above with a wide margin of discretion would be legitimate, would satisfy the tests of suitability and necessity for culture and status and the balancing exercise would come down on the side of the aim being proportionate. However, the position of human rights as the third factor above, although value-neutral under formal rationality, creates concerns as the policy aim appears to limit the unanimity principle of the doctrine of non-discrimination and confining it to Union citizens. Thus, the aim is illegitimate and cannot justify the finding of irrationality, without any need to examine the tests for suitability and necessity or to conduct the balancing exercise.

The third issue involves the principle of the freedom of movement of persons, either with another principle or within the doctrine itself. The establishment of the internal market is a major policy objective of the Union that was characterised in the EC Treaty by the removal of barriers to the free movement of persons between Member States (Article 3(1)(c) EC). The Lisbon Treaty has seen a subtle reordering of the objectives of the EU with no mention of free movement of persons relating to the internal market. Thus, Article 3(2) TEU ties free movement of persons to the AFSJ that is only offered to Union citizens. However, the literal, and wide, reading of Article 26(2) TFEU continues the approach of the former EC Treaty and implies the abolition of all frontier controls on all persons, irrespective of nationality, to create the internal market. However, the requirement of free movement of workers within the EU as specified by Article 45 TFEU, in which the term workers was intended similarly to encompass all persons irrespective of nationality, has been narrowed to nationals of Member States by secondary legislation and the ECJ. Thus the wide interpretation of persons in the doctrine of the internal market appears to stand in contradiction to that employed for the freedom of movement of workers. However, especially with the new approach to the internal market and free movement of persons in the Lisbon Treaty, this contradiction is actually tension between two doctrinal positions and the initial meaning of 'persons' has been limited by secondary legislation and the ECJ, thereby pulling in the same direction but in a more narrow vein.

The limitation of the definition of workers to nationals of Member States within the doctrine of freedom of movement of workers, first by secondary legislation and then more recently by the ECJ's case law, appears also to be a contradiction but this time with the meaning intended by the EC Treaty's founding fathers. The delay by the Court in confirming this limitation, even though it had opportunities to do so in the past, would appear to indicate a concern within the ECJ over this apparently contradictory definition in the secondary legislation with the intentions for freedom of movement of workers set out in the EC Treaty and now in the TFEU. This, it is submitted, illustrates a contradiction at the heart of the freedom of movement principle. The policy here has a number of aims. The first is legal, with Member States retaining sovereignty over decisions of entry and exit of nationals from outside the Union. The second is economic, with the objective of ensuring the benefits of the right to freedom of movement are restricted to Union citizens and their family members. A third possible aim is cultural, in that if nationals from outside the Union move to a Member State then it will be easier for them to assimilate and integrate into that Member State's community if their freedom of movement is constrained.

A third element of inconsistency appears to be evident in the use of the term 'freely' in Article 18 EC. If a citizen of the Union has a right to move and reside freely, then adopting legislative measures, and interpreting such a right of free residence, so that the right to reside is not a stand-alone principle but limited by the requirement of sickness insurance and sufficient resources not to be a burden on the host Member State contradicts the term 'freely', as movement and residence is not free. The policy aim here is clearly economic, with the responsibility of ensuring that the move from the home to the host Member State be laid on the shoulders of the individual.

A final layer of contradiction within this issue arises with Article 24(2) of the Citizens' Directive.[131] This provision permits Member States not to confer the entitlement of social assistance on applicants within the scope of the directive for the first three months of residence or longer where the individual is seeking employment. This social assistance is equivalent to the jobseeker's allowance granted to those searching for employment in the UK. However, the Court in *Collins*[132] held that, following the introduction of Union citizenship and its interpretation by the ECJ, it was no longer possible to exclude from the scope of equal treatment a benefit of a financial nature intended to facilitate access to employment in the labour market of a Member State, which included jobseeker's allowance. Therefore, there appears to be a contradiction between the

131  European Parliament and Council Directive 2004/38/EC on the right of citizens of the Union and their family members to move and reside freely within the territory of the Member States [2004] OJ L158/77.
132  Case C–138/02 *Brian Francis Collins v Secretary of State for Work and Pensions* [2003] ECR I–2703.

directive and the ECJ case law on the same subject matter. In *Vatsouras*[133] the Court attempted to square the circle by finding that benefits intended to facilitate access to the labour market could not be regarded as constituting social assistance and thus fell outside the scope of Article 24(2), thereby removing the contradiction.

As has been seen before objective justification of the contradictory approaches requires first that the aims are legitimate. The legal rationale for not extending free movement rights to TCNs will be legitimate if Member States have retained their sovereignty over controlling the entry and exit of all TCNs. The personal scope of Directive 2004/38 makes it clear that rights of freedom of movement are granted to Union citizens but that family members within the scope of Articles 2(2) and 3(2) can move with or join the Union citizen. Thus these derived rights for TCNs ensure that Member States do not retain control over entrance to their territory. Furthermore, the retention of the right of residence upon the death of a Union citizen or divorce and the right to permanent residence after five years' residing with the EU citizen in the host state create personal rights of residence for TCNs that is out of the control of Member States. Thus the legal aim is not legitimate. The economic objective is legitimate if TCNs do not also produce economic effects. This is clearly absurd as a TCN worker, purely from an economic angle, will be a unit of production providing benefit to the economy. However, there is a further element to the economic aim, which is that if an individual exercises their right to freedom of movement then there is a complementary responsibility on the individual for their and their family's wellbeing and not ensuring that they do not become a burden on the host Member State. This objective appears to be legitimate with the measures in the Citizen Directive being suitable and necessary and the *stricto sensu* test of proportionality comes down on the side of this aim, justifying the finding of formal irrationality. Finally, the cultural aim can be countered with the fact that as TCNs have already moved from a third country to a Member State in the EU then it is highly likely that they would be more willing to exercise a right of free movement within the EU than nationals of Member States because they are not as constrained by social, cultural or familial ties. Indeed, the lack of cultural ties to the host Member State can be seen as an advantage enabling the TCN to move within the EU for the greatest effect. Therefore the aims are not legitimate, even with the application of wide discretion to policy-makers, and the finding of formal irrationality cannot be justified.

### 6.3.1.2 Instrumental legal rationality

As previously outlined, there are two levels of instrumental legal rationality: generic, which is further examined through the eight Fullerian characteristics; and specific. These are both considered here, although only relevant characteristics

---

133 Joined Cases C–22 & 23/08 *Athanasios Vatsouras & Josif Koupatantze v Arbeitsgemeinschaft (ARGE) Nürnberg 900* [2009] ECR I–4585 para 45.

are discussed. It should be noted initially that the contradictions identified under formal irrationality also fall under the heading of contradictions for instrumental generic irrationality, but this time any tensions are discounted as it is the straight contradiction that is of concern. Furthermore, any analysis of objective justification has a higher standard of review, reflecting the importance of the rule of law to the concept of legitimacy but instrumental rationality is strictly value-neutral. As such, the *Gaygusuz* contradiction between the EU approach to social security and that of the ECtHR will continue to be objectively justified until the EU accedes to the ECHR as required by Article 6(2) TEU thus satisfying a legal aim, even though the economic aim for *Gaygusuz* would not be legitimate as only potential impact would not actually outweigh restrictions of rights. However, the contradictory positions involving non-discrimination and free movement of persons need more careful consideration as they are funda-mental principles that should only be justified if the reasons are narrow and specific. The legitimacy of the aims were found above to be economic. When weighing economic aims against fundamental principles, under a reasonably strict intensity of review, then the balance must come down in favour of the latter, thereby finding that the contradictions involving non-discrimination and free movement of persons are instrumentally irrational and not justified.

The first matter deals with the treatment of TCNs in comparison with that of citizens of the EU. The difference in the general treatment of TCNs by EU law compared with EU citizens could suggest that the law fails the requirement of generality, such that the law is inconsistent, and that individuals in similar posi-tions are treated differently. This could be especially the case where TCNs are economically active in the host Member State through employment and paying taxes as well as enjoying the benefits of society and so it could be thought that TCNs are treated unfairly as they are treated in a different manner to citizens of the Union. However, Union law is applied consistently and TCNs are treated equally to other individuals in a similar position, as the individuals to whom TCNs must be compared are their fellow TCNs. Furthermore, both primary and sec-ondary legislation is of general application throughout the Union so a case in one Member State will be treated in a similar manner across the EU.

The second issue deals with congruence such that the law as it is officially declared is compatible with the law as it is administered. The principles of non-discrimination on the grounds of nationality and citizenship of the Union appear to be problematic areas. The law as it is stated in Article 18 TFEU is specific that 'any discrimination on the grounds of nationality shall be prohibited' so long as the matter can be brought within the scope of the application of the EU treaties. Although TCNs had difficulty bringing themselves within the scope *ratione personae* of Article 18 TFEU, as they were outside the scope of the EU treaties, it is clear from the wording of the provision that if this hurdle could be cleared then Article 18 TFEU could be relied upon. The development of Union citizenship, and the subsequent ECJ case law, however, has shifted the principle from a human right to a citizen right, dependent on possession of the nationality of a Member State. Therefore, to rely on the principle of non-discrimination on the ground of nationality there has to be a requirement for individuals to be discriminated against on the basis of their nationality. There is also a cause for concern here in the way the law has been applied in practice and as the law specified at the time of the Treaty of Rome. The EC Treaty underwent frequent amendments and policy areas developed over time leading to the current Lisbon Treaty. However, the principle of the freedom of movement of workers as originally stated in the Treaty of Rome in 1957, and as now enunciated in Article 45 TFEU, has not been amended. It was argued in Chapter 3 that the original intention of the freedom of movement of workers was for the term 'workers' to apply to all individuals legally resident within the territory of the Union regardless of nationality, and thus to include TCNs within its *ratione personae*. Through the introduction of secondary legislation limiting this freedom of movement to nationals of Member States, and with the ECJ now confirming this limitation, the law in practice apparently contradicts the law as originally declared and a state of incongruence exists. It should be noted that findings or formal rationality over the same policy do not influence considerations of instrumental rationality as the underlying objectives are different. The aims of the policy approach towards discrimination on the basis of nationality for TCNs are legal with national interests playing a central role, that is, status based, which classifies TCNs as aliens and is linked to the legal aim, and leading to a citizenship rather than human rights objective. The legitimacy of these aims appears to be satisfied when viewed through the lens of the objectives of the Stockholm Programme, which equates fundamental rights protection with Union citizenship. However, such a limitation of fundamental rights appears to undermine the essential element of the protection of human rights that they are applicable to all on the basis of innate humanity. Thus, although the legal and status based aims are legitimate, the protection of human rights objective is not legitimate and therefore instrumental irrationality is not objectively justified. The legal and status based aims would satisfy the tests for suitability and necessity and the balancing exercise for the legal objective would objectively justify the finding of irrationality. However, the balancing exercise for the status of TCNs would need to be viewed from the different status models available and the objective in the Stockholm Programme to grant TCNs 'rights and obligations comparable to those of citizens of the Union'.[134] On that basis the status based aim would fail the proportionality test.

A further necessary element contained within instrumental rationality is that of specific instrumental rationality, which creates sufficiency for action-guidance when complementing the generic version. Three factors constitute specific instrumental rationality, of which two are applicable here. The first is that legitimate ends or goals must be promoted in a good faith manner or attempt by the legislative bodies or judiciary when acting within the legal enterprise. The ends that European legal doctrines are meant to promote are those laid down in Article 3 TEU. These do not mention TCNs specifically, although Article 3(3) TEU requires

---

134  The Stockholm Programme (n 25) 30.

the Union to establish an internal market and Article 3(2) TEU mandates the Union to 'offer its citizens an area of freedom, security and justice without internal frontiers, in which the free movement of persons is ensured in conjunction with appropriate measures with respect to external border controls, asylum, immigration'. These objectives in the Lisbon Treaty are subtly different to those set out in the previous TEU and EC Treaty, now enhancing the position of Union citizens vis-à-vis free movement of persons and the AFSJ. However, Article 26 TFEU on the internal market retains the previous position such that it is to be 'an area without internal frontiers in which the free movement of . . . persons . . . is ensured'. Moreover, aspirational societal goals are included in the preambles to the TEU and the TFEU. These include 'an ever closer union among the peoples of Europe' and, for the TEU, the facilitation of the free movement of persons in an area of freedom, security and justice. Thus, although not mentioned in the ends of the Union, TCNs legally resident within the EU could legitimately infer an expectation to be included within the personal scope of the treaties by being included in the term 'persons' and 'peoples'. The exclusion of TCNs from the right to freedom of movement for workers by secondary legislation and the ECJ's subsequent curtailment of the rights in Article 45 TFEU to nationals of Member States, which apparently contradicted the intentions of the EEC's founding fathers, would appear to fail to promote the societal goals or ends of the Union. This failure to promote the goals or ends of the Union needs to be taken into consideration when carrying out the balancing exercise and, it is submitted, would negate any legitimate aims that were preferred for such a policy. As a consequence the finding of specific instrumental irrationality could not be objectively justified.

The second factor is that legal officials must utilise the most effective legal technique to achieve societal ends, ensuring that the function of the legal act matches its effect. The function of Article 18 TFEU is to prohibit discrimination on the grounds of nationality and thereby protect the individual. The development of Article 18 TFEU as a citizen right through the ECJ's interpretation of it with reference to Articles 20 and 21 TFEU, rather than a human right, and the Race Directive's exclusion of nationality discrimination from its material scope along with its lack of application to the entry, residence or status of TCNs, ensure that discrimination for TCNs on the grounds of nationality remains possible. The effect of Article 18 TFEU fails to match its function. The aims of the development of Article 18 TFEU have been predominantly status based and on the promotion of the Union citizen rather than the human rights of all individuals as suggested by a general provision on the principle of non-discrimination on the basis of nationality. This objective cannot be considered to be legitimate as it weighs against the fundamental status of human rights. Thus, once again, the irrationality result cannot be justified objectively.

### 6.3.1.3   *Substantive legal rationality*

The rights that a TCN enjoys from the EU treaties or secondary legislation implementing the treaties' provisions are subsidiary or derivative rights. These rights are not granted directly to TCNs on the basis of their own individual capacity, nor are they possessed personally, but they depend upon the specific relationship between the TCN and the right holder, who has to be a Union citizen. Directive 2004/38 does now enable TCNs who suffer divorce from, or the death of, their EU citizen spouse to retain the right of residence already granted if certain conditions are met. Indeed, this can be turned into a permanent right of residence. This is a significant improvement on the position before, where if the relationship failed or ceased to exist then the protection afforded to the TCN through such derived rights was removed immediately from the time of the failure. In fact this can still occur if the criteria for retained residence are not satisfied. However, the right of retained residence is still dependent upon the initial relationship with an EU citizen and, as the ECJ made clear in *Carpenter*,[135] the EU citizen's wife was able to remain with her husband because to separate the couple would have negatively affected Mr Carpenter's rights to freedom of movement, not Mrs Carpenter's. Such subordination of TCNs to the will of the right holder, or the polity, objectifies non-Member State nationals and in effect dehumanises them.[136] Legal doctrine is substantively justified or legitimised through human rights norms that require the individual to be subjectified. EU legal doctrine on the right of free movement for TCNs by objectifying human beings breaches the requirement of the standards of fairness in the community and must therefore be found to be substantively irrational. The concept of substantive rationality is controversial as it applies a value-laden judgment as to the standard by which law is to be analysed but any attempt at objective justification, by the very requirements of substantive rationality, requires the highest intensity of examination equating to the US standard of strict scrutiny test. As substantive rationality requires policy to be underpinned by the values found in human rights, only values of human rights can justify any finding of irrationality and only after a particularly diligent examination of the principle of proportionality. The difficulty here for objective justification is that TCNs can claim fundamental rights but they are derived rights and thus rights pertaining to the TCN's relationship with the actual right holder. There is therefore a dislocation between the ability to claim the right and the ownership of the right that resides on the question of principle. The result is the use of an aim to justify substantive irrationality that is not grounded in human rights and is thus not legitimate.

### 6.3.1.4 Conclusions and suggested solutions

The political legitimacy of freedom of movement of persons policy and policy outputs as viewed through the lens of legal rationality is flawed with findings of irrationality at the formal, instrumental and substantive levels. Some of these flaws can be objectively justified when the rationale for the policy is examined.

---

135 Case C–60/00 *Mary Carpenter v Secretary of State for the Home Department* [2002] ECR I–6279.
136 JHH Weiler 'Thou shalt not Oppress a stranger: On the judicial protection of the human rights of non-EC nationals' (1992) 3 *EJIL* 65.

However, there are two themes in particular that emerge: those of discrimination and human rights, which cause significant concerns and are difficult to objectively justify. Suggested solutions to these issues have different objectives depending on the level of irrationality so, for example, as formal and instrumental rationalities are value-neutral then solutions do not require any improvement in the lot of TCNs, merely the removal of the irrational policy stance. This should be compared to substantive rationality, where the value-laden nature of the concept requires the practical position of TCNs to be improved, in accordance with the objectives of the Stockholm Programme.

For both formal and instrumental rationality two adjustments in policy could alleviate the issues with irrationality. The first would be clearly to state, either through legislation or jurisprudence of the ECJ, that TCNs fall within the *ratione personae* of the principle of non-discrimination on the basis of nationality such that the nationality discrimination standard applied to all persons. By bringing TCNs within the scope of the treaties this could then lead to the second solution that would see the term 'workers' extended to TCNs. To correct the finding of substantive irrationality the suggested solution would be to grant rights to TCNs, thereby empowering TCNs to enforce their rights on their own behalf rather than through a relationship with an EU citizen.

### 6.3.2   Free movement rights based on the AFSJ

#### 6.3.2.1   Formal legal rationality

Similar to the appraisal of formal rationality for free movement rights, the three possible circumstances for contradictory policy to occur are evident in the analysis of the different legislative measures conducted in Chapter 4.

There is possible contradiction between EU law and other international legal systems in six specific areas. The first field of concern is that between international law commitments and the Dublin Regulation.[137] The Dublin Regulation enables an asylum-seeker to be returned to another Member State without assessing the merits of the asylum-seeker's case, as there is an automatic presumption in recital 2 that all Member States are safe for the return of asylum applicants, in contravention of Articles 3 and 13 ECHR.[138] Furthermore, it is assumed that Member States do not return asylum-seekers or refugee applicants to third countries in breach of their Geneva Convention commitments even though there is evidence to the contrary.[139] Elements of the Dublin Regulation that have been carried over from the Dublin Convention also cause

---

137   Council Regulation 343/2003/EC establishing the criteria and mechanisms for determining the Member State responsible for examining an asylum application lodged in one of the Member States by a third-country national [2003] OJ L50/1.

138   *MSS v Belgium and Greece* (2011) 53 EHRR 2 and Joined Cases C–411 & 493/10 *NS v Secretary of State for the Home Department* and *ME, ASM, MT, KP and EH v Refugee Applications Commissioner and Minister for Justice, Equality and Law Reform* [2012] 2 CMLR 9.

139   ibid; L Kok *The Dublin II Regulation* (UNHCR 2006) 2.

contradictory concerns. Article 3(3) of the Dublin Regulation allows Member States to send an asylum-seeker, pursuant to the national legislation, to a third country, so long as it is in compliance with the Geneva Convention. However, when this is married with bilateral readmission agreements between Member States and third countries and the readmission agreements are negotiated by the Commission on behalf of the EU with third countries, then problems are produced. Union readmission agreements include a clause requiring the third country to take back a non-national TCN even if he or she only transited through that third country. This in turn has seen EU neighbour third countries either signing their own bilateral agreements with other third countries or having a policy to hand on any returnees. Directive 2005/85[140] provides a definition of a safe third country (Article 27) and a European safe third country (Article 36), which enables a Member State to waive the requirement of any examination for the return of a TCN to one of these states. The combined effect of the Dublin Regulation, readmission agreements and Directive 2005/85 is chain *refoulement*, refugees in orbit and the contravention of a state's international obligations as set out in Article 33(1) of the Geneva Convention and Articles 3 and 13 ECHR.

The objective justification of any contradiction first requires the aims behind the policy to be identified. The first is the legal situation and for the Dublin Regulation two issues are apparent. Under Article 13(2) UDHR, first, there is no right of entry to a state and, secondly, that as a principle of national sovereignty a state has control over the entry and exit of persons to its territory, which includes asylum-seekers. This is ameliorated by international obligations based on treaties or conventions and in particular the Geneva Convention. Although the EU has not signed or ratified the Geneva Convention,[141] the Stockholm Programme[142] bases the development of a Common Policy on Asylum on 'a full and inclusive application of the 1951 Geneva Convention relating to the Status of Refugees and other relevant international treaties'. The second issue is the Member States' voluntary pooling of their national sovereignty in this area resulting in the Dublin Regulation, which also results in the transfer of international obligations to the EU as reflected in recital 2 of the Dublin Regulation as 'based on the full and inclusive application of the Geneva Convention'. The economic aim for a Member State is to ensure that the asylum-seeker does not become a burden on the state and in particular the social welfare systems of that state. Indeed, an influx of asylum-seekers could potentially produce a major burden on the state's welfare system before any economic benefits accrue from the asylum-seeker through working, paying taxes and contributing to the economy,

---

140 Council Directive 2005/85/EC on minimum standards on procedures in Member States for granting and withdrawing refugee status [2005] OJ L326/13.
141 The Stockholm Programme mandates the Union to accede to the 1951 Geneva Convention and 1967 Protocol, subject to a report from the Commission on the legal and practical consequences –The Stockholm Programme (n 25) 32. The Commission's Stockholm Programme Action Plan suggests that the report is due at some point in 2013 – Commission Communication on delivering an area of freedom, security and justice (n 47) 55.
142 The Stockholm Programme (n 25) 32.

although there is very little evidence of this actually happening. In recent years it is the states with the EU's eastern and southern external borders that have shouldered the burden of receiving significant numbers of asylum-seekers, at the same time as experiencing the most demanding economic circumstances of the Union. This economic burden[143] is shared unequally across the EU,[144] a situation that could be rectified through the redistribution of asylum-seekers across the EU[145] for which the Dublin Regulation should be a key instrument but is not.[146] Dublin III also does not resolve this situation, a situation that could be described as reverse free-riding with smaller and less well-off Member States paying more than larger, richer countries.[147] The third aim, with large numbers of asylum-seekers originating from Africa, Iraq or Afghanistan, is the protection of national, or European, security rather than human security with a perceived threat from terrorism for which the Dublin Regulation can control by limiting asylum applications to a single Member State and manage the application process. This security aim is enhanced by the portrayal of asylum-seekers through their classification in status as aliens and is not ameliorated by the suspicion of the native population, fuelled by tabloid newspaper reporting[148] and based on the cultural fear of the outsider. These latter two elements of status and culture cannot be considered as direct aims of the Dublin Regulation but they are consequential or indirect outcomes. For the contradiction to be objectively justified these aims must be found to be legitimate and satisfy the principle of proportionality. The legal, economic and security aims are certainly legitimate and satisfy the tests of suitability and necessity. There is also no issue with the balancing exercise for the legal aims, although the objectives could be strengthened further by the Union acceding to the Geneva Convention. For the economic aims alternative objectives of more equal burden sharing and greater financial assistance to asylum-seekers come into the equation. However, the standard of review when assessing this gives considerable discretion to policymakers and, as such, the contradiction is justified. On the issue of security the aim again is legitimate, it cannot be construed as being unsuitable or unnecessary, and the balancing exercise, even with the status and cultural effects, must come down on the side of objective justification. As such the contradiction is formally irrational but objectively justified.

143 See G Noll 'Risky games? A theoretical approach to burden-sharing in the asylum field' (2003) 16 *JRS* 236; ER Thielemann 'Between interests and norms: explaining burden-sharing in the European Union' (2003) 16 *JRS* 253.
144 ECRE 'Sharing responsibility for refugee protection in Europe: Dublin reconsidered' March 2008 http://www.ecre.org/files/Sharing%20Responsibility_Dublin%20Reconsidered.pdf 12.
145 C Costello 'The Asylum procedures Directive and the proliferation of safe country practices: deterrence, deflection and the dismantling of international protection?' (2005) 7 *EJML* 35, 38.
146 ER Thielemann 'Why asylum policy harmonisation undermines refugee burden-sharing' (2004) 6 *EJML* 47, 58.
147 ER Thielemann, T Dewan 'The myth of free-riding: refugee protection and implicit burden-sharing' (2006) 29 *West European Politics* 351, 364.
148 J Banks 'Unmasking deviance: the visual construction of asylum seekers and refugees in English nationals newspapers' (2012) 20 *Critical Criminology* 293.

The Receptions Directive[149] also raises cause for concern for contradictions between an international legal system and EU law. When asylum-seekers apply for asylum the Member State, according to Article 13(1), must grant asylum-seekers the right to material reception conditions from when their asylum applications are made, to ensure a standard of living that is adequate for the health of the applicant and is capable of ensuring their subsistence (Article 13(2)), the aim being to secure the human dignity of the asylum-seeker.[150] These material reception conditions include housing, food and clothing, provided in kind, or as financial allowances or in vouchers, and a daily expenses allowance (Article 2(j)). However, Member States can make the provision of the material reception conditions subject to actual residence by the applicants in a specific place, as determined by the Member State (Article 7(4)). Furthermore, they may be reduced or withdrawn where the asylum-seeker inter alia abandons the prescribed place of residence without informing the competent authorities, or without gaining permission if the move had been requested (Article 16(1)(a)). The only benefit that the Member States cannot withdraw is an asylum-seeker's access to emergency health care (Article 16(4)).[151] It should be noted from the outset that the standards outlined are the minimum[152] required and Member States can choose to retain higher standards (Article 4). However, these minimum norms are markedly 'minimum'[153] and Member States have the option to lower them further if the asylum-seeker is found to be in breach of the directive's requirements. As the material reception conditions are supposedly the minimum standards required to enable an asylum-seeker to retain his or her human dignity, their withdrawal must therefore treat a human being as being less than human. Such a position appears to be in contradiction to Article 1 of the UDHR, which provides that '[a]ll human beings are born free and equal in dignity and rights' as read in accordance with the first recital: 'recognition of the inherent dignity and of the equal and inalienable rights of all members of the human family is the foundation of freedom, justice and peace in the world'.

The policy aims for the Receptions Directive are slightly different from those involving the Dublin Regulation as they involve rights of TCNs when they have

149 Council Directive 2003/9/EC laying down the minimum standards for the reception of asylum seekers [2003] OJ L31/18. It should be noted that the new directive, set out in Council Document 14112/1/12, does not add anything that may change the analysis carried out here apart from where noted.
150 See the Explanatory Memorandum in the Commission proposal for a Council Directive laying down the minimum standards for the reception of asylum seekers COM(2001) 181 final 3, 4, 15 and 16.
151 This has been extended in the new directive such that a Member State has to ensure access to health care (not emergency health care) and a dignified standard of living for all asylum seekers (new art 20(5)).
152 PJ Kuijper 'The evolution of the third pillar from Maastricht to the European constitution: Institutional aspects' (2004) 41 *CMLRev* 609, 614 notes that a minimum standards directive 'does exactly what the title announces, namely laying down rather minimal standards'.
153 D O'Keeffe 'Can the leopard change its spots? Visas, immigration and asylum following Amsterdam' in D O'Keeffe, P Twomey (eds) *Legal Issues of the Amsterdam Treaty* (Hart Publishing 1999) 271, 272.

been granted entry into the Union. The legal aims centre on the position of the UDHR in the framework of international human rights law, and the legal position of the term 'human dignity'. The UDHR is merely a declaratory or aspirational document without legal force and, as such, it could be dismissed as irrelevant. However, the Charter of Fundamental Rights has taken the UDHR's provision on human dignity and included it in Article 1, which reads: '[h]uman dignity is inviolable. It must be respected and protected'. This is given added urgency in the Explanations of the Charter,[154] where it states that '[t]he dignity of the human person is not only a fundamental right in itself but constitutes the real basis of fundamental rights' with human dignity also being recognised as a protectable principle through fundamental rights by the ECJ.[155] The economic aim is similar to that of the Dublin Regulation, that is, to provide support for TCNs through the material reception conditions but at as low a cost as possible. Any security aim must be construed from the human security dimension as the minimum reception conditions to sustain a human being's human dignity. This then leads on to the human rights aim of ensuring the protection of everyone's human rights in the EU, including Union resident TCNs. The legitimacy of these aims centres on the legal, economic and security position of the minimum reception conditions and human dignity. The aims it is suggested are legitimate as the essence of formal rationality is value-neutral. Thus, the instruments are in place to protect human dignity through the minimum reception conditions but there is no requirement to analyse if human dignity is in fact protected. The result is that any formal irrationality is objectively justified.

The Qualification Directive[156] also provides contradictions between EU and international law. Article 1A of the Geneva Convention enables refugee status to be claimed by 'any person' but Article 2(c) and (e) of the Qualification Directive restricts this to TCNs and stateless persons in contravention of the Geneva Convention's Articles 3, which requires states to apply the Convention's provisions to refugees without discrimination as to country of origin, and 42, which prohibits reservations to Article 1. Secondly, Article 33(1) of the Geneva Convention provides the right to, and the conditions for, the principle of *non-refoulement* with exceptions in Article 33(2). Article 33(2) does not authorise states to withdraw or refuse to grant refugee status but simply to allow *refoulement* in extreme circumstances. This is given effect by Article 21 of the Qualification Directive but then Article 14(4) enables Member States to withdraw refugee status and Article 14(5) sanctions Member States to refuse to grant refugee status for the reasons in Article 33(2). The criteria that make up an exhaustive list for cessation and

---

154 Explanations Relating to the Charter of Fundamental Rights [2007] OJ C303/17.
155 Case C–377/98 *Netherlands v European Parliament & Council* [2001] ECR I–7079 paras 70–77.
156 Council Directive 2004/83/EC on minimum standards for the qualification and status of third country nationals or stateless persons as refugees or as persons who otherwise need international protection and the content of the protection granted [2004] OJ L304/12. Directive 2011/95 has now replaced but does not alter the analysis in this section. It should be noted that the UK and Ireland have opted out of the new directive, and Denmark has yet to opt in, so Directive 2004/83 will continue to apply to these Member States.

exclusion from refugee status are provided for in Article 1C–F of the Geneva Convention and do not include the elements in Article 33(2). Furthermore, the exhaustive list of exclusion clauses in Article 1F of the Geneva Convention has been extended by Article 14(2)(b) and (3) of the Qualification Directive. Thirdly, these exclusion clauses have been extended in Article 17 for subsidiary protection so that a 'serious non-political crime' is replaced with a 'crime', Article 33(2) elements are included and an additional exclusion added when other crimes capable of being punished by imprisonment in the host Member State are committed or the applicant has left the country of origin to escape such punishment. This latter clause has no equivalent in the Geneva Convention. Fourthly, the Article 34 naturalisation provision of the Geneva Convention has been replaced with a requirement for Member States to provide integration programmes.

Similar to the Dublin Regulation, the Qualification Directive exhibits multiple aims and within those objectives there can be numerous issues, starting with the legal aims that can crossover with other legislative measures. This time the Qualification Directive in recital 2 calls for a 'full and inclusive application of the Geneva Convention' and a recognition in recital 3 that the Geneva Convention provides 'the cornerstone of the international legal regime for the protection of refugees'. However, as Storey[157] notes, the aim of the directive is not to override the Geneva Convention but to provide detail not included in that international treaty, although it is submitted that it fails to delineate this. A further legal element is the objective of ensuring a minimum level of international protection being available in all the Member States without disparities before advancing to full harmonisation,[158] a situation that is highly unlikely with the opt-outs of the UK, Ireland and Denmark. Finally on the legal element is the position of national sovereignty, particularly when it comes to the granting of nationality to TCNs, a matter that remains firmly within the competence of the Member States, and the opt-outs available for the UK, Ireland and Denmark. The economic aims of the Qualification Directive are to limit 'the secondary movements of applicants for international protection between Member States, where such movement is purely caused by differences in legal frameworks' (recital 13 in Directive 2011/95 and similar recital 7 of Directive 2004/83) and 'to ensure that a minimum level of benefits is available for those persons in all Member States' (recital 12, and recital 6 respectively). A further economic aim can be discerned in the lack of a right to freedom of movement for TCNs with international protection, namely to limit the extent of the benefits of the internal market to Union citizens and family members. Two further interlinked factors are the protection of human rights and the question of status. The Geneva Convention provides the basis for international protection as discussed above and human rights but the Qualification Directive

---

157 H Storey 'EU Refugee Qualification Directive: a brave new world?' (2008) 20 *IJRL* 1, 8.
158 Commission proposal for a Council Directive on minimum standards for the qualification and status of third country nationals and stateless persons as refugees or as persons who otherwise need international protection COM(2001) 510 final 6.

has an additional aim of introducing subsidiary international protection, not to coordinate or harmonise such protection already found in Member States' domestic law[159] but to introduce a new right that complements protection on the basis of refugee status. Thus, status is an essential element for determining the rights that then flow from the granting of it but there is nothing equivalent in international legal doctrine. The legitimacy of the legal aims must be considered in respect of the inconsistency that is being considered, namely between the Qualification Directive and, in particular, the Geneva Convention. As such the aims behind the directive as construed on the basis of a rational basis test give a broad discretion to policy-makers and therefore they must be considered to be legitimate. Likewise, the economic aims are designed either to benefit the TCNs concerned or to improve the working of the internal market; both aims that cannot be questioned as illegitimate. Finally, the introduction of subsidiary protection introduces a new type of protection for individuals who previously would not have been protected, and thus implements a new and higher human rights standard than previously. The result of the contradiction, although formally irrational, is to build upon and improve the level of protection under the Geneva Convention, thus objectively justifying any contradiction.

The Temporary Protection Directive[160] enables Member States in certain situations to provide for groups of persons with certain characteristics to be provided with a form of international protection significantly lower than full refugee or even subsidiary protection status. This is the case even if these individuals could establish the criteria to be classed as refugees or beneficiaries of subsidiary protection. Thus, it enables Member States to circumvent their international legal obligations, at least temporarily, and again appears to be contradictory. However, there is a tension here between the protection of refugees and providing another layer of international protection for a mass influx of displaced persons, which would only have been in place before through ad hoc Member State action. As such the Temporary Protection Directive does not appear to create a contradictory position with international law.

The numerous proposals for regional protection areas (RPAs) and transit processing centres (TPCs) further appear to create contradictions between EU and international law. If these 'camps' were situated in third countries outside the EU then the Member States would appear to relinquish their international protection obligations. Indeed, if a TCN applied for refugee status in the territory of a Member State and was then removed to a camp in another country outside the EU then there would appear to be contravention of a number of the provisions of the Geneva Convention. First, it appears to violate Article 3 on the prohibition of discrimination as to race, religion or country of origin, especially if this was

---

159 J McAdam *Complementary Protection in International Refugee Law* (OUP 2007) 55.
160 Council Directive 2001/55/EC on minimum standards for giving temporary protection in the event of a mass influx of displaced persons and on measures promoting a balance of efforts between Member States in receiving such persons and bearing the consequences thereof [2001] OJ L212/12.

because the applicant originated from a specific state, possibly included on a list of such states. Secondly, Article 31(1) requires Contracting States not to impose penalties on applicants who enter the country illegally, provided they present themselves without delay and with good reason for the illegal entry. Thirdly, Article 31(2) obligates states not to impose restrictions on the movement of applicants other than those that are necessary. As asylum-seekers held in RPAs or TPCs would not be able to reach the Contracting State then Article 31 could not bite. Another proposal to turn asylum-seekers or refugees back on the high seas before entering Member State territorial waters also appears to contradict the principle of *non-refoulement*, if, as has been cogently argued (see Chapter 4), it has *jus cogens* status. All of these ideas, namely RPAs, TPCs and turning asylum-seekers back on the high seas, could also be in breach of a number of provisions of the ECHR. In *Hirsi Jamaa v Italy*,[161] when the Italian authorities turned a boat full of asylum-seekers back to Italy, the ECtHR held that there was a breach of Articles 3 and 4 of Protocol 4 and Article 13 ECHR. Significantly, the breach of Article 13 ECHR was on the basis that the asylum-seekers were unable to ask or present their case for asylum.

For the establishment of RPAs and TPCs the legal aim is to ensure that TCNs do not enter the territory of the host Member State, thereby not engaging the legal obligations under the Geneva Convention and denying the opportunity for that TCN to claim the status of international protection or be granted asylum. The setting up of RPAs and creation of TPCs has the economic aim of 'processing' TCNs outside the Union's territory enabling reception, maintenance and subsistence costs to be saved, selection to be based on ability and in particular economic benefit to Member States' economies, as well as significant cost reductions on the social welfare systems of the Member States. Furthermore, large influxes of TCNs could be controlled from outside the region thereby regulating cultural and national security effects. These aims must be construed in a value-neutral manner and as such it must be considered that the objectives are legitimate and satisfy the tests of suitability and necessity when considering RPAs and TPCs. However, these aims of limiting rights must be balanced against other rights that will be significantly affected. Those rights are in particular human rights of the TCNs as protected under the Geneva Convention and the ECHR. As such the policy of RPAs and TPCs can be considered to be objectively justified if the areas and camps were only to be used to organise, process and introduce efficiencies into the system. However, if they were employed in a controlling manner involving selection and rejection of potential applicants before they reached the Member State's territory to claim asylum then the balancing exercise falls on the side of human rights. As for arrest or turning back on the high seas the aim may be legitimate but it would fail the test of suitability and necessity and any balancing exercise conducted, as in *Hirsi Jamaa v Italy*, would come down firmly on the side of human rights.

161 *Hirsi Jamaa and Others v Italy* (2012) 55 EHRR 21.

The EAW Framework Decision[162] provides a further concern over the contradiction between EU law and Articles 5 and 6 ECHR. Article 2(2) of the EAW Framework Decision partially abolishing the principle of *non bis in idem* has been held by the ECJ[163] to be valid and not to violate fundamental rights as the definition of criminal offences and penalties remain within the competence of the Member States. However, Article 2(2) of the EAW Framework Decision imports the partial abolition of the principle of double criminality into national law, leaving Member States no discretion over its adoption, and so could be open to challenge before the ECtHR[164] either on the basis of Article 5 ECHR (the right to liberty and security of the person) or Article 6 (the right to a fair trial). As such, there would appear to be a contradiction between the EAW Framework Decision and the ECHR.

The legal aim of the EAW Framework Directive is to ensure that any European arrest warrant is executed on the basis of the principle of mutual recognition (Article 1(2)) of judgments and judicial decisions (Article 82(1) TFEU) and is one of the central aims of the AFSJ as set out in the Stockholm Programme.[165] Thus, there is assumed to be mutual trust between the judicial authorities of the Member States and the mutual assumption that the Member States' criminal justice systems conform to the standards of the ECHR. This aim is both legitimate and proportionate and so any formal irrationality can be objectively justified.

Furthermore, possible contradiction appears to exist between doctrinal positions of EU law. This is particularly apparent for four policies.

The first area is the possible contradiction between the Long-term Residents Directive (LTR Directive)[166] and the principle of non-discrimination. Recital 5 of the LTR Directive instructs Member States to give effect to the provisions of the LTR Directive without discrimination, with a considerable list of areas of non-discrimination. However, discrimination on the basis of nationality is a marked absentee from this list, which appears to allow Member States to adopt the directive without considering the prohibition of discrimination on the basis of nationality. The result of this position enables a Member State to enact legislation to give effect to the LTR Directive whilst discriminating against TCNs on the basis of their nationality, a clear contradiction with Article 18 TFEU. The policy on rights for long term residents was outlined initially at the Tampere Council meeting in 1999, which stated that the EU must 'ensure fair treatment of third country nationals who reside legally on the territory of the Member States', that an 'integration policy should aim at granting them rights and obligations

---

162  Council Framework Decision 2002/584/JHA on the European Arrest Warrant and the surrender procedures between Member States [2002] OJ L190/1.
163  Case C–303/05 *Advocaten voor de Wereld VZW v Leden van de Ministerrad* [2007] ECR I–3633.
164  See *Matthews v United Kingdom* (1999) 28 EHRR 361; *Bosphorus Hava Yolları Turizm ve Ticaret Anonim Şirketi v Ireland* (2006) 42 EHRR 1.
165  The Stockholm Programme (n 25) 11.
166  Council Directive 2003/109/EC concerning the status of third country nationals who are LTRs [2004] OJ L16/44.

comparable to those of EU citizens'[167] and that TCNs 'should be granted in that Member State a set of uniform rights which are as near as possible to those enjoyed by EU citizens'.[168] The EC Treaty required the AFSJ to safeguard the rights of TCNs (Article 61 EC) and the TFEU now demands a policy that is 'fair to third country nationals' (Article 67(3) TFEU). The Tampere Conclusions outlined above have been reiterated in the Stockholm Programme.[169] The LTR Directive distinguishes between different classes of TCNs, in particular through the extensive exclusions from the scope of the directive in Article 3(2), thereby ensuring that there is no uniform set of rights. This lack of uniformity is even more pronounced for the UK and Ireland as they have opted out of the LTR Directive. Furthermore, the rights and obligations are significantly less than for EU citizens, reduced still further by authorising the Member States to limit or restrict the general principle of equal treatment with Member State nationals in specified areas (Article 11). If there is a right to equal treatment with nationals of the host Member State then that principle is not a right to equality if it can be limited against the rights available to the comparator. Thus, there is no fair treatment of all TCNs legally resident on the Member States' territories, and a succession of internal contradictions.

To justify contradictory policy positions objectively the aims of the policy must first be identified and analysed for their legitimacy. The legal aims of the LTR Directive and the policy towards LTR TCNs raises a number of issues. It is stating the obvious that LTR TCNs have already entered the EU, in particular their host Member State, and are legally resident there and so any free movement questions from third countries are not relevant. However, internal free movement of persons is an area on the policy agenda. Article 13(1) of the UDHR states that '[e]veryone has the right to freedom of movement and residence within the borders of each State'[170] but the EU is a collection of states rather than a single state and from this perspective the EU does not fall within Article 13(1) UDHR. From an alternative position, however, Article 13(1) could also be viewed as classifying 'State' as a political entity, in comparison with Article 13(2) that utilises the term 'country' and as the EU is the regional political entity that regulates free movement of persons then the EU should be classified as 'State' for the purposes of Article 13(1). However, this impinges on the question of national sovereignty and the right of a state to control who enters that territory. Furthermore, the nationalisation of TCNs remains solely within the competence of the Member States,[171] even though the Tampere Conclusions endorsed 'the objective that long-term legally resident third-country nationals be offered the opportunity to obtain the nationality of the Member State in which they are

---

167 Presidency Conclusions of the Tampere European Council (n 1) para 18.
168 ibid para 21.
169 The Stockholm Programme (n 25) 30.
170 See also art 12(1) ICCPR and art 2(1) of Protocol 4 to the ECHR.
171 Commission proposal for a Council Directive concerning the status of third-country nationals who are long-term residents COM(2001) 127 final 8.

resident'.[172] The second aim is economic. Recital 4 of the directive notes that the integration of LTR TCNs is 'a key element in promoting economic and social cohesion' and recital 9 emphasises that '[e]conomic considerations should not be a ground for refusing to grant long-term resident status and shall not be considered as interfering with the relevant conditions'. However, to be granted LTR status TCNs must have enough resources not to be a burden on the host Member State and have sickness insurance (recital 7). Recital 18 depicts the overall aim of the granting of LTR status to TCNs as contributing to 'the effective attainment of an internal market as an area in which the free movement of persons is ensured' and to 'a major factor of mobility, notably on the Union's employment market'. The third aim of policy formation towards LTR TCNs is that of status. As highlighted above, the Tampere Conclusions and Stockholm Programme speak of a uniform set of rights granted to LTR TCNs that are as comparable and as near as possible to those enjoyed by EU citizens to enable integration. This objective then equates the status of LTR TCNs with citizens or as near as possible to aid integration. As stated above, to justify contradictory policy objectively first requires that the underlying aims be legitimate. The legal aims here on the position of free movement within the Union and national sovereignty over entry to a Member State are legitimate and satisfy the tests of suitability and necessity from a value-neutral position. However, when considering the balancing exercise the legal aims must be set against the right that the directive is interfering with. The rights here are the fundamental principle of the free movement of persons and the principle of non-discrimination on the basis of nationality. Once this is set out clearly it becomes apparent that the attempt objectively to justify the contradictions must fail. The economic rationale of free movement of persons, and the internal market, is that individuals as labour are construed as factors of production that should be able to move within the single market to be able to exploit openings for labour and to ensure that supply matches demand as far as possible. LTR TCNs are valuable components of the labour force who, because they have moved once already from a third country, may be more willing than citizens of the EU to move within the Union's territorial borders. Furthermore, with the need to attract immigration into the EU in the future the attractiveness of being able to move and choose where to settle in the EU may encourage TCN immigration to,[173] and integration within,[174] the EU. Thus the economic aims of the LTR Directive are not legitimate, and even if they were then they would fall on the balancing exercise. The status based aim outlined in the directive is clearly legitimate and the aim satisfies the tests for suitability and necessity. However, once that aim is set against the reality of the free movement rights granted in the directive in the balancing exercise, difficulties emerge. Under the status classification model

---

172  Presidency Conclusions of the Tampere European Council (n 1) para 21.
173  A Turmann *A New Europe Agenda for Labour Mobility* (CEPS 2004).
174  A Wiesbrock 'Free movement of third-country nationals in the European Union: the illusion of inclusion' (2010) 35 *ELR* 455, 458.

of Peers[175] LTR TCNs under the directive could be considered equivalent to that of worker, which would damage the objectives of EU immigration law, or alien, which would damage the internal market.[176] It could be that LTR TCNs form a new status, appropriate to the objectives in the Tampere Conclusions and the Stockholm Programme and the economic reality of globalisation, equated to that of denizenship[177] or quasi-citizenship[178] enabling alien and citizen to converge over time. However, this is not Union policy and so the balancing exercise finds that formal irrationality cannot be objectively justified.

The principle of freedom of movement and restrictions applied to TCNs, whether they are asylum-seekers or applicants for international protection status other than LTR TCNs (the question of contradictions between the free movement of persons and LTR TCNs has been discussed above), also creates concern over possible contradictions for formal rationality. The AFSJ is designed to create a single territorial area with a common policy that regulates asylum, refugees and immigration. With the adoption of Regulation 562/2006,[179] applicable to all persons, whether citizens of the Union or TCNs, the EU has removed internal border controls between Member States. It is suggested that this creates a new territory capable of being labelled as 'Schengenland' which, as there are common asylum and immigration policies and no internal border controls, should entail freedom of movement in 'Schengenland'. However, the Receptions Directive and the Temporary Protection Directive do not provide for any free movement rights between the Member States for asylum-seekers or beneficiaries of temporary protection and even freedom of movement in a Member State for an asylum-seeker can be curtailed to an area assigned to them by the Member State or, if necessary, confinement to a particular place. The Qualification Directive does not provide any freedom of movement between Member States whilst the application is being processed, or indeed upon the grant of international protection status, although there is a right of free movement in the host Member State. It does enable refugees, once the status is granted, to be issued with travel documents to allow travel outside the host Member State territory, and beneficiaries of subsidiary protection are entitled to a national passport if their presence is required for compelling humanitarian reasons in another state (Article 25 Qualification Directive). Article 26 of the Geneva Convention specifies that Contracting States must 'accord to refugees lawfully in its territory the right to choose their place of residence to move freely within its territory, subject to any regulations applicable to aliens generally in the same circumstances'. This right of free movement is lacking within Schengenland and the right of residence

175  S Peers 'Aliens' (n 74) 291.

176  ibid 307.

177  T Hammar *Democracy and the Nation State, Aliens, Denizens and Citizens in a World of International Migration* (Avebury 1990).

178  S Castles, A Davison *Citizenship and Migration: Globalization and the Politics of Belonging* (Macmillan Press 2000) 94.

179  European Parliament and Council Regulation 562/2006/EC establishing a Community Code on the rules governing the movement of persons across borders [2006] OJ L105/1.

is only available in the host Member State that conferred refugee status (Article 24 Qualification Directive). Even a legislative instrument designed to provide rights for TCNs, the Single Permit Directive,[180] fails to include any right to freedom of movement for persons. It could be argued that the Member States are the Contracting States of the Geneva Convention and therefore limiting free movement to a Member State is in line with these international obligations. However, the Member States have chosen to pool their sovereignty in this area, and as they have transferred competence to the EU in the area of refugee law so their international obligations should now be those of the EU. Indeed, Article 20 Qualification Directive, which provides the general rules for the application of Chapter VII entitled 'Content of International Protection' and in which Article 24 on residence permits and Article 33 on freedom of movement in the Member State are contained (Article 32 of Directive 2004/83 contains the same provision), states that Chapter VII is without prejudice to the rights laid down in the Geneva Convention. It could be argued therefore that the lack of EU free movement rights for refugees or, at least, the right to choose a place of residence, contradicts Article 26 of the Geneva Convention and is thus formally irrational. The relevant aims behind this policy have been set out above with the legal aim of pooling or transferring sovereignty being the key factor. The issue here is that the Member States have chosen to relinquish an element of sovereignty to the Union but it is clear that the Member States have retained their sovereignty to determine entry to their national territory. This then is a legitimate aim that satisfies the requirements of proportionality and thus objectively justifies the contradiction. However, of more serious concern is the statement of policy in the Tampere Conclusions[181] that to deny freedom, which includes the right to move freely throughout the Union, from 'those whose circumstances lead them justifiably to seek access to our territory' would be 'in contradiction with Europe's traditions'. Thus the aim of denying freedom of movement to TCNs on the basis of national sovereignty is in conflict with the traditions of Europe and as such cannot be legitimate.

There are also restrictions on the freedom of movement that appear to produce contradictions with the Schengen Borders Code (SBC), especially over the two issues of removal of internal border controls and freedom to travel. The removal of internal border controls means that any person, whether a TCN or a citizen of the Union, is able to cross the EU's internal borders without having his or her travel documents checked. Freedom of movement, however, is heavily curtailed for TCNs, especially if they are asylum-seekers or beneficiaries of certain international protection and thus appearing to contradict the removal of internal borders. However, this is a situation where the apparent contradiction is

---

180  European Parliament and Council Directive 2011/98/EU on a single application procedure for a single permit for third-country nationals to reside and work in the territory of a Member State and on a common set of rights for third-country workers legally residing in a Member State [2011] OJ L343/1.
181  Presidency Conclusions of the Tampere European Council (n 1) para 3.

merely tension between doctrines as the SBC deals with a specific situation, namely the provision for persons, regardless of nationality, to cross internal borders at any point without border checks being carried out and does not address the right to freedom of movement, or limitations on it. The second situation concerns the apparent contradiction between the right to free movement as had been specified in Article 61(a) EC, that appeared to be a general right applicable to all, the SBC removing internal border controls and the common visa policy that limits the right to travel between Member States for TCNs to a maximum of three months with a short term visa. However, on closer reflection and with the introduction of Article 67 TFEU to replace Article 61 EC these contradictions are indeed tensions with a general free movement principle, a limited freedom to travel for TCNs and no checks required on these persons at internal borders.

The EAW Framework Decision enables individuals to be removed, either through extradition or surrender, to another Member State. Chapter VI of Directive 2004/38[182] provides the restrictions that Member States may apply on the freedom of movement of Union citizens and their family members, regardless of nationality (Article 27), with specific protections against expulsion (Article 28) and procedural safeguards (Article 31). At first blush these three provisions appear to provide significantly higher standards for individuals than the EAW Framework Decision, and thus there would appear to be contradiction between the two. However, although the two instruments appear to deal with similar situations they actually regulate alternative scenarios, with Directive 2004/38 governing expulsion from the host Member State territory on the basis of public order, health or security and the EAW controlling extradition or surrender to another Member State for the purposes of criminal prosecution. Therefore, as they regulate different situations there is tension between the policies of expulsion and restriction of free movement, and extradition but not contradiction. The second situation also involves the EAW Framework Decision and the partial abolition of the *non bis in idem* principle in Article 2(2). This appears to contravene the requirement in Article 50 of the Charter of Fundamental Rights that prohibits a person being tried and punished twice in criminal proceedings for the same criminal offence. An individual could be tried and convicted in one Member State before then being extradited under Article 2(2) to another Member State to be tried for the same offence on the same facts. Thus there is a contradiction between two legal instruments but of greater concern is the contradiction between the EAW Framework Decision and a fundamental right. Aims of the EAW Framework Decision have already been considered above but different aims will be in play for different possible contradictions between doctrines. However, the legal aim is the same as that above; mutual trust between the judicial authorities of Member States, which forms the cornerstone of judicial cooperation, and the

---

182 European Parliament and Council Directive 2004/38/EC on the right of citizens of the Union and their family members to move and reside freely within the territory of the Member States [2004] OJ L158/77.

mutual assumption that the Member States' criminal justice systems conform to the standards of the ECHR. The second element is the issue of security, as it was the terrorist attack on the World Trade Center on 11 September 2001 that precipitated the Commission to bring forward the proposal for the EAW Framework Decision. This question of security manifested itself in a desire for a single procedure to replace traditional extradition within the EU, to speed up the transfer of suspects between Member States and to remove the political dimension in extradition. Once these aims are set into the principles required for objective justification it can easily be seen that the aims are legitimate and satisfy the tests for proportionality, thus objectively justifying any possible formal irrationality.

The fourth policy area for concern is that between the Single Permit Directive and the principle of equality. Article 12(1) of the Single Permit Directive introduces the right to equal treatment for TCNs in a considerable number of areas of policy. This welcome development, however, is severely attenuated by providing significant discretion for Member States in most of these fields to limit these rights to equal treatment. The result is unequal treatment of TCNs in comparison with nationals of that Member State, and because of the wide discretion unequal treatment across different Member States. The aim of this rights limitation is grounded in national sovereignty and the desire by Member States to maintain control of the rights granted to TCNs. However, first the Tampere Conclusions[183] and now the Stockholm Programme[184] have made it an imperative objective of the Union's migration policy to grant TCNs 'rights and obligations comparable to those of citizens of the Union', placing this 'at the core of European cooperation in integration'. Even if the aim of national sovereignty is considered to be legitimate, once this is set against the aims and objectives expressed in the Tampere Conclusions and the Stockholm Programme then it cannot be proportionate and such a contraction cannot be objectively justified.

A third element of formal irrationality can occur when there is a contradiction detected within a doctrine itself, that doctrine here being the principle of the freedom of movement of persons, a stand-alone principle that provides a freedom to persons that is not limited by any notions of citizens of the EU, TCNs or specific groups of TCNs (see Chapter 2 for a discussion on the general right to free movement). However, this general principle applicable to all within the territorial borders of the EU, rather than as a global right, has been limited to citizens of the EU and their family members, with a significant curtailment of the principle for TCNs by a number of legal instruments adopted under the AFSJ, a clear contradiction within the principle of freedom of movement of persons. There are of course a considerable number of aims behind the principle of freedom of movement of persons, not least an economic aim. However, the most significant aim underpinning free movement as regards the AFSJ is the legal aim as it applies to national sovereignty. Much

---

183 Presidency Conclusions of the Tampere European Council (n 1) para 18.
184 The Stockholm Programme (n 25) 30.

of the legislation-making power has been transferred by the Member States to the EU but the decision-taking power over freedom of movement for TCNs has been retained by the Member States through the pre-eminence of the Council in the decision-making process. Following the Lisbon Treaty, the European Parliament has become an equal partner with the Council in the adoption of legislative measures using the ordinary legislative procedure (Article 294 TFEU) but the first phase legislation put in place the will of the Member States and any further legislation will mainly either be amending or recasting the measures. As the Member States retained operational control of legislation affecting TCNs within the AFSJ then their freedom of movement should still only operate within the host Member State. Of course this curtailment of free movement, and the adoption of the legislative measures for that purpose, is a legitimate process of law-making, and fulfils the requirements of the tests for suitability and necessity. However, it must be balanced against other objectives applicable in this situation, and in particular the requirement in the Tampere Conclusions and the Stockholm Programme to improve the lot of TCNs. This *stricto sensu* proportionality test comes down on the side of the latter objective, such that national sovereignty cannot objectively justify the contradictions in free movement.

### 6.3.2.2   *Instrumental legal rationality*

As has been discussed there are two elements to instrumental legal rationality, generic and specific, and they are both in evidence in free movement rights within the AFSJ. However, only the relevant criteria will be considered in the following analysis.

The first matter of concern involves the LTR Directive and clarity. The law of the AFSJ since its introduction by the Treaty of Amsterdam has evolved very rapidly, raising concerns over the constancy of the law and through its complexity and clarity. The LTR Directive is designed to provide details of the acquisition of LTR status for TCNs and the associated rights. However, its complexity is such that it has confused even the most acute legal brains.[185] For TCNs, most of whom will not speak the host Member State's language as a first language and also may not have benefited from higher education or legal training, the rights and limitations on those rights contained within the directive are unlikely to be easily accessible or enforceable. The result is that this complexity will create confusion, rights will not be enforced and the aims of the directive, as well as those set out in the Stockholm Programme, will be unattainable. The aims behind the LTR Directive have already been set out above, to which nothing more needs to be added and it is undoubtedly the case that the aims are legitimate. However, it must be questioned whether the complexity of the directive fulfils the test of suitability and a less complex measure could have been adopted so the principle of necessity

---

185  S Peers 'Implementing equality? The Directive on Long Term Resident Third Country Nationals' (2004) 29 *ELR* 437, 458.

also causes major problems. Finally, when it comes to the balancing exercise the overall objectives of the Stockholm Programme must take precedence over the aims of the LTR Directive and thus the directive will be instrumentally irrational for lack of clarity that cannot be objectively justified.

The second issue of difficulty lies with a TCN claiming international protection in a Member State and generality of the law, so that the authorities must apply the law consistently and treat individuals in similar positions equally with like cases being treated alike. It has been claimed by McAdam[186] that persons claiming international protection should be treated in the same manner, whether they are asylum-seekers, refugees or beneficiaries of subsidiary or temporary protection. In particular, they should be treated with dignity, their human rights respected and provided with a haven until their applications are assessed. However, claimants of international protection are treated in different ways in the AFSJ depending on whether they are classified as asylum-seekers, refugees, beneficiaries of subsidiary or temporary protection, or economic immigrants and depending in which state an application is made. As such there appears to be a failure of the generality of the law as individuals in similar positions may be assessed and granted alternative status that can lead to different treatment. This is even more marked across the different Member States as the legislative instruments are directives with considerable discretion for implementation by the Member States. Although with the adoption of Directive 2011/95 some differences have been ameliorated by Member States granting TCNs international protection status rather than refugee or subsidiary protection status, the fact that the UK and Ireland have opted out of this new Qualification Directive only increases the lack of generality. The aim behind this approach certainly appears to be to differentiate the circumstances of groups of TCNs and to apply legislative measures to those different groups. There are, however, two layers of generality involved. The first is that advanced by McAdam, whereby all individuals claiming international protection should receive the same treatment no matter what their status. This must be questioned as the Qualification Directive introduced the concept of subsidiarity protection for TCNs who could not bring themselves within the requirements for refugee status. This was not something envisaged by or included in the Geneva Convention, a similar situation to that of temporary protection status introduced by the Temporary Protection Directive. As such the aim of introducing these new types of international protection and their subsequent lack of generality is obviously legitimate and proportionate. The second layer of lack of generality finds that there is no single legal standard applied across Union territory to all Member States. Therefore, TCNs will be treated differently in different Member States based merely on their presence in a particular Member State. The aim in these circumstances cannot be legitimate when considered in this context and cannot objectively justify the finding of instrumental irrationality.

186 McAdam *Complementary Protection* (n 159) 90; J McAdam 'The European Union Qualification Directive: the creation of a subsidiary protection regime' (2005) 18 *IJRL* 461, 497.

The third issue is that of contradiction and, as outlined above, the contradictions identified under formal rationality will also fall under generic instrumental rationality but observed strictly as contradictions, without tensions negating those contradictions, and viewed through a higher intermediate scrutiny intensity. Any contradiction found to be formally irrational and not objectively justified will also be instrumentally irrational. For the other objectively justified contradictions the aims will remain the same but the standard of scrutiny will see some revision over the conclusions relating to those aims. First, any economic aims, particularly those involving chain *refoulement* and refugees in orbit, the Receptions Directive and Qualification Directive, will not survive the stricter review and will therefore either not be legitimate or will not be able to overcome the more fundamental aims associated with those policies in an examination of *stricto sensu* proportionality. For the Receptions Directive, just as with formal rationality, any contemplation of human dignity must be value-neutral and purely procedural. The procedures for the protection of TCNs' human dignity are clearly defined in the minimum reception conditions, thus satisfying the requirements for instrumentally rational objective justification. Similarly, the content of the Qualification Directive is designed to build on the Geneva Convention and introduces another type of international protection in subsidiary status. This would appear to satisfy the legal aim of recital 4 (Directive 2011/95, recital 3 for Directive 2004/83), which states that the Geneva Convention is the cornerstone of the international legal regime for the protection of refugees and Article 20 that declares Chapter VII on the content of international protection to be without prejudice to the rights laid down in the Geneva Convention. However, as examined in Chapter 4, there are numerous instances in the directive where there are either inconsistencies between the provisions of the directive and the rights in the Geneva Convention, or the directive does not incorporate the Geneva Convention's provisions. The result is inconsistency between the Qualification Directive and the Geneva Convention which is not possible to justify objectively considering the position and importance of the Geneva Convention in the architecture of the directive. Furthermore, by failing fully to incorporate the Geneva Convention the directive contradicts the objectives set out in the Tampere Conclusions[187] and recognised in the directive (recital 3 of Directive 2011/95 and recital 2 of Directive 2004/83). However, as the AFSJ is made up of the principles of freedom, security and justice, aims involving security, especially with the importance now attached to it following the Hague and Stockholm Programmes, will remain both legitimate and proportionate, unless they are outweighed as with the Qualification Directive. Thus any findings of instrumental irrationality for chain *refoulement* and refugees in orbit, the Receptions Directive and the EAW Framework Directive based on security objectives will continue to be objectively justified. However, the fundamental principles of non-discrimination and free movement of persons are not objectively justified by security aims and any balancing exercise

---

187 Presidency Conclusions of the Tampere European Council (n 1) para 13.

involving other objectives will be construed reasonably strictly and on the side of these fundamental principles. Contradictions involving non-discrimination and freedom of movement of persons will not be capable of being objectively justified for instrumental rationality.

The fourth issue in the difficulty of generic instrumental rationality is the issue of congruence of the law as officially declared against the law as administered in practice. This can be observed in three ways. The first involves determining the country responsible for assessing an asylum application initially under the Dublin Convention but now in the Dublin Regulation, and soon to be replaced by the new Dublin Regulation, Dublin III. The reported practices of the national authorities[188] and cases involving Greece[189] create significant incongruences with the law as officially declared in the Dublin Regulation, thereby producing a major problem for the rule of law. A similar situation is clear for the LTR Directive as outlined in strong language by the Commission in its 2011 report.[190] The third way is through the wide discretion granted to Member States in the Receptions Directive that the Member States have taken every opportunity to exploit.[191] This resulted in the Commission issuing a proposal[192] to recast the directive but the resultant recast directive does little to dispel the incongruence. Again the aims of the legislative measures are perfectly legitimate but the incongruences outlined work to undermine those aims and so cannot act as the basis for any objective justification of the irrationality.

The fifth issue involves the opt-out protocols for the UK and Ireland and the equally complex position of Denmark following negotiation of its own protocol at the Treaty of Amsterdam incorporating a number of the Fullerian elements. The protocols create a highly complex political environment made even more complex by the UK and Ireland's approach to the numerous recast directives, choosing to opt out of the recast whilst still being bound by the original directives. The result of such complexity apart from a lack of clarity means that the law will be applied inconsistently. Furthermore, cases in these states will be treated differently to those in the Schengenland states, even where the factual position is exactly the same and are thus 'like' cases. The aim behind the protocols is predominantly legal, the desire by the Member States concerned to maintain their national sovereignty and control of TCNs entering the host Member State territory. When viewed from the perspective of the UK and Ireland, the special circumstances of two island nations sitting apart from continental Europe and enjoying a special relationship as evidenced by the

---

188  Kok *The Dublin II Regulation* (n 139).
189  *MSS* and *NS* (n 138).
190  Commission Report on the application of Directive 2003/109/EC concerning the status of third-country nationals who are long-term residents COM(2011) 585 final.
191  Commission Communication of the report on the application of Directive 2003/9/EC laying down the minimum standards for the reception of asylum seekers COM(2007) 745 final 10.
192  Commission proposal for a European Parliament and Council Directive laying down the minimum standards for the reception of asylum seekers (recast) COM(2008) 215 final.

Common Travel Area,[193] then the aim must be perceived as legitimate and such a legitimate aim must satisfy the requirements of proportionality. However, this aim and legitimacy cannot be extended to Denmark and as such Denmark's position is instrumentally irrational.

Specific instrumental rationality consists of three elements, one of which requires that legislative officials promote legitimate ends or goals in a good faith manner or attempt. The goals and objectives for TCNs, and LTR TCNs in particular, were contained in the Tampere Conclusions. The LTR Directive noted in recital 2 that the objectives contained in the Tampere Conclusions were to approximate the status of LTR TCNs to those of nationals of the Member States and to provide a uniform set of rights that were as near as possible to those of EU citizens. This is confirmed in the Stockholm Programme. However, the failure to include TCNs who had obtained international protection (rectified now by Directive 2011/51), the ability of Member States to derogate from the principle of equal treatment in Article 11 and a very limited form of free movement means that the LTR Directive does not come close to meeting the aims of Tampere. The question then is to determine if those goals and objectives were promoted in a good faith manner or attempt. The legislative history would suggest that this was not the case as the final directive is a considerably watered down version of the original Commission proposal that aimed to implement the Tampere Conclusions and so the directive is an incongruent means to implement the aims underlining the policy formation. The same situation is apparent in the process of adoption of the Single Permit Directive. This failure to fulfil the objectives of the Tampere Conclusions, and now the Stockholm Programme, undermine the rule of law itself and cannot possibly be objectively justified.

The second factor in specific instrumental rationality is the use of the most effective legal technique to achieve societal ends by legal officials, ensuring that the function of the legal act matches its effect. The legal instrument that creates significant difficulties here is the Dublin Regulation. As outlined in Chapter 4 and above, the Dublin Convention did not satisfy this requirement, and although the Dublin Regulation is an improvement, it is submitted that many of the inherent weaknesses of the Dublin Convention are carried over into the Dublin Regulation, and into the new Dublin III. As this goes to the very aim of the instrument and as first the Dublin Convention[194] and now the Dublin Regulation[195] simply does not work then it is impossible objectively to justify this element of irrationality.

193 Home Office 'Joint Statement of Mr Damian Green UK Minister of State for Immigration and Mr Alan Shatter Ireland Minister for Justice and Equality regarding Co-operation on Measures to Secure the External Eommon Travel Area Border' December 2011 http://www.homeoffice. gov.uk/about-us/freedom-of-information/released-information1/foi-archive-immigration/21197-mea-sec-trav/21197-mea-sec-trav?view=Binary.
194 N Blake 'The Dublin Convention and rights of asylum seekers in the European Union in Guild, Harlow (eds) (n 74) 95.
195 Dublin Regulation (n 137).

The third element of specific instrumental rationality, which considers the judiciary's different ideologies and personal agendas when interpreting the law, is engaged when considering the inconsistency between the EAW Framework Decision and its application by Member States' national courts. It is not unreasonable to acknowledge that the judges of the ECJ comply with this element when utilising their teleological approach to interpretation. However, the different interpretations of the EAW Framework Decision and national implementing measures, by national judges, suggests that this is an area of concern when there is little guidance as yet provided by the ECJ. This is not a criticism of the ECJ but of the legislative measures that have limited the jurisdiction of the Court and thereby create the possibility of interpretative problems. This concern is particularly evident when interpreting the principle of supremacy[196] and the recent approach of the UK Supreme Court to the EAW Framework Directive in *Assange*,[197] where Lord Mance utilised the European Communities Act 1972 rather than supremacy,[198] thereby highlighting these problems. The inconsistency between the EAW Framework Directive and its interpretation by national judges can be derived from the desire by Member States to maintain their national sovereignty in the third pillar areas of the EC Treaty. This problem is likely to fade with the supranationalisation of this area under the Lisbon Treaty, although the projected opt-out by the UK could exacerbate the issue depending on the solution for the UK that is eventually adopted.

The final issue involves a series of instruments that causes concern for the specific instrumental rationality requirement that the most effective legal techniques are used to achieve societal ends by legal officials, as it applies to the criminalisation, detention and deportation of asylum-seekers. One of the targeted areas of Union policy on illegal immigration is human smuggling and trafficking,[199] which has been implemented in the Human Trafficking Directive.[200] However, the common visa policy and carrier sanctions force asylum-seekers or those claiming international protection, the majority being desperate individuals in desperate circumstances, into the arms of the human smugglers to elicit their illegal entry into the EU. Thus asylum becomes criminalised,[201] with voices raised in concern[202] and proposals to decriminalise asylum and migration.[203] The question of criminality and the policy characteristics associated with it are not part of the remit of

---

196  See A Albi 'Supremacy of EC law in the new Member States: bringing parliaments into the equation of "co-operative constitutionalism"' (2007) 3 *EuConst* 25.

197  *Assange v Swedish Prosecution Authority (Nos 1 and 2)* [2012] 2 AC 471 (SC).

198  ibid [216] (Lord Mance).

199  See Commission Communication on policy priorities in the fight against illegal immigration of third-country nationals COM(2006) 402 final and The Stockholm Programme (n 25) 30.

200  European Parliament and Council Directive 2011/36/EU on preventing and combating trafficking in human beings and protecting its victims, and replacing Council Framework Decision 2002/629/JHA [2011] OJ L101/1.

201  There has been increased academic interest in this over the last decade. For a theoretical analysis of this criminalisation see SH Legomsky 'The new path of immigration law: asymmetric incorporation of criminal justice norms' (2007) 64 *Washington and Lee Law Review* 469.

202  T Hammarberg 'It is wrong to criminalize migration' (2009) 11 *EJML* 383.

203  GS Goodwin-Gill 'The international protection of refugees: what future?' (2000) 12 *IJRL* 1, 6.

this book. However, a brief word must be said on this issue as it does impinge upon the rule of law. Article 31 of the Geneva Convention requires those entering the territory to claim refugee status not to be criminalised by having penalties imposed upon them for crossing the nation's borders. Furthermore, Article 18 of the Charter of Fundamental Rights provides that a 'right to asylum shall be guaranteed with respect to the rules of the Geneva Convention'. The strengthening of the external borders of the EU and elongating the supply lines of asylum through carrier sanctions and the common visa policy means that more asylum-seekers become involved in human trafficking, the elimination of which is an objective set out in the Stockholm Programme. The policy of criminalising the asylum supply chain can only make sense if 'asylum-seekers and refugees are characterised as deviant and dangerous',[204] a perception portrayed by media outlets to the general population[205] that perpetuates greater demand for criminalisation and restrictive policies,[206] which according to Banks means that the 'criminalisation of asylum is a self-perpetuating practice'.[207] The aim of this criminalisation approach is supposed to be to support the regulation of immigration but the underlying objective is to prevent illegal immigration resulting in the demonisation and criminalisation of asylum-seekers, which forces TCNs into the hands of human traffickers. The aims behind criminal policy are different from those behind migration policy and must be examined to determine if this instrumentally irrational position can be objectively justified. As Aliverti[208] notes, the use of criminal law in this field is instrumental and has the aim of assisting the enforcement of immigration rules, which are primarily the concern of civil or administrative law.[209] Therefore the aims of the criminal law in this area are threefold: the prevention of harm to others; punishment; and deterrence.[210] However, as Aliverti makes clear,[211] prevention of harm is difficult to justify as there is no damage to other persons or property from an asylum-seeker and punishment, criminal punishment in particular, should be reserved for censuring serious wrongdoing.[212] Criminal law should not be used to pursue a specific policy goal, here the prevention of illegal immigration, where prevention drives the decisions to criminalise, prosecute and appropriate penalty,[213] or to support the enforcement of administrative and regulatory aims. Finally, deterrence must link punishment with the individual's perception of this punishment. Criminalising asylum-seekers can lead to jail

204 J Banks 'The criminalisation of asylum seekers and asylum policy' (2008) 175 *Prison Service Journal* 43, 49.
205 Banks 'Unmasking deviance' (n 148).
206 Goodwin-Gill 'The international protection of refugees' (n 203).
207 ibid.
208 A Aliverti 'Making people criminal: the role of the criminal law in immigration enforcement' (2012) 16 *Theoretical Criminology* 417, 423.
209 JH Chacón 'Overcriminalizing immigration' (2012) 102 *The Journal of Criminal Law & Criminology* 613.
210 Aliverti 'Making people criminal' (n 208) 426.
211 ibid.
212 A Ashworth 'Is the criminal law a lost cause?' (2000) 116 *LQR* 225, 250.
213 Aliverti 'Making people criminal' (n 208) 426.

sentences followed by expulsion but there is no evidence that this deters TCNs from making further attempts at entering the Member State. Indeed, it is quite to the contrary. Kathrani notes that it is this deterrence aim that has become the predominant objective of criminalising asylum-seekers and in particular a belief has taken hold that certain asylum groups need to be deterred from their actions as they are claimed to exhibit dangerous risks against the national interests.[214] Since the terrorist attacks on New York in 2001, Madrid in 2004 and London in 2005 these asylum groups have been equated with jihadist Islamists. Unfortunately, there is no evidence that deterrence has succeeded and the criminalisation has been far wider than this particular group. As such none of the criminal aims are legitimate and so cannot objectively justify the finding of irrationality.

The detention of asylum-seekers is one of the complementary punishments to the criminalisation of asylum-seekers.[215] As has been seen in Chapter 4 the EU has embraced detention as a means to govern illegal immigration with provisions regulating it in the new Dublin Regulation (Dublin III), the Receptions Directive, the Procedures Directive and the Returns Directive. The aim of immigration detention is theoretically different from the objectives of 'normal' criminal law as it is seen as an administrative or bureaucratic, non-punitive measure that is intended to facilitate the deportation of the TCN.[216] However, as Bosworth[217] demonstrates, the conditions of detention are frequently worse than those in prison and thus the detention can be equated better with aims of criminal rather than administrative law. The three aims of criminal law of prevention of harm, punishment and deterrence display similar problems to those for criminalisation. However, it could be claimed that detention is a useful tool for the appropriate authorities preceding deportation. This pre-deportation detention has been limited by the Returns Directive to six months, with the possibility of extending this to 18 months (Article 15), thus ensuring detention cannot be unlimited,[218] although this practice will continue in the UK as the UK and Ireland have opted out of the directive (recitals 26 and 27).[219] As the Returns Directive limits detention through the principle of proportionality such that its only justified aim is 'to prepare the return or carry out the removal process and if the application of less coercive measures would not be sufficient' (recital 16), then for this purpose, if detention was to be viewed independently from other policies, it is legitimate and objectively justifies the finding of irrationality.

---

214  P Kathrani 'Asylum law or criminal law: blame, deterrence and the criminalisation of the asylum seeker' (2011) 18 *Jurisprudence* 1543, 1545.
215  M Welch, L Schuster 'Detention of asylum seekers in the US, UK, France, Germany and Italy' (2005) 5 *Criminal Justice* 331, 333.
216  A Leerkes, D Broeders 'A case of mixed motives: formal and informal functions of administrative immigration detention' (2010) 50 *British Journal of Criminology* 830, 831.
217  M Bosworth 'Subjectivity and identity in detention: punishment and society in a global age' (2012) 16 *Theoretical Criminology* 123, 130.
218  C Johnston 'Indefinite immigration detention: can it be justified?' (2009) 23 *JIANL* 351.
219  See *R (Lumba) v Secretary of State for the Home Department* [2012] 1 AC 245 (HL) for a description by the Supreme Court of the UK's approach.

Unfortunately detention cannot be viewed independently as it is, according to Bosworth,[220] the corollary to deportation and as, according to Advocate General Mazák in *Kadzoev*,[221] the Member States retain a residual competence to detain[222] 'because of aggressive behaviour, based on some other provision of national law such as legislation intended to maintain public order or the criminal law'. Therefore, deportation is the final piece of the criminalisation jigsaw, especially when the Returns Directive imposes a five year entry ban into the EU for any TCN involuntarily deported (Article 11(1)), a punishment imposed for not leaving voluntarily. The result of the EU approach in general, taking account of all the legal instruments mentioned, is to criminalise and punish TCNs. It is highly unlikely to deter desperate people in desperate situations from trying to reach the EU and thus the policy options chosen drive these individuals into the arms of human traffickers. As the Union aim is to stop human trafficking these policies, and the objectives underpinning them, perpetuate human trafficking, and the aims cannot be legitimate and cannot objectively justify the conclusion of instrumental irrationality.

### 6.3.2.3   *Substantive legal rationality*

The position of TCNs in the AFSJ is disturbing when considered against human rights norms. The violation of both the Geneva Convention and the ECHR by the legislative instruments that have been adopted and analysed in Chapter 4, and the accompanying practices of chain *refoulement*, refugees in orbit and possible breaches of individual human rights that the formulated instruments and policies, if not encourage, then at least condone, signify a marked lack of regard for TCNs as human beings with innate human rights. The instruments and the human rights infringed include the following: the Dublin Regulation and Articles 3 and 13 ECHR and 33(1) of the Geneva Convention; the Qualification Directive and Articles 1A, 1F, 3, 33(1), 34 and 42 of the Geneva Convention; RPAs and TPCs and Articles 3 and 4 of Protocol 4 and 13 ECHR and Articles 3 and 31 of the Geneva Convention; and the EAW Framework Decision and Articles 5, 6 and 50 ECHR. However, a brief focus on the material reception conditions in the Receptions Directive[223] that are designated as the minimum required to ensure the dignity of the asylum-seeker (Article 13) should be sufficient to illustrate the point. The Member States are authorised to withdraw the material reception conditions, except for emergency medical care, in the event of digressions by a TCN from prescribed activity, which can include the TCN

---

220  M Bosworth 'Deportation, detention and foreign national prisoners in England and Wales' (2011) 15 *Citizenship Studies* 583, 587.

221  Case C–357/09 PPU *Said Shamilovich Kadzoev (Huchbarov)* [2009] ECR I–11189, Opinion of AG Mazák, n 38.

222  C Costello 'Human rights and the elusive universal subject: immigration detention under international human rights and EU law' (2012) 19 *Indiana Journal of Global Legal Studies* 257, 295.

223  Council Directive 2003/9/EC laying down the minimum standards for the reception of asylum seekers [2003] OJ L31/18 art 3.

exercising freedom of movement and leaving his or her designated place of residence without informing the appropriate authorities. This means that the withdrawal of the material reception conditions must breach the statement that '[h]uman dignity is inviolable' (Article 1 of the Charter) and could lead to the risk of the individual becoming destitute in breach of Article 3 ECHR.[224] As Article 1 of the Charter goes on to hold that human dignity[225] must be respected and protected then it is difficult to see how this provision satisfies human rights norms. Even with the extension of the material reception conditions to include health care, not emergency health care, and a dignified standard of living for all asylum-seekers[226] is to be welcomed, there is no indication which of the material reception conditions are required to satisfy 'a dignified standard of living'. The effect of such an approach is to treat TCNs, or more particularly asylum-seekers, as less than human. This dehumanisation of TCNs can be characterised in the amalgamation of the term asylum/refugee and immigration, in particular when dealing with illegal immigration and the return of 'illegal' immigrants to third countries, and the utilisation of the terms 'flood', 'swamped' or 'invasion' in common parlance to describe immigration and justify their criminalisation.[227] The result is the failure not only to protect the human rights of TCNs but to fail to respect their human rights or even their humanity. There is then just a small step that is needed to be taken to classify all asylum-seekers, which can then be extrapolated to other TCNs over time, as different from Union citizens and to criminalise their attempts to enter the territory. This violates the requirements of substantive rationality where human rights of individuals must be protected through the human rights norms of the Union.

It was established in Chapter 2 and reiterated above that for a finding of substantive irrationality to be objectively justified then it can only be done so on the basis of the same value-laden test. Therefore, a finding of substantive irrationality can only be justified by a greater human rights requirement. The difficulty here is with the shifting position of the general aim towards TCNs. In the Tampere Conclusions especially, and the Hague and Stockholm Programmes to a lesser extent, there was a definite aim of the Member States acting on behalf of the Union to improve the position of TCNs resident within the Union. Those Tampere Conclusions emphasised European integration built on human rights, democratic institutions and the rule of law,[228] and the contradiction with Europe's traditions if freedom of movement was denied to legally resident TCNs.[229] By the time of the Stockholm Programme both fundamental rights and rights of

---

224 See *R (on the application of Limbuela, Tesema and Adam) v Secretary of State for the Home Department* [2006] 1 AC 396 (HL); noted in A Mackenzie 'Case comment' [2006] EHRLR 67 and A Hardiman-McCartney 'Absolutely right: providing asylum seekers with food and shelter under Article 3' (2006) 65 *CLJ* 4.
225 See J Jones 'Human dignity in the EU Charter of Fundamental Rights and its interpretation before the European Court of Justice' (2012) 33 *Liverpool Law Review* 281.
226 Council Document 14112/1/12 (n 149) art 20(5).
227 Banks 'Unmasking deviance' (n 148) 334.
228 Presidency Conclusions of the Tampere European Council (n 1) para 1.
229 ibid para 3.

freedom of movement were very much contained in the citizens section of the programme.[230] The result of this movement away from the protection of fundamental rights of everyone, and therefore protecting human rights on the basis of a person's innate humanity, is to limit the fundamental, including human, rights, of TCNs. TCNs start to be treated by policy-makers as different from Union citizens, from the aims set down for the AFSJ to the rights that they are granted in subsequent legislative measures so that they take on the mantle of 'the Other' and are open to becoming dehumanised. As the aim itself appears to limit fundamental rights protection to Union citizens then it is not an aim that is grounded in human rights and therefore is not legitimate when it comes to objective justification.

The Charter of Fundamental Rights after the Lisbon Treaty now has legal effect (Article 6(1) TEU) and its impact is only just starting to be felt. It could be that the Charter enables the human rights of all residents of the EU to be protected, and if that is the case then many of the problems identified could be ameliorated. However, the UK and Poland negotiated an opt-out from the Charter,[231] the scope of which remains unclear.[232] The ECJ has also begun to interpret the opt-out finding that the protocol in general 'does not call into question the applicability of the Charter in the United Kingdom or in Poland, a position which is confirmed by the recitals in the preamble',[233] those recitals being recitals 3 and 6. The Court went on to hold that Article 1(1) 'explains Article 51 of the Charter with regard to the scope thereof and does not intend to exempt the Republic of Poland or the United Kingdom from the obligation to comply with the provisions of the Charter or to prevent a court of one of those Member States from ensuring compliance with those provisions'.[234] Unfortunately that was as far as the Court went as it was found that there was no need to consider the other parts of the Protocol. However, Advocate General Trstenjak in her Opinion did not look into Article 1(2) in any depth[235] but decided that Article 2 of the protocol did not create a general opt-out for the UK and Poland and only applied to provisions of the Charter that made reference to national laws and practices.[236] How the ECJ will develop the scope, both material and personal, and application of the Charter will emerge over the next few years. So far with the cases considered by the Court involving TCNs there are grounds for optimism, but it does little to help ameliorate the finding of substantive irrationality as it currently stands.

230 The Stockholm Programme (n 25) 8.
231 Protocol (No 30) on the application of the Charter of Fundamental Rights of the European Union to Poland and to the United Kingdom [2012] OJ L326/313.
232 S Peers 'The "opt-out" that fell to Earth: the British and Polish Protocol concerning the EU Charter of Fundamental Rights' (2012) 12 *HRLR* 375, 378 has summarised academic opinion, which it can be stated generally as sceptical, as to any substantive opt-out from the Charter's provisions.
233 *NS* (n 138) para 119.
234 ibid para 120.
235 *NS* (n 138), Opinion of AG Trstenjak, paras 172–74.
236 ibid para 176.

Another possible positive enhancement of the protection of the principle of universality of human rights in the EU is the requirement in Article 6(2) TEU for the Union to accede to the ECHR.[237] The negotiations took place in the Council of Europe's Steering Committee on Human Rights (CDDH) and a draft agreement of accession[238] was drawn up by an informal working group consisting of 14 expert members, seven from Union Member States and seven from non-EU but ECHR Contracting States. Once the agreement was presented, problems developed on both sides[239] but these were resolved through negotiations and a final agreement was published in April 2013.[240] This will need the ECJ to confirm its compatibility with the EU treaties followed by the Council adopting the agreement unanimously,[241] the latter being a difficult task with the recent attitudes of some Member Statess towards the ECHR. Therefore, at the current time, although accession could potentially improve the position vis-à-vis substantive irrationality, such a possibility remains in the future.

### 6.3.2.4   *Conclusions and suggested solutions*

The evaluation of the legislative instruments adopted under the AFSJ establishes that there are failings of formal, instrumental and substantive legal rationality, some of which can be objectively justified but the majority of which cannot be. These findings of legal irrationality are a cause of considerable concern in such an important area of policy that affects so many individuals, many of whom are members of minority groups and all without a political voice to influence Union policy formulation and implementation through the ballot box. For formal rationality and instrumental rationality any solutions proposed would only be value-neutral and be capable of resolving the immediate concerns. However, for

237  See T Lock 'Walking on a tightrope: the draft ECHR Accession Agreement and the autonomy of the EU legal Order' (2011) 48 *CMLRev* 1025; T Lock 'End of an epic? The draft Agreement on the EU's accession to the ECHR' (2012) 31 *YEL* 162 for analysis of the drafting process. See T Lock 'EU accession to the ECHR: implications for judicial review in Strasbourg' (2010) 35 *ELR* 777; SI Sánchez 'The Court and the Charter: the impact of the entry into force of the Lisbon Treaty on the ECJ's approach to fundamental rights' (2012) 49 *CMLRev* 1565 for examination of the EU's accession on the approach to human rights of the ECtHR and ECJ respectively.

238  CDDH report to the Committee of Ministers on the elaboration of legal instruments for the accession of the European Union to the European Convention on Human Rights, CDDH(2011)009 reproduces in the appendix the most recent version of the draft legal instruments.

239  See CDDH Common paper of Andorra, Armenia, Azerbaijan, Bosnia-Herzegovina, Iceland, Liechtenstein, Monaco, Montenegro, Norway, Serbia, Switzerland, Russian Federation, Turkey and Ukraine on major concerns regarding the Draft revised Agreement on the Accession of the European Union to the European Convention on Human Rights 47+1(2013)003 and K Lundgren, B Lochbihler 'European parliamentarians "Deeply concerned" at national moves to block EU accession to the European Convention on Human Rights' PACE Press Release AP018(2012) 25 January 2012 https://wcd.coe.int/ViewDoc.jsp?id=1899615&Site=DC.

240  CDDH, Fifth Negotiation Meeting Between the CDDH Ad Hoc Negotiation Group and the European Commission on the Accession of the European Union to the European Convention on Human Rights: Final Report to the CDDH, 47+1(2013)008.

241  ibid 2.

substantive legal rationality any resolution would need to conform to the value-laden requirements contained within the notion of substantive rationality. For formal and instrumental rationality there are certain themes that are clearly apparent. The first is the requirement to comply with international legal obligations, especially those set out in the Geneva Convention, and referred to in the Tampere Conclusions, the Hague Programme, the Stockholm Programme and many of the legislative instruments adopted under the AFSJ. This is especially important for the Qualification Directive, as it provides the guidance for the national authorities when applying the Geneva Convention (recital 23 of Directive 2011/95 and recital 19 of Directive 2004/83). It is certainly welcome that much of the Qualification Directive has extended the international protection to TCN applicants but there are noticeable lacunae that should be filled, not least the ability of Union citizens to be able to claim refugee status in another Member State. It could also be claimed that responsibilities under the ECHR should also be covered but until the Union accedes to the ECHR under Article 6(2) TEU this will not be absolutely necessary. The second theme is complexity that creates considerable difficulties for the AFSJ and the vast amount of legal instruments adopted under it. Many of the measures are intricate, the language used dense and the considerable derogations for Member States from key entitlements ensures confusion for anybody unless a legal expert in the field. As Boelaert-Suominen notes, 'it takes an extremely well-informed specialist to determine the current status and rights of third-country nationals under EC law'.[242] The solution it could be suggested is trite – rationalise the legal instruments to simplify, harmonise and ensure they are clear, precise and unconditional. However, a second suggestion that goes with this has more resonance, which is to set out a catalogue of clearly defined rights that can be relied upon and enforced by TCNs. It may be that this catalogue is not as comprehensive as those available to Union citizens but it should include some form of right to freedom of movement of TCNs, the third theme from the analysis. This catalogue of rights would also feed into the fourth theme of the criminalisation and demonisation of asylum-seekers and TCNs in general, which infringes international law and Union aims and principles. The suggestion made by Goodwin-Gill[243] to decriminalise the asylum system would remove the supply of human beings from the arms of human traffickers and organised crime. The consequence would be to treat asylum-seekers humanely and remove this modern form of human slavery from Union society. A fifth theme is a familiar one with the principle of non-discrimination not applicable or available as a universal, enforceable right to all TCNs. The solution is again quite straightforward and that is to return the principle of non-discrimination to its universal rather than citizenised status and ensure that it can be relied on by all individuals resident in

---

242 S Boelaert-Suominen 'Non-EU nationals and Council Directive 2003/109/EC on the status of third-country nationals who are long-term residents: five paces forward and possibly three paces back' (2005) 42 *CMLRev* 1011, 1051.

243 Goodwin-Gill 'The international protection of refugees' (n 203) 6.

the EU. This last theme also has connotations for the theme that underpins the finding that the AFSJ is substantively irrational, the universal application and protection for all individuals of protectable human rights. The suggestion though goes further than just enabling individuals, whether they are Union citizens or TCNs, to enforce their human rights in a court of law but requires all policies to have as their moral basis the essential requirement that the legal instruments, the policies developed and the decision-making process be compliant with human rights.

### 6.3.3 Free movement rights based on association agreements

#### 6.3.3.1 *Formal legal rationality*

The first element of formal rationality, that of contradiction of Union law by a legal instrument from another legal system, does not appear to be relevant, but the other two factors in formal rationality do raise concerns over certain specific issues.

The first issue surrounds the concept of non-discrimination on the basis of nationality, which is enshrined in Article 18 TFEU and, from the analysis conducted in Chapter 5, a contradictory situation with the principle of free movement of persons exists in the various agreements. Nationals of EFTA states enjoy the right to freedom of movement of persons but there is no such right for Turkish, Maghreb or for Central and Eastern European Countries' (CEEC) nationals under the CEEC Agreements. Furthermore, the Accession Treaty for the new Member States created a contradiction between the rights associated with citizens of the Union and those of workers. Thus CEEC nationals, as citizens of the Union, are entitled to enjoy the right to freedom of movement but old Member States limited this right for workers, either by maintaining their national provisions for labour market entry in force at the time of accession or by adopting new highly restrictive measures at the time of accession, the latter self-sanctioned in the transition arrangements, which could last for the duration of the seven year transition phase. This then appears to limit the right to free movement on the basis of nationality, a situation that contradicts the principle of non-discrimination on the basis of nationality. It could be argued that this is a situation that provides for tension between principles rather than contradiction and this position has some force when the purposes of the various agreements are taken into account. However the transition arrangements in the Accession Treaty for the CEECs, particularly as distinctions are made for Cyprus and Malta, do contradict the principle of freedom of movement.

As set out above, for the contradiction to be objectively justified the aims behind the contradictory policy must be identified and then it must be determined whether they are legitimate or not. It could be claimed that there is a legal aim with the Member States retaining control over the question of the right to freedom of movement. It could also be claimed that there is an economic aim that restrictions on the freedom of movement on the basis of nationality are designed to limit the impact on the host Member State's social welfare systems such that they do not become over-burdened by the sudden influx of new Union citizens seeking work. This is exemplified by the UK's Accession (Immigration and Worker Registration) Regulations 2004,[244] which required CEEC nationals not resident in the UK at the time of accession to have to work in the UK for an uninterrupted period of 12 months and be registered as working with an authorised employer before they could claim social security.[245] A further aim, linked with the former, is that of security and in particular the protection of public order, a problem that could occur in Member States if a sudden influx of new Member State nationals destabilised the society of the host Member State. Of these three aims the legal aim is questionable as, although Article 4(2) TFEU distributes shared competence for the internal market to the Union and Member States, the principle of freedom of movement of persons is very much contained within the Union domain. For the economic aim it is reasonable to find that this is a legitimate concern of Member States, and the manner in which the restrictions on the freedom of movement have been adopted and applied satisfy the tests for suitability and necessity. When it comes to the balancing exercise then this restriction must be weighed against the actual right of freedom of movement of persons, a fundamental right of the Union. As the standard of review enables considerable discretion to be granted to the Member States then for formal rationality the balance must come down on the side of the restriction of free movement. This is also the case for the security aim.

The second issue centres round the notion of family reunification. The doctrines of family reunification and free movement of workers appear to create a contradictory situation. In the CEEC Agreements a family member who entered the EU to rejoin the CEEC worker for family reunification was able to engage in the labour market immediately, without any time restriction. The Accession Treaty for the CEEC states maintained this position for family members already resident with the worker on 1 May 2004, or 1 January 2007 for Bulgaria and Romania, but if family members following that date exercised their right to family reunification then they had to be excluded from access to the labour market for 18 months or until 30 April 2007, or 31 December 2009 for Bulgaria and Romania, whichever is the earlier. Furthermore, Article 14 of the Family Reunification Directive, Directive 2003/86,[246] only authorises Member States to set a time limit that must not exceed 12 months for TCN family members of TCN workers to take up employment. The scope of the directive means that it cannot apply to family members of a Union citizen (Article 3(3)) and is without prejudice to more favourable positions of agreements between the EU and third countries (Article 3(4)(a)). However, it highlights the contradiction between the two doctrines of the right to family reunification and the right of access to the labour market

---

244 Accession (Immigration and Worker Registration) Regulations 2004 SI 2004/1219.
245 See *Zalewska v Department for Social Development (Northern Ireland)* [2008] 1 WLR 2602 (HL).
246 Council Directive 2003/86/EC on the right to family reunification [2003] OJ L251/12.

when TCN family members, and CEEC family members under the CEEC Agreements, appear to be in a more favourable position than family members of EU citizens originating from the CEEC States. It could be that this contradiction could be ameliorated by the ECJ providing a narrow interpretation of the derogations from the right to freedom of movement, or by finding that the Accession Treaty's standstill clause ensures that family members of CEEC nationals cannot be placed in a worse position after the Accession Treaty than they were in before under the CEEC Agreements. There is, however, for the moment, a contradiction between doctrines as they apply to CEEC nationals. The contradiction also exists for family members of Turkish workers who have no Union right to family reunification in Article 7 of Decision 1/80, have a limited access to the labour market after three years and are entitled to full employment rights after five years. This would appear to sit uncomfortably with Article 14 of the Family Reunification Directive. It may be the case that Article 3(4)(a) works in favour of the Turkish worker and his family members, particularly as the directive applies to TCNs residing lawfully in the territory of the Member States (Article 1), where a TCN is defined as any person who is not an EU citizen within the meaning of Article 20(1) TFEU. However, for Maghreb nationals who have no right to family reunification in the Euro-Mediterranean Agreements (EMAs), and no right of access to the employment market, they could now benefit from the directive.

The aim behind the contradiction is difficult to identify. The aims behind family reunification are predominantly economic, in that a worker is likely to feel more at home and thus more productive if he is given close support by his family, and cultural, as the focus of society is based on the family. Freedom of movement also contains similar aims, especially when it comes to family reunification. The consequence of this is that the irrationality of the position has no legitimate aim and so cannot be objectively justified.

The second area of difficulty with formal rationality is the situation when contradiction occurs with a legal doctrine itself. There are a number of concerns for this inconsistency. Contradictions appear to arise within the principle of non-discrimination itself as the scope of the term is defined differently between the different agreements. The EEA Agreement prohibits it in the same words as Article 18 TFEU, Article 9 of the EC-Turkey Protocol refers to Article 18 TFEU, whilst the Maghreb Agreements and CEEC Agreements limit the right to working conditions, remuneration or dismissal for legally employed workers, before the CEEC Agreements ensure that this is 'subject to the conditions and modalities applicable in each Member State'. As such the general principle of non-discrimination on the grounds of nationality will differ according to the nationality of the TCN, which is an internally contradictory position and indeed tautologous.

The aims behind this are similar to those outlined above. However, there is a more significant added aim, which is the legal objective. The EU has the legal personality (Article 47 TEU) and specific powers (Articles 217 and 218 TFEU) to conclude such agreements. However, the purpose, objective and spirit of each agreement is different and therefore the ECJ will interpret them in a different manner.[247] This underlying legal aim is a legitimate one, provided for the Union in the EU treaties, and is carried out by the Union's institutions in a way that fulfils the proportionality requirement, thereby rendering the contradiction justified.

From the discussion above it is clear that there is not only contradiction between two doctrines but also a contradictory position within the right to family reunification itself. The right to family reunification is now included in the Family Reunification Directive for all TCNs. However, there is no right to family reunification in the Ankara Agreement or its implementing decisions, or in the EMAs. It may be that the directive overrules the specific rules set out for Turkey and the Maghreb countries but until the matter comes before the ECJ for interpretation this contradiction will remain.

The aim again is the same legal objective that was identified for the contradiction in the principle of non-discrimination. Like that inconsistency it must be found to be legitimate and thus the contradiction is objectively justified.

The third issue of concern lies internally within the area of free movement of persons and arises in a number of ways. The national rules regulating first entry to a host Member State for Turkish nationals may now be contradictory following the judgment in *Tum and Dari*.[248] The Ankara Agreement and implementing decisions did not interfere with a Member State's competence to regulate the first entry of Turkish nationals into that host Member State. There is therefore no right of entry to the EU for a Turkish national. However, the criteria that Member States apply will now differ depending on the intent of the Turkish national. A Turkish national intending to enter the Member State to work will be assessed using the criteria in place at the time of his or her application, but a Turkish national intending to enter the Member State to either exercise the right to freedom of establishment, or the right to provide services, will have to be assessed using the criteria for entry in force at the time that the Additional Protocol came into force in that Member State. Thus, there will be two criteria applicable in each Member State for an assessment of a Turkish national's entry and which will apply will depend on whether the Turkish national is a worker or is exercising freedom of establishment or the freedom to provide services. Although this appears to be a contradictory position on closer inspection it is clear this is merely tension between legislative measures with the ECJ providing the guidance[249] needed for domestic courts as envisaged by the preliminary reference procedure.

---

247 Case 270/80 *Polydor Ltd and RSO Records Inc v Harlequin Record Shops Ltd and Simons Records Ltd* [1982] ECR 329 paras 15–18.
248 Case C–16/05 *R v Secretary of State for the Home Department ex parte Veli Tum and Mehmet Dari* [2007] ECR I–7415.
249 See Case C–186/10 *Tural Oguz v Secretary of State for the Home Department* [2012] 1 WLR 709 and the response of the UK Court of Appeal in *KA (Turkey) v Secretary of State for the Home Department* [2013] 1 CMLR 2 (CA).

The second is in the ECJ's different approaches in the *Micheletti*[250] and *Mesbah*[251] cases that actually involve judgment based on the same principle. Here, both Mr Micheletti and Mrs Mesbah's son-in-law had dual nationality, with Mr Micheletti claiming an EC right through his Member State nationality (he also had non-Member State nationality) and Mrs Mesbah claiming an EMA right based on her son-in-law's Moroccan nationality (he also had nationality of a Member State). Mr Micheletti was able to rely on his Member State nationality, as to deny it would breach his right to free movement, whilst Mrs Mesbah could not rely on her son-in-law's Moroccan nationality, as there was no right to free movement in the EMAs. The right to confer nationality on an individual remains within the competence of the Member States but once that nationality is conferred then it is 'owned' by that national who can then use it as he or she sees fit to claim further rights. It appears contradictory to be able to rely on Member State nationality to claim an EU right but not be able to rely on non-Member State nationality to claim a right that is available on the basis of being a non-Member State national. At first blush this again looks like contradiction but on a more nuanced consideration it becomes clear that it is tension within the same principle and, indeed, even if was found to be contradictory then the legal aim of protecting national sovereignty would objectively justify it as it is legitimate and would satisfy the proportionality requirements.

The third concern again lies between judgments of the ECJ and displays a long-running problem of the ECJ when dealing with previous case law that it wishes to overrule, the origins of which lie in its civil law background. *Taflan-Met*[252] established that Decision 3/80 required supplementary measures to be adopted by the Council for any of its provisions to be directly effective. The categorical nature of this denial of direct effect was undermined in *Sürül*[253] by first claiming that the former case had not considered the provision in question and then finding that it did not require an implementing measure to be directly effective. However, the Court in *Sürül* failed to overrule *Taflan-Met* on this point. Two categorical jurisprudential points therefore conflict: implementing measures are required for any provision of Decision 3/80 to be directly effective; and no implementing measure is required for a particular provision to be directly effective. This is a clear contradiction within the doctrine and produced by the working procedure of the ECJ. There are no aims that underpin it and as such it cannot be objectively justified.

### 6.3.3.2   *Instrumental legal rationality*

As has already been established, there are two aspects to instrumental legal rationality: generic and specific. Both are evident again when analysing the impact

---

250  Case C–369/90 *Mario Vicente Micheletti and Others v Delegación del Gobierno en Cantabria* [1992] ECR I–4239.
251  Case C–179/98 *Belgium v Fatna Mesbah* [1999] ECR I–7955.
252  Case C–277/94 *Z̧ Taflan-Met and Others v Bestuur van de Social Verzekeringsbank* and *O Akol v Bestuur van de Algemene Bedrijfsvereniging* [1996] ECR I–4085.
253  Case C–262/96 *Sema Sürül v Bundestantalt für Arbeit* [1999] ECR I–2685.

of free movement rights based on association agreements. It must also be borne in mind that the findings of contradiction identified above for formal legal rationality will also fall within the inconsistency element of generic instrumental legal rationality, this time analysed with a higher level of scrutiny (intermediate scrutiny test) and discounting any tension between or within doctrine.

The first issue for generic instrumental rationality is the complexity of the legislation itself that creates problems for the clarity requirement of generic instrumental rationality that, until 2003, was reasonably transparent. The adoption of the Family Reunification Directive has created opacity in this field, especially over the interaction of the right to family reunification and the rights of entry to the Member States for family members from Turkey and the Maghreb. Furthermore, the Accession Treaties for the CEEC states are complex and difficult documents to comprehend, which not only need to be carefully interpreted but also require knowledge of Member States' national law fully to appreciate the free movement available to CEEC nationals. The aims behind this policy leading to such complexity are admirable, being predominantly legal and with the object of ensuring that a uniform law is applied, covering such issues as family reunification and freedom of movement, across the EU. As such the aims are legitimate and satisfy the test of suitability but problems occur with the principle of necessity, and then when the balancing exercise is conducted. Over-complexity of legislation leads to a situation where those who are ruled cannot comprehend or understand the law, a clear difficulty for the rule of law and clearly illustrated in the very narrow House of Lords majority ruling in *Zalewska*.[254] There is no question that rationalisation of the law would achieve the aims in a more succinct manner and when set in the balancing exercise then the rule of law means that the finding of irrationality cannot be objectively justified.

The second issue, linked with the first, is the actual wording of the different pieces of legislation themselves that impinge on the clarity, non-contradictory, generality and congruence elements of generic instrumental rationality. Legal instruments, it must be accepted, are likely to be complex documents often dealing with difficult situations and frequently intractable problems. However, from the discussion of the first issue it can be seen that the wording of, in particular, the Accession Treaty creates significant layers of intricacy leading to abstruseness. The requirement of non-contradiction in instrumental rationality simply requires the laws, cases or doctrines not to be contrary to one another, without taking into account the distinctions between contradictions and tensions in formal rationality. Thus, all the inconsistencies of legislative wording outlined above for formal rationality, regardless of tensions between doctrines, are incorporated into the assessment of this element of instrumental rationality. The language of the legislation also impinges upon the generality of the law, where the authorities must apply the law consistently and treat individuals in similar positions equally and like cases must be treated alike. This second element appears to be satisfied as the agreements apply generally across the Community, thereby ensuring that like

254 *Zalewska* (n 245).

cases within different Member States are treated alike, with interpretation of the law provided by the ECJ or the EFTA Court for the EEA Agreement. However, for the law to be applied consistently under the first part of the generality requirement, it is submitted that provisions within different legal instruments using identical or close to identical wording should be interpreted in a similar manner. The ECJ has failed to do this, albeit through the accepted international legal procedure of considering the purpose of the agreement in question, particularly in the cases *El-Yassini*[255] and *Mesbah* involving the EMA Agreements. Thus, the ECJ has introduced inconsistency into the Union legal order in which individuals are treated differently even though the different laws relied on are worded identically, or close to identically. This then impacts on the congruence of the law as officially declared and its compatibility with it as administered. For the law to be administered, such that it is congruent, then provisions that are identical or nearly identical should be interpreted by the ECJ in a similar manner. The Court does not do so, as the purpose of the agreement is considered, and thus the law appears to be administered incongruently with that officially declared. For all four elements, namely clarity, non-contradiction, generality and congruence the aim again is centred around the legal objectives that underpin the different agreements and for the first two elements, clarity and non-contradiction, the same point on the rule of law as above means that there cannot be objective justification. Indeed, for the contradictions identified under formal irrationality that are contained within the fundamental principles of free movement of persons and non-discrimination the fundamental nature of free movement and non-discrimination would outweigh competing rights in the assessment of proportionality. However, for generality and congruence there is the additional consideration of the features of freedom of movement, as seen in the EEA Agreement, or not, as in the EMA Agreements. It cannot be denied that the interpretative techniques utilised by the ECJ are perfectly legitimate and recognised by international law but this does not surmount the fact that there is inconsistency and incongruence between identically or near identically worded legal instruments. The force of such legal instruments and the economic benefits of freedom of movement outweigh the legal workings of the Court viewed from a value-neutral position and utilising an intermediate scrutiny standard of review and therefore instrumental irrationality is not objectively justified.

The third issue is the difficulty for generic instrumental rationality created by the Council failing to agree to an implementing measure for Decision 3/80. Decision 3/80 was adopted to implement Article 39 of the Protocol with the aim of coordinating the social security systems of the Member States to enable Turkish workers employed or formerly employed in the Union, their family members and survivors to qualify for social security benefits. This was supposed to have been adopted within 12 months of the protocol coming into force but it took over a decade before the Association Council approved it but then did not finish the

255 Case C–416/96 *Nour Eddline El-Yassini v Secretary of State for the Home Department* [1997] ECR I–1209.

implementation. By failing to adopt an implementing measure the law fails to satisfy the prospective requirement. Furthermore, this leads to a situation where the law as officially declared again appears to lack congruence with that administered, as evidenced in *Taflan-Met* and *Sürül*. The main policy aim is economic with the Member States desiring to protect their social welfare systems from being overburdened by Turkish nationals. This is clearly a sensitive political 'hot potato', particularly in countries such as Germany and Austria with very high Turkish working populations. However, although such an aim could be considered to be legitimate such issues must be considered in the context of the aim of Article 39 of the Protocol and the adoption of Decision 3/80 and from a value-neutral perspective. To adopt legislation to coordinate the Member States' social security schemes for Turkish nationals but then to fail to adopt legislation to enable these people to claim their rights before the courts clearly creates considerable concern for the rule of law that cannot be justified by political expediency hidden behind an economic objective.

Generally, the association agreements have few problems with specific instrumental legal rationality. However, the failure by the Council to adopt an implementing measure for Decision 3/80 means that the Council has not even attempted to accomplish the required aim in Article 39 of the protocol, thus failing to promote the legitimate ends or goals of the Ankara Agreement. Furthermore, the requirement that legal officials must use the most effective legal technique to achieve societal goals, thereby ensuring the function of the legal act matches its effect, is completely negated by the lack of this implementing measure. It is not possible objectively to justify this flagrant breach of a substantive aim and seriously undermines the rule of law as it applies, in particular, to the relationship between the EU and Turkey.

### 6.3.3.3   *Substantive legal rationality*

With the introduction of the Lisbon Treaty and adoption of Article 6(1) TEU giving legal effect to the Charter of Fundamental Rights, the human rights underpinning of the Union legal edifice is supplied by the Charter, and supported by the ECHR. At first blush the law is substantively rational as human rights underpin the legal system. However, for the law to be fully assessed for substantive rationality individuals who have their human rights violated should be able to bring a claim against the perpetrators of the breach before the courts of law of the legal system that is allegedly violating human rights.

TCNs that can bring themselves within the scope of the international agreements should be able to rely on the EU's human rights protection through the use of the Charter as they are brought under the Union legal umbrella.[256] However, these rights are not possessed by the individuals concerned on the basis

---

256 Only in Case 12/86 *Meryem Demirel v Stadt Schwäbisch Gmünd* [1987] ECR 3719 has there been an attempt to use the human rights standards of the ECHR, which the ECJ rejected as the case lay outside the EU legal domain.

of their innate humanity but because they have established an EU nexus. The EU nexus enables the Union right to be claimed under the particular international agreement that then enables a fundamental right claim to be advanced. Human rights by their very nature are rights 'owned' by human beings on the basis of their innate humanity. Thus all human beings resident in a community in which human rights norms are protected should be able to claim the benefit of that right without any further condition. By making human rights conditional then the norms cannot be protected and the legal system cannot be substantively rational. This is exemplified by TCNs of the country covered by the agreement, resident in the Union who are unable to bring themselves under the coverage of the agreement. They will not therefore be able to establish the required EU nexus and will not be able to rely on Union human rights protection.[257] It may also be the case that any TCNs within the coverage of the agreements may not be able to establish this EU nexus as they have not exercised freedom of movement,[258] a right not available under the agreements, except the EEA Agreement, or within the TFEU (see Chapter 3).

The situation with substantive rationality is controversial as there are value judgments that underlie the concept. It was seen in Chapter 2 that the protection of human rights as the key feature of substantive rationality could be justified and provided legitimate justification for legislative requirements. However, it was also acknowledged that the substitution of an alternative moral perspective, such as a utilitarian position, for such a value judgment could provide a vastly different perspective. Thus, there needs to be consideration of this position from an established policy stance, with the stance chosen being that of the Tampere Conclusions' voluntary commitment by the EU and its Member States to improve the position of the TCNs and reiterated in the provisions of the Stockholm Programme. From this policy stance, and as Article 2 TEU states the 'Union is founded on the values of respect for ... human rights, including the rights of persons belonging to minorities', then for EU law to be substantively rational it must protect the human rights of all human beings resident within the territory of the EU. To do this, individuals must be able to bring legal action to sustain any claims to violations of human rights principles, a situation that is currently not possible for all individuals legally resident in the Union. It is possible that this position is ameliorated by the legal force given to the Charter by Article 6(1) TEU after the Lisbon Treaty but this has yet to be tested before the ECJ. Furthermore, once the EU accedes to the ECHR in accordance with the requirements of Article 6(2) TEU, and as outlined above, then it could be that human rights of TCNs could be enforced at the ECtHR in Strasbourg. However, this remains speculative until definitive case law develops and so the protection of TCN rights through the association

257  These TCNs might be able to obtain protection for human rights abuses through the legal order of the Member State in which they are resident. This, however, does not negate the lack of substantive rationality within the *Union* legal order.

258  See for example Joined Cases 35 & 36/82 *Elestina Esselina Christina Morson and Sweradjie Jhanjan v Netherlands* [1982] ECR 3723.

agreements fails the test for substantive rationality and is not justified by other standards of human rights protection.

### 6.3.3.4   *Conclusions and suggested solutions*

As with the previous two areas of analysis the policy approach to TCNs under association agreements is defective for formal, instrumental and substantive legal rationality, although some findings of irrationality can be objectively justified. Although the situation for association agreements tends to be less serious for irrationality when it comes to the principle of free movement of persons than the previous two fields, identifying solutions to alleviate or ameliorate these results can again be formulated around a number of themes, which is a developing pattern. The first two themes are the recognition that discrimination on the basis of nationality should apply to all persons equally, and the requirement that all individuals should be able to enforce their human rights before the courts. By ensuring the universality of nationality discrimination and human rights enforcement then much of legal irrationality would fade away, especially the value-laden substantive irrationality. This universal protection of human rights would be relatively easy to achieve through declaratory judgments of the ECJ and it could be that as the ECJ interprets the Charter then human rights protection will be enforceable for TCNs under association agreements. However, when providing solutions over discrimination it must be noted that any solution does not need to be imbued with moral values as this falls for consideration under formal and instrumental legal rationality, both of which are value-neutral. Therefore, any solution may not necessarily improve the lot of all TCNs but must merely remove the irrational elements. The first solution would be to ensure that in all future accessions to the EU, there would be no difference in treatment based on nationality. As this would be value-neutral then it is possible that accession arrangements, especially for transition measures, could be restrictive of the principle of freedom of movement but if such a measure applied to all TCNs then there would not be a problem with discrimination. The second suggested solution would be to introduce a universal amendment for all the agreements in which a general non-discrimination article would be adopted. It is difficult to envisage this downgrading any free movement rights for TCNs and it would ensure that the principle of non-discrimination was universally applied.

The third theme that is apparent in formal and instrumental legal rationality is the complexity of the legislative measures. Unfortunately, to alleviate the problems with rationality caused by the complexity of the international agreements negotiated by the Union with third countries then they would need to be renegotiated and redrafted with simplicity of legislation as a central aim in the process.

The final theme is the failure by the Association Council to adopt an implementing legal instrument for Decision 3/80, which leads to both formal and instrumental irrationality. The solution is simple – adopt an implementing measure. The adoption of a Union position for negotiation in the Association Council through Decision 2012/776[259] would rectify the issue as Decision 3/80 would be repealed and the new instrument would not need an implementing measure. However, it needs to be adopted, a requirement that has proven difficult in the past to achieve under similar circumstances involving the CEECs.

259  Council Decision 2012/776/EU on the position to be taken on behalf of the European Union within the Association Council set up by the Agreement establishing an association between the European Economic Community and Turkey, with regard to the adoption of provisions on the coordination of social security systems [2012] OJ L340/19.

# 7  Conclusions

Third country nationals (TCNs) are an integral part of the EU, whose numbers are likely to grow over the next 50 years and whose significance, it is submitted, has still not been fully realised by the citizens and politicians of the Member States. The lives of TCN residents in the EU, just like EU citizens, are regulated by laws, laws adopted by political legislatures whose actions must be justified to those who they legislate for. This chapter will summarise the findings of the previous chapters of this book before putting forward suggestions for the adoption of the solutions outlined in Chapter 6 to ensure the output of the polity satisfies the requirements of legal rationality and thus becomes politically legitimate.

## 7.1  Conclusions

In Chapter 1 theories of legitimacy were outlined, with input and output examined and reasons provided for the decision to select output-orientated legitimacy as the standard for investigation of legitimacy in the EU. It was established that for output-orientated legitimacy to be an effective tool for analysis a model needed to be formulated against which policy areas could be benchmarked. Those benchmarks would be supplied by the model of legal rationality and the policy area selected, with the reasoning determining that selection explained, was the fundamental principle of free movement of persons in the Union as it applied to TCNs.

Chapter 2 developed the themes that were necessary principles of legal rationality and the way in which legitimate aims could objectively justify any findings of irrationality. Rationality was examined from the perspective of different disciplines, identifying a common theme applicable for an investigation of policy outputs. From the finding that law regulated human action and human social action and was the final outcome of the political process, it was established that legal outputs were the appropriate tools to measure political legitimacy. The benchmarks to provide a model for this analysis of output-orientated legitimacy were delivered by the theory of legal rationality, which was made up of three distinct elements: formal legal rationality; instrumental legal rationality; and substantive legal rationality. By viewing legal measures through the three parts of legal rationality it could be determined whether or not the law was legally rational. However, it was found that the result of this rationality determination was abstract, not necessarily infused with policy considerations and unlikely to provide useful recommendations for policy development. It was necessary therefore to situate the legal rationality outcomes within a policy context to see if any legitimate aims of policy could objectively justify findings of legal irrationality This objective justification required that the policy had to be legitimate and satisfied the full principle of proportionality analysis, with the intensity of review increasing with the seriousness of the irrationality concept. Thus, for formal rationality the aim only had to satisfy the rational basis test, which gave a wide scope of discretion to policy-makers, whilst the strict scrutiny test for substantive rationality required an aim to be for the protection of human rights, and finally an intermediate scrutiny test for instrumental rationality would come somewhere between the two. This grounded the abstract theory in the political reality of the world of EU immigration and asylum policy.

The policy area chosen for investigation was the EU free movement rights of third country nationals, which had three specific and discrete fields of competence: provisions of the treaties and their implementing legislation; the area of freedom, security and justice (AFSJ); and association agreements. Chapter 3 examined the free movement rights outlined in the provisions of the treaties and secondary legislation adopted to implement them. The objectives of the Union were outlined, especially as they applied to TCNS, before scrutinising the principle of non-discrimination and discovering that with the adoption of the Treaty of Lisbon there had been a successful attempt to constrain the universality of the principle to Union citizens. This citizenisation of non-discrimination excluded TCNs from the benefits of its application and was reflected in the directives adopted to implement Article 19 TFEU and in the case law of the ECJ. The result of this was for the principle of equal treatment to lose its essential requirement of universality and to develop a culture of 'us and them'. Union citizenship when examined was found to provide an opportunity for a new inclusive concept of citizenship to be developed exclusively for the reality of the Union situation. However, the ECJ had interpreted this restrictively, limiting the rights associated with Union citizenship exclusively to nationals of Member States. Furthermore, as the case law developed so had the connection between Union citizenship and the principle of non-discrimination, thereby supporting the transformation of the universal principle of non-discrimination into a citizen right outlined in legislation. With the adoption of the Citizens Directive TCNs enjoyed some rights that were derived exclusively from the relationship they held to the Union citizen, although over time these rights were transferred from the EU citizen to the TCN. This derived nature of piggy-backed rights was also clearly evident when considering the free movement rights of workers, services and the right to freedom of establishment. The result was a highly attenuated right of free movement for TCNs that was only granted to TCNs if they were 'owned' by a Union citizen.

Chapter 4 examined the AFSJ and the free movement rights contained within it and the legislation adopted to create it. The introduction of the AFSJ, its development and the complex and difficult opt-outs for the UK, Ireland and Denmark were examined before then considering three sections specifically of the AFSJ dealing with the free movement rights of asylum-seekers, refugees, or now after Directive 2011/95 those seeking international protection status and immigrants, before looking briefly at free movement of persons in the AFSJ, the jurisdiction of the European courts and the European Arrest Warrant (EAW) Framework Decision. The result of the opt-outs, especially for the UK and Ireland, was found to increase security and justice whilst limiting freedom for TCNs. The legal measures for asylum-seekers under the Dublin Convention, now replaced by the Dublin Regulation (Dublin II) and about to be amended by Dublin III, complemented by Eurodac and the Receptions Directive, created no rights of free movement for TCNs between Member States. In fact the right of free movement within a Member State could be totally restricted to a specific place in certain circumstances (Article 7 of the Receptions Directive), whilst the minimum reception conditions (Article 14) designed to protect an asylum-seeker's human dignity did not set out a substantive definition of human dignity. The ability of Member States to remove these minimum receptions conditions for a TCN exercising freedom of movement (Article 16) meant that human dignity could be violated owing to an individual exercising an EU fundamental principle. For refugees the provisions of the Qualification Directive, the Refugee Procedures Directive and the Temporary Protection Directive were studied and, although the introduction of new opportunities for individual protection in the form of subsidiary and temporary protection were welcomed, there were in particular worries over the mismatch with the Geneva Convention, amongst many other concerns. Furthermore, there was no right to freedom of movement for individuals with international protection status, although they were entitled to travel documents for the purposes of travel (Article 25 of Directive 2011/95). The situation was further complicated by the UK and Ireland opting out of the new Qualification Directive, leaving in place the provisions of Directive 2004/83. When it came to immigration the investigation was split into legal and illegal immigration. For legal immigration a number of legal measures were examined but it was clear that although the Blue Card and LTR TCN Directives provided for a possibility of movement for TCNs satisfying criteria that gave considerable discretion to Member States, this fell far short of an enforceable right to mobility let alone a right to freedom of movement. Furthermore, the rights guaranteed to TCNs could be easily restricted by a lengthy list of exceptions derogated to Member States. The complexity of this matrix of legislation was considered to be alarming, especially as the focus for it was TCNs most of whom would not be trained legal experts[1] and more than likely would have a different first language to that of the host Member State. Illegal immigration was examined through the provisions dealing with expulsion in the AFSJ (although this was covered in greater detail in

---

1 S Boelaert-Suominen 'Non-EU nationals and Council Directive 2003/109/EC on the status of third-country nationals who are long-term residents: five paces forward and possibly three paces back' (2005) 42 *CMLRev* 1011, 1051.

Chapter 3), the returns policy of the EU and readmission agreements with third countries. Unsurprisingly, for illegal immigrants there were no rights to freedom of movement but more disconcerting was the liberal use of detention at Member States' discretion, the criminalisation of asylum-seekers with the lengthy ban on re-entry to the Union territory after expulsion and the opportunity for human rights violations under the readmission agreements and lack of monitoring organisation. It was noted that the Schengen Borders Code removed internal borders but did not provide a right to freedom of movement as this was found elsewhere, the extension of the jurisdiction of the ECJ after the Lisbon Treaty was welcomed and it was pointed out the ease with which individuals, including TCNs, could be transferred from Member State to Member State, either to stand trial for alleged criminal activity or to serve sentences for trials in their absence in comparison with the lack of the right to freedom of movement of persons for TCNs. In conclusion, the size and complexity of the AFSJ legislative measures were noted, as was the hierarchical nature of the treatment of TCNs under the AFSJ, and finally the lack of a right to freedom of movement for persons compared with the ease of transfer of prisoners under the EAW Framework Decision.

Chapter 5 investigated the free movement rights of TCNs under the various association agreements that the EU had entered into with third countries, in particular those with the European Economic Area (EEA) countries, the Ankara Agreement with Turkey, the Maghreb Agreements with Algeria, Morocco and Tunisia, and the CEEC Agreements. The rights provided by the agreements were outlined as they applied to individuals who exercised either an opportunity to move, or a right of free movement, the latter only available for the EEA Agreement. Indeed, none of the agreements, apart from the EEA Agreement, allowed for any right to mobility within the EU once entry to the territory of the relevant Member State was allowed but rights to improved access to the labour market were provided for depending on the length of stay in a particular job and Member State. Furthermore, the right to non-discrimination had been interpreted by the ECJ teleologically and generously. The result was a series of agreements that provided rights for TCNs that fell short of free movement rights, apart from the EEA Agreement, enabling greater access to the labour market as time passed from when they first entered the Member State's territory. This was less than full Union citizenship but could be equated to market citizenship and generosity of rights depending on the purpose of the agreement and position of the third country. If the third country was European and likely to accede to the EU then the closer the accession approached the more generous the interpretation of the agreement by the ECJ.

In Chapter 6 the underlying attitudes shaping the EU's policy towards TCNs were outlined, starting with the Conclusions of the Tampere European Council in October 1999, to the Hague Programme of 2005, through the French Presidency's European Pact on Immigration and Asylum initiative of 2008 to the current Stockholm Programme of 2009. From these Union programmes that delineated EU aims for the AFSJ the underlying policy aims towards TCNs were distilled and identified as legal, economic, status, security, human rights and cultural. The findings of the three areas examined in Chapters 3–5 were observed through the lens of legal rationality to find that there were failings of irrationality at all three levels: formal; instrumental; and substantive. However, once examined for objective justifications some of these findings of irrationality were found to be objectively justified. For free movement rights under the treaties and their implementing legislation it was found that the citizenisation of the principle of non-discrimination and the restriction of TCNs from the scope of free movement rights caused formal legal irrationality and instrumental legal irrationality, the latter at both generic and specific levels. Furthermore, and most concerning, by only enabling rights for TCNs through a derived relationship to a Union citizen, EU law subordinated TCNs to the will of that right holder, objectified TCNs and effectively dehumanised non-Member State nationals, thereby breaching the requirements of fairness within the Community, which was substantively legally irrational. For free movement rights within the AFSJ the establishment of regional protection areas (RPAs) and transit processing centres (TPCs) contradicted international law and constituted formal legal irrationality. Formal legal irrationality also occurred without objective justification between the Long-term Residents (LTR) Directive and the principle of non-discrimination on the basis of nationality, the restriction of the right to freedom of movement for TCNs and the aims of the AFSJ, the Single Permit Directive and the right to equal treatment, and within the doctrine of free movement of persons itself. All of these contradictions also fell under generic instrumental legal irrationality, as did the contradictory position between the Qualification Directive and the Geneva Convention and any contradictions involving the principles of non-discrimination and freedom of movement of persons. Generic instrumental legal irrationality also occurred over: the complexity of the AFSJ legal instruments, especially the LTR Directive; the lack of generality of the law with individuals in similar situations being treated differently and the law not being consistent or being consistently applied across the different Member States, a particular problem with the opt-outs of the UK and Ireland and the Qualification Directive; the incongruence of the law as officially declared against the law as administered in practice, particularly over the Dublin Regulation, LTR Directive and Receptions Directive; and the complexity, inconsistency and lack of generality of the Danish opt-out. The law also suffered from a lack of specific instrumental legal rationality over the LTR and Single Permit Directives, the functioning of the Dublin Regulation, the criminalisation of the asylum system and the EAW Framework Decision. Finally, there was a finding of substantive legal irrationality at multiple levels, be they on the basis of violations of international human rights instruments, the Charter of Fundamental Rights or a systemic dehumanisation of TCNs. For free movement rights under the association agreements there was a finding of formal legal irrationality over contradictions between free movement and family reunification and the difficulties over the lack of an implementing measure for Decision 3/80. Again these contradictions fell within the domain of generic instrumental legal irrationality too, as did the contradictions between the principle of the freedom of movement of persons and the principle of non-discrimination on the basis of nationality but also contractions within the freedom of movement doctrine. Other generic instrumental legal irrationalities occurred over the complexity and clarity of the law, its lack of generality, incongruence and, by failing to adopt an implementing measure for Decision 3/80, the Association Council failed the prospective requirement as well as not attempting to achieve the legitimate aims and goals of the Ankara Agreement, thus absolutely failing the requirement of specific instrumental legal rationality. Finally, TCNs under the association agreements, apart from those under the EEA Agreement, did not have a right to freedom of movement and therefore could not establish an EU nexus to enable them to enforce any of their human rights before the Union courts. This was a clear breach of the requirements of substantive legal rationality.

## 7.2 Recommendations

Chapter 6 also made suggestions for solutions to these findings of legal irrationality. The remainder of this chapter will take those solutions and develop them into policy recommendations for the EU to make the free movement rights of TCNs politically legitimate. However, before putting these recommendations forward two points need to be emphasised. First, it would be wise for policy-makers to be made aware of difficulties with policy-making. As Castles[2] pointed out, evidence from history suggested that the use of migration policies to achieve certain aims and objectives often failed to achieve those objectives. A secondary reading of this historical evidence was that the policy objectives were achieved but the unintended consequences resulted in further legislative measures being required, significant changes being made to society and problems developing many years later. El-Enany[3] demonstrates a similar situation developing in the EU over the treatment of refugees in particular, with refugee law retaining its status as the 'unwanted child of States'.[4] The second point is one of optimism. If refugee law is the 'unwanted child of States' then in the Union it is a toddler. The AFSJ has existed for a very short space of time and come a considerable distance from its formation. The pace of development is heady, driven forward by the five year programmes first set in place by the Tampere Conclusions with a first phase of legislation now being further expanded in a second phase. The essential requirement for this evolution is for policy-makers to retain sight of the aims and objectives of a common policy on asylum, immigration and external border control that is 'fair towards third-country nationals' (Article 67(2) TFEU). This fairness is reflected in the Tampere declaration that the EU 'must ensure fair treatment of third country nationals who reside legally on the territory of its

2  S Castles 'Why migration policies fail' (2004) 27 *Ethnic and Racial Studies* 205; S Castles 'The factors that make and unmake migration policies' (2004) 38 *IMR* 852.
3  N El-Enany 'Who is the new European refugee?' (2008) 33 *ELR* 313.
4  R Byrne, A Shacknove 'The safe country notion in European asylum law' (1996) 9 *Harvard Human Rights Journal* 185, 187.

Member States', reflected in a 'vigorous integration policy' designed to grant them 'rights and obligations comparable to those of EU citizens' with enhanced 'non-discrimination in economic, social and cultural life'.[5] It must be emphasised therefore that TCNs can only be integrated into Member State society by ensuring 'fair treatment of third country nationals who reside legally on the territory of the Member States' and 'granting them rights and obligations comparable to those of citizens of the Union'.[6] It is with these two points in mind that the following recommendations are made.

### 7.2.1 *Complexity of legislation and opt-outs*

The size of the legislative measures that effect the situation of TCNs is considerable and continues to grow. The opt-outs for the UK and Ireland and the policy decisions of the two countries means that many of the first generation AFSJ Directives have to remain on the statute books as they retain legal force for these two countries, whilst being superseded by new legislative measures in the remaining 25 Member States (Denmark is included in the 25 as Denmark has adopted all the measures so far). Along with this vast volume of law, the provisions within the legislative measures are intensely complex, a fact reflected in the comments of Boelaert-Suominen[7] about the LTR Directive and the misinterpretation of Article 9 of that directive by Peers.[8] Most of the TCNs that this legislation applies to are not trained legal experts, and many of them will speak a first language that is not necessarily an official language of the Union. The complexity must be reduced if TCNs are going to be able to identify and enforce their rights provided in Union law and if they are to know if they are receiving the requisite fair treatment or not. Furthermore, the opt-outs, and the opportunities for opt-outs, should be enthusiastically reduced over a period of time until there is a single layer of law that applies to all individuals across all the Union's territory. The lack of this generality of the law is a major concern for the rule of law and should be actively discouraged.

### 7.2.2 *Catalogue of rights*

The first recommendation of reduced complexity feeds into the second recommendation, namely to provide a clear, precise and unconditional catalogue of rights for TCNs. This is in line with the aims of the Union set out in the Tampere Conclusions and the Stockholm Programme and which should have been reflected in the LTR, the Blue Card and Single Permit Directives. Instead,

---

5  Presidency Conclusions of the Tampere European Council 15–16 October 1999 SN 200/1/99 para 18.
6  European Council Document 'The Stockholm Programme – an open and secure Europe serving and protecting citizens' [2010] OJ C115/1, 30.
7  Boelaert-Suominen 'Non-EU nationals and Council Directive 2003/109/EC' (n 1).
8  S Peers Implementing equality? The Directive on Long Term Resident Third Country Nationals' (2004) 29 *ELR* 437, 458.

these directives produced a tangle of very limited rights with a mass of derogations for Member States. It would be disingenuous to describe these as rights comparable with the rights of EU citizens. Such a catalogue of rights must also reflect the fact that TCNs are not a homogenous group of individuals and therefore it is suggested that there should be three levels of rights: asylum-seekers; individuals with international protection; and legal immigrants. These three groups should be able to turn to a single document where their graduated rights are clearly set out, with limited derogations that are stated in a transparent manner.

### 7.2.3   Free movement of persons

The previous recommendation leads on to the third recommendation. The focus of this book has been on free movement rights of TCNs, or rather the lack of them. As the European Council stated at Tampere this right of freedom of movement is not the preserve of the Union's citizens and denying it to TCNs 'would be in contradiction with Europe's traditions'.[9] Unfortunately, that is precisely what has happened and needs to be reconsidered at the earliest opportunity. The recent economic crisis is not a fair reflection of the likely development of the EU over the next 50 years, which is projected to see a shrinking working-age population as people live longer and the birth rate continues to fall (see Chapter 1). This demographic trend will lead to an increasing number of gaps appearing in the labour market that will need to be addressed if the Union is first to return to economic growth and then to sustain it. TCNs should be a part of the solution to this uncertain situation by either being actively recruited from third countries or, more beneficially, allowed to move intra-Union to help fill the lacunae. It is recommended that the catalogue of rights described above should also include a right to freedom of movement. As with the three categories of individuals so there could be a hierarchical right to freedom of movement starting with a right to travel for asylum-seekers, moving to a right to mobility for individuals with international protection and a full right to freedom of movement for legal migrants. Within this latter category this right could be dependent on establishing a link of solidarity with the host Member State before being able to access this right, of which length of residence could be one of the factors taken into consideration.

The right of free movement, and a catalogue of rights, is also essential for the treatment of highly-skilled migrants, to the benefit of the TCN but also for Union industries, the Member States and the EU itself. Up until 1974 the German government operated a guest-worker policy, where TCNs were invited to move temporarily to Germany to fill gaps in the labour market for reduced pay, rights and working conditions compared with their German worker counterparts. The result was that instead of being temporary, these guest-workers became permanent ethnic minorities, settling in Germany and leading to more TCNs

---

9 Presidency Conclusions of the Tampere European Council (n 5) para 3.

joining them through family reunification.[10] Unfortunately, the introduction of the LTR, Blue Card and Single Permit Directives with their lack of right to freedom of movement and ability of Member States significantly to attenuate the majority of rights seeks to introduce a resurrected form of guest-worker.[11] The results are likely to be a temporary workforce that is cheaper and with fewer rights than the domestic workforce, TCN employment encouraged by industry but a secondary underclass society without opportunity for promotion, rights or, as there is no right to vote, a voice. The formula is ripe for social unrest or the return of the settlement and family reunification model of Germany's previous experience. The creation of a catalogue of rights for TCNs, which would include a sliding scale to enjoy the right to freedom of movement, would restrict the potential development of these negative situations.

### 7.2.4  *The principle of non-discrimination*

The principle of non-discrimination is a fundamental principle of the EU that has been citizenised by legislative and jurisprudential developments. This creates a significant problem for TCNs, who are unable to take advantage of the right to non-discrimination on the basis of nationality but also the concept of non-discrimination and its underlying principle of equality. Such a principle is universal in nature and as such should be available to all people resident in the Union. By limiting the right to EU citizens 'the end result is a fragmentation of equality rights with variable standards of protection'.[12] This has created problems for TCNs at every level examined in this book and has consistently been found to be legally irrational. The principle should be returned to its universal nature at the earliest opportunity, either by amending the directives dealing with non-discrimination and equal treatment, especially the Race Directive, or by the ECJ enforcing Article 21 of the Charter.

### 7.2.5  *Human rights and the dehumanisation of TCNs*

The clearest and most concerning finding of the rationality analysis was the failing of the policy on free movement rights for TCNs on the basis of substantive legal irrationality. The very quality of human rights that ensures those rights are effective is that they are owned by individuals simply on the basis of their innate humanity, which enables an individual to enforce those rights by an action in a court of law. This protection of human rights then operates at a number of levels: first, there must be a right; secondly, that right must be owned by an individual simply by being a human being; thirdly, there are no human beings that are lesser human beings; and, fourthly, an individual human being must be able to

---

10  S Castles 'The guest-Worker in Western Europe – an obituary' (1986) 20 *IMR* 761.
11  S Castles 'Guest-workers in Europe: a resurrection?' (2006) 40 *IMR* 741.
12  P Watson 'Equality between Europe's citizens: Where does the Union now stand?' (2012) 35 *Fordham International Law Journal* 1426, 1478.

enforce his or her human rights in a court. The recommendations to resolve the finding of substantive irrationality operate at all four of these levels, all of which need to be addressed for the policy to be politically legitimate.

The first level is that there must be a right. Until recently this was a problem for the EU as human rights could only be protected through general principles of EU law that had been held in a series of ECJ judgments[13] to safeguard fundamental rights. This had been entrenched in Article 6(2) TEU but to activate such a right then a Union connection had to be established, which for individuals was normally the exercise of the right to freedom of movement, a right not available to TCNs. When the Charter of Fundamental Rights was produced[14] it was only solemnly proclaimed by the Commission, Council and Parliament and therefore had no binding legal force. With the entering into force of the Lisbon Treaty on 1 December 2009 the Charter was given the same legal value as the EU treaties (Article 6(1) TEU). Unfortunately, the Charter is a mixture of rights, freedoms and principles and the body of the text does not indicate how to distinguish whether an ambiguous Charter Article was a right, freedom or principle. Therefore, to determine which of the Charter's Articles will provide actionable rights will need to await interpretation by the ECJ.

The second level is that the right must be owned simply by being a human being. This creates the situation that the individual must not have to rely on another person related to that individual exercising his or her rights before being able to claim the right. Furthermore, a TCN that would not be able to exercise a right to freedom of movement and therefore establish an EU nexus must not be excluded from being able to rely on the Charter if one of the Charter's provisions is infringed.

The third level can be classified as requiring human beings not to be dehumanised. All individuals resident within the EU need to be treated as human beings, who are able to claim and enforce their human rights merely on the basis of their innate humanity. A number of recommendations would ensure that TCNs were not treated in a dehumanised manner. The first is to introduce the catalogue of rights and the reintroduction of the universality of the principle of non-discrimination on the basis of nationality outlined above. The tautologous scenario of discriminating on the basis of nationality in a right to non-discrimination on the basis of nationality would be removed, whilst TCNs would be able to rely on their own rights of free movement rather than having to rely on derived rights. As Weiler[15] has observed, where an individual can only protect his or her human rights through establishing a sufficiently close relationship with another individual who must then choose to exercise his or her own right to freedom of movement, then those persons become subordinated to the will of the right holder and the

---

13  Case 29/69 *Erich Stauder v City of Ulm* [1969] ECR 419; Case 11/70 *Internationale Handelsgesellschaft mbH v Einfuhr- und Vorratsstelle für Getreide und Futtermittel* [1970] ECR 1125; Case 4/73 *J Nold, Kohlen- und Baustoffgroßhandlung v Commission* [1974] ECR 491.
14  Charter of Fundamental Rights of the European Union [2000] OJ C364/1.
15  JHH Weiler 'Thou shalt not oppress a stranger: on the judicial protection of the human rights of non-EC nationals' (1992) 3 *EJIL* 65, 90.

polity as a whole and they become a 'thing' 'which serves the purpose of ensuring free movement'. Thirdly, the aims of the Stockholm Programme to provide 'rights and obligations comparable to those of citizens of the Union'[16] should be fully realised in the catalogue of rights described above, with the objective of ensuring that TCNs do not become dehumanised in comparison with Union citizens. However, this requires further action to ensure that all international human rights legal commitments are fully enforced in the Dublin Regulation, the Qualification Directive, RPAs and TPCs, and the EAW Framework Decision. Furthermore, the minimum reception conditions in the Receptions Directive must ensure that human dignity is fully protected and so the possibility of withdrawal of the conditions should be repealed. Fourthly, the asylum system should be decriminalised. By criminalising, detaining and punishing asylum-seekers the right to claim asylum, set out in Article 18 of the Charter, is diminished. The result is a demonisation of asylum-seekers as a stratum of society that is less than human, which then becomes extrapolated to an ever increasing category of TCNs. This leads to the fifth suggestion that the Commission should develop a policy for mainstreaming the catalogue of rights and the universal principle of non-discrimination on the basis of nationality into all decision-making processes. Furthermore, the mainstreaming options should be accompanied by press briefings to accentuate the positive benefits of TCNs to the Union, particularly through legal migration, but also to illustrate international protection through TCNs' own stories.

The fourth recommendation is that all individuals resident in the Union should be able to enforce their human rights before a court. Now that the Charter has legal force then it is possible that individuals may be able to sue the Charter directly. However, as already outlined it is uncertain which of the Charter's provisions are rights, freedoms or principles, which of these are judiciable and which can be enforced by a TCN if they are still required to show an EU nexus. Article 6(2) TEU requires the Union to accede to the ECHR and it is strongly recommended that this happens as soon as practicably possible so that all individuals will be able to rely on the ECHR and the lengthy interpretative jurisprudence of the European Court of Human Rights (ECtHR).

## 7.3 Final conclusions

Third country nationals are valuable individuals to the EU and are likely to become a much more important factor in the EU economy over the next 50 years. They are, however, a non-homogenous group of approximately 20.1 million people who, as they are unable to vote, are without a voice. The consequence of this is that they are marginalised when it comes to policy and decision-making implementing that policy. As open borders are not a practical reality of a Union of 27 Member States (soon to become 28) then policy and decision-making lead to legislative measures that manage the EU's borders, TCNs and their activity.

16 'The Stockholm Programme' (n 6) 30.

TCNs have no input into those legislative measures that can have significant impacts on their rights and thus their lives. These legislative measures are the final outcome of the political process and to assess the legitimacy of this output (output-orientated legitimacy) against measurable benchmarks the concept of legal rationality was constructed. This proved to be an effective model for analysing a specific area or discipline of law in an abstract manner. When the legal rationality findings were set against the aims of the policy to determine if any irrationality could be objectively justified then useful policy recommendations could be made.

Ultimately, it was found that the EU's policy towards the free movement of TCNs was politically illegitimate as it failed for formal, instrumental and substantive rationality. The recommendations in this chapter for strategic changes would go some way to correcting such policy failings. It must be reinforced that the key to policy approaches towards TCNs was initially set out in the Tampere Conclusions as ensuring 'fair treatment of third country nationals who reside legally on the territory of its Member States'[17] and then reiterated in the Stockholm Programme as the Union 'must ensure fair treatment of third country nationals who reside legally on the territory of the Member States'.[18] Much complex legislation has been adopted effecting TCNs over a short space of time with the aim of managing immigration, asylum and migration flows into the EU. This book has attempted to undertake a first overall assessment of the effect of that legislation against measureable benchmarks and to provide policy recommendations for future amendments to legislative measures. The final recommendation is that all politicians and decision-makers should keep in mind the key aim of fairness towards TCNs that should underpin all future immigration and asylum policy.

17 Presidency Conclusions of the Tampere European Council (n 5) para 18.
18 'The Stockholm Programme' (n 6) 30.

# Bibliography

## Primary legislation

### European

Charter of Fundamental Rights of the European Union [2000] OJ C364/1

Consolidated Version of the Treaty Establishing the European Community (Treaty of Rome 1957 as amended by the Single European Act 1986, Treaty on European Union 1992, Treaty of Amsterdam 1997 and the Treaty of Nice) [2002] OJ C325/33

Consolidated Version of the Treaty on European Union (as amended by the Treaty of Nice) [2002] OJ C325/5

Consolidated Versions of the Treaty on European Union, the Treaty on the Functioning of the European Union and the Charter of Fundamental Rights of the European Union [2012] OJ C326

Consolidated Versions of the Treaty on European Union and the Treaty on the Functioning of the European Union, Council Document 6655/7/08, 12 November 2012

Charter of Fundamental Rights of the European Union, Council Document 6655/7/08, 12 November 2012, 482

Agreement Establishing an Association between the European Economic Community and Turkey [1973] OJ C113/2

Additional Protocol to EEC-Turkey Agreement [1973] OJ C113/18

Co-Operation Agreement – Algeria [1978] OJ L263

Co-Operation Agreement – Morocco [1978] OJ L264

Co-Operation Agreement – Tunisia [1978] OJ L265

Schengen Agreement [2000] OJ L239/13

Convention implementing the Schengen Agreement of 15 June 1985 [2000] OJ L239/19

Association Agreement with Central and Eastern European Country – Hungary [1993] OJ L347

Association Agreement with Central and Eastern European Country – Poland [1993] OJ L348

Agreement on the European Economic Area [1994] OJ L1/3

Treaty of Accession – Finland, Austria and Sweden [1994] OJ C241

Surveillance and Court Agreement (SCA) [1994] OJ L344/3

Association Agreement with Central and Eastern European Country – Romania [1994] OJ L357

Association Agreement with Central and Eastern European Country – Bulgaria [1994] OJ L358

Association Agreement with Central and Eastern European Country – Slovak Republic [1994] OJ L359

Association Agreement with Central and Eastern European Country – Czech Republic [1994] OJ L360

Association Agreement with Central and Eastern European Country – Slovenia [1996] OJ L344

Convention Determining the State Responsible for Examining Applications for Asylum Lodged in one of the Member States of the European Communities (Dublin Convention) [1997] OJ C254/1

Association Agreement with Central and Eastern European Country – Latvia [1998] OJ L26

Association Agreement with Central and Eastern European Country – Lithuania [1998] OJ L51

Association Agreement with Central and Eastern European Country – Estonia [1998] OJ L68

Euro-Mediterranean Agreement – Tunisia [1998] OJ L97

Euro-Mediterranean Agreement – Morocco [2000] OJ L70

Agreement between the Governments of the States of the Benelux Economic Union, the Federal Republic of Germany and the French Republic on the gradual abolition of checks at their common borders [2000] OJ L239/13

Convention implementing the Schengen Agreement of 15 June 1985 [2000] OJ L239/19

Charter of Fundamental Rights of the European Union [2000] OJ C364/1

Treaty of Accession – The Czech Republic, Poland, Hungary, Slovenia, Estonia, Latvia, Lithuania, Slovakia, Cyprus and Malta [2003] OJ L236/17

Stabilisation and Association Agreement between the European Communities and their Member States, of the one part, and the Former Yugoslav Republic of Macedonia, of the other part [2004] OJ L84/13

Stabilisation and Association Agreement between the European Communities and their Member States, of the one part, and the Republic of Croatia, of the other part [2005] OJ L26/3

Treaty of Accession – Bulgaria and Romania [2005] OJ L157/11

Euro-Mediterranean Agreement – Algeria [2005] OJ L265

Stabilisation and Association Agreement between the European Communities and their Member States, of the one part, and Bosnia and Herzegovina, of the other part, Council Document 8226/08

Stabilisation and Association Agreement between the European Communities and their Member States, of the one part, and the Republic of Albania, of the other part [2009] OJ L107/166

Stabilisation and Association Agreement between the European Communities and their Member States of the one part, and the Republic of Montenegro, of the other part [2010] OJ L108/3

Treaty of Accession – Croatia [2012] OJ L112/10

## *International*

Universal Declaration of Human Rights (adopted 10 December 1948 UNGA Res 217 A(III))

European Convention for the Protection of Human Rights and Fundamental Freedoms (adopted 4 November 1950, entered into force 3 September 1953) ETS 5

Convention Relating to the Status of Refugees (adopted 28 July 1951, entered into force 22 April 1954) 189 UNTS 137

International Covenant on Civil and Political Rights (adopted 16 December 1966, entered into force 23 March 1976) 999 UNTS 171

International Covenant on Economic, Social and Cultural Rights (adopted 16 December 1966, entered into force 3 January 1976) 993 UNTS 3

Protocol Relating to the Status of Refugees (adopted 31 January 1967, entered into force 4 October 1967) 606 UNTS 267

Vienna Convention on the Law of Treaties between States and International Organisations or between International Organisations (adopted 21 March 1986) (1986) 25 ILM 543

United Nations Convention on the Rights of the Child (adopted 20 November 1989, entered into force 2 September 1990) 1577 UNTS 3

International Convention on the Protection of the Rights of All Migrant Workers and Members of Their Families (adopted 18 December 1990, entered into force 1 July 2003) UNGA Res 45/158

General Agreement on Tariffs and Trade (adopted 15 April 1994, entered into force 1 January 1995) 1867 UNTS 187

General Agreement on Trade in Services (adopted 15 April 1994, entered into force 1 January 1995) 1869 UNTS 183

### *Domestic*

European Communities Act 1972

European Arrest Warrant Act 2004 [2004] BGBl.I 1748

European Arrest Warrant Act 2006 [2006] BGBl.I 1721

## Secondary legislation

### *Regulations*

Council Regulation 1612/68/EEC on freedom of movement for workers within the Community [1968] OJ Sp Ed L257/2

Council Regulation 1408/71/EEC on the application of social security schemes to employed persons, to self-employed persons and to members of their families moving within the Community (consolidated version as an annex to Regulation 118/97/EC) [1997] OJ L28/1

Council Regulation 574/72/EEC laying down the procedure for implementing Regulation 1408/71/EEC on the application of social security schemes to employed persons, to self-employed persons and to their families moving within the Community [1972] OJ L74/1

Council Regulation 1683/95/EC laying down a uniform format for visas [1995] OJ L164/1 (subsequently amended by Regulations 334/2002/EC, 1791/2006/EC and 856/2008/EC)

Council Regulation 2317/95/EC determining the third countries whose nationals must be in possession of visas when crossing the external borders of the Member States [1995] OJ L164/1

Council Regulation 574/99/EC determining the third countries whose nationals must be in possession of visas when crossing the external borders of the Member States [1999] OJ L72/2

294 The legitimacy of the EU through legal rationality

Council Regulation 2725/2000/EC concerning the establishment of 'Eurodac' for the comparison of fingerprints for the effective application of the Dublin Convention [2000] OJ L316/1

Council Regulation 539/2001/EC listing the third countries whose nationals must be in possession of visas when crossing the external borders and those whose nationals are exempt from that requirement (subsequently amended by Regulations 2414/2001/EC, 453/2003/EC, 851/2005/EC, 1791/2006/EC, 1932/2006/EC, 1244/2009/EC, 1091/2010/EU and 1211/2010/EU) [2001] OJ L81/1

Council Regulation 1091/2001/EC on freedom of movement with a long-stay visa [2001] OJ L150/4

Council Regulation 333/2002/EC on a uniform format for affixing the visa issued by Member States to persons holding travel documents not recognised by the Member State drawing up the form [2002] OJ L53/4

Council Regulation 343/2003/EC establishing the criteria and mechanisms for determining the Member State responsible for examining an asylum application lodged in one of the Member States by a third-country national [2003] OJ L50/1

Council Regulation 407/2002/EC laying down certain rules to implement Regulation 2725/2000/EC [2002] OJ L62/1

Council Regulation 859/2003/EC extending the provisions of Regulation 1408/71/EEC and Regulation 574/72/EEC to nationals of third countries who are not already covered by these provisions solely on the ground of their nationality [2003] OJ L124/1

Council Regulation 1560/2003/EC laying down detailed rules for the application of Regulation 343/2003/EC [2003] OJ L222/3

European Parliament and Council Regulation 883/2004/EC on the coordination of social security systems [2004] OJ L166/1

European Parliament and Council Regulation 562/2006/EC establishing a Community Code on the rules governing the movement of persons across borders (Schengen Borders Code) [2006] OJ L105/1

European Parliament and Council Regulation 1931/2006/EC laying down rules on local border traffic at the external land borders of the Member States and amending the provisions of the Schengen Convention [2006] OJ L405/1

European Parliament and Council Regulation 810/2009/EC establishing a Community Code on Visas (Visa Code) [2009] OJ L243/1

European Parliament and Council Regulation 987/2009/EC laying down the procedure for implementing Regulation 883/2004/EC on the coordination of social security systems [2009] OJ L284/1

European Parliament and Council Regulation 988/2009/EC amending Regulation 883/2004/EC on the coordination of social security systems, and determining the content of its Annexes [2009] OJ L284/43

European Parliament and Council Regulation 265/2010/EU amending the Convention Implementing the Schengen Agreement and Regulation 562/2006/EC as regards movement of persons with a long-stay visa [2010] OJ L85/1

European Parliament and Council Regulation 1231/2010/EU extending Regulation 883/2004/EC and Regulation 987/2009/EC to nationals of third countries who are not already covered by these Regulations solely on the ground of their nationality [2010] OJ L344/1

European Parliament and Council Regulation 1077/2011/EU establishing a European Agency for the operational management of large-scale IT systems in the area of freedom, security and justice [2011] OJ L286/1

## Directives

Council Directive 64/221/EEC on the co-ordination of special measures concerning the movement and residence of foreign nationals which are justified on grounds of public policy, public security or public health [1964] OJ Sp Ed 850/64/117

Council Directive 68/360/EEC on the abolition of restrictions on movement and residence within the Community for workers of Member States and their families [1968] OJ Sp Ed L253/13

Council Directive 73/148/EEC on the abolition of restrictions on movement and residence within the Community for nationals of Member States with regard to establishment and the provision of services [1973] OJ L172/14

Council Directive 90/364/EEC on the right of residence [1990] OJ L180/26

Council Directive 90/365/EEC on the right of residence for employees and self-employed persons who have ceased their occupational activity [1990] OJ L180/28

Council Directive 93/96/EEC on the right of residence for students [1993] OJ L317/59

Council Directive 95/46/EC on the protection of individuals with regard to the processing of personal data and on the free movement of such data [1995] OJ L281/31

European Parliament and Council Directive 96/71/EC concerning the posting of workers in the framework of the provision of services [1997] OJ L18/1

Council Directive 2000/43/EC implementing the principle of equal treatment between persons irrespective of racial or ethnic origin [2000] OJ L180/22

Council Directive 2000/78/EC establishing a general framework for equal treatment in employment and occupation [2000] OJ L303/16

Council Directive 2001/40/EC on the mutual recognition of decisions on the expulsion of third country nationals [2001] OJ L149/34

Council Directive 2001/51/EEC supplementing the provisions of Article 26 of the Convention Implementing the Schengen Agreement of 14 June 1985 [2001] OJ L187/45

Council Directive 2001/55/EC on minimum standards for giving temporary protection in the event of a mass influx of displaced persons and on measures promoting a balance of efforts between Member States in receiving such persons and bearing the consequences thereof [2001] OJ L212/12

Council Directive 2003/9/EC laying down the minimum standards for the reception of asylum seekers [2003] OJ L31/18

Council Directive 2003/86/EC on the right to family reunification [2003] OJ L251/12

Council Directive 2003/109/EC concerning the status of third country nationals who are LTRs [2004] OJ L16/44

Council Directive 2003/110/EC on assistance in cases of transit for the purposes of removal by air [2003] OJ L321/26

European Parliament and Council Directive 2004/38/EC on the right of citizens of the Union and their family members to move and reside freely within the territory of the Member States [2004] OJ L158/77

Council Directive 2004/82/EC on the obligation of carriers to communicate passenger data [2004] OJ L261/24

Council Directive 2004/83/EC on minimum standards for the qualification and status of third country nationals or stateless persons as refugees or as persons who otherwise need international protection and the content of the protection granted [2004] OJ L304/12

Council Directive 2004/114/EC on the conditions of admission of third-country nationals for the purposes of studies, pupil exchange, unremunerated training or voluntary service [2004] OJ L375/12

Council Directive 2005/71/EC on a specific procedure for admitting third-country nationals for the purposes of scientific research [2005] OJ L289/15

Council Directive 2005/85/EC on minimum standards on procedures in Member States for granting and withdrawing refugee status [2005] OJ L326/13

European Parliament and Council Directive 2006/123/EC on services in the internal market [2006] OJ L376/36

European Parliament and Council Directive 2008/115/EC on common standards and procedures in Member States for returning illegally staying third-country nationals [2008] OJ L348/98

Council Directive 2009/50/EC on the conditions of entry and residence of third-country nationals for the purposes of highly qualified employment [2009] OJ L155/17

European Parliament and Council Directive 2011/36/EU on preventing and combating trafficking in human beings and protecting its victims, and replacing Council Framework Decision 2002/629/JHA [2011] OJ L101/1

European Parliament and Council Directive 2011/51/EU amending Council Directive 2003/109/EC to extend its scope to beneficiaries of international protection [2011] OJ L132/1

European Parliament and Council Directive 2011/98/EU on a single application procedure for a single permit for third-country nationals to reside and work in the territory of a Member State and on a common set of rights for third-country workers legally residing in a Member State [2011] OJ L343/1

## *Decisions*

Decision of the Heads of State and Government, meeting within the European Council, concerning certain problems raised by Denmark on the Treaty on European Union [1992] OJ C348/2

Council and Commission Decision 94/1/ECSC & EC on the conclusion of the Agreement on the European Economic Area between the European Communities, the Member States and the Republic of Austria, the Republic of Finland, the Republic of Iceland, the Principality of Liechtenstein, the Kingdom of Norway, the Kingdom of Sweden and the Swiss Confederation [1994] OJ L1/1

Decision of the EEA Council 1/95 on the entry into force of the Agreement on the European Economic Area for the Principality of Liechtenstein [1995] OJ L86/58

Council Decision 1999/435/EC concerning the definition of the Schengen *acquis* for the purpose of determining, in conformity with the relevant provisions of the Treaty establishing the European Community and the Treaty on European Union, the legal basis for each of the provisions or decisions which constitute the *acquis* [1999] OJ L176/1

Council Decision 1999/436/EC determining, in conformity with the relevant provisions of the Treaty establishing the European Community and the Treaty on European Union, the legal basis for each of the provisions or decisions which constitute the Schengen *acquis* [1999] OJ L176/17

Council Decision 1999/437/EC on certain arrangements for the application of the Agreement concluded by the Council of the European Union and the Republic of Iceland and the Kingdom of Norway concerning the association of those two States with the implementation, application and development of the Schengen *acquis* [1999] OJ L176/31

Council Decision 1999/438/EC concerning the Joint Supervisory Authority set up under Article 115 of the Convention applying the Schengen Agreement of 14 June 1985, on the gradual abolition of checks at common borders, signed on 19 June 1990 [1999] OJ L176/34

Council Decision 2000/365/EC concerning the request of the United Kingdom of Great Britain and Northern Ireland to take part in some of the provisions of the Schengen *acquis* [2000] OJ L131/43

Council Decision 2000/750/EC establishing a Community Action Programme to combat discrimination (2001 to 2006) [2000] OJ L303/23

Council Framework Decision 2001/220/JHA on the standing of victims in criminal proceedings [2001] OJ L82/1

Council Decision 2002/192/EC concerning Ireland's request to take part in some of the provisions of the Schengen *acquis* [2002] OJ L64/20

Council Framework Decision 2002/584/JHA on the European Arrest Warrant and the surrender procedures between Member States [2002] OJ L190/1

Council Decision 2004/80/EC concerning the conclusion of the Agreement between the European Community and the Government of the Hong Kong Special Administrative Region of the People's Republic of China on the readmission of persons residing without authorisation [2004] OJ L17/23

Council Decision 2004/191/EC setting out the criteria and practical arrangements for the compensation of the financial imbalances resulting from the application of Directive 2001/40/EC [2004] OJ L60/55

Council Decision 2004/424/EC concerning the conclusion of the Agreement between the European Community and the Macao Special Administrative Region of the People's Republic of China on the readmission of persons residing without authorisation [2004] OJ L143/97

Council Decision 2004/926/EC on the putting into effect parts of the Schengen *acquis* by the United Kingdom of Great Britain and Northern Ireland [2004] OJ L395/70

Council Decision 2004/927/EC providing for certain areas covered by Title IV of Part Three of the Treaty establishing the European Community to be governed by the procedure laid down in Article 251 of that Treaty [2004] OJ L396/45

Council Decision 2005/372/EC concerning the conclusion of the Agreement between the European Community and the Democratic Socialist Republic of Sri Lanka on the readmission of persons residing without authorisation [2005] OJ L124/41

Council Decision 2006/188/EC on the conclusion of the Agreement between the European Community and Denmark extending to Denmark the provisions of Regulation 343/2003/EC and Regulation 2725/2000/EC [2006] OJ L66/37

Council Decision 2007/341/EC on the conclusion of the Agreement between the European Community and the Russian Federation on readmission [2007] OJ L129/38

Council Decision 2007/471/EC on the application of the provisions of the Schengen *acquis* relating to the Schengen Information System in the Czech Republic, the Republic of Estonia, the Republic of Latvia, the Republic of Lithuania, the Republic of Hungary, the Republic of Malta, the Republic of Poland, the Republic of Slovenia and the Slovak Republic [2007] OJ L179/46

Council Decision 2007/801/EC on the full application of the provisions of the Schengen *acquis* in the Czech Republic, the Republic of Estonia, the Republic of Latvia, the Republic of Lithuania, the Republic of Hungary, the Republic of Malta, the Republic of Poland, the Republic of Slovenia and the Slovak Republic [2007] OJ L323/34

Council Decision 2007/817/EC on the conclusion of the Agreement between the European Community and the former Yugoslav Republic of Macedonia on the readmission of persons residing without authorisation [2007] OJ L334/1

Council Decision 2007/818/EC on the conclusion of the Agreement between the European Community and the Republic of Montenegro on the readmission of persons residing without authorisation [2007] OJ L334/25

Council Decision 2007/819/EC on the conclusion of the Agreement between the European Community and the Republic of Serbia on the readmission of persons residing without authorisation [2007] OJ L334/45

Council Decision 2007/820/EC on the conclusion of the Agreement between the European Community and Bosnia and Herzegovina on the readmission of persons residing without authorisation [2007] OJ L334/65

Council Decision 2007/826/EC on the conclusion of the Agreement between the European Community and the Republic of Moldova on the readmission of persons residing without authorisation [2007] OJ L334/148

Council Decision 2007/839/EC concerning the conclusion of the Agreement between the European Community and Ukraine on readmission of persons [2007] OJ L332/46

Council Framework Decision 2008/913/JHA on combating certain forms and expressions of racism and xenophobia by means of criminal law [2008] OJ L328/55

Council Framework Decision 2009/299/JHA amending Framework Decisions 2002/584/JHA, 2005/214/JHA, 2006/783/JHA, 2008/909/JHA and 2008/947/JHA, thereby enhancing the procedural rights of persons and fostering the application of the principle of mutual recognition to decisions rendered in the absence of the person concerned at the trial [2009] OJ L81/24

Council Decision 2010/649/EU on the conclusion of the Agreement between the European Community and the Islamic Republic of Pakistan on the readmission of persons residing without authorisation [2010] OJ L287/50

Council Decision 2010/701/EU on the position to be taken by the European Union within the Stabilisation and Association Council established by the Stabilisation and Association Agreement between the European Communities and their Member States, of the one part, and the former Yugoslav Republic of Macedonia, of the other part, with regard to the adoption of provisions on the coordination of social security systems [2010] OJ L306/28

Council Decision 2010/702/EU on the position to be taken by the European Union within the Stabilisation and Association Council established by the Stabilisation and Association Agreement between the European Communities and their Member States, of the one part, and the Republic of Croatia, of the other part, with regard to the adoption of provisions on the coordination of social security systems [2010] OJ L306/35

Council Decision 2011/118/EU on the conclusion of the Agreement between the European Union and Georgia on the readmission of persons residing without authorisation [2011] OJ L52/45

Commission Decision 2011/503/EU authorising Spain to temporarily suspend the application of Articles 1 to 6 of Regulation 492/2011/EU of the European Parliament and of the Council on freedom of movement for workers within the Union with regard to Romanian workers [2011] OJ L207/22

Council Decision 2012/499/EU on the signing, on behalf of the European Union, of the Agreement between the European Union and the Republic of Turkey on the readmission of persons residing without authorisation [2012] OJ L244/4

Council Decision 2012/776/EU on the position to be taken on behalf of the European Union within the Association Council set up by the Agreement establishing an association between the European Economic Community and Turkey, with regard to

the adoption of provisions on the coordination of social security systems [2012] OJ
L340/19

Commission Decision 2012/831/EU authorising Spain to temporarily suspend the
application of Articles 1 to 6 of Regulation 492/2011/EU of the European Parliament
and of the Council on freedom of movement for workers within the Union with regard
to Romanian workers [2012] OJ L356/90

Council Decision 2013/77/EU on the signing, on behalf of the European Union, of the
Agreement between the European Union and the Republic of Cape Verde on the
readmission of persons residing without authorisation [2013] OJ L37/1

## Miscellaneous

Unilateral Declarations of Denmark, to be associated to the Danish Act of Ratification of
the Treaty on European Union and of which other Member States will take cognizance
[1992] OJ C348/4

## Domestic

Accession (Immigration and Worker Registration) Regulations 2004, SI 2004/1219

## Legislative proposals

Commission proposal for a Council Regulation to implement Decision 3/80 COM(1983)
13 final

Commission proposal for a Decision, based on Article K3 of the Treaty on European
Union, establishing the Convention on the crossing of the external frontiers of the
Member States COM(1993) 684 final

Commission proposal for a Council Act establishing the Convention on rules for the
admission of third-country nationals to the Member States COM(1997) 387 final

Commission proposal for a Council Regulation on co-ordination of social security systems
COM(1998) 779 final

Commission proposal for a Council Directive establishing a general framework for equal
treatment in employment and occupation COM(1999) 565 final

Commission proposal for a Council Directive implementing the principle of equal
treatment between persons irrespective of racial or ethnic origin COM(1999) 566 final

Commission proposal for a Council Decision establishing a Community Action Programme
to combat discrimination 2001–2006 COM(1999) 567 final

Commission proposal for a Directive on the posting of workers who are third country
nationals for the provision of cross-border services and Commission proposal for a
Directive extending the freedom to provide cross-border services to third country
nationals established within the Community COM(1999) 3 final/2, amended COM
(2000) 271 final

Commission proposal for a Council Directive concerning the status of third-country
nationals who are long-term residents COM(2001) 127 final

Commission proposal for a Council Directive laying down the minimum standards for the
reception of asylum seekers COM(2001) 181 final

Commission proposal for a Directive on the conditions of entry and residence of third
country nationals for employed and self-employed economic activities COM(2001)
386 final

Commission proposal for a Directive relating to the conditions in which third country nationals shall have the freedom to travel in the territory of the Member States for periods not exceeding three months, introducing a specific travel authorisation and determining the conditions of entry and movement for periods not exceeding six months COM(2001) 388 final

Commission proposal for a Council Directive on minimum standards for the qualification and status of third country nationals and stateless persons as refugees or as persons who otherwise need international protection COM(2001) 510 final

Commission proposal for a Regulation extending the provisions of Regulation 1408/71/ EEC to nationals of third countries who are not covered by these provisions solely on the ground of their nationality COM(2002) 59 final

Commission proposal for a comprehensive plan to combat illegal immigration and trafficking of human beings in the European Union [2002] OJ C142/23

Commission proposal for a European Parliament and Council Directive on common standards and procedures in Member States for returning illegally staying third-country nationals COM(2005) 391 final

Commission proposal for a European Parliament and Council Regulation establishing a Community Code on Visas COM(2006) 403 final

Commission proposal for a Council Directive on the conditions of entry and residence of third-country nationals for the purposes of highly qualified employment COM(2007) 637 final

Commission proposal for a Council Directive on a single application procedure for a single permit for third-country nationals to reside and work in the territory of a Member State and on a common set of rights for third-country workers legally residing in a Member State COM(2007) 638 final

Commission proposal for a Regulation listing the third countries whose nationals must be in possession of visas when crossing the external borders and those whose nationals are exempt from that requirement (codified version) COM(2008) 761 final

Commission proposal for a European Parliament and Council Directive laying down the minimum standards for the reception of asylum seekers (recast) COM(2008) 815 final

Commission proposal for a European Parliament and Council Regulation establishing the criteria and mechanisms for determining the Member State responsible for examining an application for international protection lodged in one of the Member States by a third-country national or a stateless person (recast), COM(2008) 820 final

Commission proposal for a European Parliament and Council Regulation concerning the establishment of 'Eurodac' for the comparison of fingerprints for the effective application of the Dublin Regulation (recast) COM(2008) 825/3 final

Commission proposal for a European Parliament and Council Regulation concerning the establishment of 'Eurodac' for the comparison of fingerprints for the effective application of the Dublin Regulation (recast) COM(2009) 342 final

Commission proposal for a Council Decision on requesting comparisons with EURODAC data by Member States' law enforcement authorities and Europol for law enforcement purposes COM(2009) 344 final

Commission proposal for a European Parliament and Council Directive on minimum standards on procedures in Member States for granting and withdrawing international protection (recast) COM(2009) 554 final

Draft — Decision No . . . / . . . of the Stabilisation and Association Council established by the Stabilisation and Association Agreement between the European Communities and their Member States, of the one part, and the former Yugoslav Republic of Macedonia, of the other part, of . . . with regard to the provisions on the coordination of social security systems contained in the Stabilisation and Association Agreement [2010] OJ L306/29

Draft — Decision No . . . / . . . of the Stabilisation and Association Council established by the Stabilisation and Association Agreement between the European Communities and their Member States, of the one part, and the Republic of Croatia, of the other part, of . . . with regard to the provisions on the coordination of social security systems contained in the Stabilisation and Association Agreement [2010] OJ L306/36

Commission proposal for a European Parliament and Council Directive on conditions of entry and residence of third-country nationals in the framework of an intra-corporate transfer COM(2010) 378 final

Commission proposal for a European Parliament and Council Directive on the conditions of entry and residence of third-country nationals for the purposes of seasonal employment COM(2010) 379 final

Commission proposal for a European Parliament and Council Regulation concerning the establishment of 'Eurodac' for the comparison of fingerprints for the effective application of the Dublin Regulation (recast) COM(2010) 555 final

Commission proposal for a European Parliament and Council Regulation amending Regulation 562/2006/EC COM(2011) 118 final

Commission amended proposal for a European Parliament and Council Directive on minimum standards on procedures in Member States for granting and withdrawing international protection (recast) COM(2011) 319 final

Commission amended proposal for a European Parliament and Council Directive laying down minimum standards for the reception of asylum seekers COM(2011) 320 final

Commission amended proposal for a European Parliament and Council Regulation on the establishment of an evaluation and monitoring mechanism to verify the application of the Schengen *acquis* COM(2011) 559 final

Commission proposal for a European Parliament and Council Regulation amending Regulation 562/2006/EC in order to provide for common rules on the temporary reintroduction of border control at internal borders in exceptional circumstances COM(2011) 560 final

Commission proposal for a European Parliament and Council Regulation establishing a European Neighbourhood Instrument COM(2011) 839 final

Commission proposal for a European Parliament and Council Regulation on the enforcement of Directive 96/71/EC concerning the posting of workers in the framework of the provision of services COM(2012) 131 final

Commission proposal for a Council Directive on the position to be taken on behalf of the European Union within the Association Council set up by the Agreement establishing an association between the European Economic Community and Turkey with regard to the provisions on the coordination of social security systems COM(2012) 152 final

Commission proposal for a European Parliament and Council Regulation concerning the establishment of 'Eurodac' for the comparison of fingerprints for the effective application of the Dublin Regulation (recast) COM(2012) 254 final

Commission proposal for a Council Decision concerning the signing of the Agreement between the European Union and the Republic of Cape Verde on the readmission of persons residing without authorisation COM(2012) 558 final

## Commission Communications

Commission Communication on the internal market, dated 18 May 1992 SEC(1992) 877 final

Commission Communication concerning a racism action plan COM(1998) 183 final

Commission Communication towards a common asylum procedure and a uniform status, valid throughout the Union, for persons granted asylum COM(2000) 755 final

Commission Communication on a Community immigration policy COM(2000) 757 final

Commission Communication on a common policy on illegal immigration COM(2001) 672 final

Commission Communication on a Community return policy on illegal residents COM(2002) 564 final

Commission Communication on wider Europe – neighbourhood: a new framework for relations with our Eastern and Southern neighbours COM(2003) 104 final

Commission Communication towards more accessible, equitable and managed asylum systems COM(2003) 315 final

Commission Communication on the development of a common policy on illegal immigration, smuggling and trafficking of human beings, external borders and the return of illegal residents COM(2003) 323 final

Commission Communication on immigration, integration and employment COM(2003) 336 final

Commission Communication on European Neighbourhood Policy: strategy paper COM(2004) 373 final

Commission Communication on the managed entry in the EU of persons in need of international protection and enhancement of the protection capacity of the regions of origin: improving access to durable solutions COM(2004) 410 final

Commission Communication on regional protection programmes COM(2005) 388 final

Commission Communication on a common agenda for integration: framework for the integration of third-country nationals in the European Union COM(2005) 389 final

Commission Communication on priority actions for responding to the challenges of migration: First follow-up to Hampton Court COM(2005) 621 final

Commission Communication on a policy plan on legal migration COM(2005) 669 final

Commission Communication on the Global Approach to Migration one year on: Towards a comprehensive European migration policy COM(2005) 735

Commission Communication of the report on the implementation of the Hague Programme for 2007 COM(2006) 333 final

Commission Communication on policy priorities in the fight against illegal immigration of third-country nationals COM(2006) 402 final

Commission Communication on applying the Global Approach to Migration to the Eastern and South-Eastern regions neighbouring the European Union COM(2007) 247

Commission Communication of the report on the implementation of the Hague Programme for 2006 COM(2007) 373 final

Commission Communication of the third annual report on migration and integration COM(2007) 512 final

Commission Communication of the report on the application of Directive 2003/9/EC laying down the minimum standards for the reception of asylum seekers COM(2007) 745 final

Commission Communication on a common immigration policy for Europe: principles, actions and tools (COM)2008 359 final

Commission Communication on a policy plan on asylum: An integrated approach to protection across the EU COM(2008) 360 final

Commission Communication of the report on the implementation of the Hague Programme for 2007 COM(2008) 373 final

Commission Communication of the report on the application of Directive 2003/86/EC on the right to family reunification COM(2008) 610/3 final

Commission Communication on strengthening the Global Approach to Migration: Increasing coordination, coherence and synergies COM(2008) 611 final

Commission Communication of the report on the application of Directive 2004/38/EC on the right of citizens of the Union and their family members to move and reside freely within the territory of the Member States COM(2008) 840 final

Commission Communication on Justice, Freedom and Security in Europe Since 2005: An Evaluation of the Hague Programme and Action Plan COM(2009) 263 final

Commission Communication on delivering an area of freedom, security and justice for Europe's citizens: an Action Plan implementing the Stockholm Programme COM(2010) 171 final

Commission Communication on the evaluation of EU Readmission Agreements COM(2011) 76 final

Commission and High Representative of the European Union for Foreign Affairs and Security Policy Joint Communication on a partnership for democracy and shared prosperity with the Southern Mediterranean COM(2011) 200 final

Commission Communication on migration COM(2011) 248 final

Commission and High Representative of the European Union for Foreign Affairs and Security Policy Joint Communication on a new response to a changing Neighbourhood COM(2011) 303 final

Commission Communication on the European Agenda for the Integration of Third-Country Nationals COM(2011) 455 final

Commission and High Representative of the European Union for Foreign Affairs and Security Policy Joint Communication on delivering on a new European Neighbourhood Policy JOIN(2012) 14 final

## Commission green papers

Commission Green Paper on a Community return policy for illegal immigrants COM(2002) 175 final

Commission Green Paper on an EU approach to managing economic migration COM(2004) 811 final

Commission Green Paper on the future Common European Asylum System COM(2007) 301 final

Commission Green Paper on the right to family reunification of third-country nationals living in the European Union COM(2011) 735 final

## Council documents

Council Document 10579/92

Council Resolution on limitation on admission of third-country nationals to the territory of the Member States for employment [1996] OJ C274/3

Council Resolution relating to the limitations on the admission of third-country nationals to the territory of the Member States for the purpose of pursuing activities as self-employed persons [1996] OJ C274/7

Council Resolution on the admission of third-country nationals to the territory of the Member States for study purposes [1996] OJ C274/10

Council Document 15056/01

Council Document 14673/02

Council Document 14817/02

Council Document 15895/03

Council Document 5381/04

Council Document 'The Hague Programme: Strengthening Freedom, Security and Justice in the European Union' [2005] OJ C53/1

Council Document 'Council and Commission Action Plan Implementing the Hague Programme on Strengthening Freedom, Security and Justice in the European Union' [2005] OJ C198/1

Council Document 15914/1/05

Stabilisation and Association Agreement between the European Communities and their Member States, of the one part, and the Republic of Albania, of the other part, Council Document 8164/06

Council Document 11556/06

Stabilisation and Association Agreement between the European Communities and their Member States of the one part, and the Republic of Serbia, of the other part, Council Document 16005/07

Council Document 5598/08

Stabilisation and Association Agreement between the European Communities and their Member States, of the one part, and Bosnia and Herzegovina, of the other part, Council Document 8226/08

Council Document 13440/08

Council Document 14368/08

Council Document 15903/08

Council Document 16325/08

Council Document 16151/1/08

Council Document 16325/08

Council Document 16952/08

Council Document EUCO 6/09

European Council Document 'The Stockholm Programme – An Open and Secure Europe Serving and Protecting Citizens' [2010] OJ C115/1

Council Document 8692/11

Council Document 9166/4/11

Council Document 9167/4/11

Council Document 9179/12

Council Document 14112/1/12

Council Document 15389/12

Council Document 16332/12

Council Document 18006/12

Council Document 122501/12

Council Document 128520/12

Council Document 7715/13

# Reports

## Council

European Council Consultative Commission on Racism and Xenophobia 'Final Report' ref.6906/1/95 Rev 1 Limite RAXEN 24, General Secretariat of the Council of the European Union 1995

## European Parliament and its committees

PE 374.321v02-00
P6_TA(2004)0105
A6-0082/2007
PE 409.459v02-00

## Commission

Commission Report based on Article 34 of the EAW Framework Decision COM(2006) 8 final
Commission Report on the functioning of the transitional arrangements set out in the Accession Treaty 2003 (period 1 May 2004–30 April 2006) COM(2006) 48 final
Commission Report on the evaluation of the Dublin system COM(2007) 299 final
Commission Report on the first phase (1 January 2007–31 December 2008) of the Transitional Arrangements set out in the 2005 Accession Treaty and as requested according to the Transitional Arrangement set out in the 2003 Accession Treaty COM(2008) 765 final
Commission Demography Report 2008: Meeting Social Needs in an Ageing Society SEC(2008) 2911
Commission first annual report on immigration and asylum COM(2010) 214 final
Commission Report on the application of Directive 2005/85/EC COM(2010) 314 final
Commission Report on the application of Directive 2004/83/EC COM(2010) 465 final
Commission Report on the application of Title III (Internal Borders) of Regulation 562/2006/EC COM(2010) 554 final
Commission second annual report on immigration and asylum COM(2011) 291 final
Commission Report on the application of Directive 2003/109/EC concerning the status of third-country nationals who are long-term residents COM(2011) 585 final
Commission Report on the application of Directive 2004/114/EC COM(2011) 587 final
Commission Report on the Functioning of the Transitional Arrangements on Free Movement of Workers from Bulgaria and Romania COM(2011) 729 final
Commission Report on the application of Directive 2005/71/EC COM(2011) 901 final
Commission third annual report on immigration and asylum COM(2012) 250 final

## House of Lords

European Union Committee *A Community Immigration Policy* (HL 2000–2001, 64)
European Union Committee *Defining Refugee Status and Those in Need of International Protection* (HL 2001–2002, 156)

European Union Committee *Fighting Illegal Immigration: Should Carriers Carry the Burden?* (HL 2003–2004, 29)
European Union Committee *Handling EU Asylum Claims: New Approaches Examined* (HL 2003–2004, 74)
European Union Committee *The Hague Programme: A Five Year Agenda for EU Justice and Home Affairs* (HL 2004–2005, 84)
European Union Committee *Illegal Immigrants: Proposals for a Common EU Returns Policy* (HL 2005–2006, 166)
European Union Committee *The Stockholm Programme: Home Affairs* (HL 2008–2009, 175)

## Other bodies

Committee of Ministers of the Council of Europe 'Twenty Guidelines on Forced Return' (adopted 4 May 2005) CM(2005)40
High Level Panel Report on the Free Movement of Persons, delivered 18 March 1997

## Action plans

Commission Action Plan on racism COM(1998)183 final
Council and Commission Action Plan on how best to implement the provisions of the Treaty of Amsterdam on an Area of Freedom, Security and Justice [1999] OJ C19/1

## Cases

### ECJ

Case 6/64 *Flaminio Costa v ENEL* [1964] ECR 585
Case 29/69 *Erich Stauder v City of Ulm* [1969] ECR 419
Case 11/70 *Internationale Handelsgesellschaft mbH v Einfuhr- und Vorratsstelle für Getreide und Futtermittel* [1970] ECR 1125
Case 76/72 *Michel S v Fonds National de Reclassement Social des Handicapés* [1973] ECR 457
Case 4/73 *J Nold, Kohlen- und Baustoffgroßhandlung v Commission* [1974] ECR 491
Case 181/73 *R & V Haegeman v Belgium* [1974] ECR 449
Case 2/74 *Reyners v Belgium* [1974] ECR 631
Case 9/74 *Donato Casagrande v Landeshaupstadt München* [1974] ECR 773
Case 33/74 *Johannes Henricus Maria van Binsbergen v Bestuur van de Bedrijfsvereniging voor de Metaalnijverheid* [1974] ECR 1299
Case 41/74 *Yvonne van Duyn v Home Office* [1974] ECR 1337
Case 67/74 *Carmelo Angelo Bonsignore v Oberstadtdirektor der Stadt Köln* [1975] ECR 297
Case 118/75 *Italy v Lynne Watson and Alessandro Belmann* [1976] ECR 1185
Case 40/76 *Slavica Kermaschek v Bundesanstalt für Arbeit* [1976] ECR 1669
Case 30/77 *R v Pierre Bouchereau* [1977] ECR 1999
Case 8/78 *Milac* [1978] ECR 1721
Case 120/78 *Rewe-Zentral AG v Bundesmonopolverwaltung für Branntwein* [1979] ECR 649
Case 148/78 *Pubblico Ministero v Tullio Ratti* [1979] ECR 1629
Case 207/78 *Ministère Public v Gilbert Even and ONPTS* [1979] ECR 2019
Case 110/79 *Una Coonan v Insurance Officer* [1980] ECR 1445
Case 131/79 *R v Secretary of State for Home Affairs, ex parte Mario Santillo* [1980] ECR 1585

Case 157/79 *R v Stanislaus Pieck* [1980] ECR 2171
Case 810/79 *Peter Überschär v Bundesversicherungsanstalt für Angestellte* [1980] ECR 2747
Case 270/80 *Polydor Ltd and RSO Records Inc v Harlequin Record Shops Ltd and Simons Records Ltd* [1982] ECR 329
Case 53/81 *DM Levin v Staatssecretaris van Justitie* [1982] ECR 1035
Joined Cases 62 & 63/81 *Société anonyme de droit français Seco and Société anonyme de droit français Desquenne & Giral v Etablissement d'assurance contre la vieillesse et l'invalidité* [1982] ECR 223
Case 104/81 *Hauptzollamt Mainz v CA Kupferberg & Cie KG aA* [1982] ECR 3641
Joined Cases 35 & 36/82 *Elestina Esselina Christina Morson and Sweradjie Jhanjan v Netherlands* [1982] ECR 3723
Case 77/82 *Anastasia Peskeloglou v Bundesanstalt für Arbeit* [1983] ECR 1085
Case 152/82 *Sandro Forcheri and his wife Marisa Forcheri, née Marino v Belgium and asbl Institut Supérieur de Sciences Humaines Appliquées – Ecole Ouvrière Supérieure* [1983] ECR 2323
Case 13/83 *European Parliament v Council* [1985] ECR 1513
Case 14/83 *Sabine von Colson and Elisabeth Kamann v Land Nordrhein-Westfalen* [1984] ECR 1891
Case 238/83 *Caisse d'Allocations Familiales v Mr and Mrs Richard Meade* [1984] ECR 2631
Case 267/83 *Aissatou Diatta v Land Berlin* [1985] ECR 567
Case 293/83 *Françoise Gravier v City of Liège* [1985] ECR 593
Case 94/84 *Office Nationale de l'Emploi v Joszef Deak* [1985] ECR 1873
Case 170/84 *Bilka-Kaufhaus GmbH v Weber Von Hartz* [1986] ECR 1607
Case 59/85 *Netherlands v Ann Florence Reed* [1986] ECR 1283
Case 131/85 *Gul v Regierungsprasident Dusseldorf* [1986] ECR 1573
Case 139/85 *RH Kempf v Staatssecretaris van Justitie* [1986] ECR 1741
Case 316/85 *Centre public d'aide sociale de Courcelles v Marie-Christine Lebon* [1987] ECR 2811
Case 12/86 *Meryem Demirel v Stadt Schwabisch Gmund* [1987] ECR 3719
Case 24/86 *Vincent Blaizot v University of Liège and Others* [1988] ECR 379
Case 197/86 *Steven Malcolm Brown v Secretary of State for Scotland* [1988] ECR 3205
Case 249/86 *Commission v Germany* [1989] ECR 1263
Case 263/86 *Belgium v René Humbel and Marie-Thérèse Edel* [1988] ECR 5365
Case 186/87 *Ian William Cowan v Le Trésor Public* [1989] ECR 195
Case 235/87 *Annunziata Matteucci v Communauté française of Belgium and Commissariat général aux relations internationales of the Communauté française of Belgium* [1988] ECR 5589
Case 305/87 *Commission v Greece* [1989] ECR 1461
Case C–105/89 *Ibrahim Buhari Haji v Institut national d'assurances sociales pour travailleurs indépendants* [1990] ECR I–4211
Case 106/89 *Marleasing SA v La Comercial Internacional de Alimentacion SA* [1990] ECR 4135
Case C–113/89 *Rush Portugesa Lda v Office National d'Immigration* [1990] ECR I–1417
Case C–192/89 *SZ Sevince v Staatssecretaris van Justitie* [1990] ECR I–3461
Case C–292/89 *R v IAT, ex parte Gustaff Desiderius Antonissen* [1991] ECR I–745
Case C–357/89 *VJM Raulin v Netherlands Ministry for Education and Science* [1992] ECR I–1027
Case C–3/90 *MJE Bernini v Minister van Onderwijs en Wetenschappen* [1992] ECR I–1071
Case C–18/90 *Office National de l'emploi v Bahia Kziber* [1991] ECR I–199
Case C–369/90 *Mario Vicente Micheletti and Others v Delegación del Gobierno en Cantabria* [1992] ECR I–4239
Case C–370/90 *R v Immigration Appeal Tribunal and Surinder Singh, ex parte Secretary of State for the Home Department* [1992] ECR I–4265
*Opinion 1/91* [1991] ECR I–6079

C–153/91 *Camille Petit v Office National des Pensions* [1992] ECR I–4973

Case C–237/91 *Kazim Kus v Landeshauptstadt Wiesbaden* [1992] ECR I–6781

Case C–243/91 *Belgian State v Noushin Taghavi* [1992] ECR I–4401

Joined Cases C–397–403/01 *Pfeiffer* [2004] ECR I–8835

*Opinion 1/92* [1992] ECR I–2821

Joined Cases C–92/92 & 326/92 *Phil Collins and Others v Imrat Handelsgesellschaft mbH* [1993] ECR I–5145

Case C–272/92 *Maria Chiara Spotti v Freistaat Bayern* [1993] ECR I–5185

Case C–379/92 *Peralta* [1994] ECR I–3453

Case C–43/93 *Raymond Vander Elst v Office des Migrations Internationales* [1994] ECR I–3803

Case C–58/93 *Zoubir Yousfi v Belgian State* [1994] ECR I–1353

Case C–308/93 *Bestuur van de Sociale Verzekeringsbank v JM Cabanis-Issarte* [1996] ECR I–2097

Case C–355/93 *Hayriye Eroglu v Land Baden-Württemburg* [1994] ECR I–5113

Case C–434/93 *Ahmet Bozkurt v Statssecretaris van Justitie* [1995] ECR I–1475

*Opinion 2/94* [1996] ECR I–1759

Case C–7/94 *Landesamt für Ausbildungsförderung Nordrhein-Wesfalen v Lubor Gaal* [1996] ECR I–1031

Case C–103/94 *Zoulika Krid v Caisse nationale d'assurance vieillesse des travailleurs salariés (CNAVTS)* [1995] ECR I–719

Case C–237/94 *John O'Flynn v Adjudication Officer* [1996] ECR I–2617

Case C–277/94 *Z Taflan-Met and Others v Bestuur van de Social Verzekeringsbank* and *O Akol v Bestuur van de Algemene Bedrijfsvereniging* [1996] ECR I–4085

Joined Cases C–71, 155 & 271/95 *Belgium v Commission* [1997] ECR I–687

Case C–126/95 *A Hallouzi-Choho v Bestuur van de Sociale Verzekeringsbank* [1996] ECR I–4807

Case C–171/95 *Recep Tetik v Land Berlin* [1997] ECR I–329

Case C–285/95 *Suat Kol v Land Berlin* [1997] ECR I–3069

Case C–392/95 *European Parliament v Council* [1997] ECR I–3213

Case C–351/95 *Selma Kadiman v Freistaat Bayern* [1997] ECR I–2133

Case C–386/95 *Suleyman Eker v Land Baden-Wurttemberg* [1997] ECR I–2697

Case C–36/96 *Faik Gunaydin v Freistaat Bayern* [1997] ECR I–5143

Cases Joined C–64/96 & 65/96 *Land Nordrhein-Westfalen v Kari Uecker* and *Vera Jacquet v Land Nordrhein-Westfalen* [1997] ECR I–3171

Case C–85/96 *María Martínez Sala v Freistaate Bayern* [1998] ECR I–2691

Case C–98/96 *Kasim Ertanir v Land Hessen* [1997] ECR I–5179

Case C–170/96 *Commission v Council* [1998] ECR I–2763

Case C–262/96 *Sema Sürül v Bundestantalt für Arbeit* [1999] ECR I–2685

Case C–274/96 *Criminal proceedings against Horst Otto Bickel and Ulrich Franz* [1998] ECR I–7637

Case C–275/96 *Anne Kuusijärvi v Riksförsäkringsverket* [1998] ECR I–3419

Case C–348/96 *Criminal proceedings against Donatella Calfa* [1999] ECR I–11

Case C–416/96 *Nour Eddline El-Yassini v Secretary of State for the Home Department* [1997] ECR I–1209

Case C–1/97 *Mehmet Birden v Stadtgemeinde Bremen* [1998] ECR I–7747

Case C–113/97 *Henia Babahenini v Belgian State* [1998] ECR I–183

Case C–210/97 *Haydar Akman v Oberkreisdirektor des Rheinisch-Bergischen-Kreises* [1998] ECR I–7519

Case C–230/97 *Criminal proceedings against Ibiyinka Awoyemi* [1998] ECR I–6781

Case C–321/97 *Ulla-Brith Andersson and Susanne Wåkerås-Anderson v Swedish State* [1999] ECR I–3551

Case C–329/97 *Sezgin Ergat v Stadt Ulm* [2000] ECR I–1487

Case C–337/97 *CPM Meeusen v Hoofddirectie van de Informatie Beheer Groep* [1999] ECR I–3289

Case C–340/97 *Ömer Nazli and Others v Stadt Nürnberg* [2000] ECR I–957

Case C–378/97 *Criminal proceedings against Florus Ariël Wijsenbeck* [1999] ECR I–6207

Case C–37/98 *R v Secretary of State for the Home Department, ex parte Abdulnasir Savas* [2000] ECR I–2927

Case C–65/98 *Safet Eyüp v Landesgeschäftstelle des Arbeitsmarktservice Vorarlberg* [2000] ECR I–4747

Joined Cases C–102 & 211/98 *Ibrahim Kocak v Landesversicherungsanstalt Oberfranken und Mittelfranken* and *Ramazan Ors v Bundesknappschaft* [2000] ECR I–1287

Case C–179/98 *Belgium v Fatna Mesbah* [1999] ECR I–7955

Case C–224/98 *Marie-Nathalie D'Hoop v Office National d'Emploi* [2002] ECR I–6191

Case C–281/98 *Roman Angonese v Cassa di Risparmo di Bolzano SpA* [2000] ECR–I 4139

Case C–377/98 *Netherlands v European Parliament & Council* [2001] ECR I–7079

Case C–33/99 *Hassan Fahmi and M Esmoris Cerdeiro-Pinedo Amado v Bestuur van de Sociale Verzekeringsbank* [2001] ECR I–2415

Case C–63/99 *R v Secretary of State for the Home Department, ex parte Wieslaw Gloszczuk and Elzbieta Gloszczuk* [2001] ECR I–2579

Joined Cases C–95–98 & 180/99 *Mervett Khalil, Issa Chaaban and Hassan Osseili v Bundesanstalt für Arbeit, Mohamad Nasser v Landeshauptstadt Stuttgart* and *Meriem Addou v Land Nordrhein-Westfalen* [2001] ECR I–7413

Case C–184/99 *Rudy Grzelczyk v Centre public d'aide D'Ottignies-Louvain-la-Neuve* [2001] ECR I–6193

Case C–192/99 *R v Secretary of State for the Home Department, ex parte Manjit Kaur* [2001] ECR I–1237

Case C–235/99 *R v Secretary of State for the Home Department, ex parte Eleanora Ivanova Kondova* [2001] ECR I–6427

Case C–257/99 *R v Secretary of state for the Home Department, ex parte Julius Barkoci and Marcel Malik* [2001] ECR I–6557

Case C–268/99 *Aldona Malgorzata Jany and Others v Staatssecretaris van Justitie* [2001] ECR I–8615

Case C–413/99 *Baumbast v Secretary of State for the Home Department* [2002] ECR I–7091

Case C–459/99 *Mouvement contre le racisme, l'antisémitisme et la xénophobie ABSL (MRAX) v Belgium* [2002] ECR I–6591

C–60/00 *Mary Carpenter v Secretary of State for the Home Department* [2002] ECR I–6279

Case C–162/00 *Land Nordrhein-Westfalen v Beata Pokrzeptowicz-Meyer* [2002] ECR I–1049

Case C–188/00 *Bülent Kurz, né Yüce v Land Baden-Württemberg* [2002] ECR I–10691

Case C–438/00 *Deutscher Handballbund eV v Maros Kolpak* [2003] ECR I–4135

Case C–109/01 *Secretary of State for the Home Department v Hacene Akrich* [2003] ECR I–9607

Case C–171/01 *Wählergruppe "Gemeinsam Zajedno/Birlikte Alternative und Grüne GewerkschafterInnen/UG", and Others* [2003] ECR I–4301

Joined Cases C–187 & 385/01 *Criminal proceedings against Hüseyin Gözütok and Klaus Brügge* [2003] ECR I–1345

Joined Cases C–317 & 369/01 *Erin Abatay and Others, and Nadi Sahin v Bundesanstalt für Arbeit* [2003] ECR I–12301

Joined Cases C–397–403/01 *Bernhard Pfeiffer and Others v Deutsches Rotes Kreuz, Kreisverband Waldshut eV* [2004] ECR I–8835

Case C–452/01 *Margarethe Ospelt v Schlössle Weissenberg Familienstiftung* [2003] ECR I–9743

Case C–23/02 *Office national de l'emploi v Mohamed Alami* [2003] ECR I–1399

Case C–138/02 *Brian Francis Collins v Secretary of State for Work and Pensions* [2003] ECR I–2703

Case C–148/02 *Carlos Garcia Avello v Belgium* [2003] ECR I–11613

Case C–200/02 *Kunqian Catherine Zhu and Man Lavette Chen v Secretary of State for the Home Department* [2003] ECR I–9925

Case C–224/02 *Heikki Antero Pusa v Osuuspankkien Keskinäinen Vakuutusyhtiö* [2003] ECR I–5763

Case C–275/02 *Engin Ayaz v Land Baden-Württemberg* [2004] ECR I–8765

Case C–286/02 *Bellio F.Illi Srl v Prefettura di Treviso* [2004] ECR I–3465

Case C–327/02 *Lili Georgieva Panayotova and Others v Minister voor Vreemdelingenzaken en Integratie* [2004] ECR I–11055

Case C–373/02 *Sakir Öztürk v Pensionsversicherungsanstalt der Arbeiter* [2004] ECR I–3605

Case C–441/02 *Commission v Germany* [2006] ECR I–3449

Case C–456/02 *Michel Trojani v CPAS* [2004] ECR I–7573

Case C–467/02 *Inan Cetinkaya v Land Baden-Württemberg* [2004] ECR I–10895

Case C–105/03 *Criminal proceedings against Maria Pupino* [2005] ECR I–5285

Case C–136/03 *Georg Dörr v Sicherheitsdirektion für das Bundesland Kärnten* and *Ibrahim Ünul v Sicherheitsdirektion für das Bundesland Vorarlberg* [2005] ECR I–4759

Case C–157/03 *Commission v Spain* [2005] ECR I–2911

Case C–209/03 *R v London Borough of Ealing and Secretary of State for Education, ex parte Dany Bidar* [2005] ECR I–2119

Case C–215/03 *Salah Oulane v Minister voor Vreemdelinganzaken en Integratie* [2005] ECR I–1215

Case C–230/03 *Mehmet Sedef v Freie und Hansestadt Hamburg* [2006] ECR I–157

Case C–373/03 *Ceyhun Aydinli v Land Baden-Württemburg* [2005] ECR I–6181

Case C–374/03 *Gaye Gürol v Bezirksregierung Köln* [2005] ECR I–6199

Case C–383/03 *Ergül Dogan v Sicherheitsdirektion für das Bundesland Vorarlberg* [2005] ECR I–6237

Case C–445/03 *Commission v Luxembourg* [2004] ECR I–10191

Case C–469/03 *Criminal proceedings against Filomeno Mario Miraglia* [2005] ECR I–2009

Case C–503/03 *Commission v Spain* [2006] ECR I–1097

Case C–540/03 *European Parliament v Council* [2006] ECR I–5769

Case C–95/04P *British Airways plc v Commission* [2007] ECR I–2331

Case C–144/04 *Werner Mangold v Rüdiger Helm* [2005] ECR I–9981

Case C–145/04 *Spain v UK* [2006] ECR I–7917

Case C–244/04 *Commission v Germany* [2006] ECR I–885

Case C–258/04 *Office national d'emploi v Ioannis Ioannidis* [2005] ECR I–8275

Case C–300/04 *MG Eman and OB Sevinger v College van burgemeester en wethouders van Den Haag* [2006] ECR I–8055

Case C–436/04 *Criminal proceedings against Leopold Henri van Esbroek* [2006] ECR I–2333

Case C–467/04 *Criminal proceedings against Giuseppe Francesco Gasparini and Others* [2006] ECR I–9199

Case C–471/04 *Finanzamt Offenbach am Main-Land v Keller Holding* [2006] ECR I–2107

Case C–502/04 *Ergün Torun v Stadt Augsburg* [2006] ECR I–1563

Case C–1/05 *Yunying Jia v Migrationsverket* [2007] ECR I–1

See Case C–4/05 *Hasan Güzeli v Oberbürgermeister der Stadt Aachen* [2006] ECR I–10279

Case C–16/05 *R v Secretary of State for the Home Department, ex parte Veli Tum and Mehmet Dari* [2007] ECR I–7415

C–76/05 *Herbert Schwarz and Marga Gootjes-Schwarz v Finanzamt Bergisch Gladbach* [2007] ECR I–6849

Case C–77/05 *UK v Council* [2007] ECR I–11459

Case C–97/05 *Mohamed Gattoussi v Stadt Rüsselsheim* [2006] ECR I–11917

Case C–137/05 *UK v Council* [2007] ECR I–11593

Case C–150/05 *Jean Leon van Straaten v Holland and Italy* [2006] ECR I–9327

Case C–241/05 *Nicolae Bot v Préfet du Val-de-Marne* [2006] ECR I–9627

Case C–288/05 *Criminal proceedings against Jürgen Kretzinger* [2007] ECR I–6441

Case C–291/05 *Minister voor Vreemdelingenzaken en Integratie v RNG Eind* [2007] ECR I–10719

Case C–303/05 *Advocaten voor de Wereld VZW v Leden van de Ministerrad* [2007] ECR I–3633

Case C–325/05 *Ismail Derin v Landkreis Darmstadt-Dieburg* [2007] ECR I–6495

Case C–336/05 *Ameur Echouikh v Secrétaire d'État aux Anciens Combattants* [2006] ECR I–5223

Case C–367/05 *Criminal proceedings against Norma Kraaijenbrink* [2007] ECR I–6619

Case C–432/05 *Unibet (London) Ltd and Unibet (International) Ltd v Justitiekanslern* [2007] ECR I–2271

Case C–467/05 *Criminal proceedings against Dell'Orto* [2007] ECR I–5557

Joined Cases C–11 & 12/06 *Rhiannon Morgan v Bezirksregierung Köln and Iris Bucher v Landrat des Kreises Düren* [2007] ECR I–9161

Case C–133/06 *European Parliament v Council* [2008] ECR I–3189

Case C–228/06 *Mehmet Soysal and Ibrahim Savatli v Germany* [2009] ECR I–1031

Case C–242/06 *Minister voor Vreemdelingenzaken en Integratie v T Sahin* [2009] ECR I–8465

Case C–294/06 *R (on the application of Ezgi Payir, Burhan Akyuz and Birol Ozturk) v Secretary of State for the Home Department* [2008] ECR I–203

Case C–349/06 *Murat Polat v Stadt Rüsselsheim* [2007] ECR I–8167

Case C–524/06 *Heinz Huber v Bundesrepublik Deutschland* [2008] ECR I–9705

Case C–33/07 *Ministerul Administraţiei şi Internelor – Direcţia Generalăde Pas,apoarte Bucureşti v Gheorghe Jipa* [2008] ECR I–5157

Case 92/07 *Commission v Netherlands* [2010] ECR I–3683

Case C–158/07 *Jacqueline Förster v Hoofddirectie van de Informatie Beheer Groep* [2008] ECR I–8507

Case C–297/07 *Klaus Bourquain* [2008] ECR I–9425

Case C–337/07 *Ibrahim Altun v Stadt Böblingen* [2008] ECR I–10323

Case C–453/07 *Hakan Er v Wetteraukreis* [2008] ECR I–7299

Case C–465/07 *Meki Elgafaji and Noor Elgafaji v Staatssecretaris van Justitie* [2009] ECR I–921

Case C–484/07 *Fatma Pehlivan v Staatssecretaris van Justitie* (ECJ 16 June 2011)

Case C–485/07 *Rand van bestuur van het Uitvoeringsinstituut werknemersverzekeringen v H Akdas and Others* [2011] ECR I–4499

Case C–551/07 *Deniz Sahin v Bundesminister für Inneres* [2008] ECR I–10453

Case C–19/08 *Migrationsverket v Edgar Petrosian and Others* [2009] ECR I–495

Joined Cases C–22 & 23/08 *Athanasios Vatsouras and Josif Koupatantze v Arbeitsgemeinschaft (ARGE) Nürnberg 900* [2009] ECR I–4585

Case C–66/08 *Proceedings concerning the execution of a European arrest warrant issued against Szymon Kozlowski* [2008] ECR I–6041

Case C–115/08 *Land Oberösterreich v ČEZ as* [2009] ECR I–10265

Case C–123/08 *Dominic Wolzenburg* [2009] ECR I–9621

Case C–127/08 *Blaise Baheten Metock and Others v Minister for Justice, Equality and Law Reform* [2008] ECR I–6241

Case C–152/08 *Real Sociedad de Fútbol SAD and Nihat Kahveci v Consejo Superior de Deportes and Real Federación Española de Fútbol* [2008] ECR I–6291

Case C–40/11 *Yoshikazu Iida v Stadt Ulm* (ECJ 8 November 2012)

Case C–42/11 *João Pedro Lopes Da Silva Jorge* [2012] 3 CMLR 54

Case C–61/11 PPU *Hassen El Dridi, alias Karim Souffi* [2011] ECR I–3015

Joined Cases C–71 & 99/11 *Germany v Y and Z* [2013] 1 CMLR 5

Case C–83/11 *Secretary of State for the Home Department v Muhammad Sazzadur Rahman, Fazly Rabby Islam & Mohibullah Rahman* [2012] 3 CMLR 55

Case C–141/11 *Torsten Hörnfeldt v Porsten Meddelande AB* [2012] 3 CMLR 37

Case C–179/11 *Cimade, Groupe d'information et de soutien des immigrés (GISTI) v Ministre de l'Intérieur, de l'Outre-mer, des Collectivités territoriales et de l'Immigration* [2013] 1 CMLR 11

Case C–245/11 *K v Bundesasylamt* (ECJ 6 November 2012)

Case C–256/11 *Murat Dereci, Vishaka Heiml, Alban Kokollari, Izunna Emmanual Maduike & Dragica Stevic v Bundesministerium für Inneres* [2012] 1 CMLR 45

Case C–268/11 *Atilla Gülbahce v Freie und Hansestadt Hamburg* (ECJ 8 November 2012)

Case C–277/11 *MM v Minister for Justice, Equality and Law Reform, Ireland and Attorney General* (ECJ 22 November 2012)

Case C–329/11 *Alexandre Achughbabian v Préfet du Val-de-Marne* [2012] 1 CMLR 52

Joined Cases C–356 & 357/11 *O & S v Maahanmuuttovirasto* and *Maahanmuuttovirasto v L* (ECJ 6 December 2012)

Case C–364/11 *Abed El Karem El Kott and Others v Bevándorlási és Állampolgársági Hivatal* (ECJ 19 December 2012)

Case C–396/11 *Ministerul Public – Parchetul de pe lângă Curtea de Apel Constanţa v Ciprian Vasile Radu* (Opinion of AG Sharpston 18 October 2012)

Case C–399/11 *Stefano Melloni v Ministerio Fiscal* (ECJ 26 February 2013)

Case C–430/11 *Criminal proceedings against Md Sagor* (ECJ 6 December 2011)

Case C–451/11 *Natthaya Dülger v Wetteraukreis* [2012] 3 CMLR 50

Joined Cases C–523 & 585/11 *Lawrence Prinz v Region Hannover and Philipp Seeberger v Studentenwerk Heidelberg* (Opinion of AG Sharpston 21 February 2013)

Case C–529/11 *Olaitan Ajoke Alarape and Olukayode Azeez Tijani v Secreatry of State for the Home Department* (Opinion of AG Bot 15 January 2013)

Case C–278/12 PPU *Atiqullah Adil v Minister voor Immigratie, Integratie in Asiel* (ECJ 19 July 2012)

## General Court

T–115/94 *Opel Austria GmbH v Council* [1997] ECR II–39

Case T–112/98 *Mannesmannröhren-Werke AG v Commission* [2001] ECR II–729

Case T–54/99 *max.mobil Telekommunikation Service GmbH v Commission* [2002] ECR II–313

## EFTA Court

Case E–1/94 *Ravintoloitsijain Liiton Kustannus Oy Restamark* [1994] EFTA Court Report 1

Case E–2/97 *Mag Instrument Inc v California Trading Company (Maglite)* [1997] EFTA Court Report 127

Case E–9/97 *Erla Maria Sveinbjornsdottir v Iceland* [1998] EFTA Court Report 95

Case E–3/98 *Herbert Rainford-Towning v Liechtenstein* [1998] EFTA Court Report 205

Case E–1/01 *Hörður Einarsson v Iceland* [2002] EFTA Court Report 1

Case E–2/01 *Dr Franz Martin Pucher v Liechtenstein* [2002] EFTA Court Report 44

Case E–4/01 *Karl K Karlsson hf v Iceland* [2002] EFTA Court Report 240

Case E–1/03 *EFTA Surveillance Authority v Iceland* [2003] EFTA Court Report 143

Case E–3/04 *Tsomakas Athanasios and Others v Norway* [2004] EFTA Court Report 97
Case E–8/04 *EFTA Surveillance Authority v Liechtenstein* [2005] EFTA Court Report 48
Case E–1/06 *EFTA Surveillance Authority v Norway* [2007] EFTA Court Report 7
Case E–3/06 *Ladbrokes Ltd v Norway* [2007] EFTA Court Report 86
Case E–1/07 *Criminal proceedings against A* [2007] EFTA Court Report 246
Case E–8/07 *Celina Nguyen v Norway* [2008] EFTA Court Report 224
Case E–2/10 *Þór Kolbeinsson v Iceland* [2010] EFTA Court Report 234
Case E–4/11 *Arnulf Clauder* [2011] EFTA Court Report 216

## ECHR

*Ireland v United Kingdom* (1979–80) 2 EHRR 25
*Soering v United Kingdom* (1989) 11 EHRR 439
*Vilvarajah v United Kingdom* (1992) 14 EHRR 248
*Gaygusuz v Austria* (1996) 23 EHRR 364
*Chahal v United Kingdom* (1997) 23 EHRR 413
*Assenov v Bulgaria* (1999) EHRR 652
*Matthews v United Kingdom* (1999) 28 EHRR 361
*TI v United Kingdom* [2000] INLR 211
*Jabari v Turkey* [2001] INLR 136
*Boultif v Switzerland* (2001) 33 EHRR 50
*Conka v Belgium* (2002) 34 EHRR 54
*Koua Poirrez v France* (2005) 40 EHRR 2
*Bosphorus Hava Yolları Turizm ve Ticaret Anonim Şirketi v Ireland* (2006) 42 EHRR 1
*Üner v Netherlands* (2007) 45 EHRR 14
*Keles v Germany* (2007) 44 EHRR 12
*Mubilanzila Mayeka and Kaniki Mitunga v Belgium* (2008) 46 EHRR 23
*Saadi v United Kingdom* (2008) 47 EHRR 17
*Maslov v Austria* (2008) 47 EHRR 20
*NA v United Kingdom* (2009) 48 EHRR 15
*KRS v United Kingdom* (2009) 48 EHRR SE8
*A v United Kingdom* (2009) 49 EHRR 29
*Saadi v Italy* (2009) 49 EHRR 30
*Gebremedhin v France* (2010) 50 EHRR 29
*Medvedyev and Others v France* (2010) 51 EHRR 39
*MSS v Belgium and Greece* (2011) 53 EHRR 2
*SH v United Kingdom* (2012) 54 EHRR 4
*Sufi and Elmi v United Kingdom* (2012) 54 EHRR 9
*Hirsi Jamaa and Others v Italy* (2012) 55 EHRR 21

## Domestic courts

### UK

*R v Secretary of State for the Home Department, ex parte Sandhu (Amirjit Singh)* [1983] 3 CMLR 131 (CA)
*Mandla (Sewa Singh) and Another v Dowell Lee and Others* [1983] AC 548 (HL)
*Council of Civil Service Unions and Others v Minister for the Civil Service* [1985] AC 374 (HL)

*Gwynedd County Council v Jones and Another* [1986] ICR 833 (EAT)

*R v Director of Labour and Social Security, ex parte Mohamed* [1992] 2 CMLR 481 (Supreme Court of Gibraltar)

*R v Secretary of State for the Home Department, ex parte Marchon* [1993] 2 CMLR 132 (CA)

*Crown Suppliers (Property Services Agency) v Dawkins* [1993] ICR 517 (CA)

*R v Ministry of Defence, ex parte Smith and Grady* and *R v Admiralty Board of the Defence Council, ex parte Beckett and Lustig-Prean* [1996] QB 517 (CA)

*R v Secretary of State for the Home Department, ex parte Adan, Subaskaran and Aitsegeur* [2001] 2 AC 477 (HL)

*R (on the Application of A) v Secretary of State for the Home Department* [2002] 3 CMLR 14 (CA)

*R (on the application of Zeqiri) v Secretary of State for the Home Department* [2002] Imm AR 296 (HL)

*R (on the application of Yogathas and Thangarasa) v Secretary of State for the Home Department* [2003] 1 AC 920 (HL)

*R (on the application of Razgar) v Secretary of State for the Home Department* [2004] 2 AC 368 (HL)

*R (on the application of European Roma Rights Centre and Others) v Immigration Officer, Prague Airport* [2004] QB 811 (CA)

*R (on the application of European Roma Rights Centre and Others) v Immigration Officer, Prague Airport* [2005] 2 AC 1 (HL)

*A and Others v Secretary of State for the Home Department* [2005] 2 AC 68 (HL)

*Secretary of State for Work and Pensions v Carlos Bobezes* [2005] 3 All ER 497 (CA)

*Office of the King's Prosecutor, Brussels v Cando Armas and Another* [2006] 2 AC 1 (HL)

*R (on the application of Limbuela, Tesema and Adam) v Secretary of State for the Home Department* [2006] 1 AC 396 (HL)

*Oliver v Secretary of State for the Home Department* [2006] 3 CMLR 46 (QB)

*R (on the Application of Ozman Taskale) v Secretary of State for the Home Department* [2006] EWHC 712 (Admin)

*R (on the application of Ibrahim Aksoy) v Secretary of State for the Home Department* [2006] EWHC 1487 (Admin)

*R (on the application of Temiz) v Secretary of State for the Home Department* [2006] EWCH 2450 (Admin)

*LB and MB v Secretary of State for the Home Department* [2006] UKAIT 15 (AIT)

*DA v Secretary of State for the Home Department* [2006] UKAIT 27 (AIT)

*MG and VC v Secretary of State for the Home Department* [2006] Imm AR 619 (AIT)

*LC v Secretary of State for the Home Department* (IAT 17 August 2007)

*Dabas v High Court of Justice, Madrid* [2007] 2 AC 31 (HL)

*R (on the application of Yusuf Aldogan) v Secretary of State for the Home Department* [2007] EWHC 2586 (Admin)

*TR v Secretary of State for the Home Department* [2008] UKAIT 4 (AIT)

*RZ v Secretary of State for the Home Department* [2008] UKAIT 7 (AIT)

*Hilali v Governor of Whitemoor Prison and Another* [2008] 1 AC 805 (HL)

*EA v Secretary of State for the Home Department* [2008] UKAIT 17 (AIT)

*R (on the application of Zego) v Secretary of State for the Home Department* [2008] EWHC 302 (Admin)

*Pilecki v Circuit Court of Legnica, Poland* [2008] 1 WLR 325 (HL)

*LG (Italy) v Secretary of State for the Home Department* [2008] EWCA Civ 190 (CA)

*R (on the application of Nasseri) v Secretary of State for the Home Department* [2008] 2 WLR 523 (QB)

*IS (Serbia) v Entry Clearance Officer, Skopje* [2008] UKAIT 31 (AIT)

*Germany*

*Poland*

*Cyprus*

*Attorney General of the Republic of Cyprus v Konstantinou* [2007] 3 CMLR 42

*Greece*

*Re Execution of a German Arrest Warrant: Tsokas and Another* [2007] 3 CMLR 24
*Re Enforcement of a European Arrest Warrant Against Tzoannos* [2008] 2 CMLR 38

*Czech Republic*

*Re Constitutionality of Framework Decision on the European Arrest Warrant* [2007] 3 CMLR 24

*Republic of Ireland*

*Minister for Justice, Equality and Law Reform v Stapleton* [2007] IESC 30

*Third countries*

*Sale, Acting Commissioner, Immigration and Naturalization Service v Haitian Centers Council* 509 US 155 (1993) (SC)
Case 10.675 *The Haitian Centre for Human Rights v United States* Report 51/96 [1998] 5 IHRR (Inter-American Commission for Human Rights)

# Books

Adams J, Brownsword R *Key Issues in Contract* (Butterworths 1995)
Allan TRS *Constitutional Justice: A Liberal Theory of the Rule of Law* (OUP 2001)
Amnesty International *The State of the World's Human Rights Report 2007* (Amnesty International 2007)
Anderson B *Imagined Communities* (Verso 1991)
Arnull A *The General Principles of EEC Law and the Individual* (Leicester University Press 1990)
Arnull A, Wincott D (eds) *Accountability and Legitimacy in the European Union* (OUP 2002)
Arnull AM, Dashwood AA, Ross MG and Wyatt DA *Wyatt & Dashwood's European Union Law* (4th edn Sweet & Maxwell 2000)
Arnull AM, Dashwood AA, Dougan M, Ross MG, Spaventa E and Wyatt DA *Wyatt & Dashwood's European Union Law* (5th edn Sweet & Maxwell 2006)
Arnull A, Eeckhout P and Tridimas T (eds) *Continuity and Change in EU Law* (OUP 2008)
Ashiagbor D, Countouris N and Lianos I (eds) *The European Union After the Treaty of Lisbon* (CUP 2012)
Balzacq T, Carrera S (eds) *Security Versus Freedom? A Challenge for Europe's Future* (Ashgate 2006)
Barak A *Proportionality: Constitutional Rights and their Limitations* (CUP 2012)
Barry B, Goodin RE (eds) *Free Movement: Ethical Issues in the Transnational Migration of People and of Money* (Harvester Wheatsheaf 1992)
Battjes H *European Asylum Law and International Law* (Brill 2006)
Beetham D *The Legitimation of Power* (Macmillan 1991)
Beetham D, Lord C *Legitimacy and the European Union* (Longman 1998)

Begg I, Peterson J and Weiler JHH (eds) *Reassessing the Fundamentals* (Blackwell Publishing 2003)

Bell M *Anti-Discrimination Law and the European Union* (OUP 2002)

Bellamy R (ed) *Constitutionalism, Democracy and Sovereignty: American and European Perspectives* (Avebury 1996)

Benhabib S *The Rights of Others: Aliens, Residents and Citizens* (CUP 2004)

Beyleveld D, Brownsword R *Law as a Moral Judgment* (Sweet & Maxwell 1986)

Beyleveld D *The Dialectical Necessity of Morality: An Analysis and Defence of Alan Gewirth's Argument to the Principle of Generic Consistency* (University of Chicago Press 1991)

Bingham T *The Rule of Law* (Allen Lane 2010)

Boccardi I *Europe and Refugees: Towards an EU Asylum Policy* (Kluwer Law International 2002)

Borjas GJ, Crisp J (eds) *Poverty, International Migration and Asylum* (Palgrave 2005)

Brownsword R *Contract Law: Themes for the Twenty-First Century* (2nd edn OUP 2006)

Brubaker R *The Limits of Rationality* (George Allen and Unwin 1984)

Bunyon T (ed) *Statewatching the New Europe: A Handbook on the European State* (Statewatch 1993)

Cane P, Tushnet M (eds) *The Oxford Handbook of Legal Studies* (OUP 2003)

Carens JH *Culture, Citizenship and Community* (OUP 2000)

Castles S, Davison A *Citizenship and Migration: Globalization and the Politics of Belonging* (Macmillan Press 2000)

Chalmers C, Davies G and Monti G *European Union Law* (2nd edn CUP 2010)

Cholewinski R *Migrant Workers in International Human Rights Law* (Clarendon Press 1997)

Coleman J, Shapiro S (eds) *The Oxford Handbook of Jurisprudence and Philosophy of Law* (OUP 2002)

Collins H *Regulating Contracts* (OUP 1999)

Commission on Human Security *Human Security Now* (Commission on Human Security 2003)

Cottingham J *Rationalism* (Thoemmes Press 1984)

P Craig, G de Búrca (eds) *The Evolution of EU Law* (1st edn OUP 1999)

Craig P, de Búrca G (eds) *The Evolution of EU Law* (2nd edn OUP 2011)

Craig P, de Búrca G *EU Law: Texts, Cases, and Materials* (5th edn OUP 2011)

Craig P, Rawlings R (eds) *Law and Administration in Europe: Essays in Honour of Carol Harlow* (OUP 2003)

Cranston M *What are Human Rights?* (2nd edn Bodley Head 1973)

Curtin D *Postnational Democracy: The European Union in Search of a Political Philosophy* (Kluwer Law International 1997)

Dahl RA *On Democracy* (Yale University Press 1998)

Dine J, Watt B (eds) *Discrimination Law: Concepts, Limitations and Justifications* (Longman 1996)

Dougan M, Spaventa E (eds) *Social Welfare and EU Law: Essays in European Law* (Hart Publishing 2005)

Dworkin R *Taking Rights Seriously* (Duckworth 1978)

Dworkin R *A Matter of Principle* (Clarendon Press 1985)

Ellis E *EU Anti-Discrimination Law* (OUP 2005)

European University Institute (ed) *Collected Courses of the Academy of European Law Vol. VI-1* (Nijhoff 1998)

Eurostat *Living Conditions in Europe Data 2003–2006: 2008 Edition* (Office for Official Publications of the European Communities 2008)

Feller E, Türk V and Nicholson F (eds) *Refugee Protection in International Law: UNHCR's Global Consultations on International Protection* (CUP 2003)

Finnis J *Natural Law and Natural Rights* (Clarendon Press 1980)

Franck TM *Fairness in International Law and Institutions* (Clarendon Press 1995)

Fredman S (ed) *Discrimination and Human Rights: The Case of Racism* (OUP 2001)

Freeman S *The Cambridge Companion to Rawls* (CUP 2002)

Fuller LL *The Morality of Law* (Yale University Press 1969)

Gamberale C *European Citizenship and Political Identity* (University of Sheffield unpublished thesis No 9481 1998)

Gewirth A *Reason and Morality* (University of Chicago Press 1978)

Gewirth A *The Community of Rights* (University of Chicago Press 1986)

Gibney M *The Ethics and the Politics of Asylum: Liberal Democracy and the Response to Refugees* (CUP 2004)

Griffith JAG *The Politics of the Judiciary* (5th edn Fontana 1997)

Guild E, Harlow C *Implementing Amsterdam: Immigration and Asylum Rights in EC Law* (Hart Publishing 2001)

Guild E, Carrera S and Eggenschwiler A (eds) *The Area of Freedom, Security and Justice Ten Years On: Successes and Future Challenges Under the Stockholm Programme* (Centre for European Policy Studies 2010)

Gulman C (ed) *Scritti in Onore di Giuseppe Federico Mancini, Volume II* (Guiffrè 1998)

Habermas J *Legitimation Crisis* (Heinemann 1976)

Habermas J *Communication and the Evolution of Society* (Heinemann Educational 1979)

Habermas J *The Theory of Communicative Action Volume One* (Polity Press 1984)

Haldane ES, Ross GTR *The Philosophical Works of Descartes* (CUP 1911)

Hammar T *Democracy and the Nation State, Aliens, Denizens and Citizens in a World of International Migration* (Avebury 1990)

Harden I, Lewis N *The Noble Lie: The British Constitution and The Rule of Law* (Hutchinson 1986)

Hayek FA *The Road to Serfdom* (London 1944)

Hayter T *Open Borders: The Case Against Immigration Controls* (Pluto Press 2000)

Held D *Models of Democracy* (2nd edn Polity 1996)

Heukels T, Blokker N and Brus M (eds) *The European Union after Amsterdam* (Kluwer Law International 1998)

Hirst P, Khilnani S (eds) *Reinventing Democracy* (Blackwells Publishers 1996)

Hoekman BM, Kostecki MM *The Political Economy of the World Trading System* (OUP 1995)

Howard E *The Race Directive: Developing the Protection Against Racial Discrimination Within the EU* (Routledge 2010)

Human Security Centre *Human Security Report 2005: War and Peace in the 21st Century* (OUP 2005)

Hume D *A Treatise of Human Nature* (Selby-Bigge LA ed, 3rd edn OUP 1975)

Jackson JH *The Jurisprudence of GATT and the WTO: Insights on Treaty Law and Economic Relations* (CUP 2000)

Hvidt N, Mouritzen H *Danish Foreign Policy Yearbook 2012* (Danish Institute for International Studies 2012)

Joerges C, Mény Y and Weiler JHH (eds) *Mountain or Molehill? A Critical Appraisal of the Commission White Paper on Governance* (European University Institute, Harvard Law School and NYU School of Law 2001)

Juss SS *International Migration and Global Justice* (Ashgate 2006)

Kant I *The Critique of Pure Reason* (Kemp Smith N (ed) The Macmillan Press Ltd 1929)

Klatt M, Meister M *The Constitutional Structure of Proportionality* (OUP 2012)

Kok L *The Dublin II Regulation* (UNHCR 2006)

Kramer MH *In Defense of Legal Positivism* (OUP 1999)

Kymlicka W *Multicultural Citizenship: A Liberal Theory of Minority Rights* (OUP 1995)

Majone G *Dilemmas of European Integration: The Ambiguities and Pitfalls of Integration by Stealth* (OUP 2005)

Lindseth P *Power and Legitimacy: Reconciling Europe and the Nation-State* (OUP 2010)

Maresceau M (ed) *Enlarging the European Union: Relations between the EU and Central and Eastern Europe* (Longman 1997)

Marquand D *Parliament for Europe* (Jonathan Cape 1979)

Marshall TH *Citizenship and Social Class* (CUP 1949) reprinted in Marshall TH, Bottomore T *Citizenship and Social Class* (Pluto Press 1992)

Martin D, Guild E *Free Movement of Persons in the European Union* (Butterworths 1996)

McAdam J *Complementary Protection in International Refugee Law* (OUP 2007)

Meilaender PC *Toward a Theory of Immigration* (Palgrave 2001)

Miles R, Thränhardt D (eds) *Migration and European Integration: The Dynamics of Inclusion and Exclusion* (Pinter Publishers 1995)

Miller D *Citizenship and National Identity* (Polity Press 2000)

Neuwahl N, Rosas A (eds) *The European Union and Human Rights* (Kluwer Law International 1995)

Nozick R *The Nature of Rationality* (Princeton University Press 1993)

O'Keeffe D, Twomey P (eds) *Legal Issues of the Amsterdam Treaty* (Hart Publishing 1999)

O'Leary S *The Evolving Concept of Community Citizenship* (Kluwer Law International 1996)

Ott K (ed) *Croatian Accession to the European Union: Facing the Challenges of Negotiation* (Institute of Public Finance 2005)

Pavlakos G (ed) *Law, Rights and Discourse: The Legal Philosophy of Robert Alexy* (Hart Publishing 2007)

Pécoud A, de Guchteneire P (eds) *Migration Without Borders: Essays on the Free Movement of People* (UNESCO Publishing/Berghahn Books 2007)

Peers S *EU Justice and Home Affairs Law* (Longman 2000)

Peers S *EU Justice and Home Affairs Law* (3rd edn OUP 2011)

Preschal S *Directives in EC Law* (2nd edn OUP 2005)

Rawls J *A Theory of Justice* (2nd edn OUP 1999)

Rawls J *Political Liberalism* (expanded edn Columbia University Press 2005)

Regis Jr E (ed) *Gewirth's Ethical Rationalism: Critical Essays with a Reply by Alan Gewirth* (University of Chicago Press 1984)

Rogers N *A Practitioner's Guide to the EC-Turkey Association Agreement* (Kluwer Law International 2000)

Rogers N, Scannell R *Free Movement of Persons in the Enlarged European Union* (Sweet & Maxwell 2005)

Scharpf FW *Governing in Europe: Effective and Democratic* (OUP 1999)

Schumpeter JA *Capitalism, Socialism and Democracy* (Routledge 1976)

Shaw J, More G (eds) *New Legal Dynamics of European Union* (Clarendon Press 1995)

Shaw J *Law of the European Union* (3rd edn Palgrave 2000)

Shaw J *The Transformation of Citizenship in the European Union: Electoral Rights and the Restructuring of Political Space* (CUP 2007)

Simmonds NE *Central Issues in Jurisprudence* (3rd edn Sweet & Maxwell 2011)

Simpson JA, Weiner ESC (prepared) *The Oxford English Dictionary Vol.XIII* (2nd edn Clarendon Press 1989)

Soysal Y *Limits of Citizenship – Migrants and Postnational Membership in Europe* (University of Chicago 1994)

Toddington S *Rationality, Social Action and Moral Judgment* (Edinburgh University Press 1993)

Tridimas T *The General Principles of EU Law* (2nd edn OUP 2006)

Turmann A *A New Europe Agenda for Labour Mobility* (CEPS 2004)

Turner S (ed) *The Cambridge Companion to Max Weber* (CUP 2000)

UNHCR *Handbook on Procedures and Criteria for Determining Refugee Status under the 1951 Convention and the 1967 Protocol relating to the Status of Refugees HCR/IP/4/Eng/REV.1* (2nd edn United Nations Publications 1992)

United Nations Development Programme (UNDP) *New Dimensions of Human Security* (OUP 1994)

United Nations *Replacement Migration: Is it a Solution to Declining and Aging Populations? ST/ESA/SER.A/206* (United Nations Publications 2000)

Veil S et al *Report of the High Level Panel on the Free Movement of Persons* (Office for Official Publications of the European Communities 1998)

Walzer M *Spheres of Justice: A Defence of Pluralism and Equality* (Basic Books 1983)

Weale A, Nentwich M (eds) *Political Theory and the European Union: Legitimacy, Constitutional Choice and Citizenship* (Routledge 1998)

Weber M *Economy and Society: An Outline of Interpretative Sociology* (Roth G, Wittich C (eds) University of California Press 1968)

Weiler JHH *The Constitution of Europe: "Do the New Clothes have an Emperor?" and other Essays on European Integration* (CUP 1999)

Weiler JHH (ed) *The EU, the WTO and the NAFTA: Towards a Common Law of International Trade* (OUP 2000)

Wilhelmsson T (ed) *Perspectives of Critical Contract Law* (Dartmouth 1993)

Wolf M *Why Globalisation Works* (Yale University Press 2004)

## Journal articles

Abell NA 'The compatibility of readmission agreements with the 1951 Convention relating to the status of refugees' (1999) 11 *IJRL* 60

Abu-Akeel AK 'The MFN as it applies to service trade: new problems for an old concept' (1999) 33 *Journal of World Trade* 103

Acierno S 'The *Carpenter* judgment: fundamental rights and the limits of the Community legal order' (2003) 28 *ELR* 398

Ackerman T 'Case note' (2007) 44 *CMLRev* 141

Achermann A, Gattiker M 'Safe third countries: European developments' (1995) 7 *IJRL* 19

Acosta D 'The good, the bad and the ugly in EU migration law: is the European Parliament becoming bad and ugly? (The adoption of Directive 2008/115: the Returns Directive)' (2009) 11 *EJML* 19

Adam S, van Elsuwege P 'Citizenship rights and the federal balance between the European Union and its Member States: comment on *Dereci*' (2012) 37 *ELR* 176

Adamo S 'The legal position of migrants in Denmark: assessing the context around the "cartoon crisis"' (2007) 9 *EJML* 1

Addo MK, Grief N 'Does Article 3 of the European Convention on Human Rights enshrine absolute rights?' (1998) 9 *EJIL* 510

Addo MK, Grief N 'Some practical issues affecting the notion of absolute right in Article 3 ECHR' (1998) 23 *Supp (Human Rights Survey) ELR* 17

Addo MK, Grief N 'Is there a policy behind the decisions and judgments relating to Article 3 of the European Convention on Human Rights?' (1995) 20 *ELR* 178

Adinolfi A 'Free movement and access to work of citizens of the new Member States: the transitional measures' (2005) 42 *CMLRev* 469

Adler-Nissen R 'Behind the scenes of differentiated integration: circumventing national opt-outs in justice and home affairs' (2009) 16 *JEPP* 62

Afzal M 'Rethinking asylum: the feasibility of human security as new *ratione personae* protection' (2005) 3 *Journal of International Law & Policy* 2:1

Albi A 'Supremacy of EC law in the new Member States: bringing parliaments into the equation of "co-operative constitutionalism"' (2007) 3 *EuConst* 25

Albors-Llorens A 'The role of objective justification and efficiencies in the application of Article 82 EC' (2007) 44 *CMLRev* 1727

Alegre S, Leaf M 'Mutual recognition in European judicial co-operation: a step too far too soon? Case study – the European arrest warrant' (2004) 10 *ELJ* 200

Alexander W 'Free movement of non-EC nationals: a review of the case law of the Court of Justice' (1992) 3 *EJIL* 53

Aliverti A 'Making people criminal: the role of the criminal law in immigration enforcement' (2012) 16 *Theoretical Criminology* 417

Allain J 'The *jus cogens* nature of *non-refoulement*' (2002) 13 *IJRL* 534

Allan TRS 'Human rights and judicial review: a critique of "due deference"' (2006) 65 *CLJ* 671

Allan TRS 'Deference, defiance, and doctrine: defining the limits of judicial review' (2010) 60 *University of Toronto Law Journal* 41

Allan TRS 'Judicial deference and judicial review: legal doctrine and legal theory' (2011) 127 *LQR* 96

Anker D, Fitzpatrick J and Shacknove A 'crisis and cure: a reply to Hathaway/Neve and Schuck' (1998) 11 *Harvard Human Rights Journal* 295

Anon 'Case comment' [1997] EHRLR 172

Anon 'Case comment' [1999] EHRLR 225

Anon 'Case comment' [2002] EHRLR 276

Anon 'Case comment' [2002] EHRLR 691

Anon 'Case comment' [2007] EHRLR 103

Anon 'Case comment' [2007] EHRLR 468

Anon 'Case comment' [2008] EHRLR 422

Mrabet EA 'Readmission agreements: the case of Morocco' (2003) 5 *EJML* 379

Arena N 'The concept of "mass influx of displaced persons" in the European Directive Establishing the Temporary Protection Scheme' (2005) 7 *EJML* 435

Arnull A 'Arrested development' (2005) 30 *ELR* 605

Arnull AM 'Family reunification and fundamental rights' (2006) 31 *ELR* 611

Aron R 'Is multinational citizenship possible?' (1974) 41 *Social Research* 638

Ashworth A 'Is the criminal law a lost cause?' (2000) 116 *LQR* 225

Aus JP 'Eurodac: A solution looking for a problem?' ARENA Working Paper 9/06

Azoulai L, Coutts S 'Restricting Union citizens' residence rights on grounds of public security: where Union citizenship and the AFSJ meet' (2013) 50 CMLRev 553

Baldaccini A 'The return and removal of irregular migrants under EU law: an analysis of the Returns Directive' (2009) 11 *EJML* 1

Baldaccini A 'The EU Directive on Return: principles and protests' (2010) 28 *Refugee Survey Quarterly* 114

Balkin JM 'Respect-worthy: Frank Michelman and the legitimate constitution' (2004) 39 *Tulsa Law Review* 485

Ball R, Dadomo C 'Case comment' (2009) 15 *EPL* 335

Banks J 'The criminalisation of asylum seekers and asylum policy' (2008) 175 *Prison Service Journal* 43 at 49

Banks J 'Unmasking deviance: the visual construction of asylum seekers and refugees in English national newspapers' (2012) 20 *Critical Criminology* 293

Banner C, Thomson A 'Human rights review of state acts performed in compliance with EC law' [2005] EHRLR 649

Bantekas I 'The principle of mutual recognition in EU criminal law' (2007) 32 *ELR* 365

Barber NW 'Citizenship, nationalism and the European Union' (2002) 27 *ELR* 241

Barbera M 'Not the same? The judicial role in the new Community anti-discrimination law context' (2002) 31 *ILJ* 82

Barnard C 'The United Kingdom, the "social chapter" and the Amsterdam Treaty' (1997) 26 *ILJ* 275

Barnard C 'The principle of equality in the Community context: *P, Grant, Kalanke* and *Marschall*: four uneasy bedfellows?' (1998) 57 *CLJ* 352

Barnard C 'Case note' (2005) 42 *CMLRev* 1465

Barnett RE 'Constitutional legitimacy' (2003) 103 *Columbia Law Review* 111

Battjes H 'A balance between fairness and efficiency? The Directive on International Protection and the Dublin Regulation' (2002) 4 *EJML* 159

Battjes H 'The *Soering* threshold: why only fundamental values prohibit refoulement in ECHR case law' (2009) 11 *EJML* 205

Battjes H 'In search of a fair balance: the absolute character of the prohibition of refoulement under Article 3 ECHR reassessed' (2009) 22 *Leiden Journal of International Law* 583

Baudenbacher C 'The EFTA Court – an example of the judicialisation of international economic law' (2003) 28 *ELR* 880

Baudenbacher C 'The EFTA Court: an actor in the European judicial dialogue' (2005) 28 *Fordham International Law Journal* 353

Bell M 'The new Article 13 EC: a sound basis for European anti-discrimination law?' (1999) 6 *MJ* 5

Bell M 'Article 13 EC: The European Commission's anti-discrimination proposals' (2000) 29 *ILJ* 79

Bell M 'Beyond European labour law? reflections on the EU Racial Equality Directive' (2002) 8 *ELJ* 384

Bell M 'Civic citizenship and migrant integration' (2007) 13 *EPL* 311

Bellamy R, Castiglione D 'Legitimizing the Euro-"polity" and its "regime": the normative turn in EU studies' (2003) 2 *EJPT* 7

Bellamy R 'Still in deficit: rights, regulation, and democracy in the EU' (2006) 12 *ELJ* 725

Bennett RW '"Mere" rationality in constitutional law: judicial review and democratic theory' (1979) 67 *California Law Review* 1029

Berkowitz N 'Case comment' (2006) 20 *IANL* 51

Berkowitz N 'Case comment' (2007) 27 *JIANL* 43

Berkowitz N 'Case comment' (2008) 22 *JIANL* 371

Besselink LFM 'Case note' (2008) 45 *CMLRev* 787

Betts A 'Towards a Mediterranean solution? Implications for the region of origin' (2006) 18 *IJRL* 652

Bierbach JB 'Case note' (2008) 4 *EuConst* 344

Bignani FE 'The democratic deficit in European Community rulemaking: a call for notice and comment in comitology' (1999) 40 *Harvard International Law Journal* 451

Billet C 'EC readmission agreements: a prime instrument of the external dimension of the EU's fight against irregular immigration. An assessment after ten years of practice' (2010) 12 *EJML* 45

Bingham T 'The rule of law' (2007) 66 *CLJ* 67

Birkinshaw P 'Supranationalism, the rule of law, and constitutionalism in the draft Union constitution' (2004) 23 *YEL* 199

Blackstock J 'The EU Charter of Fundamental Rights: scope and competence' 18 April 2012 http://eutopialaw.com/2012/04/18/the-eu-charter-of-fundamental-rights-scope-and-competance-2/

Blom-Hansen J, Brandsma GJ 'The EU comitology system: intergovernmental bargaining and deliberative supranationalism?' (2009) 47 *JCMS* 719

Boelaert-Suominen S 'Non-EU nationals and Council Directive 2003/109/EC on the status of third-country nationals who are long-term residents: five paces forward and possibly three paces back' (2005) 42 *CMLRev* 1011

Boeles P, Bruins M 'Case reports of the European Court of Human Rights and the Human Rights Committee' (2007) 9 *EJML* 253

Boeles P 'Case reports of the European Court of Human Rights, the Human Rights Committee and the Committee Against Torture' (2008) 10 *EJML* 105

Bogusz B 'Regulating the right of establishment for accession state nationals: reinforcing the "buffer zone" or improving labour market flexibility?' (2002) 27 *ELR* 474

Bond J 'Excluding justice: the dangerous intersection between refugee claims, criminal law, and "guilty" asylum seekers' (2012) 24 *IJRL* 37

Borchelt G 'The safe third country practice in the European Union: a misguided approach to asylum law and a violation of international human rights standards' (2002) 33 *Columbia Human Rights Law Review* 473

Borjas GJ 'Economic theory and international migration' (1989) 23 *IMR* 457

Borjas GJ 'The economics of immigration' (1994) 32 *Journal of Economic Literature* 1667

Borjas GJ 'The economic benefits from immigration' (1995) 9 *Journal of Economic perspectives* 3

Borjas GJ 'Immigration and welfare magnets' (1999) 17 *Journal of Labor Economics* 607

Bossuyt M 'Belgium condemned for inhuman or degrading treatment due to violations by Greece of EU asylum law' [2011] EHRLR 582

Bossuyt M 'The Court of Strasbourg acting as an asylum court' (2012) 8 *EuConst* 203

Boswell C 'Theorizing migration policy: is there a third way?' (2007) 41 *International Migration Review* 75

Bosworth M 'Deportation, detention and foreign national prisoners in England and Wales' (2011) 15 *Citizenship Studies* 583

Bosworth M 'Subjectivity and identity in detention: punishment and society in a global age' (2012) 16 *Theoretical Criminology* 123

Bouteillet-Paquet D 'Passing the buck: a critical analysis of the readmission policy implemented by the European Union and its Member States' (2003) 5 *EJML* 359

Boutillon S 'The interpretation of Article 1 of the 1951 Convention Relating to the Status of Refugees by the European Union: toward harmonisation' (2003) 18 *Georgetown Immigration Law Journal* 111

Boyle J 'Legal realism and the social contract: Fuller's public jurisprudence of form, private jurisprudence of substance' (1993) 78 *Cornell Law Review* 371

Bradley M 'Back to basics: the conditions of just refugee returns' (2008) 21 *JRS* 285

Brandsma GJ, Curtin D and Meijer A 'How transparent are EU 'comitology' committees in practice?' (2008) 14 *ELJ* 819

Brandtner B 'The drama of the "EEA": comments on Opinions 1/91 and 1/92 (1992) 3 *EJIL* 300

Brinkmann G 'Case note' (1999) 1 *EJML* 131

Brinkmann G 'Opinion of Germany on the single permit proposal' (2012) 14 *EJML* 351

Brochman G 'The current traps of European immigration policies' Willy Brandt Series of Working Papers in International Migration and Ethnic Relations 1/03

Brouwer ER 'Eurodac: its limitations and temptation' (2002) 4 *EJML* 231

Brouwer E 'Case note' (2008) 45 *CMLRev* 1251

Brouwer E 'Mutual trust and the Dublin Regulation: protection of fundamental rights in the EU and the burden of proof' (2013) 9 *Utrecht Law Review* 135

Brown C 'The Race Directive: towards equality for all the peoples of Europe?' (2002) 21 *YEL* 195

Browne-Wilkinson N 'The infiltration of a bill of rights' [1992] PL 397

Bruch EM 'Open or closed: balancing border policy with human rights' (2007) 96 *Kentucky Law Journal* 197

Buckley J 'Case comment' [2012] EHRLR 205

Bulterman M 'Case note' (1997) 34 *CMLRev* 1497

Bulterman M 'Case note' (1999) 36 *CMLRev* 1325

Bulterman M 'Case note' (2008) 45 *CMLRev* 245

Bunyan T 'Commission: Action Plan on the Stockholm Programme – a bit more freedom and justice and a lot more security' April 2010 http://www.statewatch.org/analyses/no-95-stockholm-action-plan.pdf

Bürgin A 'European Commission's agency meets Ankara's agenda: why Turkey is ready for a readmission agreement' (2012) 19 *Journal of European Public Policy* 883

Burrows N 'The rights of Turkish workers in the Member States' (1994) 19 *ELR* 305

Byrne R, Shacknove A 'The safe third country notion in European asylum law' (1996) 9 *Harvard Human Rights Journal* 185

Caldwell PJ 'Case comment' (2011) 36 *ELR* 135

Cambien N 'Case note' (2009) 15 *Columbia Journal of European Law* 321

Canetta E 'The EU policy on return of illegally staying third-country nationals' (2007) 9 *EJML* 435

Canor I '*Primus inter pares*: who is the Ultimate guardian of fundamental rights in Europe?' (2000) 25 *ELR* 3

Caraoshi LI, Ndoci N 'Do EU Member States need readmission agreements? Analysis of the EC-Albania readmission agreement' (2011) 25 *JIANL* 12

Carens JH 'Aliens and citizens: the case for open borders' (1987) 49 *Review of Politics* 250

Carens JH 'Realistic and idealistic approaches to the ethics of migration' (1996) 30 *IMR* 156

Carens JH 'Who should get in? The ethics of immigration admissions' (2003) 17 *Ethics & International Affairs* 95

Carlier J-Y 'Case note' (2005) 42 *CMLRev* 1121

Carrera S 'What does free movement mean in theory and practice in an enlarged EU?'(2005) 11 *ELJ* 699

Carrera S, Guild E 'The French Presidency's European Pact on Immigration and Asylum: intergovernmental vs. Europeanisation? security vs. rights?' September 2008 http://www.ceps.be/book/french-presidency%E2%80%99s-european-pact-immigration-and-asylum-intergovernmentalism-vs-europeanisatio

Carrera S, Wiesbrock A 'Whose European citizenship in the Stockholm Programme? The enactment of citizenship by third country nationals in the EU' (2010) 12 *EJML* 337

Castles S 'The guest-worker in Western Europe – an obituary' (1986) 20 *IMR* 761

Castles S 'Why migration policies fail' (2004) 2 *ERS* 205

Castles S 'The factors that make and unmake migration policies' (2004) 38 *IMR* 852

Castles S 'Guest-workers in Europe: a resurrection?' (2006) 40 *IMR* 741

Cernic JL 'National security and expulsion to a risk of torture' (2008) 12 *Edin LR* 486

Chacón JH 'Overcriminalizing immigration' (2012) 102 *The Journal of Criminal Law & Criminology* 613

Chan C 'Proportionality and invariable baseline intensity of review' (2013) 33 *LS* 1

Chang HF 'Migration as international trade: the economic gains from the liberalized movement of labor' (1998) 3 *UCLA Journal of International Law & Foreign Affairs* 371

Chang HF 'The economics of international labor migration and the case for global distributive justice in liberal political theory' (2008) 41 *Cornell International Law Journal* 1

Cheyne I 'International agreements and the European Community legal system' (1994) 19 *ELR* 581

Chia J 'Immigration and its imperatives' (2009) 15 *ELJ* 683

Chido CJ 'Peril of movement: migrating Roma risks expulsion as EU Member States test the limits of the Free Movement Directive' (2011) 20 *Tulane Journal of International and Comparative Law* 233

Cholewinski R 'The protection of the right of economic migrants to family reunion in Europe' (1994) 43 *ICLQ* 568

Cholewinski R 'Migrants as minorities: integration and inclusion in the enlarged European Union' (2005) 43 *JCMS* 695

Cicekli B 'The rights of Turkish migrants in Europe under international law and EU law' (1999) 33 *IMR* 300

Clayton G 'Asylum seekers in Europe' (2011) 11 *HRLR* 758

Closa C 'Citizenship of the Union and nationality of the Member States' (1995) 32 *CMLRev* 487

Cohen-Eliya M, Porat I 'Proportionality and the culture of justification' (2011) 59 *American Journal of Comparative Law* 463

Coman GI 'European Union policy on asylum and its inherent human rights violations' (1998) 64 *Brooklyn Law Review* 1217

Cornelisse G 'Case comment' (2011) 48 *CMLRev* 925

Costello C 'Case note' (2000) 37 *CMLRev* 817

Costello C 'The Asylum Procedures Directive and the proliferation of safe country practices: deterrence, deflection and the dismantling of international protection?' (2005) 7 *EJML* 35

Costello C 'The *Bosphorus* ruling of the European Court of Human Rights: fundamental rights and blurred boundaries in Europe' (2006) 6 *HRLR* 87

Costello C '*Metock*: free movement and "normal family life" in the Union' (2009) 46 *CMLRev* 587

Costello C 'Dublin case *NS/ME*: finally, and end to blind trust across the EU?' [2012] *Asiel & Migrantenrecht* 83

Costello C 'Human rights and the elusive universal subject: immigration detention under international human rights and EU law' (2012) 19 *Indiana Journal of Global Legal Studies* 257

Costello C 'Courting access to asylum in Europe: recent supranational jurisprudence explored' (2012) 12 *HRLR* 287

Cox S 'Case comment' (2011) 25 *JIANL* 293

Craig P 'Case note' (2009) 46 *CMLRev* 1265

Cremona M 'The "dynamic and homogenous" EEA: Byzantine structures and variable geometry' (1994) 19 *ELR* 508

Cremona M 'Citizens of third countries: movement and employment of migrant workers within the European Union' (1995) 2 *LIEI* 87

Currie S '"Free" movers? The post-accession experience of Accession-8 migrant workers in the UK' (2006) 31 *ELR* 207

Currie S 'Case note' (2007) 51 *(Sum) SLR* 28

Currie S 'Accelerated justice or a step too far: residence rights of non-EU family members and the Court's ruling in *Metock*' (2009) 34 *ELR* 310

Curtin D 'The constitutional structure of the Union: a Europe of bits and pieces' (1993) 30 *CMLRev* 17

Cygan A, Szyszczak E 'Case note' (2006) 55 *ICLQ* 977

Damjanovic D 'Case note' (2010) 47 *CMLRev* 847

Davies G 'The Services Directive: extending the country of origin principle, and Reforming public administration' (2007) 32 *ELR* 232

Davies P 'Posted workers: single market or protection of national labour law systems?' (1997) 34 *CMLRev* 571

de Baere G 'Case note' (2012) 106 *AJIL* 616

de Búrca G 'The quest for legitimacy in the European Union' (1996) 59 *MLR* 349

Deen-Racsmány Z, Blekxtoon R 'The decline of the nationality exception in European extradition?' (2005) 13 *European Journal of Crime, Criminal Law and Criminal Justice* 317

Deen-Racsmány Z 'The European arrest warrant and the surrender of nationals revisited: the lessons of constitutional challenges' (2006) 14 *European Journal of Crime, Criminal Law and Criminal Justice* 271

De Giorgi G, Pellizzari M 'Welfare migration in Europe' (2009) 16 *Labour Economics* 353

de Groot GR, Seiling A 'The consequences of the *Rottmann* judgment on Member State autonomy: the European Court of Justice's avant-gardism in nationality matters' (2011) 7 *EuConst* 150

Del Sarto RA, Schumacher T 'From EMP to ENP: what's at stake with the European neighbourhood policy towards the southern Mediterranean' (2005) 10 *EFAR* 17

Dembour MB '*Gaygusuz* revisited: the limits of the European Court of Human Rights' equality agenda' (2012) 12 *HRLR* 689

den Boer M, Corrado L 'For the record or off the record: comments about the incorporation of Schengen into the EU' (1999) 1 *EJML* 397

den Heijer M 'Whose rights and which rights? The continuing story of *non-refoulement* under the European Convention on Human Rights' (2008) 10 *EJML* 277

den Heijer M 'Case note' (2012) 49 *CMLRev* 1735

Devuyst Y 'The European Union's institutional balance after the Treaty of Lisbon: "community method" and "democratic deficit" reassessed' (2008) 39 *Georgetown Journal of International Law* 247

de Waele H 'EU citizenship: revisiting its meaning, place and potential' (2010) 12 *EJML* 319

Dickson B 'Safe in their hands? Britain's law lords and human rights' (2006) 26 *LS* 329

d'Oliveira HUJ 'Case note' (1993) 30 *CMLRev* 623

d'Oliveira HUJ 'Decoupling nationality and Union citizenship' (2011) 7 *EuConst* 138

Doppelhammer M 'Expulsion: a test case for European Union citizenship' (1999) 24 *ELR* 621

Dougan M, Spaventa E 'Educating Rudy and the non-English patient: a double bill on residency rights under Article 18 EC' (2003) 28 *ELR* 699

Dougan M 'The court helps those who help themselves: the legal status of migrant work-seekers under Community law in the light of the *Collins* judgment' (2005) 7 *EJSS* 7

Dougan M 'Fees, grants, loans and dole cheques: who covers the costs of migrant education within the EU?' (2005) 42 *CMLRev* 943

Dougan M 'The constitutional dimension to the case law on Union citizenship' (2006) 31 *ELR* 613

Dougan M '"And some fell on stony ground . . . " a review of Giandomenico Majone's *Dilemmas of European Integration*' (2006) 31 *ELR* 865

Dougan M 'Cross-border educational mobility and the exportation of student financial assistance' (2008) 33 *ELR* 723

Douglas-Scott S 'The rule of law in the European Union – putting the security into the "area of freedom, security and justice"' (2004) 29 *ELR* 219

Douglas-Scott S 'Case note' (2006) 43 *CMLRev* 243

Douglas-Scott S 'The EU's area of freedom, security and justice: a lack of fundamental rights, mutual trust and democracy' (2009) 11 *CYELS* 53

Drywood E 'Giving with one hand, taking with the other: fundamental rights, children and the Family Reunification Decision' (2007) 32 *ELR* 396

Dubey J-P 'Case note' (2005) 42 *CMLRev* 499

Duffy A 'Expulsion to face torture? *Non-refoulement* in international law' (2008) 20 *IJRL* 373

Dunstan R 'Playing human pinball: the Amnesty International United Kingdom section report on UK Home Office "Safe third country" practice' (1995) 7 *IJRL* 606

Durieux JF 'Of war, flows, laws and flaws: a reply to Hugo Storey' (2012) 31 *Refugee Survey Quarterly* 161

Eaton J 'The internal protection alternative under European Union law: examining the recast Qualification Directive' (2012) 24 *IJRL* 765

Eckes C 'Does the European Court of Human Rights provide protection from the European Community?' (2007) 13 *EPL* 47

Editorial 'Freedoms unlimited? Reflections on *Mary Carpenter v Secretary of State*' (2003) 40 *CMLRev* 537

Editorial 'The EU as an area of freedom, security and justice: implementing the Stockholm Programme' (2010) 47 *CMLRev* 1307

Edwards A 'Human security and the rights of refugees: transcending territorial and disciplinary borders' (2009) 30 *Michigan Journal of International Law* 763

Edwards RA 'Judicial deference under the Human Rights Act' (2002) 65 *MLR* 859

Ehin P 'Competing models of EU legitimacy: the test of popular expectations' (2008) 46 *JCMS* 619

Ehrling L '*De facto* discrimination in world trade law: national and most-favoured-nation treatment – or equal treatment?' (2002) 36 *Journal of World Trade* 921

Eichenhofer E 'How to simplify the co-ordination of social security' (2000) 2 *EJSS* 231

Eisele K, van der Mei AP 'Portability of social benefits and reverse discrimination of EU citizens vis-à-vis Turkish nationals: comment on *Akdas*' (2012) 37 *ELR* 204

El-Enany N 'Who is the new European refugee?' (2008) 33 *ELR* 313

Ellis E 'Recent developments in European Community sex equality law' (1998) 35 *CMLRev* 379

Ellis E 'Social advantages: a new lease of life?' (2003) 40 *CMLRev* 639

Elsen C 'From Maastricht to The Hague: the politics of judicial and police cooperation' (2007) 8 *ERA Forum* 13

Elsmore MJ, Starup P 'Union citizenship – background, jurisprudence, and perspective: the past, present, and future of law and policy' (2007) 26 *YEL* 57

Elsmore M, Starup P 'Case note' (2007) 44 *CMLRev* 787

Eriksen EO, Fossum JE 'Europe in search of legitimacy: strategies of legitimation assessed' (2004) 25 *IPSR* 435

Errera R 'The CJEU and subsidiary protection: reflections on *Elgafaji* – and after' (2010) 23 *IJRL* 93

Errera R 'Case comment' (2011) 23 *IJRL* 521

Etzioni A 'The Community deficit' (2007) 45 *JCMS* 23

Eyjólfsson M 'Case note' (2000) 37 *CMLRev* 191

Fahey E 'Interpretive legitimacy and the distinction between "social advantage" and "work seeker's allowance"' (2009) 34 *ELR* 933

Farraj A 'Refugees and the biometric future: the impact of biometrics on refugees and asylum seekers' (2011) 42 *Columbia Human Rights Law Review* 891

Feldman D 'Deporting suspected terrorists to face torture' (2008) 67 *CLJ* 225

Feller E 'Carrier sanctions and international law' (1999) 1 *IJRL* 48

Feller E 'Asylum, migration and refugee protection: realities, myths and the promise of things to come' (2006) 18 *IJRL* 510

Fennelly N 'The area of "freedom, security and justice" and the European Court of justice – a personal view (2000) 49 *ICLQ* 1

Fichera M 'The European arrest warrant and the sovereign state: a marriage of convenience?' (2009) 15 *ELJ* 70

Fichera M 'Case note' (2009) 46 *CMLRev* 241

Fisher E 'The European Union in the age of accountability' (2004) 24 *OJLS* 495

Fitzpatrick J 'Temporary protection of refugees: elements of a formalised regime' (2000) 94 *AJIL* 279

Fletcher M 'Some developments to the *ne bis in idem* principle in the European Union' (2003) 66 *MLR* 769

Fletcher M 'Extending "indirect effect" to the third pillar: the significance of *Pupino*' (2005) 30 *ELR* 862

Fletcher M 'Schengen, the European Court of Justice and flexibility under the Lisbon Treaty: balancing the United Kingdom's "ins" and "outs"' (2009) 5 *EuConst* 71

Flynn L 'The implications of Article 13 EC – after Amsterdam, will some forms of discrimination be more equal than others?' (1999) 36 *CMLRev* 1127

Foblets M-CSFG 'Europe and its aliens after Maastricht: the painful move to substantive harmonisation of Member States' policies towards third country nationals' (1994) 42 *American Journal of Comparative Law* 783

Føllesdal A 'Survey article: the legitimacy deficits of the European Union' (2006) 14 *Journal of Political Philosophy* 441

Forman J 'The EEA Agreement five years on: dynamic homogeneity in practice and its implementation by the two EEA Courts' (1999) 36 *CMLRev* 751

Foster S 'Case comment' (1997) 31 *Law Teacher* 238

Franck TM 'Legitimacy in the international system' (1988) 82 *AJIL* 705

Franck TM 'Clan and superclan: loyalty, identity and community in law and practice' (1996) 90 *AJIL* 359

Fredriksen HH 'The EFTA Court 15 years on' (2010) 59 *ICLQ* 731

Fredriksen HH 'Bridging the widening gap between the EU Treaties and the Agreement on the European Economic Area' (2012) 18 *ELJ* 868

Fries S, Shaw J 'Citizenship of the Union: first steps in the European Court of Justice' (1998) 4 *EPL* 533

Garlick M 'The EU discussions on extraterritorial processing: solution or conundrum?' (2006) 18 *IJRL* 601

Garman JJ 'The European Union combats racism and Xenophobia by forbidding expression: an analysis of the Framework Decision' (2008) 39 *University of Toledo Law Review* 843

Geddes A 'Immigrant and ethnic minorities and the EU's "democratic deficit"' (1995) 33 *JCMS* 197

Gerards JH 'Intensity of judicial review in equal treatment cases' (2004) 51 *NILR* 135

Gilbert G 'Is Europe living up to its obligations to refugees?' (2004) 15 *EJIL* 963

Gill M, Ahluwalia NS 'Case comment' (2011) 25 *JIANL* 304

Giuffre M 'Case comment' (2012) 61 *ICLQ* 728

Giulietti C, Guzi M, Kahanec M and Zimmerman KF 'Unemployment benefits and immigration: evidence from the EU' (2013) 34(1) *International Journal of Manpower* 24–38

Goldston JA 'Race discrimination in Europe: problems and prospects' [1999] EHRLR 462

Golynker O 'Partial migration in the EU after the *Baumbast* case: bringing social and legal perspectives together' (2004) 15 *KCLJ* 367

Golynker O 'Jobseekers' rights in the European Union: challenges of changing the paradigm of social solidarity' (2005) 30 *ELR* 111

Golynker O 'Student loans: the European concept of social justice according to *Bidar*' (2006) 31 *ELR* 390

Golynker O 'Case note' (2009) 46 *CMLRev* 2021

Goodwin-Gill GS 'The international protection of refugees: what future?' (2000) 12 *IJRL* 1

Goodwin-Gill GS 'The right to seek asylum: interception at sea and the principle of non-refoulement' (2011) 23 *IJRL* 443

Gosalbo-Bono R 'The significance of the rule of law and its implications for the European Union and the United States' (2010) 72 *University of Pittsburgh Law Review* 229

Grafstein R 'The failure of Weber's conception of Legitimacy: its causes and implications' (1981) 43 *The Journal of Politics* 456

Graver HP 'Mission impossible: supranationality and national legal autonomy in the EEA Agreement' (2002) 7 *EFAR* 73

Greer S '"Balancing" and the European Court of Human Rights: a contribution to the Habermas-Alexy debate' (2004) 63 *CLJ* 412

Grief N 'Non-discrimination under the European Convention on Human Rights: a critique of the United Kingdom Government's refusal to sign and ratify Protocol 12' (2002) 27 *ELR (Human Rights Survey)* 3

Griffiths JAG 'The brave new world of Sir John Laws' (2000) 63 *MLR* 159

Grimm D 'Does Europe need a constitution?' (1995) 1 *ELJ* 282

Groenendijk K 'Legal concepts of integration in EU migration law' (2004) 6 *EJML* 111

Groenendijk K 'Reinstatement of controls at the internal borders of Europe: why and against whom?' (2004) 10 *ELJ* 150

Groenendijk K 'Family reunification as a right under Community law' (2006) 8 *EJML* 215

Gross T 'Integration of immigrants: the perspective of European Community law' (2005) 7 *EJML* 145

Grynberg R, Qalo V 'Migration and the World Trade Organization' (2007) 41 *Journal of World Trade* 751

Guild E 'Between persecution and protection: refugees and the new European asylum policy' (2000) 3 *CYELS* 169

Guild E 'The EC Directive on Race Discrimination: surprises, possibilities and limitations' (2000) 29 *ILJ* 416

Guild E 'Seeking asylum: storm clouds between international commitments and EU legislative measures' (2004) 29 *ELR* 198

Guild E 'The European geography of refugee protection – exclusions, limitations and exceptions from the 1967 Protocol to the present' [2012] EHRLR 413

Gümüs YK 'EU Blue Card scheme: the right step in the right direction?' (2009) 11 *EJML* 435

Hailbronner K, Thierry C 'Schengen II and Dublin: responsibility for asylum applications in Europe' (1997) 34 *CMLRev* 957

Hailbronner K 'Union citizenship and access to social benefits' (2005) 42 *CMLRev* 1245

Hailbronner K 'Detention of asylum seekers' (2007) 9 *EJML* 159

Hailbronner K, Thym D 'Case note' (2011) 48 *CMLRev* 1253

Hall S 'Loss of Union citizenship in breach of fundamental rights' (1996) 21 *ELR* 129

Halleskov L 'The Long-term Residents Directive: a fulfilment of the Tampere objective of near-equality?' (2005) 7 *EJML* 181

Hamilton B, Whalley J 'Efficiency and distributional implications of global restrictions on labour mobility: calculations of policy implications' (1984) 14 *Journal of Development Economics* 61

Hammarberg T 'It is wrong to criminalize migration' (2009) 11 *EJML* 383

Hamood S 'EU-Libya cooperation on migration: a raw deal for refugees and migrants?' (2008) 21 *JRS* 19

Hansen JD 'Immigration and welfare redistribution in welfare states' (2003) 19 *European Journal of Political Economy* 735

Hansen R 'Asylum policy in the European Union' (2000) 14 *Georgetown Immigration Law Journal* 779

Hardiman-McCartney A 'Absolutely right: providing asylum seekers with food and shelter under Article 3' (2006) 65 *CLJ* 4

Harvey A 'Expulsion and exclusion' (2007) 21 *JIANL* 208

Harvey CJ 'Expulsion, national security and the European Convention' (1997) 22 *ELR* 626

Harvey C 'The right to seek asylum in the European Union' [2004] EHRLR 17

Hathaway JC, Neve RA 'Making international refugee law relevant again: a proposal for collectivised and solution-orientated protection' (1997) 10 *Harvard Human Rights Journal* 115

Hathaway JC 'The meaning of repatriation' (1997) 9 *IJRL* 551

Hatzopoulos V 'With or without you . . . judging politically in the field of area of freedom, security and justice' (2008) 33 *ELR* 44

Hedemann-Robinson M 'Third-country nationals, European Union citizenship, and free movement of persons: a time for bridges rather than divisions' (1997) 12 *YEL* 321

Hepple B 'Race and law in Fortress Europe' (2004) 67 *MLR* 1

Herlin-Karnell E 'In the wake of *Pupino*' (2007) 8 *German Law Journal* 1147

Herlin-Karnell E 'European arrest warrant cases and the principles of non-discrimination and EU citizenship' (2010) 73 *MLR* 824

Herlin-Karnell E 'From mutual trust to the full effectiveness of EU law: 10 years of the European arrest warrant' (2013) 38 *ELR* 79

Hillion C 'Case note' (2003) 40 *CMLRev* 465

Hillion C 'The European Union is dead. Long live the European Union: a commentary on the Treaty of Accession 2003' (2004) 29 *ELR* 583

Hinarejos A 'Recent human rights developments in the EU courts: the Charter of Fundamental rights, the European arrest warrant and terror lists' (2007) 7 *HRLR* 793

Hinarejos A 'Extending citizenship and the scope of EU law' (2011) 70 *CLJ* 309

Hinarejos A 'Citizenship of the EU: clarifying 'genuine enjoyment of the substance' of citizenship rights' (2012) 71 *CLJ* 279

Hinarejos A, Spencer JR and Peers S 'Opting out of criminal law: what is actually involved?' CELS Working Paper New Series 1 September 2012 http://www.cels.law.cam.ac.uk/Media/working_papers/Optout%20text%20final.pdf

Hobbing P 'A farewell to open borders? The Danish approach' November 2011 http://www.ceps.eu/book/farewell-open-borders-danish-approach

Hoogenboom A 'Moving forward by standing still? First admission of Turkish workers: comment on *Commission v Netherlands (Administrative Fees)*' (2010) 35 *ELR* 707

Hoogenboom T 'Integration into society and free movement of non-EC nationals' (1992) 3 *EJIL* 51

Horeth M 'No way out for the beast? The unsolved legitimacy problem of European governance' (1999) 6 *JEPP* 249

Howard-Hassman RE 'Human security: undermining human rights?' (2012) 34 *Human Rights Quarterly* 88

Hublet C 'The scope of Article 12 of the Treaty of the European Communities vis-à-vis third-country nationals: evolution at last?' (2009) 15 *ELJ* 757

Hurwitz A 'The 1990 Dublin Convention: a comprehensive assessment' (2000) 11 *IJRL* 464

Huysmans J 'The European Union and the securitization of migration' (2000) 38 *JCMS* 751

Ibrahim M 'The securitization of migration: a racial discourse' (2005) 43 *International Migration* 163

Iliopoulou A, Toner H 'Case note' (2002) 39 *CMLRev* 609

Iliopoulou A, Toner H 'A new approach to discrimination against free movers' (2003) 28 *ELR* 389

Jacqueson C 'Union citizenship and the Court of Justice: something new under the sun? Towards social citizenship' (2002) 27 *ELR* 260

Jančić D 'Caveats from Karlsruhe and Berlin: whither democracy after Lisbon?' (2010) 46 *Columbia Journal of European Law* 337

Janssens C 'Case note' (2007) 14 *Columbia Journal of European Law* 169

Johnson KR 'Open borders?' (2003) 51 *UCLA Law Review* 193

Johnston C 'Indefinite immigration detention: can it be justified?' (2009) 23 *JIANL* 351

Joly D 'The porous dam: European harmonisation on asylum in the nineties' (1994) 6 *IJRL* 159

Jones J 'Human dignity in the EU Charter of Fundamental Rights and its interpretation before the European Court of Justice' (2012) 33 *Liverpool Law Review* 281

Jones TD 'Case note' (1994) 88 *AJIL* 114

Jorgensen CW, Sorensen KA 'Internal border controls in the European Union: recent challenges and reforms' (2012) 37 *ELR* 249

Jørgensen S 'The right to cross-border education in the European Union' (2009) 46 *CMLRev* 1567

Juss SS 'Free movement and the world order' (2004) 16 *IJRL* 289

Juss SS 'Complicity, exclusion, and the "unworthy" in refugee law' (2012) 31 *Refugee Survey Quarterly* 1

Kaldor M, Martin M and Selchow S 'Human security: a new strategic narrative for Europe' (2007) 83 *International Affairs* 273

Kalverboer ME, Zijlstra AE and Knorth EJ 'The development consequences for asylum-seeking children living with the prospect for five years or more of enforced return to their home country' (2009) 11 *EJML* 41

Karayigit MT 'Why and to what extent a common interpretative position for mixed agreements?' (2006) 11 *EFAR* 445

Kathrani P 'Asylum law or criminal law: blame, deterrence and the criminalisation of the asylum seeker' (2011) 18 *Jurisprudence* 1543

Kavanagh A 'Defending deference in public law and constitutional theory' (2010) 126 *LQR* 222

Kerber K 'Temporary protection in the European Union: a chronology' (1999) 14 *Georgetown Immigration Law Journal* 35

King G, Murray CJL 'Rethinking human security' (2002) 116 *Political Science Quarterly* 585

King T 'Ensuring human rights review of intergovernmental acts in Europe' (2000) 25 *ELR* 79

Klepp S 'A contested asylum system: the European Union between refugee protection and border control in the Mediterranean Sea' (2010) 12 *EJML* 1

Klug A 'Harmonization of asylum in the European Union – emergence of an EU refugee system?' (2004) 47 *GYIL* 594

Kochenov D 'Case note' (2010) 47 *CMLRev* 1831

Kochenov D 'A real European citizenship: a new jurisdiction test: a novel chapter in the development of the Union of Europe' (2011) 18 *Columbia Journal of European Law* 55

Kochenov D, Plender R 'EU citizenship: from an incipient form to an incipient substance? The discovery of the Treaty text' (2012) 37 *ELR* 369

Kochenov D 'The essence of EU citizenship emerging from the last ten years of academic debate: beyond the cherry blossoms and the moon?' (2013) 62 *ICLQ* 97

Komárek J 'European constitutionalism and the European arrest warrant: in search of the limits of "contrapunctual principles"' (2007) 44 *CMLRev* 9

Komárek J 'In the court(s) we trust? On the need for hierarchy and differentiation in the preliminary ruling procedure' (2007) 32 *ELR* 467

Konstadinides T '*La fraternité européene*? The extent of national competence to condition the acquisition and loss of nationality from the perspective of EU citizenship' (2010) 35 *ELR* 401

Koser K, Walsh M and Black R 'Temporary protection and the assisted return of refugees from the European Union' (1998) 10 *IJRL* 444

Koser K 'New approaches in asylum?' (2001) 39 *International Migration* 85

Kostakopoulou T '"Integrating" non-EU migrants in the European Union: ambivalent legacies and mutating paradigms' (2002) 8 *Columbia Journal of European Law* 181

Kowalik-Bańczyk K 'Should we Polish it up? The Polish Constitutional Tribunal and the idea of supremacy of EU law' (2005) 6 *German Law Journal* 1355

Kramer MH 'On the moral status of the rule of law' (2004) 63 *CLJ* 65

Kuijper PJ 'Some legal problems associated with the communitarisation of policy on visas, asylum and immigration under the Amsterdam Treaty and incorporation of the Schengen *acquis*' (2000) 37 *CMLRev* 345

Kuijper PJ 'The evolution of the third pillar from Maastricht to the European constitution: institutional aspects' (2004) 41 *CMLRev* 609

Kunoy B 'A Union of national citizens: the origins of the court's lack of *avant-Gardisme* in the *Chen* case' (2006) 43 *CMLRev* 179

Kunoy B, Mortansson B 'Case comment' (2010) 47 *CMLRev* 1815

Kurayigit MT '*Vive la clause de standstill*: the issue of first admission of Turkish nationals into the territory of a Member State within the context of economic freedoms' (2011) 13 *EJML* 411

Lahuerta SB 'Race equality and TCNs, or how to fight discrimination with a discriminatory law' (2009) 15 *ELJ* 738

Lambert H 'The European Court of Human Rights and the right of refugees and other persons in need of protection to family reunion' (2000) 11 *IJRL* 427

Lambert H 'The EU Asylum Qualification Directive, its impact on the jurisprudence of the United Kingdom and international law' (2006) 55 *ICLQ* 161

Lambert H, Farrell T 'The changing character of armed conflict and the implications for refugee protection jurisprudence' (2010) 22 *IJRL* 237

Lambert H '"Safe third country" in the European Union: an evolving concept in international law and implications for the UK' (2012) 26 *JIANL* 318

Lane R, Shuibhne NN 'Case note' (2000) 37 *CMLRev* 1237

Langrish S 'The Treaty of Amsterdam: selected highlights' (1998) 23 *ELR* 3

Lansbergen A '*Metock*, implementation of the Citizens' Rights Directive and lessons for EU citizenship' (2009) 31 *Journal of Social Welfare & Family Law* 285

Lansbergen A, Miller N 'European citizenship in internal situations: an ambiguous revolution?' (2011) 7 *EuConst* 287

Laredo AT 'The EEA Agreement: an overall view' (1992) 29 *CMLRev* 1199

Laws J 'Is the High Court the guardian of fundamental constitutional rights?' [1993] PL 59

LaViolette N '"UNHCR guidance note on refugee claims relating to sexual orientation and gender identity": a critical commentary' (2010) 22 *IJRL* 173

Lawson R 'Case note' (2007) 3 *EuConst* 32

Lax VL 'Must EU borders have doors for refugees? On the compatibility of Schengen visas and carriers' sanctions with EU Member States' obligations to provide international protection to refugees' (2008) 10 *EJML* 315

Lazowski A 'Poland: constitutional tribunal on the surrender of Polish citizens under the European arrest warrant' (2005) 1 *EuConst* 569

Lazowski A 'Conformity of the Accession Treaty with the Polish Constitution. Decision of 11 May 2005' (2007) 3 *EuConst* 148

Lazowski A 'And then they were twenty-seven: a legal appraisal of the Sixth Accession Treaty' (2007) 44 *CMLRev* 401

Lebeck C 'National constitutional control and the limits of European integration: the European arrest warrant in the German Federal Constitutional Court' [2007] PL 23

Lebeck C 'Sliding towards supranationalism? The constitutional status of EU Framework decisions after *Pupino*' (2007) 8 *German Law Journal* 501

Leczykiewicz D 'Case note' (2006) 43 *CMLRev* 1181

Leczykiewicz D 'Constitutional conflicts and the third pillar' (2008) 33 *ELR* 230

Leerkes A, Broeders D 'A case of mixed motives: formal and informal functions of administrative immigration detention' (2010) 50 *British Journal of Criminology* 830

Legomsky S 'Secondary refugee movements and the return of asylum seekers to third countries: the meaning of effective protection' (2003) 15 *IJRL* 567

Legomsky SH 'The USA and the Caribbean interdiction program' (2006) 18 *IJRL* 677

Legomsky SH 'The new path of immigration law: asymmetric incorporation of criminal justice norms' (2007) 64 *Washington and Lee Law Review* 469

Lenaerts K 'The contribution of the European Court of Justice to the area of freedom, security and justice' (2010) 59 *ICLQ* 255

Lenaerts K 'Exploring the limits of the EU Charter of Fundamental Rights' (2012) 8 *EuConst* 375

Lester A, Beattie K 'Risking torture' [2005] EHRLR 565

Levy C 'Refugees, Europe, camps/state of exception: "into the zone", the European Union and extraterritorial processing of migrants, refugees, and asylum-seekers (theories and practice)' (2010) 29 *Refugee Survey Quarterly* 92

Lichtenberg H 'The rights of Turkish workers in Community law' (1995) 24 *ILJ* 90

Lieven S 'Case comment' (2012) 14 *EJML* 223

Lock T 'EU accession to the ECHR: implications for judicial review in Strasbourg' (2010) 35 *ELR* 777

Lock T 'Walking on a tightrope: the draft ECHR Accession Agreement and the autonomy of the EU legal order' (2011) 48 *CMLRev* 1025

Lock T 'End of an epic? The draft agreement on the EU's accession to the ECHR' (2012) 31 *YEL* 162

Lord C, Beetham D 'Legitimising the EU: is there a "post-Parliamentary" basis for its legitimation?' (2001) 39 *JCMS* 443

Loughran G, Short H 'Somalia: indiscriminate risk' (2012) 26 *JIANL* 175

Lynskey O 'Complementing and completing the common European Asylum system: a legal analysis of the emerging extraterritorial elements of EU refugee protection policy' (2006) 31 *ELR* 230

Mackarel M 'The European arrest warrant – the early years: implementing and using the warrant' (2007) 15 *European Journal of Crime, Criminal Law and Criminal Justice* 37

Mackarel M '"Surrendering" the fugitive: the European arrest warrant and the United Kingdom' (2007) 71 *Journal of Criminal Law* 362

Mackenzie A 'Case comment' [2006] EHRLR 67

Majone G 'Europe's "democratic deficit": the question of Standards' (1998) 4 *ELJ* 5

Mallia P 'Case note' (2011) 30(3) *RSQ* 107

Mancini GF 'Politics and the judges: the European perspective' (1980) 43 *MLR* 1

Mancini GF 'Europe: the case for statehood' (1998) 4 *ELJ* 29

Mantu S 'European Union citizenship Anno 2011: *Zambrano, McCarthy* and *Dereci*' (2012) 26 *JIANL* 40

Marguery TP 'The protection of fundamental rights in European criminal law after Lisbon: what role for the Charter of Fundamental Rights?' (2012) 37 *ELR* 444

Marmor A 'Are constitutions legitimate?' (2007) 20 *Canadian Journal of Law and Jurisprudence* 69

Martin D 'Case note' (1999) 1 *EJML* 149

Martin D 'Case note' (2000) 2 *EJML* 101

Martin D 'Case note' (2000) 2 *EJML* 431

Martin D 'Case note' (2002) 4 *EJML* 127

Martin D 'Case note' (2003) 5 *EJML* 143

Martin D 'Case note' (2003) 5 *EJML* 155

Martin D 'Case note' (2006) 8 *EJML* 231

Martin D 'Case note' (2007) 9 *EJML* 457

Martin D 'Case note' (2008) 10 *EJML* 365

Martin D 'Case note' (2009) 11 *EJML* 95

Martinson DS 'Who has the right to intra European social security? From market citizens to European citizens and beyond' EUI Working Paper, Law, 2003/13

Marx R 'Adjusting the Dublin Convention: new approaches to Member State responsibility for asylum applications' (2001) 3 *EJML* 7

Marzo C 'A new method of interpretation linked to European citizenship' [2010] 3 Web JCLI

Mavronicola N 'What is an 'absolute right'? Deciphering absoluteness in the context of Article 3 of the European Convention on Human Rights' (2013) 12 *HRLR* 723

McAdam J 'The European Union Qualification Directive: the creation of a subsidiary protection regime' (2005) 18 *IJRL* 461

McAdam J 'An intellectual history of freedom of movement in international law: the right to leave as a personal liberty' (2011) 12 *Melbourne Journal of International Law* 27

Melis B 'Case note' (1999) 36 *CMLRev* 1357

Meloni A 'The development of a common visa policy under the Treaty of Amsterdam' (2005) 42 *CMLRev* 1357

Meloni A 'The Community Code on Visas: harmonisation at last?' (2009) 34 *ELR* 671

Menon A, Weatherill S 'Transnational legitimacy in a globalising world: how the European Union rescues its states' (2008) 31 *Western Union Politics* 397

Michelman FI 'Constitutional legitimation for political acts' (2003) 66 *MLR* 1

Michelman FI 'Is the constitution a contract for legitimacy?' (2003) 8 *Review of Constitutional Studies* 101

Michelman FI 'Ida's way: constructing the respect-worthy governmental system' (2003) 72 *Fordham Law Review* 345

Mincheva E 'Case comment' (2010) 12 *EJML* 361

Mink J 'EU asylum and human rights protection: revisiting the principle of non-refoulement and the prohibition of torture and other forms of ill-treatment' (2012) 14 *EJML* 119

Mitsilegas V 'The constitutional implications of mutual recognition in criminal matters in the EU' (2006) 43 *CMLRev* 1277

Mölders S 'European arrest warrant is void – The decision of the German Federal Constitutional Court of 18 July 2005' (2005) 7 *German Law Journal* 45

Möller K 'Proportionality: challenging the critics' (2012) 10 *International Journal of Constitutional Law* 709

Moore J 'Whither the accountability theory: second-class status for third-party refugees as a threat to international refugee protection' (2001) 13 *IJRL* 32

Moore M 'Case note' (1997) 34 *CMLRev* 727

Moreno-Lax V 'Dismantling the Dublin system' (2012) 14 *EJML* 1

Morris R 'Case note' (2011) 18 *MJ* 179

Morris R 'European citizenship: cross-border relevance, deliberate fraud and proportionate responses to potential statelessness' (2011) 17 *EPL* 417

Moses WL, Letnes B 'The economic costs to international labor restrictions: revisiting the empirical discussion' (2004) 32 *World Development* 1609

Muir E 'Enhancing the protection of third-country nationals against discrimination: putting EU anti-discrimination law to the test' (2011) 18 *MJ* 136

Murphy C 'Lon Fuller and the moral value of the rule of law' (2005) 24 *Law & Philosophy* 239

Nafzinger JAR 'The general admission of aliens under international law' (1983) 77 *AJIL* 804

Nannestad P 'Immigration and welfare states: a survey of 15 years of research' (2007) 23 *European Journal of Political Economy* 512

Nascimbene B, Di Pascale A 'The 'Arab Spring' and the extraordinary influx of people who arrived in Italy from North Africa' (2011) 13 *EJML* 341

Nathwani N 'The purpose of asylum' (2000) 12 *IJRL* 354

Nett R 'The civil right we are not ready for: the right of free movement of people on the face of the Earth' (1971) 81 *Ethics* 212

Nettesheim M 'Developing a theory of democracy for the European Union' (2005) 23 *Berkeley Journal of International Law* 358

Neuberger DE 'General, equal and certain: law reform today and tomorrow' (2012) 33 *Statute Law Review* 323

Neuman GL 'Extraterritorial violations of human rights by the United States' (1994) 9 *American University Journal of International Law and Policy* 213

Neuwahl N 'Freedom of movement for workers under the EEC Treaty Association Agreement' (1988) 13 *ELR* 360

Neyer J 'Justice, not democracy: legitimacy in the European Union' (2010) 48 *JCMS* 903

Nohlen N 'Germany: the European arrest warrant case' (2008) 6 *IJCL* 153

Noll G 'Formalism v. empiricism: some reflections on the Dublin Convention on the occasion of recent European case law' (2001) 70 *NJIL* 161

Noll G 'Risky games? A theoretical approach to burden-sharing in the asylum field' (2003) 16 *JRS* 236

Noll G 'Visions of the exceptional: legal and theoretical issues raised by transit processing centres and protection zones' (2003) 5 *EJML* 303

Oberleitner G 'Human security: a challenge to international law?' (2005) 11 *Global Governance* 185

Oberleitner G 'Porcupines in love: the intricate convergence of human rights and human security' [2005] EHRLR 588

O'Brien C 'Real links, abstract links and false alarms: the relationship between the ECJ's "real link" case law and national solidarity' (2008) 33 *ELR* 643

O'Brien C 'Case note' (2011) 48 *CMLRev* 203

O'Keeffe D 'The Schengen Convention: a suitable model for European integration?' (1991) 11 *YEL* 185

O'Keefe D 'The Agreement on the European Economic Area' (1992) 19 *LIEI* 1

O'Leary S 'Nationality law and Community competence: a tale of two uneasy bedfellows' (1992) 12 *YEL* 353

O'Leary S 'Putting flesh on the bones of European Union citizenship' (1999) 24 *ELR* 68

O'Leary S 'Equal treatment and EU citizens: a new chapter on cross-border educational mobility and access to student financial assistance' (2009) 34 *ELR* 612

Olivier B, Reestman JH 'Case note' (2007) 3 *EuConst* 463

Oliver P 'Non-Community nationals and the Treaty of Rome' (1985) 5 *YEL* 57

Oliver P 'Case note' (2011) 48 *CMLRev* 2023

Oosterom-Staples H 'Case note' (2005) 42 *CMLRev* 205

Padfield N 'The implementation of the European arrest warrant in England and Wales' (2007) 3 *EuConst* 253

O'Sullivan M 'Acting the part: can non-state entities provide protection under international refugee law?' (2012) 24 *IJRL* 85

Ott A 'The *Savas* case – analogies between Turkish self-employed and workers?' (2000) 2 *EJML* 445

Ott A 'Case note' (2004) 10 *Columbia Journal of European Law* 379

Owen T 'Human security – conflict, critique and consensus: colloquium remarks and a proposal for a threshold-based definition' (2004) 35 *Security Dialogue* 373

Pallis M 'Obligations of states towards asylum seekers at sea: interactions and conflicts between legal regimes' (2002) 14 *IJRL* 329

Palmer S 'A wrong turning: Article 3 ECHR and proportionality' (2006) 65 *CLJ* 438

Panizzon M 'Readmission agreements of EU Member States: a case for EU subsidiarity or dualism?' (2012) 31 *Refugee Survey Quarterly* 101

Pardo S, Zemer L 'Towards a new Euro-Mediterranean neighbourhood space' (2005) 10 *EFAR* 39

Parga AH '*Bosphorus v Ireland* and the protection of fundamental rights in Europe' (2006) 31 *ELR* 251

Parga AH 'Case note' (2006) 43 *CMLRev* 583

Paris R 'Human security: paradigm shift or hot air?' (2001) 26 *International Security* 87

Parra J 'Stateless Roma in the European Union: reconciling the doctrine of sovereignty concerning nationality laws with international agreements to reduce and avoid statelessness' (2011) 34 *Fordham International Law Journal* 1666

Pech L '"A Union founded on the rule of law": meaning and reality of the rule of law as a constitutional principle of EU law' (2010) 6 *European Constitutional Law Review* 359

Pécoud A, de Guchteneire P 'International migration, border controls and human rights: assessing the relevance of a right to mobility' (2006) 21 *Journal of Borderlands Studies* 69

Pedain A 'A hollow victory: the ECJ rules on direct effect of freedom of establishment provisions in Europe agreements' (2002) 61 *CLJ* 284

Pedain A '"With or without me": the ECJ adopts a pose of studied neutrality towards EU enlargement' (2002) 51 *ICLQ* 981

Pedersen PJ, Pytlikova M and Smith N 'Selection and network effects: migration flows into OECD countries 1990–2000' (2008) 52 *European Economic Review* 1160

Peers S 'Indirect rights for third-country service providers confirmed' (1994) 19 *ELR* 303

Peers S 'Towards equality: actual and potential rights of third-country nationals in the European Union' (1996) 33 *CMLRev* 7

Peers S 'Case note' (1996) 33 *CMLRev* 103

Peers S 'Equality, free movement and social security' (1997) 22 *ELR* 342

Peers S 'ILPA European update' December 1999

Peers S 'Case note' (1999) 39 *CMLRev* 1027

Peers S 'Social security equality for Turkish nationals' (1999) 24 *ELR* 624

Peers S 'Case note' (2002) 39 *CMLRev* 1395

Peers S 'Readmission agreements and EC external migration law' Statewatch Analysis No 17, May 2003 http://www.statewatch.org/news/2003/may/readmission.pdf

Peers S 'Mutual recognition and criminal law in the European Union: has the Council got it wrong?' (2004) 41 *CMLRev* 5

Peers S 'Implementing equality? The Directive on Long-term Resident Third country nationals' (2004) 29 *ELR* 437

Peers S 'Double jeopardy and EU law: time for a change?' (2006) 8 *Eur JL Reform* 199

Peers S 'Salvation outside the church: judicial protection in the third pillar after the *Pupino* and *Segi* judgments' (2007) 44 *CMLRev* 883'

Peers S 'Finally "fit for purpose"? The Treaty of Lisbon and the end of the third pillar legal order' (2008) 27 *YEL* 47

Peers S 'In a world of their own? Justice and home Affairs opt-outs and the Treaty of Lisbon' (2008) 10 *CYELS* 383

Peers S 'Free movement, immigration control and constitutional conflict' (2009) 5 *EuConst* 173

Peers S 'Turkish visitors and Turkish students: new rights from the European Court of justice' (2009) 29 *JIANL* 197

Peers S 'Legislative update: EC immigration and asylum law attracting and deterring labour migration: the Blue Card and Employer Sanctions Directives' (2009) 11 *EJML* 387

Peers S 'EC immigration law and association agreements: fragmentation or integration' (2009) 34 *ELR* 628

Peers S 'Legislative update, EC immigration and asylum law: the new Visa Code' (2010) 12 *EJML* 105

Peers S 'Legislative update EU immigration and asylum law 2010: extension of long-term residence rights and amending the law on trafficking in human beings' (2011) 13 *EJML* 201

Peers S 'An EU immigration code: towards a common immigration policy' (2012) 14 *EJML* 33

Peers S 'A proposal for an EU immigration code', Statewatch Analysis No 167 January 2012 http://www.statewatch.org/analyses/no-167-immigration-code-steve-peers.pdf

Peers S 'Expulsion of Turkish citizens: a backward step by the Court of Justice' (2012) 26 *JIANL* 56

Peers S 'Legislative update 2011, EU immigration and asylum law: the recast Qualification Directive' (2012) 14 *EJML* 199

Peers S 'The "opt-out" that fell to Earth: the British and Polish Protocol Concerning the EU Charter of Fundamental Rights' (2012) 12 *HRLR* 375

Peers S, Costa M 'Accountability for delegated and implementing acts after the Treaty of Lisbon' (2012) 18 *ELJ* 427

Peers S 'Transfer of international protection and European Union law' (2012) 24 *IJRL* 527

Peers S 'The Court of Justice lays the foundations for the Long-term Residents Directive' (2013) 50 *CMLRev* 529

Pennings F 'The European Commission proposal to simplify regulation 1408/71' (2001) 3 *EJSS* 45

Phuong C 'Persecution by non-state agents: comparative judicial interpretation of the 1951 Refugee Convention' (2003) 4 *EJML* 521

Phuong C 'The removal of failed asylum seekers' (2005) 25 *LS* 117

Phuong C 'Minimum standards for return procedures and international human rights law' (2007) 9 *EJML* 105

Pickup A 'Case comment' (2012) 26 *JIANL* 289

Piotrowicz R, van Eck C 'Subsidiary protection and primary rights' (2004) 53 *ICLQ* 107

Pippan C 'The rocky road to Europe: the EU's stabilisation and association process for the Western Balkans and the principle of conditionality' (2004) 9 *EFAR* 219

Pirjola J 'Shadows in paradise: exploring *non-refoulement* as an open concept' (2007) 19 *IJRL* 639

Plachta M 'European arrest warrant: revolution in extradition?' (2003) 11 *European Journal of Crime, Criminal Law and Criminal Justice* 178

Plender R 'Competence, European Community law and nationals of non-Member States' (1990) 39 *ICLQ* 599

Pollicino O 'The new relationship between national and European Courts after the enlargement of Europe: towards a unitary theory of jurisprudential supranational law?' (2010) 29 *YEL* 65

Poole T 'Questioning common law constitutionalism' (2005) 25 *LS* 142

Pop V 'New Danish government rolls back border controls' 4 October 2011 http://euobserver.com/justice/113809

Pratt AN 'Human trafficking: the nadir of an unholy trinity' (2007) 13 *European Security* 55

Raffaelli R 'Criminalizing irregular immigration and the returns Directive: an analysis of the *El Dridi* case' (2011) 13 *EJML* 467

Raz J 'Multiculturalism' (1998) 11 *Ratio Juris* 193

Raz J 'The myth of instrumental rationality' (2005) 1(1) *Journal of Ethics and Social Philosophy*

Reid AS, Doherty M 'Voting rights for the European Parliament: whose responsibility?' [1999] EHRLR 420

Rijpma JJ 'Case note' (2008) 45 *CMLRev* 835

Rivers J 'Proportionality and variable intensity review' (2006) 65 *CLJ* 174

Roberts A 'Righting wrongs or wronging rights? The United States and human rights Post-September 11' (2004) 15 *EJIL* 721

Roberts S '"Our view has not changed": the UK's response to the proposal to extend the co-ordination of social security to third country nationals' (2000) 2 *EJSS* 189

Rogers N 'Case note' (1999) 1 *EJML* 365

Rogers N 'Minimum standards for reception' (2002) 4 *EJML* 215

Rogers N 'Immigration and the European Convention on Human Rights: are new principles emerging?' [2003] EHRLR 53

Rogers N 'Turkish Association Agreement applications – a myriad of problems and some solutions' (2006) 20 *Journal of Immigration Asylum and Nationality Law* 283

Roig A, Huddleston T 'EC readmission agreements: a re-evaluation of the political impasse' (2007) 9 *EJML* 363

Rosas A 'Justice in haste, justice denied? The European Court of Justice and the area of freedom, security and justice' (2009) 11 *CYELS* 1

Rosenow K 'The Europeanisation of integration policies' (2009) 47 *International Migration* 133

Rotaeche CG, Lloréns FB 'Case note' (1999) 1 *EJML* 357

Rousseva E 'The concept of "objective justification" of an abuse of a dominant position: can it help to modernise the analysis under Article 82 EC?' (2006) 2(2) *CompLRev* 27

Ryan B 'The common travel area between Britain and Ireland' (2001) 64 *MLR* 855

Sánchez SI 'Free movement of third country nationals in the European Union? Main features, deficiencies and challenges of the new mobility rights in the area of freedom, security and justice' (2009) 15 *ELJ* 791

Sánchez SI 'The Court and the Charter: the impact of the entry into force of the Lisbon Treaty on the ECJ's approach to fundamental rights' (2012) 49 *CMLRev* 1565

Sarmiento D 'The European arrest warrant and the quest for constitutional coherence' (2008) 6 *IJCL* 171

Satzger H, Pohl P 'The German Constitutional Court and the European arrest warrant: "cryptic signals" from Karlsruhe' (2006) 4 *JICC* 686

Scharpf FW 'Economic integration, democracy and the welfare state' (1997) 4 *JEPP* 18

Schermers HG 'Case note' (1999) 36 *CMLRev* 673

Schiltz C '*Akrich*: a clear delimitation without limits' (2005) 12 *MJ* 241

Schmitter PC, Karl TL 'What democracy is . . . and is not' (1991) 2 *Journal of Democracy* 75

Schrauwen A 'People in the Community: a recurring fraction' (1998) 25 *LIEI* 93

Schuck PH 'Refugee burden-sharing: a modest proposal' (1997) 22 *Yale Journal of International Law* 243

Schutte JJE 'Schengen: its meaning for the free movement of persons in Europe' (1991) 28 *CMLRev* 549

Seglow J 'The ethics of immigration' (2005) 3 *Political Studies Review* 317

Sevon L, Johansson M 'The protection of the rights of individuals under the EEA Agreement' (1999) 24 *ELR* 373

Shah P 'British nationals under Community law: the *Kaur* case' (2001) 3 *EJML* 271

Shaw J 'The interpretation of European Union citizenship' (1998) 61 *MLR* 293

Shaw J 'Postnational constitutionalism in the European Union' (1999) 6 *JEPP* 579

Shaw J 'The political representation of Europe's citizens: developments' (2008) 4 *EuConst* 162

Sherlock A 'Asylum seekers and the Convention' (1992) 17 *ELR* 281

Sherlock A 'Deportation of aliens and Article 8 ECHR' (1998) 23 *ELR* HR62

Shuibhne NN 'Legal implications of EU Enlargement for the individual: EU citizenship and free movement of persons' (2004) 5 *ERA Forum* 355

Shuibhne NN 'Derogations from the free movement of persons: when can EU citizens be deported?' (2006) 8 *CYELS* 187

Shuibhne NN 'Seven questions for seven paragraphs' (2011) 36 *ELR* 161

Shuibhne NN '(Some of) the lids are all right' (2012) 49 *CMLRev* 349

Simmonds NE 'Straightforwardly false: the collapse of Kramer's positivism' (2004) 63 *CLJ* 98

Singer M 'Legitimacy criteria for legal systems' (2006) 17 *KCLJ* 229

Sinn A, Wörner L 'The European arrest warrant and its implementation in Germany – its constitutionality, laws and current developments' [2007] ZIS 204

Skordas A, Sitaropoulos N 'Why Greece is not a safe host country for refugees' (2004) 16 *IJRL* 25

Skordas A 'Immigration and the market: the Long-term Residents Directive' (2006) 13 *Columbia Journal of European Law* 201

Slot PJ, Bulterman M 'Harmonization of legislation on migrating EU citizens and third country nationals: towards a uniform evaluation framework?' (2006) 29 *Fordham International Law Journal* 747

Smith T 'Neutrality isn't neutral: on the value-neutrality of the rule of law' (2011) 4 *Washington University Jurisprudence Review* 49

Solanke I 'Using the citizen to bring the refugee in' (2012) 75 *MLR* 78

Spaventa E 'On discrimination and the theory of mandatory requirements' (2000) 3 *CYELS* 457

Spaventa E 'Case note' (2005) 42 *CMLRev* 225

Spaventa E 'Opening Pandora's box: some reflections on the constitutional effects of the decision in *Pupino*' (2007) 3 *EuConst* 5

Spencer JR 'The European arrest warrant' (2003–2004) 6 *CYELS* 201

Stalker P 'Migration trends and migration policy in Europe' (2002) 40 *International Migration* 151

Starup P, Elsmore MJ 'Taking a logical step forward? Comment on *Ibrahim* and *Teixeira*' (2010) 35 *ELR* 571

Steinorth C 'Case comment' (2008) 8 *HRLR* 185

Storey H 'EU Refugee Qualification Directive: a brave new world?' (2008) 19 *IJRL* 1

Storey H 'Armed conflict in asylum law: the "war-flaw"' (2012) 31 *Refugee Survey Quarterly* 1

Sunstein CR 'Naked preferences and the constitution' (1984) 84 *Columbia Law Review* 1689

Taggart T 'Proportionality, deference, *Wednesbury*' [2008] NZLR 423

Tayleur T 'Schengen: opting in – but how far?' (2001) 151 *NLJ* 482

Tchorbadjiyska A 'Case note' (2004) 10 *Columbia Journal of European Law* 549

Teitgen-Colly C 'The European Union and asylum: an illusion of protection' (2006) 43 *CMLRev* 1503

Teubner G 'Substantive and reflexive elements in modern law' (1983) 17 *Law & Society Review* 239

Tezcan/Idriz N 'Free movement of persons between Turkey and the EU: to move or not to move? The response of the judiciary' (2009) 46 *CMLRev* 1621

Thielemann ER 'Between interests and norms: explaining burden-sharing in the European Union' (2003) 16 *JRS* 253

Thielemann ER 'Why asylum policy harmonisation undermines refugee burden-sharing' (2004) 6 *EJML* 47

Thielemann ER, Dewan T 'The myth of free-riding: refugee protection and implicit burden-sharing' (2006) 29 *West European Politics* 351

Thomas N, Tow WT 'The utility of human security: sovereignty and humanitarian intervention' (2002) 33 *Security Dialogue* 177

Thym D 'Respect for private and family life under Article 8 ECHR in immigration cases: a human right to regularize illegal stay?' (2008) 57 *ICLQ* 87

Tiedemann P 'Subsidiary protection and the function of Article 15(c) of the Qualification Directive' (2012) 31(1) *RSQ* 123

Tomuschat C 'Case note' (2000) 37 *CMLRev* 449

Tomuschat C 'Inconsistencies – the German Federal Constitutional Court on the European arrest warrant' (2006) 2 *EuConst* 209

Toner H 'Case note' (2002) 39 *CMLRev* 881

Toner H 'Case note' (2003) 5 *EJML* 163

Traser J 'Who's afraid of the EU's latest enlargement? The impact of Bulgaria and Romania joining the Union on free movement of persons' ECAS Report 2008 http://www.ecas-citizens.eu/content/view/84/178

Trebilcock MJ 'The law and economics of immigration policy' (2003) 5 *American Law & Economics Review* 271

Tryfonidou A 'The beginning of a new era in the European Union?' (2003) 14 *KCLJ* 81

Tryfonidou A 'Further cracks in the "great wall" of the European Union?' (2005) 11 *EPL* 527

Tryfonidou A 'Family reunification rights of (migrant) Union citizens: towards a more liberal approach' (2009) 15 *ELJ* 634

Tsakyrakis S 'Proportionality: an assault on human rights?' (2009) 7 *International Journal of Constitutional Law* 468

UNHCR 'Advisory Opinion on the extraterritorial application of non-refoulement obligations under the 1951 Convention relating to the Status of Refugees and its 1967 Protocol' [2007] EHRLR 484

van den Bogaert S 'And another uppercut from the European Court of Justice to nationality requirements in sports regulations' (2004) 29 *ELR* 267

van der Mei AP 'Freedom of movement and financial aid for students' (2001) 3 *EJSS* 181

van der Mei AP 'Residence and the evolving notion of European Union citizenship' (2003) 5 *EJML* 419

van der Mei AP 'Case note' (2004) 6 *EJML* 277

van der Mei AP 'Union citizenship and the "de-nationalisation" of the territorial welfare state' (2005) 7 *EJML* 203

van der Mei AP 'The Bozkurt-interpretation rule and the legal status of family members of Turkish workers under Decision 1/80 of the EEC-Turkey Association Council' (2009) 11 *EJML* 367

van Eijken H, de Fries SA 'A new route into the promised land? Being a European citizen after *Ruiz Zambrano*' (2011) 36 *ELR* 704

van Elsuwege P 'European Union citizenship and the purely internal rule revisited' (2011) 7 *EuConst* 308

van Gerven W 'The genesis of EEA law and the principles of primacy and direct effect' (1992) 16 *Fordham International Law Journal* 955 van Ginkel H, Newman E 'In quest of "human security"' (2000) 14 *Japan Review of International Affairs* 79

van Ooik R 'Freedom of movement of self-employed persons and the Europe agreements' (2002) 4 *EJML* 377

van Selm J 'Access to procedures: "safe third countries", "safe countries of origin" and "time limits"' June 2001 UNHCR http://www.unhcr.org/protect/PROTECTION/3b39a2403.pdf

van Selm J 'Return seen from a European perspective: an impossible dream, and improbable reality, or an obstruction to refugee policy?' (2005) 28 *Fordham International Law Journal* 1504

van Vooren B 'A case-study of "soft law" in EU external relations: the European neighbourhood policy' (2009) 34 *ELR* 696

Velluti S 'Case note' (2005) 45 *(Sum) SLR* 35

Velluti S 'What European Union strategy for integrating migrants? The role of OMC soft mechanisms in the development of an EU immigration policy' (2007) 9 *EJML* 53

Verschueren H 'EC social security co-ordination excluding third country nationals: still in line with fundamental rights after the *Gaygusuz* judgment?' (1997) 34 *CMLRev* 991

Waddington L 'Article 13 EC: mere rhetoric or a harbinger of change?' (1999) 1 *CYBELS* 175

Wagner E 'The integration of Schengen into the framework of the European Union' (1998) 25 *LIEI* 1

Wagner W 'Building an internal security community: the democratic peace and the politics of extradition in Western Europe' (2003) 40 *Journal of Peace Research* 695

Walker N 'The White Paper in constitutional context' Jean Monnet Working Paper No 6/01

Walker N 'Denizenship and the deterritorialization in the EU' EUI Working Paper Law 2008/08

Wang Y 'Most-favoured-nation treatment under the General Agreement on Trade in Services – and its application in financial services' (1996) 30 *Journal of World Trade* 91

Ward I 'Identifying the European other' (2002) 14 *IJRL* 219

Watson P 'Equality between Europe's citizens: where does the Union now stand?' (2012) 35 *Fordham International Law Journal* 1426

Weber A 'Case note' (1994) 31 *CMLRev* 423

Weidlich S 'First instance asylum proceedings in Europe: do bona fide refugees find protection?' (2000) 14 *Georgetown Immigration Law Journal* 643

Weiler JHH 'The transformation of Europe' (1991) 100 *YLJ* 2403

Weiler JHH 'Thou shalt not oppress a stranger: on the judicial protection of the human rights of non-EC nationals' (1992) 3 *EJIL*

Weiler JHH 'Europe: the case against the case for statehood' (1998) 4 *ELJ* 43

Weiner M 'Ethics, national sovereignty and the control of immigration' (1996) 30 *IMR* 171

Welch M, Schuster L 'Detention of asylum seekers in the US, UK, France, Germany and Italy' (2005) 5 *Criminal Justice* 331

Westen P 'The empty idea of equality' (1982) 95 *HLR* 537

White RCA 'Free movement, equal treatment, and citizenship of the Union' (2005) 54 *ICLQ* 885

Whittle R, Bell M 'Between social policy and Union citizenship: the Framework Directive on equal treatment in employment' (2002) 27 *ELR* 677

Wiener A 'Forging flexibility: the British "no" to Schengen' (2000) 1 *EJML* 441

Wiesbrock A 'Free movement of third-country nationals in the European Union: the illusion of inclusion' (2010) 35 *ELR* 455

Wiesbrock A 'Case comment' (2010) 6 *EuConst* 462

Wiesbrock A 'Disentangling the "Union citizenship puzzle"? The *McCarthy* case' (2011) 36 *ELR* 861

Wilsher D 'Non-state actors and the definition of a refugee in the United Kingdom: protection, accountability or culpability?' (2003) 15 *IJRL* 68

Wintamute R '"Within the ambit": how big is the "gap" in Article 14 European Convention on Human Rights? Part 1' [2004] EHRLR 366

Wintamute R 'Filling the Article 14 "gap": government ratification and judicial control of Protocol No 12 ECHR: Part 2' [2004] EHRLR 484

Woods L 'Family rights in the EU – disadvantaging the disadvantaged?' (1999) 11 *Child & Family LQ* 17

Wouters J, Naert F 'Of arrest warrants, terrorist offences and extradition deals: an appraisal of the EU's main criminal law measures against terrorism after "11 September"' (2004) 41 *CMLRev* 909

Xuereb K 'European cultural policy and migration: why should cultural policy in the European Union address the impact of migration on identity and social integration?' (2011) 49 *International Migration* 28

Yack B 'Popular sovereignty and nationalism' (2001) 29 *Political Theory* 517

York S, Fancott N 'Enforced destitution: impediments to return and access section 4 "hard cases" support' (2008) 22 *JIANL* 5

York S 'Case comment' (2012) 26 *JIANL* 283

Yorke J 'Europe's judicial inquiry in extradition cases: closing the door on the death penalty' (2004) 29 *ELR* 546

Yorke J 'The right to life and abolition of the death penalty in the Council of Europe' (2009) 34 *ELR* 205

Yorke J 'Inhuman punishment and abolition of the death penalty in the Council of Europe' (2010) 16 *EPL* 77

Young AL 'In defence of due deference' (2009) 72 *MLR* 554

Zieck M 'Doomed to fail from the outset? UNHCR's Convention Plus initiative revisited' (2009) 21 *IJRL* 387

Zuleeg M 'Case note' (1996) 33 *CMLRev* 93

## Other materials

Amnesty International 'Out of the spotlight: the rights of foreigners and minorities are still a grey area' EUR 25/016/2006 http://www.amnesty.org/en/library/asset/EUR25/016/2005/en/dom-EUR250162005en.html

Anan K '*International Migration* and Development: Report of the Secretary General' A/60/871 18 May 2006 http://www.un.org/esa/population/migration/hld/Text/ReportoftheSGJune2006_English.pdf

CDDH report to the Committee of Ministers on the elaboration of legal instruments for the accession of the European Union to the European Convention on Human Rights, CDDH(2011)009

CDDH Common paper of Andorra, Armenia, Azerbaijan, Bosnia-Herzegovina, Iceland, Liechtenstein, Monaco, Montenegro, Norway, Serbia, Switzerland, Russian Federation, Turkey and Ukraine on major concerns regarding the Draft revised Agreement on the

Accession of the European Union to the European Convention on Human Rights 47+1(2013)003

CDDH, Fifth Negotiation Meeting Between the CDDH Ad Hoc Negotiation Group and the European Commission on the Accession of the European Union to the European Convention on Human Rights: Final Report to the CDDH, 47+1(2013)008

Commission Staff Working Paper, Revisiting the Dublin Convention: Developing Community legislation for Determining which Member State is Responsible for Considering an Asylum Application Submitted in One of the Member States SEC(2000)522 final Commission Staff Working Paper, Evaluation of the Dublin Convention SEC(2001)756 final

Conclusions of the Danish Presidency *Bull. EC* 6-1993

Council Information concerning the declarations the declarations by the French Republic and the Republic of Hungary on their acceptance of the jurisdiction of the Court of Justice to give preliminary rulings on the acts referred to in Article 35 of the Treaty on European Union [2005] OJ C318/1 and L327/19

Economic Policy Committee and the European Commission (DG ECFIN) 'The impact of ageing on public expenditure: projections for the EU25 Member States on pensions, health care, long term care, education and unemployment transfers (2004–2050)' Special Report 1/2006 http://ec.europa.eu/economy_finance/publications/publication6654_en.pdf

ECRE 'Information Note on Council Directive 2005/85/EC' October 2006 http://www.ecre.org/topics/areas-of-work/protection-in-europe/118.html

ECRE 'Sharing Responsibility for Refugee Protection in Europe: Dublin Reconsidered' March 2008 http://www.ecre.org/files/Sharing%20Responsibility_Dublin%20Reconsidered.pdf.

ECRE 'Comments on Commission Proposal for a European Parliament and Council Directive laying down minimum standards for the reception of asylum seekers' April 2009 http://www.ecre.org/topics/areas-of-work/protection-in-europe/142.html

ECRE 'Comments from the European Council on Refugees and Exiles on the European Commission Proposal to recast the Dublin Regulation' April 2009 http://www.ecre.org/topics/areas-of-work/introduction/133.html

ECRE 'Information Note on the Returns Directive' January 2009 http://www.ecre.org/topics/areas-of-work/returns/171.html

ECRE 'Comments on Amended Commission Proposal to recast Reception Conditions Directive' September 2011 http://www.ecre.org/component/content/article/57-policy-papers/253-ecre-comments-and-recommendations-on-the-amended-commission-proposal-to-recast-the-reception-conditions-directive-com2011-320-final.html

ECRE 'Amended Commission Proposal to recast the Asylum Procedures Directive' September 2011 http://www.ecre.org/component/content/article/57-policy-papers/248-ecrecommentsrecastapd2011.html

ECRE 'Dublin II Regulation: lives on hold' February 2013 http://www.ecre.org/component/content/article/56-ecre-actions/317-dublin-ii-regulation-lives-on-hold.html

EDPS 'Opinion on the amended Proposal for a European Parliament and Council Regulation concerning the establishment of "Eurodac" for the comparison of fingerprints for the effective application of the Dublin Regulation (recast)' September 2012 http://www.edps.europa.eu/EDPSWEB/webdav/site/mySite/shared/Documents/Consultation/Opinions/2012/12-09-05_EURODAC_EN.pdf

Europa 'Integration of third country nationals' (1 September 2005) MEMO/05/290 http://europa.eu/rapid/press-release_MEMO-05-290_en.htm

Explanations Relating to the Charter of Fundamental Rights [2007] OJ C303/17

GCIM 'Migration in an interconnected world: new directions for action – Report of the Global Commission on international Migration' GCIM 2005 http://www.gcim.org

Home Office 'Joint Statement of Mr Damian Green UK Minister of State for Immigration and Mr Alan Shatter Ireland Minister for Justice and Equality Regarding Co-operation on Measures to Secure the External Common Travel Area border' December 2011 http://www.homeoffice.gov.uk/about-us/freedom-of-information/released-information1/foi-archive-immigration/21197-mea-sec-trav/21197-mea-sec-trav?view=Binary

Joint Supervisory Body of Europol 'Opinion 12/52with respect to the amended proposal for a Regulation of the European Parliament and of the Council on the establishment of EURODAC' October 2012 http://www.statewatch.org/news/2012/oct/europol-jsb-opinion-eurodac.pdf

Lundgren K, Lochbihler N 'European Parliamentarians "deeply concerned" at national moves to block EU accession to the European Convention on Human Rights' PACE Press Release AP018(2012) 25 January 2012 https://wcd.coe.int/ViewDoc.jsp?id=1899615&Site=DC

Novinite.com 'Dutch Govt Stalls Bulgaria, Romania Schengen bids till 2013' 17 September 2012 http://www.novinite.com/view_news.php?id=143320

Novinite.com 'Dutch Govt to block again Bulgaria, Romania Schengen bids – Report' 9 January 2013 http://www.novinite.com/view_news.php?id=146699

PRO ASYL 'The truth may be bitter, but it must be told: the situation of Refugees in the Aegean and the Practices of the Greek Coast Guard' October 2007 http://www.statewatch.org/news/2007/oct/greece-proasyl-refugees.pdf

PRO ASYL 'The situation in Greece is out of control' October 2008 http://www.proasyl.de/fileadmin/proasyl/fm_redakteure/Asyl_in_Europa/Griechenland/Out_of_contol_Eng_END.pdf

Standing Committee of Experts on International Immigration, Refugee and Criminal Law 'Note of the Meijers Committee on the proposal for a Regulation on the establishment of Eurodac' October 2012 http://www.statewatch.org/news/2012/oct/eu-meijers-committee-eurodac-proposal.pdf

Study Group on Europe's security capabilities 'Barcelona Report: a human security doctrine for Europe' September 2004 http://www2.lse.ac.uk/international Development/research/CSHS/humanSecurity/barcelonaReport.pdf

Tampere European Council Presidency Conclusions SN200/99

The Sofia Globe 'Decision on Bulgaria and Romania joining Schengen Visa Zone unlikely before autumn' 7 March 2013 http://sofiaglobe.com/2013/03/07/decision-on-bulgaria-and-romania-joining-schengen-visa-zone-unlikely-before-autumn/

UNHCR 'Convention Plus at a glance' June 2005 http://www.unhcr.org/cgi-bin/texis/vtx/protect/opendoc.pdf?tbl=PROTECTION&id=403b30684

UNHCR 'Statement on Subsidiary Protection under the EC Qualification Directive for People threatened by indiscriminate violence' January 2008 http://www.unhcr.org/refworld/docid/479df7472.html.

UNHCR 'Position on the Return of asylum-seekers to Greece under the "Dublin Regulation"' 15 April 2008 http://www.unhcr.org/cgi-bin/texis/vtx/refworld/rwmain?docid=4805bde42

UNHCR 'Guidance Note on Refugee Claims Relating to Sexual Orientation and gender identity' November 2008 http://www.unhcr.org/refworld/pdfid/48abd5660.pdf

UNHCR 'Comments on Commission Proposal for a European Parliament and Council Directive laying down minimum standards for the reception of asylum seekers' March 2009 http://www.unhcr.org/cgi-bin/texis/vtx/refworld/rwmain?docid=49ba8a192

UNHCR 'Comments on the Commission's Proposals for recast Dublin and Eurodac Regulations' March 2009 http://www.unhcr.org/refworld/docid/49c0ca922.html

UNHCR 'Statement on Article 1F of the 1951 Convention' July 2009 http://www.unhcr.org/refworld/pdfid/4a5de2992.pdf

UNHCR 'Comments on the European Commission's proposal for a Directive of the European Parliament and of the Council on minimum standards on procedures in Member States for granting and withdrawing international protection' August 2010 http://www.unhcr.org/4c640eee9.pdf

UNHCR 'Safe at last? Law and practice in selected EU Member States with respect to asylum-seekers fleeing indiscriminate violence' July 2011 http://www.unhcr.org/refworld/pdfid/4e2ee0022.pdf

UNHCR 'Comments on the European Commission's Amended Proposal for a Directive of the European Parliament and of the Council on common procedures for granting and withdrawing international protection status' January 2012 http://www.unhcr.org/4f35256c9.pdf

UNHCR 'An efficient and protective Eurodac' November 2012 http://www.unhcr.org/refworld/pdfid/50ad01b72.pdf

# Index

abuse of power 12
abuse of rights 183–4
accession: association agreements 175,
    180, 198–9, 203–4, 211–12, 268–70,
    273, 282;
European Convention on Human Rights
    173, 225, 228–30, 236, 266–7, 289
accountability 3–4, 7, 21, 119
action guidance 9, 13–14, 227, 237–8
Addo, MK 78
Adler-Nissen, R 83–4
affectual orientation 9–10
AFSJ *see* area of freedom, security
    and justice
Afzal, M 223
age of criminal responsibility 163
Algeria 198, 201, 282
Aliverti, A 261
Allan, TRS 13
amnesties 163
Ankara Agreement *see* Turkey-EEC
    Association Agreement and
    Council Decisions
Arab Spring 116, 118, 123, 199
area of freedom, security and justice
    (AFSJ) 7, 77–174, 240–68: citizenship
    217, 233; contradiction 240–55, 257–8,
    283; equal treatment 217; European
    Convention on Human Rights 91,
    263–4, 266–7; formal rationality 230,
    233, 240–55, 266, 283; free movement
    rights 23–4, 27, 76, 154–8, 173–4, 233,
    240–68, 280; Geneva Convention 78,
    160, 240–2, 261, 263, 267, 281; Hague
    Programme 214–16, 257, 254, 267,
    282; hierarchical rights 20, 173, 282;
    human rights 213–14, 216–18, 233,
    263–6, 268, 283; immigration 146–54,
    281–2; instrumental rationality 238,
    255–63, 266, 283; integration 213–17;

international protection status, persons
    with 173–4, 256–7, 281; introduction
    of AFSJ 77, 80–4; nationality
    discrimination 230, 233, 283; non-
    discrimination 29–30, 267–8, 283;
    objective justification 233, 264–6, 283;
    opt-outs 81–4, 159, 173, 218–20,
    258–9, 281, 283; policy 213–20, 280–3,
    284–5 ; Qualification Directive 256–7,
    263, 267, 281, 283; Receptions
    Directive 257, 258, 283; Schengen
    Protocol 80–4; Stockholm Programme
    215–17, 257, 259, 264–5, 282;
    substantive rationality 263–6, 283;
    Tampere Conclusions 173, 213–16,
    259, 267, 274, 282–5; terrorism 214
    *see also* asylum seekers; European Arrest
    Warrant (EAW) Framework Decision;
    immigration; refugees
arrest *see* European Arrest Warrant (EAW)
    Framework Decision
Aruba, voting rights of persons in 40
assimilation 225, 227, 232, 234
association agreements 175–212: accession
    175, 180, 198–9, 203–4, 211–12,
    268–70, 273, 282; aims of agreements
    205–6, 215, 270–1; binding nature 176;
    Charter of Fundamental Rights of the
    EU 275–7, 284; citizenship 209, 282;
    contradiction 268–74, 283–4; direct
    effect 207; European Convention on
    Human Rights 275–6; family members
    206, 210–11, 269–71, 273; formal
    rationality 268–72, 277–8, 283–4; free
    movement rights 7, 176–212, 268–74,
    277, 280, 282, 284; general non-
    discrimination article, proposal for 277;
    instrumental legal rationality 272–5,
    277–8, 284; legitimacy 268–9, 271;
    nationality discrimination 176, 205–7,

For Product Safety Concerns and Information please contact our EU
representative  GPSR@taylorandfrancis.com
Taylor & Francis Verlag GmbH, Kaufingerstraße 24, 80331 München, Germany

www.ingramcontent.com/pod-product-compliance
Lightning Source LLC
Chambersburg PA
CBHW071352290326
41932CB00045B/1542